W9-DEV-012

BBC Music Magazine
Top 1000 CDs Guide

Edited by Erik Levi and Calum MacDonald

BBC Books

Published by BBC Books,
an imprint of BBC Worldwide Publishing,
BBC Worldwide Limited, Woodlands,
80 Wood Lane, London W12 0TT

First published 1996

© BBC Music Magazine 1996

ISBN 0 563 38709 2

Designed by Ben Cracknell

Set in Garamond and Franklin Gothic

Printed and bound in Great Britain by Clays Ltd, St Ives plc
Cover printed by Clays Ltd, St Ives plc

CONTENTS

Biographical Notes

Managing Editor

Barry Millington: Reviews Editor of *BBC Music Magazine* and music critic for *The Times*; author/editor of five books on Wagner.

Principal contributors

Robert Cowan: Critic, journalist and broadcaster; formerly co-presenter of Classic FM's *Classic Verdict*, now a frequent contributor to BBC Radio 3's *Record Review*.

Michael Jameson: Cellist, broadcaster, lecturer and author of a study on Mozart's piano concertos.

Erik Levi: Senior Lecturer in Music at Royal Holloway, University of London, critic, broadcaster, accompanist and author of the book *Music in the Third Reich*.

Calum MacDonald: Author of books on Brahms, Schoenberg, Havergal Brian, Foulds and Ronald Stevenson; composer and editor of *Tempo* magazine.

David Nice: Critic and regular contributor to BBC Radio 3's *Record Review*; author of books on Tchaikovsky, Elgar and Strauss.

Charles Osborne: Critic, broadcaster and author of books on Bel canto opera and the complete operas of Mozart, Puccini, Strauss, Verdi and Wagner.

George Pratt: Professor of Music at the University of Huddersfield, co-presenter of BBC Radio 3's weekly programme *Spirit of the Age* and frequent contributor to *Record Review* and the BBC World Service.

Anthony Pryer: Senior Lecturer in Music, Goldsmiths' University of London, and author of numerous articles on early music.

Jeremy Siepmann: Musician and broadcaster; formerly Head of Music at BBC World Service; author of books on Chopin and the history of the piano.

Foreword

Many readers of *BBC Music Magazine* have asked for a digest of all the CD reviews the magazine has carried since its inception in 1992. Since this would mean around 10,000 reviews so far, we felt it more sensible to try a more contained – yet still compendious – approach; hence these specially comissioned reviews of 1000 CDs from both the well-trodden and scarcely explored ends of the repertoire.

Conceived by Barry Millington, *BBC Music Magazine*'s Reviews Editor, together with the guide's own editors, Calum MacDonald and Erik Levi, *Top 1000 CDs Guide* offers a path through the bewildering thicket of recordings now available. Full price or budget, new recording or old, authentic or not, the selection is intentionally eclectic. Our team of reviewers has faced the daunting prospect of comparing sometimes as many as fifty versions of the same piece. The results are inevitably highly personal, but *BBC Music Magazine* has always played host to a variety of voices and tastes within its pages. It is natural that this outlook should extend to this, its first CD guide.

In addition, the guide proper is preceded by four stimulating essays by Calum MacDonald, Robert Cowan, Anthony Pryer and David Nice on various aspects of recordings. These articles, a distinctive feature of a CD guide such as this, complement the main body of material in the book and reflect closely the spirit of *BBC Music Magazine*.

Private passions combined with authority are finally the best, perhaps the only, tools for good criticism. With today's high level of recording standards, we can usually assume a technically accurate performance. But does a disc move or delight or thrill? You may be sure that all the selections here, often weeded out from hundreds of possibles, will be acclaimed as something very special by their reviewers. I hope this gives you the confidence to follow their enthusiasm and discover new pleasures for yourself.

Fiona Maddocks

Editor, *BBC Music Magazine*

Preface

Since the advent of the compact disc during the 1980s, music lovers have been faced with an ever-increasing stream of releases from the recording companies, now totalling several hundred new titles per month. Among the bewildering profusion of current CD issues, you will encounter new recordings of the standard repertoire, which compete against refurbished releases of classic performances dating back through the last eighty years of recording history. Then there are also so-called 'authentic' performances presenting listeners with a radical choice of playing styles and editions, as well as a great deal of unfamiliar music that deserves to be more widely heard.

Wading through this torrent of activity in the recording field requires expert guidance, and this is where the *BBC Music Magazine Top 1000 CDs Guide* will provide all the informed assistance you should ever need. Our guide offers the widest possible conspectus – not only the finest CDs in terms of performance of the standard repertoire, but also the finest performances throughout the broadest range of pieces, composers and musical styles. From collecting the discs recommended in our guide, you will build up a truly comprehensive collection of excellence that spans the entire spectrum of classical music, from the medieval period to the present day.

The logic of encompassing such a wide range of repertoire has demanded a fresh approach in the writing of reviews. Quite clearly, we have avoided imposing any uniformity of taste, or undue veneration for works and performances just because they happen to be widely admired. On the principle that writers are generally most illuminating when discussing the things they love, we have allowed our reviewers' choices to be entirely personal and driven by their specialised knowledge and individual enthusiasms. The result, we feel, gives the collector an unusually stimulating insight into the musical treasures that are currently available on CD.

Just as the latest recording of a given work is not necessarily the best, neither is the most expensive. The vigorous growth of budget and super-budget labels, whether they present new recordings or recycle old ones, is an important feature of the current CD scene. It is hardly surprising, therefore, that many of our first choices come into these budget categories, but when they do not – especially in standard repertoire – we have often indicated the existence of competitive budget versions for collectors of limited financial means.

While the vast majority of the reviews have been specially written by the editors and a team of expert reviewers, a number have been reprinted directly from past issues of *BBC Music Magazine*, particularly when the existing review accords entirely with our own assessment of the disc. Thus you will find, in these pages, some examples of the work of nearly all *BBC Music Magazine*'s regular reviewers. In most cases, the review in question was awarded five stars (the *BBC Music Magazine*'s highest rating) for performance. However, we have not felt ourselves bound to reproduce the verdicts of the magazine, so after our considered evaluation, some discs which may have received a lower rating there, are nevertheless included here.

One of the special features of the guide is the inclusion of a number of fascinating articles on issues concerned with recording – the growth of the repertoire, the case for historic recordings and for authenticity, and an examination of composers as recording artists. Alongside the reviews, we hope that you will find these articles will further enhance your appreciation of the recording process, and of the critical decisions made by our reviewers in the following pages.

How to use this guide

Following the procedure adopted in the reviews section of *BBC Music Magazine*, the *Top 1000 CDs Guide* divides the repertoire into the standard five categories of Chamber music, Choral and Song, (solo) Instrumental, Opera, and Orchestral. Ballet music is included in the Orchestral section: music for piano duet/two pianos is included in the Instrumental section.

All entries in each category are in alphabetical order of the composer's surname. Since a number of discs contain music by more than one composer, or from more than one of these categories, cross-references have been provided to facilitate the location of a specific work.

We have also included an appendix containing a list of works that are better known by a title or nickname.

We have read, checked and re-checked the contents of the book but in the event of any oversights, the Editors welcome correspondence regarding factual errors that may be contained in this guide.

The reviews themselves are laid out in the same accessible style as that of *BBC Music Magazine*. The order and layout have been kept as simple as possible, with minimal use of technical terms and symbols, not only to help the reader locate particular reviews quickly but to encourage exploration of other works. Each entry contains information on the following:

Composers: Composers' forenames have been omitted except where two composers share the same surname.

Works: Titles of works are generally presented in their original language, sometimes with a translation in the review itself.

Performers: The following abbreviations have been adopted: CO (Chamber Orchestra), PO (Philharmonic Orchestra), RSO (Radio Symphony Orchestra) and SO (Symphony Orchestra). In addition, the London Philharmonic and Symphony orchestras and the Royal Philharmonic Orchestra have been abbreviated to LPO, LSO and RPO respectively.

Record label and number: A great deal of care has gone into checking the catalogue numbers. Despite our best efforts, errors may occur for which the publisher cannot be held responsible.

Attention has been paid to new recordings and deletions and, where possible, reviews have been incorporated or deleted immediately before going to press. Given the fluidity of the market, however, we cannot guarantee that all discs will remain available. Readers are advised that some record companies have introduced a special import service, and it may also be worth trying specialist retailers.

Recording process: All CDs reviewed are fully digital (DDD) unless otherwise shown; the abbreviation ADD is used for analogue recording. AAD for analogue recording and editing/mixing. Where a disc is wholly or partially mono this has also been indicated.

Disc timing

Price range: 🎵🎵🎵: full price; 🎵🎵: mid price; 🎵: budget price.

Contributors' names: The names of the principal contributors (see page 4) have been abbreviated to their initials.

Erik Levi and *Calum MacDonald*

An Expanding Universe

CDs and the classical repertoire

Calum MacDonald

When compact discs first began to appear on the market, the earliest releases featured – by and large, and inevitably – the most standard of standard repertoire: favourite opera with big-name stars, greatest symphonies, popular concertos, cleaned-up reissues of historic performances. Those of us with more adventurous tastes feared that, if CD became the dominant form of commercially available classical music, it would inevitably narrow the available repertoire. The LP catalogues offered, at that time, perhaps the widest diversity in the history of recorded music. As companies invested in more expensive CD technology, hoping to attract new listeners previously unfamiliar with classical music, they would surely – so the argument ran – limit their horizons to the more familiar items, the tried and true mainstream, requiring little rehearsal time and guaranteeing steady sales.

Well, we were wrong. The 'CD revolution' has coincided with – or been the catalyst for – an exponential explosion in the number of composers and works that find their way on to disc. The 'revolution' is a real one, its effects still becoming felt. The chance to hear, in the comfort of one's home, all sorts of hitherto obscure or even unknown works is breaking down the tidy accounts of music history in the textbooks, with their hierarchies of great composers, the not so great, and the largely anonymous mass of also-rans. So this guide, reflecting the way things are, features CDs of composers whose very names would have been largely unknown a decade or so ago: Carver, Langgaard, McEwen, Truscott, Veracini, *et al*...

There are many reasons for this explosion. Maybe no one wholly understands their complex interaction. But it seems significant that this is largely a phenomenon of recorded as opposed to live music. In a lifetime of frequent concert-going, you might never hear a work of Langgaard or McEwen, and there's little sign that the CD repertoire revolution has had much effect on concert programmes. Are concert-goers and record buyers two increasingly separate publics? Promoters, who must recoup the costs (artists' fees, hire of hall, promotion) of a single event in a single place, tend increasingly to play safe, to offer the comfortingly and enticingly familiar. But discs continue earning over a period of years, as far afield as they can be distributed. Even if the unfamiliar repertoire turns out not to the buyer's tastes, at least he or she doesn't have to sit in embarrassed silence with hundreds of strangers and fellow sufferers. You listen to something else.

But maybe you try again another day. The very fact that record companies find some commercial sense in recording out-of-the-mainstream repertoire argues the existence of a public with tastes more adventurous than the live concert season caters to. There's an opportunity to capitalise on established tastes by offering that public new brands. You like Vivaldi? Try some Locatelli. If you enjoy Mahler, you just have to hear Hans Rott's Symphony. You want stirring, tuneful English music: how about some George Lloyd. And so on. Reassuring the customer that the unfamiliar is really the familiar, differently packaged, is an important element in marketing.

Of course, the rediscovery of old music, and the discovery of new, is a process that has been going on since the antiquarian instincts of the 19th century led people to take an educated interest in the past, and the first great musicologists began publishing complete editions of Bach, Handel and Schütz. But it was enormously accelerated by the arrival of the gramophone record. Witness Vivaldi's *Four Seasons* concertos, among the most popular and most-recorded music of all time. Literally nobody heard these works for nearly 200 years after the composer's death. The first modern edition didn't appear until 1927 (with a dedication to Mussolini!). It was recorded on six 78rpm discs in 1942 – and nowadays there are upwards of 150 recorded versions. But there are also dozens and dozens of other Vivaldi concertos on the market. At least one CD company has embarked on the awesome task of recording Vivaldi's complete works – including his multitudinous operas. (These have so far failed to enthuse the international musical consciousness in the wake of *The Four Seasons*, despite the now invincible attractions of the near-contemporary operas of Handel and Rameau – fifty years ago *they* weren't thought worth listening to, either.)

The New Completeness is a phenomenon in itself. Perhaps it's a subliminal result of the nature of the CD medium, able to accommodate up to twenty minutes' more music than an LP and thus better suited for, say, a back-to-back coupling of two symphonies. Though much exploration beyond the frontiers of the standard repertoire still occurs in haphazard fashion and with one-off pet projects, there's an increasing trend towards recording complete *oeuvres* – or sections of *oeuvres* – in integral series, or 'complete editions'. Formerly extended only to the very famous indeed, this privilege (which itself suggests a measure of authority and critical standing) now encompasses composers who ten years ago were hardly more than dictionary entries. Complete editions of Bach's organ music, of Haydn symphonies and string quartets, are – if not two a penny – no longer the stuff of adventure. Hyperion's determination to record Liszt's entire piano output, a series which had reached Volume 37 at the time of writing, is certainly worthy of note. Purcell's complete vocal music (from the same company) is perhaps inevitable given his recent tercentenary. But who would have anticipated a complete cycle, still in progress, of the 32 symphonies of Havergal Brian (on Marco Polo)? The 16 symphonies of Rued Langgaard (from Danacord)? Two competing cycles (on BIS and CPO) of the 16 by Allan Pettersson? The piano sonatas of Clementi (Altarus)? The complete player-piano studies of Conlon Nancarrow (Wergo)? The extant choral music of the Renaissance Scottish polyphonist Robert Carver (ASV)? Every work of William Walton (Chandos), including items the composer himself suppressed?

Significantly, all the companies named are small to medium operations. Sometimes all that a small producer can offer initially, to establish a reputation and market identity, is a repertoire not served by the big conglomerates. But the latter, whose fortunes were made in the mainstream, and who possess vast back catalogues of historic performances, have tended to follow where the independents lead. Some have set up subsidiary labels (like Catalyst, a creation of BMG/RCA, or Decca's Argo) specifically to carry more adventurous programmes. But in general the main catalogues of Decca, DG, EMI, Philips and Sony are much more varied than they were a decade ago.

The passion for completeness has repercussions on musical scholarship. It may involve performing works that were never actually published, or for which no satisfactory modern edition exists. Archives and attics are being ransacked to provide yet more repertoire for the medium. A project to record the works of Nicholas Ludford, the most prolific Tudor composer of Masses, has stimulated new research and uncovered much biographical material on a previously very shadowy figure. In the 20th-century field, Decca's admirable Entartete Musik (Degenerate Music) series is designed to disinter the works of composers condemned and suppressed by the Nazis, many of whom perished in the gas-chambers and have been forgotten for half a century. The remarkable revaluation of the jazz-influenced Czech Erwin Schulhoff and of the still-surviving Berthold Goldschmidt to the status of important European composers is a symptom of this new awareness.

Such ventures may or may not involve an exercise of critical discrimination about the works to be recorded. An unquantifiable proportion of the unfamiliar music now on CD is undoubtedly mediocre by the ultimate canons of artistic greatness. But that's hardly the point. All this activity can only be healthy: music only really exists when it's being heard, and the more of it we hear the more we find it's possible to second-guess those critical canons.

Record companies, however, are neither charitable nor scholastic institutions. Into the equation comes what we might call the 'Górecki factor'. As if to confirm the view that for many people music is now a substitute for religion, certain contemporary works – mainly of the melodiously minimal and expressively spiritual variety – have achieved a quite unparalleled commercial success in terms of record sales. This tendency started perhaps with the works of the Estonian Arvo Pärt, and such scores as the cello concerto *The Protecting Veil* by John Tavener. It reached its climax with Nonesuch Records' record-breaking sales (not unassisted by the airtime of Classic FM, a radio station partly owned, like Nonesuch, by Time-Warner) of the Dawn Upshaw/David Zinman recording of Symphony No. 3 for soprano and orchestra, by the erstwhile Polish avant-garde composer Henryk Mikolaj Górecki: a highly untypical work by a figure whose identification with minimalism is coincidental and misleading. Worldwide sales have topped 700,000 – an amazing total in a market where it's whispered that even some top-line Mozart opera sets have difficulty in selling into three figures. The resulting scramble to find 'the next Górecki Third' and to anticipate the CD-buying public's taste has benefited a great deal of contemporary and not-so-contemporary music. Not only of the 'Holy Minimalist' tendency, either, although the 'next Górecki' turned out to be Pope Gregory and his medieval Latin Chants. It seems that simple music with an odour of sanctity will always sell: in this age, Mammon discovers it's God who has the best tunes.

But at least they're different tunes; and the fact that the public will buy, in bulk, the unfamiliar and/or the contemporary is a lesson CD producers aren't about to unlearn. Performers have a stake in all this too. Some are genuinely exploratory themselves, enthusiastic to promote their own discoveries or music outside the standard repertoire that they happen to admire. Such laudable impulses can even assist a career. A conductor's ability to deliver, say, an internationally admired cycle of Beethoven symphonies may still be the most reliable yardstick by which his greatness may be judged. But the competition is multitudinous and intense. Unfamiliar repertoire may offer a better chance of being noticed. Your Beethoven cycle will be one of fifty: your Tubin cycle could be the only one in the catalogue. If your reputation is already established, your flexibility in repertoire is increased. Artists under contract can sometimes swing specific items (like Nicholas Maw's *Odyssey*) on an unwilling major company.

Another by-product is a steady erosion of the distinction between 'standard' and 'obscure' repertoire. No catalogue illustrates this better than that of the former Hong Kong-, now New-Zealand-based company HNH, whose market leader was and is the budget Naxos label, originally established to bring the mainstream repertoire into supermarkets, to people who didn't usually buy CDs. Founded on a core of mainly Eastern European performers, none of them household names but mostly musicians of high quality and eager for international exposure, Naxos built up a remarkable following, its competitive budget-price versions of standard classics quite often becoming top critical recommendations. Naxos profits helped to fund more esoteric programming on the stablemate Marco Polo, 'the label of discovery'. Marco Polo has, indeed, a distinguished record of discoveries and first recordings. But Naxos itself has found buyers gaining enough confidence in the label's identity to be willing to experiment with the unfamiliar at its low price – especially in the fields of Baroque and Renaissance music, where even this 'supermarket label' is bringing previously unrecorded repertoire on to CD. Currently, Naxos is recording its own cycles of the complete symphonies of Arnold Bax and Malcolm Arnold, previously thought to appeal only to dedicated aficionados of British music – the Arnold will, in fact, be the first-ever complete cycle. Even contemporary music is now 'budget' property; as I write this article I hear that Naxos has just issued those prime documents of serial modernism, the three piano sonatas of Pierre Boulez, in performances by the Turkish pianist Idil Biret, one of their house artists, who has already recorded a complete Brahms cycle for them. (Even this included some Brahms never before heard on disc.)

I single out Naxos only as an example. But its message seems profound. Despite the crushing and volatile financial pressures which beset much of the recording industry, every important producer realises they must diversify in repertoire or die. To which the collector need only echo Amen. Adventure and exploration are the stuff of life, and classical music isn't a museum but an entire cosmos. The CD repertoire should reflect not just a few big names but a thousand points of light.

Old Friends for New

A cautionary tale

Robert Cowan

First loves are rarely lifelong, but musical first loves have an irritating habit of staying put. And when records are involved, the problem seems particularly complex. Most of us learn major works from the repertoire through recordings, and our tendency to cling loyally to the version we first heard can be due to any one of numerous excuses – reluctance to change, unwillingness to explore, lack of time, lack of money, etc. But there's another potential reason that's not quite so easy to disregard: our first love might also happen to be a great performance. To give a specific example, I first heard Tchaikovsky's Fifth Symphony through an old set of 78s by the Philadelphia Orchestra conducted by Leopold Stokowski. It was a constant companion: I'd listen before school, after school, at weekends and at dead of night. Tchaikovsky's essay had become the soundtrack of my puberty; it alone seemed privy to my oscillating emotions, doubts, ambitions and desires; it somehow reflected them too. But there was a minor snag in that this forty-minute masterpiece occupied ten 78rpm sides rather than the two sides of an LP. So I resolved to save time and money by investing in a cheap 'long-player' version by an unknown orchestra and conductor (at least unknown to me at the time) – although as far as I was concerned Tchaikovsky's Fifth was Tchaikovsky's Fifth and it would surely sound the same *whoever* played it. How wrong I was! In fact, the experience was something of a mini-trauma: gone was the passion, the warmth, the exultant finale and the wonderful string sound. What took their place was a sort of dusty waxwork, worthy and vaguely recognisable, but unalive and therefore unyielding.

And the experience wasn't unique. I'd buy LPs of Chopin only to find none of the flair or fervour that leaped from my grandfather's 78s of Alfred Cortot and Solomon. Anodyne violin LPs were already in abundance, but where was the individuality and tear-jerking eloquence of Jascha Heifetz, Fritz Kreisler or the teenage Yehudi Menuhin? And then there were the singers and their personalities – Wagnerian heroics from Lauritz Melchior, outsize theatrical declamations from Feodor Chaliapin, then the great divas, Amelita Galli-Curci and Rosa Ponselle. 'Old' had in fact become an epithet for 'great'. It was an ominous sign. I even bought an anorak, and could frequently be seen scouring market stalls for dusty old records.

Listening beyond history

The phase was brief but intense, and it taught me a great deal. Friends and colleagues had long criticised me for what they recognised as an unhealthy preoccupation with the past. 'Surely our own contemporaries are doing an equally good job,' some would say, 'and newer recordings have the added advantage of stereo definition.' But the nagging suspicion that these old records *did* offer something unique prompted me to analyse what seemed like palpable interpretative superiority. Of paramount importance was the fact that individual 78s were, in a sense, complete performances. Before the Forties and the arrival of magnetic tape, you couldn't re-record odd bars unless you were willing to have a second shot at an entire 4–5-minute 78rpm side. That's one of the reasons why the best old records have an engaging, seat-of-the pants spontaneity. Some artists would replay a whole work or passage ten or more times before they were satisfied with the results, and in many cases their first attempts actually survive in record archives. Then there's the question of musical tradition, where individual performers learned from their teachers or peers, and not from other people's records. Before the war, making a record was something of an event, and many musicians were still highly sceptical about the process, claiming (as did conductor Wilhelm Furtwängler and violinist Bronislaw Huberman) that interpretation is a spontaneous art and that no one performance can ever prove definitive.

History, too, is of the essence – though to call old records merely 'historical' is to identify only a very minor aspect of their musical appeal. Still, it does well to consider that both Kreisler and Huberman played the Brahms Violin Concerto to Brahms, that Willem Mengelberg received advice on conducting Tchaikovsky's Fifth Symphony from the composer's brother, that Bruno Walter premiered two works by Mahler (*Das Lied von der Erde* and the Ninth Symphony), and that baritone Victor Maurel was Verdi's first Iago. All these musicians recorded the works in question and were therefore able to suggest how the composers themselves might have expected their music to be played, conducted or sung. But the most compelling reasons for returning to old records are both nebulous and fraught with conceptual complications. If the First World War felled the heart of Romanticism, the Second World War and its attendant horrors buried it for ever. All manner of inspired naivety vanished and a calculated sophistication arrived in its train. This is a very broad generalisation, I know, but it may help explain why the great Romantic composers (and I include Beethoven among them) were best served while the values and illusions they held sacred still had some credibility. Does that sound like a tenable theory? Well, to find out you'll need to listen for yourself.

Reducing the crackle

But before starting my initial recommendations, I must tell you that making old mono tapes and 78s into respectable CDs is a complicated business, and preferences among transfer techniques are about as varied as tastes in musical performance. Died-in-the-wool record collectors (and 'collector' CD labels, such as Pearl and Biddulph) tend to favour the 'purist' approach, which, roughly speaking, means tracking down mint copies of the original 78s, splicing the sides together so that longer works play continuously, and avoiding anything in the way of excessive filtering. By 'filtering' I mean reducing the 78 (shellac) surface noise (or, in the case of tape, 'hiss') that so many people find off-putting. However, if you filter *too* much, the upper frequencies of the original recordings become dulled and the tonal properties of the performances distorted.

One possible solution to the surface noise problem is to search out the original 78rpm 'masters' and prepare new pressings – not on gritty shellac but on quiet vinyl (the plastic substance used in the manufacture of LPs). This, of course, means that the new pressing will have only a fraction of the crackle of a standard shellac disc. The major record companies, such as RCA and EMI (or its official historical offshoot, Testament), have this facility easily to hand, and in some cases are even able to re-record directly from the original master shell. The trouble here is that a great number of masters were destroyed either during the war or, as storage space-saving became more crucial, in the wake of stereo recording.

A novel alternative to re-pressing on to vinyl is the use of original reproducing equipment, an option that Nimbus uses for its Prima Voce CD series. Nimbus lines up a huge, painstakingly refurbished horn gramophone, then places a sensitive microphone in front of it and spices the resulting transfer with a smidgeon of reverberation (much as you'd hear in the opera house). This can work exceptionally well when the 78s so treated were originally recorded via a horn (as all discs were prior to the advent of microphones), but tends to minimise the dynamic range of electrical recordings. Then there are the computerised 'noise reduction' systems, mainly 'NoNoise' (a patented system, usually applied to excess and not recommended by me) and the vastly superior CEDAR, now CEDAR-2, which is selectively used by the likes of EMI and Testament and has been so imaginatively utilised by Dutton Labs. Unlike, say, Pearl and Biddulph, Dutton Labs aim to reduce surface noise to an absolute minimum and to 'restore' the 78s much as one might restore an old painting. This involves adding a certain amount of reverberation and extending the frequency range of the original recordings, with results that can be either startlingly realistic or mildly synthetic.

All these systems are effective in one way or another. But no amount of refurbishing or technical wizardry will mask the fact that these old recordings require a certain degree of tolerance on behalf of the listener. The list below is a sort of basic starter-pack, a sampling of the honest, committed music-making that was particularly prevalent during the pre-stereo era. That's not to underestimate the many marvellous records that have emerged during the last forty or so years; rather, it's a reminder that music-making has a past as well as a present, and that a thorough knowledge of both will help secure the good health of its future.

Recordings of a lifetime: some initial recommendations

BEETHOVEN

Symphony No. 3 in E flat (Eroica) (c/w Symphony No. 8 in F)

NBC SO/Arturo Toscanini

RCA Victor Gold Seal GD 60269 □ **ADD** □ 🎵🎵

The most intensely moving of Toscanini's numerous *Eroicas*, a heroic confrontation that retains its power to this day. Both recordings date from 1939.

CHOPIN

Piano Works

Solomon

Testament SBT 1030 □ **ADD** □ 🎵🎵

Poetic, manful and quietly perceptive, this is surely the sort of playing that Chopin himself would have favoured.

ELGAR

Violin Concerto (c/w Cello Concerto)

Yehudi Mehuhin (violin); LSO/Edward Elgar

EMI CDC 5 55221 2 □ **ADD** □ 🎵🎵🎵

The fifteen-year-old prodigy in musical communion with English music's elder statesman: a magnificent achievement, beautifully transferred.

SCHUBERT

Impromptus (c/w Fantasy in C (Wanderer))

Edwin Fischer (piano)

Appian APR 5515 □ **ADD** □ 🎵🎵

Intuitive music-making at its most compelling, the Impromptus in particular having never been equalled (and only approached by Fischer's eloquent successor, Alfred Brendel).

TCHAIKOVSKY

Symphony No. 5 in E minor (c/w 1812 Overture; 'encores')

Philadelphia Orchestra/Leopold Stokowski

Biddulph WHL 015 □ **ADD** □ 🎵🎵

A freewheeling but wonderfully supple performance featuring one of the great virtuoso ensembles of all time.

TCHAIKOVSKY

Symphony No. 6 in B minor (Pathétique) (c/w works by Wagner, Beethoven & Furtwängler)

Berlin PO/Wilhelm Furtwängler

Biddulph WHL 006/7 □ ADD □ (2 discs) □ 🕑🕑

A performance of overwhelming impact and emotional force, recorded during the dark days of Nazi rule.

VAUGHAN WILLIAMS

A London Symphony; Serenade to Music (c/w Greensleeves Fantasia; The Wasps Overture)

Soloists; Queen's Hall Orchestra, BBC SO/Henry Wood

Dutton Laboratories CDAX 8004 □ ADD □ 🕑🕑

An exhilarating account of the *London Symphony* – incisive, eloquent and played with tremendous panache. The *Serenade to Music* is sung by the singers for whom it was originally composed.

FEODOR CHALIAPIN

Russian opera arias

Feodor Chaliapin (bass); various orchestras & choirs

EMI Références CDH 7 61009 2 □ ADD □ 🕑🕑

Including a live Covent Garden recording (1928) of Mussorgsky's 'Death of Boris', one of the most riveting operatic characterisations in gramophone history.

ROSA PONSELLE

The Columbia Acoustic Recordings

Rosa Ponselle (soprano), etc

Pearl GEMM CDS 9964 □ AAD □ (2 discs) □ 🕑🕑🕑

The greatest soprano of them all, recorded at the very height of her considerable powers.

AMELITA GALLI-CURCI

Galli-Curci, Vol. 2

Amelita Galli-Curci (soprano), etc

Nimbus Prima Voce NI 7852 □ ADD □ 🕑🕑

Glorious coloratura singing, presented both solo and in duet with some of Galli-Curci's most revered contemporaries.

Settling Old Scores

The authentic performance argument

Anthony Pryer

In an atmosphere of some secrecy, several major art galleries are now exploring ways of replacing with copies their most admired but constantly breathed-over paintings. It is hoped that these replicas will be indistinguishable from their originals. The difficulties come not with the design and colouring of the pictures (which can be reproduced accurately by digitalised scanning techniques) but with the fabrication of their surface textures and the copying of the materials used to construct them. Even more difficult is the reproduction of those aspects that are part of the ageing process of an artwork – aspects that we have come to think of as part of the 'charm' of the *Mona Lisa*, and which used to be part of the 'charm' of Michelangelo's *Last Judgement* until it was recently cleaned and 'restored'.

Of course, in music things are rather different: nobody has to plan in secret to present to the public an inauthentic version of a work by Bach or Machaut. Indeed, many people positively prefer, for example, Leopold Stokowski's heavily romanticised transcriptions of Bach's Preludes and Fugues (reissued on the Pearl label in 1994) to what they think of as the authentic but anaemic tinklings of a harpsichord; and doubtless many prefer performances of 14th-century dances that sound as though they are accompanied by the massed spoons of the Sheffield Stainless-Steel Band to those that employ the modest sonorities of early strings and percussion. But if you are one of those people, should you feel guilty? or ignorant but happy? or knowledgeable but unconcerned?

The problem is that the issue of period performance in music concerns not just one question, but three – and the three questions need to be treated in sequence. First, can we accurately reconstruct past performances at all? Secondly, if we can, will authentic performances lead to authentic experiences? Thirdly, whether they will or not, ought we at least try to get some sense of what went on in the past – in other words, do we have a duty towards the past?

The reconstruction of past performances can be a difficult matter. In the first place, for music written before 1600 it is rare to find autograph scores or sources that are known to have been supervised by the composer. For this music we cannot be sure of the authority of the copy in front of us, and the few exceptions – manuscripts linked to Machaut, Isaac, Cipriano da Rore and one or two others – prove the rule. Even in the case of later music, errors, omissions and variant versions are not uncommon. Mozart's Rondo in E flat for horn, K371, for example, in spite of being recorded more than once and discussed by music analysts as a 'coherent work', has recently been discovered to have sixty bars missing, and to be part of another work (his earliest attempt at a horn concerto). Again, the problems of constructing definitive versions of operas (which were frequently adapted by composers for particular singers and opera houses) are a well-known musicological nightmare. For example, there is not, and nor could there ever be, a 'definitive' score of Bizet's *Carmen* – and all recordings to date make cuts to the original material (some of which is self-contradictory anyway).

But even if we could establish in every case exactly what music the composer intended there to be in the 'definitive' version, this would not be the end of the matter. At various stages throughout its history, almost all aspects of music – exact pitch, instrumentation, rhythmic detail, performance context, pace, expression and form – have been left to chance or to convention, rather than notated in the score, even if that score had been sanctioned by the composer. Recordings of Monteverdi's Vespers, for example, vary widely in the details of their instrumentation, the relative speed of each movement, the application of vocal ornaments and even the order and inclusion of certain movements. Moreover, some sing the final Magnificat at written pitch, others transpose it up because they think the original notation implies this, and yet others transpose it up because they want to produce a bright, high-voiced climax at the end whether or not it is authentic. Finally, some attempt to present Monteverdi's music within the context of an actual vespers service (with plainsongs, etc), and others do not.

No doubt there can be difficulties in establishing an authentic edition, style, sonority and context for a work from the past. What is abundantly clear is that these difficulties have led many to lose patience with the notion of authenticity altogether. They assert that the authenticist approach is little more than a time-wasting attempt to mind-read the thoughts of the dead (though they are not averse to claiming to know, for example, that 'Bach would have welcomed inauthentic performances of his works'). Moreover, they charge that such an approach would put performers in a ridiculous strait-jacket, endlessly committing them to reproducing One True Particular Past Performance. Finally, they argue that what really matters is 'the music itself', which flourishes with each new interpretation: composers, after all, cannot know everything about the music they create. This was put very neatly by the pianist Jorge Bolet when he was asked why he did not play Chopin's music as Chopin intended: 'Well,' he replied, 'I have been playing Chopin longer than Chopin.'

At this point we might well need to return to our earlier comparison between music and painting for further illumination. After all, there is only one *Mona Lisa*, and the reason why forgers and art galleries have the troubles they do is because, to fool anyone, they have to find ways to reconstruct the work in every detail. Moreover, any such reconstruction would have to be able to be compared with the original without fear of detection.

Those against period performance have a tendency to talk about music in this way too – but music is not like this. Musical compositions are not rigid archives of meaning but strategies for performance, and this is true from the moment that they are created. There is little doubt, for example, that Monteverdi's operas appeared in as many versions during his lifetime as the occasions upon which they were performed. Thus, those interested in authentic performance might well wish to see his *Orfeo* played in accordance with the stylistic norms of its period, but that is a long way from a belief in there being One True Particular Past Performance of the work. Moreover, we may not be able to mind-read dead composers, but the general attitudes and the stylistic norms which governed performances of the past are often reassuringly broad and richly documented in a variety of ways.

It seems clear that, on some occasions at least, we are able to re-create accurately sounds from the past. But why should we bother? Can authentic performance, for example, re-create the original experience? Of course, taking all the evidence together, we might sometimes be able to imagine some of the things that people of the past experienced in the presence of their music. But, for us, this would still be an *imagined* experience, and we could not eradicate from that experience the pleasure of delving into the past. So we are left with the paradox that our pleasure in historical reconstruction is among the least authentic of our attitudes to music. For us the 'pastness' of the music is part of its charm, rather like the grime of ages which now forms part of the *Mona Lisa* experience for us. In trying to live with this problem, we are caught rather like the masochist who enjoyed taking a cold shower in the morning – so he had to take a hot one.

In fact, the justification for authentic performance does not come from a simple belief that the past can be made present. Instead, it is part of a wider desire to reach an authentic understanding of the complexity of our musical experiences. When we listen to the music of Machaut or Monteverdi, of Chopin or Shostakovich, we are not just taking in a soundscape; we are also (perhaps unconsciously) admiring a musical personality. We want to know what is meant by the music, and whether it contains elements of parody, or irony, or the imprint of personal suffering. To do this we need to know about the original intentions behind a work – irrespective of whether it is ancient or modern. Again, we hear early music stripped of Romantic sonorities and gestures we are then artistically refreshed; we have been given a rare chance to experience the most complete possible match between the music and its probable aesthetic purpose – surely a worthy aim for the performance of music from any age. In such performances our faith in the ability of works to be renewed through new interpretations, far from being denied, is confirmed. Finally, present-day musicians provide a link between past performers and future ones. Through their attempts at authentic performance, they preserve responsibly what we know of the past for comparison and use by future musicians. This is not to say that all performances should be authentic ones, but at least some of them should be. In this way the present generation of performers will be able to serve not only an aesthetic purpose but an ethical one, as it acts out the role of curator as well as creator on the stage of history.

The Composer as Conductor

David Nice

Tchaikovsky would have called it fate, the rest of us sheer historical bad timing, that the art of recording came too late to capture his talents as a conductor. Too late, equally regrettably, for Brahms (whose well-known comment that he conducted his own works quite differently from performance to performance would be much more welcome with documentary evidence) or Wagner; much too late for Berlioz. And though each of these geniuses, heralds of conducting as we know it, was able to pass on the wisdom of interpreting their works to a younger generation who did record their thoughts for posterity, there can be no substitute for the way in which the composer puts into practice his own ideas and feelings about his own music – or, in a select few cases, the music of others. If he has perfected the conductor's technique (again, the lot of a select few), then so much the better. There are plenty of examples in the 20th-century recorded legacy both of the 'natural' and of the inspired communicator putting the point across with limited technical skills.

The three great late Romantics – Mahler, Elgar and Strauss – all have something to teach us; though while Strauss and Elgar made good use of recording, albeit relatively late in their careers, Mahler sneaks in, by proxy as it were, with four piano rolls made in 1905. They do scant justice to a man who was, by all accounts, one of the most phenomenally gifted conductors of his or any age. Two of the rolls, as featured on a fascinating issue promoted by that passionate Mahlerian Gilbert Kaplan, reproduce piano-playing of astonishing ineptitude. Never mind the wrong notes; the rhythms and the tempi are so uncertain that in adding her voice to the piano roll of the second of the *Lieder eines fahrenden Gesellen*, 'Ging heut' morgen', the mezzo soloist on the disc, Claudine Carlson finds it impossible to keep up with the composer-pianist. Mahler's jerky interpretation of the song finale to his Fourth Symphony, the charming child's view of heaven, also tells us little, I feel, about how he might have conducted the work.

One of the early songs, 'Ich ging mit Lust', is steadier; but what makes it all worthwhile is the composer's much more concentrated piano transcription of the Fifth Symphony's funeral-march first movement. This, too, is hardly free of wrong notes; but the underlying feeling for the lyrical lines and the implicit power of the climaxes shine through. Above all, there are some valuable indications as to the kind of precise articulation Mahler wanted. When Andrew Litton turned to the recording after having prepared his own interpretation of the Fifth Symphony, he was relieved to have a 'hunch' confirmed: 'I went for a slight delay on the triplet in the trumpet solo, as well as in the double-dotted rhythm, and Mahler plays it the same way – everything is pulled back just that slight amount. Here is proof that he means what he says on the printed page – but you never know how far to go until you hear an historic document like that.'

Litton is by no means the only one among today's more interesting interpreters to return to the composer's thoughts. Charles Mackerras was quite unabashed to acknowledge that his performances, and subsequent recordings, of the Elgar symphonies were inspired by listening to the composer's own interpretations. His Elgar Second Symphony, he warned the critics before a Barbican concert performance, would be faster as well as more flexible than usual, following the composer's ever-fluctuating tempi on the 1929 recording, and he would even attempt to re-create something of the original sound: more portamento (carrying the sound from note to note) and vibrato from the strings, and a brighter, more open brass timbre. Mackerras being Mackerras, of course, the performance was far from a pale carbon copy; but the pell-mell approach to the first movement's strenuous abundance of themes will not be to all tastes (nor was it the approach of that great Elgar disciple, Adrian Boult, in later years).

Certainly keen, nervous forward movement remains the keynote in both symphonies on the first of EMI's ambitious three volumes covering all the composer's electrical recordings (the acoustic recordings made between 1925, with reduced forces and the attendant re-orchestration as well as the occasional abridgement – fascinating in their own right – are available on a Pearl five-CD set). Inevitably, the piecemeal nature of the recording sessions means that white heat can't always be sustained; the Second, for instance, begins bracingly before temperatures momentarily drop at what would have been a 78 side-turn. But there are stretches in both symphonies that have never been equalled, like the last four minutes of the First's finale (the motto theme emerging with unparalleled power), the first of the great heart-on-sleeve tidal waves of the Second's funeral march, and the sonorous full strings of its terrifying Rondo. For a sample of Elgar as the great, effortless connector we have to turn to a live recording from 1927. The prelude to *The Dream of Gerontius* might have been moulded by Furtwängler; not even the exceptionally bronchitic Royal Albert Hall audience can halt its hallowed progress. Other gems on subsequent issues are the infinitely detailed *Enigma* Variations and an account of *In the South* which suggests that the opening exuberance, as realised with exceptional vividness by the 73-year-old composer-conductor, might be another self-portrait of the composer at his most self-confident.

More in the way of masterly conducting technique, and sometimes less in the way of sheer love and affection, come across in the performances of the veteran Richard Strauss. We have no recorded evidence of the wild youth upbraided by his father for 'serpentine gestures' unbecoming in 'a beanpole like you'. Yet three of the fresh and finely engineered recordings he made of his own music towards the end of the Twenties, with the Berlin Staatskapelle have appeared on Pearl, with a few seconds disastrously shorn off Till Eulenspiegel's 'Grosse Grimasse' in the transfer. The economical master Strauss had become by the last years of his life, with the volcano audibly bubbling below the surface, is extensively documented. Strauss was accused of indifference to his tone poems on occasions, and brisk speeds tend to fuel that impression: after a miraculously flexible opening, the 1944 Vienna *Heldenleben* rushes uncomfortably towards its mid-point. Yet the hero's home-coming, like the brilliant high-noon of the *Don Juan* from the same year, reminds us of how far the music has come, and the sustained tempo of the hero's withdrawal from the world has an absolute rightness no conductor since has been able to match. The *Zarathustra* shows us Strauss prepared to be magisterially broad when he feels the subject-matter requires it, and his faithfulness to his own metronome markings in keeping the *Symphonia domestica* on the move vindicates this most berated of the tone poems as a masterpiece, in spite of the very roughest sound. The detail is very often clearer than on many an artificially adjusted digital recording, and expressively so much more to the point.

Strauss is one of the few masters to leave us some of his thoughts on other composers. Mozart, one of his two musical gods (Wagner was the other), can sound surprisingly fresh in his hands. At times, this is an approach of which our own authenticists might approve for its swiftness and clarity, especially when those virtues flow untrammelled in Symphony No. 40; but the frequent ritards into lyrical second subjects, equating a change of tempo with a change of mood, are relics of the 19th century (Wagner began the practice, apparently, as an individualist's response to the uniform tempi and single dynamic levels maintained by another composer-conductor, Mendelssohn, simply to cover up orchestral defects). Never mind; Strauss's Mozart, even when it threatens to break all bounds, is always alive, the violin tone is a supremely focused hallmark of the Strauss style and in the *Jupiter* finale the performance lets all the myriad ideas hold sway before the resplendent final tying of threads. One other performance, of music by the other Straussian god, Wagner, is not to be missed. The prelude to *Tristan und Isolde* unfolds in that single breath that Strauss admired in the great Hans von Bülow's conducting of the piece, and which listeners in turn praised in his own performance; though there is also some masterly rubato allowed for the cellos' phrasing along the way.

If Strauss's conducting has any parallel among other composers, it's an unlikely one – with Igor Stravinsky. Both Strauss and Stravinsky favoured fast-ish, padding-free performances of their works, with excellent rhythmic definition. Although Stravinsky claimed that the rhythmic aspect was by far the most important in his self-interpretations, he shares Strauss's ability to give just the right amount of leeway to the melodic high points. And there are plenty of them in his early ballets, as his marvellously clear and alive performances of *Petrushka* and *The Rite of Spring* made in 1960 vividly proclaim. Earlier composer-conducted *Rites* – the first of them marked Stravinsky's recording debut with an orchestra in 1928 – offer a striking contrast, proving that even the composer is a different animal at various stages in his life. But although these recordings may be more exciting, the 1960 performance does bear out the composer's strictures about rhythmic definition. The same balance between passion and precision is highlighted in his approach to the pearly instrumental beauties of *Perséphone* and the second of his two unsurpassable recordings of *The Rake's Progress*; emotion is bounded, not repressed. Like Hindemith in his Fifties recordings of three great orchestral works (the *Konzertmusik* for brass and strings, *Nobilissima visione* and *Symphonia serena*), Stravinsky the conductor reminds future interpreters that the lyrical aspect of his music, the shaping of a line to make it sing, should never be underestimated.

With the extensive Stravinsky edition and the Hindemith performances, we move into the stereo era and what should, to all intents and purposes, be rightful territory for the main body of reviews. It is hard, even so, to resist one observation on Benjamin Britten's invaluable legacy of recordings, since it begs a question seldom raised by other composer-conductors. Technically accomplished and expressively eloquent as these great interpretations undoubtedly are, repeated listening – as well as the new-generation Britten performances that are beginning to emerge – suggests that the composer often toned down the sensuous high points and the moments of high drama in his operas: is this the disciplined prerogative of the well-tempered conductor, a point of view rather than a fault? Perhaps; but anyone engrossed in the Decca recording of *Billy Budd* may well find the malignant underswell rather muted – which is not to deny one of the great *frissons* of recording, the thrilling orchestral rush up to the interlude of 34 shattering chords at the heart of the work.

Perhaps as something of a corrective, I offer a personal choice – from a very long list – of two very different interpretations which do seem to realise the full emotional power of the works in question. In both cases the recordings were fairly close to the time of composition. One is Vaughan Williams's account of his seething, almost self-consciously dissonant Fourth Symphony. Reports of his conducting suggest no outstanding technical gifts, but all the same this is a quite astonishingly assured performance, moving from one angry peak to another with quicksilver orchestral precision. It puts Holst's 1926 recording of *The Planets* on the same disc quite in the shade: only compare Holst's scratchy 'Mercury' and Vaughan Williams's crackling Scherzo. Above all, there is a real sense of a special event, of a sustained strength of feeling which surely only the composer could achieve.

The same is true of Rachmaninov conducting his Third Symphony, where the first movement, shot through with the melancholy spirit of the homesick composer's native Russia, carries the same unique conviction. Here, though, the conducting technique is unquestionable. Rarely a bar passes without magisterial command both of every dynamic nuance and of the Romantic rubato built into the score; and yet it never sound mannered.

Rachmaninov's fame as a pianist turned out to be double-edged sword in the United States; his recordings of the four piano concertos, outside the scope of the present article, are peerless, and yet interest in Rachmaninov the virtuoso tended to obscure the achievements of the orchestral master. Only three specimens are left of Rachmaninov conducting (the other two, featured on the same RCA disc, are the orchestral version of the *Vocalise* and the tone poem chiller *The Isle of the Dead*). Even the Third Symphony, a desperate bid to prove the worth of his latest large-scale work, was recorded only on the strength of a promise that he would return to the studio as soloist in the First Piano Concerto. Its orchestral successor, the haunting Symphonic Dances which turned out to be the composer's swan-song and which he valued highest, should have furnished the last opportunity to hear Rachmaninov conducting in the recording studio; but a company executive, judging the work 'insignificant', vetoed the composer's request. Posterity curses this little man's judgement; but dwelling on the might-have-beens of recording history gets us nowhere.

There is at least one Rachmaninov-related happy ending. The premiere of the young composer's First Symphony in 1895 was a notorious fiasco, miserably under-prepared and by all accounts conducted in a drunken stupor by Rachmaninov's fellow conductor Alexander Glazunov. Posterity's curse in this instance has to be mitigated by a little miracle, even though it hardly helps Rachmaninov's case. In 1928 Glazunov, never to return to the Russian motherland he no longer recognised, visited London, where he was persuaded by a more enlightened record-company manager (Columbia's Joe Batten) to record his ballet *The Seasons*. Shabby and alcoholic he may have been, but Glazunov must have conveyed all the charm and wit of his score to the orchestra, and with considerable technique: for there is no other way to account for the magic of such moments as the whirling start of 'Spring'. Without this legacy – a one-off, like so many that space forbids a mention of here – we should have been in danger of consigning Glazunov to the rank and file of a composer who should never have conducted. As it is, he joined the roll of honour in the nick of time.

Top recordings mentioned above; outstanding performances are in *italics*

MAHLER

Mahler Plays Mahler – The Welte-Mignon Piano Rolls: *Symphony No. 5 – first movement: Trauermarsch*; Lieder eines fahrenden Gesellen – 'Ging heut' morgen'; Lieder und Gesänge – 'Ich ging mit Lust'; Symphony No. 4 – fourth movement: Sehr behaglich ('Das himmlische Leben'); Mahler remembered

Gustav Mahler (Welte-Mignon piano rolls), Claudine Carlson (mezzo-soprano), Yvonne Kenny (soprano)

Carlton Golden Legacy GLRS 101 □ 🎵🎵

ELGAR

The Elgar Edition, Vol. 1: *Symphonies Nos 1 & 2*; Falstaff; *The Dream of Gerontius – Prelude*; excerpts from two live recordings of 1927; The Music Makers (excerpts)

Margaret Balfour (mezzo-soprano), Steuart Wilson, Tudor Davies (tenor), Herbert Heyner, Horace Stevens (bass); Royal Choral Society, Three Choirs Festival Chorus, LSO, Royal Albert Hall Orchestra/Edward Elgar

EMI CDS 7 54560 2 □ ADD mono □ (3 discs) □ 🎵🎵🎵

Vol. 2, including *Enigma Variations*: EMI CDS 7 54564 2 (3 discs)

Vol. 3, including *In the South*: EMI CDS 7 54568 2 (3 discs)

STRAUSS

Richard Strauss conducts his own tone poems, Vol. 2: *Don Juan*; Till Eulenspiegel; *Also sprach Zarathustra*; Ein Heldenleben; Le bourgeois gentilhomme – Suite; Tod und Verklärung; *Symphonia domestica*

Vienna PO/Richard Strauss

Preiser 90216 □ ADD mono □ (3 discs) □ 🎵🎵🎵

Vol. 1: Preiser 90205 (2 discs)

STRAUSS

Mozart: Symphonies Nos 39, 40 & 41 (Jupiter)

Berlin State Opera Orchestra/Richard Strauss

Koch Legacy 3-7076-2 □ ADD mono □ 🎵🎵

STRAUSS

Wagner: The Flying Dutchman Overture; *Tristan und Isolde – Prelude to Act I***; Gluck (arr. Wagner): Iphigénie en Aulide Overture;** *Mozart: Symphony No. 40***; The Magic Flute Overture: Cornelius (ed. Liszt): The Barber of Baghdad Overture**

Berlin PO, Berlin State Opera Orchestra/Richard Strauss

Koch Legacy 3-7119-2 □ ADD mono □ ⨀⨀

STRAVINSKY

Ballets, Vol. 1: The Firebird; *Petrushka***;** *The Rite of Spring***; Les Noces; Renard; The Soldier's Tale – Suite**

CBC SO, Columbia SO/Igor Stravinsky

Sony SM3K 46291 □ ADD □ (3 discs) □ ⨀⨀

STRAVINSKY

The Rake's Progress

Alexander Young, Judith Raskin, John Reardon, Regina Sarfaty; Sadler's Wells Opera Chorus, RPO/Igor Stravinsky

Sony SM2K 46299 □ ADD □ (2 discs) □ ⨀⨀

STRAVINSKY

*Perséphone***; Oedipus rex; Ode;** *Monumentum pro Gesualdo***; The Flood**

Vera Zorina (speaker), Michele Molese (tenor); Columbia SO, Washington Opera Society/Igor Stravinsky

Sony SM2K 46300 □ ADD □ (2 discs) □ ⨀⨀

HINDEMITH

*Nobilissima visione – Suite***;** *Symphonia serena***;** *Konzertmusik for brass and strings***; Sonata for solo viola; Scherzo for violin and cello; String Trio No. 2; Clarinet Concerto; Horn Concerto**

Emanuel Feuermann (cello), Louis Cazuhac (clarinet), Dennis Brain (horn), Szymon Goldberg (violin); Philharmonia Orchestra/Paul Hindemith (viola)

EMI CDS 5 55032 2 □ ADD stereo/mono □ (2 discs) □ ⨀⨀

BRITTEN

*Billy Budd***; The Holy Sonnets of John Donne; Songs and Proverbs of William Blake**

Peter Pears, Peter Glossop, Michael Langdon, Dietrich Fischer-Dieskau; Wandsworth School Boys Choir, Ambrosian Opera Chorus, LSO/Benjamin Britten (piano)

Decca 417 428-2 □ ADD □ (3 discs) □ ⨀⨀

HOLST/VAUGHAN WILLIAMS

Holst: The Planets; *Vaughan Williams: Symphony No. 4*

LSO/Gustav Holst; BBC SO/Ralph Vaughan Williams

Koch Legacy 3-7018-2 □ ADD mono □ ⨀⨀

RACHMANINOV

The Complete Recordings, Vol. 2: *Symphony No. 3*; The Isle of the Dead; Vocalise; transcriptions, violin sonatas & piano music by other composers

Fritz Kreisler (violin); Philadelphia Orchestra/Sergei Rachmaninov

RCA Victor Gold Seal 09026 61265 2 □ ADD mono □ (4 discs) □ 🕑🕑

GLAZUNOV

The Seasons (c/w Symphony No. 7)

SO/Alexander Glazunov

Pearl GEMM CD 9404 □ ADD mono □ 🕑🕑

This performance is also available on EMI CDC 5 55223 2, c/w Prokofiev playing his Piano Concerto No. 3 and piano pieces

Chamber

ARENSKY

Piano Trios Nos 1 & 2

Beaux Arts Trio

Philips 442 127-2 □ 63:15 mins □ ⊘⊘⊘

Tempered by Rimsky-Korsakov's orientalism and Tchaikovsky's eclectic refinement, Anton Arensky's pristine, elevated style is nowhere more arresting than in his two splendid piano trios. These richly sonorous, predominantly elegiac compositions are magnificently played by the Beaux Arts Trio. Recorded sound is of demonstration quality, and these sensational accounts deserve the strongest conceivable recommendation. *MJ*

BACH

Flute Sonatas, BWV 1030–5; Partita, BWV 1013

Stephen Preston (flute), Trevor Pinnock (harpsichord), Jordi Savall (viola da gamba)

CRD 33145 □ ADD □ 97:46 mins (2 discs) □ ⊘⊘⊘

Preston is master of the distinctive expressiveness of the Baroque flute – gentle tone, clear open notes contrasting with veiled cross-fingering, flexible intonation, differences between registers. The scale of his sound is critical in the three works where Bach squeezes a trio sonata's four players – two soloists, bass and continuo – into the hands of two. Flute and harpsichord treble must balance as equal soloists above the keyboard bass. Preston and Pinnock duet subtly in the heartfelt B minor Sonata, specially poignant because the flute cannot reach the lower key-note, but floats wistfully above it.

The second disc presents the conventional solo sonatas, gamba reinforcing harpsichord bass. Flute and multi-stopped gamba alone begin BWV 1033, stretching to the limit the search for colouristic variety. After the E minor Adagio, using every trick of intonation and vibrato, Preston rises superbly to a challenge

from Quantz in his treatise on playing the flute: 'No matter how difficult the notes performed may be, this difficulty must not be apparent in their performer.'

The minimal forces – a lone solo flute – in the final Partita creates, in the Sarabande especially, the most limpid of lyrical melodies, containing within it the substance of its own harmony. Time hangs suspended. *GP*

BACH

Die Kunst der Fuge; Clavier-Übung, Part 2

Gustav Leonhardt, Bob van Asperen (harpsichord)

Deutsche Harmonia Mundi GD 77013 □ ADD □ 131:51 mins (2 discs) □ ⊘⊘

Die Kunst der Fuge

Amsterdam Bach Soloists

Ottavo OTR C 48503 □ 70:25 mins □ ⊘⊘⊘

Bach never specified the instruments for *The Art of Fugue*. It has been recorded on harpsichord, organ, piano, string quartet, viols, brass ensemble, orchestra, wind band and mixed consorts. Perhaps it should not even be played at all: Albert Schweitzer described it as 'purely theoretical', Wilfrid Mellers dubbed it 'an abstract *demonstratio* of contrapuntal principle… Bach plays to God and himself in an empty church…'

In a fascinating note, Leonhardt spells out his reasons for choosing the harpsichord. Some arise directly from the score – additional parts in final bars, impossible for solo ensemble but no problem for keyboard. The clefs provide further clues, as does Bach's own description of a mirror fugue as 'for two keyboards'. For Leonhardt, the additional part here ensures 'that the second player does not have to play with one hand in his pocket'! His playing, with van Asperen, has an electrifying vitality. But the sheer contrapuntal wizardry, too, begins to spill over from cerebral to emotional appreciation – you can't after all wholly divorce structure from gesture. Leonhardt omits the final, incomplete fugue, but this mid-price box includes the partita and the *Italian Concerto* which constitute the second part of the *Clavierübung*.

The Amsterdam Bach Soloists, by contrast, describe their mixture of modern wind and strings as 'an undogmatic use of authentic interpreting practice'. They prove that *The Art of Fugue* isn't simply the apotheosis of an outmoded age, nor is Bach 'alone with God in an empty church' but speaking with an immediacy to appeal to us all. *GP*

BACH
Musikalisches Opfer

Davitt Moroney, Martha Cook (harpsichord), Janet See (flute), John Holloway (violin), Jaap ter Linden (cello)

Harmonia Mundi HMC 901260 □ 51:09 mins
□ ⊘⊘⊘

The Musical Offering – two contrapuntal ricercars (one in three parts, one magnificently in six), ten canons of varying complexity, and a trio sonata – is bound together by the theme of Frederick the Great. He gave it to Bach to improvise on when the composer visited Berlin in 1747. Frederick was a fine musician – a flautist. He clearly had a sense of musical humour too: his theme is subtly constructed with powerfully directional harmony at the beginning and end and a sinuous chromatic middle. Bach, too, displayed a sophisticated musical wit: one canon has the upper voice in double-length note-values – augmentation – and the sycophantic annotation 'May the king's fortune augment like the augmented notes', while beside the canon which creeps ever upwards he wrote 'May the king's glory mount with the ascending modulation'.

Not all the devices are audible – no ear can pick out a 'crab' canon, one voice imitating the other but backwards! Yet the performers approach them with such overt affection that contrivance does not mask musicality, while the trio sonata is rhythmically springy and gracefully shaped. A rather rumbly ambience, a little intrusive between movements, at least gives a sense of 'presence' to this challenging disc. *GP*

BACH
Musikalisches Opfer – Ricercar a 6 (arr. Webern)
see **ORCHESTRAL**: WEBERN: Passacaglia

BACH
Violin Sonatas, BWV 1014–19, 1021 & 1023

Elizabeth Blumenstock (violin), John Butt (harpsichord)

Harmonia Mundi HMU 907084/85 □ 119:55 mins
(2 discs) □ ⊘⊘⊘

The six Sonatas for Violin and Harpsichord, BWV 1014–19, contain some of Bach's loveliest music. These graceful, flowing duets were also among the most revolutionary works of their time, the first such pieces to free the harpsichord from its accompanying continuo role and grant it equal prominence with the violin. Sometimes the two are equal melodists, most strikingly in the canonic third movement of BWV 1015. Harpsichord right hand and violin copy each other so effortlessly that you could easily miss the contrivance, distracted, too, by the continuous semiquavers below. Elsewhere the relationship is less close, the violin singing its own line above a written-out accompaniment in BWV 1016. Sometimes each plays two independent lines above the bass – so the opening movement of the First Sonata achieves five real parts at times.

Blumenstock and Butt, playing Baroque instruments, highlight the music's sparkling charm while doing splendid justice to its more expressive moments such as the captivating Andantes in each of the first two sonatas. The second disc includes two traditionally disposed continuo sonatas, the bass-line augmented by Elisabeth le Guin (cello) and Steven Lehning (viola da gamba) respectively to create a refreshing contrast in timbre. *Graham Lock*

BARRAQUE
Concerto
see **CHORAL & SONG**: BARRAQUE: Le temps restitué

BARTOK
Sonata for Two Pianos and Percussion; Concerto for Two Pianos, Percussion and Orchestra (c/w Mozart: Andante with Five Variations, K501; Rachmaninov: Suite No. 2; Debussy: En blanc et noir; Lutosławski: Variations on a Theme of Paganini; Saint-Saëns: Carnaval des animaux; Ravel: La valse)

Martha Argerich, Stephen Kovacevich, Nelson Freire (piano), Willy Goudsward, Michael de Roo, Jan Labordus, Jan Pustjens (percussion); Amsterdam Concertgebouw Orchestra/David Zinman; Gidon Kremer, Isabelle van Keulen (violin), Tabea Zimmermann (viola), Mischa Maisky (cello), Georg

Hörtnagel (double bass), Irena Grafenauer (flute), Eduard Brunner (clarinet), Markus Steckeler, Edith Salmen-Weber (percussion)

Philips Duo 446 557-2 □ ADD/DDD □ 138:30 mins (2 discs) □ *🎵🎵*

Although it may seem somewhat extravagant to have both the Bartók Sonata for Two Pianos and Percussion and the later Concerto arrangement coupled on the same set, there are obvious attractions in being able to compare the respective merits of each version in such a convenient format. But even had Philips opted to separate the two works, I would still nominate the Argerich–Kovacevich performance of the Sonata as being pretty well unbeatable. Where in the opening, for example, other front runners, such as the impressive Heisser–Pludermacher partnership on Erato, seem content merely to explore the colouristic aspects of Bartók's dense chordal patterns, Argerich and Kovacevich achieve the same level of atmosphere, yet bring an added sense of harmonic logic to the proceedings. And, of course, with this particular partnership the sparks well and truly fly during the more percussive sections of the music.

The rest of the programme offers equally stunning playing with the Rachmaninov, Lutosławski and Ravel items from Argerich and Freire proving to be an absolute *tour de force* that never fails to take one's breath away. *EL*

String Quartets Nos 1–6

Tokyo String Quartet

DG 20th Century Classics 445 241-2 □ ADD □ 159:11 mins (3 discs) □ *🎵🎵*

In their breadth of expression and sophistication of means, Bartók's six quartets represent one of the pinnacles of the chamber music repertoire. It's hardly surprising, therefore, that their musical and technical challenges have attracted the attention of many a leading ensemble. Yet choosing the ideal recorded cycle has never been a straightforward process. One's instincts might suggest that recordings by native Hungarians, such as the legendary Végh Quartet (Astrée), get nearer to understanding the very essence of Bartók's musical language. Then again, those opting for technical bravado and amazing rhythmic precision would incline towards the Emerson Quartet's much-praised DG set, which in financial terms offers a particularly attractive proposition for incorporating all six quartets on to two CDs. Most convincing of

all, however, is the Tokyo Quartet. Technically every bit as impressive as the Emersons, their interpretations are far more probing, encompass a greater range of emotions and capture the native accents of the music to the manner born. *EL*

Violin Sonatas Nos 1 & 2; Contrasts

György Pauk (violin), Jenő Jandó (piano), Kálmán Berkes (clarinet)

Naxos 8.550749 □ 75:04 mins □ *🎵*

Bartók's Violin Sonatas must rank among the most challenging duo works in the repertoire, both for performers, whose technical and interpretative powers are stretched to the very limit, and for listeners, who have to grapple with music of uncompromising harshness. Over the years Gidon Kremer (on DG and Hungaroton) has proved to be a staunch ambassador for these works, but György Pauk and Jenő Jandó offer equally powerful renditions, and they appear to be perfectly attuned to the local inflections of Bartók's rhapsodic style. Together with *Contrasts*, in which Kálmán Berkes provides some stunningly virtuosic clarinet-playing, this disc represents wonderful value for money and should be snapped up without delay by all aficionados of 20th-century chamber music. *EL*

Cello Sonata in E flat; Legend-Sonata in F sharp minor; Sonatina in D; Folk-Tale

Bernard Gregor-Smith (cello), Yolande Wrigley (piano)

ASV CD DCA 896 □ 76:09 mins □ *🎵🎵🎵*

Arnold Bax is best known for his orchestral music, and his symphonies in particular, but in truth his output ranged across practically all the main forms, with the exception of opera. This disc, which adds some fine music to the catalogue, confirms the importance of chamber music at every stage of Bax's career.

All the pieces are works of quality. The *Folk-Tale* (1918) builds up to a fierce climax and is generally 'melancholy and expressive', the large-scale Sonata (1923) recalls the power of Bax the symphonist, particularly in the driving rhythms which open the finale, while the Sonatina (1934) is rather more modest in its scope. The *Legend-Sonata* (1943) has a splended sweep, looking back in style to the tone poem *The Garden of Fand* (1916), which it quotes. And the finale features one of Bax's finest tunes.

Bernard Gregor-Smith, best known as the Lindsay Quartet's cellist, brings a commanding assurance to this repertoire, aided by his wife and regular accompanist Yolande Wrigley. With its well-balanced recording and excellent documentation, this disc can be recommended to anyone wishing to explore some of the hidden treasures of British chamber music. *Terry Barfoot*

BAX

Legend for viola and piano
see Collection: English Music for Viola

BEETHOVEN

Cello Sonatas (complete); Variations on 'See, the Conquering Hero Comes' from Handel's Judas Maccabaeus, WoO 45; Variations on 'Ein Mädchen oder Weibchen' from Mozart's Die Zauberflöte, Op. 66; Variations on 'Bei Männern, welche Liebe fühlen', from Mozart's Die Zauberflöte, WoO 46

Joel Krosnick (cello), Gilbert Kalish (piano)

Arabesque Z 6656-2 □ 145:00 mins (2 discs)
□ *❂❂❂*

Joel Krosnick is best known as cellist of the world-renowned Juilliard Quartet, a position he has held since 1983, though he has concertised and recorded independently, both as recitalist and concerto soloist, throughout a long and distinguished career. Partnered by pianist Gilbert Kalish, Krosnick delivers the five sonatas at face value, allowing the music to speak for itself, unimpeded by received performing conventions. The first two, of 1796, a summation of rococo formulas, are deftly and imaginatively presented. The ground-breaking A major Sonata, Op. 69, came 11 years later, in the wake of the first three symphonies and much else; it was truly a work reflecting the ideology and aspirations of a new, revolutionary epoch, and these artists treat it as nothing less – their account is thrilling. Beethoven returned to the medium again in 1815; the two sonatas of Op. 102 are perhaps more economical and compressed in form, yet explore vast expressive horizons; Krosnick and Kalish probe far beyond the notes, inflecting phrase after phrase with sublime gravity and weight. This two-disc edition also includes deliciously pointed readings of the three sets of variations: Handel's *Conquering Hero* has rarely enjoyed such winning ceremonial at his home-coming, and seldom have the two sets of *Zauberflöte* variations been delivered with such zest, coyness and warmth. The recordings, too, are first class.

A highly attractive mid-price alternative offering all these works will be found on a two-disc set from DG Dokumente – miraculous performances from Pierre Fournier, recorded with pianist Friedrich Gulda in the Brahms-Saal of the Vienna Musikverein in 1959. Even by modern standards, the digitally refurbished CD sound is perfectly acceptable, given the prowess and inimitable authority of their musicianship. *MJ*

BEETHOVEN

Piano Trios (complete)

Beaux Arts Trio

Philips 438 948-2 □ ADD □ 174:58 mins (3 discs)
□ *❂❂*

The Beaux Arts Trio's more recent cycle of Beethoven's complete works for piano trio is unfortunately deleted at present, though one cannot believe that it will be out of the catalogue for very long. In the meantime, there's much to recommend in this earlier set which features the original personnel of the Beaux Arts Trio. Admittedly neither the engineering nor the interpretations are quite as sophisticated as on their subsequent recordings, though as always, this outstanding ensemble invests the music with great authority, offering insights not only in the familiar *Ghost* and *Archduke* Trios, but also in the equally inventive earlier works. *EL*

BEETHOVEN
Quintet for Piano and Wind, Op. 16
see MOZART: Quintet for Piano and Wind in E flat

BEETHOVEN

Septet in E flat, Op. 20; Quintet in E flat, H19; Sextet in E flat, Op. 81b

Jenő Keveházi, János Keveházi, Sándor Berki (horn), Otto Rácz (oboe), József Balogh (clarinet), József Vajda (bassoon), Ildikó Hegyi, Péter Popa (violin), Győző Máthé (viola), Péter Szabó (cello), István Tóth (double bass)

Naxos 8.553090 □ 74:15 mins □ *❂*

Another winner from Naxos, offering over seventy minutes of wonderful music, excellently played, and in superb digital sound. The performance of the Septet is genial, gracious and utterly in accord with the lordly demeanour of the work itself. These Hungarian artists play it with captivating vitality and idiomatic flair, and the CD sound is both naturally balanced and admirably detailed. The fillers, the seldom-heard Sextet for two horns and string quartet, Op. 81b, and the even rarer Quintet in E flat for three horns, oboe and bassoon, H19, receive athletic and committed performances. Beethoven is known to have presented a copy of the first horn part of the Sextet to Gustav Nottebohm, carrying the words: 'Sextet by me. God knows where the other parts are.' The taxing, high-register horn writing, perilously difficult using the modern valve horn, and still more elusive on the primitive natural horns of Beethoven's day, holds few terrors for these fine players, and happily there's no trace of the vibrato-laden woolliness often associated with Eastern European horn-playing. An outstanding budget release, in demonstration-quality sound – why pay more? *MJ*

BEETHOVEN

Septet in E flat, Op. 20
see also MENDELSSOHN: Octet in E flat

BEETHOVEN

String Quartets, Op. 18

Quatuor Turner

Harmonia Mundi HMN 911540/41 □ 148:30 mins
(2 discs) □ 🎵🎵

Listening to Beethoven's ground-breaking early string quartets played on period instruments, in an attempt to return to the spirit of so-called 'authentic' performance, can often prove more a disappointment than a revelation. Wavering intonation, scrappy, unrefined attack of lightweight bows upon recalcitrant plain gut strings, and a niggling concern that this is surely not the way the composer envisioned these works in performance, have all fuelled controversy, with most collectors opting for one or another of a plethora of 'safer' modern instrument versions. But now things have changed; the apocryphal notion of Beethoven as iconoclastic revolutionary infuses this outstanding cycle from the Turner Quartet, staunch authenticists who consistently outflank rival period accounts (even those of the Smithson Quartet, also on Harmonia Mundi). These are bristling, curtly doctrinaire readings; the emphatic urgency propelling the opening Allegro con brio of No. 6, and the heroic muscularity of No. 2 underscore another familiar dictum, as 'Napoleon bursts into the Classical drawing-room' (or rather his musical *alter ego*, the young Beethoven) with these works. The Turners proclaim his triumphant arrival, and assert that he's in no hurry to leave. The recordings, produced in association with France-Musique, are superb, and this remarkable two-disc set is yet more enticing at mid-price. *MJ*

BEETHOVEN

String Quartets in F, Op. 59/1 (Razumovsky) & in B flat, Op. 18/6; String Quartets in E minor, Op. 59/2 & in C, Op. 59/3 (Razumovsky)

Cleveland Quartet

Telarc CD-80229, CD-80268 □ **64:14 mins,**
69:26 mins □ 🎵🎵🎵

By the time Beethoven revisited the quartet genre some four years after the publication of the six works of his Op. 18, his own world, and indeed the world at large, had been shaken to its very foundations. But while the libertarian spirit of a new age rampaged across Europe, Beethoven's inner cosmos had been turned in on itself by the tragedy of encroaching deafness.

Each of the *Razumovsky* Quartets pays individual homage to the eponymous Russian count for whom they were written; it has often been suggested that Op. 59/1 (its finale is marked 'Theme russe', ensuring that no one could possibly miss the point) achieved for the string quartet much that the *Eroica* had already made a living reality for the symphony. The Clevelanders evidently share such a viewpoint in this nobly expansive performance, full of blinding insight and aspiration. This is coupled with their account of the final Op. 18 work. The second disc includes the remaining *Razumovsky* Quartets; the more cerebral entreaties of the E minor Quartet, Op. 59/2, contrast with a spell-binding performance of the Quartet in C, Op. 59/3; the finale of the latter, in which Beethoven extends virtuoso writing to unprecedented limits, is both majestic and physically exciting. Throughout these readings the Cleveland Quartet reflect our current *fin de siècle* perceptions of Beethoven, as did the legendary Busch and Végh Quartet documentations in former decades. Sadly, Telarc's projected integral survey of the Beethoven quartets will remain incomplete, as this phenomenal ensemble disbanded at the end of their 1994/5 season, although the remaining Op. 18 works have now been released. Since the journey remains unfinished, these performances merit the strongest possible commendation, and Telarc's state-of-the-art sonics deliver the music with awesome power and presence. *MJ*

BEETHOVEN

String Quartets in F, Op. 59/1 (Razumovsky), in F minor, Op. 95 (Quartetto serioso), in C sharp minor, Op. 131 & in A minor, Op. 132

Busch Quartet

Preiser 90172 □ ADD mono □ 131:25 mins (2 discs) □ 😊😊

The wonder of these accounts by the legendary Busch Quartet is that the spirituality of their music-making shines across sixty years of history, its Herculean power and authority undiminished, and its energy and integrity as spellbinding as ever. There's an air of sublime communion about the 1937 recording of Op. 132, and I doubt that any performance, before or since, has mirrored more poignantly the mood of benediction and gratitude of the great *Heiliger Dankgesang*. The C sharp minor Quartet, Op. 131, was recorded a year earlier; again, the galvanism and refinement of the Busch approach seems uniquely telling. Two middle-period works, Op. 59/1 and Op. 95 (the *Quartetto serioso*), receive monumentally powerful performances of rare heroism. So gripping and addictive is playing of this stature that one very soon grows to tolerate the inevitable limitations of the primitive HMV masters from which these excellent CD transfers have been produced. These recordings have a place in the collections of all who revere these cornerstones of western civilisation. Indispensable, and good value at mid-price. *MJ*

BEETHOVEN

String Quartets in E flat, Op. 74 (Harp) & in F minor, Op. 95 (Quartetto serioso)

Cleveland Quartet

Telarc CD-80351 □ 64:14 mins □ 😊😊😊

Beethoven's Op. 74 and Op. 95 string quartets are traditionally viewed as the bridging link, both structurally and spiritually, between the Op. 59 *Razumovsky* set and the series of late masterpieces. Though differing from one another in countless details, the pair form a very serviceable coupling, fitting comfortably on a single CD, and you're unlikely to find performances of greater stature and dignity than those recorded here by the Cleveland Quartet. Their playing is vibrantly idiomatic and technically superb: they have the collective and individual finesse and virtuosity to generate playing of galvanic impulse and contrasting other-worldly melancholia, though they are in superlative form (even by their own devastatingly high standards) in their uncompromising and highly dramatic approach to the F minor work, the so-called *Quartetto serioso*. The *Harp* Quartet is played with equal refinement and spirituality, and the Cleveland Quartet have been most beautifully and atmospherically recorded by Telarc. The shame of it is that, by the time this review appears in print, this world-beating ensemble will have disbanded, leaving incomplete what would surely have become one of the finest recent cycles of the Beethoven quartets. But what does exist of this projected series is phenomenally good. *MJ*

BEETHOVEN

String Quartets in E flat, Op. 127, in C sharp minor, Op. 131, in B flat, Op. 130, in A minor, Op. 132 & in F, Op. 135; Grosse Fuge

Tokyo String Quartet

RCA Victor Red Seal RD 60975 □ 202:06 mins (3 discs) □ 😊😊😊

From every standpoint these are exceptional performances, not necessarily supplanting those treasured traversals from the Talich and Végh Quartets in terms of overall grandeur of conception and freedom from contrived artifice, but often more polished and technically secure, and offering immeasurably superior recorded sound. The late quartets are transcendent masterpieces, having the greatest subjective impact on the widest cross-section of listeners, and the very public demeanour of these Tokyo performances won't suit everybody; neither will the heaven-storming intensity of the playing, particularly that of first violinist Peter Oundjian – his virtuosity and facility are amazing, though he does occasionally seem to work a little too hard to beautify textures aurally in a way that is sometimes at odds with the musical line.

But the glories of this set would be difficult to enumerate. To cite just one instance, the ethereal *Heiliger Dankgesang* from Op. 132, music somehow above and beyond any notion of time and place, bespeaks the empathy and intelligence of the Tokyo readings, in which the music, and not four individual personalities putting forward their views on a great work of art, is what registers most powerfully on the listener. The C sharp minor Quartet, Op. 131, is masterfully played, and few accounts rival this one in terms of raw emotionalism and breathtaking eloquence. The *Grosse Fuge*, Beethoven's alternative finale for Op. 130, demonstrates the superlative technical accomplishments of the Tokyo Quartet, and has been banded conveniently after the 'official' finale of Op. 130. Op. 135 receives a deftly intuitive yet profoundly questioning performance, again superbly insightful and tonally luxuriant. These are glorious realisations of works that changed the course of western art music, and continue to challenge and ennoble the human spirit almost two centuries later.

Recorded sound is magnificent throughout. While other quartets offer greater intimacy of expression – and arguably deeper, more profoundly spiritual interpretations – very few can rival the technical excellence of these performances. A highly recommendable mid-price alternative is the Lindsay Quartet's four-disc set on ASV. *MJ*

BEETHOVEN

Violin Sonatas (complete)

Itzhak Perlman (violin), Vladimir Ashkenazy (piano)

Decca Ovation 421 453-2 □ ADD □ 139:00 mins (4 discs) □ 🎵🎵

Collectors seeking a complete edition of the Beethoven violin sonatas in fine modern sound, offering performances of aristocratic compulsion and enraptured intimacy, should look no further than this set. The phenomenally detailed remastered sonics impart extra clarity and presence to Decca's original analogue masters, which yielded excellent results, even on LP. Perlman's playing is a model of precision and elegance; his fine-spun tone is never forced or ungratifying, while Ashkenazy's contributions are as apposite, eloquent and powerful as one could wish. What impresses, perhaps above all else here, is the high degree of intimacy and freshness in each of these performances; the pair are at their most volatile and extrovert in the heroic *Kreutzer* Sonata, where the fervour and magnanimity of their playing say much about the way this music threatens to burst free of the formal restraints imposed upon it, aspiring towards true symphonic utterance. But less imposing horizons, perhaps in the courtly Op. 12 works, are no less touchingly surveyed by these master performers, who dance and charm the listener into delighted submission by the sheer elegance and wit of their approach. Nonetheless, the warmth and grace are always masterfully controlled, and the authority and eloquence of these performances remain highly compelling. *MJ*

BEETHOVEN

Violin Sonatas (complete)
see also MOZART: Violin Sonatas

BEETHOVEN

Violin Sonatas in F, Op. 24 (Spring), in G, Op. 30/3 & in A, Op. 47 (Kreutzer)

Henryk Szeryng (violin), Artur Rubinstein (piano)

RCA Victor Gold Seal 09026 61861 2 □ ADD □ 68:56 mins □ 🎵🎵

Distinguished readings of the best loved of Beethoven's violin sonatas, coupled with the marginally less familiar G major Sonata, Op. 30/3. Szeryng's playing – high-flown, visionary yet never charmless or casual – is the perfect foil to Rubinstein's colossal presence at the keyboard. Rubinstein proves himself a willingly compliant and sensitive accompanist in the *Spring* Sonata, allowing Szeryng's captivating interpretation free rein. Their *Kreutzer* is memorable for its verve and corporate passion; athleticism and dignity unite in a splendid tribute to this unique artistic collaboration. CD transfers are a delight; the sound is brightly lit, though never coarse or edgy, and instrumental balance and perspective are sensitively judged. A fine mid-price reissue of these outstanding performances. *MJ*

BEETHOVEN

Violin Sonatas in A, Op. 30/1, in C minor, Op. 30/2 & in G, Op. 30/3

Gidon Kremer (violin), Martha Argerich (piano)

DG 445 652-2 □ 64:28 mins □ 🎵🎵🎵

Dazzlingly incisive, authoritative and eruptively impassioned accounts of the three sonatas Beethoven composed concurrently with the trilogy of piano sonatas (Op. 31) in 1802. The fine Sonata in C minor, the most compelling and mysterious of the set, is framed by more modest three-movement siblings in A and G major respectively. Kremer and Argerich address this intellectually demanding creation with deep understanding of everything that C minor tonality signifies in Beethovenian terms: the urgency, drama and gravity of their account is unforgettably persuasive. Kremer and Argerich astonish with the clarity and pulsating energy of their playing, at once confrontationally argumentative and provocative, yet always so blithely self-effacing and true to the intentions of the composer that one could hardly imagine this music played better. A remarkable feat, and splendidly recorded too. *MJ*

BERG

Lyric Suite
see also VERDI: String Quartet in E minor

String Quartet; Lyric Suite

Alban Berg Quartet

EMI CDC 5 55190 2 □ 47:18 mins □ 🍥🍥🍥

It was over twenty years ago that the Alban Berg Quartet first recorded their namesake's chamber output for Teldec with characteristically impressive results. Although those performances are still available as part of a mid-price boxed set, they are largely superseded by these 1992 re-makes, which bring an even greater emotional intensity to the impassioned lovesick music of the *Lyric Suite*. In addition, the Alban Bergs make light of the fearsome technical demands of the two-movement String Quartet and the manic fourth movement, Presto delirando, of the *Lyric Suite*. Definitive accounts by any standards, although it's regrettable that EMI could not have found some room for a few of the Webern chamber pieces. *EL*

Harmonia artificiosa-ariosa: diversi mode accordata (Partitas Nos 1–7)

Purcell Quartet

Chandos Chaconne CHAN 0575/6 □ 90:21 mins (2 discs) □ 🍥🍥🍥

If the 350th anniversary of the birth of Heinrich von Biber, the leading Austro-German composer before Bach, didn't quite take off in 1994 as the Purcell tercentenary did in the following year, this can only be due, surely, to Anglocentric chauvinism rather than to any musical inferiority on Biber's part. His range of activity may have been a little circumscribed, but within the field of violin-dominated instrumental music his imagination and resource are second to none.

Famed for their dazzling virtuosity and above all their 'wrong tunings' (*scordatura*), Biber's partitas maintain an astonishingly high level of invention, melodic freshness and quirkiness. Of these seven partitas, five use such abnormal tuning with remarkable effects on the natural resonance of the strings.

The playing of the Purcell Quartet is simply stunning: virtuosity so effortless as to be unnoticeable, and a sense of capricious fantasy so vital to the convincing projection of such highly personal music, veering from mind-blowing complexity to artless simplicity, often in the space of a few seconds. *Antony Bye*

Tragoedia; Five Distances; Three Settings of Celan; Secret Theatre

Christine Whittlesey (soprano); Ensemble InterContemporain/Pierre Boulez

DG 439 910-2 □ 76:01 mins □ 🍥🍥🍥

Tragoedia and *Secret Theatre* are two of Harrison Birtwistle's finest compostions. The former is the work by which he firmly established himself; like *Punch and Judy*, the opera it spawned, the piece is immediate in impact, often aggressive, its block-like, almost symmetrical structure makes it surprisingly easy to follow.

Secret Theatre, from what must now be viewed as this composer's middle period, was an important step towards a more complex and goal-directed approach. Its 'instrumental theatre' is further dramatised and clarified by the movement of players on stage. But, on disc at least, the piece is still a greater challenge; I suppose increased separation of the players would have sounded too artificial.

Two shorter, recent pieces for smaller forces complete a compelling disc. *Five Distances* for wind quintet finds Birtwistle in an uncommonly relaxed mood: more breathing space, more audible connections between lines. The first of the *Three Settings of Celan*, for soprano, two clarinets and three lower strings, is almost indulgent; elsewhere Birtwistle uses spare textures to more elusive ends. Sharply etched, responsive performances; in the songs, Whittlesey is passionate but clean and clear. *Keith Potter*

Violin Sonatas Nos 1 & 2 (Poème mystique); Baal Shem

Leonard Friedman (violin), Alan Schiller (piano)

ASV CD DCA 714 □ 68:55 mins □ 🍥🍥🍥

This was one of the last recordings that Leonard Friedman made before his death, and it is testimony to a fine violinist as well as to Bloch's extraordinarily evocative and understanding writing for the instrument. All three works date from the early Twenties, when Bloch wrote much of his strongest music. *Baal Shem* is his best-known violin work, a three-movement suite inspired by aspects of Orthodox Jewish life, its central movement the famous 'Nigun', a classic instance of this composer's powers of wild, improvisatory rhapsody. The Violin Sonatas are, however, equally characteristic. The extended and ambitious No. 1 is a work of considerable dramatic power, and the more frankly 'oriental' No. 2 might justly be compared to the great violin works of Szymanowski and Enescu. All in all this is a superb disc, with performances of utter commitment in vibrant and natural sound. *CM*

BOCCHERINI

String Quartets, Op. 2/1–6

Sonare Quartet

CPO 999 123-2 □ 69:09 mins □ 𝄞𝄞

Boccherini (1743–1805) is by no means as under-played and under-recorded as he once was, but he still awaits serious discovery by the record-buying public, and where his chamber music is concerned this must surely be due to the fact that few really first-rste ensembles have taken up his cause. That may well be about to change. On the evidence of this disc (and another superb one of early Mozart quartets), the Sonare Quartet are an *absolutely* first-rate group whose relative neglect by record companies is difficult to understand. In sweetness and variety of tone, in eloquence (and elegance) of line, as in their masterly control of instrumental blend, and their superbly coordinated individuality, they fulfil all the prerequisites of string-quartet playing at its finest. Of all current recordings of Boccherini's chamber music (and I've heard the lot), this strikes me as the only one deserving of a place in the top 1,000 with the one possible exception of the three-volume survey of the delightful guitar quintets by Zoltan Tokos and the Danubius Quartet on Naxos. *JS*

BOCCHERINI

String Quintets in F minor, Op. 11/4 in E, Op. 11/5 & in D, Op. 11/6

Smithsonian Chamber Players

Deutsche Harmonia Mundi RD 77159 □ 67:00 mins □ 𝄞𝄞𝄞

Guitar Quintets (complete)

Pepe Romero (guitar); Academy of St Martin in the Fields Chamber Ensemble

Philips Duo 438 769-2 □ ADD □ 156:15 mins (2 discs) □ 𝄞𝄞

Virtuoso cellist, chamber music collaborator and technical innovator, Luigi Boccherini wrote a vast quantity of chamber music, mostly at the behest of one or other of the various patrons who commissioned works from him, and much of which has now fallen into general oblivion. The neglect occasioned by the popularity of the string quartet and piano trio genres perfected by the Viennese Classical masters is only now being redressed, with many of Boccherini's finest works emerging on disc. His string quintets (he is generally credited with the invention of the format of the string quartet plus second cello, a format ennobled by Schubert) make attractive listening, especially when delivered with the kind of élan and authority brought to bear upon three of the best of them by the Smithsonian Chamber Players. The Op. 11 Quintets date from 1775, though in fact Boccherini composed well over 100 works in the form, the vast majority of which have not survived to find places in the repertoire; among those that have, the D major work, Op. 11/6, is perhaps the most imaginative and enjoyable of all. Subtitled 'dello l'ucceleria' (From the Aviary), its imitations of bird-song effects, huntsmen's horns, and even pan pipes are of great interest. The Guitar Quintets, written for the Marquis de Benavente, are no less attractive, particularly when played by Pepe Romero and the ASMF Chamber Ensemble; most were adapted from earlier chamber works, and this fine recording leaves one wondering why we hear so little of this composer today. Recorded sound and performances are exemplary in the case of both issues. *MJ*

BORODIN

String Quartets Nos 1 in A & 2 in D

Borodin String Quartet

EMI CDC 7 47795 2 □ ADD □ 66:22 mins □ 𝄞𝄞𝄞

No string quartet has a higher stock of sinuous and beguiling melodies than Borodin's Second, as Broadway and Hollywood so cannily acknowledged (*Kismet* is hardly a favourite of mine among musicals, but that's not to deny its effectiveness as a new home for many of Borodin's themes). This eponymous team's special virtue is to present the work not as a parade of good tunes but rather as a generous, seamless flow of melody; the performance is unsurpassable for grace of phrasing and a suppleness that is always subtly at the service of the music.

What the First Quartet lacks in sheer inspiration it makes up for in a wider, if sometimes more contrived scope; when a spontaneous Russian composer turns to academic devices, the result is never entirely happy. Still, the players make the most of the radiant special effects in slow movement and

Scherzo, and once again their carefully polished sweep helps to paper over any structural cracks. An earlier recording of the Second by the same quartet, though with previous violin personnel, forms part of an ideal Russian string quartet survey on Decca, flanked by Tchaikovsky's simple First Quartet – with the famous Andante cantabile that moved Tolstoy to tears – and Shostakovich's lamentatory Eighth. *DN*

BRAHMS/SCHUMANN

Brahms: Cello Sonatas Nos 1 in E minor, Op. 38 & 2 in F, Op. 99

Schumann: Adagio and Allegro, Op. 70

János Starker (cello), Rudolf Buchbinder (piano)

RCA Victor Red Seal 09026 61562 2 □ 64:43 mins □ 𝄞𝄞𝄞

BRAHMS

Cello Sonatas Nos 1 in E minor, Op. 38 & 2 in F, Op. 99; Sonata in D, Op. 78 (transcribed from Violin Sonata No. 1)

Maria Kliegel (cello), Kristin Merscher (piano)

Naxos 8.550656 □ 77:06 mins □ 𝄞

The 68-year-old János Starker brings a dignified naturalness of phrasing, and exceptional tonal refinement to both sonatas, though his account of Op. 38 has a severity and stoicism which bring the valedictory element in this work into sharper relief than is usual, providing stark, unblenching endorsement of the composer's searching remit in composing the piece. The Scherzo, aptly fleet of foot, sighs nostalgically in the central trio section, while the fugal finale has real breadth and authority. Starker's one-time teaching assistant at Bloomington, Maria Kliegel, plays with great imagination, and is less unyielding in approach; her accompanist, Kristin Merscher, though wholly competent, is no real match for Rudolf Buchbinder, yet the credentials of the Naxos are boosted by inclusion of the 'third' Brahms Cello Sonata, the transcription by Paul Klengel of the Op. 78 Violin Sonata. But Starker storms heavenwards in his heroically impassioned reading of the F major Sonata; this is intellectually taxing music, with an alarming plethora of balance problems to be overcome in performance, and Buchbinder handles the titanic piano part with compelling ease. Starker's coupling, the *Adagio and Allegro* by Schumann, an effective foil to the Brahms sonatas, is eruditely delivered in his incomparably majestic and forceful style. This

outstanding disc should satisfy every listening need, though Kliegel's impressive Naxos release offers fine performances costing less than half as much. *MJ*

BRAHMS/WEBER

Brahms: Clarinet Quintet in B minor, Op. 115

Weber: Clarinet Quintet in B flat

Richard Stoltzman (clarinet); Tokyo String Quartet

RCA Victor Red Seal 09026 68033 2 □ 67:16 mins □ 𝄞𝄞𝄞

The clarinet quintets of Brahms and Weber form an ideal coupling; stylistically and idiomatically polarised, the true character of each is abruptly crystallised when, as with this fine Stoltzman and Tokyo Quartet collaboration, both works can be appraised side by side. Both were created for great clarinettist-contemporaries of their composers; Weber's theatrically extrovert quintet of 1815 was intended as a vehicle for the skills of Munich-based virtuoso Heinrich Bärmann, while the autumnal valediction of the Brahms quintet would honour Richard Mühlfeld's artistry 76 years later. Stoltzman's account of the Weber, with the Tokyo Quartet, is an enthralling *tour de force* – his technical control in bravura passagework and elegant liquidity of tone and phrasing seem all but unsurpassable. His Brahms, too, is radiantly played; the burgeoning lyricism and grandeur are admirable, and this performance may be commended without significant reservation. Recorded sound is also excellent. A compelling alternative to Stoltzman, however, will be found coupled with Brahms's three string quartets on Sony (see p42): Charles Neidich's rapturously introspective partnership with the Juilliard Quartet emerges as more intuitive and affecting than Stoltzman's performance, and bears that rare hallmark of charismatic greatness. *MJ*

BRAHMS

Clarinet Sonatas Nos 1 in F minor, Op. 120/1 & 2 in E flat, Op. 120/2; Clarinet Trio in A minor, Op. 114

Michel Portal (clarinet), Boris Pergamenschikov (cello), Mikhail Rudy (piano)

EMI CDC 7 54466 2 □ 69:35 mins □ 𝄞𝄞𝄞

It was the 'polish and almost feminine sensitivity' displayed in the playing of Meiningen Court clarinettist Richard Mühlfeld which impelled an ageing, ailing Johannes Brahms towards the creation of his late, autumnally fruitful chamber works for clarinet: the Quintet in B minor, Op. 115, and the trilogy recorded here. Michel Portal's sensitive ears and creditable taste vouchsafe eloquence and plenteous incident in accounts of the two sonatas, Op. 120, which Brahms wrote expressly for Mühlfeld, and in which they frequently appeared together. Partnered by Mikhail Rudy, who scarcely puts a foot wrong throughout this disc, Portal's glowing tone and fervent commitment and understanding of this music support interpretations of stature and shapeliness. The pair are joined by cellist Boris Pergamenschikov in a heroic and strivingly urgent reading of the Clarinet Trio, Op. 114. First-rate playing, fresh and articulate, though the recording is slightly recessed, which minimises the risks of over-dominant piano sound, and contributes to the plush, well-upholstered sonic impression created by this disc. *MJ*

BRAHMS

Horn Trio in E flat, Op. 40; Clarinet Trio in A minor, Op. 114

Michael Thompson (horn), James Campbell (clarinet); Borodin Trio

Chandos CHAN 8606 □ **60:00 mins** □ ⊘⊘⊘

Splendid, ripe-toned accounts of the Horn and Clarinet trios by Brahms, from artists who clearly understand each other and, more important, appreciate the radiance and reserve of these works. Michael Thompson is heard to fine advantage in the Op. 40 Horn Trio, never an easy work to bring off, particularly if its full, expressive range is to be addressed without the piece sounding effortful and over-taxing. Thompson and the Borodins face searching rivalry from Barry Tuckwell, Itzhak Perlman and Vladimir Ashkenazy on Decca; the trio comes off quite magnificently here, though sits rather obtusely beside the César Franck Violin Sonata – strange bedfellows indeed, but illustrious performances nonetheless. Thompson's horn sounds deep both from Black Forest Glade and from the troubled psyche of a composer still expressing grief at the loss of his mother; a noble, often passionate reading from these performers. If you wish to obtain the Horn Trio on disc, then chances are that you'll also seek the Op. 114 Clarinet Trio as part of the same package. Canadian-born James Campbell plays authoritatively, and is very ably supported by the Borodins; cellist Yuli Turovsky gives notice of an eloquent, warmly idiomatic account to

follow in his superb first-movement soliloquy – as fine and compelling a start as anyone could wish, and early promise is never disappointed throughout the remainder of this performance. *MJ*

BRAHMS

Piano Quartets Nos 1–3

Isaac Stern (violin), Jaime Laredo (viola), Yo-Yo Ma (cello), Emanuel Ax (piano)

Sony S2K 45846 □ **128:00 mins (2 discs)** □ ⊘⊘⊘

Stern, Laredo, Ma and Ax, all world-class soloists, bring to the early pair of piano quartets, written during 1861–2, a grand, open-hearted manner and eloquent tonal refinement; the sweep and passion never preclude moments of introspection and seriousness, and every textual detail of these scores registers with pinpoint accuracy. Emanuel Ax is among the world's finest Brahms interpreters; his imposing presence at the keyboard is telling, for the power and dignity of his contribution lend imperious weight to these accounts. What is more remarkable, perhaps, is the sense of integration among the three string players, each of whom seems to share intuitively a common view of how the music should be performed – vibrato and tone coloration are sensitively matched, and the unanimity of weight, resolution and impact throughout their collaboration is outstanding. The C minor Quartet, Op. 60, the most urgently rhetorical of the series, receives striking advocacy here; there is much that disturbs in this work, bespeaking the composer's private aspirations and anxieties, and these artists debate such emotions with maximum conviction. Incomparable performances, and warmly, if rather closely recorded. *MJ*

BRAHMS/SCHUMANN

Brahms: Piano Quintet in F minor, Op. 34

Schumann: Piano Quintet in E flat, Op. 44

Jenő Jandó (piano); Kodály Quartet

Naxos 8.550406 □ **67:00 mins** □ ⊘

Another outstanding budget issue from Naxos, offering capable, dependably rewarding performances in serviceable digital sound. Jenő Jandó is a remarkable artist; he has the true measure of each of these works. The opening of the Brahms, with its repressed angst summarily released as the exposition gets under way, is strikingly atmospheric and powerful, although this massive movement loses something of its architectural cohesion and rigour when, as happens here, the big exposition repeat is omitted. The Kodály Quartet lack the tonal voluptuousness of their more glamorous rivals, but the *frisson* and energy of their playing is always impressive, and their urgency of commitment is never at issue. Jandó plays magnificently, and is probably at his finest in the Scherzo and finale, and in the stirring opening movement of the Schumann Quintet. Recorded sound is a little distant and un-focused, and the chosen venue, though warm and natural, is slightly over-reverberant; this tends to favour the piano in fortissimo passages, occasionally to the detriment of the strings. But the general impression created is inviting, and the performances are quite superb. At bargain price, this is a most appealing offering. *MJ*

<hr>

BRAHMS

Piano Trios Nos 1–3; Piano Trio in A, Op. posth. (attributed to Brahms)

Beaux Arts Trio

Philips Duo 438 365-2 □ 119:00 mins (2 discs) □ 🕫🕫

Now available at mid-price on the excellent Philips Duo label, the Beaux Arts's Brahms performances have a distinctive largesse of spirit and sonority which makes their accounts immediately attractive. This two-disc set has the added virtue of completeness; the Beaux Arts Trio have also recorded the A major Trio unearthed in manuscript form in Bonn during 1924, and issued posthumously in 1938, which most authorities now consider to be a work from the pen of the young Brahms. The performance of the B major Trio, Op. 8 (written 1853–4, but here in its substantially revised version of 1889), is spacious, impassioned and sensitive – Bernard Greenhouse's Stradivari cello lends plush support to Isidore Cohen's serenely cultured violin lines, and Menahem Pressler is commanding and compliant at the piano. The C major Trio, perhaps the freshest and most gratifying of Brahms's piano trios, is equally fine here; the Scherzo, in particular, is a delight. In the case of the imposing C minor Trio, there are valid alternative viewpoints, particularly from the famous partnership of Stern, Rose and Istomin, who recorded these works in the mid-Sixties (their performances have been reissued by Sony); although the Beaux Arts's performance is consistently well played, and is admirably warm and intuitive, other accounts focus deliberately upon the dramatic and volatile nature of this work. Still,

the sense of deep involvement and shared delight at revealing the many joys of these scores will ensure a wide and grateful audience for these recordings – at mid-price, there's nothing to touch them. *MJ*

<hr>

BRAHMS

String Quartets, Op. 51/1 & 2, Op. 67; Clarinet Quintet in B minor, Op. 115

Charles Neidich (clarinet); Juilliard String Quartet

Sony S2K 66285 □ 148:59 mins (2 discs) □ 🕫🕫🕫

The Juilliard Quartet, heard in the acoustically inviting Savings Bank Music Hall, Troy, NY, has phenomenal empathy with the Brahmsian idiom; these accounts are eloquently considered, passionately argued, and possess an opulent tonal sheen ideal in this music. Op. 51/1, its turbulent emotions repressed behind austere polyphonic formalism, is admirably calculated. Brahms's personal maxim 'Frei aber froh' (Free, but joyful), the dictum of his majestic A minor Quartet, Op. 51/2, assumes lyrically imploring gravity here; first violinist Robert Mann, one of the great quartet leaders of the century, has seldom sounded so beguiling. The Quartet in B flat, Op. 67, the summit of Brahms's attainments in the genre, receives playing of resounding impact and eloquence from these artists, who partner clarinettist Charles Neidich in a fastidiously cerebral account of the Clarinet Quintet, Op. 115. This is an exemplary reading, full of lush autumnal radiance, and a fine coupling for the Juilliard's charismatic performances of the three string quartets. *MJ*

<hr>

BRAHMS

String Quartet in B flat, Op. 67
see also SCHUMANN: String Quartet in A minor, Op. 41/1

<hr>

BRAHMS

String Sextets Nos 1 in B flat, Op. 18 & 2 in G, Op. 36

Academy of St Martin in the Fields Chamber Ensemble

Chandos CHAN 9151 □ 77:55 mins □ 🕫🕫🕫

String Sextets Nos 1 in B flat, Op. 18 & 2 in G, Op. 36; Theme and Variations for Piano, in D minor (arranged from 2nd movement of Sextet, Op. 18)

Isaac Stern, Cho-Liang Lin (violin), Jaime Laredo, Michael Tree (viola), Yo-Yo Ma, Sharon Robinson (cello), Emanuel Ax (piano)

Sony S2K 45820 □ 90:07 mins (2 discs) □ 🕫🕫🕫

Ardent, robust and nobly wrought versions of the two Brahms sextets from the ASMF Chamber Ensemble on a well-filled, radiantly recorded Chandos disc, and incomparably beautiful playing from Isaac Stern and friends, somewhat extravagantly dispersed over two full-price discs from Sony, no more generous a proposition for the inclusion of the piano transcription of the variation movement from Op. 18, played by Emanuel Ax. In truth, I shouldn't wish to be without either version; the Chandos disc offers palmy, luxuriant performances, heard in a fine acoustic setting (the Snape Maltings Concert Hall) whose distinctive properties enhance one's enjoyment of these accounts. The Op. 18 Sextet appeared in 1862; more public and celebratory in tone than its companion, it nonetheless demands minute attention to details if inner lines are to register as Brahms intended. Nothing is left to chance here, in a reading of compelling, unforced grandeur. Particularly memorable is the six-variation Andante, whose measured, processional tread has an inevitability ably revealed by Stern *et al.* The Academy team is very fine in the bucolic Scherzo, and in the finale (which Joachim felt lacking in both weight and rhetoric). Stern and company give a masterly performance of Op. 36. Published in 1866, this G major Sextet recalls the mixed emotions that followed Brahms's abortive engagement to Agathe von Siebold (her Christian name is enshrined in the opening movement) seven years earlier in 1859. Superbly recorded, but these Sony discs are less than well filled, so cash-conscious collectors will probably plump for the distinguished ASMF accounts from Chandos. *MJ*

BRAHMS

Viola Sonatas Nos 1 in F minor, Op. 120/1 & 2 in E flat, Op. 120/2; Two Songs, Op. 91

Marilyn Horne (mezzo-soprano), Pinchas Zukerman (viola), Martin Katz, Marc Neikrug (piano)

RCA Victor Red Seal 09026 61276 2 □ 56:32 mins □ 🎵🎵🎵

Incandescent beauty and commanding eloquence from Zukerman and Neikrug in Brahms's two Op. 120 Sonatas. The mellifluous, autumnal radiance of Zukerman's tone (aided by his exceptional 1670 Andrea Guarneri instrument) adds poignancy and gravitas to these readings. Like his 1974 DG survey with Barenboim, these performances were taped at New York's Manhattan Center. They are urgent, lavishly detailed interpretations, broad in concept and

emphasis, yet never vulgarised or overblown. The patrician ardour has mellowed somewhat, though these new performances prove the more satisfying option.

The F minor work is imbued with inner tensions which less probing musical intellects might readily overlook; these artists leave nothing unsaid, and the playing has its own blend of sinewy vigour, resignation and rhetoric. The E flat Sonata, a work suffused with a nostalgia and lyricism wholly typical of late Brahms, draws playing of intoxicating intensity and amplitude from this expert duo. These sonatas were originally written for clarinet in 1891, and the composer might well have reeled in astonishment at the glories revealed here in what is, after all, a secondary incarnation for them.

His reaction might have been similar had he heard Marilyn Horne's affectionate delivery of the two songs, Op. 91, fruits of a previous, though equally catalytic musical friendship with the Joachims. The earlier song anticipated the arrival of their first child, and features a medieval carol set as viola obbligato. The Rückert setting came much later, yet it became the first panel of this unusual diptych. These are coercively beautiful performances, and I can only endorse this release with unqualified admiration and gratitude. *MJ*

BRAHMS

Violin Sonatas Nos 1–3

Augustin Dumay (violin), Maria João Pires (piano)

DG 435 800-2 □ 71:50 mins □ 🎵🎵🎵

Augustin Dumay's patrician view of the Brahms sonatas gives his performances an irresistible inner compulsion and fervour. But even if the architectural and formal demands of the music can, in some measure, be served through mere rhetoric, no amount of hectoring and theatrics could ever prepare the listener for the crystalline beauty and logic of this playing. The G major Sonata, Op. 78, arguably the least demonstrative of the three, responds well to Dumay's relative understatement, with the result that its thematic unity is clarified. Pires is quite superb here, and the empathetic spirit of true communion displayed by this duo is uncannily affecting.

Dumay's bounding, surgingly vivacious reading of the A major Sonata never lacks intimacy and introspection, but remains above all else a triumphantly songful, persuasively nuanced interpretation of a work containing references to three of Brahms's early Lieder.

Contrastingly defiant and challenging in mood, the Sonata in D minor receives a performance of intense drama and resolution; the repressed tensions of the work are seldom relieved, even during the sublime Adagio. With just over 70 minutes of music, DG might have included the Scherzo from the *FAE* Sonata, though completeness is sacrificed at minimal cost, given the magisterial rewards of this disc. *MJ*

BRIDGE

Pensiero; Allegro appassionato
see Collection: English Music for Viola

BRIDGE

Piano Trio No. 2; Phantasie Trio in C minor; Phantasie Piano Quartet in F sharp minor

Dartington Piano Trio; Patrick Ireland (viola)

Hyperion CDA 66279 □ 65:54 mins □ 𝄢𝄢𝄢

Frank Bridge's late chamber works probably represent his most profound and individual contribution to the repertoire. The deep expressive feelings aroused by his attempts to come to grips with the stylistic advances of contemporary European music, and to orientate himself in the restless, brittle postwar world of the Twenties and Thirties are embodied in particularly powerful and cogent form in the Second Piano Trio (1929). Though his last two string quartets are equally important, this is quintessential 'late Bridge'. Its two movements are visionary but also deeply shadowed, intensely evocative of haunted landscapes on moonless nights, composed in an attenuated manner of almost crystalline clarity, where a few notes count for much. Yet it's conceived on a large scale, and its climaxes have a heroic sweep.

The Dartington Trio's advocacy of this difficult work is superbly sensitive, outclassing the Borodin Trio's rival version on Chandos. Their coupling – the early Phantasie Trio (1907) and the Piano Quartet of 1911 – show the vast distance Bridge had travelled in the intervening years, for these mellifluous and enjoyable works reveal him as, of all the British composers of his time, the nearest to Fauré in his aesthetic. Hyperion's recording is outstanding. *CM*

BRITTEN

Cello Sonata; Cello Suites Nos 1 & 2

Mstislav Rostropovich (cello), Benjamin Britten (piano)

Decca London 421 859-2 □ ADD □ 68:18 mins
□ 𝄢𝄢

It's a matter of some regret that as yet Rostropovich hasn't recorded the third of Britten's three Suites for Unaccompanied Cello, and for those who prefer to hear this work alongside its neighbours, I would strongly recommend Timothy Hugh's outstanding performances on Hyperion. Indeed, there are moments, particularly in the First Suite's recurring Canto, where Hugh shapes the awkward double-stop passages in an even more convincing manner than Rostropovich, though nobody quite brings off the technical high jinks of the work's concluding Moto perpetuo with the same degree of aplomb as the Russian master. In the Cello Sonata, few present-day performers rival Rostropovich and Britten in extracting so much from this emotionally elusive music. For this alone, the present release is absolutely mandatory. *EL*

BRITTEN

String Quartets Nos 2 & 3

Britten Quartet

Collins 10252 □ 63:35 mins □ 𝄢𝄢𝄢

Both these quartets are crowned by magnificent and powerful finales in variation form – the Second paying homage to Purcell with a wonderfully sustained chacony, the Third culminating in an extended passacaglia that reverberates with haunting echoes of the composer's final opera, *Death in Venice*. Over the years there have been some impressive recordings of these works, not least those from the Amadeus Quartet (on Decca) and the Lindsays (on ASV) whose account of the Third is exceptionally moving. But for the most stimulating playing of all I would turn to the Britten Quartet. Not everyone will appreciate their red-blooded approach to the music. But the extreme intensity of expression generated by such interpretations causes one to look anew at these works, realising that a more fragile mode of expression lies beneath their surface brilliance. *EL*

BRUCKNER

String Quintet; String Quartet; Intermezzo in D minor; Rondo in C minor

L'Archibudelli

Sony SK 66251 □ 75:37 mins □ 𝄢𝄢𝄢

A magnificent issue devoted to Bruckner's complete string chamber music. Bruckner contemptuously described the Quartet and Rondo of 1862 as 'exercises', but each emerges with greater substance in admirable readings from the splendid Dutch ensemble, L'Archibudelli. Its account of the String Quintet is arguably the finest available, and instantly eclipses the Raphael Ensemble's recent Hyperion performance. An essential purchase for all dedicated Brucknerians. *MJ*

Trio Sonatas, Op. 1/2, 4 & 6, Op. 2/2 & 3

Trio Sonnerie

ASV Gaudeamus CD GAU 110 □ 47:00 mins
□ ❷❷❷

Although Buxtehude's reputation rests now, as in his lifetime, on his organ music, his only publications were some sets of trio sonatas. They are structurally quite conservative – up to a dozen short sections rather than three or four extended movements. Their scoring, though, is quite unusual. Instead of two equal treble instruments above a continuo, they employ violin and viola da gamba. Sometimes these play as treble partners, meeting at the overlap between their respective ranges. Elsewhere they foreshadow in texture, though not of course in style, the Classical piano trio – treble in dialogue with tenor, as in the first Vivace movement on the disc. At times, there are a few bars of conventional solo sonata layout as the gamba reverts to its more normal role of doubling the bass-line.

The novelty of the instrumental timbres and the variety of their distribution make these five sonatas a constant delight – if too brief at only 47 minutes. Trio Sonnerie play them with a sense of great involvement and some mischievous humour – they're full of quirky motifs and witty exchanges – all within a nicely intimate recorded sound. *GP*

Eight Compositions (1948–93): Gra; Enchanted Preludes; Duo; Scrivo in vento; Changes; Con leggerezza pensosa; Cello Sonata; Riconoscenza per Goffredo Petrassi

Charles Neidich (clarinet), Harvey Sollberger (flute), Fred Sherry (cello), Rolf Schulte (violin), David Starobin (guitar), Martin Goldray, Charles Wuorinen (piano)

Bridge BCD 9044 □ 78:39 mins □ ❷❷❷

Elliott Carter's two major string/piano duos – the Cello Sonata of 1948 and the 1974 Duo for Violin and Piano – here balance six of the short works for one, two or three players, tributes and playful arabesques, which have so unexpectedly thronged his latest years of creativity. The result is an invaluable,

kaleidoscopic introduction to one of the liveliest instrumental minds of our time.

Fred Sherry and Charles Wuorinen fluently dispatch the four-movement Cello Sonata, the earliest and apparently most 'traditional' work in the collection. Yet this is where Carter first refined his ideas of metrical modulation, conflict and cross-purpose between players: mainstream Americana turning Cubist and many-dimensional. It's also eloquent, even gabby, and volatile in the sense of forever aspiring to flight. In the single-movement, mosaic-like Duo the torrential discourse continues without any reference to traditional tonality or structure, but Rolf Schulte and Martin Goldray here turn in a far more amiable and beguiling version of this rugged, mercurial work than Robert Mann and Christopher Oldfather on Sony.

The short pieces, from the guitar study *Changes* (1983) to 1993's *Gra* for clarinet in homage to Lutosławski, aren't exactly miniatures, but relaxed fantasies of tone colour and technique: 'tennis matches for the imagination' is the striking image in David Schiff's booklet notes. Amiably and insistently the pieces test the virtuosity of the individual instrumentalists, and the members of the Group for Contemporary Music rise joyfully to their challenges in nicely realistic, not over-bright sound. *CM*

Concert for piano, violin and string quartet
see RAVEL: Piano Trio in A minor

Chopin: Cello Sonata in G minor, Op. 65

Franck: Sonata in A (arr. Delsart from Violin Sonata)

Jacqueline du Pré (cello), Daniel Barenboim (piano)

EMI Studio CDM 7 63184 2 □ ADD □ 56:56 mins
□ ❷❷

Barenboim plays excellently, as one would expect, but it's Du Pré who reaches out and grabs you. From the moment of her first entry the immediacy is almost eerie, especially as this is no over-the-top 'throwing herself about' (a complaint often made in the earliest years of her celebrity) but a deeply considered and measured performance – almost excessively so. Chopin, despite countless corrupt performing traditions, was never a man to wear his heart on his sleeve, and this is one of his most concentrated and least ingratiating works. It cost him untold effort, and his interpreters here pay him the compliment of approaching the work with the utmost seriousness. The result, however, sounds strangely inhibited, despite its powerful intensity, and in purely instrumental terms Du Pré is not at her peak. The tone lacks something of its customary sheen, and the intonation is uneven – and yet, and yet... the performance stays with one, drawing one back again and again to the music itself. And that's one measure of a *great* performance. The Franck is more obviously engaging, though the composer knew just what he was doing when he wrote the work for violin, but next to the Chopin it sounds rather too much like a curiosity. *JS*

CLARKE

Viola Sonata; Lullaby; Morpheus
see Collection: English Music for Viola

CORELLI

Violin Sonatas, Op. 5

Elizabeth Wallfisch (violin), Richard Tunnicliffe (cello), Paul Nicholson (organ, harpsichord)

Hyperion CDA 66381/2 □ 127:11 mins (2 discs)
□ *❷❸❹*

Corelli's reputation as a violinist is well documented by his admiring contemporaries, even though his sight-reading was apparently flawed – he's reported to have twice begun in C major a piece in C minor! As a composer his fame rests on a mere six collections, including this set of twelve sonatas for violin and continuo. Highly decorated versions of the simple solo lines of the first six pieces, supposedly 'composed by Mr A Corelli as he plays them' and published in 1710, provide a precious glimpse of his own practice.

The first six pieces are cast in the tradition of 'Church sonatas', alternating slow and fast movements, including some multiple-stopping. For these Paul Nicholson uses organ continuo, changing the colour to harpsichord for the following five sonatas – 'da camera' (chamber) sonatas with dances following an opening preludio – and the final one, a set of variations on the Spanish tune *La folia*.

The recording is intimate, the performance full of wit and nuance – coquettish delays at cadences, flexible tempi that never lose a sense of dancing pulse. Although such an archival collection is meant for dipping into, I found myself listening to the complete discs in two sittings. *GP*

COUPERIN

Concerts Royaux

Trio Sonnerie

ASV Gaudeamus CD GAU 101 □ 59:12 mins
□ *❷❸❹*

In his *Apothéose de Lully* published three years after these *Concerts*, François Couperin ('Le Grand') had Apollo declare: 'The combining of French and Italian taste must create perfection in music.' These four suites may owe their harmonic drive and impetus to Corelli but they remain thoroughly French in their grace, decoration and moods – *gracieusement, tendrement* (in a charming *Échos* movement), *naïvement*. Couperin published them on two staves, advertising them as suitable for keyboard alone. With right hand taking the upper part, the amount of continuo filling would be left to the taste – and available fingers – of the harpsichordist. Clearly, though, they are solo sonatas for violin (or flute/oboe) with the accompanying harpsichord bass reinforced by gamba. This is the solution here, very stylishly played by the Trio Sonnerie.

The *Concerts*, played at court to entertain the king, are elegant rather than profound. Yet some movements are very affecting – the Sarabande of the third *Concert* for instance, nearly five minutes of absorbingly gentle reflection. We sit, as presumably did Louis XIV, quite close to the trio, in a nicely intimate acoustic. (A warning – you need to add the incorrectly advertised index numbers together to find your way around the disc.) *GP*

DEBUSSY

Première rapsodie
see **INSTRUMENTAL**: Collection: The Glenn Gould Edition

DEBUSSY

Sonata for Flute, Viola and Harp
see FRANCK: Violin Sonata in A

DEBUSSY/RAVEL

Debussy: String Quartet in G minor

Ravel: String Quartet in F

Carmina Quartet

Denon CO-75164 □ 53:19 mins □ *❷❸❹*

A familiar pairing indeed. Debussy was approaching 31 and Ravel just 27 when these atmospherically polarised yet refreshingly congruent works were written. These irresistibly beautiful performances from the award-winning Carmina Quartet are outstanding. Indeed, there has not been a finer recording of these works since the legendary Quartetto Italiano LP version appeared some thirty years ago (their accounts made a welcome reappearance in the Philips mid-price Silver Line series – worth considering if Denon's higher price-tag is a deterrent). The

Carmina's virtuosity and its coercive sensuality during the slow movements ensures that you're soon bewitched by this CD, which will spend most of its time in, rather than out of your CD player. An unfathomable, wellnigh symbiotic alchemy is at work between these artists and these particular works, and Denon's recording seduces the ear as beguilingly as the music-making itself. *MJ*

DEBUSSY

String Quartet in G minor
see also RAVEL: String Quartet in F

DEBUSSY/FAURE/SAINT-SAENS

Debussy: Violin Sonata

Fauré: Violin Sonata No. 1 in A, Op. 13

Saint-Saëns: Violin Sonata No. 1 in D minor, Op. 75

Chee-Yun (violin), Akira Eguchi (piano)

Denon CO-75625 □ 63:04 mins □ 𝄞𝄞𝄞

Viscerally intense, compellingly assertive accounts of three masterpieces of French Romanticism, spanning the turn of the last century and, in the case of Debussy's Sonata, proclaiming a novel course and wider vistas of emotional concentration within this tried and tested genre. Debussy's final composition (he died in 1918, having written half of the projected series), his Violin Sonata is elaborate in range and style yet remarkably concise and economical, lasting around 15 minutes in all. The young Korean virtuoso Chee-Yun plays it superbly; it's a performance full of driving insight and incident, rich in tone and sensitivity, and immaculately accompanied by Akira Eguchi. The work is framed by a chaste, crystalline reading of the Op. 13 Sonata by Fauré, and by Chee-Yun's account of the first, and perhaps greatest, of Saint-Saëns's Sonatas, Op. 75, of 1885. Cast in a typically Beethovenian four-movement form, this tempestuous work demands much from both players; this performance is quite excellent in every way, and recorded sound is magnificent. *MJ*

DEBUSSY

Violin Sonata
see also FRANCK: Violin Sonata in A
and RAVEL: Violin Sonatas

DOWLAND

Lachrimae; Songs

Caroline Trevor (alto), Jacob Heringman (lutes); Rose Consort of Viols

Amon Ra CD-SAR 55 □ 62:37 mins □ 𝄞𝄞𝄞

Lachrimae

Parley of Instruments Renaissance Violin Consort/Peter Holman

Hyperion CDA 66637 □ 68:46 mins □ 𝄞𝄞𝄞

Although both these discs include the *Lachrimae* 'or seaven teares figured in seaven passionate pavans', they differ markedly in performance and in the selection of additional music. The Rose Consort alternate pavans and songs: '... though the title doth promise tears... yet no doubt pleasant are the teares which Musicke weeps, neither are teares shed alwayes in sorrowe, but sometime in joy and gladness...'

Caroline Trevor's clean, countertenor-ish quality, intonation spot on throughout, expresses perfectly Dowland's yearning chromaticism. Her words are coloured by a West Country burr, now believed to approximate to Elizabethan courtly speech. The Rose Consort accompany her and play the *Lachrimae* pavans at low pitch (modern G minor), creating with their superb tuning a rare richness of sonority.

The Parley Consort give you Dowland's 1604 publication complete: the seven *Lachrimae* together with 'divers other Pavans, Galiards, and Almands', played by Renaissance violins, Dowland's other option. A fifth higher than the Rose viols, the poignant pavans have a lighter character: the violins, though Dowland was self-confessed as 'semper dolens' (ever sorrowful), are more searing and less reconciled to despair than the viols. Both are wonderful accounts of this extraordinary indulgence in grief, illustrating vividly the capacity of great music to respond to contrasting interpretations. *GP*

DVORAK

Piano Quartet in E flat
see SCHUMANN: Piano Quartet in E flat

DVORAK

Piano Quintets in A, Opp. 5 & 81

Sviatoslav Richter (piano); Borodin Quartet

Philips 412 429-2 □ 68:22 mins □ 𝄞𝄞𝄞

Recorded live at the 1982 Prague Spring Festival, in the city's beautiful and historical Rudolfinum, these fine performances of Dvořák's two piano quintets first appeared in rather coarse-sounding LP format. It should be stressed that, even on CD, sonics aren't ideal; the Czech audience, though respectfully attentive, isn't totally quiet, and there's still a certain astringency and harshness about these transfers which might well prompt recourse to the tone controls of your amplifier. But the performances are incomparable. Richter, that most quixotically wayward among contemporary pianists, is heard at his brilliant best here, and the Borodins support him magnificently. Another plus here is the inclusion of the slighter Op. 5 work, premiered in 1872 but never published during the composer's lifetime, and rescued from obscurity fifty years later. Its more familiar successor, the great Op. 81 Quintet, was written in 1887; it receives spirited and mercurial playing here, with much thought given to the characterisation of individual movements – a stomping, earthily rustic Scherzo, and a tranquil, invitingly paced and glowingly reflective slow movement. The finale brims over with energy and local colour, and, despite certain reservations about the sound, this is a disc I wouldn't willingly part with. The Czech pianists Panenka and Firkušný, on Supraphon and Sony respectively, have their share of problems, too, and regardless of any nationalistic credentials their recordings vary in quality, and neither eclipses Richter and the Borodins. *MJ*

DVORAK

Piano Quintet in A, Op. 81

see also FRANCK: Piano Quintet in F minor

DVORAK

Piano Trios Nos 3 in F minor, Op. 65 & 4 in E minor, Op. 90 (Dumky)

Young Uck Kim (violin), Yo-Yo Ma (cello), Emanuel Ax (piano)

Sony Masterworks MK 44527 □ 72:00 mins □ 🎧🎧

Dvořák's piano trios have never enjoyed the widespread popularity they surely deserve; they are strongly idiomatic works, often with a fair helping of local Bohemian colour, and elaborately conceived with more than a hint of gratitude to Brahms, as in the case of the first to be heard on this outstanding disc, Dvořák's Trio in F minor, Op. 65. Compared to the *Dumky* Trio (which follows it here), this is an unjustly marginalised work, but a most enjoyable one nonetheless, and made more compelling by the insistent advocacy of the Kim–Ma–Ax trio, who perform it with electrifying panache and authority. Gloriously expansive and passionate playing from Kim and Ma constantly illuminates moments of rare genius throughout the score, while Ax is magnificent, particularly in his graceful under-characterisation of the charming second movement. Dvořák composed his Fourth (and last) Piano Trio in 1891. The work has never

been so well served on disc as here; these artists play with superb insight and authority, and there is no lack of either nostalgic melancholy or sheer power in their interpretation. *MJ*

DVORAK

String Quartets (complete); Cypresses; Two Waltzes, Op. 54; Quartet Movement, B120; Andante appassionata, B40a

Prague Quartet

DG 429 193-2 □ ADD □ 589:00 mins (9 discs) □ 🎧🎧

You'll unearth no finer large-scale survey of Dvořák's works for string quartet than this; and at mid-price this comprehensive edition, running to some nine CDs in all, represents excellent value for money. The performances, from the Prague Quartet (who, not surprisingly, have this music in their blood), are memorably full-blooded and consistent, though the sound varies in quality throughout the discs. What does become clear, though, is the fact that Dvořák found this medium difficult to master; that's apparent in the first three works recorded here. However, these discs provide the patient listener with the opportunity to trace Dvořák's growing mastery of structural and instrumental aspects of quartet writing. Still, with playing of such fire and steadfastness, not even the grossly over-inflated Third Quartet (some seventy minutes in length!) outstays its welcome and, besides, you'd be fortunate indeed to hear it, or any of its apprentice siblings, in the concert hall. The atmospheric miniatures Dvořák issued under the title *Cypresses* and the two Waltzes are welcome inclusions, but the quartet fragment in F, B40a, and Quartet Movement are no less fascinating, and recordings, while somewhat dated and occasionally erratic in quality, are wholly serviceable. For the Dvořák specialist there are rare prizes among these reissued Prague Quartet offerings. *MJ*

DVORAK

String Quartets in E flat, Op. 51 & in C, Op. 61

Chilingirian Quartet

Chandos CHAN 8837 □ 63:00 mins □ 🎧🎧🎧

These are able, warmly agreeable accounts of two fine Dvořák quartets, both of which have been to some extent overshadowed by the *American*. The E flat Quartet is spaciously conceived and presages something of the pastoral/lyric quality of Dvořák's Sixth Symphony, composed three years afterwards in 1880. The melodic material is never less than charming, though the Chilingirians feel its underlying earthiness and energy too; the first movement has forwardness and breadth, the second subject-group the more telling for its comparative ease and simplicity of expression. The mandatory folk-inspired Dumka draws a contemplative and poised response, though there's bustle and energy aplenty in the finale. The C major Quartet was written in 1881; predominantly high-spirited and strongly nationalistic in character (the Czech ambience is stronger here than in Op. 51), it receives a keenly responsive and intelligent performance from the Chilingirian Quartet who, if marginally less authoritative than the Prague or Talich Quartets, have the edge as far as recording quality is concerned. The Chandos sound is refreshingly natural and beautifully detailed, and the music-making is splendidly refined and well judged. *MJ*

DVORAK/SMETANA

Dvořák: String Quartet in F, Op. 96 (American)

Smetana: String Quartet No. 1 in E minor (From my Life)

Alban Berg Quartet

EMI CDC 7 54215 2 □ **54:00 mins** □ 🌑🌑🌑

At rather under an hour's duration, this disc might seem an expensive proposition at full price, but make no mistake – these performances are worth every penny, and more! The recordings were made at the Vienna Konzerthaus in 1989 and 1991, during live public concerts, and are of excellent technical quality throughout; audience noise is minimal, and the entirely natural acoustic aura surrounding the players is a delight to experience. From the outset one senses that the Alban Berg Quartet mean business in Dvořák's best-known quartet, the *American*. Thomas Kakuska's introductory viola melody has palpable excitement and intensity, matched impeccably as the theme is distributed among the other players. After an electrifying reading of the first movement, the nostalgically songful Lento finds just the right mood and pace; the impassioned central episode is unusually diverting, and the quiet soulfulness and resignation of the cello's concluding reprise of the main idea are affecting and appealing, as only a live performance can be. The Scherzo is cheerfully muscular, but coolly overcast during the Trio section, while the splendid finale is as bracing, vibrant and colourful as one could imagine. Smetana's autobiographical First String Quartet is made of sterner stuff: challenging, yet often disconcertingly

introspective in character, it provides an apposite foil to the *American* and receives a startlingly frank and tempestuous performance here. An expensive issue, but an indispensable one, offering playing of the highest calibre, and a fine recording to match. *MJ*

ELGAR

Piano Quintet in A minor; String Quartet in E minor

John Bingham (piano); Medici String Quartet

Medici-Whitehall MQCD 7002 □ **63:00 mins** □ 🌑🌑🌑

Wood Magic – The Life of Sir Edward Elgar in Words and Music (Violin Sonata in E minor, etc)

Paul Robertson (violin), John Bingham (piano), Barbara Leigh-Hunt, Richard Pasco (speaker); Medici String Quartet

Medici-Whitehall MQCD 7001 □ **73:00 mins** □ 🌑🌑🌑

Two outstanding discs devoted to the best of Elgar's chamber works, in splendid modern sound. Like the Cello Concerto, these works voiced Elgar's revulsion and dismay at the atrocities of the First World War, nostalgically, as in the A minor Quintet for Piano and Strings ('full of old times,' according to the composer), and with the noble, sonorous resignation of the String Quartet and Violin Sonata. Pianist John Bingham is impressively poised and thorough in the Piano Quintet; this grandly proportioned account is glowingly recorded, and contributions from the Medici Quartet are highly charged and utterly distinguished. They are also heard in an impassioned version of Elgar's E minor String Quartet, completing the first of these two discs; there is simply no better currently available recording of either work, and sound quality is magnificent. The Violin Sonata, Op. 82, is played by the Medici's first violinist Paul Robertson, accompanied by John Bingham; this affectionate and purposeful performance has more fibre and intellectual focus than Nigel Kennedy's Chandos version, and the disc is completed by a moving entertainment in words and music recounting events in the composer's life. Two splendid issues which no Elgarian would want to miss. *MJ*

ENESCU/BARTÓK/YSAŸE

Enescu: Violin Sonata No. 3 (dans le caractère populaire roumain)

Bartók: Sonata for Solo Violin

Ysaÿe: Solo Violin Sonatas, Op. 27/3 & 6

Sherban Lupu (violin), Claude Cymerman (piano)

Continuum CCD 1003 □ ADD □ 61:35 mins □ 𝄞𝄞𝄞

Enescu's Third Violin Sonata (1926), composed 'in the spirit of Romanian folk-music' but entirely on original themes, is one of his most individual masterpieces. Quite as uncompromising as the Bartók sonatas, and seductively impressionistic as Szymanowski's *Mythes*, it distils an extremely complex idiom, both harmonically and contrapuntally. Streams and flurries of rhythmically and melodically ornate decoration, notated with almost fanatical precision and often using quarter-tones, paradoxically re-create the wayward rubato, improvisational freedom and fantasy of the folk fiddler, within a highly sophisticated musical design.

Enescu himself recorded the work with Dinu Lipatti; Menuhin, his pupil, did so for EMI. There's a fine account by Adelina and Justin Oprean on Hyperion, coupled with the early, Fauréian Second Sonata and one fascinating movement from an unfinished sonata. But for virtuosic insight in thoroughly atmospheric modern sound my first choice would be Lupu and Cymerman. Lupu's solo couplings are first rate too: a thrilling, utterly authoritative account of Bartók's Sonata, and equally superb interpretations of two from Ysaÿe's set of six flamboyant unaccompanied Sonatas, published in 1924 and the nearest thing this century has produced to parallel the Bach solo sonatas and partitas. *CM*

FAURÉ

Cello Sonatas Nos 1 in D minor, Op. 109 & 2 in G minor, Op. 117; Serenade; Sicilienne; Élégie; Romance; Papillon; Après un rêve; Morceau de lecture, for two cellos

Steven Doane, Kurt Fowler (cello), Barry Snyder (piano)

Bridge BCD 9038 □ 61:13 mins □ 𝄞𝄞𝄞

Steven Doane is among the most interesting yet paradoxically most under-recorded of today's cellists. Direct comparison with the acclaimed RCA issue from Steven Isserlis and Pascal Devoyon finds Doane consistently more alluring and meditative, and Bridge's sound more immediate and transparent in texture, within a wider dynamic range. The accounts of the two sonatas are assured and impassioned; pianist Barry Snyder provides lithe, watchful accompaniments, and both artists approach this music with committed panache and intensity. Doane (an acclaimed solo and chamber musician, and former principal cello with the Rochester Philharmonic and Milwaukee Symphony orchestras) navigates his way through these uncompromisingly revealing scores with extraordinary subtlety, producing an exquisitely beautiful legato and breathtaking tone that few cellists (Isserlis included) have equalled on disc. The shorter works, such as the stirring *Élégie* and the mercurial *Papillon*, are delivered with outstanding insight and exemplary technical skill, though close microphone placement does convey some extra-musical sounds (such as Doane's periodically cavernous intakes of breath), as well as the magnificent sonority of the 1720 Tecchler cello used for this production, with exceptional fidelity. This release concludes with the seldom-heard *Morceau de lecture* (for two cellos) and is thus marginally more comprehensive than its RCA rival. *MJ*

FAURÉ

Piano Quartets Nos 1 in C minor, Op. 15 & 2 in G minor, Op. 45

Isaac Stern (violin), Jaime Laredo (viola), Yo-Yo Ma (cello), Emanuel Ax (piano)

Sony SK 48066 □ 66:54 mins □ 𝄞𝄞𝄞

More from this award-winning team of virtuosi, who prove as compelling in the two Fauré Piano Quartets as previously they did in Brahms's works for this combination. These are lithe, polished and, above all, deeply felt accounts of compositions that seldom appear entirely spontaneous on disc, probably as a result of the fastidiousness and chaste refinement of the material, and the obvious challenges of balancing rhetoric and weight of utterance without obscuring the contributions of the three string players involved. There are no such problems here, for these accounts are as cultivated yet passionately urgent as one could wish, and, moreover, recorded sound is in a class apart. Improbable as it may seem over a century after the event, the C minor Quartet, a work of profound grandeur and seriousness, at whose premiere Fauré himself appeared at the piano, was described as 'noisy and discordant', and rejected by two eminent Parisian publishing houses on the grounds of its avowed inaccessibility and vulgarity. But these artists reveal the boldness of a work which Florent Schmitt considered to be 'a masterpiece of taste and vivacity'. The Second Quartet, written in 1885, again receives an exemplary performance, combining dramatic incident and characterfully idiomatic lightness of texture, notably from Emanuel Ax, whose unforced yet authoritative approach is a delight. Masterful performances, and brilliantly recorded, though in a bright and occasionally over-reverberant acoustic. *MJ*

Piano Quintets Nos 1 in C minor, Op. 89 & 2 in D minor, Op. 115; Piano Quartets Nos 1 in C minor, Op. 15 & 2 in G minor, Op. 45; String Quartet in E minor, Op. 121; Piano Trio in D minor, Op. 120

Jean Hubeau (piano), Raymond Gallois-Montbrun (violin), Colette Lequin (viola), André Navarra (cello); Quatuor Via Nova

Erato 4509-96953-2 □ ADD □ 168:22 mins (3 discs) □ 𝄐𝄐

Erato's three-CD set under review here brings together Fauré's finest chamber works. The performances are generally superb, though there is a measure of disappointment concerning the rather harsh sound in these recordings dating from 1969 and 1970. But this set is attractively presented and most intelligently annotated – an unmissable bargain at mid-price.

Pianist Jean Hubeau features in all but one of these performances: an uncommonly perceptive, adroit and compelling artist. His readings of the large-scale Piano Quintets, Opp. 89 and 115, are superb. He is partnered by the Quatuor Via Nova, who contribute their own strongly idiomatic account of Fauré's three-movement String Quartet. Hubeau's impressively understated pianism adds distinction to refined performances of the two piano quartets, and the fine, emotionally turbulent D minor Piano Trio. All are performances of uniform excellence and genuine affinity with the intimate, deeply personal character of these works, the sole caveat being the dry, slightly harsh sound quality of these transfers. Piano timbre especially tends to be slightly tinny and bright, but judicious handling of the tone controls quickly puts matters right, and in any event the quality of playing throughout this set ably compensates for its sonic shortcomings. Highly recommended. *MJ*

Violin Sonatas Nos 1 in A, Op. 13 & 2 in E minor, Op. 108

Krysia Osostowicz (violin), Susan Tomes (piano)

Hyperion CDA 66277 □ 50:15 mins □ 𝄐𝄐𝄐

Forty years separate the two violin sonatas of Gabriel Fauré; the first, composed when he was 31 years old, is a volatile and affectingly lyrical work, redolent of the sensuality and optimism aroused by early romantic involvement, while its successor is contrastingly defeatist and introspective in character, occasioned as much by increasingly frail health as by the onset of the First World War. Violinist Krysia Osostowicz probes deeply into the mood of disquieted anxiety of the later E minor Sonata, though there are moments of optimism and nostalgia, too, particularly in her ebullient, impassioned reading of the finale. Osostowicz and her erudite partner Susan Tomes convey the ardour and exuberance of the First Sonata very ably; the playing is effortlessly nuanced and delectably rich-toned, and Hyperion's beautifully focused recording is demonstrably superior to the Philips CD transfers of classic accounts from Arthur Grumiaux and Paul Crossley. That mid-price release also includes Grumiaux's magnificent performance of the César Franck Sonata in an unquestionably distinguished package of the greatest French Romantic violin sonatas; that said, the comfortable intimacy of Hyperion's sonics and the keenly intuitive playing from Osostowicz and Tomes make their fine disc a more appealing choice. *MJ*

Violin Sonata No. 1 in A
see DEBUSSY: Violin Sonata

Quartetto intimo; Aquarelles; Lento quieto

Endellion String Quartet

Pearl SHECD 9564 □ AAD □ 53:03 mins □ 𝄐𝄐𝄐

Pungent, utterly original and torrentially inventive, John Foulds's *Quartetto intimo* (1931–2) is perhaps the greatest British string quartet of the inter-war period, surpassing even Frank Bridge's late quartets for incipient modernism with its polytonality, quarter-tones and Bartókian instrumental bravura, yet set in the context of an effervescent and wholehearted Romanticism. The quarter-tones turn up again (or rather much earlier) in 'The Waters of Babylon', the central movement of *Aquarelles* (1905–14), otherwise an irrepressibly tuneful suite of miniatures; and the *Lento quieto*, the only completed movement of the quartet Foulds was working on in India in the late Thirties, is a hymn-like nocturne of sublime and plangent beauty. This disc – the only version of all three works – was the Endellion Quartet's recording debut, and it has quite special qualities of fire and atmosphere in amazingly vivid sound. An unqualified recommendation to all interested in British music or the 20th-century string quartet. *CM*

FRANCK/DVORAK

Franck: Piano Quintet in F minor

Dvořák: Piano Quintet in A, Op. 81

Clifford Curzon (piano); Vienna Philharmonic Quartet

Decca 421 153-2 □ ADD □ 69:24 mins □ 🎵🎵

Although these recordings were made over thirty years ago, they have stood the test of time remarkably well – the Dvořák in particular has remained a top recommendation ever since it was first released on LP. The performance of the Franck Quintet, on the other hand, is more controversial. Some may prefer a more full-blooded approach to the first movement, but the relative restraint of Curzon and the Vienna Philharmonic Quartet is welcome, particularly in those passages that can so easily sound overblown. The players' lack of self-indulgence also pays musical dividends in the slow movement, and serves to make the finale, performed here with tremendous energy and commitment, a more structurally convincing conclusion to the work. By today's standards, the recorded sound is a little boxy, but with performances of this quality, any lingering reservations are quickly swept aside. *EL*

FRANCK

Violin Sonata in A; Pièce héroïque in B minor; Chorale No. 2 in B minor; Panis angelicus; Symphonic Variations; Les Éolides, Prélude, Choral et Fugue; Cantabile in B; Symphony in D minor

Arthur Grumiaux (violin), István Hajdu, Eduardo del Pueyo, Marie-Françoise Bucquet (piano), Pierre Cochereau (organ), José Carreras (tenor); Vienna SO/Uwe Christian Harrer, Amsterdam Concertgebouw Orchestra/Willem van Otterloo, Monte Carlo National Opera Orchestra/Paul Capolongo

Philips Duo 442 296-2 □ ADD □ 130:00 mins (2 discs) □ 🎵🎵

FRANCK/DEBUSSY/RAVEL

Franck: Violin Sonata in A

Debussy: Violin Sonata in G minor; Sonata for Flute, Viola and Harp

Ravel: Introduction and Allegro

Kyung-Wha Chung (violin), Radu Lupu (piano), Osian Ellis (harp); members of the Melos Ensemble

Decca 421 154-2 □ ADD □ 67:00 mins □ 🎵🎵

Few recorded versions of the César Franck Violin Sonata can realistically compete with these magnificent accounts from Chung and Grumiaux, either in terms of musical distinction or value for money. The performance of Chung and Lupu is electrifying; it comes on what is, to my mind, one of the finest examples of digital remastering of original analogue material, taped with the Debussy works during 1980. There's some dazzling fiddle-playing here; Chung plays with searing authority and commitment throughout, and she is wonderfully supported by Radu Lupu, for whom the titanic piano part clearly holds few terrors. This most attractive offering also includes the classic Melos Ensemble performance of the seductive *Introduction and Allegro* by Ravel; as improbable as it may seem, this account was committed to tape, and then to vinyl LP during the early Sixties, yet the sound is as fresh and natural as one could wish for, and the performance is utterly beguiling. Chung and Lupu, then, command a strong recommendation in the Franck Sonata, while the subtlety and variety of expression in their reading of the Debussy Sonata is hardly less compelling.

Arthur Grumiaux, surely one of the greatest interpreters of the Franck Sonata – an artist thoroughly steeped in the great traditions of the Franco-Belgian school of violin-playing, and heir apparent of the work's dedicatee Eugène Ysaÿe (for whom the sonata was written as a wedding gift in 1886) – made a memorable recording in December 1961 with the pianist István Hajdu. This nobly impassioned performance, a reading of sublime intellectual mastery and phenomenal architectural cohesion, sounds particularly impressive, despite its vintage, in the recent Philips Duo double-disc issue, *The Best of César Franck*. The Bitstream digitisation techniques applied to the original masters have added freshness and brilliance to the sound, which is nothing less than sensationally vivid and realistic, while the performance is utterly exceptional in all its aspects. You'd pay substantially more for any premium digital version of the Franck Sonata, but compared to the Chung and especially Grumiaux versions considered above, both of which are outstanding in every way, it would be difficult to justify any increased outlay. *MJ*

FRANCK

Violin Sonata in A (arr. for cello)
see CHOPIN: Cello Sonata in G minor

GADE

String Quartet in F (Willkommen und Abschied); Allegro in A minor; Andante and Allegro molto in F minor; String Octet in F, Op. 17

Kontra Quartet; Anne Egendal, Per Lund Madsen (violin), Sune Ranmo (viola), Hans Nygaard (cello)

BIS CD-545 □ 76:14 mins □ 🎵🎵🎵

Niels W Gade (1817–90) was one of the great figures of an illustrious 19th-century revivalist epoch in the history of Danish culture, popularly referred to as Denmark's 'golden age'. Born in Copenhagen, the son of a carpenter and instrument-maker, the young Gade developed an early affinity for the chamber works of Beethoven, Schumann and Mendelssohn, as second violinist of a student quartet. At 26, with a significant number of compositions already to his credit, Gade settled in Leipzig, where he developed associations with Robert and Clara Schumann, Joachim and Mendelssohn, whom he succeeded as director of the Gewandhaus Orchestra. His String Octet (1848) is a masterpiece of its genre; taking Mendelssohn's work for the same instrumental combination as his inspiration, Gade produced a work of outstanding quality and strength, though the remaining works featured on this superb BIS disc will prove even less familiar. The quartet movements included here were unpublished apprentice efforts, though they are tuneful and cohesive enough to warrant inclusion alongside the Octet and the Goethe-inspired F major Quartet *Willkommen und Abschied* of 1840. Eloquent and highly sophisticated playing from the acclaimed Kontra Quartet, ably augmented by four extra players for the Op. 17 String Octet. A magnificent release, which can only further a revival of interest in Gade's music. *MJ*

GIBBONS

Consort & Keyboard Music; Songs & Anthems

Rose Consort of Viols, Red Byrd

Naxos 8.550603 □ 68:24 mins □ 🎵

Gibbons was a master of dense webs of counterpoint; two six-part fantasias for viol consort on this disc tease and engross the ear. But best of all are the ten variations on 'Go from my Window', the opening phrase haunting the texture at unpredictable pitches.

Much of the playing and singing is lively in pace – techniques, and attitudes to period performance, no longer dictate a stately, reverential approach. The six voices of Red Byrd are very lively in timbre too, not least because they use a broad Dorset pronunciation, currently favoured as an authentic sound before the 17th-century 'great vowel shift'. So words, however clearly articulated, aren't always immediately comprehensible, and the booklet rather unhelpfully omits the texts. But it's good to have singers taking such matters seriously at last – as instrumentalists have been doing for years.

Another delightful texture is Tessa Bonner's solo voice amid the viol consort, taking one of the options of music specifically 'apt for Viols and Voyces'. Tim Roberts plays harpsichord, virginal and organ pieces with transparently detached articulation and fluent decorations. The whole assortment makes an ideal introduction to one of England's finest composers, still under-represented on record. *GP*

GLINKA

Viola Sonata
see SHOSTAKOVICH: Viola Sonata

GRAINGER

The Sussex Mummers' Christmas Carol; Arrival Platform Humlet
see Collection: English Music for Viola

GRIEG/SCHUMANN

Grieg: String Quartets in G minor, Op. 27 & in F, Op. posth.

Schumann: String Quartet in A minor, Op. 41/1

Petersen Quartet

Capriccio 10 476 □ 75:11 mins □ 🎵🎵🎵

Unheeded in the concert hall and neglected on disc, Grieg's G minor String Quartet, his only completed essay in the genre, receives unflinching advocacy from the Petersen Quartet. Their galvanic new performance eclipses rival versions from both the English and Guarneri Quartets. Widely censured for its quasi-orchestral effects and occasionally routine invention, the work is remarkable for its original (though much-maligned) scoring. It opens with a 12-part chord, dispersed throughout the voices using the double-stop techniques that give the work its unusually sonorous concentration and intensity. A thematic motto, taken from the 35-year-old composer's Ibsen setting 'Spillemaend' (The Fiddlers) provides a unifying focus throughout the quartet; the charming Intermezzo (in place of the customary Scherzo) includes traditional 'Hardanger' fiddle melodies. The posthumous F major Quartet was abandoned in 1891; the two extant movements were published in 1908 by Grieg's Dutch colleague Julius Röntgen. Both the Quartet in F and the youthful Op. 41/1 Quartet by Schumann receive performances which leave little to be desired. The Petersens are an excellent quartet, accorded a warmly atmospheric and frequently spectacular recording. A superb offering. *MJ*

GRIEG

Violin Sonatas Nos 1 in F, 2 in G & 3 in C minor

Dong-Suk Kang (violin), Roland Pöntinen (piano)

BIS CD-647 □ 69:04 mins □ ☺☺☺

'These three works are among my best, and represent periods in my development; the first, naive and rich in role-models; the second, national; and the third, having the widest horizons.' Grieg's personal observations, recorded in a letter to the poet Björnstjerne Björnson dated 16 January 1900, still serve us well in assessing these compositions objectively. Two decades separate the first two sonatas from the masterly C minor work, the finest of the set. Following Augustin Dumay's admirable DG release comes this one from Kang and Pöntinen; an outstanding issue, it now leads the field by a clear margin. Dong-Suk Kang plays with sweeping ardour, passion and admirable warmth. Tempi are alert, textures dutifully clarified (all credit to Pöntinen's superb handling of the piano parts), and the music is treated with a degree of commitment and instinctive authority which makes these creditable pieces sound a good deal more profound and thoroughgoing than one might normally imagine. The artists benefit from the entirely natural perspectives created by the BIS engineers; internal balance and clarity of piano voicings could scarcely be improved. An issue of technical excellence and absolute musical credibility. *MJ*

GUILLEMAIN

Violin Sonata in A, Op. 1/4
see LECLAIR: Violin Sonatas

HAAS/KRASA

Haas: String Quartets Nos 2 (From the Monkey Mountains) & 3

Krása: String Quartet

Hawthorne String Quartet

Decca Entartete Musik 440 853-2 □ 75:46 mins □ ☺☺☺

The music of the lost generation which died in Auschwitz is at last coming to wider public attention. Haas and Krása, both born in 1899, produced music of vision, humour and poignancy, much of which is touched by genius. This addition to Decca's Entartete Musik series of music suppressed by the Third Reich, which features string quartets by the two composers, is a revelation. Both men in their early twenties had an imagination and technical facility matching that of their compatriot Martinů; that they did not live to fulfil this promise and further enrich the Czech and European tradition is but one of the many crimes of Nazism.

Haas's Second Quartet (1925) often leans heavily on his teacher Janáček, but it is unfailingly ear-catching and shot through with true originality. Krása, four years earlier, is in his First Quartet even more challenging, though his musical language never turns the listener away. Haas's Third Quartet (1938) is both stirring and more integrated in style – a moving testament to Slavonic courage in the face of approaching tyranny. The Hawthorne Quartet play this music with a passion and feeling for idiom which radiates from every bar. Excellently recorded and presented, this is an issue which no one who cares about 20th-century music can afford to ignore. *Jan Smaczny*

HANDEL

Recorder Sonatas; Trio Sonata in F, HWV 405

L'École d'Orphée: Philip Pickett, Rachel Beckett (recorder), Susan Sheppard (cello), Lucy Carolan (harpsichord)

CRD 3378 □ ADD □ 67:56 mins □ ☺☺☺

I assume the seven sonatas for solo recorder and continuo here are all played by Pickett with Beckett joining him only for the last item, a trio sonata – the booklet isn't specific. Whoever is playing has quite remarkable breath control: after 25 seconds of continuous energetic semiquavers in the opening Allegro of the G minor Sonata, the phrase ends are given generous value where mere mortals would be gasping. I've yet to hear a continuo cellist get nearer than does Susan Sheppard to surmounting the extraordinary scramble in the A minor *Fitzwilliam* Sonata, and the last movement is very engaging, dancing at a lively tempo with light-footed ease.

Much of the music is borrowed. Anthony Hicks's notes include full details of whence – and whither much of it was later to go: Handel was never loath to reuse a good idea. The final Trio Sonata, though, has re-emerged through a happy find in the Library of Congress. Originally thought to be a duo for two unaccompanied recorders, Christopher Hogwood found its bass part, conjuring into existence a delightful ensemble, unique in Handel's output. *GP*

HANDEL
Sonatas, 'Op. 1'

Rachel Beckett (recorder), Lisa Beznosiuk (flute), Paul Goodwin (oboe), Elizabeth Wallfisch (violin), Paul Nicholson (harpsichord), Richard Tunnicliffe (cello)

Hyperion CDA 66921/3 □ 171:34 mins (3 discs) □ ❷❷❷

'Op. 1' is in quotation marks because there were two publications so titled. In the Seventies one was found to be a blatant forgery, made by the publisher Walsh to circumvent a royal copyright granted to Handel. Further research has weeded out some spurious pieces and added some more, producing twenty sonatas in all.

The scholarship is transmuted into sound of the highest quality here. Peter Holman's notes make the significant point that Handel wrote many of his sonatas while immersed in composing and presenting operas: the solo lines seem to reflect the virtuosity of his professional orchestral players rather than suiting amateurs in domestic performance. The flute sonata HWV 379, for instance, has a strikingly taxing Allegro, its single line leaping constantly beyond an octave to create two parts in one. Lisa Beznosiuk's slow playing is no less entrancing as she bends pitch and flexes phrasing with sensuous passion. Elizabeth Wallfisch generates tremendous off-the-string vitality, most of all in a remarkably high sonata, HWV 358 – perhaps meant for violino piccolo.

Here is all the 'Op. 1' you could ever want, in performances which, in the present state of the art, I cannot see beaten. *GP*

HANDEL
Trio Sonatas for two violins & basso continuo

L'École d'Orphée: John Holloway, Micaela Comberti, Alison Bury (violin), Susan Sheppard (cello), Robert Woolley, Lucy Carolan (harpsichord)

CRD 3377 □ ADD □ 66:42 mins □ ❷❷❷

L'École d'Orphée devoted six discs to Handel's chamber music, recorded in the early Eighties and thoroughly worth reissuing despite some problems with sound quality. The analogue original is rather astringent when transferred to CD – hi-fi buffs have a legitimate excuse to play with filters and graphic equalisers. Then, reasonably generous length is achieved by combining two recording occasions, not at quite the same pitch. So allow time between sonatas for pitch-awareness to dissipate.

These details can't mask the spirited playing, beginning with a mercurial performance of an early sinfonia in B flat. The notes point out a 'tendency to over-extend its musical material', which dates the piece but, for me, creates a hypnotic focus on the violins – and the cello, fully involved in the textures.

A trio in F minor is also an early work with angular lines, bizarre harmonic twists and dazzling virtuosity. It's an instance of Handel's bold, adventurous spirit revelling in the experience of Italy. Not that he became dull in his maturity, as the C major Trio from 1738 makes clear, beginning unconventionally fast rather than slow, and with a strange pre-echo of the 'Lift up your Heads' rhythm in *Messiah*. *GP*

HAYDN
Piano Trios (complete)

Beaux Arts Trio

Philips 432 061-2 □ ADD □ 754:00 mins (9 discs) □ ❷❷

This universally acclaimed survey of Haydn's piano trios was recorded over virtually a decade by the Beaux Arts Trio, for whom the Herculean undertaking was clearly a labour of love. These legendary performances do, of course, reflect performing conventions firmly rooted in our own era, rather than in Haydn's, but nonetheless the consistency and quality of playing is beyond reproach, and for once the virtues of completeness seem to override any concerns about stylistic or interpretative provenance. Now available in glowing digital transfers (the original Philips LPs could be relied on to offer superb sound in any event), and deployed across nine mid-price CDs, this set will provide a lifetime of unadulterated listening pleasure. Haydn composed 14 breathtaking masterpieces of the genre in the 1790s, and it is to this mature corpus of works that most attention has been directed over the years. But the Beaux Arts team lavishes as much care and affection on the slighter works of the cycle as it imparts to the readings of the great, mature trios; the performances are massively distinguished, and no other ensemble has assayed these decisive pieces with such unwavering authority and interpretative vision. *MJ*

HAYDN

Piano Trios, Hob. XV:12 in E minor, 13 in C minor & 14 in A flat; Piano Trios, Hob. XV:24 in D, 25 in G & 26 in F sharp minor

Patrick Cohen (piano), Erich Höbarth (violin), Christophe Coin (cello)

Harmonia Mundi HMC 901277, HMC 901514
☐ 69:52 mins, 47:15 mins ☐ 𝄞𝄞𝄞

Two exemplary discs devoted to six of the finest of Haydn's 45 piano trios, from this outstanding team of authenticists. The first disc includes searching, highly concentrated works dating from 1788–90. The second features trios dating from the period of Haydn's second sojourn in London in 1794–5, all of which were dedicated to Rebecca Schroeter, a young widow with whom Haydn had established a warm friendship during his previous visit to England in 1791. The music is exquisitely crafted; Hob. XV:24 is described by Rosemary Hughes as 'the most beautiful of all the trios… irradiated by that sunset calm that is so peculiarly Haydn's'. Its successor contains the aptly named *Gypsy* Rondo, while No. 26 includes a serene Adagio cantabile (unquestionably one of Haydn's greatest musical conceptions) of intense pathos and dignity. These discs form links into a complete survey of Haydn trios from these artists, using instruments of the period. Cohen, Höbarth and Coin astutely balance vigour, subtlety, elegance and fiery passion in readings of praiseworthy consistency and excellence. No Haydn aficionado should miss these fabulous offerings, in sound that's quite as brilliant and pithy as the playing itself. *MJ*

HAYDN

The Seven Last Words of Our Saviour on the Cross; String Quartet in D minor, Op. 103

Kodály Quartet

Naxos 8.550346 ☐ 64:29 mins ☐ 𝄞

Haydn's *Seven Last Words* are an adjunct to his great canon of string quartets. They began life in orchestral guise, following an invitation from a Canon of Cádiz to provide music for the Lenten devotions of 1786. Haydn directed the work in Vienna during 1803 at what proved to be his last public performance. You probably won't encounter finer playing than this, though I should not wish to be without the distinguished Astrée Auvidis performance, on authentic instruments, from the Quatuor Mosaïques; beware, however, for the price-tag will be significantly more than double the price of the Kodály Naxos issue! Now increasingly frail, Haydn wrote two movements of the last of his great series of string quartets (he never finished the work) later in the same year. These were issued in 1806 as Haydn's Op. 103; Haydn proposed a sad postscript in the shape of a pitiful canon to the words 'Hin ist alle meine Kraft, alt und schwach bin ich' (Gone is all my strength, old and weak am I). The two solitary movements sit eloquently aside the *Seven Last Words* here; it would be difficult to contemplate performances of greater intensity than these, from the superb Naxos edition of Haydn quartets played by the Kodály Quartet. The recording quality, too, is first class; rich, wide-ranging and beautifully atmospheric, complementing performances of serene, ritualistic gravity. Superb. *MJ*

HAYDN

String Quartets, Op. 20

Quatuor Mosaïques

Astrée Auvidis E 8784 ☐ 147:00 mins (2 discs) ☐ 𝄞𝄞𝄞

Haydn's six string quartets, Op. 20, collectively known as the *Sun* Quartets, were composed in 1772 and represent the summation of his earliest efforts in a genre which he created, to all intents and purposes, single-handedly. Inevitably overshadowed by the illustrious magnificence of his later quartets, Haydn's Op. 20 series was decisive, though perhaps more limited in both scale and historical influence – even so, the music is charming, and these performances will provide unalloyed listening pleasure. Outstanding here are No. 2, with its riveting, declamatory Capriccio; No. 4, memorable for its structural finesse and zestful final Presto; and No. 5, a work of searing intensity that finds restful solace in its exquisitely tender Adagio. The performers here are the French period-instrument ensemble, the Quatuor Mosaïques, who play these works with winning alacrity and natural, often deeply felt authority. The erudite and typically compelling insert notes by the distinguished Haydn scholar HC Robbins Landon are joyfully illuminating, and serve to give these already exemplary readings an imprimatur of scholastic respectability that's so often lacking these days. Strongly recommended. *MJ*

HAYDN

String Quartets, Op. 33

Coull Quartet

CRD 34956 □ 125:58 mins (2 discs) □ ⓐⓐⓐ

Illustrious music-making, displaying great refinement and unimpeachable technical mastery from the Coull Quartet, in their two-disc survey of Haydn's six string quartets, Op. 33. Haydn described the set, written in 1781, as having been written 'in an entirely new and special way', while the celebrated British musicologist Donald Tovey affirmed that 'no later set of Haydn quartets, not even Op. 76, is, on its own plane, so uniformly weighty and so varied in substance'. Two of the six quartets, Nos 2 in E flat and 3 in C, have, through the acquisition of epithets (the *Joke* and the *Bird* respectively), earned somewhat wider popularity than their peers, each of which contains countless master strokes of Haydnesque felicity of invention and sheer genius. The Coull Quartet have an uncommon affinity with this music; their performances are as fresh, amiable and thoroughly charming as any in the catalogues, but reveal the depth and magnanimity of each work with tremendous flair and authority. Slow movements are a particular joy, played with a purposeful gravity and flair that most of their rivals don't attain; the capriciousness, ardour and sighing melancholy of much of their material is deeply affecting. Roger Coull's imaginative cadenza in the concluding bars of the D minor Andante of Quartet No. 6, and naturally spontaneous embellishments in the thematic reprises elsewhere, are delightfully apposite, and these winning interpretations have been warmly and spaciously recorded. *MJ*

HAYDN

String Quartets, Op. 64; The Seven Last Words of Our Saviour on the Cross

Amadeus Quartet

DG 431 145-2 □ ADD □ 164:15 mins (3 discs) □ ⓐⓐⓐ

String Quartets, Op. 64

Kodály Quartet

Naxos 8.550673, 8.550674 □ 63:56 mins, 55:48 mins □ ⓐ

Haydn composed his six quartets listed as Op. 64 during 1790. These outstanding works have been frequently recorded, though never more brilliantly and perceptively than when addressed during the mid-Seventies by the Amadeus Quartet, then at the height of its fame. The DG recordings have been superbly re-processed for CD release of these memorable performances. The music sounds utterly beguiling, and playing is sensitive and highly distinguished, with the celebrated high-lying opening paragraph of Op. 64/5, the *Lark* Quartet, revealing just how fine these players were in their collective heyday. The set also includes an imposing account of the *Seven Last Words*, in the string quartet version of 1787, again excellently played and recorded. From the outstanding Naxos series devoted to Haydn's complete quartets come two superlative discs from the Kodály Quartet; this is perhaps the most impressive survey of the quartets to emerge in recent years, with phenomenal playing and particularly warm, atmospheric recordings presented at bargain price. Unless you particularly value the utterly distinctive Amadeus performing style as fundamental to the enjoyment quotient here, or require the Op. 64 works conveniently packaged as a complete set, then have no reservations about purchasing these astonishing Naxos discs, which offer performances of stature and superb sound quality at minimal cost. *MJ*

HAYDN

String Quartets, Op. 71

Kodály Quartet

Naxos 8.550394 □ 61:54 mins □ ⓐ

Written in 1793, and dedicated to Count Anton Georg Apponyi (hence the collective epithet sometimes given to this trio of Haydn string quartets), a member of an illustrious circle of Viennese intellectuals dominated by Baron von Swieten, the Op. 71 quartets occupy another generously filled bargain offering from Naxos. Taped in June 1989 at Hungaroton's Rottenbiller studios in Budapest, these accounts from the Kodály Quartet are largely beyond criticism; the flair and intelligence of the playing is a delight, and in matters of technical execution, style and precision these performances can confidently hold their own in the company of any in the catalogues. These are felicitous and admirably conceived interpretations; the players have a keen judgement of style, and the music is delivered with consummate good taste. There is, moreover, a palpable sense of joy and spontaneity which is sustained throughout every instalment of this remarkable series, and it is worth pointing out that, as budget issues, these Naxos disc offer stunning sound quality and first-rate documentation. From this present issue one need hear only the wonderful variation movement (Andante con moto) of Op. 71/3 to perceive the calibre of playing on offer in this irresistibly priced series. *MJ*

HAYDN

String Quartets, Op. 76

Kodály Quartet

Naxos 8.550314, 8.550315 □ 67:05 mins, 68:18 mins □ ⊘

More from the Kodálys, with superb accounts of Haydn's six quartets, Op. 76, dispersed across two phenomenal budget-priced discs. One can but marvel at the sheer inventiveness, wit and contrapuntal genius of these fabulous works. Three of the series, Nos 2, 3 and 4, have acquired nicknames, with the austere and dramatic D minor Quartet, known popularly as the *Fifths* (by reason of its constant preoccupation with this interval), generating a powerful response from these players. The *Emperor* Quartet, so called because its slow movement takes Haydn's own 'Emperor's Hymn' (then Austria's anthem) as the theme for a fine variation movement, and the so-called *Sunrise* Quartet, Op. 76/4, among Haydn's most harmonically sophisticated works in this form, receive performances of remarkable insight and brilliance. The Naxos recordings, too, are astoundingly good; admirably clear, warmly atmospheric and impeccably balanced. Why even consider paying more, when so much is offered for so little? *MJ*

HAYDN

String Quartets, Op. 77

Kodály Quartet

Naxos 8.553146 □ 51:22 mins □ ⊘

Just as Haydn completed these works, cautionary tremors presaging the most radical upheaval of the entire history of the quartet medium began to pervade the musical world. Artaria of Vienna published two quartets of a projected series of six commissioned by Prince

Franz Joseph Maximilian Lobkowitz (to whom Haydn's Op. 77 quartets were dedicated) in September 1802; it is generally conceded that Haydn's concerns over radical aspects of Beethoven's recent Op. 18 quartets (another Lobkowitz commission) precipitated his decision to abandon the undertaking. Thus, Haydn's Op. 77 quartets would be the last he ever completed; masterful, yet tinged with an element of nostalgic regret that's so often detectable in late Haydn, these lovely works are very ably presented by the Kodály Quartet. Their playing is robust, compellingly articulate and tonally opulent; there's no lack of expressive charm and warmth, and sound quality is first class. Illuminating, involving and splendidly charismatic performances. *MJ*

HINDEMITH

Septet for Wind
see **ORCHESTRAL**: WEILL: Violin Concerto

HINDEMITH/PROKOFIEV/WALTON

Hindemith: String Quartet No. 3 in C

Prokofiev: String Quartet No. 2 in F

Walton: String Quartet in A minor

Hollywood String Quartet

Testament SBT 1052 □ ADD mono □ 73:37 mins □ ⊘⊘⊘

These performances date from the earliest Fifties (the Walton partly from 1949), but they've never been bettered; you won't expect state-of-the-art sound, but what you get is a perfectly acceptable aural image and playing of wonderful insight, fire and intensity. Hindemith's Third Quartet is perhaps the finest of the seven he composed, and one of his most impressive creations of the Twenties. It was also one of the first scores to announce to the world that he was an intensely serious-minded musician, not just the expressionist shocker and satirist of his early operas and the *Kammermusiken*. Prokofiev's delightful quartet on Kabardinian folk-themes, one of his nearest approaches to the ambience of Bartók and Janáček, is given a performance of infectious vivacity and rhythmic spring. The Walton alternates soulful lyricism with spiky rhythmic pointing; these extremes have seldom, if ever, been as strongly conveyed as here. Walton told the Hollywood Quartet after their performance: 'I hope no one ever records my quartet again, because you captured so exactly what I wanted.' Among contemporary Quartets, the Britten (Collins), Coull (Hyperion), Endellion (Virgin) and Gabrieli (Chandos) all stand up well, but none surpasses this version; the Gabrieli, uniquely, also offer Walton's ambitiously experimental and abrasive early quartet, suppressed after its ISCM performance in 1922. The expert CD transfer puts the Hollywood's marvellous performances in the best possible perspective. *CM*

HUMMEL

Quartet in E flat for Clarinet, Violin, Viola and Cello
see WEBER: Clarinet Quintet in B flat

IRELAND

Violin Sonatas Nos 1 & 2; Fantasy Sonata; Cello Sonata; The Holy Boy; Phantasie Trio; Piano Trios Nos 2 & 3

Lydia Mordkovitch (violin), Karine Georgian (cello), Ian Brown (piano), Gervase de Peyer (clarinet), Gwenneth Pryor (piano)

Chandos CHAN 9377/8 □ 147:25 mins (2 discs) □ 🕭🕭🕭

When will the world of music reawaken to John Ireland? It's incredible that, at present, this is the sole recording available of some of these glorious, expansive Romantic works, brimming with memorable melodies. Ireland's most profound and personal voice is found in his piano music, songs and chamber works, the latter mostly dreamily gentle and softly free-flowing. The violin sonatas and trios are especially notable, containing serene, meditative passages that stir the heart deeply; the First Sonata (1909) is tuneful and genial, the Second (1917) a more vigorous, darker protest against the First World War, but with a radiant, affirmative slow movement second subject.

The darker mood also informs the Second Trio, which evokes war in the trenches. Interestingly, the collection shows themes developing from work to work; for example, the wistfully Romantic theme of the First Violin Sonata's final movement flowers fully in the meltingly beautiful Phantasie Trio. Ensemble playing by the three instrumentalists is very fine, the performances well shaped, relaxed and spacious (Ireland hated his music hurried and wanted all his many notes to be heard). Until Lyrita reissues the warm and inspired readings of Neaman, Parkin and Lloyd Webber, this splendid Chandos set is indispensable. *Ian Lace*

JANACEK

Capriccio; Concertino
see OPERA: JANACEK: Katya Kabanova

JANACEK

Mládí
see OPERA: JANACEK: From the House of the Dead

JANACEK/WOLF

Janáček: String Quartets Nos 1 (Kreutzer Sonata) & 2 (Intimate Letters)

Wolf: Italian Serenade

Hagen Quartet

DG 427 669-2 □ 51:29 mins □ 🕭🕭🕭

Janáček was nearly seventy when he embarked on the first of his two masterly string quartets in 1923, yet there is something profoundly adolescent about the searing passions – the musical expression of his overwhelming love for Kamila Stösslová, 27 years his junior – only just contained within such unconventionally satisfying frameworks. A complementary paradox informs the playing of the Hagen Quartet: old heads on young shoulders, so alert to all the subtleties of Janáček's poignant Romanticism and yet tougher than any other contenders with the hair-raisingly modern disruptions that continually break across its path. No quartet, for instance, saws into the *sul ponticello* (close-to-the-bridge) attacks of the First Quartet's inner movements more uncompromisingly than the Hagens, and only the Britten Quartet (EMI) realise more introspective heartbreak in the playing out of both love-affairs (the Tolstoyan tale of Quartet No. 1, the less fraught but even more passionate autobiography of No. 2).

Compared to the Britten's extra offerings (*Pohádka* for cello and piano and the Violin Sonata) or Radoslav Kvapil's performance of the half-hour piano suite *On an Overgrown Path* which follows the excellent Talich Quartet's readings on Calliope, Wolf's *Italian Serenade* may be short measure as a companion piece, but its lightly ironic perspective on love comes as a well-chosen relief after so much harrowing reflection. *DN*

JANACEK

Violin Sonata
see RAVEL: Violin Sonatas

KODALY/VERESS

Kodály: Duo for Violin and Cello; Sonata for Solo Cello

Veress: Sonata for Solo Violin

Sergiu Luca (violin), Roel Dieltiens (cello)

Harmonia Mundi HMC 901560 □ 70:21 mins □ 🕭🕭🕭

The vast majority of Kodály's chamber works date from the first two decades of the 20th century, a period when the composer, along with his compatriot, Bartók, was engaged in the study and assimilation of Hungarian folk-song. It's hardly surprising, therefore, that folk-idioms strongly inflect the writing of these two works, though their seemingly rhapsodic mode of expression is invariably balanced by a rigorous control of musical structure.

Many performers fail to convey this equilibrium, hoping that technical brilliance and intense emotional expression will simply carry them through. Fortunately, Luca and Dieltiens never fall into this trap – their performances are amazingly alive to all Kodály's expressive nuances, but they never allow indulgence to get in the way of musical logic. This is particularly true of the magnificent Sonata for Solo Cello, which is given a performance that is fully equal to the legendary Starker recording on EMI.

The inclusion of the short Sonata for Solo Violin by Sándor Veress, composed in 1935, is particularly welcome for demonstrating the fruitful continuation of folk influences in a younger generation of Hungarian composers. It, too, receives a dazzling rendition from Sergiu Luca, and makes me impatient to hear more from this unjustly neglected composer. *EL*

KODALY

Duo for Violin and Cello
see also RAVEL: Sonata for Violin and Cello

KORNGOLD/SCHOENBERG

Korngold: String Sextet in D

Schoenberg: Verklärte Nacht

Raphael Ensemble

Hyperion CDA 66425 □ 65:14 mins □ *♪♪♪*

These two works were premiered by an ensemble led by Mahler's brother-in-law, Arnold Rosé, concert-master of the Vienna Philharmonic and one of the leading advocates of the radical innovations of the Second Viennese School. Schoenberg's *Verklärte Nacht* is the seminal and in many senses the definitive harbinger of musical modernism, and is still widely perceived as having been decades in advance of its time. Yet while Viennese audiences found it hard to accept its unconventional and licentious style (Richard Dehmel's text, around which the work is constructed, provoked a scandal), Erich Wolfgang Korngold's lavish scores, with their overtly Romantic gestures and expansive melodies, were willingly accepted by contemporary audiences. The Sextet, one of the landmarks of 20th-century chamber music, was premiered in May 1917; its enraptured intensity and radiant optimism

presaged sinister developments in European politics – within years, Korngold (and Schoenberg) were victimised as 'non-Aryan' figures by the new Nazi regime. While Korngold would become one of Hollywood's greatest composers, the Sextet would not be heard again until rediscovered by the present performers in 1987. The Raphael Ensemble are superb in every respect; their performances have blazing commitment and integrity, and Hyperion's recording is in the demonstration category. *MJ*

KRASA

String Quartet
see HAAS: String Quartets Nos 2 & 3

LACHENMANN

String Quartet No. 2 (Reigen seliger Geister); Tanzsuite mit Deutschlandlied

Arditti Quartet, Deutsches SO, Berlin/Olaf Henzold

Auvidis Montaigne MO 782019 □ 64:53 mins
□ *♪♪♪*

Only for the strongest constitutions, perhaps. Or the most delicate? Few composers, apparently, are more suspicious of musical tradition than the contemporary German Helmut Lachenmann. An unreconstructed avant-gardist, he feels that our ideas of the beautiful are irredeemably fouled with cliché; he strives to reject all sounds with familiar qualities, comfortable or recognisable associations. His remarkable String Quartet No. 2 (1989) is half over before the first normally bowed tone is sounded; even then we hear the merest wisps of melody and ornamentation, against a continuous subliminal background of unpitched sonorities, *flautando* harmonics, ephemeral percussions with wood or fingers, or the bows' metal tension-screws on the strings. Yet the subtitle, 'Dance of the Blessed Spirits', alludes, surely, to Gluck's *Orfeo* – perhaps also to the wider legend of Orpheus, subduing furies and conjuring music from inanimate matter. The quartet's uncanny, spectral melancholy, its small, swarming sounds tremulous on the brink of musical speech, are ultimately very moving, and astonishingly interpreted here by the Arditti.

Musical history is further deconstructed in *Tanzsuite mit Deutschlandlied*, an 18-section work that filters the shards and bones of traditional dance movements (waltz, siciliano, tarantella and so on) through an orchestral fabric which, like the writing of the quartet, is largely percussive and alienated from itself. Much of the material derives, however distantly, from 'Deutschland über alles', and there are sidelong references to Bach and Schoenberg. In its rebarbative fashion this is a virtuoso work on the furthest reaches of orchestral sound, and the performance does it full justice. *CM*

LECLAIR

Overtures and Trio Sonatas, Op. 13

Purcell Quartet

Chandos Chaconne CHAN 0542 □ 70:11 mins
□ 🕓🕓🕓

Op. 13 was the last work published by Leclair before his murder in 1764. The leading pioneer of French violin music, he began his career as a dancer at the Lyon opera, and the elegance instilled by this training remained central to his music. When he was later attracted by the technical brilliance of the Italian violin school, his compositions developed into exquisite blends of French charm and Italian brio.

His mastery of both styles is evident in Op. 13, whose three *ouvertures* begin in characteristically French fashion – a courtly introduction followed by a fugal movement – while their companion *sonates en trio* adhere to the Italian slow–fast–slow–fast pattern. All six compositions are arrangements of earlier Leclair pieces, the third overture deriving from his only opera, *Scylla et Glaucus*. Its dramatic opening and scintillating second Allegro arrest the ear, and all three overtures have sweetly yearning slow movements. The third sonata is very attractive too, its Gratioso featuring the two violins in unaccompanied dialogue.

The Purcell Quartet specialise in Baroque chamber music. They mesh together beautifully here, and the closely entwined violin parts allow Catherine Mackintosh and her new partner Catherine Weiss to display their rapport to winning effect. *Graham Lock*

LECLAIR/MONDONVILLE/GUILLEMAIN

Leclair: Violin Sonatas in A minor, Op. 5/7 & in A, Op. 9/4

Mondonville: Violin Sonata in G, Op. 3/5

Guillemain: Violin Sonata in A, Op. 1/4 (c/w harpsichord works by Duphly & Forqueray)

Simon Standage (violin), Lars Ulrik Mortensen (harpsichord)

Chandos Chaconne CHAN 0531 □ 68:20 mins
□ 🕓🕓🕓

Leclair's music is more than the satisfyingly simple mingling of French and Italian styles

common in France in the first few decades of the 18th century. There are moments of harmonic and melodic richness which assert themselves independently of both traditions; always rich in effect, this music has a pleasing unpredictability. Nevertheless, spotting the Gallicisms and Italianisms can be fun, particularly when, for example, the former is so beguilingly apparent in the Tempo Gavotta finale of Op. 5/7.

Leclair's sonatas are joined on this disc by two enormously appealing works by his younger contemporaries Mondonville and Guillemain, along with two characteristically extravagant harpsichord solos by Duphly and one more moderate one from the younger Forqueray.

In terms of virtuosity and feeling for effect, Simon Standage is a near-ideal interpreter. His ability to tinker with the metrical fabric of these sonatas without doing violence to the music is a delight. The violin sound, perhaps as a result of the recording, is a touch acetic, but the ear soon adjusts. Lars Ulrik Mortensen makes imaginative use of the two manuals of the Blanchet copy he plays in accompaniments, and shines in his solos. Whether for dipping into or listening *en suite*, this is a highly recommendable issue. *Jan Smaczny*

LEIFS

String Quartets Nos 1–3

Yggdrasil Quartet

BIS CD-691 □ 75:37 mins □ 🕓🕓🕓

These three quartets epitomise Icelandic composer Jón Leifs (1899–1968) as the musical pioneer and free-thinker that he was. Written without preconception, they demand the same of their listeners. The First is an austere, ever-unpredictable single movement, based on the parallel fifths of the medieval *tvísöngur*, the passionate and searching Second, in memory of his drowned daughter, perhaps the greatest of them all. The Swedish Yggdrasil Quartet does Leifs proud in performances of real understanding and conviction.
Hilary Finch

LIGETI

String Quartet No. 1
see LUTOSLAWSKI: String Quartet

LUTOSLAWSKI/LIGETI/SCHNITTKE

Lutosławski: String Quartet

Ligeti: String Quartet No. 1 (Métamorphoses Nocturnes)

Schnittke: Canon in memoriam I Stravinsky

Hagen Quartet

DG 431 686-2 □ **54:00 mins** □ *⊘⊘⊘*

When it was first performed during the Sixties, Lutosławski's String Quartet raised many eyebrows for its use of aleatoric techniques where the individual parts were not synchronised in the conventional manner of the bar-line, but through a series of carefully designed instructions and cues. Yet far from creating a sense of anarchy, such freedoms actually enhanced the dramatic impact of the whole – a feeling that is triumphantly conveyed in the present performance. Equally compelling, though less obviously characteristic of its composer, is the early String Quartet of Ligeti – a work so imbued with the spirit and musical manner of Bartók that it could almost qualify for the honour of being labelled the Hungarian master's Seventh Quartet! Once again, the Hagen Quartet make light work of its formidable technical difficulties, and the disc as a whole serves as one of the best possible introductions to the world of contemporary chamber music. *EL*

MACMILLAN

... as others see us...; Three Dawn Rituals; After the Tryst; Untold

see **ORCHESTRAL:** MACMILLAN: Veni, veni, Emmanuel

MARTINU

Cello Sonatas Nos 1–3

János Starker (cello), Rudolf Firkušný (piano)

RCA Victor Red Seal 09026 61220 2 □ **54:21 mins** □ *⊘⊘⊘*

Martinů seems to have drawn particular inspiration from the solo cello, for these three sonatas find him at the height of his creative powers. This urgency is especially apparent in the first two sonatas written during the dark days of the Second World War. Here, the driving rhythms, anguished melodic lines and pungent harmonies attest to the composer's own anxiety in the face of the Nazi occupation of his native Czechoslovakia. In contrast, a more reflective and nostalgic vein runs through the Third Sonata of 1952, though a current of unease still penetrates the surface from time to time. Needless to say, both these performers serve the music to its best advantage. Starker's approach may strike some

as uninvolving, but this is a superficial impression which fails to take account of the cellist's overwhelming mastery of tonal colouring and the subtlety of his phrasing. Firkušný proves to be the ideal partner, understanding Martinů's language from the inside and investing the piano writing with a delicacy of touch that eludes most performers. *EL*

MENDELSSOHN/BEETHOVEN

Mendelssohn: Octet in E flat, Op. 20

Beethoven: Septet in E flat, Op. 20

Vienna Octet

Decca 421 093-2 □ **ADD** □ **74:06 mins** □ *⊘⊘*

The classic Vienna Octet performance of Mendelssohn's prodigally brilliant Octet for strings, Op. 20, has maintained its own place in the catalogues for well over three decades. The performance is electrifying, while the recording itself, made at one of Decca's choice locations, the Vienna Sofiensaal (source of many legendary productions, including the first complete *Ring* cycle, with Solti and the Vienna Philharmonic), is altogether remarkable for its vivid transparency and broad dynamic range. That this incredibly fertile and original composition was the work of a boy of 16 remains one of the great enigmatic wonders of musical history. This disc also includes another great Op. 20, the Septet by Beethoven, again marvellously cultured and elegant playing, characterised by that peculiarly Viennese warmth that proves so endearing a feature of these great Vienna Octet accounts. An indisputable classic, and one that continues to wear its years as lightly and unobtrusively as the music itself. Glorious sound and incomparable playing; a disc I'd be happy to pay many times more than the asking price to acquire. *MJ*

MENDELSSOHN

Piano Trios Nos 1 in D minor, Op. 49 & 2 in C minor, Op. 66

Israel Piano Trio

CRD 3459 □ **60:00 mins** □ *⊘⊘⊘*

Schumann spoke of Mendelssohn's emotionally charged D minor Trio as 'the master trio of our time' when he first heard the work shortly after its completion in 1839. Its successor, written six years later, inhabits the no less tempestuous tonality of C minor; both works are remarkable for their expressive passion and severity, demonstrating

Mendelssohn's phenomenal mastery of the genre, and inviting enquiry as to why he did not explore the medium (of which he was absolute master) more frequently. There's no shortage of admirable recordings to choose from, though none of them displaces these electrifying performances from the Israel Piano Trio. Their approach is leonine and powerful; the sweep and gravity of the opening movement of No. 1 is stormily vehement, though the performance is intelligently conceived, with no lack of inner warmth. If the combined strengths of these artists bear occasionally rather broodingly on the music, then it does so to fine advantage; there is tempestuous rhetoric and passion aplenty, while the slow movement of the C minor Trio is richly charged and eloquently austere in manner. These are strongly compelling performances, at once eminently prepared and executed, and gloriously, occasionally rather fulsomely recorded. *MJ*

MENDELSSOHN
String Quartets, Opp. 12, 13, 44 & 80
Cherubini Quartet

EMI CDS 7 54514 2 □ 172:58 mins (3 discs) □ *◐◑◒*

As these discs were issued during the summer of 1993, the Carmina and Coull Quartets were commencing rival cycles to join established surveys from the Melos, Artis and Bartholdy Quartets. But the Cherubini performances are particularly alluring; they exhibit missionary zeal and eloquence, and rare dedication to this music. Moreover, these artists have lived long with these scores before venturing to commit them to disc. Several of these compositions acknowledge Mendelssohn's debt to Beethoven (Opp. 12 and 13 especially), though, unlike their recent rivals, the Ysaÿe Quartet (on Decca), the Cherubinis give clear notice that this is not Beethoven but something wholly original in concept and idiom. Where the Ysaÿes sound hectoringly aggressive, it is the Cherubini Quartet who reveal the blitheness of quintessentially Mendelssohnian inspiration. Their reading of the Op. 80 work, Mendelssohn's last essay in the genre, composed following the death of his sister Fanny, is unquestionably the finest I've yet heard on disc, and recording quality is likewise superb. *MJ*

MESSIAEN
Quatuor pour la fin du temps
Luben Yordanoff (violin), Albert Tétard (cello), Claude Desurmont (clarinet), Daniel Barenboim (piano)

DG 20th Century Classics 423 247-2 □ ADD □ 49:07 mins □ *◐◑*

Messiaen's *Quartet for the End of Time*, written when the composer was incarcerated in a prisoner-of-war camp in Germany, makes almost superhuman demands on its interpreters. One particular stumbling block is the notoriously difficult unison passagework in the 'Danse de la fureur, pour les sept trompettes' which all too rarely presents absolute unanimity of ensemble and perfect intonation. And then there are those slow movements – for clarinet solo, cello and piano, and violin and piano – that test to the very limits the performers' ability both to sustain and give direction to a seemingly endless line of melody. Few currently available recordings really satisfy all these musical criteria, but this 1979 recording, made in the presence of the composer, has great immediacy, and is distinguished by some wonderfully insightful playing from Daniel Barenboim. *EL*

MIASKOVSKY
String Quartets in A minor, Op. 33/1 & in F minor, Op. 33/4
Taneyev Quartet

Russian Disc RD CD 11 013 □ AAD □ 58:42 mins □ *◐◑*

Partly contemporary with Shostakovich's string quartet cycle was another such Soviet musical epic, the 13 quartets of Miaskovsky, spanning from the first decade of the century to just before his death in 1951. If Miaskovsky's quartet output is more uneven, and some works more derivative, than Shostakovich's, they still include some of the supreme achievements of Russian chamber music. Finest of all, perhaps, is the magnificent A minor Quartet published as No. 1. (The numbering of Miaskovsky's quartets is highly misleading, and so are Russian Disc's notes. This quartet, which they imply is a student work, dates from 1929–30 and is really his fourth or fifth, while the official Fourth, coupled here, is a revision of his Conservatoire graduation work, written twenty years earlier!)

Op. 33/1 is the culminating score in Miaskovsky's 'modernist' period, a wild, passionate and deeply disturbed effusion of Blochian eloquence and near-Bergian chromaticism, densely but thrillingly written and more dissonantly expressionistic than any of Shostakovich's quartets. The more nostalgic and bucolic No. 4, by contrast, as befits an early work, vividly illustrates Miaskovsky's early debt to Tchaikovsky and represents a direct link back to the 19th-century Romantic national tradition. The splendid Taneyev Quartet, who have recorded all Miaskovsky's quartet output, expound both works with vibrant dedication in a vivid acoustic. *CM*

MONDONVILLE
Violin Sonata in G, Op. 3/5
see LECLAIR: Violin Sonatas

MOZART

Clarinet Quintet in A, K581; Trio in E flat, K498 (Kegelstatt)

Wolfgang Meyer (basset clarinet), Patrick Cohen (fortepiano); Quatuor Mosaïques

Astrée Auvidis E 8736 □ 51:30 mins □ ⊘⊘⊘

There's been much musicological cap-doffing towards the valedictory pronouncements of the A major Clarinet Concerto, K622, Mozart's last orchestral work, and his final Piano Concerto, K595 in B flat, also of 1791. Historical fact suggests that these works pursue a strand of resignation eloquently debated two years previously, in the Clarinet Quintet, K581. This version from Wolfgang Meyer and the Quatuor Mosaïques offers rich insight into the pathos of the work. Meyer's tonal opulence, notably in the oft-exploited 'chalumeau' register perfected by Anton Stadler, for whom Mozart wrote the Quintet and the Concerto K622, is only occasionally marred by the rattling key-work of his reproduction basset clarinet. But Meyer's is an ineffably beautiful reading of K581; I hope to be returning to this disc with reverential gratitude for many years to come! *MJ*

MOZART

Divertimento in E flat for String Trio, K563; Six Preludes and Fugues (after Bach), K404a

L'Archibudelli

Sony Vivarte SK 46497 □ 62:41 mins □ ⊘⊘⊘

Hands up, all Mozart lovers who know this wonderful work! Amazingly, there are many who don't. And why? Can it simply be the relative rarity of string trios as opposed to string quartets? Perhaps. Be that as it may, here is a superlatively civilised, penetrating and unfailingly euphonious opportunity to discover the work – and if you already know it, to rediscover it, again and again. L'Archibudelli are an ensemble founded by the

pioneering cellist-scholar Anner Bylsma, and their playing is of a quality that should win over even the most dedicated opponent of period performance. But no one performance can reveal everything, and listeners preferring a more traditional approach may find equal but different revelations in the version by the Grumiaux Trio on Philips, though this suffers occasionally from an excessive symmetry of phrase which impedes the music's inner song. Both recordings give you Mozart's fascinating preludes to his own arrangements (but *are* they?) of six fugues by Bach. *JS*

MOZART

Piano Quartets in E flat, K493 & in G minor, K478; Horn Quintet, K407

Clifford Curzon (piano), Dennis Brain (horn); members of the Amadeus Quartet, Griller Quartet

Decca 425 960-2 □ ADD mono □ 62:01 mins □ ⊘⊘

There's enough choice here to satisfy virtually any taste. Those who like a good old-fashioned, robust, pre-authenticist approach may find Rubinstein and the Guarneri on RCA more to their taste than I do; those who favour the modern piano and up-to-date recorded sound but prefer a more carefully honed stylistic approach should be happy with Previn and friends (also on RCA: a very attractive release indeed), while listeners bent on a period-instrument version can turn either to Bilson *et al* on DG (with all concerned in top form) or, as I'd do, to the Mozartean Players on Harmonia Mundi (at their stylish best, blending scholarship, vitality and imagination with a sense of spontaneity and continuous development all too rare in any sphere). But for sheer, timeless musicianship, untainted by any sense of dogma and informed by an unsurpassed subtlety which in no way emasculates the music, it has to be Curzon and the Amadeus who lead the field here, never mind that the recording is more than forty years old. And as if that weren't enough, you also get an account of the Horn Quintet from Brain and the Griller Quartet which has still not been bettered more than half a century later. *JS*

MOZART

Piano Trios (complete)

The Mozartean Players

Harmonia Mundi HMU 907033/34 □ 136:18 mins (2 discs) □ ⊘⊘⊘

Fortunately, the listener is wonderfully well served in this repertoire, be it in the realm of so-called authenticity or in that (implicitly inauthentic) performing tradition exemplified by the first-class Beaux Arts Trio. Their own traversal of the trios, available in a three-disc box from Philips, is musicanly, delightful and moving to its figurative fingertips. The lion's share of the material (and in this case the microphone balance) goes to the pianist, and there are few such sensitive and capable Mozart pianists around as the Beaux Arts's Menahem Pressler, whose lively urbanity is never tinged with glibness. But my most lasting and illuminating pleasure in the hearing of these works recently has come from the rather presumptuously named group cited above (*The* Mozartean Players, notice) – an American period-instrument ensemble of outstanding excellence, whose fortepianist, Steven Lubin, may be familiar as the pianist in L'Oiseau-Lyre's Beethoven concerto cycle with Hogwood and the Academy of Ancient Music. This is playing of the utmost grace and elegance, replete with a most beautiful textural translucency, impeccably refined phrasing and articulation, and a rhythmic profile of continuous suppleness and perfectly judged momentum. *JS*

Mozart: Quintet for Piano and Wind in E flat, K452

Beethoven: Quintet for Piano and Wind, Op. 16

Murray Perahia (piano); members of the English CO

Sony SK 42099 □ 53:00 mins □ ❷❷❷

One is really spoiled for choice here. With excellent versions featuring Ashkenazy, Barenboim, Brendel, Gulda, Jandó, Lupu, Perahia and Previn, to name some but not all, it's hard to go too far wrong. At that level of musicianship it really all boils down to personal taste. For my own part, I find Brendel and Co. on Philips a little too self-consciously intelligent and point-making, Barenboim on Erato excessively high-pressured, Previn a little bland, and so on. The hardest choice for me is between Ashkenazy, Perahia and Lupu, but in the end it's to Perahia and his friends from the English Chamber Orchestra that I keep returning with the fullest sense of satisfaction. Immaculate, urbane, stylish, lively, poignant and effortlessly expressive, they combine an entrancing instrumental blend with musical conversation at its most sophisticated and entrancing. This is chamber music-making at its most engaging – polished but never slick, flexible but never slack, poetic but never

precious. Of budget-priced versions I've enjoyed none more than Jandó *et al* on Naxos. *JS*

String Quartets in G, K387, in D minor, K421, in E flat, K428, in B flat, K458 (The Hunt), in A, K464 & in C, K465 (Dissonance) (The Six 'Haydn' Quartets)

Emerson Quartet

DG 431 797-2 □ 185:56 mins (3 discs) □ ❷❷❷

Unfortunately, all my favourite recordings of these six wonderful works are currently available only as part of much bigger sets. Nothing subsequently released has shifted my enthusiasm for the Quartetto Italiano, which remains undimmed after fully three decades. These are performances whose artistic integrity, spiritual warmth, innate aristocracy and conversational vitality transcend all fashions, musicological or otherwise, and every penny spent in acquiring their set of the complete Mozart quartets (eight mid-price CDs on Philips) will be repaid a thousand times over. The Alban Berg Quartet on Teldec are also richly satisfying, and characteristically euphonious, but they too come only in an eight- or a four-disc box. Not, mind you, that you'll be slumming if you go for the Emersons. They're very good indeed, if a little impersonal for my tastes, and excellently recorded too. And if you prefer a period approach, the Salomon Quartet on Hyperion are exceptionally attractive and attentive. *JS*

String Quintets (complete)

Grumiaux Ensemble

Philips Complete Mozart Edition 422 511-2 □ ADD □ 120:50 mins (3 discs) □ ❷❷

This is some of the warmest, most lyrical, most searching and sweetest-sounding music-making you're ever likely to come across. And in the late 20th century, with all its bustle, stress and tension, playing like this comes as balm to the soul. Nothing is hurried, there's always time to breathe, to sing, to reflect, to savour what may well be Mozart's most perfectly realised chamber music. If *Sturm und Drang* gung-ho vitality is your scene, you may find this unbearably bland and leisurely. This is playing that puts up no flags, grinds no axes, and is so centred upon the music itself that the notion of an audience just doesn't come into it. This is 'the music of friends' *par excellence*. It's quite simply the kind of playing that makes the world a better place. If period instruments are a must for you, it's a shame you have to miss out on this, but you should find much to admire and enjoy in the playing of the Salomon Quartet with Simon Whistler on Hyperion. *JS*

MOZART

String Quintets in C, K515 & in G minor, K516

L'Archibudelli

Sony SK 66259 □ 62:50 mins □ 〇〇〇

Mozart was the supreme operatic composer of all time, and not just in his operas. His music is almost always a continuous tapestry of cause and effect, a series of conversations and ensembles which constantly enrich our perception of increasingly familiar material. In no composer's music can it more rightly be said that context alters content – a fact beautifully exemplified by L'Archibudelli throughout these outstanding performances. While adopting a very wide dynamic range, they never over-dramatise the music, spurning exaggeration of every kind. Theirs is playing of the greatest stylishness, keenly alert to the expressive and structural power of even the slightest details and maintaining simultaneous coherence at every level. This is 'period' performance at its best, in which scholarship and instinct combine as indissoluble elements of whole artistic experience. It's performances like these, still far too rare, which demonstrate beyond a shadow of doubt that 'authenticity' means nothing without imagination. Listeners preferring a more modern sound, on the other hand, may turn with confidence to the Takács Quartet with György Pauk on Decca and the Tokyo Quartet with Pinchas Zukerman on RCA. *JS*

MOZART/BEETHOVEN

Mozart: Violin Sonatas in C, K301, in E minor, K304, in F, K376, in B flat, K378, in B flat, K454 & in A, K526

Beethoven: Violin Sonatas (complete)

Arthur Grumiaux (violin), Clara Haskil (piano)

Philips 442 625-2 □ ADD □ 309:55 mins (5 discs) □ 〇〇

For sheer artistry these recordings remain in a class of their own. This isn't to say that there aren't others of comparable quality, but I know of none that so consistently combines Classical restraint with poetic eloquence. Unfortunately, the engineers have added to Haskil's fabled

discretion by sonically removing her to another room, or at least to a remote corner of the studio, thereby rendering her a mere accompanist. More's the pity, since these are works in which the piano writing is often the dominant feature (indeed, they were originally billed specifically as sonatas for piano with violin accompaniment). Happily, her immaculately phrased and pianistically refined contribution survives the treatment. For some, however, she may seem restrained to the point of austerity. These might be happier with Barenboim and Perlman on DG, though one will look in vain there for comparable refinement. *JS*

NONO

La lontananza nostalgica utopica futura; 'Hay que caminar' soñando

Gidon Kremer, Tatiana Grindenko (violin), Sofia Gubaidulina (sound projection)

DG 435 870-2 □ 60:01 mins □ 〇〇〇

Luigi Nono's last decade found him still the least compromising of modernists; renouncing the serial tradition, he embarked on new explorations of the expressive nature of sound. Most of his late works allude to a medieval graffito in Toledo Cathedral: 'Caminantes, no hay caminos, hay que caminar' (Travellers, there are no roads, but we must go on). By comparison, most other composers since Varèse have been faint-hearts.

La lontananza nostalgica utopica futura (Nostalgia for the distant, future Utopia) was written for Gidon Kremer. Magnetic tapes transform sounds from a pre-recorded improvisation session by Kremer under Nono's direction. Kremer provides a memoir of Nono's nerve-racking way of working: the 'live' solo part was completed scant hours before the premiere. Yet the result is both one of the most challenging works in the violin repertoire, and a richly imaginative electronic composition. The violin duo *'Hay que caminar' soñando*, Nono's last work, explores the interface of sound and silence with passion and mercurial spontaneity. Kremer's advocacy of *La lontananza*, in a richly resonant ambience, is stunning, though he uses only about sixty per cent of Nono's taped material. (Note that Irvine Arditti, similarly eloquent on Auvidis Montaigne in a drier acoustic, uses it all.) *CM*

ONSLOW

String Quintets in C minor (Bullet), in E, Op. 39 & in B minor, Op. 40

L'Archibudelli, members of the Smithsonian Chamber Players

Sony Vivarte SK 64308 □ 77:03 mins □ 𝄞𝄞𝄞

Three quintets by Georges Onslow (1784–1853) receive convincing advocacy here. That the finest of them, his C minor work, Op. 38, the *Bullet* Quintet, once enjoyed wide currency was due in large measure to its tragic origins. JF Halévy's *Notes sur Onslow* (1855) relate how the composer sustained a bullet wound to the neck (with resultant partial hearing loss) during a hunt held in his honour in 1829. Descriptive titles ('pain', 'fever and delirium', 'convalescence' and 'recovery') for individual movements enshrine the tragedy in music which is fitfully melodramatic.

In all three quintets, the thematic distinction and contrapuntal ingenuity of Onslow's style are apparent. But the pronounced melancholia and air of resignation which inform these quintets underscore a pathological condition common to most of Onslow's music.

This quality emerges powerfully in these performances. Indeed, the playing is exemplary, and recorded sound is of the highest order.

Georges Onslow's music (and that of many of his contemporaries) became outmoded and marginalised as the floodgates of Lisztian Romanticism burst open in the 1840s and 50s. It has much ground to reclaim, and issues of this calibre can only help. *MJ*

PANUFNIK

'Messages' – String Quartets Nos 1–3; Song to the Virgin Mary; String Sextet (Trains of Thought)

Chilingirian String Quartet

Conifer 74321 16190 2 □ 72:23 mins □ 𝄞𝄞𝄞

Andrzej Panufnik (1914–91) is best known for his orchestral music, particularly his ten symphonies. He lived in Britain from 1954, and was principal conductor of the City of Birmingham Symphony Orchestra, having previously worked with the Kraków and Warsaw Philharmonics. As his career developed, he devoted himself increasingly to composition.

This disc contains his three string quartets, along with two sextets, one of which is an arrangement of a vocal piece. These chamber works offer a distillation of Panufnik's methods, and those who are familiar with his orchestral works may be surprised by the frequently spare textures. But the tendency to move from introspection to affirmation brings a full range of emotion and sound, a striking example being the postlude of the First Quartet (1976), with its inexorable sense of growth.

The recording, like the music, is clean and precise: the Chilingirian Quartet's sensitive pianissimo playing is captured perfectly, while the climaxes are rich in tone. In his excellent notes, Bernard Jacobson refers to Panufnik's search for 'human emotion and cosmic mystery', and this personal, intimate music is well served in these performances. As an introduction to the art of this underrated composer, I recommend this disc, and especially the sextet arrangement of the moving *Song to the Virgin Mary*. *Terry Barfoot*

PROKOFIEV

String Quartets Nos 1 in B minor & 2 in F

Britten Quartet

Collins 11892 □ 50:29 mins □ 𝄞𝄞𝄞

As so often with Prokofiev, the more simple the end result seems, the more lasting the impact. The First Quartet of 1931, shaped by Prokofiev's careful examination of the late Beethoven quartets, boasts as its crowning glory a sustained and serious Andante – played here with suitably vocal eloquence by the Britten Quartet. The extrovert Second Quartet, however, tends to outshine all serious considerations. A vibrant and zestful attempt to catch the inflections in the folk-music of the Kabardinia region to which the composer was evacuated in 1941, it never smacks of the compulsion to examine ethnic music which every Soviet composer felt during the Stalin years. The Brittens relish the muscular, gritty string writing with its occasional exultant discords, giving the folk-songs room to swagger and showing off the skill of Prokofiev's detailed accompaniment. A few carefully chosen tempi, slower than recommended, help to underline the integrity of the exercise, bringing us closer to the world of Bartók's middle-period quartets – and there can be no higher compliment to Prokofiev's underrated *jeu d'esprit* than that. *DN*

PROKOFIEV

String Quartet No. 2 in F
see HINDEMITH: String Quartet No. 3 in C

Violin Sonatas Nos 1 in F minor & 2 in D; Five Melodies for Violin and Piano, Op. 35bis

Gidon Kremer (violin), Martha Argerich (piano)

DG 431 803-2 □ 64:52 mins □ *ΘΘΘ*

The most ominous of Prokofiev's chamber works and the one most likely to reveal his true feelings in the bleak Forties, the First Violin Sonata needs a certain austerity of tone to reach its true heart of darkness. The acerbic Gidon Kremer, partnered rather than merely supported by the mesmerising Martha Argerich, certainly maintains that across the span of the first movement's terse melodic ideas; and no one captures better the hallucinatory quality of the muted violin runs (marked *freddo* – cold – in the score) against bell-like chords from the piano at the end of the movement, returning crucially in the finale – 'like the wind in a graveyard', Prokofiev described them.

Kremer and Argerich also capture the nostalgic quality of the watery, *Ondine*-like Andante, though its beauty sounds even more unearthly in the hands of the young Itzhak Perlman and Vladimir Ashkenazy on RCA. Perlman's sweetness of tone makes him a preferable option to Kremer in the Second Sonata, transcribed by the composer from the original for flute, and a far less probing piece of undeniable melodic charm. If your affections are divided more equally than mine between the two sonatas, then the RCA disc is the one to have; but there's no doubt that Kremer and Argerich have the edge (literally) in the undeniable masterpiece. *DN*

Fantasias for 3 & 4 Viols; Two In Nomines; Chacony in G minor

Concentus Musicus Wien/Nikolaus Harnoncourt, The English Concert/Trevor Pinnock

Archiv 447 153-2 □ ADD/DDD □ 56:36 mins □ *ΘΘ*

Purcell's sublime Fantasias for viols must be regarded as among the finest chamber works of the Baroque period. Essentially intimate musical statements in a genre that had all but gone out of fashion at the time they were written, the Fantasias sometimes invoke the spirit of Dowland, but also demonstrate a striking and individual approach to sonority and harmony. The Concentus Musicus's recording of these masterpieces dates from the early sixties and was originally issued on the Austrian Amadeo label. Archiv's remastering has given the original fuzzy sound a new lease

of life, and the performances get to the heart of the music, balancing scholarly performing principles with interpretative intuition. The masterly Chacony in G minor, recorded in 1985 by the English Concert, makes an appropriate and attractive bonus. *EL*

Pièces de clavecin en concerts

Christophe Rousset (harpsichord), Ryo Terakado (violin), Kaori Uemura (viola da gamba)

Harmonia Mundi HMC 901418 □ 73:35 mins □ *ΘΘΘ*

This single disc of five *concerts* represents the whole of Rameau's output of original chamber music. (A sixth *concert* is a transcription of some solo harpsichord pieces.) Each suite consists of three to five movements, many of them character pieces with descriptive titles – 'La timide', 'L'indiscrète' – or the names of people who, Rameau explains in his preface, had selected a particular piece with which to be associated – a familiar 20th-century sponsorship ploy.

The *concerts* are very versatile, for harpsichord with violin and gamba (as performed here) or with flute replacing violin and/or with second violin replacing gamba. Finally, they are self-sufficient for harpsichord alone – its music is fully written out and, Rameau insists, leaves 'nothing to be desired'. Although this is clearly an exaggeration, the virtuosic demands on the harpsichordist are extreme. Hands cross, play octaves, and cover the whole register of the (extended) French instrument. These techniques, not overtly germane to the harpsichord, put the spotlight on Christophe Rousset, whose playing is in places breathtakingly exciting.

This is a hidden corner of the later French Baroque repertoire which eminently repays exploration. *GP*

Introduction and Allegro
see FRANCK: Violin Sonata in A

Ravel: Piano Trio in A minor

Chausson: Concert for piano, violin and string quartet

Joshua Bell (violin), Steven Isserlis (cello), Jean-Yves Thibaudet (piano); Takács Quartet

Decca 425 860-2 □ 62:15 mins □ *ΘΘΘ*

Ravel's Piano Trio has been comprehensively recorded over the years. The finest account may quite possibly be that from the Beaux Arts Trio, coupled with the trio by Chausson, though this Decca release, featuring the superb *Concert* by Chausson, offers other and no less attractive benefits. Chausson's Trio, an early but unexpectedly fine piece in its own right, seems a less appealing foil to the Ravel Trio than the sensational *Concert*, which receives a magnificent performance from Bell, Thibaudet and the Takács Quartet. The Ravel Trio, with Steven Isserlis as cellist, could scarcely be better played; this thrilling account, warmly sensitive and prudently judged by this expert team, lacks none of the fire and atmosphere of the Beaux Arts's Philips performance, and is comparable in terms of recording quality. It must be stated that each version is patently self-recommending. *MJ*

RAVEL/KODALY

Ravel: Sonata for Violin and Cello

Kodály: Duo for Violin and Cello

Jean-Jacques Kantorow (violin), Mari Fujiwara (cello)

Denon CO-1005 □ 45:13 mins □ 🎵🎵🎵

Slightly short in overall duration, though more than generous in terms of its musical and sonic virtues, this disc brings together two wholly unique, and phenomenally demanding, compositions for violin and cello. The Ravel work, composed in 1922, is explosively virtuosic in manner. Kodaly's Duo, Op. 7, an electrifying study in bravura and physical powers of execution, dates from 1909–10. It, too, makes fearsome demands on the performers, and if the Bartókian resonances of the piece seem at times almost too obvious, one should remember that Bartók's shattering Third String Quartet lay some time ahead, although the fundamental elements of spirited aggression and defiant resistance were focal issues for both composers. These are astonishing performances; the bite and *frisson* of the playing of Kantorow and Fujiwara are reproduced with startling clarity (the presence and focus of Denon's recording is perhaps a little too close for comfort at times!) on this excellent CD. *MJ*

RAVEL/DEBUSSY

Ravel: String Quartet in F

Debussy: String Quartet in G minor

Quartetto Italiano

Philips Silver Line 420 894-2 □ ADD □ 57:00 mins □ 🎵🎵

This is the classic recording of the Ravel and Debussy string quartets, now well over thirty years old, but sounding as fresh and as alluring as ever in this Philips reissue. CD transfers are admittedly at an uncomfortably high level; you may need to reduce the volume to enjoy this disc in comfort, though that's the sole caveat here. The playing is highly atmospheric, yet the cultured refinement and unanimity of approach in both works are unusually coercive. The coupling, of course, is a familiar and totally predictable one, though the degree to which these outwardly polarised quartets complement each other, in ways which neither composer could have contemplated, is engrossingly apparent in these hugely distinguished performances. The expressivity, tonal radiance and consummately skilled ensemble playing throughout these demanding works underscores Debussy's own musical dictum, aimed at revealing an ultimate degree of 'Freedom within discipline' in this medium, and others. An unmissable offering! *MJ*

RAVEL

String Quartet in F
see also DEBUSSY: String Quartet in G minor

RAVEL/DEBUSSY/JANACEK

Ravel: Violin Sonatas (1897, 1923–7)

Debussy: Violin Sonata

Janáček: Violin Sonata

Frank Peter Zimmermann (violin), Alexander Lonquich (piano)

EMI CDC 7 54305 2 □ 66:00 mins □ 🎵🎵🎵

Zimmermann and Lonquich give strongly expressive accounts of four highly contrasting works in this recital programme. It makes admirable sense to include Ravel's two violin sonatas rather than just the more familiar later one, and this playing is forceful, yet readily attuned to the Gallic contouring of these scores. The Second Sonata, written and modified extensively between 1923 and 1927, draws fine response from these artists. Zimmermann delivers the work with steely panache and never demurs from characterising the work in broadly expansive gestures, though there's never any appreciable lack of intimacy in this reading. The earlier sonata, thought to have vanished following the 1897 premiere (given by George Enescu with Ravel accompanying), surfaced again as recently as 1975; less distinguishable in manner as typical Ravel, it is, nonetheless, a fine, strongly idiomatic composition. The pair are equally compelling in the Debussy Sonata and the Violin Sonata by Leoš Janáček. Excellent playing, urgently though pliably communicative, and warmly if somewhat brightly recorded. *MJ*

Music for a Large Ensemble; Violin Phase; Octet

Shem Guibbory (violin); Steve Reich and Musicians

ECM 827 287-2 □ ADD □ 48:06 mins □ *♪♪♪*

By now we can call this 'classic' minimalism. Of the American composers who started the Minimal Music revolution, Steve Reich remains the most alive to the idea that varied repetition should mean tension and expectancy, not boredom. The sheer rhythmic life in works such as these allows long-term phase-shifts and gradual change in melodic figures to become active, engrossing musical experiences. The early *Violin Phase* (1967), in which a single violinist plays with one, two then three pre-recorded tapes of himself, dances on the very edge between tedium and unbearable tension. The ensemble works are more expansive and invigorating, especially the Octet (1979), a bouncy, zingy, open-air piece if ever there was one. Its close cousin, *Music for a Large Ensemble*, has a greater range of colour including wordless voices, but is perhaps slightly softer-centred. These 1980 performances, supervised by the composer, have infectious bite and spring; the recording, rather close and very bright, is ideal for the music. If you want to investigate how Reich's music has developed, try the orchestral Variations (coupled with John Adams's *Shaker Loops* under Edo de Waart on Philips), his Hebrew psalm-setting *Tehillim* (also on ECM), or the extraordinary string quartet with voices, *Different Trains*, with the Kronos Quartet on Nonesuch. *CM*

Clarinet Quintet in B flat
see WEBER: Clarinet Quintet in B flat

Viola Sonata
see SHOSTAKOVICH: Viola Sonata

Carnaval des animaux
see BARTOK: Sonata for Two Pianos and Percussion

Violin Sonata No. 1 in D minor
see DEBUSSY: Violin Sonata

Piano Quartet; Piano Trio No. 2

Seta Tanyel (piano), Levon Chilingirian (violin), Ivo-Jan van der Werff (viola), Garbis Atmacayan (cello)

Collins 14192 □ 76:11 mins □ *♪♪♪*

Until very recently the name of the Polish-born composer Xaver Scharwenka (1850–1924) was practically unknown except to connoisseurs of late 19th-century virtuoso piano music. Yet in his day Scharwenka was a much-admired musical figure whose works frequently graced the concert halls of Europe. That he should have fallen into almost complete neglect seems inexplicable when one is faced with chamber music of such high musical quality. True, Scharwenka was no musical pioneer, and his idiom owes much to Schumann. But this seeming lack of individuality should not blind us to the fact that these works are not only written with consummate craftsmanship but show immense powers of inventiveness. Start with the arresting Piano Trio, and I guarantee you will be hooked. It seems unnecessary to add that the performances are superb. Quite clearly, the players, too, were utterly enchanted by the discovery of this wonderful music. *EL*

À Paganini
see **ORCHESTRAL**: SCHNITTKE: Concerto Grosso No. 1

Canon in memoriam I Stravinsky
see LUTOSLAWSKI: String Quartet

Violin Sonatas Nos 1 & 2; Suite in the Old Style

Mark Lubotsky (violin), Ralf Gothóni (piano)

Ondine ODE 800-2 □ 53:15 mins □ *♪♪♪*

With well over half a dozen currently available recordings, Schnittke's First Violin Sonata must be well on the way to attaining the status of a 20th-century classic. Although an early work, dating from 1963, its disturbing mixture of anxiety, irony and religious symbolism (the deeply affecting chorale) presage the world of the mature composer, and the material as a whole carries both a distinctiveness and an economy of means which are not always conspicuous in Schnittke's other music.

The Second Sonata (subtitled 'Quasi una sonata') followed its predecessor after a gap of three years, and is a much more anarchic composition which in its day challenged Soviet authoritarianism with its no-holds-barred use of avant-garde techniques. Despite the passing of time, the deliberately provocative nature of musical argument still has the capacity to astound the listener, especially in a performance as gripping as this, in which the original dedicatee, Mark Lubotsky, delivers breathtakingly urgent performances. *EL*

SCHOENBERG

Serenade, Op. 24
see **CHORAL & SONG**: SCHOENBERG: A Survivor from Warsaw

SCHOENBERG

String Quartets Nos 1–4

Dawn Upshaw (soprano); Arditti String Quartet

Auvidis Montaigne MO 782024 □ **138:44 mins (2 discs)** □ *♪♪♪*

The quartets of Schoenberg are at last promising to join the mainstream of the string-quartet tradition, but the Ardittis' superb collection of performances is only the third complete cycle to arrive in the CD catalogue. Their set omits the posthumously published D major Quartet that Schoenberg composed in 1897, but for the four numbered quartets it is, for my money, the one to recommend above all others.

For the Arditti, of course, Schoenberg is the baseline of their repertory rather than its most rarefied extension: they specialise in the music of the 20th century and so bring to these quartets a comprehension of what followed them as well as what came before; these are never performances that look wistfully back to the world of Brahms and Wagner, out of which Schoenberg developed his musical language, but instead take each work on its stylistic merits. So the First Quartet has a Romantic luxuriance and breadth of phrase, while the Second trembles on the boundary of two worlds, one tonal and assertive, the other atonal and far less certain. Dawn Upshaw is the solo soprano in the last two movements here, radiant and absolutely secure.

It's the Third and Fourth Quartets that demonstrate the Arditti's clarity and strength of purpose most impressively. These can be elusive works to bring off, for Schoenberg's 12-note technique has to be reconciled to the Classical cut of his rhythmic invention, but the Arditti bring such spring and vividness to every phrase, understand the form and its dynamic working so completely, that the music seems utterly integrated and utterly convincing. This is a most important issue. *Andrew Clements*

SCHOENBERG

Verklärte Nacht; String Trio, Op. 45

Juilliard Quartet; Walter Trampler (viola), Yo-Yo Ma (cello)

Sony SK 47690 □ **48:12 mins** □ *♪♪♪*

Schoenberg's early, intensely passionate string sextet *Verklärte Nacht* (Transfigured Night), a chamber music tone poem, is his first masterpiece and a defining work of the end of the late-Romantic era in music. It's also his most popular piece, with many competing versions of this original form and his arrangement for string orchestra. No modern performance outclasses the one by the expanded Hollywood Quartet, rehearsed in the presence of the perfectionist composer, who could find no criticism to make. (Currently available on Testament, with an equally outstanding Schubert String Quintet.) But this Juilliard recording is perhaps the finest in state-of-the-art sound, by a vastly experienced team who have lived with and love its yearning and voluptuous melodies, its evocative textures.

The coupling is the best available interpretation of one of Schoenberg's greatest and toughest scores, the late String Trio, a high-pressure fusion of expressionistic phantasmagoria and post-tonal serenity, written after a heart-attack that nearly killed him. This is a performance of tremendous understanding as well as technical skill, bringing out the deep humanity beneath this craggy, formidable and sometimes tortured music. *CM*

SCHOENBERG

Verklärte Nacht
see also KORNGOLD; String Sextet in D *and* **ORCHESTRAL**

SCHUBERT

Fantasie in C, D934; Rondo in B minor, D895; Sonata in A minor, D821 (Arpeggione)

Raphael Oleg (violin, viola), Gerard Wyss (piano)

Denon CO-75636 □ **65:46 mins** □ *♪♪♪*

Raphael Oleg and Gerard Wyss enter a fiercely contested area, emerging honourably in these excellent, technically adroit and credibly witty performances. But do we really need another *Arpeggione*, albeit one as fine as this? This disc might have been better served by the A major Duo (Sonata), D574, possibly Schubert's greatest work for violin and piano. But the truth is that Oleg's readings of the C major Fantasie, D934, and B minor Rondo, D895, far exceed customary expectations. If some collectors find Gidon Kremer and Valery Afanassiev (DG) more tempting, then programme-planning, and manifestly not musicianship, will have been the decisive factor. Denon's sonics are superior, however, and piano timbre and inner balance between the instruments could scarcely be bettered. *MJ*

Piano Quintet in A, D667 (Trout); Lieder

Steven Lubin (fortepiano), John Mark Ainsley (tenor); Academy of Ancient Music Chamber Ensemble

L'Oiseau-Lyre 433 848-2 □ 60:20 mins □ 🕐🕐🕐

The authentic *Trout* is hardly a novelty these days; another fine performance appeared quite recently from the British ensemble Hausmusik, joining a trend established long ago by Jörg Demus and members of Collegium Aureum. Most recent, and probably finest of all, are Steven Lubin (who plays a modern copy of a Conrad Graf fortepiano of c1824) and the Academy of Ancient Music Chamber Ensemble. Now that period performance has finally come of age, there's little here to offend even the most hardened armchair sceptic; this is a performance that meets every need, whether scholarly or purely self-indulgent! Lubin's fortepiano sounds superb, and accords perfectly with the string group, all of whom employ the expected gut strings. Vibrato is minimal, though the innocent and unprejudiced ear soon adjusts to leaner textures and lower pitch. Questions of phrasing, articulation and tempo have been reappraised, but there's nothing remotely dry or joyless about this playing. Speeds are on the fast side: Schubert's Andante marking for the slow movement is taken very much at face value, while the bucolic Scherzo romps along splendidly. To complete this disc, tenor John Mark Ainsley joins Steven Lubin in seven familiar Schubert Lieder, all of which predate the quintet but share its watery connotation. *MJ*

The Complete Trios – Piano Trios in B flat, D581 & in E flat, D929; Piano Trio in one movement in B flat, D28; Notturno, D897; String Trio in B flat, D581; String Trio Movement in B flat, D471

Beaux Arts Trio; Grumiaux Trio

Philips Duo 438 700-2 □ ADD □ 127:16 mins (2 discs) □ 🕐🕐

Schubert's great masterworks for piano trio date from his final year, 1828. These are monumental creations, and receive stunningly authoritative performances from the Beaux Arts Trio, an ensemble which has undergone several major personnel changes since these recordings were made by the original players, Daniel Guilet, Bernard Greenhouse and Menahem Pressler, during the Sixties. Despite the fact that in today's Beaux Arts line-up only Pressler remains of the founding team (Isidore Cohen and Ida Kavafian have occupied the violinist's seat, with cellist Peter Wiley succeeding Bernard Greenhouse), the ensemble's more recent accounts of the Schubert trios have lost none of the charisma and depth of these early performances, and will cost considerably more than this outstanding double-disc set of reissues from Philips, which also offers matchless versions of the works for string trio from the Grumiaux Trio. These Philips Duo discs combine Schubert's entire *oeuvre* for both trio combinations, including rarities such as the String Trio Movement, D471, the early Piano Trio Movement, D28, composed in August 1812, and the sublime *Notturno* for piano trio, D897. Performances of utmost distinction, in excellent remastered sound, and all for less than the cost of a single full-priced disc – who could ask for more? *MJ*

Schubert: Sonata in A minor, D821 (Arpeggione)

Schumann: Fantasiestücke, Op. 73; Stücke im Volkston, Op. 102; Adagio and Allegro, Op. 70

Maria Kliegel (cello), Kristin Merscher (piano)

Naxos 8.550654 □ 67:36 mins □ 🕐

The arpeggione, an ill-conceived instrumental dinosaur, was invented by the Viennese instrument-maker Johann Georg Staufer in 1823, who engineered this cumbersome, six-stringed, fretted hybrid of guitar and cello, played using a conventional bow. The sole arpeggionist of note was one Vincenz Schuster, for whom Schubert composed the only significant work ever written for the instrument. The so-called *Arpeggione* Sonata, written in 1824, is a masterpiece, deeply felt and often broodingly eloquent, yet also endowed with much fresh and exuberant melody which is unmistakably Schubertian. Today, the work figures in the violin, viola and even double-bass repertoires, yet its mood and register transfer ideally to the cello, and it is in this version that the work is best known. Maria Kliegel's account is deliciously pointed and vital; the opening movement is serenely nostalgic in character, and the slow movement is most affectingly played. The Rondo finale follows without a break, and demonstrates Kliegel's effortless virtuosity and insight. This well-filled disc also includes powerfully idiomatic readings of several of Schumann's cello compositions, in fine, full-blooded digital sound. Another superb bargain from Naxos. *MJ*

String Quintet in C, D956; String Trio Movement in B flat, D471

Raphael Ensemble

Hyperion CDA 66724 □ **64:51 mins** □ *♪♪♪*

Superlatives become ephemeral and critical criteria moulder into hollow pedantry when applied to an issue of this stature. The Raphael Ensemble's account of Schubert's String Quintet joins a small but illustrious pantheon of truly exceptional recordings of this masterwork. (No other is more illustrious than the historic 1952 Prades Festival performance with Stern, Schneider, Katims, Tortelier and Casals on Sony. The intimacy and serene concentration projected across the years are deeply moving, despite the rather primitive recording.) Keenly responsive to the breadth and grandeur of the opening movement, the Raphael team have an intuitive grasp of the natural gait and eloquence of contrasting incident during the Adagio. The outraged central episode sounds awesome; fine engineering allows each strand of these histrionic obsequies to register with maximum impact. The Scherzo has phenomenal verve, while the finale is suitably muscular, although darker premonitions are never deeply concealed. This is a performance of unquestionable distinction, though the filler, the delectable Trio Movement, D471, seems ill matched beside such earth-shattering revelations. A triumph, nonetheless, for Hyperion and the Raphaels. *MJ*

String Quartets in C minor, D703 (Quartettsatz), in A minor, D804 (Rosamunde), in D minor, D810 (Death and the Maiden) & in G, D887

Melos Quartet

Harmonia Mundi HMC 901408/09 □ **124:00 mins (2 discs)** □ *♪♪♪*

Magnificent performances of Schubert's final works for string quartet from the fine Melos Quartet of Stuttgart, an ensemble who know this music as well as any of their contemporaries, and inject into these recordings all the angst and pathos one would normally expect only in the concert hall. There's tension and physical stress abroad in their account of the D minor Quartet, *Death and the Maiden*, which seldom makes for

particularly relaxed listening; indeed, this is a performance that places the listener at the edge of his seat and keeps him there. Few readings convey with such palpable apprehension and alarm the haunted terror behind this, probably Schubert's greatest work in the medium, and fewer still embrace its poignant regret and profound dismay with such total conviction. The remaining performances are of similar stature; the A minor Quartet is songful in character, but here the charming world of *Rosamunde* is invested with tortured, febrile passion and forcefulness. Similarly, the D887 work, the last of Schubert's quartets, has rarely emerged so potently, or remained so fastidiously enigmatic in character. The sound, from Harmonia Mundi, has ample breadth and clarity, conveying this tempestuously beautiful music-making to maximum effect. *MJ*

Adagio and Allegro, Op. 70
see BRAHMS: Cello Sonatas
and SCHUBERT: Sonata in A minor (Arpeggione)

Fantasiestücke, Op. 73
see also SCHUBERT: Sonata in A minor (Arpeggione)

Schumann: Piano Quartet in E flat, Op. 47
Dvořák: Piano Quartet in E flat, Op. 87

Los Angeles Piano Quartet

IMP Masters MCD 34 □ **64:56 mins** □ *♪♪*

These are heart-warming, lavishly expansive readings of two great works for piano quartet by Schumann and Dvořák. The Schumann is an engagingly fresh, beautifully lyrical composition, whose powerful ideas and structural prowess are self-evidently of Beethovenian descent. The mercurial Scherzo has something of the elfin character of Mendelssohn's examples, though cast in darker, more ominous colours. Dvořák's Op. 87, the second of his works in this form, is a virile, powerfully motoric work, with more than a dash of regional Bohemian colour and, in the stirring finale, an indefatigable power and resolve. Dvořák began sketches for the quartet on 10 August 1889, and barely a month afterwards he wrote to his friend Alois Gobl, thankful for the fact that 'the melodies just soared upon me... praise God!' You'll find no more committed and polished accounts of either work; the Los Angeles Piano Quartet play with tremendous aplomb, and the budget-priced IMP Masters recording is amply resonant and detailed. Collectors also requiring the apprentice C minor Piano Quartet, written in Schumann's 18th year, played once and left unpublished for 150 years, shouldn't miss the RCA Victor Red Seal disc from Young Uck Kim, Heiichiro Ohyama, Gary Hoffmann and André Previn, though the IMP issue should satisfy most needs with a memorable account of Op. 47. *MJ*

(As this book went to press we were informed this disc is currently unavailable, but these fine performances will surely reappear before long. *Eds*)

SCHUMANN

Piano Quintet in E flat
see BRAHMS: Piano Quintet in F minor

SCHUMANN

Piano Trio No. 1 in D minor
see **INSTRUMENTAL**: SCHUMANN: Carnaval

SCHUMANN/BRAHMS

Schumann: String Quartet in A minor, Op. 41/1

Brahms: String Quartet in B flat, Op. 67

Vogler Quartet

RCA Victor Red Seal 09026 61438 2 □ 59:16 mins □ 𝟃𝟃𝟃

Schumann's detailed study of the great Classical quartets, during 1842, found utterance in his own series of three string quartets, Op. 41. These are refined, assured, highly individual, yet curiously elusive works, not played nearly as often as they should be. Even the first of the series, the A minor work recorded here, has its share of problems, notably in the first movement, with its unusual key relationships and abrupt changes of mood. What follows is a Scherzo recalling Mendelssohn, a serene Adagio set within recitative-like episodes, and an unusually virtuosic finale. The Vogler Quartet turn in a deeply committed, accurately tight-reined account of a work which, in the wrong hands, can all too readily fall foul of its own idiosyncracies. The Voglers are on familiar ground in Brahms's last and certainly greatest quartet, his Op. 67. Their performance is particularly impressive, and skilfully attuned to the long-breathed paragraphs of this work. A fine disc from the young Vogler Quartet, whose technical accomplishments might well be the envy of rival groups already in their dotage! Richly and expansively recorded. *MJ*

SCHUMANN

String Quartet in A minor, Op. 41/1
see also GRIEG: String Quartets

SCHUMANN

Stücke im Volkston, Op. 102; Fantasiestücke, Op. 73; Märchenerzählungen, Op. 132; Märchenbilder, Op. 113; 3 Romanzen, Op. 94

Mikhail Rudy (piano), Michel Portal (clarinet), Gérard Caussé (viola), Boris Pergamenschikov (cello)

EMI CDC 7 54824 2 □ 74:41 mins □ 𝟃𝟃𝟃

The year 1849 was a decisive one for Robert Schumann; the political upheavals that precipitated Wagner's hasty departure from Dresden heralded a prolific period in Schumann's creativity. His five *Stücke im Volkston*, of April 1849, receive alert and eloquent treatment from Boris Pergamenschikov; his bold, highly charged approach is particularly impressive. The *Fantasiestücke* date from February 1849, and were probably envisioned as a continuous three-movement suite. Clarinettist Michel Portal plays with rich lyrical intensity; his suave Gallic timbre suits the music well, though he is heard to fuller advantage in the 1853 *Märchenerzählungen*, dedicated to Schumann's disciple Albert Dietrich. The Op. 94 Romances, heard here in a version for clarinet, were written in early December 1849, the oboe being Schumann's specified instrument. Portal is intuitively musical, and finds an ideal equilibrium between sentiment and seriousness. Gérard Caussé, who joins Portal and the fine supporting pianist Mikhail Rudy in Op. 132, also plays the four Märchenbilder, Op. 113, for viola and piano (1851). These highly contrasted miniatures (Florestan and Eusebius revisited, perhaps?) afford expressive as well as virtuosic opportunity, to which both artists respond adroitly. *MJ*

SCHUMANN

Stücke im Volkston, Op. 102
see also SCHUBERT: Sonata in A minor (Arpeggione)

SHOSTAKOVICH

String Quartets Nos 1–15; Two Pieces, Op. 36

Shostakovich Quartet

Olympia OCD 531/5 □ ADD □ 379:17 mins (5 discs, also available separately) □ 𝟃𝟃

An obvious first choice here might have been the Borodin Quartet's EMI cycle. Yet this eponymous Russian team is at once less consistently stylish and more dangerous in the whirlwinds that so often sweep across Shostakovich's steady 37-year odyssey (he began the First Quartet in 1938, a year after the Fifth Symphony; the death dirges of the Fifteenth in 1974 were followed only by the

Michelangelo Suite and the Viola Sonata). I opt for that danger, and for the supreme soloistic, as well as corporate, prowess of the players. Shostakovich wrote much of this music for personalities – Nos 11 to 14 are dedicated respectively to each of the members of the Beethoven Quartet, and slanted accordingly – and Andrei Shishlov, the team's outstanding first violinist, is supremely charismatic. Capable of extreme muted tenderness, he can also produce the most uncompromisingly steely tone, and it is not his fault if some of the earlier, rougher recordings catch that too harshly. Still, one has to be prepared for much necessary unpleasantness *en route* to the very different endgames of the last three quartets. The shared experience of this Fifteenth is quite the most haunting I know, notwithstanding other dedicated shrivings of the soul over the years; choose the disc which features it alongside Quartets Nos 10 and 11 if you seek a single-CD sample of this achievement. *DN*

SHOSTAKOVICH

String Quartets Nos 4 in D, 11 in F minor & 14 in F sharp

Hagen Quartet

DG 445 864-2 □ 71:06 mins □ 𝄞𝄞𝄞

The private and public testament of suffering that is Shostakovich's Eighth Quartet has been conventionally perceived as a gateway to appreciating the series – you can hear the Borodin Quartet's performance of it on the disc recommended above for the Piano Quintet – but there are many other paths to be taken, and the ever-vital Hagen Quartet choose an especially fascinating one for starters.

Their capacity for abrasiveness and acerbity – especially searing in the nastier moments of the quizzical Eleventh Quartet – come hand in hand with a withdrawn, almost unearthly beauty that casts new perspectives on the Fourth (which the Shostakovich of *Testimony* claimed to be a protest against enduring Soviet anti-Semitism; and there are certainly fleeting impressions of Jewish music to contribute to the complex fabric of the whole). That wistfulness is also indispensable in the closing pages of the Fourteenth – nostalgic, deeply moving and so evidently at one with the world that if Shostakovich had written nothing more thereafter it would have been easy to say that he was serenely reconciled to death. There are fascinating parallels here, too, with the Hagen's no less remarkable performances of the Janáček quartets. *DN*

SHOSTAKOVICH/ROSLAVETS/GLINKA

Shostakovich: Viola Sonata, Op. 147

Roslavets: Viola Sonata

Glinka (compl. Borisovsky): Viola Sonata

Yuri Bashmet (viola), Mikhail Muntian (piano)

RCA Victor Red Seal 09026 61273 2 □ 67:24 mins □ 𝄞𝄞𝄞

The longer he lived, the more Shostakovich composed with the specific instrumental talents of the greatest string-players in mind, among them violinist David Oistrakh, cellists Natalia Gutman and Mstislav Rostropovich, and the members of the Shostakovich Quartet. Had the composer lived a few years longer, there can be no doubt that the interpretative genius of Yuri Bashmet would have joined the distinguished list. Here he carries on his shoulders the supreme interpretative challenge of the Viola Sonata completed a month before Shostakovich's death in 1975. The skeletal lines of the first movement, bearing a minimum of dynamic instruction in the score, are carefully fleshed out with the subtlest hints of passing warmth and colour, while in the swan-song final Adagio, touching with extreme poignancy on the triplets and dotted rhythms of Beethoven's *Moonlight* Sonata, Bashmet and his partner Mikhail Muntian (the pianist at the premiere) find the right distant voices for this whispered deconstruction.

The route to this last word in spare sonata writing is reached via the Scriabinesque rhapsody of Nikolai Roslavets's example and the torso of a work written by 'the father of Russian music' in his youth. Here it proves impossible to tell – and pointless to judge – whether Glinka's Romantic subject-matter is generic or not, so spellbindingly does Bashmet project every aspect of instrumental line and tone. *DN*

SIMPSON

String Quartets Nos 3 & 6; String Trio

Delmé Quartet

Hyperion CDA 66376 □ 72:13 mins □ 𝄞𝄞𝄞

Robert Simpson's 15 string quartets constitute the most important extended quartet cycle by any British composer. They have all been recorded, in various couplings, on separate Hyperion discs by the Delmé Quartet, dedicated and assured exponents of Simpson's trenchantly post-Beethovenian music. It's difficult to choose a single disc as the most outstanding, so consistent is the composer's invention, the standard of playing and finely natural recorded sound. (As with Simpson's symphonies, there is a huge one-movement Ninth with a disc to itself, which may be the greatest of the quartets.) This CD perhaps gives the widest conspectus. The comparatively early Third Quartet (1954) is in a characteristic Simpsonian two-movement design, slow and fast – the latter a hugely virtuosic Allegro deciso finale. The rich and powerful Sixth (1975), with its profoundly atmospheric slow movement, is the last of a triptych of quartets that forms his commentary on and personal exploration of the forms and processes of Beethoven's *Razumovsky* Quartets. And there is a bonus in the late, concise String Trio (1987), cast as a sequence of Prelude, Adagio and Fugue. *CM*

SKALKOTTAS

Quartets Nos 1 & 2 for Piano & Wind; Concertinos for Oboe & Piano and for Trumpet & Piano, etc

Håkan Hardenberger (trumpet), Heinz Holliger (oboe), Klaus Thunemann (bassoon), Bruno Canino (piano)

Philips 442 795-2 □ 48:59 mins □ 🎵🎵🎵

Nikos Skalkottas is one of those hard-to-pin-down figures that 20th-century music has made into a speciality. Born on the Greek island of Evia in 1904, he was a pupil of Schoenberg in Berlin in the late Twenties, before he was forced to leave Germany when the Nazis came to power. He returned to Greece and spent the rest of his life isolated from the musical world, composing prodigiously. He died in 1949.

The wealth of music he wrote in his last decade has only gradually been unearthed since. The late Hans Keller was a vociferous champion of Skalkottas's achievement, but it's been hard to assess those claims: much of his music has remained unpublished, performances of what are often fiendishly difficult works are rare and recordings of them rarer still. The collection on this disc was in fact conceived as a cycle by Skalkottas, who in the early Forties framed the three works for solo wind and piano with the two quartets for oboe, bassoon and trumpet with piano. It makes a satisfying, neatly shaped sequence: Skalkottas's technique is formidable, his understanding of instrumental capabilities outstandingly perceptive and the performances, it almost goes without saying with this line-up, are first class.
Andrew Clements

SMETANA

String Quartet No. 1 in E minor (From my Life)
see **DVORAK**: String Quartet in F, Op. 96

STRAVINSKY

Concertino for Twelve Instruments; Octet
see **CHORAL & SONG**: STRAVINSKY: *Perséphone*

SZYMANOWSKI

Mythes; Nocturne and Tarantella; Violin Sonata in D minor

Lydia Mordkovitch (violin), Marina Gusak-Grin (piano)

Chandos CHAN 8747 □ 51:55 mins □ 🎵🎵🎵

The *Mythes*, three gorgeously and sensuously impressionistic studies for violin and piano inspired by Classical mythology, were the work in which Szymanowski himself believed he found his personal identity as a composer, and they have remained – especially the opening number 'The Fountain of Arethusa' – among his most widely admired pieces. They are sumptuously treated in this stunning Szymanowski recital, one of Lydia Mordkovitch's finest recordings. She invests the music with a dark, intense, lustrously resinous sound, creating the powerful emotional punch which his exotic middle-period idiom really requires if its impressionist elegance and complexly textured harmonic style are not to sound over-refined.

The *Nocturne and Tarantella*, composed shortly before the *Mythes* and often dismissed by critics as salon music, is transformed in this interpretation into a great virtuoso showpiece, its first movement like a voice of nature, the second a staggeringly dionysiac piece of bravura. The Violin Sonata is an early work, too redolent of Franck and Richard Strauss to be wholly individual, but most enjoyable when treated in such full-bloodedly Romantic fashion. Gusak-Grin is Mordkovitch's match in fire and expressivity, and draws every nuance from each phrase of Szymanowski's note-filled piano writing. A marvellously full-bodied recording too. *CM*

TAILLEFERRE

Image for eight instruments; String Quartet; Violin Sonatas Nos 1 & 2; Sonata for Solo Clarinet; Arabesque for Clarinet and Piano; Forlane for Flute and Piano; Piano Trio

Ulrike Siebler (flute), Deborah Marshall (clarinet), Heiko Stralendorff (celesta), Angela Gassenhuber (piano), Fanny Mendelssohn Quartet

Trouba Disc TRO-CD 01406 □ 66:42 mins □ 🎵🎵🎵

Utter delight. Germaine Tailleferre is usually remembered as a deeply Twenties figure, the woman member of Les Six: but she survived them all, dying in 1983 aged over ninety. Her works are compact, generally unassuming, quintessentially French, irresistibly tuneful and perfectly written for their media. Wit, elegance and pastoral languor abound; the pieces are nicely contrasted, but the style (superficially Poulenc with an undertow of Debussy and Ravel) doesn't change much from the little 1918 *Image* to the Piano Trio written sixty years later. Instead it deepens, becomes ever richer in expressive effect, as in the sensuous, profoundly lyrical slow movement of Violin Sonata No. 2. By the end we're dealing with a composer whose no-nonsense concision encompasses real wisdom: the radiant Piano Trio is one of the masterly French essays in the genre, matching Ravel and Fauré. Tailleferre has been taken up largely by German performers (the Clementi Trio of Cologne have a rival version of the Piano Trio on Largo, less well recorded but enterprisingly coupled with trios by Milhaud, Shostakovich and Nikolai Roslavets); these are wholly in sympathy with her music. Here's proof that Gallic charm survived, undimmed, into the late 20th century! *CM*

<hr>

Violin Sonata in G minor (Devil's Trill); Violin Sonatas, Op. 1/2, 8, 10 & 12; Pastorale in A

Locatelli Trio

Hyperion CDA 66430 □ 73:17 mins □ *● ● ●*

Tartini has been better known by reputation – as a virtuoso violinist and founder of an influential violin school in Padua – than by his music. This disc, five sonatas and a pastorale, is clear evidence that the music is undeservedly neglected.

Four sonatas are from the dozen of Tartini's Op. 1. This set starts with 'Church sonatas', including fugal second movements and no explicit dances. No. 2 in F more or less sustains a three-voice fugue, violin double-stopping and bass: the technical demands are far beyond Corelli's earlier Op. 5, often seen as the model for high Baroque Violin Sonatas.

The remaining items are 'chamber sonatas', including the heartfelt pathos of *Didone abbandonata*, Dido bewailing her lost Aeneas in cold, despairing fragments of harmony, three or four chords at a time. The later *Devil's Trill* ends the disc, supposedly written after a dream in which the devil played Tartini's fiddle – and devilishly well played here. In fact, Elizabeth Wallfisch's technical prowess makes all these sonatas sound easy – which

they are not – and leaves room for innumerable expressive nuances. Both this and a second collection of later sonatas are discs to treasure and enjoy through many a repeated listening. *GP*

<hr>

String Quartets Nos 1–3; String Quartet in B flat; Souvenir de Florence

Borodin Quartet; Yuri Yurov (viola), Mikhaïl Milman (cello)

Teldec 4509-90422-2 □ 151:06 mins (2 discs) □ *● ● ●*

While everyone knows and loves the ubiquitous Andante cantabile from Tchaikovsky's First Quartet, the rest of his chamber output remains surprisingly neglected. The problem cannot be attributed to any lack of musical inspiration on the part of the composer, although the fearsome technical demands of works like the masterly Third String Quartet, cast in the unusual key of E flat minor, may well be an inhibiting factor. A more plausible explanation lies with a tendency among non-Russian performers to interpret the music in an overtly Classical manner, thereby smoothing out the dramatic quality of Tchaikovsky's conceptions. Fortunately, no such criticisms can be levelled against the Borodin Quartet, whose definitive renditions of these works are gloriously captured in this excellent release. Having steeped themselves in this repertoire for many years, the Borodin Quartet have an instinctive understanding of Tchaikovsky's emotional world and produce playing of profound intensity in the heart-rending slow movements of the Second and Third Quartets. *EL*

<hr>

Chamber music

Amsterdam Baroque Soloists/Ton Koopman

Erato 4509-94355-2 □ 60:00 mins □ *● ● ●*

Telemann's easy facility as a composer has led to accusations of a lack of originality which this disc does much to challenge. He was a master of integrating not only sharply contrasting melodic ideas but also the highly distinctive tone colours of contrasting instruments playing them. When Koopman turns from harpsichord to organ, the click of its action adds a further percussive impetus to Telemann's powerful rhythmic drive.

Bright, playful passagework in the first of two G major quartets and the C major Recorder Sonata establishes this Amsterdam group's excellent ensemble and crisp articulation and, with more sombre instrumentation in the B flat minor Trio Sonata and a Bassoon Sonata which recorder-players will recognise (Telemann offers both options), they vividly demonstrate their broad range of tonal variety and mood. This is Telemann at his most diverse and exhilarating. *GP*

TELEMANN

Musique de table

Musica Antiqua Köln/Reinhard Goebel

Archiv 427 619-2 □ 253:25 mins (4 discs) □ ❷❷❷

While music such as this could possibly have accompanied a banquet, the term *Musique de table* actually delineates a musical genre, equivalent to sacred or theatre music. Telemann organised this huge variety of instrumental groupings, textures and moods into three 'Productions'. Each begins with a suite – an extended French *ouverture* and a set of galant dances, some (réjouissances, postillons) highly characterised. The following *quatuors* are outstanding – the conventional trio sonata is immensely enriched by the addition of another instrumental 'voice'.

Then in each 'Production' comes a concerto for imaginative ensembles of soloists – three violins, a pair of horns... – before a trio sonata, a solo sonata and a brief *conclusion*.

Recorded quality is good, though I could have done with less harpsichord in the smaller-scaled pieces. Goebel and Musica Antiqua Köln captivate with their characteristic energy and exuberance. If all three 'Productions' on four discs is too daunting, try Il Fondamento's performance of Part Three on a single Accent disc. It's a touch blander, but also thoroughly recommendable.

Full of delightful surprises, this is far too arresting to use as the mere background music that its title may suggest. *GP*

TIPPETT

String Quartets Nos 1–5

Lindsay Quartet

ASV CD DCS 231 □ ADD □ 122:36 mins (2 discs) □ ❷❷❷

A most intelligent and welcome compilation from the Lindsays' 1975 LP of Tippett's first three quartets (originally on Decca) and ASV's own recordings of the Fourth and Fifth Quartets, which were composed for this distinguished ensemble. Bringing to all five a dedication and wealth of experience which

result in almost ideal performances of these by no means straightforward works, Peter Cropper and his team display once again why they are one of the premier quartets active in Britain today. Nos 1–3, comparatively early works, contain some of Tippett's most attractive music. The Lindsays know perfectly how to let the intricate counterpoint of the fast movements dance as it should; they find a wealth of emotion in such lyrical effusions as the Andante of the Third Quartet. Not even their advocacy, I fear, can quite reconcile me to the subfusc invention of the Fourth, where everything somehow seems only an approximation of quartet writing: even the finale (with its direct allusions to Beethoven's *Grosse Fuge*) seems thrown together in a recklessly slapdash way. Yet the eloquence of the playing is admirable in itself, and the more relaxed mosaic of the fantasia-like Fifth Quartet, a welcome return to form, receives a performance of the deepest affection. You wouldn't guess the recordings spanned twenty years, so beautifully natural is the sound quality. A mandatory purchase. *CM*

TIPPETT

String Quartet No. 1
see also **ORCHESTRAL**: TIPPETT: Concerto for Double String Orchestra

VAUGHAN WILLIAMS

Romance for viola and piano
see Collection: English Music for Viola

VERDI/BERG

Verdi: String Quartet in E minor

Berg: Lyric Suite

Vogler Quartet

RCA Victor Red Seal RD 60855 □ 52:00 mins □ ❷❷❷

No, this isn't a deliberately perverse example of maladroit programme-planning, despite the fact that externally these two works have absolutely nothing in common! True enough, the Berg *Lyric Suite* has a frantic delirium and an ardour which are overtly provocative, but Verdi's Quartet, written in 1873, has both heady drama and lustily singable good tunes normally expected of his stage works. The Vogler Quartet are winsome Verdians; they play the affectingly lyrical slow movement (Andantino) warmly, and as Verdi directs, *con eleganza*. There's splendid wit and vitality, too, in their reading of the technically complex finale, an unusual Scherzo-Fugue. This is a particularly fine performance from these young artists of a work that is still seriously marginalised in both the concert hall and on disc. Alban Berg's *Lyric Suite* is one of the cornerstones of the Second Viennese School repertoire for strings; this is a formidably controlled account, never overbearing or truculent, yet keenly responsive to the plethora of performance directions which litter this fiendishly difficult score. Attractively natural recordings of compositions which are widely polarised in style, in readings as cultivated and imaginative as you're likely to hear anywhere. Incidentally, I'd avoid what, on paper at least, promised to be *the* prime Verdi Quartet recommendation; Sony's hard-edged sonics for the Juilliard Quartet's coupling with Sibelius's *Voces intimae* Quartet is a major disappointment. *MJ*

VIVALDI

Cello Sonatas (complete)

David Watkin (solo cello), Helen Gough (continuo cello), David Miller (theorbo, archlute, guitar), Robert King (organ, harpsichord)

Hyperion CDA 66881/2 □ 115:37 mins (2 discs)
□ 🟢🟢🟢

David Watkin's integral survey of Vivaldi's authenticated cello sonatas ranks honourably among the best available. Several rival contenders may be safely passed over. Anthony Pleeth (ASV) and Susan Sheppard (CRD) endorse CPE Bach's time-honoured, universal palliative for Baroque accompaniment – just keyboard and cello continuo alone. Christophe Coin, Pieter Wispelwey, and now David Watkin spice that hitherto drab concoction with additional parts for theorbo, archlute and Baroque guitar. Julius Berger (on Orfeo) plays a modern instrument accompanied throughout by chamber organ, and includes a tenth Sonata in A, of dubious provenance and consequently omitted from Ryom's catalogue. Watkin and Coin (L'Oiseau-Lyre), then, emerge decisively amid a very mixed field.

Finest among these works is the E minor Sonata, RV 40 (given wider currency in emasculations by Bazelaire and d'Indy), readily highlighting Watkin's purposeful style, uncluttered by intrusive gesture, though adept, emphatic and serene. Coin, altogether more sanguine and athletic, has greater spontaneity and allure alongside Watkin's decorum, impeccable clarity and relative restraint. Coin ornaments melodic lines more liberally, and collectors who prefer their Vivaldi agile, daring and occasionally a touch cavalier will find him enthralling. The dutifully introspective Watkin has the advantage of outstanding continuo support, and a recording of surpassing beauty

and unexaggerated perspectives. Pieter Wispelwey's Channel issue is competent though incomplete, so if faced with a choice I'd opt for David Watkin's consistently articulate playing, the decisive criterion being Hyperion's rapturously seductive sound. *MJ*

VIVALDI

Chamber Sonatas, RV 53, 58, 59, 81 (Lund) & 779 (Salmoè)

Paul Goodwin, Gail Hennessey (oboe), John Holloway (violin), Colin Lawson (chalumeau), Nigel North (archlute, guitar), Susan Sheppard (cello), Frances Eustace (bassoon), John Toll (harpsichord, organ)

Harmonia Mundi HMU 907104 □ 50:01 mins
□ 🟢🟢🟢

This CD collects together some attractive Vivaldi rarities. They include his only surviving sonatas for solo oboe, RV 81, plus the little-heard quartet sonata for oboe, violin, organ and chalumeau (single-reed instrument, related to the clarinet), RV 779, which was discovered in a library in Dresden as recently as the mid-Seventies.

The disc's two remaining pieces, RV 58 and RV 59, are not by Vivaldi at all! Though published under his name in 1737, they are now known to be the work of the Frenchman Nicolas Chédeville, who, nevertheless, composed his forgeries with such flair that they passed as genuine Vivaldi for two centuries. A listen to the lovely, lilting Pastorale of RV 59 will help to explain why.

Of the authentic pieces, the haunting RV 779 shares its lead voices between oboe, violin and gently exuberant organ. In RV 53 and RV 81, however, the oboe is in the limelight itself, exerting its charms most winningly in the former's opening Adagio, with its melting lyricism, and in the latter's elegant Largo, where the two oboes entwine with an exquisite delicacy. Paul Goodwin plays these pieces with a disarming finesse that exactly fits the Baroque chamber repertoire. He receives sensitive support from his fellow musicians, and the sound is excellent. A delightful release. *Graham Lock*

WALTON
String Quartet in A minor
see HINDEMITH: String Quartet No. 3 in C

WEBER/HUMMEL/REICHA

Weber: Clarinet Quintet in B flat

Hummel: Quartet in E flat for Clarinet, Violin, Viola and Cello

Reicha: Clarinet Quintet in B flat

Charles Neidich (clarinet); L'Archibudelli

Sony Vivarte SK 57968 □ 78:09 mins □ 🄋🄋🄋

Weber, the father of German Romantic opera, wrote his theatrically extrovert Clarinet Quintet in 1815 as a display vehicle for the executant skills of the Munich-based clarinet virtuoso Heinrich Bärmann. Playing on instruments of the period, clarinettist Charles Neidich and the members of the string ensemble L'Archibudelli turn in a splendid performance, which strikes a happy equilibrium between dramatic posturing and riotous, high-spirited buffoonery. This hugely enjoyable disc also includes winning performances of the Clarinet Quartet in E flat by Hummel and, from the Bohemian (later naturalised French) master of the Classical wind quintet, Antonín Reicha, a sparklingly tuneful Clarinet Quintet in B flat, dating from c1810. L'Archibudelli play with their customary flair and imagination; Neidich's instrument (modelled on an early 19th-century clarinet by Grenser) has a breadth of sonority and distinctive timbre which will astonish, while the Sony engineering is in the demonstration bracket. *MJ*

WEBER
Clarinet Quintet in B flat
see also BRAHMS: Clarinet Quintet in B minor

WEBERN
Concerto for Nine Players, Op. 24
see **INSTRUMENTAL**: Collection: The Glenn Gould Edition

WEBERN

Music for String Quartet and String Trio

Mary Ann McCormick (mezzo-soprano); Emerson Quartet

DG 445 828-2 □ 67:55 mins □ 🄋🄋🄋

Very nearly Webern's entire output for string quartet and trio: in terms of duration, more than half the disc is given up to music unheard and unpublished in his lifetime. Yet the string medium seems always to have inspired him, and these are all in one sense or another finished and significant creations. The early String Quartet and *Langsamer Satz* of 1905 and the waltz-time Rondo, all written while he was studying with Schoenberg, show what

gorgeous late-Romantic ideas Webern had at that time.

After these warmly expansive early tonal pieces we hear the clipped and powerful Op. 5 Movements, the tiny, aphoristic Op. 9 Bagatelles, and the sculptural yet explosive 'official' String Quartet, Op. 28. Minus one violin, the Emerson players also essay the masterly Op. 20 String Trio, and another, posthumously discovered trio movement. Plus female voice, they give the tremulous, suffused quartet-song *Schmerz, immer blick' nach oben* in its intended combination with early forms of two of the Bagatelles. In these brief works sensitive expressivity is all, welded in the 12-note scores to an intense structural logic, every nuance of every note having meaning.

Although recorded in four different venues, the studio sound is uniformly excellent, as are the interpretations. *CM*

WIENIAWSKI

Polonaises in D & A; Obertass Mazurka; Scherzo Tarantelle; Kuyawiak; Capriccio Valse; Légende; Souvenir de Moscow; Variations on an Original Theme

Ruggiero Ricci (violin), Joanna Gruenberg (piano)

Unicorn-Kanchana Souvenir Series UKCD 2048 □ 52:54 mins □ 🄋🄋

Henryk Wieniawski (born in Lublin, Poland, on 10 July 1835) may be said to rival Paganini in stature as one of the seminal Romantic violinist-composers of the 19th century. He began a triumphant career as an itinerant virtuoso in 1848, and became court violinist to Tsar Alexander II in 1860. The majority of his hair-raising compositions were designed as vehicles for his own legendary technique, though Wieniawski's pedagogic contributions to modern violin-playing, and his pioneering involvement with Beethoven's string quartets, make him a figure of particular interest. This CD brings together nine of Wieniawski's most familiar recital pieces, including the splendid Polonaises in D and A, the Scherzo Tarantelle, and the beautiful *Légende*, in performances of palpitating energy and bravura from Ruggiero Ricci, accompanied by Joanna Gruenberg. The recording itself, though mastered digitally, appeared on LP in 1980, and the sound of this CD reissue is somewhat first-generation in terms of overall sound quality; piano timbre is rather thin, and there's an abrasive shrillness to Ricci's sound which is occasionally unflattering. But Ricci's artistry is ideally tailored to meet the needs of this repertoire. The disc is something of a classic, and should not be missed by lovers of the grand Romantic traditions of virtuoso violin-playing. *MJ*

WOLF

Italian Serenade
see JANACEK: String Quartets

WOLPE

Suite im Hexachord; Quintet with Voice; Piece in Three Parts

Peter Serkin (piano), Jan Opalach (bass-baritone); Chamber Music Society of Lincoln Center, Speculum Musicae/Oliver Knussen, William Purvis

Bridge BCD 9043 □ 50:50 mins □ 𝄞𝄞𝄞

If any composer deserves to be regarded as the true heir to the aesthetic of Anton Webern it is Stefan Wolpe (1907–72), whose music has very slowly but surely begun to establish itself in the twenty years since his death. From 1938 onwards the German-born Wolpe lived in the United States, and it is as an American composer that he is now celebrated, for he fits nicely into that category of independent-spirited composers, fiercely uncompromising, who seem to define the history of music in the New World. He had grown up among modernists in music and the visual arts, and studied briefly in Vienna with Webern; early pieces like the *Suite im Hexachord* show austere serial working elaborated within a scheme of constant rhythmic surprise.

The great music, though, came later, after Wolpe had established himself in the USA. The 1957 *Quintet with Voice*, the main work on the Bridge disc, belongs to the years when Wolpe taught at Black Mountain College, where his colleagues included John Cage. Sometimes the music seems to reflect something of the anarchic spirit of that time, but the argument is always a thoroughly musical one, conducted with clarity and rigour. The performances, from musicians who have consistently championed and promoted Wolpe's cause, are outstanding, true labours of love. *Andrew Clements*

WOOD

String Quartets Nos 1–4

Chilingirian Quartet

Conifer 75605 51239 2 □ 77:35 mins □ 𝄞𝄞𝄞

Hugh Wood's four string quartets add up to a substantial corpus of music both in duration and in expressive range. In the Third Quartet, a dynamic transition from despair and inertia to rebirth of strength and joy is written into the music through a programmatic structure of quotes from the poetry of Donne and

Herbert, and an oblique reference to the composer's earlier setting of a Laurie Lee poem.

Elsewhere, the honest utterance of feeling seems a natural outcome of the musical processes, which range from a profound Schoenbergian working out of materials to an absorption with intricate semi-aleatoric textures, probably inspired by the example of Roberto Gerhard.

The Second Quartet mixes rhythmically measured sections with unsynchronised passages to brilliant effect, and with a sense of organic growth that is felt throughout its 39 brief sections. In contrast, the Fourth Quartet is a four-movement work in the Classical pattern, finely contrapuntal, and with a slow movement of Mahlerian intensity. As in the First Quartet, a short introduction provides ideas that prove important for the rest of the piece. The Chilingirians play this music, written for them in 1992–3, with understanding and commitment – qualities that apply equally to the other quartets on the disc. *Nicholas Williams*

COLLECTION: A CONCORDE OF SWEETE SOUNDE

Renaissance recorder music by Parsons, Tallis, Taverner, Carver, Aston, Byrd, White, etc

Amsterdam Loeki Stardust Quartet

L'Oiseau-Lyre 436 155-2 □ 58:18 mins □ 𝄞𝄞𝄞

The Amsterdam Loeki Stardust Quartet have already recorded repertory for recorder consort which ranges from the English Baroque to *Misty*. This disc, devoted to music of Renaissance England, offers a fine example of this group's freshness and startling emotional range.

Much of the music recorded here was not originally written for the recorder, but the musical arrangements throughout sound appropriate and natural. The programming is also excellent. The timbral variety of the instruments and the choice of music, which is varied both in mood and texture, effectively maintain interest and concentration. Contrast, for example, the sombre darkness of the 14th-century *Inter chorus paradiscolum* with the sparkling vigour of Aston's *Maske*. A most enjoyable recital. *Nicholas Rast*

Works by Britten, Clarke, Grainger, Bax, Bridge & Vaughan Williams

Paul Coletti (viola), Leslie Howard (piano)

Hyperion CDA 66687 □ **66:55 mins** □ *① ② ③*

Many British composers of the earlier part of the century found a special inspiration in the uniquely mellow tone of the viola, often encouraged in their endeavours by the remarkable playing of Lionel Tertis. In his first recital recording, Paul Coletti, who was born in Scotland but now lives in the United States, proves an eloquent advocate for music which is little known, but offers rewards in abundance.

For example, the three contrasted pieces by Rebecca Clarke are real discoveries. The charming *Lullaby*, the Romantically atmospheric *Morpheus* and the larger-scale Sonata reveal a talent that was based upon an intimate understanding of the instrument.

Like Clarke, Bridge was a fine viola-player; his two pieces, *Allegro appassionato* and *Pensiero*, combine sensitivity with passion and technical command, while Bax's *Legend* has a typically Celtic Romanticism. The Vaughan Williams *Romance*, an undated piece discovered after the composer's death, generates considerable emotional power; and Britten's *Elegy* is another recent discovery, first performed in 1984, but composed 55 years before.

Two unusual items by Percy Grainger complete a most stimulating programme, which is performed with distinction by both artists – it seems a pity, therefore, that pianist Leslie Howard goes unacknowledged in the biographies contained in the insert notes. *Terry Barfoot*

English chamber music of the 17th century by Byrd, Jenkins, Lawes, Matteis, Baltzar, Schop, Farinel, Simpson, Brade & Anon.

Trio Sonnerie; Stephen Stubbs (theorbo, guitar), Andrew Lawrence-King (harp, organ)

Teldec Das Alte Werk 4509-90841-2 □ **69:48 mins** □ *① ② ③*

This delightful collection of Baroque chamber music celebrates the variation-form known as 'divisions', which was very popular in 17th-century England. A largely improvisatory genre, divisions required the player to extemporise variations on a repeating 'ground' (usually a melody in the bass). The leading exponent of the music was Christopher Simpson, author of the definitive *The Division-Violist* (published in 1659): the CD takes its title from his declaration that 'invention is a gift of nature'.

In the 17th century many well-known composers and instrumentalists were tempted to test their invention at divisions. This recording includes pieces by William Byrd, William Lawes and Nicola Matteis, the latter's brief suite here being full of the most charmingly extravagant, plangent music for violin.

Since variety was of the essence in divisions, many of these works call for mercurial, even florid, virtuoso skills from the soloists. Others, such as Johann Schop's *Lachrimae* or William Brade's lovely *Coral*, touch, albeit fleetingly, on deeper feelings.

The Trio Sonnerie, abetted by Stephen Stubbs and Andrew Lawrence-King, give an excellent account of this repertoire. In particular, violinist Monica Huggett, who takes the lead on many tracks, plays with great zest and fluency. A thoroughly engaging release. *Graham Lock*

Choral and Song

De Staat

Schoenberg Ensemble/Reinbert de Leeuw

Nonesuch 7559-79251-2 □ 35:24 mins □ 🎵🎵🎵

Louis Andriessen's hard-edged and rhythmically insistent music is a politically engaged kind of minimalism very far removed from the iconic contemplation of a Pärt or a Tavener. There are similarities to John Adams or Steve Reich, but Andriessen is more uncompromising, and *De Staat*'s audible parentage includes Indonesian gamelan, jazz and the brutal ostinato rhythms of Stravinsky's *The Rite of Spring*. Andriessen himself has since moved on from the style of this work to something at once more complex and less overtly aggressive, but *De Staat* remains probably his best-known work. It's a polemical setting for chorus, oboes, brass, guitars, pianos, harps and violas of passages from Plato's *Republic*, forbidding the alteration of musical laws lest they affect the political stability of a hierarchically ordered state. It packs a visceral punch, a tremendously baleful cumulative power, and this performance has the necessary sinister discipline in dark and splendid sound. The lack of a coupling is to be regretted on this quite short disc. *CM*

ANDRIESSEN

De Stijl; M is for Man, Music, Mozart

Gertrude Thomas (voice), Astrid Seriese (voice); Schoenberg Ensemble, Asko Ensemble/Reinbert de Leeuw; Orkest de Volharding/Jurjen Hempel

Nonesuch 7559-79342-2 □ 54:13 mins □ 🎵🎵🎵

De Stijl, a portrait of the painter Mondrian, must be regarded as one of the most rhythmically exhilarating scores of recent years. Like much of Andriessen's work, it draws its inspiration from a wide variety of musical sources, including American minimalism, jazz, rock and Stravinsky. But these elements are fused into an entirely individual and powerful conception that carries the listener along with a sureness of touch that is all too rare in contemporary music. The work's impact is certainly enhanced by the outstandingly committed performance under Reinbert de Leeuw.

As a coupling, the music-theatre work *M is for Man, Music, Mozart*, commissioned originally as a soundtrack to a BBC Television bicentenary tribute to Mozart, strikes a somewhat different musical pose. The witty and sardonic sequence of songs and instrumental interludes suggests a conscious tribute to the idiom of Kurt Weill, though, as always, Andriessen manages to incorporate this stylistic reference without diluting his own clearly defined identity. Once again, the performance by the Volharding Orchestra and jazz singer Astrid Seriese is quite brilliant, and the sound is of demonstration quality. *EL*

BACH

Complete Cantatas, Vol. 1 (BWV 4, 21, 31, 71, 106, 131, 150, 185 & 196)

Barbara Schlick (soprano), Kai Wessel (alto), Guy de Mey (tenor), Klaus Mertens (bass); Amsterdam Baroque Orchestra & Choir/Ton Koopman

Erato 4509-98536-2 □ 180:18 mins (3 discs) □ 🎵🎵🎵

This is the first volume of Koopman's projected recording of all the Bach cantatas, due to be completed by the end of the millennium. Rilling has done it before, but with modern instruments that constantly demonstrate how sensitive Bach was to colour, texture and balance. Harnoncourt used Bach's own instruments, though not the small-scale forces suggested by recent research. We are inexpressibly indebted to both, but time moves on, as do techniques of instrument-making and -playing.

Koopman is approaching the challenge chronologically, here with nine cantatas, including the earliest, BWV 150 (the numbering system has nothing to do with dates of composition). Written before 1707, the most striking contrast with the mature works isn't in Bach's contrapuntal skill – wholly secure, and tested with some remarkably sinuous chromaticism – but in its kaleidoscopic changes of pace and mood. The musical invention is no less varied: the festive *Gott ist mein König* brilliantly scored for huge forces; the Actus Tragicus, *Gottes Zeit*, pure chamber music, with recorders, gambas and continuo; *Christ lag in Todesbanden* based throughout on a chorale; *Ich hatte viel Bekümmernis* including a blatantly operatic love duet.

Koopman uses (authentically) a high pitch, and the strain sometimes tells on voices, de Mey's in particular. But if you want to commit yourself to the whole of this incredibly rich repertoire, this new enterprise looks as if it will be hard to beat. *GP*

BACH

Cantatas: Liebster Gott, wenn werd ich sterben, BWV 8; Jesu, der du meine Seele, BWV 78; Was Gott tut, das ist wohlgetan, BWV 99

Julianne Baird (soprano), Allan Fast (alto), Frank Kelley (tenor), Jan Opalach (bass); The Bach Ensemble/Joshua Rifkin

L'Oiseau-Lyre 443 188-2 □ 57:59 mins □ *● ●*

This is the minimalist approach to Bach – voices and instruments one to a part. Certainly Bach was reduced at times to such limited forces, through under-funding by the Church establishment, presumably exacerbated at times by a flu epidemic on a winter weekend. Rifkin has put the arguments cogently, and others have accepted them enthusiastically. The results, in as carefully balanced a recording as here, are refreshingly transparent.

All three cantatas are from 1724, fully mature Leipzig works, beginning with elaborate movements built around a chorale, ending with the same chorale in a simple four-part setting, and with a series of recitatives and arias between. As always, the musical invention is staggering: in BWV 8, a flute depicts the tolling of a high-pitched funeral bell; in BWV 78, a dancing duet above a pizzicato violone suggests 'faint but eager steps'; in BWV 99, a vertiginous flute obbligato – Bach must have been served by an exceptional player to have risked this. *GP*

BACH

Cantatas: Ich hatte viel Bekümmernis, BWV 21; Am Abend aber desselbigen Sabbats, BWV 42

Barbara Schlick (soprano), Gérard Lesne (alto), Howard Crook (tenor), Peter Harvey, Peter Kooy (bass); La Chapelle Royale, Collegium Vocale/Philippe Herreweghe

Harmonia Mundi HMC 901328 □ 64:31 mins □ *● ● ●*

Although this recording duplicates BWV 21, recommended in the first volume of Koopman's projected recording of the complete cantatas, it earns its place here on two grounds. First, BWV 21 itself is very differently performed, yet no less convincingly – great music lends itself to constant re-interpretation. Herreweghe's approach is more reflective throughout, the performance heard from a little further away. He reinstates the tenor, too, as soloist in two arias, which Koopman gives without explanation to soprano.

Secondly, and most telling, is the presence of BWV 42. This begins with an exquisite orchestral movement, surely rescued from a lost concerto. Its solo group of two oboes and bassoon creates a unique colour – and the concerto's second movement may also be here, concealed as an aria for the same instruments accompanying an alto voice. The final aria, for bass, is no less remarkable, with three wholly unconnected musical ideas bound together in superbly inevitable counterpoint. The performance is exemplary. *GP*

BACH

Cantatas: O ewiges Feuer, BWV 34; Nun ist das Heil und die Kraft, BWV 50; Herz und Mund und Tat und Leben, BWV 147

Gillian Fisher (soprano), David James (alto), Ian Partridge (tenor), Michael George (bass), Paul Nicholson (organ); The Sixteen/Harry Christophers

Collins 13172 □ 55:59 mins □ *● ● ●*

All three of these cantatas date from Bach's later years in Leipzig, yet so consistent was his craftsmanship throughout his life that they all include music from earlier periods, leaving their outstanding quality unimpaired. BWV 50, *Nun ist das Heil*, is a single powerful movement, almost certainly from an earlier lost cantata. The other two are, in the words of the pastor-poet Neumeister, 'like a piece from an opera, composed of arias and *stylo recitativo*', with BWV 147 including the chorale setting 'Wohl mir…', familiarly 'Jesu, joy of man's desiring'.

The 18 voices of The Sixteen (*sic*!) are almost exactly what Bach described as his ideal number, though he didn't get them – hence the arguments about the scale of Bach choral performance today. The excellent solo quartet and their accompanying obbligato instruments craft lines thoughtfully, and Paul Nicholson frames the cantatas with two organ chorale preludes. *GP*

BACH

Christmas Oratorio

Lynda Russell (soprano), Catherine Wyn-Rogers (alto), Mark Padmore (tenor), Michael George (bass); The Sixteen, Orchestra of The Sixteen/Harry Christophers

Collins 70282 □ 147:38 mins (2 discs) □ 𝄞𝄞𝄞

This recording is superlative, demonstrating all The Sixteen's familiar virtues: precise, musical choral singing, crisply articulated playing by the orchestra, and a historically informed approach. Simon Heighes's informative note emphasises the devotional, rather than concert, nature of the *Christmas Oratorio*, and this is the key to Christophers's interpretation. Lilting rhythms in the arias reflect the intimacy of the nativity episodes, while the choruses radiate the joy of belief, rather than the clamour of ceremonial. Contributing to that feeling are the muted, even delicate, yet still exuberant tones of the natural trumpet (expertly played by Crispian Steele-Perkins), not least in the final chorus and in the bass aria 'Grosser Herr'. Michael George is the outstanding bass soloist; Lynda Russell, Catherine Wyn-Rogers and Mark Padmore also give pleasure in the remaining solo roles. *Barry Millington*

BACH

Magnificat, BWV 243; Ein feste Burg ist unser Gott, BWV 80

Barbara Schlick, Agnès Mellon (soprano), Gérard Lesne (alto), Howard Crook (tenor), Peter Kooy (bass); La Chapelle Royale, Collegium Vocale/Philippe Herreweghe

Harmonia Mundi HMC 901326 □ 53:00 mins □ 𝄞𝄞𝄞

This, it must be said, is a noisy recording, with a lot of 'presence' between the movements and the clatter of organ trackers behind Lesne's glorious singing of 'Esurientes'. The 21 voices, 12 strings and wind lift phrases exultingly in the opening Magnificat. Soloists match them –

Mellon's 'Exultavit' is ecstatic, Schlick's 'Humilitatem' poignant, bathed in a golden oboe glow, and Kooy is 'mighty', not weighty.

Although I've identified another fine Magnificat (reviewed with Christophers's recording of Vivaldi's Gloria; see entry), a compelling reason for recommending Herreweghe's disc is his account of *Ein feste Burg*, deservedly one of the most familiar of Bach's 200 extant cantatas. He chooses the version in which Bach's eldest son, Wilhelm Friedemann, added trumpets and timpani, greatly strengthening the mighty canon between top and bottom which Bach devised, with astonishing ingenuity, from the successive lines of the chorale melody. In the second choral movement, the power of the Burg – the stronghold – against a world peopled with devils, is magnificently portrayed in the pace of the rattling orchestral counterpoint around the unison chorale – a rare texture for Bach. In contrast, 'How Blessed are They', the double duet of alto/tenor and of violin/oboe da caccia, floats with an effortless lilt. *GP*

BACH

Magnificat, BWV 243

see also VIVALDI: Gloria

BACH

Mass in B minor

Lynne Dawson, Carol Hall, Nancy Argenta, Patrizia Kwella (soprano), Mary Nichols (mezzo-soprano), Michael Chance (alto), Howard Milner (tenor), Stephen Varcoe, Richard Lloyd Morgan (bass); Monteverdi Choir, English Baroque Soloists/John Eliot Gardiner

Archiv 415 514-2 □ 106:22 mins (2 discs) □ 𝄞𝄞𝄞

Current recordings of the B minor Mass range from 1929 to the present and encompass a variety of different approaches, from the Berlin Philharmonic and Vienna Singverein (Karajan) to the one to a part employed by Rifkin. So much of this compilation of recycled earlier music is for choir that the quality is crucial in selecting a recommendation. For me, the clarity, vitality and lyricism of the 1985 Monteverdi Choir remains unsurpassed, despite recent persuasive offerings from Koopman (Erato), Hickox (Chandos) and Christophers (Collins).

Gardiner takes liberties, though. Solo voices sing the 'Crucifixus', inviting more passion than the conventional choral *sotto voce* and generating a shattering contrast at 'Et resurrexit', full until the notorious 12 bars in the middle (where, it's assumed, the vocal bass-line is transcribed from a lost instrumental concerto). Elsewhere, too, a solo group, mostly from this immensely talented choir, varies the choral textures.

The arias are superbly managed, not only by singers – Michael Chance's countertenor cutting edge, Nancy Argenta ecstatic yet unhurried in 'Laudamus' – but by obbligato instrumentalists too: an artless and flexible violin duetting with Argenta; colourful horn hand-tuning in 'Quoniam; the ethereal flute of Lisa Beznosiuk; a vibrant richness in the oboes d'amore and da caccia. So far, challenged but unmatched. *GP*

BACH

Motets, BWV 225–230; Cantatas, BWV 50 & 118

Monteverdi Choir, English Baroque Soloists/John Eliot Gardiner

Erato 4509-99613-2 □ ADD □ **101:00 mins (2 discs)**
□ 🎵🎵

Four double-choir motets by Bach survive. Though funeral pieces, Bach's confidence in the contemplation of death gives them a sense of radiant joy. They are performed here most stylishly, not a cappella but with the kind of unspecified instrumental support which research suggests Bach would automatically have granted them. So a continuo line strengthens the bass – otherwise diluted by as many as seven parts above, with solo instruments doubling the voices in two of the motets.

As well as the remaining two explicitly titled motets, *Lobet den Herrn*, in four festively vigorous parts, and the five-part *Jesu, meine Freude*, Gardiner includes one quasi-motets. One, listed as Cantata 118, is a particular gem. Two 'litui', obsolete brass instruments here taken by natural trumpets, with four-part strings and choir, create a magnificently rich texture, in perfectly crafted counterpoint. Although Gardiner recorded this again in 1989, I've been haunted by the grippingly plangent quality of his earlier performance.

As well as being available separately, this pair of discs contributes to a boxed set including more cantatas and the orchestral suites, all wearing very well after over a decade. Only the price has changed – to our advantage. *GP*

BACH

St John Passion

The Scholars Baroque Ensemble

Naxos 8.550664/5 □ **109:40 mins (2 discs)** □ 🎵

Bach's Passions have been neatly described as unfolding on four levels: narrative, lyrical,

devotional, monumental. Yet there is nothing weightily monumental from this handful of singers and instrumentalists. The opening chorus moves at a sparkling pace, four in a bar as Bach wrote it, voices as cleanly articulated as instruments.

The Scholars' concept leans strongly towards dramatic narrative – sacred opera as opposed to sanctimonious devotion. Recitatives convey vivid realism, despite delayed cadences after the voice has finished. Robin Doveton is an involved Evangelist, David van Asch a very human Jesus. The soloists become the eight-voice chorus, especially impressive as the angry crowd lusting for blood. The narrative pace, from Evangelist to mob and back again, is unstoppable. In contrast, their devotional contribution in the chorales is beautifully shaped.

The lyrical element lies in the exceptionally colourful arias – Bach scored no two alike. They are highly charged here, from Julian Podger's impassioned outburst of remorse after Peter's denial of Christ to Kym Amps's heart-broken sobbing in 'Zerfliesse, mein Herze'.

Intimate recording exposes occasional roughness of intonation (and audible edits), but the dramatic power – and the budget price – makes this an exceptional bargain. *GP*

BACH

St Matthew Passion

Barbara Schlick (soprano), Kai Wessel (alto), Guy de Mey, Christoph Prégardien (tenor), Peter Kooy, Klaus Mertens (bass); De Nederlandse Bachvereniging, Sacramentskoor Breda, Amsterdam Baroque Orchestra/Ton Koopman

Erato 2292-45814-2 □ **164:00 mins (3 discs)**
□ 🎵🎵🎵

Bach's Passion settings are, above all, musical dramas. Unlike opera, the action, reported by the Evangelist, is in the past, reflected on in the present by the congregation in the chorales. The arias are operatic, releasing the emotional tension built up in their preceding recitatives. Koopman has a superb sense of timing for each of these elements. De Mey's narrative is vivid, with an underlying pulse despite its flexible speech rhythm, and the links with the crowd choruses and individual characters are seamless. The chorales too are forward-moving, lines marked by breaths rather than pauses.

In the arias, Wessel creates an exquisitely ethereal sound, wrapped within the weeping violin line of 'Erbarme dich'. Schlick dances delightfully with oboes d'amore in 'Ich will hier', and Koopman's own organ continuo is highly colourful, full of characterisation and wit, in his dismissive gesture towards the two false witnesses.

Consider, too, Christoph Spering's period performance (on Opus 111) based upon Mendelssohn's 1841 performing version. Tenors rather than trebles cut through the texture of the monumental first chorus with the chorale; the Evangelist is accompanied by two cellos and double-bass; clarinets replace missing oboes d'amore and da caccia – a remarkable vignette of 19th-century taste. *GP*

BACH

Chorale Variations on 'Vom Himmel Hoch' (arr. Stravinsky)
see **ORCHESTRAL**: STRAVINSKY: Dumbarton Oaks

BARBER

Knoxville – Summer of 1915; Adagio for Strings; Essays for Orchestra Nos 1 & 2; Medea's Meditation and Dance of Vengeance; The School for Scandal Overture

Sylvia McNair (soprano); Atlanta SO/Yoel Levi

Telarc CD-80250 □ 65:20 mins □ *① ① ①*

This is a fabulous disc! The performances are strikingly virtuosic and committed and Yoel Levi's Atlantans are miraculously served by Telarc's engineering. But exceptionally fine as are the accounts of the orchestral works (indeed, you'll have difficulty bettering Levi in the two orchestral *Essays*, the Sheridan-inspired overture that was Barber's graduation piece at Curtis, and the familiar *Adagio for Strings* and *Medea* items), they must yield to the ravishing and deeply moving performance of *Knoxville – Summer of 1915*, in which the soprano soloist is Sylvia McNair. The music and texts recall balmy summer days spent at Knoxville, Tennessee, in 1915; sultry evocations of an epoch and place lost amid the mists of time. McNair's delivery is deeply affecting. There is something utterly beguiling in her enunciation of 'now is the night one blue dew', yet her rhapsodic intensity, in passages such as 'who shall ever tell the sorrow of being on this earth', is profoundly haunting in its gorgeously ecstatic remorse. This *Knoxville* is the highlight of an altogether sensational release. *MJ*

BARBER

Knoxville – Summer of 1915; Two Songs, Op. 13
see COPLAND: Eight Poems of Emily Dickinson

BARBER

Songs (complete)

Cheryl Studer (soprano), Thomas Hampson (baritone), John Browning (piano); Emerson String Quartet

DG 435 867-2 □ 109:50 mins (2 discs) □ *① ① ①*

Among 20th-century composers, Samuel Barber was almost unique in possessing a natural lyricism that remained untainted by any hints of self-conscious modernism. Not surprisingly, he was drawn to the writing of songs from a very early age, and he remained devoted to the medium until the end of his life. DG's chronological survey of his vocal output offers a marvellous opportunity to savour his development as a vocal composer, the journey incorporating a number of substantial works, including the atmospheric *Dover Beach*, set imaginatively for baritone and string quartet, the more complex *Hermit Songs*, the valedictory Joyce and Graves settings from *Despite and Still*, and, most moving of all, the tender and whimsical Songs Op. 45. Cheryl Studer and Thomas Hampson prove to be staunch advocates of this music, projecting Barber's songs with unfailing commitment and sensitivity. There's wonderful support from John Browning, who voices the piano accompaniments with clarity and beauty of tone. *EL*

BARRAQUE

Le temps restitué; Concerto

Anne Bartelloni (mezzo-soprano); Groupe Vocal de France, Ensemble 2e2m/Paul Méfano

Harmonia Mundi HMA 905199 □ 64:33 mins □ *① ①*

A contemporary of Pierre Boulez, the young Jean Barraqué was hailed by the critic André Hodeir as the greatest composer since Beethoven. He wasn't, but he was one of a kind. Most of his (very few) works belong to a vast, deliberately incompleteable cycle based on and around texts from Hermann Broch's novel *The Death of Vergil*, itself so dense as to be almost unreadable. Barraqué's music, too, is texturally dense and wholly serial, continually dismantling and evolving new structures with sometimes terrible passion but always with a wholly French delight in colour, sonority and vivacious rhythm (he was a noted expert on Debussy). The choral work *Le temps restitué* is the most ambitious score in the part of the Broch cycle he was able to finish. The concerto (for clarinet, vibraphone and ensemble) is his last work, semi-detached from the cycle but even more invigorating and effervescent a play of colour and association, the clarinet wheeling and shrieking like some great hawk in mountain ravines. The performances are dedicated, near ideally faithful; the recording can't quite cope with information overload, but you get much more than a general picture of a true original of modern music. *CM*

BEETHOVEN
Choral Fantasy
see **ORCHESTRAL**: BEETHOVEN: Piano Concertos

BEETHOVEN
Missa solemnis in D

Charlotte Margiono (soprano), Catherine Robbin (mezzo-soprano), William Kendall (tenor), Alastair Miles (bass); Monteverdi Choir, Orchestre Révolutionnaire et Romantique/John Eliot Gardiner

Archiv 429 779-2 □ 71:39 mins □ 🟡🟡🟡

If you want a period approach to this great masterpiece, then Gardiner is the obvious – one might even say the only – choice. By any standards this is a release of quite extraordinary magnificence, excitement, pathos and spiritual resonance, matched by a quality of recording that has never been bettered. The period instruments and forces (smaller than in most traditional performances) obviously play an important part, giving a textural clarity and colouristic weave not easily achieved with modern hardware, but, unlike so many path-breaking 'authentic' performances, it's the sheer intensity and drive, the innate as well as the scholarly musicianship (notwithstanding some startlingly fast tempi), and the vibrant yet controlled emotional aura which give this recording its truly exceptional stature. The singing by all concerned is first rate, and Gardiner's combination of split-second precision and broad dramatic vision is positively luminous. Yet it would be a shame if this splendid recording were to supersede such masterly and moving accounts as those given by Karajan in the first of his DG versions, Jochum on Philips, Bernstein on DG (an overpoweringly intense and radiant reading), Barenboim on Erato, Colin Davis on RCA and the long-revered Klemperer version on EMI, which I find less captivating than many but which, like Davis's, has the added advantage of an outstanding *Choral Fantasy* (in this case with Barenboim, in Davis's with Gerhard Oppitz). *JS*

BERLIOZ
La damnation de Faust

Nicolai Gedda (tenor), Jules Bastin (bass), Josephine Veasey, Gillian Knight (mezzo-soprano), Richard Van Allan (bass); Wandsworth School Boys Choir, Ambrosian Singers, LSO & Chorus/Colin Davis

Philips 416 395-2 □ ADD □ 131:00 mins (2 discs) □ 🟡🟡🟡

There have been fine versions of Berlioz's quasi-operatic Mephistophelean morality tale from Inbal (Denon), Solti and Dutoit (Decca) during recent years. While all offer certain sonic advantages over this legendary Philips performance, recorded over twenty years ago, none probe the surreal machinations of Goethe's epic, re-interpreted in the febrile imagination of Hector Berlioz, with anything approaching Colin Davis's epic vision and charismatic theatricality. In Nicolai Gedda, Davis has an ideal Faust, aspiring, heroic and reckless. Jules Bastin's Méphistophélès is the epitome of nihilistic, ironic malice, while Josephine Veasey makes a suitably chaste Marguerite. I doubt that the LSO issued many more electrifying records than those of the pioneering Davis/Philips Berlioz cycle of the Seventies; they sound magnificent here, particularly when given their head in the celebrated Rakóczy March, while choral singing throughout is adroitly powerful. If the sound isn't quite up to current state-of-the-art technical standards, it's more than adequate, and conveys every gripping moment of this classic performance with creditable accuracy. Other *Fausts* come and go, but I suspect that Davis's account will continue as a bench-mark of excellence for many years to come. *MJ*

BERLIOZ
La damnation de Faust (excerpts); La marseillaise
see **ORCHESTRAL**: BERLIOZ: Benvenuto Cellini Overture

BERLIOZ
L'enfance du Christ

Anthony Rolfe Johnson, Michel Fockenoy (tenor), José van Dam (bass-baritone), Anne Sofie von Otter (mezzo-soprano), Gilles Cachemaille, Rene Schirrer (baritone), Jules Bastin (bass); Monteverdi Choir, Lyon Opera Orchestra/John Eliot Gardiner

Erato 4509-99767-2 □ 96:00 mins (2 discs) □ 🟡🟡

A capable and often highly individual account of Berlioz's *L'enfance du Christ*, presented not as drama, nor yet as oratorio, but rather in total accord with the composer's notion of the piece as a series of tableaux 'in the manner of old illuminated missals'. Among a strong team of soloists, it is the radiantly beautiful voice of

Anne Sofie von Otter, as Mary, which imparts special lustre to John Eliot Gardiner's performance. Von Otter's singing, in its jubilant simplicity, equates as closely to the notion of divine enunciation as one could possibly wish for. There's also much to admire in Gilles Cachemaille's authoritative portrayal of Joseph, with Jules Bastin as an excellent Herod. Gardiner secures fine playing from the Lyon Opera Orchestra, which, if not quite the equal of Eliahu Inbal's Frankfurt RSO (Denon) or Davis's LSO (Philips), are nonetheless keenly responsive. The Erato recording, made at the Church of St Madeleine, Perouges, is wonderfully atmospheric, thus enhancing the fundamental charm of Berlioz's amplified review of the Gospel narratives. A most attractive issue. *MJ*

BERLIOZ/BOITO/VERDI

Berlioz: Grande messe des morts

Boito: Mefistofele – Prologue

Verdi: Four Sacred Pieces – Te Deum

John Aler (tenor), John Cheek (bass); Morehouse-Spelman Chorus, Young Singers of Callanwolde, Atlanta SO & Chorus/Robert Shaw

Telarc CD-80109 □ 124:45 mins (2 discs) □ 🎧🎧🎧

Much admired for hi-fi demonstration purposes, there's no disputing the technical credentials of this spectacular Telarc production; no other version of Berlioz's Requiem conveys the apocalyptic splendour of the work to such stunning effect. True enough, the massed phalanxes of brass and additional batteries of timpani thundering sequentially from the cardinal points of the compass envelop the listener in a cataclysmic, awe-inspiring vision of impending judgement during the Dies Irae, but Robert Shaw, one of the master choral conductors of the century, reveals the penitential vulnerability behind this misrepresented masterpiece to full advantage. The Atlanta SO, transformed under Shaw, and now Yoel Levi, into one of America's foremost virtuoso ensembles, sounds magnificent; choral contributions are hardly less distinguished, though tenor soloist John Aler's diction doesn't always register clearly enough. Yet with the added attraction of blockbusters by Boito and Verdi, one would need very little persuasion to purchase this set – a sonic spectacular *par excellence*, and Telarc's legendary digital engineering has seldom realised more volcanic results. A magnificent achievement. *MJ*

BERLIOZ

Les nuits d'été; Mélodies

Diana Montague, Catherine Robbin (mezzo-soprano), Brigitte Fournier (soprano), Howard Crook (tenor), Gilles Cachemaille (baritone); Lyon Opera Orchestra/John Eliot Gardiner

Erato 4509-99768-2 □ 65:00 mins □ 🎧🎧

There's much to relish here. Under Eliot Gardiner's ever-watchful direction, Berlioz's familiar vocal cycle *Les nuits d'été* assumes sterner proportions than usual, and the recording, produced in association with Radio France, is altogether finer than the classic 1969 performance from Janet Baker and the New Philharmonia Orchestra under Barbirolli (EMI Studio), which, incidentally, includes neither texts nor annotations of any kind. Gardiner's singers are admirable; Catherine Robbin is a noble and passionate Ophelia, and there are valid aesthetic arguments for apportioning *Les nuits d'été* among several voices. The result is always refreshingly vital, and orchestral contributions from the Lyon Opera Orchestra are entirely sympathetic. A Berlioz disc of considerable eminence, this offers compellingly idiomatic accounts of material that rarely elicits performances of such stature, commitment and dramatic intuition. Unhesitatingly recommended. *MJ*

BERLIOZ

Les nuits d'été
see also Collection: French Song

BERLIOZ

Roméo et Juliette; Symphonie funèbre et triomphale

Florence Quivar (mezzo-soprano), Alberto Cupido (tenor), Tom Krause (bass); L'Ensemble Vocal Tudor de Montréal; Montreal SO & Chorus/Charles Dutoit

Decca 417 302-2 □ 130:31 mins (2 discs) □ 🎧🎧🎧

Berlioz composed his dramatic symphony *Romeo and Juliet* in 1838–9. The double-headed thunderbolt that impelled him towards this fine work was his first encounter with Shakespearian drama and, in the roles of both Ophelia and Juliet, the young Irish actress Harriet Smithson. Few performances proclaim its subtle amalgamation of symphony, cantata and opera with such understanding and commitment as this, from Charles Dutoit and his outstanding Montreal forces. Orchestral playing and vocal contributions are exceptionally fine; Florence Quivar and Alberto Cupido sing most affectingly in the principal solo roles, and the massed choral forces are admirably disciplined in their presentation of the combative dialogue between the rival Montagues and Capulets. The Montreal SO is splendid, too, in a spectacular performance of the *Symphonie funèbre et triomphale*, and the recordings were made at Decca's favoured Montreal location, the church of St Eustache, whose remarkable acoustic ambience has yielded many of the best recordings of the digital era. Highly recommended. *MJ*

BERLIOZ

Te Deum

Francisco Araiza (tenor), Martin Haselböck (organ); London Symphony Chorus, London Philharmonic Choir, Wooburn Singers, European Community Youth Orchestra/Claudio Abbado

DG 410 696-2 □ 46:53 mins □ 𝄞𝄞𝄞

This spectacular performance, recorded live in St Albans Cathedral, was among DG's earliest clutch of CD releases, finding its way on to the new medium (the original LP was already of demonstration quality) in 1984, just months after the worldwide launch of the new technology. It's not difficult to appreciate why, since, even by current standards, it would be difficult to find more compelling evidence of the potential of compact disc. The recording conveys a most vivid impression of the cavernous acoustic ambience of this great cathedral – a useful factor, of course, in the case of a work of gargantuan and visionary proportions. Martin Haselböck's organ registrations resound impressively across the sound field, and the projection and clarity of the massed choirs are strikingly realistic. Tenor Francisco Araiza sings splendidly, and one cannot praise too highly the young players of the ECYO, who give of their very considerable best under their founding music director, Claudio Abbado. With the additional dimension of a live audience, this account is thrillingly vital, and the impact of this remarkable work has never registered so magnificently as here. *MJ*

BERNSTEIN
Chichester Psalms
see **ORCHESTRAL**: BERNSTEIN: Symphonies Nos 1–3

BIRTWISTLE
Three Settings of Celan
see **CHAMBER**: BIRTWISTLE: Tragoedia

BLACHER
Three Psalms
see **ORCHESTRAL**: Collection: Testimonies of War

BOULEZ

Pli selon pli; Livre pour cordes

Halina Lukomska (soprano), Maria Bergmann (piano), Paul Stingl (guitar), Hugo d'Alton (mandolin); BBC SO, New Philharmonia Orchestra/Pierre Boulez

Sony SMK 68335 □ ADD □ 70:50 mins □ 𝄞𝄞

Pli selon pli must be regarded as one of Boulez's most impressive and absorbing compositions. A vocal cycle based upon poems by Stéphane Mallarmé, it is conceived on the grandest scale and utilises an orchestral ensemble of considerable proportions. Yet apart from the turbulent musical discourse that infuses the final movement, 'Tombeau', the overriding impression remains one of intimacy, especially in the three 'Improvisations', where the delicate sonorities of tuned percussion, guitar, mandolin and harp punctuate the predominantly lyrical vocal line.

Boulez recorded the work for Erato in 1980 with the same orchestra, but this earlier version, retailing at mid-price, is equally recommendable, and enjoys the added benefit of including the pithy if more abstruse *Livre pour cordes* of 1968, an extensive re-working of material originally used in a string quartet composed twenty years before. *EL*

BRAHMS

Alto Rhapsody; Schicksalslied; Marienlieder; Nänie; Gesang der Parzen

Nathalie Stutzmann (contralto); Bavarian Radio Chorus & SO/Colin Davis

RCA Victor Red Seal 09026 61201 2 □ 67:00 mins □ 𝄞𝄞𝄞

Nathalie Stutzmann's serenely purposeful account of Brahms's *Alto Rhapsody* is the prime focus of this issue. Her plangent, deeply affecting manner with this elusive work is outstanding; her voice has depth and sonorous amplitude, making it the perfect expressive vehicle for such sublimity. Hers is ardently responsive singing, having the fullest regard for idiomatic and textual priorities, without losing touch with the underlying emotionalism of the piece. Colin Davis ensures that choral and orchestral contributions are totally sympathetic, and the recording itself, naturally balanced, has an autumnal bloom and reverberance which serve to underscore the heroic valediction of this music. *Schicksalslied* (Song of Destiny), Op. 54, receives a performance fortified as much by enduring hope as it is also vulnerable to characteristically Brahmsian uncertainty and resignation; there's a similarly stoical quality about Davis's *Nänie*, Op. 82, which proves equally compelling. But life and death, the fundamentals of the human condition, remain; Brahms's exhortation, 'Let all mankind fear the gods' (perhaps the deliberate plurality of deities reflected his personal agnosticism), from the *Gesang der Parzen*, Op. 89, is intoned with massive commitment. *MJ*

Alto Rhapsody
see also **ORCHESTRAL**: BRAHMS: Symphony No. 3 in F

Ein deutsches Requiem

Cheryl Studer (soprano), Andreas Schmidt (baritone); Swedish Radio Chorus, Eric Ericson Chamber Choir; Berlin PO/Claudio Abbado

DG 437 517-2 □ **73:37 mins** □ *♪♪♪*

A German Requiem is a work of deeply moving consolatory power, written by a composer not blessed with profound religious faith, and occasioned in no small measure by the death of his mother in February 1865, and the loss of his friend and mentor, Robert Schumann, nine years earlier. Brahms himself remained a lifelong agnostic, claiming that, in this profound meditation upon mortality, he 'had the whole of humanity in mind'. The Requiem has received many fine recordings in the past; Otto Klemperer's sublime EMI version still figures prominently in the catalogues, wearing its 33 years in admirable CD transfers, though among several excellent digital newcomers Claudio Abbado's live Berlin account is unrivalled. Soloists Cheryl Studer and Andreas Schmidt both sing most eloquently; the Swedish choruses enunciate the German texts with commitment and authority, while the Berlin PO is heard in serene and magisterial form. Were cash no object, I'd also commend Robert Shaw's Telarc version, whose superbly drilled Atlanta forces are joined by the late Arleen Auger (in one of her finest recordings) and baritone Richard Stilwell; it represents a valid alternative view of this philosophical/humanist masterpiece. Those collectors requiring the work in a memorable period performance, re-creating choral and orchestral styles several degrees closer to the composer's intentions, will find John Eliot Gardiner's Philips account a secure and musically compelling recommendation, again at full price. *MJ*

Liebeslieder Waltzes; Neue Liebeslieder Waltzes; Three Vocal Quartets, Op. 64

Edith Mathis (soprano), Brigitte Fassbaender (mezzo-soprano), Peter Schreier (tenor), Dietrich Fischer-Dieskau (baritone); Karl Engel, Wolfgang Sawallisch (piano)

DG 423 133-2 □ **54:46 mins** □ *♪♪♪*

If a more wonderful account of this entrancing music has ever been given, then perhaps the moon really is made of cheese. So drop this book (only for the moment, of course), rush out to your nearest record shop and urge the manager to order you a copy of this superb CD at once. If he stocks it, buy two and send the other to a friend. Given the personnel, it would have been amazing if this hadn't turned out well, but each and every participant is on top form, the mutual sympathy is so immediate you could reach out and grab it, the vitality is all but overpowering, and the range of mood, colour, accentuation, blend and individuality is almost infinite. One of the things that all these performers clearly understand is the extent to which the secret of Brahms is polyphonic. There's no stodge here from beginning to end, and the recorded sound is impeccable. *JS*

Lieder

Jessye Norman (soprano), Daniel Barenboim (piano)

DG 413 311-2 □ **69:45 mins** □ *♪♪♪*

Jessye Norman's deep soprano voice (no contradiction in terms there) is perfectly suited to Brahms's music, and she brings to her very considerable artistry not only penetrating spiritual and psychological insights, a natural flair for undercover drama, and a great wit ('Vergebliches Ständchen' is pure delight in that regard) but also a profound sense of dignity. Barenboim's Brahmsian credentials go back a long way, and he's obviously in his element here, enhanced by a rapport with his partner which is evident in every bar. But why, years after it was made, is this the only solo recording of Norman in Brahms? *JS*

Lieder
see also SCHUMANN: Frauenliebe und -leben

Two Songs, Op. 91
see **CHAMBER**: BRAHMS: Viola Sonatas
and **ORCHESTRAL**: BRAHMS: Piano Concerto No. 1 in D minor

BRIAN
Symphony No. 1 in D minor (Gothic)

Eva Jenisová (soprano), Dagmar Pecková (mezzo-soprano), Vladimír Doležal (tenor), Peter Mikuláš (bass); Slovak Philharmonic Choir, Slovak Opera Chorus, Slovak Folk Ensemble Chorus, Lucnica Chorus, Bratislava City Choir & Children's Choir, Youth Echo Choir, Czechoslovak RSO (Bratislava), Slovak PO/Ondrej Lenard

Marco Polo 8.223280/1 □ **111:30 mins (2 discs)** □ ❷❷❷

The first of Havergal Brian's 32 symphonies (completed in 1927, first performed in 1961) is a legend of 20th-century music. Its length and enormous orchestral and choral requirements consigned it to *The Guinness Book of Records* long before a recording was seriously contemplated. But the forces are justified by the sweep and scope of the music: a thrilling, visionary experience that unites the late-Romantic symphonic traditions at their most grandiose with a Berliozian sense of space and a modern re-invention of the most incandescent Renaissance polyphony. It's Brian's tribute to the Gothic age as a period of intense spiritual striving, and to its matchless monuments, the great cathedrals of Europe.

Three purely orchestral movements for large orchestra introduce three choral ones, which together constitute a seventy-minute setting of the Te Deum for vocal quartet, multi-divided choruses, children's voices, even larger orchestra and four extra brass bands. The range of invention is staggering, as is the technical difficulty, and some effects – the choral clusters in the fifth movement, the wild dissonance and heterophony of the last one – go beyond any of Brian's British and most of his international contemporaries. The music feels very Central European in this Slovak performance – the only recording, and despite a few compromises and uncertainties entirely recommendable. The confidence of the choirs, their ability to sustain intonation, is particularly impressive, and Lenard directs the gigantic ensemble in a true interpretation of desperate fire. The studio recording conjures up a surprisingly realistic sound image. Recommended for hi-fi demonstrations: nothing else will tax your speakers quite like it. *CM*

BRITTEN
Cantata misericordium
see **ORCHESTRAL**: BRITTEN: Cello Symphony

BRITTEN
Complete Folk-song Arrangements

Felicity Lott (soprano), Philip Langridge (tenor), Thomas Allen (baritone), Carlos Bonell (guitar), Osian Ellis (harp), Christopher van Kampen (cello), Graham Johnson (piano); Wenhaston Boys Choir/Christopher Barnett, David Owen Norris (piano); BBC Singers/Simon Joly; Northern Sinfonia/Steuart Bedford

Collins 70392 □ **198:47 mins (3 discs)** □ ❷❷❷

Over three hours of folk-song settings might seem too much of a good thing, even for regular frequenters of Cecil Sharp House, but unlike the cosy, romanticised versions of Vaughan Williams, Holst, Moeran and others, Britten's folk-songs, like Grainger's before him, are as much original compositions as arrangements. In their own utterly perfect way they are as representative of his genius as anything else he wrote.

Even to Brittenophiles, this collection will spring some pleasant surprises. Here is every surviving example of Britten the arranger's art, including the various orchestral versions Britten made of some of these and a wealth of material which, inexplicably, still remains unpublished, not least of which is a magical setting of 'The Bitter Withy' for tenor, boys choir and piano.

If Felicity Lott, Philip Langridge and Thomas Allen can't quite match Peter Pears's unique range of colour and wry humour, even with the sterling and authoritative support provided by Steuart Bedford, Osian Ellis and Graham Johnson, they are as finely attuned and varied in response to this absorbing, challenging music as one could today reasonably hope for. *Antony Bye*

BRITTEN
Holy Sonnets of John Donne; Songs and Proverbs of William Blake
see **OPERA**: BRITTEN: Billy Budd

BRITTEN
Les illuminations; Quatre chansons françaises; Serenade for Tenor, Horn and Strings

Felicity Lott (soprano), Anthony Rolfe Johnson (tenor), Michael Thompson (horn); Royal Scottish National Orchestra/Bryden Thomson

Chandos CHAN 8657 □ **58:55 mins** □ ❷❷❷

For those who prefer to hear the vocal part of Britten's masterpiece, *Les illuminations*, performed, as originally intended, by a soprano, Felicity Lott's 1989 recording deserves special commendation. From the very outset, Lott commands our attention with extraordinarily forceful enunciation of Rimbaud's colourful imagery. But later she allows sufficient breadth of tonal colouring to capture to perfection the sensuality of 'Antique'. Bryden Thomson and the Royal Scottish National Orchestra provide superbly incisive and atmospheric accompaniments, and the engineering combines warmth with clarity of texture.

Britten's early flirtation with the French language is further represented here by the *Quatre chansons françaises*. Composed when Britten was only 15 years of age, these are astonishingly assured settings of Verlaine and Hugo. Once again, Lott's vast experience of performing Fauré and Ravel is particularly telling, and she treats these exquisite miniatures with great sensitivity. In the Serenade, Anthony Rolfe Johnson and Michael Thompson effect an impressive and youthful-sounding partnership, though in the last resort Pears still has the edge in this particular work. *EL*

BRITTEN

Phaedra
see **OPERA**: BRITTEN: The Rape of Lucretia

BRITTEN

Serenade for Tenor, Horn and Strings; Les illuminations; Nocturne

Peter Pears (tenor), Barry Tuckwell (horn); LSO, English CO/Benjamin Britten

Decca London 436 395-2 □ ADD □ 72:49 mins □ ⊘⊘

Because the vast majority of Britten's vocal music was written specifically for the tenor Peter Pears, it's sometimes difficult to imagine it sounding more convincing when performed by other singers. This is particularly true of the Serenade, a work that has been blessed with a number of impressive recordings, most notably one by Philip Langridge that appears conveniently in a boxed set of the complete orchestral song cycles from Collins. Yet time and time again I find myself returning to Pears and to Britten for interpretative insights that seem to elude rival interpreters. The 1960 version of this masterpiece may not present Pears in the freshest of voices, but it's nonetheless compelling and boasts some outstanding horn-playing from Barry Tuckwell. The other two cycles are equally atmospheric and incisive, and Decca's engineering is first class throughout. *EL*

BRITTEN

Seven Sonnets of Michelangelo; Canticle I; Winter Words; Four Folk-song Arrangements

Anthony Rolfe Johnson (tenor), Graham Johnson (piano)

Hyperion CDA 66209 □ 59:26 mins □ ⊘⊘⊘

Britten's numerous song cycles for voice and piano may form an integral part of his vocal output, but as yet no company has recorded them complete. For this reason the present disc fills a vital gap, while serving as an admirable introduction to Britten's art. Perhaps the most conspicuous aspect of the programme is its illustration of the versatility of the composer's poetic settings. Thus, the Italianate warmth of the *Michelangelo Sonnets* provides an admirable foil to the bleakness of the Hardy cycle, *Winter Words*. Similarly, one can draw contrasts between the highly stylised melismatic writing of the First Canticle and the unaffected simplicity of the folk-songs. I need hardly stress that both performers on this warmly recorded disc respond with great sensitivity to the varying demands of each work, and their interpretations are thankfully devoid of any unwarranted affectations. *EL*

BRITTEN

War Requiem; Ballad of Heroes; Sinfonia da requiem

Heather Harper (soprano), Philip Langridge, Martyn Hill (tenor), John Shirley-Quirk (bass-baritone); Choristers of St Paul's Cathedral, LSO & Chorus/Richard Hickox

Chandos CHAN 8983/4 □ 125:24 mins (2 discs) □ ⊘⊘⊘

It would be fair to say that all of the currently available versions of Britten's *War Requiem* offer some special qualities. For example, I could not imagine any Britten aficionado being without the composer's own Decca recording – a classic Sixties performance whose defiant message of peace, delivered against the bleak climate of the Cold War, inspired a whole generation of listeners. And then there's Simon Rattle, whose Eighties EMI recording contains moments of great poignancy. But overall, Richard Hickox provides the most convincing appraisal of this masterpiece. The choral singing is particularly outstanding, achieving a thrilling intensity throughout the climaxes of the Dies Irae, while providing a marvellous feeling of solace in the work's closing pages. Praise should also be given to the soloists, particularly Langridge and

Shirley-Quirk, who really rise to the occasion in the moving Owen settings.

Add to this package Chandos's brilliantly clear engineering, the generous inclusion of two closely related works, with a performance of the *Sinfonia da requiem* that more than matches the composer's own recording in terms of urgency and variety of orchestral colouring, and you have a clear winner. *EL*

BRUCKNER

Masses Nos 1–3; Te Deum; Psalm 150; Motets

Soloists; Bavarian Radio Chorus & SO, Chorus of the Deutsche Oper, Berlin, Berlin PO/Eugen Jochum

DG 423 127-2 □ ADD □ 227:00 mins (4 discs)
□ *QQ*

Eugene Jochum recorded these works from Bruckner's extensive choral *oeuvre* between 1963 and 1972. Soundwise, digital remastering hasn't improved things vastly, particularly in the case of the F minor Mass (No. 3) and the Te Deum, where textures become heavily congested at fortissimo climaxes, although the choral motets, again recorded during the late Sixties, have emerged with marginally greater transparency. In other respects, transfers of the two earlier Masses (Nos 1 in D minor and 2 in E minor) are generally more successful, and deserve consideration because of the resolution and grandiloquence of the performances. At mid-price, this four-disc set of illustrious reissues represents good value, and the very fact that these performances have survived in the catalogues over several decades offers positive proof of their importance. *MJ*

BRUCKNER

Te Deum; Mass No. 1 in D minor

Joan Rodgers (soprano), Catherine Wyn-Rogers (alto), Keith Lewis (tenor), Alastair Miles (bass); Corydon Singers & Orchestra/Matthew Best

Hyperion CDA 66650 □ 67:27 mins □ *QQQ*

Under their music director Matthew Best, the Corydon Singers and their eponymous orchestra have garnered impressive credentials in Bruckner's choral music; this Hyperion release celebrates their 21st anniversary season. In recording any large-scale choral work, and particularly those by Bruckner, the chosen venue makes its own contribution to the undertaking. That's emphatically the case here, as the Westminster Cathedral organ blazes imperiously above the orchestra in the visionary invocation to the work. Elsewhere, the solo vocal quartet is admirable, and the *ad*

hoc Corydon Orchestra acquits itself well, though highest honours must go to the outstanding 140-voice chorus, who sing with earth-shattering conviction, utmost clarity of diction and enviable precision of ensemble and intonation. The coupling, Bruckner's Mass in D minor, is an apposite choice. The premiere, given under the composer's direction in the great cathedral of Linz in 1864, was one of his few major triumphs prior to the appearance of the Fourth and Seventh Symphonies. Matthew Best secures a fine response from his Corydon forces, and if his account doesn't have quite the serenity or authority of Eugen Jochum's classic DG recording (Jochum's Te Deum is less spectacular, though the solo violinist is more refined and expressive than his Corydon counterpart; see entry above), the combined strengths of this Hyperion version guarantee prime recommendation. *MJ*

BRUCKNER

Te Deum
see also **ORCHESTRAL:** BRUCKNER: Symphony No. 5

BUSNOIS

Victimae paschali laudes
see OCKEGHEM: Missa Mi-Mi

BUTTERWORTH/VAUGHAN WILLIAMS

Butterworth: A Shropshire Lad

Vaughan Williams: Songs of Travel; 10 Blake Songs; Linden Lea; Orpheus with his Lute; The Water Mill; Silent Noon

Robert Tear (tenor), Benjamin Luxon (baritone), Neil Black (oboe), David Willison, Philip Ledger (piano)

Decca 430 368-2 □ ADD □ 72:46 mins □ *QQ*

The bitter brew and ballad-like verbal irony of AE Housman's volume of poems, with lovelorn youths and soldiers set apart from their fellows among the natural beauty of a half-imaginary Shropshire landscape, inspired a whole generation of British composers. Out of innumerable *Shropshire Lad* settings, George Butterworth's cycle of six songs is one of the two definitive musical incarnations (the other is Vaughan Williams's *On Wenlock Edge*). Benjamin Luxon's darkly eloquent singing uncovers the depressive core under the almost Schubertian perfection of Butterworth's songs. He's coupled with Robert Tear, sometimes rough-voiced but always powerful, in Vaughan Williams's youthful, ardent RL Stevenson cycle *Songs of Travel* (seldom heard as given here, complete) and his late, austere set of Blake songs with solo oboe, as well as a selection of other characteristic songs mainly from Vaughan Williams's earlier period. Decca's recordings are beautifully balanced, and at mid-price in the British Collection this is a notable bargain. *CM*

BYRD

Gradualia, Vol. 1: The Marian Masses

William Byrd Choir/Gavin Turner

Hyperion CDA 66451 □ 79:39 mins □ ⊘ ⊘ ⊘

In the difficult years of the late 16th century, William Byrd managed to remain a Roman Catholic and stay alive. These pieces are selected from the various Catholic services throughout the year which celebrated the Virgin Mary, and into them Byrd has poured all his skill and understanding. Many of them set the same texts: just for fun I listened to all nine Alleluia settings one after the other and was astonished at the variety and interest of the music – though no single item lasted for more than 47 seconds (track 16 is the best). Byrd is at his most impressive and sublime here in the glorious 'Nunc dimittis' and in the delicate intricacy of 'Optimam partem'. The recording and performances are superb, producing a mature and assured sound with an exquisite sense of line and formal repose. *AP*

BYRD

Music for voice and viols

Rachel Platt (soprano); Concordia

Meridian CDE 84271 □ 60:27 mins □ ⊘ ⊘ ⊘

William Byrd described his songs as 'apt for Voyces or Viols'. But his intention was for 'instruments to expresse the harmonie and one voyce to pronounce the dittie', as nine songs are performed here. They come from a shamefully neglected repertory of over 100, with barely a handful on record.

Rachel Platt has a captivating voice, full of colour, yet finely drawn to match the transparency of the viols around her. She articulates words perfectly, yet they never fragment her fine, purposeful legato line. Her songs range from 'My mistress had a little dog' (which died, though the words are full of political double meanings) to Byrd's anguished elegy on the death of Thomas Tallis, 'Ye sacred muses'. Viols occasionally mask the singer, who appears sometimes to wander about rather distractingly – through headphones, you can't always be sure where the next phrase is coming from.

The four viols of Concordia (with Laurence Dreyfus) play several consort pieces, including a magnificent Fantasy. While its two upper parts lead and follow each other in strict canon throughout, the other three parts are so

ingeniously involved that countless listenings will still leave new discoveries to be made – as will all this delightful disc. *GP*

CALDARA

Stabat mater
see VIVALDI: Gloria

CANTELOUBE

Chants d'Auvergne (Songs of the Auvergne)

Arleen Auger (soprano); English CO/Yan Pascal Tortelier

Virgin Ultraviolet CUV 5 61120 2 □ 49:20 mins □ ⊘

Throughout the first half of this century the composer Joseph Canteloube, who was born in the Auvergne, travelled around France collecting and arranging folk-songs. Most of his settings with orchestral accompaniment of songs from the Auvergne, dating from the mid-Twenties, were memorably recorded fifty years later by Victoria de los Angeles. Her EMI collection is still available, and has been joined over the years by equally treasurable recordings by Jill Gomez (EMI), Kiri Te Kanawa (Decca) and Anna Moffo (RCA), for these songs seem to bring out the best in their interpreters. My first choice, however, would be the delectable voice of Arleen Auger in 18 of the most admired songs, among them such favourites as the haunting 'Baïlèro' and the high-spirited 'Malurous qu'o uno fenno'. *CO*

CARISSIMI

Jephte; Jonah; The Judgement of Solomon

Gabrieli Consort & Players/Paul McCreesh

Meridian CDE 84304 □ 53:27 mins □ ⊘ ⊘ ⊘

This competes with an attractive performance, directed by Erik van Nevel (on Accent) of *Jephte*, coupled with *Vanitas vanitatum* and *Ezechia* – so you could safely buy both discs on grounds of repertoire alone.

Where they coincide, with *Jephte*, they are very different. McCreesh omits dubious instrumental parts: van Nevel includes them, creates additional ritornelli from them, and ends up twice the length of McCreesh's performance. These oratorios are overtly operatic, supposedly didactic but clearly delighting congregations denied opera during Lent. So the deciding factor is vocal quality – and here, for me, McCreesh wins, above all with Janet Coxwell as Jephtha's daughter. Her plaint, meditating in the wilderness before she is sacrificed by her rash father, is one of the great musical laments, matching Penelope's in Monteverdi's *Il ritorno d'Ulisse* from the same era. No less moving is the wonderful stillness at the end of the final chorus, which moved Handel deeply – he too treated Jephtha's daughter with great compassion in his last oratorio, 100 years later.

Carissimi seems doomed to appalling documentation: booklets for both discs are in tiny print and barely readable. The single folded page offered by Meridian has room only for a translation, omitting the original Latin text. *GP*

CARVER

Missa Dum sacrum mysterium; O bone Jesu; Gaude flore virginali

Cappella Nova/Alan Tavener

ASV Gaudeamus CD GAU 124 □ 61:45 mins □ 😊😊😊

The Scottish Reformation, even more vicious in virtuous zeal than its English counterpart, deliberately destroyed a dazzling and sophisticated culture of high polyphonic church music, 'Musick Fyne'. Among the few surviving manuscripts is the so-called Carver Choirbook, containing the complete authenticated works of Robert Carver (c1487–1566), canon of the Augustinian abbey of Scone – perhaps Scotland's greatest composer and an indubitable master of the European Renaissance, peer of Josquin, Dufay, Fayrfax and Taverner.

The incandescent ten-part Mass *Dum sacrum mysterium* of about 1506 is one of Carver's most breathtaking achievements, as much for its haunting quality of ecstatic vision as for the immense scale on which its flowing counterpoint, motivic working, decorative elaboration and infinite variety of texture are conceived. The two motets are equally fine: the 19-part *O bone Jesu* is the most remarkable polyphonic *tour de force* in British music apart from Tallis's *Spem in alium*, while the gentler five-part *Gaude flore virginali* shows a more intimate, lyrical personality, allied to remarkable textural invention. The Scottish vocal group Cappella Nova have become the prime exponents of Carver's music: this is the most spectacular disc from its series of his complete works for ASV. *CM*

CAVALLI

Salve regina
see Collection: Marian Music

CEREROLS

Missa pro defunctis; Vespers

Guillemette Laurens (soprano); Currende/Erik van Nevel

Accent ACC 94106 D □ 78:28 mins □ 😊😊😊

This Spanish Benedictine monk, who lived from 1618 to 1680, is awarded barely half a column of biography in *New Grove* and, before this revealing disc, a mere half-dozen items on record. Yet his music is highly distinctive. The abbey of Montserrat supported an Escolania, an ecclesiastical conservatoire, where, as choirboy, novice and finally monk, Joan Cererols was steeped in the music of Spain's greatest Renaissance composer, Victoria. Overlaid on this rich polyphony is the harmonic pace and drive of the mid-17th century and a revelling in spatial dialogue inherited from Gabrieli's Venice.

The Requiem Mass alternates timeless plainchant with four-part singing from the 21 voices of Currende. Contrasts are more vivid in the Vespers, where plainchant intonations alternate with an eight-part choir, sometimes in dense counterpoint, sometimes in a vigorously syllabic chordal homophony; but, most dramatically, exchanging short fragments with solo soprano – Guillemette Laurens – in the glorious acoustic of a church in Ghent.

The guitarist Fernando Sor, hearing a piece by Cererols performed at Montserrat a century after the composer's death, wrote: 'On leaving the church I thought only of all this religious harmony which was so grandiose.' The impact is no less today. *GP*

CHARPENTIER

Canticum ad Beatam Virginem Maria

Le Concert des Nations/Jordi Savall

Astrée Auvidis E 8713 □ 74:30 mins □ 😊😊😊

An exceptional proportion of Charpentier's church music is on the Marian theme. Savall and his gifted international group of six singers, four violists, theorbo and keyboard continuo have selected here a musical history of the Virgin's life – *Salve regina*, Magnificat, *Stabat mater* and the Litanies, punctuated by brief instrumental preludes.

This is most beautifully reflective and expansive music, with dissonances gently melting one into the next – the long chromatic descent into 'this vale of tears' being astonishingly intense. The opening 'Hymn... between men and angels' is a dialogue between male voices asking in lively ritornellos, 'What is most praiseworthy after God himself?' Here two exquisitely beautiful angels compare the Virgin to everything else in creation, until all join together in a hymn of praise.

Most absorbing of all is a *Stabat mater* setting, twenty short verses alternating solo soprano and men's voices to create a timeless reflection of Mary at the foot of the cross.

The music, the performance and the distant recording bathed in resonance create an overwhelming effect. A recording to treasure. *GP*

CHARPENTIER
Messe des morts; Litanies; Psalms 110, 112 & 126; Transfige dulcissime Jesu

Le Concert Spirituel/Hervé Niquet

Naxos 8.553173 □ 61:23 mins □ ⊘

Charpentier wrote most of this varied repertoire – a Requiem Mass, Litanies of the Virgin and Psalms of Praise – for use in the Jesuit church of St Louis in Paris. Twenty-five years later, such music was being taken out of its liturgical context and given in concert performances by Le Concert Spirituel. The ensemble was re-created in 1988 and incorporates 17 voices, strings and a colourful range of continuo instruments, all directed by Hervé Niquet. This, their first recording for Naxos, is very welcome.

The church of Notre-Dame du Liban provides a warm acoustic. The performance is cool rather than overtly passionate, the music itself creating powerful images, from the dark pathos of De Profundis, which ends the Requiem, to the dancing gaiety of the strings introducing Psalm 112, 'Praise the name of the Lord'.

The downside of Naxos's super-budget price has often been the skimpy accompanying notes. Here the booklet is substantial and informative, confirming the outstanding value for money of the label as well as its imaginative programming. *GP*

CLEMENS NON PAPA
O Maria, vernans rosa
see Collection: Marian Music

COMPERE
Choral Works

Orlando Consort

Metronome MET CD 1002 □ 57:41 mins □ ⊘⊘⊘

In 1501, when Petrucci published the first-ever printed collection of music, it was the works of Loyset Compère that featured most frequently in his anthology. This CD is a marvellous addition to the catalogue,

incorporating ten of his works, most of them never recorded before. Several of the songs are newly furnished with their recently discovered complete texts – among these I was particularly struck by the long spinning sequence at the end of 'Ne vous hastez pas', sung with a gravity-defying poise and a wonderful sense of inner momentum. 'Ave Maria' gives us a rather different style, with more weight placed on the individual phrases and a slower pace. The churchy acoustic used throughout is generally fine, though it does not suit the songs with Italian words. Finally, Compère's *Missa in nativitate* is a profound and interesting composition, and is sung here with beautiful control and with the utmost attention to detail. *AP*

COPLAND/BARBER
Copland: Eight Poems of Emily Dickinson; Quiet City

Barber: Knoxville – Summer of 1915; Two Songs, Op. 13; Adagio for Strings

Barbara Hendricks (soprano); LSO/Michael Tilson Thomas

EMI CDC 5 55358 2 □ 63:17 mins □ ⊘⊘⊘

Aaron Copland wrote surprisingly few songs; and the young Michael Tilson Thomas conducted the premiere of his orchestrated Emily Dickinson settings on the composer's seventieth birthday in 1970. He returns to them now, with soprano Barbara Hendricks: both musicians understand Copland as well as he, in turn, understood and partnered the strange and plain-speaking compassion of Dickinson's poetry.

The woodwind soloists of the LSO tangle in the heat-haze of Copland's string writing in 'Nature, the gentlest mother', and Hendricks's soprano competes feistily with her orchestral counterparts in the gusty 'There came a wind like a bugle'.

Two of Samuel Barber's four Op. 13 songs sound, by contrast, felicitous and luxuriant. Hendricks reveals the radiant ecstasy of James Agee's 'Sure on this shining night'; and the bloom of her voice brings sensuous nostalgia to Barber's great setting of that poet's *Knoxville*.

In between these fine song performances, the LSO brings sophistication and flair to Copland's *Quiet City* and Barber's *Adagio for Strings* in an unusually satisfying programme. Its enjoyment is enhanced by Michael Tilson Thomas's own apposite and anecdotal programme notes. *Hilary Finch*

COUPERIN

Leçons de ténèbres; Victoria, Christo resurgenti; Magnificat

Miecke van der Sluis (soprano), Guillemette Laurens (mezzo-soprano), Pascal Monteilhet (lute), Marianne Muller (viola de gamba), Laurence Boulay (harpsichord, organ)

Erato MusiFrance 2292-45012-2 □ **60:43 mins**
□ 🟐🟐🟐

François Couperin set these Lessons to be sung in Holy Week at the service of Tenebrae (darkness) when 15 candles are extinguished one by one, symbolising the sufferings of Christ. Written in the sensuous, affective tradition inherited from the early Baroque, these Lamentations of Jeremiah must have been among the most passionate music ever heard by the French nobility, who flocked to convents to hear them sung by the nuns. Here, they're no less beautifully sung by these two distinctive yet matched voices.

Each verse begins with an extended vocalisation on a letter of the Hebrew alphabet, the voices curving and twining in supple counterpoint in the third Lesson. The other two, for solo voice, are no less affective – the fifth letter, 'HE', is utterly entrancing. Then the words create the structure, in powerful rhetoric and description. Jerusalem 'plorans…', 'weeping sore in the night…', is but one of innumerable heart-rending moments.

The penitential mood is relieved by the Motet for Easter Day, and the Magnificat setting, in which both voices illuminate each verse with vividly descriptive word-setting. A less familiar corner of the Baroque, this richly deserves exploring. *GP*

DALLAPICCOLA

Canti di prigionia; Cinque frammenti di Saffo; Due liriche di Anacreonte; Sex carmina Alcaei; Tempus destruendi – Tempus aedificandi; Due cori di Michelangelo Buonarroti il giovane

Julie Moffat (soprano); New London Chamber Choir/ James Wood, Ensemble InterContemporain/ Hans Zender

Erato 4509-98509-2 □ **72:30 mins** □ 🟐🟐🟐

At last a first-rate recording of some of Dallapiccola's masterpieces. Here is some of the most beautiful and perfectly crafted music of the 20th century – a purity of utterance of a kind that is rare indeed. The *Canti di prigionia* and the Greek Lyrics represent obverse sides of Dallapiccola's reaction to the rise of fascism in Italy. The *Canti* are universal pleas for freedom

from oppression: choral settings of Latin texts by three condemned prisoners, with an ensemble – at once translucent and apocalyptic – of two pianos, two harps and percussion.

In the darkest war years Dallapiccola also found solace in the serenity of the Greek poets. His three sets of Greek Lyrics are exquisite miniatures charting the progress of his journey towards 12-note music in a country which had scarcely progressed beyond *verismo* opera.

Hans Zender and the Ensemble InterContemporain are admirable interpreters of this music, though Julie Moffat lacks the purity – and at times the sheer power and intensity – the *Liriche greche* demand. The two fine a cappella works are superbly performed by James Wood's New London Chamber Choir. *Misha Donat*

DALLAPICCOLA

Canti di prigionia
see also **OPERA**: DALLAPICCOLA: Il prigioniero

MAXWELL DAVIES

The Turn of the Tide; Worldes Blis; Sir Charles His Pavan

Children's choirs from Manchester Cathedral, Manchester Grammar School Choir, RPO, BBC Philharmonic/Peter Maxwell Davies

Collins 13902 □ **72:56 mins** □ 🟐🟐🟐

This disc is a useful introduction to Maxwell Davies's music, as it shows his contrasting private and public faces. *Worldes Blis* is a very private piece which spins itself broodingly out of the opening plainsong melody, announced by a solo trombone. Over the next forty minutes it gradually accumulates a darkly intense energy and momentum that's discharged in the final climax. The sense of concentrated inwardness instilled by trombonist Christopher Mowat's opening solo is sustained until the very end in this blazing performance, conducted by the composer himself.

The Turn of the Tide is a public piece, both in its scoring – a combination of professional orchestra and schoolchildren – and its theme: the threat of man-made environmental disaster. To my ears the piece seems a rather uneasy combination of Maxwell Davies's own brand of lean, angular counterpoint, and a picturesquely tonal style. The combined forces of four children's choirs from Manchester acquit themselves magnificently in the final hymn to unsullied nature, but the piece itself is too self-conscious and contrived to hit the right jubilant note. *Ivan Hewett*

DEBUSSY/RAVEL

Debussy: Ariettes oubliées; Cinq poèmes de Baudelaire; Chansons de Bilitis

Ravel: Histoires naturelles

Nathalie Stutzmann (contralto), Catherine Collard (piano)

RCA Victor Red Seal RD 60899 □ 67:21 mins
□ ❷❷❷

It's somewhat surprising that so many singers tend to fight shy of performing Debussy. But the music makes such tremendous demands on the interpreter, who must achieve both subtlety of nuance and flexibility of line while at the same time generating an atmosphere of understated intensity. Little wonder, then, that recordings of Debussy's vocal works are few and far between when compared, say, with those devoted to Fauré or Poulenc.

Yet among the slender number of recommendable recordings of this repertoire, Nathalie Stutzmann's ravishing performances of the *Ariettes oubliées*, the *Chansons de Bilitis* and the neo-Wagnerian *Cinq poèmes de Baudelaire* certainly deserve special mention. Admittedly, Stutzmann's rich and creamy contralto tone may be far removed from the more ethereal sounds originally envisaged by Debussy. But Stutzmann overcomes any potential heaviness in her voice by creating the widest possible variety of colours, and responding with sensitivity to the underlying meaning of each text. Her pianist, Catherine Collard, appears perfectly attuned to this approach and achieves a wonderful delicacy of touch in songs like 'C'est l'extase' from *Ariettes oubliées* and 'La flûte de Pan' from *Chansons de Bilitis*. The Ravel cycle of animal portraits, more extrovert in character, provides an admirable contrast to the rest of the disc. *EL*

DEBUSSY

Chansons de Bilitis
see also Collection: French Song

DEBUSSY

La damoiselle élue; Nocturnes; Le martyre de Saint Sébastien (symphonic fragments)

Dawn Upshaw (soprano), Paula Rasmussen (mezzo-soprano); Los Angeles Master Chorale (women's voices), Los Angeles PO/Esa-Pekka Salonen

Sony SK 58952 □ 68:01 mins □ ❷❷❷

This disc shows quite how long a shadow Wagner's *Parsifal* cast over Debussy's career: its influence can be detected in the instrumentation of the early cantata *La damoiselle élue* (The Blessed Damozel) and more particularly in the subject-matter of the late *Le martyre de Saint Sébastien*. The recording also reveals just how far Debussy had forged his own idiom in the intervening decades: while both works share a certain luminosity, the lush Romantic gestures of the Rossetti setting are pared down to a more abstract austerity in *Le martyre*. The latter work is here represented by the suite of four symphonic fragments, so that the music is denuded of its dramatic context – it would be interesting to see how Esa-Pekka Salonen, who largely adopts a cool and measured approach, coped with the fuller version that was recorded so successfully by Michael Tilson Thomas with the LSO. That said, Salonen on this disc elicits accomplished performances from orchestra and chorus alike, and what Dawn Upshaw, as the Blessed Damozel, lacks in sensuality (compared with Jessye Norman, for example) she makes up for in innocence. The account of 'Nuages' from the *Nocturnes* is impressively controlled and affectingly stark.
William Humphreys-Jones

DELALANDE

Regina Coeli; De Profundis; Cantate Domino

Ex Cathedra Chamber Choir & Baroque Orchestra/Jeffrey Skidmore

ASV Gaudeamus CD GAU 141 □ 56:10 mins
□ ❷❷❷

In the court of Louis XIV at Versailles, Mass was said daily – but so quietly that it did not disturb the extended music being performed simultaneously. You can understand why, when presented with this wonderful choral and instrumental sound, sometimes in five rich and sumptuous parts, sometimes solos and duets in dancing expressions of joy. The animation of the music is matched by the performers. Many are young, recently graduated, singing with great freshness and infectious enthusiasm. Outstanding among the soloists, all drawn from this talented choir, are Paul Agnew, with a real *haut-contre* tenor (top C without the aid of falsetto), and the artless and unaffected soprano of Helen Groves.

'De profundis' is a funeral motet, used at Louis XIV's own burial service. Its counterpoint is dense and powerful, as it rises gradually 'out of the depths', with ardent, rhetorical harmonies at the pleading, 'Hear my voice'. The final 'Requiem aeternam' is overwhelming as one searing dissonance melts into the next, before the promise of perpetual light brings a final sense of rejoicing. At under an hour long, the disc is less than generous –

but the music and the performance of it are a revelation. *GP*

DELIUS

A Mass of Life; An Arabesque; Songs of Sunset

Heather Harper (soprano), Helen Watts (contralto), Robert Tear (tenor), Benjamin Luxon (bass), Janet Baker (mezzo-soprano), John Shirley-Quirk (baritone); LPO & Choir, Liverpool Philharmonic Choir, Royal Liverpool PO/Charles Groves

EMI CMS 7 64218 2 □ ADD □ 141:15 mins (2 discs) □ 🔊🔊

The vast canvas of the Nietzschean *A Mass of Life*, with its exhilarating opening invocation to the Will, wild dancing choruses, fluidly organic handling of solos, chorus and large orchestra, and culmination in the great 'Wanderer's Night Song', among the most profound music Delius ever wrote, mark out this work as one of his supreme masterpieces. Its problems of balance and articulation are notorious, but they're as nearly solved as they ever will be in this classic account by Charles Groves: more measured and literal-sounding, at first, than the famous mono Beecham recording, but gaining in the long run from the solidity and definition the account brings to some of Delius's most remarkable textural writing. *Songs of Sunset* (1906–7), to poems of Ernest Dowson, is less well known than it deserves, an almost archetypal expression of *fin de siècle* languor ('They are not long, the days of wine and roses') in Delius's most gorgeous vein. This, too, is a most successful version, graced by the voices of Janet Baker and John Shirley-Quirk at the peak of their form. The later *An Arabesque* (1915) is a perfect foil – chill and bleak, lamenting lost bliss, and most eloquently sung by Shirley-Quirk. An essential item for any collection of British music. The recordings, from the late Sixties, have come up very well. *CM*

DELIUS

Sea Drift; Songs of Farewell; Songs of Sunset

Sally Burgess (mezzo-soprano), Bryn Terfel (baritone); Waynflete Singers, Southern Voices, Bournemouth SO & Chorus/Richard Hickox

Chandos CHAN 9214 □ 77:08 mins □ 🔊🔊🔊

Delius's preoccupation with the transience of life and love links these three works. *Sea Drift* (1903–4), written at the height of his powers, is regarded by many as his greatest achievement. It concerns two mating birds: the death of the female and the male's bewilderment and grief. The music is a setting of poetry by Walt Whitman. So too, is *Songs of Farewell* (1929–30), the finest achievement of Delius's final years. Again, the images are principally of the sea and voyages as metaphors for acceptance of death and the journey into the hereafter.

This is an intelligent programme and an outstanding issue. Terfel seizes every opportunity and colours his voice in perfect accord with the texts. In the marvellously evocative *Songs of Sunset* (1906–7), both he and Sally Burgess sing with passion the Ernest Dowson lines of dying love. The choir is first class too: jubilant in the rapturous 'Shine, shine' chorus of *Sea Drift* and radiantly confident in the demanding 'Joy, Shipmate Joy' of *Songs of Farewell*. Hickox captures the spirit and atmosphere of these haunting scores beautifully, and the sound is full with wide perspectives. A must for Delius lovers. *Ian Lace*

DOWLAND

The First Book of Songs

Rufus Müller (tenor), Christopher Wilson (lute)

ASV Gaudeamus CD GAU 135 □ 74:32 mins □ 🔊🔊🔊

Thurston Dart called 1597 'a year of wonders' for English music: it saw the publication of various madrigal books, tutors, collections of vocal music from France and Italy, and Dowland's *First Book of Songs*, the first substantial collection of a genre that was to dominate English music for the next quarter-century – the lute-song. So successful was the *First Book* that it was reprinted four times during the next decade, and several contemporary plays lift quotations from the texts Dowland set. All 21 songs have been included on this delightful disc (the only exclusion being the single lute solo).

Rufus Müller is clearly a most intelligent singer with a warm, agile tenor, well suited to this repertoire, yet with a potential power that produces an intense undercurrent in the more weighty songs. His diction is impeccable, and he responds with great sensitivity to every nuance of these fine poems. (Using original pronunciation may have added a further dimension – perhaps next time?)

Christopher Wilson's distinctive, soft-toned lute-playing goes from strength to strength: few players would handle this music better. *Kate Bolton*

DOWLAND

Flow My Teares; First & Second Books of Songs (excerpts)

Paul Agnew (tenor), Christopher Wilson (lute)

Metronome MET CD 1010 □ 58:36 mins □ *ΦΦΦ*

Dowland's songs are the finest jewels in the crown of Elizabethan music. Celebrated specially for their pathos and melancholy, they were immensely popular, with 5,000 copies printed. Agnew and Wilson have recorded eight songs from each book, a programme I was gradually drawn into hearing at one sitting. They're by no means an unremitting portrayal of 'Dowland *dolens*', as he was dubbed, including original dances – galliards with added words; that wonderful expression of lovers' heightening passion, 'I see… hear… touch… kisse… die…'; as well as the song version of the familiar *Lachrimae*.

Agnew's alluring voice has a French *haut-contre* gentleness in its highest register. His tone can be chillingly empty – the start of 'I saw my Lady weepe'. Elsewhere he is full of fun, playing with the pun on 'love' – the singer's love and the sleeping girl who is the object of it – in 'Sleep, Wayward Thoughts'. Wilson is far more than mere accompanist as words and allusions permeate his lute-playing. I cannot imagine a more persuasive Dowland recital than this. *GP*

DOWLAND

Songs
see also **CHAMBER**: DOWLAND: Lachrimae

DUPARC

Mélodies

José van Dam (baritone), Florence Bonnafous (soprano), Maciej Pikulski (piano)

Forlane UCD 16692 □ 67:30 mins □ *ΦΦΦ*

A disease of the nervous system, contracted early in his career, prevented Henri Duparc from playing a leading role in 19th-century French musical life. Yet Duparc was anything but a *petit maître*, his output of just 17 songs constituting one of the glories of the entire vocal repertoire. Perhaps the most remarkable aspect of his achievement lies in its diversity, each song inhabiting a quite distinctive emotional world. Likewise, the musical influences are varied yet subtly assimilated, not least those of Wagner and Liszt, whose chromatic harmonies seem to take on a decidedly French accent in songs such as 'Extase' and 'Le manoir de Rosemonde'.

There are persuasive arguments for hearing Duparc's songs in their later orchestrated versions, but the original piano accompaniments allow for greater intimacy of expression. Certainly, these qualities are brought to the fore in this outstanding recording in which José van Dam confirms his position as the finest interpreter of French song since Gérard Souzay. *EL*

DURUFLE/FAURE

Duruflé: Requiem
Fauré: Requiem

Jennifer Larmore (soprano), Thomas Hampson (baritone); Ambrosian Singers, Philharmonia Orchestra/Michel Legrand

Teldec 4509-90879-2 □ 77:42 mins □ *ΦΦΦ*

Maurice Duruflé's noble Requiem is the true successor to Fauré's, likewise imbued with the spirit of the old Church modes and infused with a similar spirit of aching serenity. The two settings of the 'Pie Jesu' are directly comparable. It makes excellent sense to couple their Requiems together. Like Fauré's, too, Duruflé's can be performed with large or small orchestral forces, or with organ. If you want it small and intimate, look no further than Matthew Best's refined and deeply sympathetic version on Hyperion, with Ann Murray, Thomas Allen and the Corydon Singers, coupled with some of Duruflé's fine Latin motets. The organ version, coupled with the Fauré, is available at mid-price in Philip Ledger's excellent King's College performance (with Janet Baker among the soloists) on EMI. The resplendent full-orchestral version, however, is how I prefer to hear this radiant work, and Teldec's vibrant, passionately committed version, in absolutely top-notch sound, seems to me unrivalled. Legrand finds more drama here (and, indeed, in the Fauré) than any other conductor; his soloists sing with utter conviction, and the forces are ideally balanced. A clear first choice. *CM*

DVORAK

Stabat mater; Biblical Songs

Kaaren Erickson (soprano), Claudine Carlson (mezzo-soprano), John Aler (tenor), John Cheek, Manfred Hemm (bass); Westminster Symphonic Choir, New Jersey SO/Zdeněk Mácal

Delos DE 3161 □ 106:37 mins (2 discs) □ *ΦΦΦ*

Recorded using the Delos twenty-bit digital system and Dolby Surround Sound technique, Zdeněk Mácal's authoritative account of Dvořák's *Stabat mater* was released in 1994. Mácal's team of four soloists sings with eloquence and understanding, not least the soprano Kaaren Erickson, who outshines her most recent rival, Livia Aghova, on the Bělohlávek recording (Chandos). The New Jersey SO may be the least-recorded orchestra in the New York hinterland, but it is nonetheless a formidable ensemble, refined and rich-toned in every section; under Zdeněk Mácal, it consistently impresses, and plays with a flair and zeal that should be the envy of its better-known compatriots. The Westminster Choir is among the most prodigious of American vocal ensembles, and its contributions here are highly distinguished. In the Biblical Songs, Manfred Hemm displays a fine sense of line and impressively controlled phrasing, and his performance as a whole deserves the highest praise. *MJ*

ELGAR

The Apostles

Alison Hargan (soprano), Alfreda Hodgson (contralto), David Rendall (tenor), Bryn Terfel, Stephen Roberts, Robert Lloyd (bass); LSO & Chorus/Richard Hickox

Chandos CHAN 8875/6 □ **127:00 mins (2 discs)**
□ ✪✪✪

This 1990 performance of Elgar's oratorio *The Apostles* does not wholly eclipse Adrian Boult's largely unimpeachable EMI version, but it is, on balance, a finer option. Richard Hickox evidently holds this work in high esteem, and conveys his affection and enthusiasm in dramatic fashion throughout a lengthy composition which can outstay its welcome in the wrong hands. Among the soloists, Robert Lloyd is particularly impressive as Judas, with Bryn Terfel a fine Peter. Chandos has elicited many plaudits over the years for its excellent recordings of large-scale choral repertoire for reasons much in evidence here: dynamic range and spatial clarity are effortlessly reproduced, and the large choral and orchestral forces involved are ideally balanced. *MJ*

ELGAR

The Dream of Gerontius; Sea Pictures

Janet Baker (mezzo-soprano), Richard Lewis (tenor), Kim Borg (bass); Sheffield Philharmonic Choir, Ambrosian Singers, Hallé Choir & Orchestra/John Barbirolli

EMI CMS 7 63185 2 □ **ADD** □ **122:01 mins (2 discs)**
□ ✪✪

Elgar's ground-breaking oratorio has been well served on record in the past half-century, from Sargent's passionate 1945 account with Heddle Nash and Gladys Ripley (now available on Testament). But if a gun were at

my head I think I'd still choose this unforgettable Barbirolli version. By common consent, Janet Baker's Angel, her voice in its absolute prime, is incomparable. Richard Lewis is a Gerontius of moving intensity. The standard criticism is that Kim Borg's English pronunciation is deeply unconvincing, but what a voice, dark and agonised: his 'Proficiscere' is as powerful as might fall from the lips of a foreign priest, and the slightly alien quality makes his Angel of the Agony somehow all the more moving. Barbirolli's knowledge and love of the score are without parallel; he draws an intensely luminous quality of sound from the orchestra. His is the most mystical *Gerontius*, yet the big massed moments have astonishing grandeur, and the emotion he wrings from the score is overwhelming. The CD transfer is first rate. If you absolutely must have a modern recording, Hickox on Chandos offers much, but not this kind of miracle. This is also the clear first recommendation for *Sea Pictures*: a further definitive example of Baker's artistry. She had made the cycle very much her own and never sang it better than here. And all at mid-price! *CM*

ELGAR

The Kingdom; Coronation Ode

Margaret Price (soprano), Yvonne Minton (mezzo-soprano), Alexander Young (tenor), John Shirley-Quirk (baritone), Felicity Lott (soprano), Alfreda Hodgson (contralto), Richard Morton (tenor), Stephen Roberts (bass); LPO & Choir/Adrian Boult; King's College Choir, Cambridge University Music Society, Kneller Hall Band, New Philharmonia Orchestra/Philip Ledger

EMI CMS 7 64209 2 □ **ADD** □ **129:57 mins (2 discs)**
□ ✪✪

Slatkin on RCA and Hickox on Chandox offer excellent modern accounts of Elgar's third and last oratorio, but this magisterial Boult recording – the first, which revealed the work's glories when it had utterly fallen out of the repertoire – remains the clear first choice for me. Though the score isn't without staid passages in the outer sections, the central portions, including the thrilling Pentecost scene and Peter's sermon, are among Elgar's most inspired music. Shirley-Quirk is the noblest Peter on record, and Margaret Price's delivery of 'The Sun Goeth Down' (with its seraphic violin obbligato) remains one of the greatest moments in Elgar recording. The CD transfer has improved the definition of the chorus, which was a little recessed on the LP. Elgar's setting of AC Benson's *Coronation Ode* for the coronation of Edward VII turns ceremonial flummery into magnificent, passionate musical pageantry. This was where the trio of the first *Pomp and Circumstance* March had its fateful meeting with the words 'Land of Hope and Glory'. The result is very nearly a major work; Ledger and his team, in one of the most brilliant-sounding recordings ever made in King's College Chapel, play it for all its (considerable) worth in surging excitement and lyric nostalgia. *CM*

The Music Makers; Sursum corda; Salut d'amour; Chanson de matin; Chanson de nuit; Dream Children; Elegy; Sospiri

Jean Rigby (mezzo-soprano); BBC SO & Chorus/Andrew Davis

Teldec 4509-92374-2 □ 75:49 mins □ 𝄞𝄞𝄞

In setting O'Shaughnessy's ode about the 'dreamers of dreams', Elgar created some of his most personal music. *The Music Makers*, seldom estimated at its true worth, is a kind of concentrated act of farewell to the musical grandeurs of the Edwardian era: he quotes several of his most famous works, but in an unmistakable spirit of elegy. Boult's EMI recording, with Janet Baker on top form, was long the only recommendation (it's currently available coupled with his *Gerontius*, characteristically fine but not quite comparable with the Barbirolli reviewed above). There's now a very good version on Chandos by the late Bryden Thomson, with Linda Finnie as soloist (coupled with a *Sea Pictures* somewhat below the standard of the peerless Baker–Barbirolli account). But Andrew Davis's Teldec recording emerges as my first choice. No other version conjures the piece's dream-like atmosphere so convincingly, and Rigby, less commanding than Baker, is nevertheless intensely appealing in lyricism. The coupling is an imaginative selection of Elgar's shorter and lighter orchestral works, including the rarely heard *Dream Children*. *CM*

Sea Pictures
see also **ORCHESTRAL**: ELGAR: Cello Concerto in E minor

La chanson d'Eve; Mélodies

Janet Baker (mezzo-soprano), Geoffrey Parsons (piano)

Hyperion CDA 66320 □ 66:17 mins □ 𝄞𝄞𝄞

Janet Baker was a devotee of Fauré's songs throughout her career, and this recording displays her perfect sympathy with his rapt, searchingly lyrical voice-writing. This varied and generous selection of 28 songs is perhaps the best general introduction on disc to this important side of Fauré's output and is also one of Geoffrey Parsons's finest recordings: voice and piano seem always utterly at one. Though the programme includes none of the aching existential rapture of Fauré's last years, its centrepiece is the marvellous and seldom-heard 11-song *Chanson d'Eve* cycle (composed 1907–10) which opens his final period. The 17 others are well chosen and include a goodly proportion of the best loved, including 'Après un rêve' and 'Le secret', as well as several of the finest settings of Verlaine (for whose poetry Fauré possessed a deep affinity), such as 'Mandoline' and 'En sourdine'. A magical disc. *CM*

Requiem; Pelléas et Mélisande

Mathias Usbeck (treble), Gilles Cachemaille (baritone); Romand Chamber Choir, Pro Arte Choir, Suisse Romande Orchestra/Armin Jordan

Erato 2292-45813-2 □ 52:41 mins □ 𝄞𝄞𝄞

This recording of Fauré's Requiem has flair and a robust honesty that is immediately captivating. Mathias Usbeck is tender and expressive in the 'Pie Jesu', even if not flawless. The baritone Gilles Cachemaille shows admirable control. The women of the chorus have a pure, youthful tone that is enviable. The organ is real and sensitively positioned in the orchestral perspective. There is a good sense of place and of real, wholehearted performance.

The incidental music for *Pelléas et Mélisande* is ravishingly played. From the opening bars of the prelude and its surging, pleading melody it is clear that Armin Jordan's treatment of these four short pieces is anything other than incidental. *Christopher Lambton*

Requiem
see also DURUFLE: Requiem

Missa O quam glorifica; Ave Dei patris filia; Sumwhat musyng; To complayne me, alas; That was my joy (anonymous), etc

The Cardinall's Musick/Andrew Carwood

ASV Gaudeamus CD GAU 142 □ 74:26 mins □ 𝄞𝄞𝄞

Having completed an excellent four-volume survey of Nicholas Ludford's masses, The Cardinall's Musick turned its attention to Ludford's greatest contemporary, Robert Fayrfax (1464–1521). This first volume of Fayrfax's music features the Mass, *O quam glorifica*, which the composer offered for his doctoral examination at Cambridge in 1504. Despite its academic origins, listeners will be struck by this complex work's seductive mellifluousness and ingenious rhythmic diversity. The Cardinall's Musick's finely proportioned account highlights this music's rich harmony and highly ornate melismas, expressing the emotion rather than the sub stance of the text. Try the hypnotic textural patterns of the Gloria and Credo, the sumptuous harmonies of the Sanctus, the spiritual purity of the two-part counterpoint between soprano and bass at the words 'in nomine Domini' in the Benedictus, or the inspirational quality of the Agnus Dei's exultant final phrases.

Fayrfax's majestic *Ave Dei patris filia* is also particularly effective. Here, The Cardinall's Musick luxuriates in the composer's vivid text setting, in which the score's imaginatively varied vocal groupings culminate in strict imitation in all voices, emphasising the eternal purity of the Virgin Mary. *Nicholas Rast*

FRANCK

Panis angelicus
see **CHAMBER**: FRANCK: Violin Sonata in A

GABRIELI

Four Christmas Motets
see SCHUTZ: *The Christmas Story*

GESUALDO

Ave, dulcissima Maria
see Collection: Marian Music

GESUALDO

Madrigals

Les Arts Florissants/William Christie

Harmonia Mundi HMC 901268 □ 54:54 mins □ *♪♪♪*

Carlo Gesualdo is one of the most colourful eccentrics in western music. As a prince he was above the law for murdering his adulterous wife and her lover, discovered *in flagrante*. As a composer he violated musical laws, taking descriptive word-painting to its extreme. While others, such as Monteverdi and Gabrieli, were developing large-scale structures based on strong, directional harmony and broad schemes of tonality, Gesualdo focused obsessionally on isolated ideas. Successive intervals, each representing rhetorically a single word, add up to grotesquely angular lines;

chords chosen for their own descriptive sake flow in a continuous chromatic stream. Nor is rhythm immune, with, for example, pauses within 'sospirava' ('sighed') – single words disintegrating into a series of momentary still-life images.

The subject-matter of this selection from Books Three to Six is all-consuming love, obsessive to the point of stupefaction. No ensemble could be more persuasive – or accurate – than the singers of Les Arts Florissants, with theorbo, lirone and harp providing three interludes. The fixed-pitch harp shows vividly the limitations of unequal temperament when melodic and vertical intervals become, for a moment, virtually incomprehensible.

Not for the faint-hearted, but a striking example of music which can go no further. *GP*

GESUALDO

Sacrarum Cantionum Liber Primus (1603)

Oxford Camerata/Jeremy Summerly

Naxos 8.550742 □ 68:12 mins □ *♪*

The infamous Gesualdo is best known for the wayward and expressive harmonies of his madrigals. Here we have a marvellous chance to hear the other side of his work, mostly unrecorded before. In *Tribulationem* and *O vos omnes*, there is fulsome attention to the ravishing harmonic effects while retaining the necessary vocal line, and everywhere there is clarity of texture and subtle phrasing. Not all of these pieces are of equal quality, but the variety is sometimes pleasing. The lively and beautifully articulated *Sancti spiritus Domine* comes towards the end as a joyous surprise. An enterprising and enriching disc. *AP*

GIBBONS

Songs & Anthems
see **CHAMBER**: GIBBONS: Consort & Keyboard Music

GOLDSCHMIDT

Mediterranean Songs
see **OPERA**: GOLDSCHMIDT: Der gewaltige Hahnrei

GOLDSCHMIDT

Two Psalms
see **ORCHESTRAL**: Collection: Testimonies of War

GORECKI

Symphony No. 3 (Symphony of Sorrowful Songs)

Dawn Upshaw (soprano); London Sinfonietta/David Zinman

Nonesuch 7559-79282-2 □ 52:52 mins □ *♪♪♪*

This was the disc that put the contemporary Polish composer Henryk Mikolaj Górecki firmly into the mainstream repertoire, its sales – running into hundreds of thousands – shattering all previous records for a contemporary musical work. It wasn't the symphony's first recording (the work is twenty years old), and there are by now many rivals, some with more idiomatic Polish singers (and some with interesting couplings). Yet there's no doubt that this performance has a special aura and carries a huge emotional charge.

In his setting of three laments (not specifically connected with Auschwitz, as much of the publicity has suggested, even though one of the texts is by a prisoner of the Gestapo (who survived), but rather as a timeless meditation on the human condition), Górecki appears simple and direct. But he is by no means a simple composer (as explorers of his other works soon discover) and Symphony No. 3 is in its own way as rigorous and logical as any of his more avant-garde scores. The canonic structure of the first movement creates a polyphony of exceptional richness, and this and all the succeeding, sumptuous string sonorities are vibrantly captured in Nonesuch's studio recording. The three movements, all 'sorrowful' and 'slow', are nevertheless very different, allowing Upshaw to span a very wide interpretative range with magisterial intensity. *CM*

GRIEG

Peer Gynt; Sigurd Jorsalfar (complete incidental music)

Barbara Bonney (soprano), Marianne Eklöf (mezzo-soprano), Kjell Magnus Sandve (tenor), Urban Malmberg, Carl Gustaf Holmgren (baritone), Wenche Foss, Toralv Maurstad, Tor Stokke (speaker); Gösta Ohlin Vocal Ensemble, Pro Musica Chamber Choir, Gothenburg SO/Neeme Järvi

DG 423 079-2 □ 123:44 mins (2 discs) □ *① ① ①*

This is a particularly impressive two-disc set from DG, containing the first-ever complete recordings of Grieg's incidental music for Ibsen's *Peer Gynt* and Bjørnson's *Sigurd Jorsalfar*, heard as they left the composer's writing-desk in the years 1875 and 1872 respectively. Its chief joy is the inspirational and assertive way in which Järvi and his forces bring these scores to life. Barbara Bonney is an ideal Solveig in *Peer Gynt*, and is supported by Marianne Eklöf (Anitra) and – in the title role – the fulsomely voiced Urban Malmberg. One normally hears only those fragments of the complete score which comprise the familiar *Peer Gynt* Suite; the opportunity to experience 'Morning Mood', 'In the Hall of the Mountain King', 'The Death of Aase', and

'Anitra's Dance' within the overall framework of Ibsen's text is constantly engrossing. The incidental music composed by Grieg for Bjørnstjerne Bjørnson's historical drama concerning the life and loves of two sibling joint rulers of 12th-century Norway, *Sigurd Jorsalfar*, is but little known today, only the patriotic Homage March has attained any lasting familiarity. Suffice it to say that, by the close of the work, the two monarchs have pledged to advance their nation's cause, both at home and abroad. The music is well worth experiencing and is particularly well played here. Neeme Järvi's accounts of both scores leave absolutely nothing to be desired, and the Gothenburg SO plays with splendid refinement and brilliance throughout. *MJ*

GRIEG

Songs

Anne Sofie von Otter (mezzo-soprano), Bengt Forsberg (piano)

DG 437 521-2 □ 67:30 mins □ *① ① ①*

Debussy's barbed comment that Grieg's music was merely 'pink bon-bons stuffed with snow' is triumphantly refuted by this recital, which brings together a healthy mixture of the familiar ('Jeg elsker dig' and 'En svane') and the unjustly neglected aspects of the Norwegian composer's song output. Among the major discoveries are the *Haugtussa* cycle of 1898. This set of eight songs about the visionary mountain maid who seeks solace in nature after being rejected by her lover represents Grieg at his very finest. Kirsten Flagstad was a staunch advocate of the work, but Anne Sofie von Otter proves to be her equal, probing the emotional depths of the final extended song with heartaching poignancy. Elsewhere, both she and her excellent partner deliver performances of exceptional sensitivity and freshness which avoid any temptation towards excessive sentimentality. *EL*

GURNEY

The Western Playland; Ludlow and Teme
see VAUGHAN WILLIAMS: On Wenlock Edge

HANDEL

Acis and Galatea; Look Down, Harmonious Saint

Claron McFadden (soprano), John Mark Ainsley, Rogers Covey-Crump (tenor), Michael George (bass); The King's Consort/Robert King

Hyperion CDA 66361/2 □ 106:12 mins (2 discs) □ *① ① ①*

Handel set the fable of *Acis and Galatea* four times – as an Italian serenata, an English 'masque', a curious bilingual amalgamation of the two, and finally the masque again with minor alterations. It was immensely popular, with 71 performances in Handel's own lifetime. The English versions were refreshingly accessible to an 18th-century London audience that was tired, a contemporary put it, of 'a parcel of Italian Eunuches, like so many Cats, [who] squall out somewhat you don't understand'.

Whether or not it was staged is unsure but, like the dramatic oratorios, it was certainly staged in the 'theatre' of Handel's mind, and dramatic pacing and convincing characterisation are crucial. McFadden is a loving Galatea, Ainsley a charming Acis, and Covey-Crump a finely polished Damon. Michael George is magnificent – a nimble but ferocious Polyphemus, whose every note is absolutely centred.

If you already have a period recording, try Mozart's K566, his 1788 arrangement of Handel in a German translation. It's a fascinating insight into Classical taste, the harmony filled out with added clarinets, bassoons and horns. Christopher Hogwood's woodwind are wonderfully grainy – and prominent – in a highly commended recording on L'Oiseau-Lyre. *GP*

HANDEL

Alexander's Feast

Donna Brown (soprano), Carolyn Watkinson (contralto), Ashley Stafford (countertenor), Nigel Robson (tenor), Stephen Varcoe (bass); Monteverdi Choir, English Baroque Soloists/John Eliot Gardiner

Philips 422 053-2 □ 98:16 mins (2 discs) □ *❷❷❷*

Alexander's Feast stands halfway between opera and oratorio. It was not staged, and the secular text is narrative rather than dramatic, yet Handel's music is full of imagery and surprises. Sometimes these features are realised in the setting of a phrase – the tragic pathos of 'fall'n is the foe' – sometimes through a striking orchestral colour – for example, three bassoons, doubled violas, cellos and bass representing a 'ghastly band' of 'Grecian ghosts that were in battle slain'. But freed of operatic demands from both singers and audience for a sequence of self-contained arias, the very first aria, 'Happy Pair', breaks down into an unexpected chorus interspersed with solo sections; later, the chorus repeats the words of a solo recitative and a duet.

This is a live recording from the Göttingen Handel Festival before an impeccably behaved audience. Only the slightly dry acoustic gives it away. But these forces don't need the help of a generous resonance, and the reward is an exciting sense of spontaneity in the performance. Warmly recommended – and best listened to after total immersion in a Handel opera or two, to enjoy fully the novelty of his remarkable structural innovations. *GP*

HANDEL

Apollo e Dafne; Crudel tiranno Amor

Nancy Argenta (soprano), Michael George (bass); Collegium Musicum 90/Simon Standage

Chandos Chaconne CHAN 0583 □ 58:07 mins
□ *❷❷❷*

The most prolifically tuneful of Handel's early works, *Apollo e Dafne* is forty minutes of flowing melodic invention. Completed in Hanover in around 1710, soon after his return from Venice, the cantata displays the fruits of Handel's years in Italy, with its graceful arias, variety of instrumental colour (flute, oboe, bassoon, cello and violin are featured) and a mythological subject taken from Ovid's *Metamorphoses*.

Michael George and Nancy Argenta sing superbly, realising both the music's limpid sensuality and its dramatic frissons, while Collegium Musicum 90 provides elegant, spirited support.

The solo cantata *Crudel tiranno Amor*, composed in London in around 1721, comprises three delightful arias. Nancy Argenta's singing is again beautiful and affecting, especially in 'O dolce mia speranza', with its heart-rending vocal line and echoing violin. Though both cantatas are relatively small-scale works, Handel's zip and finesse make them a joy, and the performances here come close to perfection. In a word, bliss! *Graham Lock*

HANDEL

Chandos Anthems: My Song shall be alway; O Come let us Sing unto the Lord; O praise the Lord with one consent

Patrizia Kwella (soprano), James Bowman (alto), Ian Partridge (tenor), Michael George (bass); The Sixteen, Orchestra of The Sixteen/Harry Christophers

Chandos Chaconne CHAN 0505 □ 75:00 mins
□ *❷❷❷*

The 11 Chandos Anthems clearly reflect the circumstances of their composition. The Duke of Chandos, immensely wealthy from lining his pockets as paymaster-general, built a magnificent Palladian mansion, Cannons, in Edgware, living there like a European princeling and maintaining his own musical establishment. At first, this ran to only a three-part choir, oboe, bassoon and string orchestra without violas, and this scale is matched in Christophers's elegant interpretation, which is the epitome of Georgian refinement.

I choose these three anthems (all 11 are available) because they use the richer sonority of a four-part choir. *O Come let us Sing unto the Lord* has two recorders to colour the pastoral tenor aria 'O come let us worship', and two of them are recorded, astonishingly, for the first time ever.

The soloists are excellent, particularly Kwella, who has the clarity of a boy treble supported by the maturer artistry of a soprano. Throughout, their singing is light and understated, and both choir and orchestra are highly polished. They certainly match Handel's own refinement, for example in *My Song shall be alway* opening with strings of suspensions entwined above a timeless walking bass (which expose a couple of careless edits). *GP*

HANDEL

Four Coronation Anthems
see **ORCHESTRAL**: HANDEL: Music for the Royal Fireworks

HANDEL

Deborah

Yvonne Kenny, Susan Gritton (soprano), Catherine Denley (mezzo-soprano), James Bowman (countertenor), Michael George (bass); Choir of New College, Oxford, Choristers of Salisbury Cathedral, The King's Consort/Robert King

Hyperion CDA 66841/2 □ **139:41 mins (2 discs)** □ *✪✪✪*

Quite why *Deborah* has never achieved the popularity of some of Handel's other oratorios is hard to fathom. Perhaps it has something to do with the story-line: the drama, though less than gripping for most of its course, reaches its grisly climax when the Canaanite commander, Sisera, has his head nailed to the floor with a tent-peg. That the fair heroine, Jael, who steels herself to the task, is merely fulfilling a prophecy – that of the seeress Deborah – does little to make it all any more palatable.

However, *Deborah* contains some of the most glorious music Handel ever wrote. Even if many of the numbers have been recycled from earlier works, the invention is still staggering.

Handel devotees can thus amuse themselves spotting the tunes, while everyone else can revel in the sumptuous scoring (including flutes, oboes, bassoons, horns, organs, trumpets and timpani) and in the sheer vitality and humanity of the piece, all superbly conveyed in Robert King's recording. *Barry Millington*

HANDEL

Dixit Dominus; Nisi Dominus; Salve regina

Arleen Auger, Lynne Dawson (soprano), Diana Montague (contralto), Leigh Nixon, John Mark Ainsley (tenor), Simon Birchall (bass); Choir & Orchestra of Westminster Abbey/Simon Preston

Archiv 423 594-2 □ **56:22 mins** □ *✪✪✪*

Handel, aged 22, was received with tremendous enthusiasm on his first visit to Italy, and he responded with some of his most spontaneous and uninhibited music. *Dixit Dominus* is his first surviving choral work, yet it displays a sure hand throughout. The orchestral opening is striking – flashing broken string chords outlining irresistible rhythms, introducing insistent choral 'dixits'. But it's a concerto, too, with dazzling virtuosity needed from contrasting soloists. And Handel's gift for description continues – vicious string and choral blows depicting the words 'shatter heads', with mysterious pulsing chords behind the voices who 'drink of the brook'.

Equally unforgettable are the hypnotically repeated broken chords above a descending bass which introduce the simplest of choral statements – a monophonic chant – at the opening of *Nisi Dominus*, returning, punningly and to great effect, at 'as it was in the beginning'.

There are moments of great tenderness too, such as the end of Auger's beautiful *Salve regina* – and a chance to share Handel's own delight in the solo organ part he played in the third movement.

I was tempted by the high polish of Christophers (Chandos), but the raw enthusiasm of Preston's forces are worth a noisy background and rather assertive recording balance. *GP*

HANDEL

Israel in Egypt; The Ways of Zion Do Mourn

Soloists; Monteverdi Choir & Orchestra/John Eliot Gardiner

Erato 4509-99758-2 □ **ADD** □ **138:00 mins (2 discs)** □ *✪✪*

Israel in Egypt was a flop at its first performance, offending because of its scriptural language in a theatre and, with its preponderance of choruses, disappointing a London audience with a taste for athletic soloists. Put aside these prejudices, anticipating instead 'a vast series of frescos painted by a giant on the walls of some primeval temple' (a 1909 description), and Gardiner's 1979 recording still succeeds magnificently. It has the power and fervour to thrill in the huge double choruses, the delicacy to delight in the picturesque descriptions, such as jumping frogs, falling hailstones, a 'thick darkness' of bassoons and unpredictable harmony. With such allusions, it's no surprise that a contemporary letter in the *Daily Post* urged audiences to study the word-book so that they would not miss any of Handel's vivid aural imagery.

Gardiner includes the funeral anthem for Queen Caroline, *The Ways of Zion*, and this provides the chance to relive the first performance, when the anthem served as Part One of a *three*-part *Israel in Egypt*. Reordering the tracks to hear first the tribulations of the Israelites before their exodus from Egypt and Moses's great hymn of praise makes for an intensely satisfying and revealing musical experience. *GP*

HANDEL

Judas Maccabaeus

Jamie MacDougall (tenor), Emma Kirkby (soprano), Catherine Denley (mezzo-soprano), James Bowman (countertenor), Michael George, Simon Birchall (bass); Choir of New College, Oxford, The King's Consort/Robert King

Hyperion CDA 66641/2 □ 149:34 mins (2 discs) □ ❶❷❸

Handel's *Judas Maccabaeus* has been disparaged for its libretto – a 'decline into claptrap' – for dramatic weakness and for its militarism. Hear it in the context of the victory celebrations for Culloden, however, and you'll discover a profusion of colourful delights.

The King's Consort, with many of our new, second-generation period instrumentalists, exhibits all the benefits of authentic timbre and texture – there is no need nowadays to make allowances for uneven tone or bad intonation. The New College Choir is spot on, poignant in mourning, exultant in victory. The whole ensemble is recorded over a wide stereo spectrum which leaves every detail clearly audible.

Emma Kirkby's Israelitish Woman enlivens even the most pedestrian numbers. Catherine Denley contrasts but blends in their five duets,

and has great facility over an impressive range. Bowman is superb in 'Father of Heav'n'. Jamie MacDougall rises to the virtuoso challenge of the warlike hero, and Michael George focuses with no less clarity as Simon.

Any weaknesses in this, the first ever complete recording, are Handel's. As a performance, it's persuasive evidence indeed that what may seem mediocre on the page can spring to life, given the artistry and conviction of performers of this calibre. *GP*

HANDEL

Messiah

Barbara Schlick, Sandrine Piau (soprano), Andreas Scholl (alto), Mark Padmore (tenor), Nathan Berg (bass); Les Arts Florissants/William Christie

Harmonia Mundi HMC 901498/99 □ 142:40 mins (2 discs) □ ❶❷❸

Messiah (arr. Mozart)

Felicity Lott (soprano), Felicity Palmer (contralto), Philip Langridge (tenor), Robert Lloyd (bass); Huddersfield Choral Society, RPO/Charles Mackerras

ASV CD DCS 230 □ 136:57 mins (2 discs) □ ❶❷❸

Messiah's librettist, Jennens, thought Handel's setting 'not near so good as he might & ought to have done'. But now that this oratorio is uniquely popular, one might ask what a French choir and orchestra and a polyglot team of soloists can add to the 33 *Messiahs* currently available. In fact, this is a stunning performance, from singers and instrumentalists alike.

Its only distinctively national quality is the assured approach to French rhythms. Christie's speeds are refreshingly lively, particularly in the section 'For behold…', here performed in Handel's 4/4 rather than its customary turgid eight. Choral textures are translucent – details new to me emerged from the delicately drawn counterpoint, enhanced by exceptional choral phrasing that manifests great concern for the meaning of the words. The soloists respond vividly to the changing dramatic demands, their English surely freer of accent than were Handel's Italians.

The Huddersfield recording sustains a contrasting tradition. The 1784 Handel commemoration *Messiah* already had '513 performers, the Harmony so unbroken that it was like the fall of Waters from one source, imperceptibly blended'. Mozart's 1789 re-orchestration is an absorbing vignette of later 18th-century taste – clarinets entwined chromatically above Handel's unison in 'The people that walked in darkness', a woodwind 'rod of iron' at the start of 'Thou shalt break them'.

Handel, already enlarging his own forces in later performances, might surely have revelled in the sheer power of the Huddersfield Choral Society, and its magnificent sound makes seats for its Christmas *Messiah* much sought after. *GP*

HANDEL

Semele

Norma Burrowes, Patrizia Kwella, Elisabeth Priday (soprano), Della Jones, Catherine Denley (mezzo-soprano), Timothy Penrose (alto), Anthony Rolfe Johnson, Maldwyn Davies (tenor), Robert Lloyd, David Thomas (bass); Monteverdi Choir, English Baroque Soloists/John Eliot Gardiner

Erato 4509-99759-2 □ 154:00 mins (2 discs) □ 🟢🟢

Semele is not a secular oratorio but an unstaged opera. Handel reveals the theatre of his imagination in striking scenic descriptions and stage directions which Gardiner's excellent forces reflect vividly in sound. Orchestral and choral textures are bright, rhythms lightly sprung, and his singers match Handel's characters superbly: Lloyd as a majestic king yet solicitous father, Della Jones as the goddess Juno scorned, fearsome and breathtakingly virtuosic in her anger. Handel paints intensely colourful musical pictures, like Iris's description of dragons that 'lash their forky stings' and 'disclose a thousand fiery eyes'.

It's no surprise that Jupiter fell for such a beguiling Semele as Norma Burrowes, bathed in an ethereal resonance once she reaches her heavenly palace. Her transformation from naive infatuation to scheming ambition – which ultimately causes her death – is managed with great subtlety.

This is a rare view of Handel creating Italianate opera in accessible English and enriched with chorus. 'Endless pleasure' sings Semele – and here it's guaranteed. *GP*

HARTMANN
Gesangsszene
see ORCHESTRAL: HARTMANN: Sinfonia tragica

HAYDN

Die Jahreszeiten (The Seasons)

Barbara Bonney (soprano), Anthony Rolfe Johnson (tenor), Andreas Schmidt (baritone); Monteverdi Choir, English Baroque Soloists/John Eliot Gardiner

Archiv 431 818-2 □ 127:00 mins (2 discs) □ 🟢🟢🟢

Two versions vie with each other for top place here, and your choice will probably depend on whether you prefer period instruments or modern ones. As one who isn't a card-carrying member of either camp, I find it particularly difficult to choose between Gardiner and Marriner (on Philips), but in this case there's a level of drama and an incisiveness of rhythmic and textural 'bite' in Gardiner's account which just tip the scales in its favour. As ever with this acutely intelligent and imaginative conductor, the pacing is spot on, the phrasing galvanic without being mannered, and the overall sound picture both opulent and lean (a tricky balance, of which Gardiner is a master). Contrasts are often razor sharp, yet the effect is not excessively angular but, rather, cohesively kaleidoscopic. As so often before, Gardiner demonstrates that size is not synonymous with bulk. His forces are, if anything, more modest than might be expected, but the vision is large, and realised through far-sighted phrasing and an imaginative use of textural 'families' – be they polyphonic, harmonic, instrumental or vocal. Marriner, on the other hand, using modestly scaled modern forces, is hardly less exhilarating, and his trio of soloists (Fischer-Dieskau, Mathis and Jerusalem) is everything you could hope for. Either way, you're on to a winner here. *JS*

HAYDN

Mass in D minor (Nelson); Te Deum in C, Hob. XXIIIc:2

Felicity Lott (soprano), Carolyn Watkinson (mezzo-soprano), Maldwyn Davies (tenor), David Wilson-Johnson (baritone); The English Concert & Choir/Trevor Pinnock

Archiv 423 097-2 □ ADD □ 50:00 mins □ 🟢🟢🟢

If you buy only one recording of a Haydn Mass in your lifetime, let it be this one. With his extraordinary ear for colour, texture and pregnancy of phrasing, it's no wonder that Pinnock felt constrained by the limitations of the harpsichord (on which no one plays better) and embarked on a career as a conductor. Yet the very constraints of the harpsichord may have been responsible for sharpening and refining his altogether exceptional control of rhythm and articulation and for his acute understanding of their functions. Taking his cue from the Mass's subtitle ('Mass in Times of Fear'), he reminds us time and again that there is music in which beauty is a false goddess. His lean, sinewy, sometimes implacable use of string tone, for instance, looks forward, in its comfortless way, to 20th-century music. At the same time he catches the ceremonial, even joyful aspects of the work with wonderful vividness and spontaneity, and draws from his singers (choir and soloists alike) both a resplendent sonority and a naturalness of rhythm which almost defy the bar-line. *JS*

HAYDN

Die Schöpfung (The Creation)

Arleen Auger (soprano), Philip Langridge (tenor), David Thomas (bass); City of Birmingham SO & Chorus/Simon Rattle

EMI CDS 7 54159 2 □ 99:32 mins (2 discs)
□ 🌑🌑🌑

At least three considerations jostle for position here, before the performance even arises. For instance, do you want your *Creation* in German or in English? On period instruments or modern? And in what combination? For a modern version in English, Rattle's seems to me to be in a class by itself. Intensely dramatic, impeccably paced, awesome and humorous in equal measure, and colourful without ever being gaudy, this is a reading that should stand the test of time without difficulty. If it has an Achilles' heel it may be in the choice of soloists, but this is always going to be a very personal thing, and there's no way of second guessing it. As an alternative, Hogwood and his Academy, on L'Oiseau-Lyre, give a performance in English on period instruments. This is no slimline version, but an extravaganza such as Haydn himself admired when he heard similarly grandiloquent mountings of Handel on his visits to London. And *his* soloists – Kirkby, Rolfe Johnson and Michael George – are perfect for their respective roles, and in peak form. Of modern performances in German, Karajan's sensational account on DG is wellnigh unbeatable – indeed, in the mid-price range it has no rivals. *JS*

HILDEGARD OF BINGEN

Canticles of Ecstasy

Sequentia

Deutsche Harmonia Mundi 05472 77320 2
□ 72:53 mins □ 🌑🌑🌑

In anticipation of the 900th anniversary of Hildegard's birth, this disc offers an admirable introduction to her output, including her songs for the Virgin Mary, her works in praise of the Holy Spirit, and her exhortations to the ecclesiastical community. The approach is uncluttered rather than purist: our modern reception of the plainsong is helped along with some discreetly added drones, and with some tinkling haloes of string accompaniment. 'O

tu suavissima' is, to my ears, the best track, its vaulting melody presented here with great beauty. The song 'O viridissima virga' is also found on Hildegard issues from EMI and from Gothic Voices (on Hyperion), while Sequentia uses a restrained chorus of female singers, and Gothic Voices opts for a male ensemble with an impeccable medieval pronunciation of the Latin text. The EMI recording misses out a chunk of the music, although it zaps us with its electronic atmospherics. And so, on balance, I go for Sequentia. *AP*

HOLST

First Choral Symphony; A Choral Fantasia

Lynne Dawson (soprano); Guildford Choral Society, RPO/Hilary Davan Wetton

Hyperion CDA 66660 □ 67:36 mins □ 🌑🌑🌑

Holst's First Choral Symphony comprises settings of Keats's poetry, including 'Ode on a Grecian Urn' as the slow second movement and 'To Fancy' and 'Folly's Song' as the Scherzo. This quicksilver-like movement scurries along breathtakingly and strongly recalls 'Mercury' from *The Planets*, the Guildford choir rising magnificently to the stiff challenges of the tongue-tripping texts and the shifting harmonies. Lynne Dawson's pure tone is a delight, and she colours her voice convincingly to the varying moods of the text. Holst's orchestrations are brilliantly colourful and draw you right into the forest revelries or the mysteries of creation. An impressive and portentous concertante organ part adds *gravitas* and a sense of transcendental mystery to the *Choral Fantasia*, a setting of Robert Bridges's 'Ode to Music'.

Neither of these imaginative works impressed critics, performers or audiences at their premieres, so they languished. With Davan Wetton drawing a first-class performance from the choir and the Royal Philharmonic Orchestra, plus a splendidly detailed and spacious recording, home audiences can now appreciate their full worth. *Ian Lace*

HOLST

The Hymn of Jesus; The Cloud Messenger

Della Jones (mezzo-soprano); LSO & Chorus/Richard Hickox

Chandos CHAN 8901 □ 65:43 mins □ 🌑🌑🌑

The Hymn of Jesus, to a mystical text from the Gnostic gospels, is one of the most visionary and totally original of all Holst's creations. From the opening trombone recitative on the plainsong 'Vexilla regis', through the great mutter of speaking choruses forty years before Britten's *War Requiem*, to the dionysiac rhythms of the dance itself and the searing dissonances of Christ's choral utterances, this is truly inspired music of powerful spirituality. Recorded versions have been few: for grandeur of sound and fidelity to Holst's intentions, this Chandos version is by some way the best ever. Hickox secures an admirably taut ensemble and shapes the music with a true sense of its architectural mass.

Twice the length of *The Hymn of Jesus*, the coupling is a real bonus: *The Cloud Messenger*, based on a classic Sanskrit poem, is the climax of Holst's 'Indian' period and the last major work he wrote before *The Planets*. After a disastrous premiere in 1913, it was sorely neglected, but this first recording, in stupendous sound and performance, shows how powerful and prophetic a piece it is, despite occasional sub-Wagnerian passages. *CM*

HONEGGER

Jeanne d'Arc au bûcher

Françoise Pollet, Michèle Command (soprano), Nathalie Stutzmann (contralto), John Aler (tenor), Jean-Philippe Courtis (bass), Marthe Keller, Georges Wilson, Pierre-Marie Escourrou (speaker); Radio France Choir & Children's Choir, French National Orchestra/Seiji Ozawa

DG 429 412-2 □ 69:04 mins □ ⊘⊘⊘

Honegger's oratorios (indeed, Honegger's works in general) are probably undervalued, and are rarely heard. Yet they were courageous and successful attempts to imbue a moribund form with new relevance. *King David* is most often recorded, but this eloquent version of *Joan of Arc at the Stake* shows the composer at the height of his powers and, sheerly as a performance, ranks above any of the earlier work. Claudel's sometimes too-clever text, with the action moving backwards in time, Joan's accusers turning into animals, and playing-cards turning into kings, has its difficulties; and mingling speech and song always brings problems of its own, not to mention Honegger's importation of such exotica as an ondes martenot into his large forces. But the result is vivid, dramatic and touching: the music has a tremendous range of colour and invention, spanning medievalism to touches of jazz and attaining tremendous power in the big choruses. This is a live recording, of a festival performance at the Basilique de St Denis in Paris, and conveys the excitement of a real event with a minimum of

audience noise. The actress Marthe Keller is magnetic as the protagonist reviewing her life while she awaits burning, and Ozawa directs a performance of terrific impact and humanity. *CM*

HOWELLS

Missa sabrinensis

Janice Watson (soprano), Della Jones (contralto), Martyn Hill (tenor), Donald Maxwell (baritone); LSO & Chorus/Gennady Rozhdestvensky

Chandos CHAN 9348 □ 76:05 mins □ ⊘⊘⊘

The *Missa sabrinensis* (1953–4) is Herbert Howells's largest work, the grand summation of a creative lifetime, much of which was dedicated to choral and liturgical music. The title 'Mass of the Severn' reflects the landscape of his native Gloucestershire which inspired so many of his works, and which made him, in some senses, the most direct artistic heir of Vaughan Williams. The result is, however, not gently pastoral but passionate, ecstatic and sometimes brazenly mystical, more in the manner of Vaughan Williams's *Sancta civitas*, the handling of the large forces often reaching heights of polyphonic complexity rarely visited in Howells's better-known and smaller works. Particularly impressive is the way in which the sense of rapture is sustained across such large architectural spans.

This triumphant performance, despite occasional textural roughnesses, has a fire and refulgent grandeur that make out the best possible case for this work as one of the major utterances of the British choral repertoire. The strong team of soloists and the chorus sing their hearts out, and Rozhdestvensky's direction has a firm and confident grasp of the large structures. Chandos's recording deals vividly with even the densest textures and the biggest climaxes. *CM*

D'INDIA

Il primo libro de madrigali a cinque voci, 1607
see Collection: Consort of Musicke

IPPOLITOV-IVANOV

Four Poems of Rabindranath Tagore
see Collection: Russian Song

ISAAC

Angeli, archangeli
see OCKEGHEM: Missa Mi-Mi

Complete Songs, Vol. 3

Dora Ohrenstein (soprano), Mary Ann Hart (mezzo-soprano), Paul Sperry (tenor), William Sharp (baritone), Philip Bush, Dennis Helmrich, Irma Vallecillo, Steven Blier, Gerard Hecht (piano), Les Scott (fife), Jay Rosenfeld (piccolo)

Albany TROY 079 □ 78:05 mins □ ✪✪✪

Ives's songs constitute one of the most original aspects of his art. He had an entirely fresh view of what a song might be, and spanned an amazing gamut from sentimental ballads to outpourings of uncompromising modernism, slice-of-life Americana and passionate philosophical or political statements that sometimes seem to burst the bounds of the medium (as in 'Lincoln, the Great Commoner' recorded here). There are various CD selections, but you need to hear many songs to appreciate the full spectrum of Ives's astonishing imagination. Unicorn-Kanchana has issued two useful discs with the dependable baritone Henry Herford and Robin Bowman at the piano, but Albany has surveyed almost the entire song output, more than 160 items, on four separately available discs, using a sensible range of voices and the various instrumental extras Ives sometimes demands. Vol. 3 gives, by a narrow margin, the most stimulating conspectus: 36 items, including early settings of German poetry, both versions of the irrepressible war march 'He Is There!', the famous glory trance 'General William Booth Enters into Heaven', affectionate parlour ballads like 'My Native Land', exquisite impressionistic fantasies like 'Mists' and 'The Children's Hour', hypnotic songs of memory, the abrasive cowboy ballad 'Charlie Rutlage', experimental works ('The Cage', 'Soliloquy') and the political satire 'Vote for Names!'. The performers are uniformly excellent; the recording has wonderful immediacy and beautiful piano tone. *CM*

Janáček: Glagolitic Mass

Kodály: Psalmus hungaricus

Tina Kiberg (soprano), Randi Stene (mezzo-soprano), Peter Svensson (tenor), Ulrik Cold (bass), Per Salo (organ), Copenhagen Boys Choir, Danish National RSO & Choir/Charles Mackerras

Chandos CHAN 9310 □ 62:44 mins □ ✪✪✪

This is the first recording of Janáček's searing masterpiece as the composer originally conceived it – and all praise to Janáček scholar Paul Wingfield's vital restoration-work.

Mackerras's labour of love also happens to be the most urgent and finely honed *Glagolitic Mass* on disc. Fleeting regrets that soprano Tina Kiberg is hardly the fervent equal of Elisabeth Söderström in Mackerras's earlier, Czech-based version (Supraphon), or that the solo voices seem unevenly matched in the Sanctus quickly vanish when confronted with the focused might of the Danish National Radio Choir and the layered ensemble of brass. Both of them are given unrivalled depth and richness by the excellent Chandos recording. Besides the most important of the restorations is revelatory. Timpani now break violently across the tortured organ solo preceding the crucifixion sequence in the Credo: a further turn of the screw all the more terrifying following the tenderness Mackerras urges in the early stages of this riveting orchestral interlude.

A lengthy emotional breathing-space is needed before facing Kodály's near-contemporary (1923) *Psalmus hungaricus*. The Hungarian's musical representation of weeping, anger and consolation may be less blindingly distinctive, but it draws an equally vivid response from this outstanding choir and from the finest of the disc's four soloists, heroic tenor Peter Svensson. *DN*

Říkadla
see: **OPERA**: JANÁČEK: From the House of the Dead

Le chant des oyseaulx

Ensemble Clément Janequin

Harmonia Mundi HMC 901099 □ ADD □ 45:10 mins □ ✪✪✪

These varied little songs were published in Paris between 1528 and 1552. They invite us to delight in simple and basic pleasures – the perkiness of 'M'y levay', the naughtiness of 'Il estoit', the warm dream of love in 'Toutes les nuictz' and the mindless twittering of 'Le chant des oyseaulx'. These performers are well established and accomplished in this repertory, and their approach is well judged on the whole. 'A ce joly moys de may' seems a little slow to me, and 'Hélas, mon Dieu' rather stolid, but the others are marvellous and diverse. I enjoyed particularly the poise and suppleness of 'Le chant du rossignol' and the folksy harshness of 'Ung jour Colin'. Janequin's witty music deserves to be known more widely. *AP*

Six Joyful Songs
see Collection: Russian Song

Psalmus hungaricus; Missa brevis; Pange lingua; Psalm 114

Elizabeth Gale, Sally Le Sage, Hannah Francis (soprano), Alfreda Hodgson (contralto), Ian Caley, Lájos Kozma (tenor), Michael Rippon (bass), Gillian Weir, Christopher Bowers-Broadbent (organ); Brighton Festival Chorus, Wandsworth School Boys Choir, LSO/István Kertész, Lászlo Heltay

Decca 433 080-2 □ ADD □ **70:04 mins** □ ⊘⊘

Kodály's *Psalmus hungaricus* of 1923, setting a free Hungarian translation of Psalm 55 shortly after the newly independent Hungary had succumbed to a right-wing putsch, is his choral masterpiece: a fervent choral-orchestral plea for deliverance from enemies, with national, personal and political overtones. It's best heard in the language in which it was composed, and this excellent version by Kertész, in vintage Seventies Decca sound, remains supreme. The three other works, including the austerely expressive a cappella Mass, are typical of Kodály's later music and are conducted by László Heltay, an inspiring director of the Brighton Festival Chorus.

The most stunning *Psalmus hungaricus* on disc, however, is in German – DG's historic recording of the first stereo broadcast on Berlin Radio after the war, conducted by Ferenc Fricsay, with Ernst Haefliger as tenor soloist. Worth searching out, and the coupling includes a rare recording of Kodály's only symphony. *CM*

Psalmus hungaricus
see also JANACEK: Glagolitic Mass

Abschiedslieder
see ORCHESTRAL: KORNGOLD: Symphony in F sharp

The Rio Grande; Aubade héroïque; Summer's Last Will and Testament

Sally Burgess (mezzo-soprano), William Shimell (baritone), Jack Gibbons (piano); Chorus of Opera North, Leeds Festival Chorus, English Northern Philharmonia/David Lloyd-Jones

Hyperion □ **CDA 66565** □ **75:15 mins** □ ⊘⊘⊘

A brilliant, workaholic conductor, Constant Lambert's output is small but strongly defined in personality, often mingling black humour with dionysiac energy in a way that sets him apart from his contemporaries such as Walton.

The Rio Grande (1927), his biggest public success, remains his best-loved work. Part choral fantasy, part piano concerto, its inspired mating of jazz, blues harmony, South American rhythms, post-Lisztian piano technique and sophisticated orchestral and vocal writing is a unique and potent achievement. The crisp, electrically charged nature of this, one of Hyperion's finest recordings, is near ideal.

Strongly in its favour is the coupling: the only recording of Lambert's largest and probably greatest work. Based on a masque by Thomas Nashe, and radically transforming 16th-century dance and madrigal styles into something vibrantly contemporary, *Summer's Last Will* is a huge, colourful, rhythmically intoxicating, lyrically tender and ultimately chilling fresco of Elizabethan London in the plague years. Less a true choral work than a virtuoso orchestral score with important choral contributions, it unites the many aspects of Lambert's personality, and this performance is nothing short of a triumph. With the bitter-sweet *Aubade héroïque* as makeweight, no disc makes a better case for Lambert's importance. *CM*

Lagrime di San Pietro

Ensemble Vocal Européen/Philippe Herreweghe

Harmonia Mundi HMC 901483 □ **59:30 mins** □ ⊘⊘⊘

The Tears of St Peter, settings of twenty non-liturgical Italian poems, are spiritual madrigals, with the delicate imagery of the words subtly reflected in the music. Unusually, these pieces are in seven parts, allowing dramatic contrasts of range and density. The symbolism of 'seven' for the suffering and sorrows of the Virgin Mary is extended by an additional Latin motet at the end to make seven times the Trinity, 21 pieces in all, further integrated by working their way systematically round the modes so that each has a fresh colour.

The performance, one voice to a part, is superb. Minimal vibrato and fine intonation create the richest of sonorities. The singing is flexibly paced, involved and very expressive, reflecting Lassus's deeply human concern for personal salvation in this, his last work. He died three weeks after its dedication. *GP*

LASSUS

Masses for five voices; Infelix ego

Oxford Camerata/Jeremy Summerly

Naxos 8.550842 □ 68:24 mins □ 🎵

Lassus is one of those composers who is widely recorded on the Continent as well as by British singers. I have chosen this particular disc for its bright, clear sound, its musicianship and its bargain price. Also, the *Missa Entre vous filles* has not been recorded before and so we get a new work which is displayed here with a transparent blend of voices and a bell-like warmth of tone. The *Missa Susanne un jour* is also included; it is an old favourite and is serviced well on this recording, growing in depth as the music proceeds. The Oxford Camerata can sound a little young and raw, in spite of their tunefulness, but they reach the highest standards in the superb *Infelix ego*. The sound-world of this recording is much to be preferred to the hectic noise of the Lassus disc by Philippe Herreweghe (Auvidis) or the curiously fuzzy subdued atmosphere of The Sixteen's Lassus recording for Collins. *AP*

LINLEY

Lyric Ode on the Fairies; Aerial Beings and Witches of Shakespeare

Lorna Anderson, Julia Gooding (soprano), Richard Wistreich (bass); The Parley of Instruments Baroque Orchestra & Choir/Paul Nicholson

Hyperion CDA 66613 □ 60:05 mins □ 🎵🎵🎵

Among the many discoveries revealed by Peter Holman, the major inspiration behind Hyperion's series The English Orpheus, is Thomas Linley junior. Born into a musical Gloucestershire family, he studied in Florence, where he became a boyhood companion of Mozart, his exact contemporary. This charming ode shows him sharing with Mozart something of that barely definable but unmistakable gift of melodic genius. The text, by a schoolboy at Winchester, is a truly dreadful example of bowdlerised Shakespeare worship – of the fairies in *A Midsummer Night's Dream*: 'Some pant with nobler war T'invade the hostile rear mice crew' (*sic!*).

The music is as beautiful as the text is absurd, full of shapely tunes that, once heard, linger hauntingly in the memory. Matching the fresh voices of Anderson, Gooding and Wistreich are a fine horn obbligato, some sparkling oboe-playing, and the near-immaculate strings of the Parley's forces.

Linley died at the age of 22, in a holiday boating accident. Had he lived, this highly original genius would, as a newspaper report prophesied, have stood 'foremost in the list of modern [1776] composers' – a powerful reason to revel in what little of his music remains. *GP*

LISZT

Songs

Brigitte Fassbaender (mezzo-soprano), Jean-Yves Thibaudet (piano)

Decca 430 512-2 □ 57:39 mins □ 🎵🎵🎵

In the liner notes to this absorbing disc, Brigitte Fassbaender argues that performing Liszt is 'for the singer a source of immense pleasure, since there are no limits to what is expected of the voice'. Following this principle, it is hardly surprising that the performances sound totally committed, for Fassbaender manages to squeeze the last drop of emotion from each musical phrase. Occasionally, the voice shows signs of strain, with some rather wide vibrato in the highest notes, but these are minor shortcomings when measured against the forceful nature of her interpretations.

The music itself is of maddeningly variable quality. I could quite happily dispense with the melodramatic posturings of 'Ich möchte hingehn', the most extended song on the disc, but the macabre 'Und wir dachten der Toten', its chromatic harmonies pointing forward to Debussy and Schoenberg, is quite remarkable.

Despite Liszt's propensity towards virtuosity, his piano accompaniments make relatively few technical demands. The major exception is the brilliant 'Die drei Zigeuner', a Lenau poem which inspired the composer to write a veritable Hungarian rhapsody for voice and piano. Here the pianist, Jean-Yves Thibaudet, really comes into his own, providing bravura playing that presents a fitting conclusion to a most stimulating release. *EL*

LOCKE

Anthems, motets and the Oxford Ode

Choir of New College, Oxford, The Parley of Instruments/Edward Higginbottom

Hyperion CDA 66373 □ 66:59 mins □ 🎵🎵🎵

Matthew Locke, a Catholic, found several opportunities to write Latin church music in Protestant England after Charles II's restoration in 1660. Some was for Edward Lowe, an Oxford professor of music, and his students, as was the *Oxford Ode*, a distinctive and delightful secular piece for a degree day ceremony in the Sheldonian theatre; Lowe and his musicians earned £3.19s.4d for performing it.

Locke also wrote magnificent Anglican church music. The anthem *Be thou exalted, Lord* had three choirs and two instrumental groups placed around the Chapel Royal, and is reproduced in splendid stereo here. Striking, too, is Locke's special effect in *Lord, let me know mine end*, where the precise dynamic markings of 'soft' and 'softest of all' underline the final contemplation of death. Elsewhere, Locke constantly surprises with sudden stabs of dissonance and contorted lines.

While the recording faithfully reflects the layout and the intimacy of the original performing spaces, New College Choir provides authentic English tone-colour – all male voices, boy trebles – as does the Parley's violin band, without 16-foot tone. This was the third in Hyperion's series The English Orpheus, which extends now to well over thirty discs with no end to the treasures it continues to reveal. *GP*

The Festal Masses (Vol. 1: Missa Videte miraculum; Ave cuius conceptio; Vol. 2: Missa Benedicta et venerabilis; Magnificat Benedicta; Vol. 3: Missa Christi Virgo dilectissima; Domine Ihesu Christe; Vol. 4: Missa Lapidaverunt Stephanum; Ave Maria ancilla trinitatis)

The Cardinall's Musick/Andrew Carwood

ASV Gaudeamus CD GAU 131, 132, 133, 140 □ **69:21 mins, 79:39 mins, 66:57 mins, 69:18 mins** □ *🎵🎵🎵*

There are nearly five hours of music here, and this is less than half of the surviving works of Ludford – a remarkable composer from the 16th century who worked at St Stephen's, Westminster. The first two volumes contain his Masses for six voices, and the full potential of this texture comes to fruition in the finely paced and deeply resonant *Missa Benedicta*. For control of line and sensitively matched imitative voices we must turn to the marvellous performance of the *Magnificat Benedicta*. Vol. 3 is more varied, with a lighter Mass setting placed alongside the dramatic (almost theatrical) *Domine Ihesu*. The best music, I think, comes in Vol. 4 in the Agnus Dei of the *Missa Lapidaverunt*. Throughout, the recording is clear and firm but supple; the plainsongs are occasionally a little rough-edged, but the polyphony will sing in your ears and your imagination for some time. This is a winning combination of scholarship, discovery and sheer musical pleasure. *AP*

The Lay of the Last Minstrel
see **ORCHESTRAL**: MACCUNN: Land of the Mountain and the Flood

Motets
see Collection: Music of the Middle Ages

Kindertotenlieder; Rückert Lieder; Lieder eines fahrenden Gesellen

Janet Baker (mezzo-soprano); Hallé Orchestra, New Philharmonia Orchestra/John Barbirolli

EMI CDC 7 47793 2 □ **ADD** □ **64:29 mins** □ *🎵🎵🎵*

A Mahler collection without peer. Striking a perfect poise between hallowed realisation of the composer's most refined dynamics and lacerating, open-voiced cries from the heart at key expressive points, Janet Baker might have been born to sing these Lieder. And the empathy between Baker and Barbirolli is total. Even when the tempi are dangerously slow, Baker seems to be ideally supported by her colleagues; and when the voice yields to the orchestra's extended comment, she always sets it up selflessly – witness the almost unbearable suspense between her last phrase in the second of the *Kindertotenlieder* and the final chord. Tears are never far away; and if 'Ich bin der Welt abhanden gekommen', that spellbindingly poignant celebration of the artist's withdrawal in the *Rückert Lieder*, merits its status as the composer's finest song, then these great artists' astonishing sensitivities leave us in no doubt that the entire cycle of *Songs on the Death of Children* – so harrowingly related to Mahler's experiences, both past and still to come at the time of composition – fathoms even more complex depths. *DN*

Kindertotenlieder
see also NONO: Il canto sospeso
and **ORCHESTRAL**: MAHLER: Symphony No. 7

Lieder eines fahrenden Gesellen
see also **ORCHESTRAL**: MAHLER: Symphony No. 1

Das klagende Lied

Joan Rodgers (soprano), Linda Finnie (mezzo-soprano), Hans Peter Blochwitz (tenor), Robert Hayward (baritone); Bath Festival Chorus, Waynflete Singers, Bournemouth SO/Richard Hickox

Chandos CHAN 9247 □ **70:56 mins** □ *🎵🎵🎵*

No apologies need be made for Mahler's earliest large-scale work, begun nearly ten years before the completion of the First Symphony, but the composer evidently had his doubts and excised the lengthy first movement, 'Waldmärchen', before the cantata's belated premiere; it was not to join its companions until 1970, and has since been convincingly championed by Boulez, Rattle, Chailly and now Hickox. Its blend of folk-song, wood-magic and elegy strikes us as authentically, if rather nebulously, Mahlerian, so was it perhaps a painful personal note that Mahler wanted to suppress? The fate of the youth in the Grimm-based fairy-tale, slain by his jealous sibling, may have echoed, in some strange way, the death of the composer's younger brother six years before the work's composition. Certainly, the way in which 'Waldmärchen' shies away from the murder to lament in gently elegiac tones suggests as much.

The wonderful Linda Finnie's first entry at this crucial point strikes movingly home alongside the warm, woody Bournemouth sound. Hickox never apologises for the leisurely telling of the tale; beguiling phrases from the fine team of singers and atmospheric woodwind solos keep impatience at bay. The sound has handsome natural presence, so be prepared for a vivid pay-off to the murdered brother's beyond-the-grave revenge. *DN*

<hr>

MAHLER

Das Lied von der Erde

Christa Ludwig (mezzo-soprano), Fritz Wunderlich (tenor); Philharmonia Orchestra, New Philharmonia Orchestra/Otto Klemperer

EMI CDC 7 47231 2 □ ADD □ 63:45 mins □ *❷❷❷*

Music's most sparely moving farewell, the half-hour 'Abschied' that lays Mahler's shattering song-symphony to rest, poses the supreme challenge to any partnership of mezzo (or contralto) and orchestra. There are too many great performances of it to be ignored here, chiefly the heart-rending performance from Kathleen Ferrier with Bruno Walter in 1952 (Decca) and the more appropriately introspective Janet Baker and Bernard Haitink (now on bargain-price Philips).

These are transcendent experiences that Ludwig and Klemperer touch, but cannot surpass, in their agonisingly human interpretation of the Chinese poems Mahler sets so lovingly. What raises the Klemperer *Lied von der Erde* as a whole above all others is his choice of tenor, Fritz Wunderlich, who died tragically young not long after this recording was made: a lighter timbre than the heroic one usually unleashed on the cruelly taxing drinking-songs, but a magnetic singer

with a real ache in the voice who perfectly reflects all of Mahler's emotional moods with unsurpassable musicianship. *DN*

<hr>

MAHLER

Rückert Lieder – Ich bin der Welt abhanden gekommen
see NONO: Il canto sospeso

<hr>

MENDELSSOHN

Elijah

Elly Ameling (soprano), Peter Schreier (tenor), Theo Adam (baritone); Leipzig Radio Chorus, Leipzig Gewandhaus Orchestra/Wolfgang Sawallisch

Philips Duo 438 368-2 □ ADD □ 131:17 mins (2 discs) □ *❷❷*

Although Kurt Masur's Teldec recording of Mendelssohn's masterpiece has received justified accolades for the conductor's inspirational treatment of the score, this 1968 recording, sung in German, provides formidable competition, especially at mid-price. Like Masur, Sawallisch adopts a highly charged approach to this work, rejecting any temptation towards excessive sentimentality or bathos. But Sawallisch enjoys the benefit of a better team of soloists in which Theo Adam is outstanding. His anguished portrayal of the Old Testament prophet may appear too operatic to those who prefer a more sober conception, but it really strikes at the heart in the great arias. Among the other singers, Peter Schreier and Elly Ameling make particularly distinguished contributions, and Mendelssohn's own orchestra is in sterling form throughout. The recording may not offer the immediacy of Teldec's digital sound, but it is more than acceptable. On the other hand, it's a pity that Philips doesn't provide texts or translations. *EL*

<hr>

MENDELSSOHN

Lieder

Dietrich Fischer-Dieskau (baritone), Wolfgang Sawallisch (piano)

EMI CMS 7 64827 2 □ ADD □ 95:00 mins (2 discs) □ *❷❷*

If Mendelssohn's *Songs without Words* have fallen into a period of relative neglect (an arguable point), his songs *with* words have suffered still more grievously – and this despite championing by some very distinguished singers, Fischer-Dieskau and Janet Baker foremost among them (the prolonged absence from the catalogue of Baker's excellent EMI recital with Geoffrey Parsons remains a mystery). Despite admirable recent recordings by Margaret Price (Hyperion), Barbara

Bonney (Teldec) and Nathalie Stutzmann (Erato) – all of whom, however, suffer from imperfect intonation – Fischer-Dieskau's is the only collection of Mendelssohn's Lieder that earns my own vote for inclusion in the top 1,000 (not least for Sawallisch's contribution). As they make abundantly and repeatedly clear, Mendelssohn's songs, while not ranking with those of Schubert, Schumann, Brahms or Wolf, are for the most part jewels of craftsmanship, whose emotional range is considerable and whose word-setting is quite exceptionally sensitive. As ever, the great baritone's diction is not only crystal clear but as innately musical as his treatment of line and colour, and if the voice isn't always at its burnished best and intonation is occasionally a little off-beam, these are small prices to pay for such a feast of musical enlightenment. *JS*

MENDELSSOHN

A Midsummer Night's Dream; Die erste Walpurgisnacht

Pamela Coburn (soprano), Elisabeth von Magnus (contralto), Birgit Remmert (mezzo), Uwe Heilmann (tenor), Thomas Hampson (baritone), René Pape (bass), Christoph Bantzer (narrator); Arnold Schönberg Choir, CO of Europe/Nikolaus Harnoncourt

Teldec 9031-74882-2 □ 77:55 mins □ 😊😊😊

This disc should come as a revelation to most listeners, bringing together the very substantial bits of *A Midsummer Night's Dream* that we don't usually hear, and a cantata of surpassing strangeness, originality and power which relatively few music lovers have ever heard at all. *Die erste Walpurgisnacht* (The First Walpurgis Night) is a setting of a ballad by Goethe, Mendelssohn's friend and mentor from childhood, depicting the violent, nightmarish chastisement and banishment of Christians by pagan Druids. Given Mendelssohn's own ambivalence concerning his family's expedient conversion from Judaism to Christianity in 19th-century Berlin, the work is fraught with multi-layered symbolic significance. Of the three versions of the work currently in the catalogue, the otherwise excellent Dohnányi performance on Decca is hamstrung by some surprisingly inadequate singing, and that of the lesser-known Francesco D'Avalos on IMP Masters, though far better sung, suffers, for me, from an excess of theatricality. Harnoncourt trusts his composer and poet, as he can well afford to do, and his more restrained, less heavily 'interpreted' account appeals to the mind

perhaps more than to the heart, and is the more disturbing for it. *JS*

MESSIAEN

Trois petites liturgies de la Présence Divine; Cinq rechants; O sacrum convivium

Cynthia Millar (ondes martenot), Rolf Hind (piano); London Sinfonietta Chorus & Voices, London Sinfonietta/Terry Edwards

Virgin VC 7 59021 2 □ 60:25 mins □ 😊😊😊

Listening to the swooning harmonies that colour the outer sections of the first of the *Trois petites liturgies* (1943–4), it seems scarcely credible that music of such yearning, sensuousness and bold optimism could have been composed in wartime occupied France. But here, as in many of his other compositions, religious fervour appears to hold the clue as to Messiaen's capacity to transcend external circumstances. Setting a text that proclaims love and total devotion to God, the work makes a striking impact in its juxtaposition of naive and sophisticated musical techniques, and in its unique and voluptuous instrumentation of female voices supported by ondes martenot, piano, tuned percussion and strings.

In contrast, the *Cinq rechants*, composed four years later for an unaccompanied choir of 12 mixed voices, is a much more complex work demanding performers of consummate virtuosity. The text explores aspects of secular love, and even invokes in places an invented language with affinities to both Sanskrit and ancient Peruvian. It provides an admirable foil to the ecstatic simplicity of the short Communion motet *O sacrum convivium*. I need hardly add that outstanding performances and a warmly balanced recording make this a wholly enticing release. *EL*

MESSIAEN

Trois petites liturgies de la Présence Divine
see also **ORCHESTRAL**: MESSIAEN: Réveil des oiseaux

MONTEVERDI

Second Book of Madrigals, 1590

Concerto Italiano/Rinaldo Alessandrini

Opus 111 OPS 30-111 □ 58:05 mins □ 😊😊😊

The madrigals in Monteverdi's Second Book of Madrigals, published in 1590, are in what he himself described as his 'first style' ('prima prattica'); unaccompanied voices singing polyphonic settings of vividly colourful poems. Ten of the 21 texts here are by the immensely popular poet Torquato Tasso of Ferrara. They invite detailed description, some of it purely verbal – 'interrupted' being split into its separate syllables and thrown between alternating voices – while some is specifically musical – lustrous chord-changes depicting 'sweeter harmony'. With music and words so inextricably integrated, it's essential to follow the texts, helpfully translated virtually word for word.

The solo voices of Concerto Italiano are outstanding. They give a very flexible performance, bringing such attention to details that the counterpoint sometimes becomes intensely complex. When the setting demands, though, they achieve total homogeneity, as in a single instrument in five parts. Their tuning is similarly responsive and in a constant state of flux – true 'just intonation'. The five lower voices, bass to bottom D, are breathtaking as the sun sets in 'Quell' ombra'. Equally compelling are the graphic descriptions of murmuring waves, trembling leaves and singing birds in the pastoral idyll 'Ecco mormorar l'onde'. *GP*

MONTEVERDI

Madrigali concertati

Viveca Axell (soprano), John Potter, Douglas Nasrawi (tenor), Harry van der Kamp (bass); Tragicomedia/ Stephen Stubbs

Teldec Das Alte Werk 4509-91971-2 □ 73:35 mins □ ❷❷❷

Too many ensembles seem in awe of Monteverdi and treat his madrigals with an almost liturgical reverence inappropriate to their often frivolous nature. It is refreshing therefore to hear these *canti amorosi* and *guerrieri* performed with the spirit and passion their texts imply. Songs like 'Tornate, o cari baci' (its chorus repeats *baci* [kisses] ten times consecutively) or the exquisitely lilting 'Zefiro torna' sound absurd if taken too seriously, but the tenors John Potter and Douglas Nasrawi – both sweet-voiced – inject a perfect lightness of tone, rendering them impassioned, foolish even, but never earnest.

The mood changes radically with the three-part 'Lamento della ninfa' – altogether more sorrowful, as Viveca Axell's plangent soprano soars above the voices of the two tenors and a bass (Harry van der Kamp) expressing their pity for her plight. And by the darker, warlike 'Ogni amante è guerrier', with its fanfares, and the bellicose 'Gira il nemico insidioso', it is powerfully dramatic.

But not only the singers deserve credit. The ensemble Tragicomedia (Stephen Stubbs, Andrew Lawrence-King and Erin Headley) gives a performance, on a range of instruments, that is subtle, incisive, engaging and in all ways exemplary. *Claire Wrathall*

MONTEVERDI

Sacred Vocal Music

Emma Kirkby (soprano), Ian Partridge (tenor), David Thomas (bass); The Parley of Instruments/Roy Goodman, Peter Holman

Hyperion CDA 66021 □ 42:17 mins □ ❷❷❷

This music, drawn from the *Selva morale e spirituale* of 1640 and the *Messa et salmi concertati* of 1651, reflects the changing tastes of the period of musical revolution through which Monteverdi lived. For one to three solo voices, with solo strings and continuo, far from the huge demands of the Vespers, thirty to forty years earlier, they are strongly structured pieces, with ground basses and recurring ritornellos – Monteverdi's solution to a style so florid that it risked being obscured by its own embroidery. Especially appealing are string echoes of vocal phrases, imitating every nuance, so that the violins seem to acquire the power of speech.

Three settings of the Psalm 'Confiteor tibi' demonstrate vividly Monteverdi's inexhaustible imagination. Word-painting abounds – closely follow the text at your first hearing to pick up, for instance, the pun of repeating the opening music for 'as it was in the beginning'.

The still-familiar voices were less overtly expressive in 1981, when this entrancing disc first appeared. Their purity still appeals, the passion no less for being understated.

Conceived as an LP, it makes a short CD at 42 minutes. But this is a small price to pay for such a gem. *GP*

MONTEVERDI

Vespers

Taverner Consort, Choir & Players/Andrew Parrott

EMI CDS 7 47078 8 □ 105:32 mins (2 discs) □ ❷❷❷

For all the scholarship devoted to them, Monteverdi's Vespers are still clouded in mystery. Questions inevitably abound. Is the work a unified one or a compendium? Was it composed for a Marian festival or honouring another saint? For single voices throughout or for widely contrasting textures? Intended for concert performance or requiring a liturgical context? And for which acoustic – St Peter's echoing vaults (the Vespers were dedicated to the pope), St Mark's vast cupolas (Monteverdi was job-hunting in Venice) or the more modest but still magnificent scale of Santa Barbara, the chapel within the ducal palace at Mantua?

Gardiner (Archiv) chooses St Mark's and is awe-inspiringly spacious. Pickett's interpretation (L'Oiseau-Lyre) is liturgical, immediate, full of dance. But for me the liturgical time-span is important; plainchant antiphons space out the riches of Monteverdi's opulent vocal and instrumental polyphony – up to ten independent parts in the Psalm 'Nisi Dominus' – and the intensely sensuous solo pieces – 'Nigra sum' and the love duet from the Song of Songs, 'Pulchra es'. Parrott's enlightened concept, persuasively unaffected, his luxuriantly coloured though quite modest forces coupled with the luminous quality of the recorded sound are still unbeatable.

It's worth considering a bargain alternative from Capriccio – Ralf Otto fitting a concert performance on to a single disc. *GP*

MONTEVERDI

Vespro in II. Vesperis in Festis B. Mariae V; Magnificat secondo à quattro voci; motets

Concerto Italiano/Rinaldo Alessandrini

Opus 111 OPS 30-150 □ 75:27 mins □ ⊘⊘⊘

This stunning disc begins with Vespers, not Monteverdi's own collation of 1610 but music selected from collections published thirty years and more later. The scale is smaller – the elegant proportions of solo voices with colourful continuo rather than the familiar vocal and instrumental choirs, and plainchant antiphons replacing the earlier solo motets. The following Magnificat is more severe still, alternating plainchant with four-part voices self-consciously demonstrating the composer's skill in archaic Palestrinian counterpoint. In total contrast, the disc ends with eight motets ranging from vividly descriptive six-part psalm settings to erotic solos from the Song of Songs.

Concerto Italiano meet these contrasting demands superbly, crisp in ensemble, energetic and fluent. Individual voices are full of personality in the impassioned solo and duo motets such as 'Laudate Dominum', with spectacular ornamentation over its near-ostinato continuo, and a bounding graphic bass. Recording balance leaves nothing to be desired in the ideal acoustic of a room in an Italian villa. A Monteverdi experience not to be missed. *GP*

MOZART

Mass in C, K317 (Coronation); Exsultate, jubilate; Vesperae solennes de confessore, K339

Barbara Bonney (soprano), Catherine Wyn Rogers (contralto), Jamie MacDougall (tenor), Stephen Gadd (bass); English Concert & Choir/Trevor Pinnock

Archiv 445 353-2 □ 67:50 mins □ ⊘⊘⊘

Trevor Pinnock doesn't have the benefit of the kind of star-studded line-up of soloists often chosen for Mozart choral works, but his performances have great freshness and rhythmic dynamism. The clear textures of period instruments, as well as the employment of a small choir, are obvious advantages, and the generous programme, which includes a stunning account of the much-loved *Exsultate, jubilate* from Barbara Bonney, makes this an irresistible release by any standards. *EL*

MOZART

Mass in C minor, K427

Sylvia McNair (soprano), Diana Montague (mezzo-soprano), Anthony Rolfe Johnson (tenor), Cornelius Hauptmann (bass); Monteverdi Choir, English Baroque Soloists/John Eliot Gardiner

Philips 420 210-2 □ 54:00 mins □ ⊘⊘⊘

Good period versions now abound, with excellent and spirited contributions from Gardiner, Harnoncourt, Herreweghe, Hogwood and Neumann (outstandingly good on Virgin). Nor can one complain about much in the so-called traditional versions by Abbado, Bernstein, Fricsay, Karajan, Levine, Marriner and Schreier, all of whom respond with great freshness and gleaming professionalism to the ceremonial splendour and not-so-hidden depths of this wonderful work. Of these, I've been most moved by Bernstein's fervent, indeed sometimes over-fervent, account on DG, most excited by Karajan, also on DG (the quality of the solo singing alone is thrilling in itself), and perhaps most stimulated and provoked by Harnoncourt on Teldec. But it's Gardiner who seems to me to have brought the music most spontaneously alive, despite an occasionally exaggerated angularity of rhythm. For some, his highly dramatic approach may seem too theatrical by half, but I can't say it bothers me much. Few conductors are so attentive to the shaping effects of sung language, irrespective of its contextual meanings, or more keenly attuned to the energising properties of silence. If you want a less high-octane but no less musical version, using modern forces, you're likely to find all you want in Abbado's splendidly sumptuous but never overstated rendering on Sony – a triumph of enlightened traditionalism, and beautifully recorded. *JS*

Requiem; Kyrie in D minor, K341

Barbara Bonney (soprano), Anne Sofie von Otter (mezzo-soprano), Hans Peter Blochwitz (tenor), Willard White (bass); Monteverdi Choir, English Baroque Soloists/John Eliot Gardiner

Philips 420 197-2 □ 54:00 mins □ ❷❷❷

On period instruments Gardiner is unlikely to disappoint, though Ton Koopman on Erato provides a compelling, if rather more idiosyncratic alternative. As in his superb version of Beethoven's *Missa solemnis*, authentic instruments and smaller forces play an important but not finally a decisive part, yielding ultimately to the sheer musicianship and technical excellence of all concerned. Played by a traditional orchestra, the performance would still retain most of its greatest qualities, though there's no gainsaying the effectiveness of the lower-than-usual pitch and the translucency of the scoring. The singing, by choir and soloists alike, is first rate, and Gardiner's unerring sense of balance – textural, colouristic and emotional – conveys with exceptional vividness both the intensity and the spaciousness of this great if mysterious work (he opts, incidentally, for Süssmayr's completion). Among the traditional versions, any kind of definitive choice is quite impossible. Marriner's vibrant account on Philips is immensely impressive, magnificently sung and paced with the psychological insight of a born dramatist. Alternatively, Hickox, at bargain price on Virgin, is equally rewarding. Nor would I want to be without Schreier's unfailingly musical and superlatively sung version for Philips. *JS*

Mussorgsky: Six Songs (orch. Markevitch); Songs and Dances of Death

Prokofiev: Five Songs to Texts by Anna Akhmatova

Tchaikovsky: None but the lonely heart; Not a word, oh my friend; Do not believe, my friend

Galina Vishnevskaya (soprano), Mstislav Rostropovich (piano); Moscow Philharmonic SO/Igor Markevitch

Philips 446 212-2 □ ADD □ 67:12 mins □ ❷❷

An ideal single-CD collection of Mussorgsky songs would need to include both the *Songs*

and Dances of Death and its polar opposite in everything except the composer's habitually faithful word-setting, *The Nursery*. At present only the scaled-down histrionic talents of the great Bulgarian bass Boris Christoff embrace the two cycles, and few listeners will want all three CDs in his classic EMI set.

So *Songs and Dances of Death* must take the grim upper hand – and preferably in Galina Vishnevskaya's mesmerising interpretation, recorded at the peak of her career (if you prefer a dark male voice in these songs, then Dmitri Hvorostovsky is partnered by Gergiev and the Kirov Orchestra in Shostakovich's lean orchestration, also on Philips). Vishnevskaya embraces the extremes of brother death's decrees and is never more impressive than in following the whispered laying to rest of the peasant in 'Trepak' with the stentorian commands of 'The Field Marshal' – inspiration for Britten when he composed the soprano role in the *War Requiem* for Vishnevskaya. The other Mussorgsky songs hauntingly orchestrated by Igor Markevitch, a popular Tchaikovsky selection and the movingly restrained account of Prokofiev's Akhmatova settings, reinforce admiration for the artistry of Russia's most charismatic soprano. *DN*

Nono: Il canto sospeso

Mahler: Kindertotenlieder; Ich bin der Welt abhanden gekommen

Barbara Bonney (soprano), Susanne Otto, Marjana Lipovšek (mezzo-soprano), Marek Torzewski (tenor); Berlin Radio Chorus, Berlin PO/Claudio Abbado

Sony SK 53360 □ 70:25 mins □ ❷❷❷

Live performances from the 1992 Berlin Festival, given in protest against resurgent racism, xenophobia and anti-Semitism in Germany. The choice of repertoire is bold, and just. Luigi Nono's luminously uncompromising memorial of human tragedy, *Il canto sospeso*, may justly be claimed as an enduring classic of Fifties modernism. Passages from letters written by anti-fascist Resistance fighters in the hours before their deaths are set in a way that extends the serial techniques of Webern's late cantatas into new and intensely human areas of the metaphysical. Anyone who thinks serial music can't express profound personal emotion should listen to the seventh movement, the farewell of the Russian girl 'going down into the damp earth'.

Abbado uses reciters to read the original letters from which Nono drew the most pregnant phrases, perhaps unnecessarily breaking the cantata's continuity. In contrast to this difficult and seldom-heard work, Marjana Lipovšek's poised accounts of the *Kindertotenlieder* and the Rückert song have great purity and simplicity – some of the most beautifully restrained Mahler I've heard in years. *CM*

NOTARI

Prime musiche nuove, 1613
see Collection: Consort of Musicke

OBRECHT

Quod chorus vatum/Haec Deum caeli
see OCKEGHEM: Missa Mi-Mi

OCKEGHEM

Missa Mi-Mi; Salve regina; Alma redemptoris mater (c/w Busnois: Victimae paschali laudes; Isaac: Angeli, archangeli; Obrecht: Quod chorus vatum/Haec Deum caeli)

The Clerks' Group/Edward Wickham

ASV Gaudeamus CD GAU 139 □ **63:26 mins** □ *♪♪♪*

This version of Ockeghem's *Missa Mi-Mi* replaces all previous recordings with its calm, clean textures and enduring sense of purpose. If one had to make a criticism one might say that it is slightly too much in the tradition of anonymous quietude that one finds in cathedral music. For example, the Credo text has a definite potential for drama and word-painting, and Ockeghem does not fail to bring all the voices together in imitation at the words 'one holy Catholic and Apostolic Church', but the relationship between the voices at this point seems to be lost on the singers. On the other hand, the treatment of the lithe and tensile duets throughout this work provides wonderful examples of the singer's art. Two works not recorded before are Ockeghem's *Salve regina* and Isaac's *Angeli, archangeli*. This last piece will surely become a favourite, with its dazzling textures and word-painting: if so, then its current popularity will match that which it enjoyed in earlier centuries. *AP*

ORFF

Carmina burana

Gundula Janowitz (soprano), Gerhard Stolze (tenor), Dietrich Fischer-Dieskau (baritone); Schöneberg Boys Choir, Chorus & Orchestra of the Deutsche Oper, Berlin/Eugen Jochum

DG Originals 447 437-2 □ **ADD** □ **56:09 mins** □ *♪♪*

The great virtues of Eugen Jochum's classic recording of Orff's much-performed choral work are the freshness and exhilaration of the choral singing, the beauty and subtlety of the soloists, among whom Dietrich Fischer-Dieskau is quite outstanding, and the power and rhythmic precision of the orchestral playing. In comparison, most recent and more sonically spectacular recordings seem flabby and colourless, particularly as DG's newly remastered transfer brings added brilliance and definition to the original. *EL*

PALESTRINA

Canticum canticorum Salomonis

Pro Cantione Antiqua/Bruno Turner

Hyperion CDA 66733 □ **79:43 mins** □ *♪♪♪*

The 'Motets for Five Voices', as Palestrina first advertised *The Songs of Solomon*, are spiritual madrigals, chamber music for devotional use. The poems reflect the eroticism of madrigals, allegorically applied to the Virgin. Pro Cantione Antiqua sing one to a part, voices matching without losing the individuality that clarifies textures and imitations. Textures are transparent, tuning wellnigh immaculate and, by selecting different voices from the ten available, colour varies subtly among the 29 pieces. *GP*

PALESTRINA

Christmas Mass in Rome
Palestrina: Missa Hodie Christus natus est, with music by Josquin, Frescobaldi, Victoria, Pasquini & Anerio; Christmas motets by Mazzocchi & Carissimi

Gabrieli Consort & Players/Paul McCreesh

Archiv 437 833-2 □ **77:08 mins** □ *♪♪♪*

Paul McCreesh is fast building a formidable reputation for his liturgical reconstructions from the Italian Renaissance. This disc re-creates a Christmas Mass, based around Palestrina's Mass *Hodie Christus natus est*, interspersing it with chant, motets by Josquin, Victoria and others, and organ toccatas by Frescobaldi.

It may at first seem strange to mix music from such a wide time-span – Josquin was born in around 1440, Anerio died in 1630 – but in his booklet note McCreesh assures us that Roman congregations of the day would have taken this in their stride. Even to listeners of today, the stylistic differences seem strangely slight.

Perhaps this is due to the Gabrieli Consort's homogeneous singing; there is nothing exaggerated in the performance, each element of the service – chant, instrumental, choral – flows gently into the next, yet the changes in texture, and a careful use of effects (the processional Introit, for instance), maintain the interest.

Palestrina's Christmas Mass is suitably joyful and receives a rhythmic and cheerful performance. But for me the musical treats lie in the instrumental pieces, especially in the contemplative organ toccatas, and the Frescobaldi Canzona for violin, cornett and continuo. That said, the singing is of a high standard, and the whole disc is highly recommended. *Edward Kershaw*

PALESTRINA

Missa O sacrum convivium; Magnificat; motets by Palestrina & Morales

Christ Church Cathedral Choir, Oxford/Stephen Darlington

Nimbus NI 5394 □ 57:57 mins □ ⨀⨀⨀

Renaissance polyphony is one of classical music's growth markets. There are regular releases from The Sixteen and the Tallis Scholars, plus an increasing number of new groups recording for the smaller companies. Invariably, the top line in these new choirs is taken by women, so it is interesting to see how the ancient male-only choral foundations compare with the new competition.

This disc proves that boy choristers *can* stand up to the demands of Palestrina's music. And why not? After all, the music was written for boys to sing. The at times slightly unrefined sound of their voices (presumably there are new voices among the 'old hands') adds to the impression that this is a working cathedral choir which does more than just make records.

The men (including male altos) of the choir are also excellent, providing just the right balance of blending and, where necessary, soloistic singing. The Agnus Dei, sung predominantly by solo voices, is one of the highlights of the disc. Stephen Darlington has included not only a pair of Palestrina's Corpus Christi motets and his imposing six-voice Magnificat, but also the original motet *O sacrum convivium* by Morales from which Palestrina drew the musical ideas for his gentle and contemplative Mass. *Edward Kershaw*

PALLAVICINO

Il sesto libro de madrigali a cinque voci, 1600

The Consort of Music/Anthony Rooley

Musica Oscura 070976 □ 63:57 mins □ ⨀⨀⨀

This is a real discovery. Pallavicino, a contemporary of Monteverdi, shows us here just exactly what made his rivals nervous. His settings of texts from Guarini's comic play *Il pastor fido* are full of variety: 'Crud'Amarilli' is certainly the equal of Monteverdi's setting, and the self-parody of 'Ohimè! se tanto amate' is caught here to a melodramatic nicety. In 'A poco, a poco' the performers evoke a genuine despair, and elsewhere there is lightness, fire and gentleness. Another distinctive, delightful and quietly instructive offering from this indispensable group of performers. *AP*

PARRY/STANFORD

Parry: Songs of Farewell

Stanford: Three Motets, Op. 38; Eternal Father; Magnificat in B flat

Choir of Trinity College, Cambridge/Richard Marlow

Conifer 75605 51155 2 □ 58:15 mins □ ⨀⨀⨀

Parry's *Songs of Farewell*, a set of unaccompanied motets enshrining some of his most ardent and idealistic music, were among his last completed works; they constitute one of the few monuments of British a cappella music since the Renaissance. In range of expression they span from the comparatively familiar 'My Soul, there is a Country' to the elaborate polyphony and trumpet imitations of the magnificent seven-part Donne setting 'Round Earth's Imagin'd Corners', and the sombre yet inspiring final number, the eight-part 'Lord, let me know mine end'. They should be in any collection of British choral music, and these fine performances from Trinity College Choir do them entire justice. Marlow uses women's voices instead of trebles for the upper lines, a procedure that Parry would have approved of.

Stanford's a cappella music is less artistically rewarding, though it contains beautiful things. The elaborate motet *Eternal Father*, interestingly enough, is a setting of a text by Parry's frequent collaborator Robert Bridges, and the Magnificat for double choir certainly makes a sumptuous culmination to the disc. Conifer's sound captures the chapel atmosphere to a nicety. *CM*

PARRY

The Soul's Ransom; The Lotos Eaters

Della Jones (soprano), David Wilson-Johnson (bass); London Philharmonic & Choir/Matthias Bamert

Chandos CHAN 8990 □ 79:52 mins □ ⨀⨀⨀

Parry devoted a large part of his composing career to choral music; having tried oratorios for the late-Victorian 'cantata market', he changed the nature of the genre by setting important poetic texts and devising ethical, non-doctrinal ones – in the process laying the foundations for the flowering of British choral music at the hands of Elgar and his own pupils Vaughan Williams and Howells. For a long time after his death, his most celebrated choral-orchestral works were the noble Milton setting *Blest Pair of Sirens* and the coronation anthem *I Was Glad*. But these two much more ambitious choral works give a better idea of Parry's range and mastery of large vocal-orchestral forces. The Tennyson setting *The Lotos Eaters*, surprisingly voluptuous and *Parsifal*-ish, is a wonderful swoon. But it's the 'Sinfonia sacra' *The Soul's Ransom* which is the masterpiece here – a tough-minded 'Psalm for the Poor' (Parry's politics were radical), inspired and glowing, which scales heights comparable to Elgar's *The Kingdom* in its vision of the dry bones whom God causes to stand up (Parry saw these as symbolising society's rejects) and in the blazingly ardent setting of 'God is a Spirit'. No collector of British music should be without this disc, one of the highlights of Bamert's Parry series, and possibly the best recording of the lot. *CM*

PERGOLESI/VIVALDI

Pergolesi: Stabat mater

Vivaldi: Gloria in D, RV 589

Eva Mei, Sylvia McNair, Elisabeth von Magnus (soprano), Marjana Lipovšek (contralto); Arnold Schönberg Choir, Concentus Musicus Wien/Nikolaus Harnoncourt

Teldec Das Alte Werk 9031-76989-2 □ 65:00 mins □ 🟡🟡🟡

While my preferred recording of the Gloria remains that of Christophers and The Sixteen, Mei and Lipovšek bring great pathos to Pergolesi's setting of the Latin sequence reflecting on the Virgin Mary at the foot of the cross. Both singers have full-scale operatic voices rather than the lighter quality often favoured for such a period performance, but they are used with discretion and great artistry. Both can sing delicately, as they do in the profoundly moving duet, 'Quis est homo...' ('Who would not weep... at such distress'). Both sing powerfully in the alla breve Handelian counterpoint, set against rushing strings, to depict a heart ablaze with love, 'Fac, ut ardeat cor meum'.

Pergolesi died a mere 26 years old, yet he wrote in a style that was to far outlive him. Here it is full of a bitter-sweet character, voices and strings often almost in unison until a poignant dissonance, heightening the

'torments', and the 'agony' in the duet movement, 'Sancta Maria'. The range of colours in these two voices, and the uninhibited vigour of the Concentus Musicus strings, create a deeply felt account of this familiar and much-loved music. *GP*

PEROTIN

Organa
see Collection: Music of the Middle Ages

POULENC

Mass in G; Quatre motets pour le temps de Noël; Litanies à la vierge noire; Notre dame de Rocamadour; Quatre petites prières de Saint François d'Assise; Quatre motets pour un temps de pénitence; Salve regina; Exultate Deo

Choir of Westminster Cathedral/James O'Donnell; Iain Simcock (organ)

Hyperion CDA 66664 □ 70:10 mins □ 🟡🟡🟡

Poulenc's music is as steeped in the Catholic tradition as Palestrina's. It was with the Litanies that the composer returned to the religious fold in the mid-Thirties, deeply traumatised by a friend's tragic death in a car accident.

The Litanies' invocations are pierced by an anguish that makes them some of the most searing pieces in the repertoire. The same can be said of the Mass. Into his own modern style Poulenc absorbs plainsong, medieval organum and a troubadour-like French folk-idiom, alternately sad and joyous like the two faces of a clown, merging the sacred with the soil to produce music of deep, passionate conviction.

The Westminster boys display an uncanny empathy with these miniature masterpieces. Their musicianship shines through every carefully measured phrase and dynamic. Their brittle sound – here like a plaintive oboe, at other times more akin to a crumhorn, or some awesome tolling bell – could not be more apt.

For those who prefer their Poulenc with women's voices on the top line, there is also the evocative choir of Trinity College, Cambridge (Conifer), or the distinctive readings by The Sixteen (Virgin).
Roderic Dunnett

POULENC

Mélodies, incl. Le bestiaire; Cocardes; Trois poèmes de Louise Lalanne; Tel jour, telle nuit; Banalités; Métamorphoses

Felicity Lott (soprano), Graham Johnson (piano)

Forlane UCD 16730 □ 64:20 mins □ 🟡🟡🟡

Poulenc loved the medium of the human voice. He composed for it with intense devotion, writing operatic and choral works and over 150 songs. As a member of Les Six, Poulenc became the epitome of the sophisticated Parisian, but he never lost touch with his intrinsic humour and sense of childlike wonder. With acute creative antennae he chose the finest writers and poets – Apollinaire, Eluard and Cocteau – for his *mélodies*, and wove round their words atmospheric musical lines evocative of Paris in the Twenties, Thirties and Forties. Wit and irony vie with nostalgia and sensuality.

This recording is a chronological programme of songs from 1918 to 1961. Some were originally for voice and orchestra, and Poulenc later transcribed them for voice and piano. The French idiom is one in which Lott excels. Added to her linguistic flair is her vocal form, which is glorious. From the early *Le bestiaire* and *Cocardes*, through the beautiful Eluard song cycle *Tel jour, telle nuit*, to the monologue 'La dame de Monte Carlo', Lott and Johnson cascade through melancholy, frivolity, shimmering elegance and biting humour. They revel in Poulenc's mesmerising sound-world with Lott's voice often soaring and floating on the cushioning effect of Johnson's superb piano-playing – exquisite writing, described by the composer himself as 'a halo of pedals'. *Elise McDougall*

POULENC

7 Mélodies
see Collection: French Song

POULENC

Stabat mater
see SZYMANOWSKI: Stabat mater

PRAETORIUS/SCHEIDT/SCHEIN

Lutheran Mass for Christmas Morning

Gabrieli Consort & Players; Roskilde Cathedral Congregational & Boys Choirs/Paul McCreesh

Archiv 439 250-2 □ 79:00 mins □ 🕭🕭🕭

Following his two recordings of Venetian music, Paul McCreesh turned his sights northwards in this ambitious project to reconstruct a Lutheran Mass for Christmas Morning as it might have been celebrated around 1620, with music by Praetorius, Scheidt and Schein. If all that sounds rather dry and scholarly, don't be put off: the Lutheran Christmas service is a joyful and festive affair, and this recording presents a kaleidoscope of constantly changing colours, textures and sounds.

Congregational involvement is essential to Lutheran worship and, to avoid too pristine and Protestant a sound, the Gabrieli Consort and Players have joined forces with the Boys Choir and Congregational Choir of Roskilde Cathedral, Denmark. The result is fresh and vigorous, and will no doubt please critics of the 'emasculated' English choral tradition. *Kate Bolton*

PROKOFIEV

Alexander Nevsky; Scythian Suite

Linda Finnie (mezzo-soprano); Scottish National Orchestra & Chorus/Neeme Järvi

Chandos CHAN 8584 □ 59:49 mins □ 🕭🕭🕭

This is very much a wide-screen version of the cantata Prokofiev fashioned from his first collaboration with the great film maker Sergei Eisenstein, realising like no other recording the technicolour essence of this prominent accompaniment to a black and white pageant (and going on to cap it with an unapologetically brazen account of the earlier *Scythian Suite*). From the atmospheric opening whiplash of icy high and low frequencies through to the glittering final victory songs, Järvi and his vividly characterising Scottish National Orchestra never falter in the breadth of their sympathies, even if the often spectacular but undeniably broad canvas of the recording occasionally diffuses the impact.

The cantata's crucial centre of gravity, the sombre song of a patriotic girl crossing the field of the dead, is delivered with authentically Slavonic-sounding richness and feeling by Linda Finnie, while the SNO Chorus phrases the big Russian melodies with plenty of heart. For those who think that only the genuine native article is good enough, Svetlanov's trenchant Russian forces should be pursued on a long-unavailable Chant du Monde disc, and there's always the curiosity of Temirkanov's St Petersburg-based project to provide a soundtrack for the film, best seen on video rather than merely heard on a stop–start CD. *DN*

PROKOFIEV

Five Songs to Texts by Anna Akhmatova
see MUSSORGSKY: Six Songs

PROKOFIEV

Ivan the Terrible (concert scenario by Christopher Palmer)

Linda Finnie (mezzo-soprano), Nikita Storojev (bass); Philharmonia Orchestra & Chorus/Neeme Järvi

Chandos CHAN 8977 □ 59:06 mins □ 🕭🕭🕭

Musically, this is as vivid a cross-section of Prokofiev's deepest and darkest film music as any, though some may lament that Christopher Palmer's sensible 'concert scenario' finds no room for the Russian narrator of Stasevich's original oratorio version; the powerfully morbid scene where the tsar comes close to death was written as melodrama – spoken voice over orchestra – and needs to be heard as such. Still, we are spared the inaccuracies of Michael Lankaster's narrative, ruining a musically fine performance under Rostropovich (Sony), and Palmer lets Järvi score over Muti's electrifying (and inexplicably deleted) EMI adherence to Stasevich with the inclusion of a polonaise and the climactic sequence of Eisenstein's Part Two where Ivan sends the pretender to his murder in the cathedral.

The black drama of such moments is skilfully offset by Järvi's fire and drive in battles and celebrations; here the recording captures all the brilliance of the higher-pitched instruments. Finnie follows her *Nevsky* triumph with further heartfelt impersonations of the Russian sound, and the chorus is impeccable – not least in its hummed reprise of the great 'Tartar steppes' theme, the melody that Prokofiev turned into the anthem of *War and Peace*. DN

PURCELL

Complete Anthems & Services, Vol. 4

Susan Gritton (soprano), James Bowman (alto), Rogers Covey-Crump, Charles Daniels (tenor), Michael George, Stephen Varcoe, Robert Evans (bass), etc; Choir of New College, Oxford, The King's Consort/Robert King

Hyperion CDA 66644 □ 70:48 mins □ *♪♪♪*

After the extended anthems of the first three volumes in Hyperion's magnificent 11-disc undertaking, this selection develops the small-scale devotional songs – eight of them – contrasted with three more verse anthems and the mighty forces of the coronation anthem *My Heart is Inditing*. It is a tribute to Purcell's boundless imagination, to ingenious programming, and to the consistently high quality of the musicians that an archival anthology can be so enjoyable as a continuous performance.

Every number brings new riches, and two have never been recorded before. Indeed, *The Way of God* is a revelation: Michael George sings with effortless ease the wide-ranging, warlike declamation originally designed for the 'stupendous' John Gostling, James Bowman and Rogers Covey-Crump wring out agonised suspensions from the defeated enemies.

No less outstanding is the devotional song 'Since God so Tender a Regard', tied to a

ground bass yet floating free of it with extraordinary ingenuity.

Instrumentalists play one to a part and are crystal clear in the Chapel Royal pieces. In the final coronation anthem they are scaled up to match the original forces in Westminster Abbey. *GP*

PURCELL

Funeral Music for Queen Mary, etc

The Sixteen, Orchestra of The Sixteen/Harry Christophers

Collins 14252 □ 79:42 mins □ *♪♪♪*

This magnificent recording breaks new ground in scholarship, matching it with performances of the highest order.

Bruce Wood has discovered that, for the queen's funeral, Purcell composed his second setting of 'Thou Knowest, Lord' to replace Thomas Morley's missing setting in the burial service. It draws tears now as it is said to have done then. No less moving is Wood's reconstruction of the processional music from Whitehall to Westminster Abbey, three linked marches for oboes and trumpets respectively, played over muffled military drums.

An amazing feat from the 13-year-old Purcell is 'In the midst of Life' from the early *Funeral Sentences*. Its angular opening lines and chromatic harmony, spiralling ever higher, are masterly.

Christophers and The Sixteen are as polished in plaiting these lines as in expressing carefree joy above the hypnotic ground bass of 'Many Such Days' in the ode – exquisite music except for one crudely witty air using a folk-song as its ungainly bass. But, for me, the elegy 'O dive custos', with the astonishingly boy-like voices of Libby Crabtree and Carys Lane, is the unforgettable high point in this superb tribute to Purcell and his queen. *GP*

PURCELL

Odes and Welcome Songs (complete)

Soloists; Choir of New College, Oxford, The King's Consort/Robert King

Hyperion CDS 44031/8 □ 545:00 mins (8 discs) □ *♪♪*

This was the first of Hyperion's series of large-scale tributes to Purcell, shamefully neglected until the tercentenary of his death in 1995. The performances are the very best of period practice – scholarly and authentic in scale and style, unfailingly warm and persuasive in spirit. Of the fine soloists, Rogers Covey-Crump's high tenor makes striking sense of those frustrating parts which for so long seemed too high for traditional tenors and yet too low for male altos; in addition, Gillian Fisher and Tessa Bonner are a particularly attractive pair of duetting sopranos. The Choir of New College, Oxford, sings the choruses in the two large-scale odes, very grand and very English – *Hail! Bright Cecilia* and *Come, Ye Sons of Art*. Elsewhere an ensemble of soloists reflects the scale of Purcell's original forces.

Despite the often third-rate – and embarrassingly obsequious – texts, these pieces are an unparalleled union of 17th-century Italian modernism, the archaic harmonic daring of an earlier English tradition, and a choral technique without which Handel would not have 'invented' the dramatic oratorio.

Begin, perhaps, with Vol. 8 (CDA 66598 when separate), *Come, Ye Sons of Art* and two Welcome Songs, or possibly Vol. 6 (CDA 66494), which includes three recording 'firsts' – but every disc is such a treasure-house of wonderful invention that the whole set must be an irresistible temptation. *GP*

RACHMANINOV

The Bells; Three Russian Songs

Natalia Troitskaya (soprano), Ryszard Karczykowski (tenor), Tom Krause (bass-baritone); Amsterdam Concertgebouw Orchestra & Chorus/Vladimir Ashkenazy

Decca 436 482-2 □ 50:17 mins □ *🎵🎵*

The bells that strike a metaphysical chord in Edgar Allan Poe's mostly lugubrious imagination also happen to be the bells of Rachmaninov's Russian youth in this haunting meeting of words and music, fantasy and feeling. Ashkenazy takes an obvious delight in the work's felicitous orchestration, and the recording discreetly assists him in pinpointing the finesse of the woodwind writing. His vocal urging may be audible in the first, aching climax of the ambiguous 'wedding bells' movement, but so sumptuous is the pay-off that it hardly matters.

Previn's pioneering EMI version – now in the useful company of Prokofiev's *Alexander Nevsky* – sometimes has the edge in the work's disorientating moments of mystery and panic, especially in the fiendish third movement (the Concertgebouw Chorus is admirably precise in this difficult music, but hardly driven). Ashkenazy scores, however, with an extra degree of luminous orchestral colouring, and a more idiomatic soprano soloist in the powerful but never coarse Natalia Troitskaya. His choice of companion piece should be of special interest to

anyone bewitched by Rachmaninov's more obsessive cast of thought: the Three Russian Songs, composed (or should one say arranged?) during his American exile, view simple folk-melodies through a selectively scored gauze of nostalgia and homesickness. *DN*

RACHMANINOV

Vespers (All-Night Vigil)

St Petersburg Academic Cappella (Glinka State Choir)/Vladislav Chernushenko

Saison Russe LDC 288 050 □ 61:50 mins □ *🎵🎵🎵*

To hear Russia's oldest and most prestigious professional choir 'live' is to witness one of the concert-hall wonders of the world, and this recording goes some way towards conveying the full richness of the experience. The famous Slavonic weight of the basses – 'as rare as asparagus in winter', wrote Rachmaninov – is matched by the burnished sound of the middle voices and the sopranos' open-throated brilliance; together they move with astonishing fluidity from the most hallowed pianissimo to an overwhelmingly rich fortissimo.

Rachmaninov's masterly fusion of flexible old Russian chant with a style very much his own taxes those virtues to the limits. The Vespers had the deepest significance for him; he quoted the bracing 'resurrection' sequence in his orchestral swan-song, the Symphonic Dances of 1940. There are moments here when the choir sounds like the most joyous of gospel singers and others when time stands still – most movingly in the Song of Simeon, where the sweetest of tenor voices (shamefully uncredited) unfolds his spellbinding melody against a rocking choral background. For absolutely perfect pitching throughout, you need to turn to the British Corydon Singers on Hyperion, but their admirable performance remains within the pure English cathedral-choir tradition; this, the genuine Russian article, is something that can never be simulated. *DN*

RAVEL

Histoires naturelles
see DEBUSSY: *Ariettes oubliées*

RAVEL

Shéhérazade
see Collection: French Song

ROSSINI

Petite messe solennelle; Stabat mater

Lucia Popp, Catherine Malfitano (soprano), Brigitte Fassbaender, Agnes Baltsa (mezzo-soprano), Nicolai Gedda, Robert Gambill (tenor), Dimitri Kavrakos, Gwynne Howell (bass); Choir of King's College,

Cambridge, Katia & Marielle Labèque (piano), David Briggs (harmonium)/Stephen Cleobury, Chorus & Orchestra of the Maggio Musicale, Florence/Riccardo Muti

EMI CZS 5 68658 2 □ **147:02 mins (2 discs)** □ *Ⓐ*

Not at all *petite* (at 85 minutes), and genial rather than *solennelle*, Rossini's 'solemn little Mass' is one of the masterpieces of his old age. In a note appended to the score, the composer confessed to the Almighty that he was really born for comic opera and wondered whether his Mass was 'sacred music or damned music'. Written for soloists and chorus accompanied by two pianos and a harmonium (preferable to the orchestral version Rossini produced three years later), this engaging and melodious work clearly comes from the heart. It could hardly be better performed than by EMI's starry quartet and the Choir of King's College, Cambridge. *CO*

ROSSINI

Stabat mater

Pilar Lorengar (soprano), Yvonne Minton (mezzo-soprano), Luciano Pavarotti (tenor), Hans Sotin (bass); LSO & Chorus/István Kertész

Decca 417 766-2 □ **ADD** □ **54:02 mins** □ *ⒶⒶ*

The text of Rossini's gloriously tuneful *Stabat mater* may be religious but the worldly spirit of the piece is the very opposite of solemn. The tenor's 'Cujus animam' swings along happily, while the setting for all four soloists of 'Sancta mater' is positively jaunty. Pavarotti sings most beautifully throughout, from his contribution to the opening movement, through his forthright 'Cujus animam' with its confident high D flat, to the quiet serenity of the 'Quando corpus' for quartet and chorus. The other soloists, though they may lack the tenor's Latin exuberance, are all first rate, and the conductor keeps the work's delightful vulgarity from getting out of hand. *CO*

SCARLATTI
Stabat mater
see Collection: Marian Music

SCHEIDT
Lutheran Mass for Christmas Morning
see PRAETORIUS: Lutheran Mass for Christmas Morning

SCHEIN
Lutheran Mass for Christmas Morning
see PRAETORIUS: Lutheran Mass for Christmas Morning

SCHOENBERG

Gurrelieder

Sharon Sweet (soprano), Marjana Lipovšek (mezzo-soprano), Siegfried Jerusalem, Philip Langridge (tenor), Hartmut Welker (bass), Barbara Sukowa (reciter); Vienna State Opera Concert Chorus, Arnold Schönberg Choir, Slovak Philharmonic Choir, Vienna PO/Claudio Abbado

DG 439 944-2 □ **106:59 mins (2 discs)** □ *ⒶⒶⒶ*

Schoenberg, not Mahler or Strauss, is the pinnacle of musical late-Romanticism: in his mid-twenties, in one gigantic work, he summed it all up for all time, and went on his way elsewhere. *Gurrelieder*, part songfest, part cantata, part post-Wagnerian operatic Liebestod, embraces such a diversity of styles and textures, and demands so titanic a choral-orchestral apparatus, that such a thing as an ideal performance is perhaps unrealisable. Abbado's heroic reading, recorded live in the Vienna Musikverein, where the work received its premiere under Franz Schreker in 1913, has a boldness and sweep and an astonishing textural clarity which – perhaps – just give it the edge; this despite the extraordinary vocal antics of Barbara Sukowa, unusually a female-voice Speaker, in the melodrama of Part Three, and Sharon Sweet, an affecting but slightly lightweight and anonymous Tove. Otherwise, this is a very strong cast, with Jerusalem a real Wagnerian Heldentenor for King Waldemar, Lipovšek a magnificent Wood Dove, and Langridge a wonderfully vinegary Klaus the Fool.

Riccardo Chailly's powerful studio reading with the Berlin RSO (Decca), which also features Jerusalem as a slightly less agonised Waldemar, is a very strong rival, even better recorded: but it misses, in the last analysis, the final ounce of heaven-storming abandon. Boulez's mid-price version (Sony) remains highly competitive, a bit slow to warm up but building to visceral climaxes that are still of demonstration standard. And he offers a precious coupling: Yvonne Minton in Schoenberg's bejewelled and rarely encountered Op. 22 Orchestral Songs. *CM*

SCHOENBERG

Pierrot lunaire; Erwartung; Lied der Waldtaube

Yvonne Minton (reciter), Janis Martin (soprano), Jessye Norman (mezzo-soprano); ensemble, BBC SO, Ensemble InterContemporain/Pierre Boulez

Sony SMK 48466 □ **ADD** □ **76:24 mins** □ *ⒶⒶ*

Recorded between 1978 and 1983, these are bench-mark accounts of works that created the whole concept of musical modernism. For *Pierrot*, Boulez assembled a distinguished team of soloists (Barenboim and Zukerman among them) who unerringly located its rich seam of indulgent irony. This elegant performance stresses the lyrical aspects of Schoenberg's surrealist cabaret fantasy – Yvonne Minton knows that the Sprechstimme ('speech-song') vocal line, which has provided generations of modern-music sopranos with excuses for overacting, sounds better the nearer it approaches the condition of song.

Erwartung, if in the last analysis less seductive and fascinating than the more recent Bryn-Julson/Rattle version on EMI, is as one would expect sung and played with great intelligence and iridescent colour, and remains a highly recommendable account of a formidable modern masterwork. Jessye Norman's account of the Song of the Wood Dove from *Gurrelieder*, in Schoenberg's own fascinating arrangement for 22 instruments, remains one of the outstanding recordings of this great artist. Altogether a superb bargain. *CM*

SCHOENBERG

A Survivor from Warsaw; Five Pieces for Orchestra, Op. 16, Accompaniment to a Cinematographic Scene; Herzgewächse; Serenade, Op. 24

Simon Callow (narrator), Eileen Hulse (soprano), Stephen Varcoe (baritone); London Voices, LSO/Robert Craft

Koch International 3-7263-2 □ 68:49 mins □ 🅟🅟🅟

A Survivor from Warsaw, to a text Schoenberg constructed from accounts of the ghetto and the gas-chambers, is one of the most dramatically effective scores ever written for speaking voice and orchestra. It's also one of the most searing musical indictments of tyranny, and a harbinger of mysterious hope, as the male chorus go to their doom singing a Hebrew psalm. Here the dissonant and fractured language of expressionism and 12-note serialism find their most compelling expressive justification. Though the piece has had many imitators, its blazing humanity has never been equalled. Robert Craft, who produced a revelatory account of the piece with Robert Horton as speaker in the days of LP, revisits it with equal success in this fascinatingly varied Schoenberg programme. Simon Callow's narration, beginning low key, holds one with an eye as glittering as Coleridge's Ancient Mariner; this is a performance to treasure.

Craft is a Schoenberg conductor of unusual experience and authority. Two other items – the *Begleitmusik zu einer Lichtspielszene* (*Accompaniment to a Cinematographic Scene*), Schoenberg's gripping foray into the world of music for the expressionist silent film, and the very rarely heard *Herzgewächse* for stratospheric soprano with harp, harmonium and celesta – are as well done here as they have ever been on disc. The remaining two are certainly recommendable, though there are finer versions elsewhere. *CM*

SCHUBERT

Lieder (Hyperion Schubert Edition, Vol. 15)

Margaret Price (soprano), Graham Johnson (piano)

Hyperion CDJ 33015 □ 72:02 mins □ 🅟🅟🅟

Margaret Price has one of the most distinctive and attractive voices of any soprano before the public today, and her contribution to the Hyperion Schubert Edition easily maintains the extraordinarily high level set by the singers elsewhere in the series.

Her technical control is wellnigh unassailable (some slightly worrying intonation in the first and last songs apart) and her enunciation impeccable. Her strength is not so much the colouring of individual words (as with Fischer-Dieskau, for example), but the establishing of a mood for the whole song: the longing of 'Der Morgenkuss', the agitation of 'Sehnsucht', the striding swagger of the walking song 'Der Wanderer an den Mond', or the sober reflection of 'Am Fenster'.

And yet she does occasionally arrest the ear with little details: the light fall of silver flakes on the tree in 'Im Freien' or the broadening of tone for the swelling of the heart later in the same song. The suppressed sexual ecstasy of 'Die junge Nonne' is her finest moment, as it is that of her partner, Graham Johnson, at the piano.

Johnson is far more than mere accompanist. He is the mastermind behind the series and his intelligent interpretations inform every song. His notes are a model blend of wit and scholarship, and greatly enhance one's appreciation of the works. *Barry Millington*

SCHUBERT

Lieder

Elisabeth Schwarzkopf (soprano), Edwin Fischer (piano)

EMI Références CDH 7 64026 2 □ ADD □ 42:32 mins □ 🅟🅟

Schwarzkopf's approach may sound a little dated now, but with a voice and musicianship like these, who cares? And with a partner like this! Fischer is incomparable – near the end of his life and at the peak of his magical powers. 'Gretchen' is ravishing, 'Die junge Nonne' terrifying, 'Der Musensohn' irresistibly joyful, and, as with them, it seems to me all but inconceivable that 'Auf dem Wasser zu singen' could ever receive a better performance. The warmth and spiritual nobility of Fischer are wonderfully complemented by Schwarzkopf's fantastic precision-enunciation and breath control. If you're new to Lieder, you could do a lot worse than start from here. *JS*

SCHUBERT

Lieder

see also SCHUMANN: Frauenliebe und -leben and **CHAMBER**: SCHUBERT: Piano Quintet in A

SCHUBERT

Die schöne Müllerin; Winterreise; Schwanengesang

Dietrich Fischer-Dieskau (baritone), Gerald Moore (piano)

DG 437 235-2 □ **ADD** □ **184:15 mins (3 discs)** □ 🔊🔊

There can be no such thing as a definitive performance of a masterpiece, let alone three, but these come as close as any. Fischer-Dieskau, probably the pre-eminent Lieder singer of our century, lived with and pondered this music throughout his career. He returned to it repeatedly, both in concert and in the studio, each time bringing new insights and approaches. No singer has more consistently brought together a voice of extraordinary beauty and flexibility, a profound sensitivity to the musical character and meaning of words, an implacable integrity and a first-hand experience of music that extends far beyond the vocal (he is, by the way, a very fine pianist as well as a conductor). These particular performances find him at the height of all his powers, and have things to reveal to every listener, however experienced or naive. *JS*

SCHUMANN

Dichterliebe; Liederkreis, Op. 24; Lieder nach Heinrich Heine

Wolfgang Holzmair (baritone), Imogen Cooper (piano)

Philips 446 086-2 □ **66:42 mins** □ 🔊🔊🔊

Two qualities distinguish the singing of Wolfgang Holzmair. He has the exact measure of his light, high baritone, breathing freely, without a moment of strain, so that the voice

can really *sing*. And his performances have possibly the closest focus of any baritone of his generation: imagination and intelligence have clearly worked long on every word, its placing and its tone of voice. Both qualities come into their own in Schumann's settings of Heinrich Heine in which tenderness is invariably shadowed by bitterness, even irony. The secret of the second *Tragödie*, for instance, is barely revealed; and in 'Du bist wie eine Blume' the worm of mortality is already i' th' bud.

Dream predominates in Holzmair's responses to the Op. 24 *Liederkreis*. As in Schubert's *Die schöne Müllerin*, we eavesdrop on the extreme emotions of youth in a half-waking, half-sleeping sensibility. Dream is of the essence, too, in *Dichterliebe*. Holzmair's meticulous shaping of the melodic underlay of words like 'birdsong' and 'longing' only throw into relief the anger of reality confronted in a searing 'I'll not complain' (Holzmair resolutely dares the high-register option here), and in the bleak bitterness of the last four songs. *Hilary Finch*

SCHUMANN

Dichterliebe; Liederkreis, Op. 39; Myrthen (excerpts)

Dietrich Fischer-Dieskau (baritone), Christoph Eschenbach (piano)

DG 415 190-2 □ **ADD** □ **63:47 mins** □ 🔊🔊🔊

If a more beautiful, compelling and profound recording of these two great cycles has ever been made, then I've missed it. Fischer-Dieskau's later partnership with Brendel on Philips is no less searching and in some ways more dramatic, but there's a touch of Shakespearian realism about it that renders it almost uncomfortable at times, and it hasn't the sheer beauty of this version, which is related at every moment to the meaning of the words and music at hand. It's a performance to treasure for a lifetime. Following not far behind it, however – in quality and flexibility of voice, in clarity and finesse of diction, in smoothness of phrase and integrity of vision – is Olaf Bär on EMI, with Geoffrey Parsons, though some may feel that beauty is sometimes achieved at the expense of musical truth, or that Bär occasionally teeters on the brink of blandness. Not so Eschenbach and Peter Schreier (perhaps the most probing and insightful of present-day tenors) on Teldec, though the voice is past its prime – nor should anyone overlook the enraptured singing of Fritz Wunderlich on DG, who repeatedly overcomes the obstacle of a distinctly pedestrian accompanist. *JS*

SCHUMANN/SCHUBERT/BRAHMS

Schumann: Frauenliebe und -leben
Schubert: Lieder
Brahms: Lieder

Janet Baker (mezzo-soprano), Martin Isepp (piano)

Saga SCD 9001 □ AAD □ 47:00 mins □ 🎵🎵

Despite formidable competition from Brigitte Fassbaender on DG, Kathleen Ferrier and the treasurable Lotte Lehmann, on Decca and Sony respectively (both with an inspired Bruno Walter at the piano), Janet Baker remains for me a clear choice for the top honours in *Frauenliebe*. The immediacy of emotion, the subtlety of response, the colouring of the voice and the acute sensitivity to words are all of an exceptional order (all the more so, in a way, when you consider that this comes from the dawn of her career). Sure, the voice is wonderful, like the innate musicianship, but one of the greatest charms of the singing here is its complete lack of narcissism – an all-too-rare virtue. One is never imposed upon by the 'voice beautiful': that's part of the directness and the deceptive simplicity. And a word must be said for the excellent Martin Isepp, whose talents as a Lieder partner have never been given their due. *JS*

SCHUMANN

Liederkreis, Opp. 24 & 39; Myrthen; Zwölf Gedichte, Op. 35; Zwölf Gedichte aus Rückerts 'Liebesfrühling' (excerpts); Dichterliebe; Spanisches Liederspiel (excerpts); Lieder und Gesänge, Op. 98 (excerpts); Spanisches Liebeslieder (excerpts)

Dietrich Fischer-Dieskau (baritone), Christoph Eschenbach (piano)

DG 445 660-2 □ ADD □ 66:21, 71:33, 57:11, 63:39, 76:59, 66:37 mins (6 discs) □ 🎵🎵

This account of the *Liederkreis*, Op. 24, is the only current recording that I myself would put into the top 1,000, despite the fact that it's available only in this not cheap treasure-trove of a box. My great admiration for Brigitte Fassbaender's single-disc account on DG is offset by my discomfort at her very variable and distracting struggles with intonation. But *Liederkreis* aside, this amazing collection of Fischer-Dieskau in Schumann should really be in any serious record collection, most of the recordings included being among the greatest

ever made – thanks in no small part to Eschenbach's contribution, which is unsurpassed in my experience. *JS*

SCHÜTZ/GABRIELI

Schütz: The Christmas Story
Gabrieli: Four Christmas Motets

Ruth Holton (soprano), John Mark Ainsley (tenor), Michael George (bass); The King's Consort/Robert King

Hyperion CDA 66398 □ 57:03 mins □ 🎵🎵🎵

Schütz spent two periods in Venice, and his *Christmas Story* reflects both very clearly. From Gabrieli, who taught him from 1608 for four years, come the colourful, richly scored tableaux, the 'Intermedii'. Here he sets direct speech, angels in triple time with violins, earthlings in 4/4 with wind – shepherds running to recorders and buzzing dulcian, high priests interpreting prophesies in stately brass. Twenty years later, Monteverdi introduced him to the means to represent drama in a single melodic line – recitative – for which Schütz himself claimed a German 'first'.

Delightfully though the King's Consort illuminates the tableaux – Ruth Holton the purest of angels and Michael George a magnicently insincere Herod – John Mark Ainsley's Evangelist is the central role. He is so subtle with the words that even non-German-speakers barely need the written translation.

The climax is the final chorus of thanksgiving, when the king leaves Schütz's ambiguous rhythms dancing – in three- or four-time? We're meant to be not sure! *GP*

SCHÜTZ

Psalms of David

Stuttgart Chamber Choir, Musica Fiata Köln/Frieder Bernius

Sony S2K 48042 □ 129:53 mins (2 discs) □ 🎵🎵🎵

Schütz was at the impressionable age of 14 when he went to Venice, where he was taught by Giovanni Gabrieli for four years and continued to absorb his teacher's style for a further five years in the city. Returning to the opulent Protestant court of Dresden, he grafted his Italian experience on to German church music with a result that is unique, and shown to magnificent effect in these psalm settings of 1619.

On paper, the music looks unpromising if not plain dull: continuous German text declaimed, often in simple, repeated chords, and with little musical structure. However, it's certainly brought to life in performance, not least by its timbral brilliance. Bernius's choice of instruments, not clearly specified by Schütz, is on the scale of a Renaissance court festival: cornetts and sackbuts, recorder and reedy dulcians, strings, with continuo organ, spinet, regal, chitarrone and lute. The music is driven by a powerful constant pulse, divided choirs and virtuoso soloists creating a spatial impact which is all-enveloping.

This is music to listen to with the text, packed full of *Figuren*, musical descriptions and allusions. The opening of 'Out of the Deep' matches the most expressive Italian madrigal – 'sitteth' is repeated sedentarily, five times – while the Lord 'slew famous kings' is depicted with razor-sharp rhythms, Psalm 150 likewise evoking a kaleidoscope of descriptive patterns. *GP*

SHAPORIN

5 Songs
see Collection: Russian Song

SHEPPARD

Western Wind Mass
see TAVERNER: Western Wind Mass

SHOSTAKOVICH

From Jewish Folk Poetry
see Collection: Russian Song

SHOSTAKOVICH

The Song of the Forests; Symphony No. 2 (To October)
see **ORCHESTRAL**: SHOSTAKOVICH: Festival Overture

SHOSTAVOVICH

Symphony No. 13 (Babi Yar)

Anthony Hopkins (narrator), Sergei Alexashkin (bass); Chicago SO & Chorus/Georg Solti

Decca 444 791-2 □ 72:40 mins □ 🔵🔵🔵

To mention Hopkins's recitation of the Yevtushenko poems before the performance of the symphony might seem like putting the cart before the horse, but somehow hearing them reinforces the breadth and the daring of the subject-matter that Shostovokich was able, in the relative thaw of 1962, to set and have performed.

Readings and performance complement each other beautifully. Hopkins's tone is reasoned and patient, with only the occasional furious outburst. He has worthy counterparts in true Russian bass Sergei Alexashkin and the well-drilled men of the Chicago Symphony Chorus (certainly the next best thing to the genuine Russian article). The orchestra will never sound quite right in Shostakovich, but light, incisive qualities bring peculiar virtues to the jackbooted horrors of 'Babi Yar' and Solti's swiftly effective way with 'Humour'. There are

a few unsteadinesses of tempo in the later stages, but the brooding strings of 'In the Store' are certainly atmospheric, and there is apt refreshment in the opening flute duet of 'A Career', one of Shostokovich's most startlingly beautiful inspirations. Hopkins visited a studio to read the poems; the symphony was recorded live in Chicago – the audience is so attentively discreet that you'd never know it. *DN*

SHOSTAKOVICH

Symphony No. 14; Six Poems of Marina Tsvetayeva

Julia Varady (soprano), Dietrich Fischer-Dieskau (baritone), Ortrun Wenkel (contralto); Amsterdam Concertgebouw Orchestra/Bernard Haitink

Decca 425 074-2 □ 72:04 mins □ 🔵🔵

Shostakovich's paradoxically life-affirming songs and dances of death take their cue from Mussorgsky and his naturalistic setting of the Russian language. Perhaps something is lost when the poems are returned to their native tongues – Spanish (Lorca), French (Apollinaire) and German (Brentano, adapted by Apollinaire and Rilke) – and only one, the crucial apostrophe to Delvig, happens to be in Russian. But when the singers happen to be as vivid in communicating the texts as Fischer-Dieskau and Varady, and the orchestral playing of exceptional vividness, then that exception (sanctioned by the composer) to the general performing rule is worth it.

The baritone may push a smooth line out of shape in order to achieve the more savage moments of expression, but the restraint of his bass-like colourings sunk in meditation is always profoundly moving, while Varady plays up the Spanish malagueña with cutting chest-voice and convinces us that 'trois grand lys', though changing the note-values of a memorable phrase, can be just as moving in French as Vishnevskaya made 'tre lillii' in her unforgettable creation of the soprano part (unfortunately not easily found on CD at present). Contralto Ortrun Wenkel's intelligent nuancing of the Tsvetayeva settings may not be quite in the same league, but this even later cycle (orchestrated just before the composer's death in 1975) makes a fascinating addition, to be heard in the still of another evening's listening. *DN*

SHOSTAKOVICH

Symphonies Nos 13 & 14
see also **ORCHESTRAL**: SHOSTAKOVICH: Symphonies Nos 1–15

SIBELIUS

Luonnotar
see **ORCHESTRAL**: SIBELIUS: Finlandia

STANFORD

Three Motets: Eternal Father; Magnificat in B flat
see PARRY: Songs of Farewell

STRADELLA

L'anime del Purgatorio
see Collection: Consort of Musicke

STRAUSS

Four Last Songs; Capriccio – Final Scene; Tod und Verklärung

Gundula Janowitz (soprano); Berlin PO/Herbert von Karajan; Bavarian RSO, Dresden Staatskapelle/Karl Böhm

DG Originals 439 467-2 □ **65:23 mins** □ *🍎🍎*

There is a dilemma here: not the familiar one concerning the rival claims of words and music which dominates Strauss's final opera *Capriccio*, but a simpler question of priorities – which comes first, the soprano or the conductor? In an ideal performance, of course, the two should be equally at the service of the composer – and that would surely have been the case had Janowitz recorded the *Four Last Songs* with Karl Böhm, a master of supple forward movement (as his live *Tod und Verklärung* here reveals), and of characterful support for the singer (witness the serene interplay in the closing scene from *Capriccio*, taken from the ideal complete performance of the opera).

As it turns out, Karajan's ponderous tempi simply have to be endured for the sake of the most supernaturally luminous Straussian soprano voice in the business. Janowitz's control of phrasing is astonishing, and her Lieder-singer's intelligence makes very impressive sense of the third song's first two stanzas; a pity the rest of the poetry has to take a back seat, given the slow speeds, to sheer beauty of tone. Response to the interpretation of these moving swan-songs, the happiest of final curtains from the octogenarian Strauss, is bound to be intensely personal; I can only suggest the one closest to my heart. *DN*

STRAUSS

Lieder

Dietrich Fischer-Dieskau (baritone), Gerald Moore (piano)

EMI CMS 7 63995 2 □ **ADD** □ **354:15 mins (6 discs)** □ *🍎🍎*

Strauss wrote so many of his songs to suit the formidable technique and stylish phrasing of his wife Pauline, singer and termagant *extraordinaire*, that the entire output tends to be associated with the soprano voice – and so to plump for a baritone interpreter (with piano

rather than orchestral accompaniment to boot) might seem perverse. The one truly outstanding Strauss collection from a female singer, however – the unsurpassable Margaret Price on EMI, who matches warmth of tone with intelligence of diction – has not been available for some time, and remains so at the time of writing. Besides, Fischer-Dieskau's comprehensive collection, by no means unaffordable at mid-price, reveals so much more than the usual familiar settings of love-lyrics. Most startling of all is the cycle *Krämerspiegel* (Shopkeeper's Mirror) – textually a rather arcane swipe at the greed of music publishers, but musically rich in witty turns of phrase and the occasional surprising depth of feeling. Recorded just before an occasional hectoring tone crept in to the voice, Fischer-Dieskau offers wide-ranging intelligence and sympathy, subtly but not over-discreetly matched by pianist Gerald Moore – certainly sufficient to permit one or two discs being heard at a single sitting. More likely, though, the set will serve as a long-term investment, to be dipped in to for several songs at a time during idle evenings. *DN*

STRAUSS

Zueignung; Die heiligen drei Könige
see **ORCHESTRAL**: STRAUSS: Symphonia domestica

STRAVINSKY

Les noces; Mass

Anny Mory (soprano), Patricia Parker (mezzo-soprano), John Mitchinson (tenor), Paul Hudson (bass), Martha Argerich, Krystian Zimerman, Cyprien Katsaris, Homero Francesch (pianos); English Bach Festival Chorus, Trinity Boys Choir, English Bach Festival Orchestra & Percussion Ensemble/Leonard Bernstein

DG 423 251-2 □ **ADD** □ **44:29 mins** □ *🍎🍎*

The combination of an all-star line-up of pianists and Bernstein's magnetic personality is simply irresistible in Stravinsky's ballet. From the very outset, the performance fizzes and crackles with rhythmic zest, and the physical immediacy of the playing is guaranteed to lift you out of your seat. In comparison, most alternative versions, including the composer's own, operate at a much lower voltage and fail to communicate the same level of exhilaration.

The Mass, scored for mixed chorus and double wind quintet, explores a much more emotionally restrained manner. Bernstein resists any obvious temptation to sensationalise the music with unwarranted interpretative idiosyncrasies, the overriding impression remaining one of dignity and reticence. Even at only 45 minutes' duration, this disc is a must. *EL*

STRAVINSKY

Les noces
see also **ORCHESTRAL**: STRAVINSKY: Ballets, Vol. 1

STRAVINSKY

Perséphone; Zvezdoliki; Symphonies of Wind Instruments; Concertino for Twelve Instruments; Octet

Irène Jacob (reciter), John Aler (tenor); Gregg Smith Singers, Newark Boys Chorus, Orchestra of St Luke's/Robert Craft

MusicMasters 01612-67103-2 □ **73:34 mins**
□ *⊘⊘⊘*

One of the best discs in Robert Craft's ongoing exploration of his mentor's output. The highlight is a revelatory performance of *Perséphone* which challenges the composer's unusually lethargic metronome marks, thus intensifying the dramatic power of Gide's text without destroying its lyrical beauty. The tenor John Aler copes pretty well with the extremely demanding high tessitura of Stravinsky's writing, but it's the chorus that really shine, and they are equally magnificent in the highly chromatic *Zvezdoliki*, a work which the composer dedicated to Debussy. The Debussy connection is further reinforced with a vital performance of the *Symphonies of Wind Instruments*, its inclusion enhanced for giving us the most accurate reading of Stravinsky's original manuscript. High-spirited renditions of the Concertino, originally conceived for string quartet, and the delightful Octet, complete an enthralling programme. *EL*

STRAVINSKY

Pulcinella
see **ORCHESTRAL**: STRAVINSKY: Petrushka
and **ORCHESTRAL**: STRAVINSKY: Ballets, Vol. 2

STRAVINSKY

Symphony of Psalms; Symphony in C; Symphony in Three Movements

LSO & Chorus/Michael Tilson Thomas

Sony SK 53275 □ **71:13 mins** □ *⊘⊘⊘*

Tilson Thomas delivers an incandescent performance of the *Symphony of Psalms*. The pacing of each movement is excellently judged in balancing monumentality of expression with dramatic urgency. Furthermore, the conductor manages to achieve a unique sense of timelessness in the closing pages without in any way sounding indulgent. The London Symphony Chorus respond with superb singing and crystal-clear diction, and the

performance as a whole benefits from Sony's marvellously spatial recording. Alas, the rest of the disc doesn't quite reach this exalted level. While the *Symphony in Three Movements* is pretty impressive, with some powerhouse orchestral playing in the outer movements, Tilson Thomas seems to lose his way in the Symphony in C, which somehow never quite operates with the same degree of involvement. *EL*

SZYMANOWSKI

Harnasie; Mandragora

Jozsef Stepien, Paulos Raptis (tenor); Chorus & Orchestra of the Polish National Opera, Warsaw/Robert Satanowski

Koch Schwann Musica Mundi 311064 □ **62:18 mins**
□ *⊘⊘⊘*

The choral ballet *Harnasie* (The Highland Robbers), based on the folk-songs and dances of the Tatra mountain region of Szymanowski's native Poland, is the cornerstone of his later period, just as *King Roger* is the summation of his earlier opulent, orientalist vein. The orchestral style is of astonishing virtuosity, and the elemental melodies and rhythms are handled in a way that sets the blood racing: it's a joyous, earthy, life-affirming score with quieter sections of magical beauty.

There's no perfect version, but Robert Satanowski's account comes much the nearest of the few available performances. The coupling is Szymanowski's only other ballet, *Mandragora*, a mannered and perfumed essay in *commedia dell'arte* humour for a much smaller orchestra, written for an adaptation of Molière's *Le bourgeois gentilhomme*, and not unreminiscent of Strauss's music on the same theme. Both works are very well recorded. *CM*

SZYMANOWSKI/POULENC

Szymanowski: Stabat mater

Poulenc: Stabat mater

Christine Goerke (soprano), Marietta Simpson (mezzo-soprano), Victor Ledbetter (baritone); Atlanta SO & Chorus/Robert Shaw

Telarc CD-80362 □ **58:24 mins** □ *⊘⊘⊘*

Poulenc's setting was composed more than twenty years after Szymanowski's inter-war masterpiece. Several of its 12 sections share features with the French composer's better-known Gloria and Organ Concerto. This is an exciting, beautifully disciplined performance, sustained by splendid brass and lower strings from an orchestra alert to the challenge of its accompanying role.

But it is the Szymanowski, sung in Polish, which provides the surprises. Gone is much of the lushness of the composer's wartime compositions. Shaw's reading achieves a purity and clarity which affect players, chorus and soloists alike. He lets the simple, thinned textures speak for themselves, unadorned. The soprano opening is less desolate than Barbara Zagorzanka on Marco Polo, and more imprecatory, but it compares well with Stefania Woytowicz on Koch, and is preferable to Elzbieta Szmytka on EMI.

One disappointment is the slightly muddy central duets, which EMI carries off so well. But the mezzo, Marietta Simpson, is admirable on her own. The chorus's shifts are so subtle, the whispers beneath bass solo (close to Szymanowski's opera *King Roger*) so dramatic, and the closing two minutes of postponed Mahlerian cadence so powerful and atmospheric, that this dedicated reading will give you great pleasure. *Roderic Dunnett*

SZYMANOWSKI

Symphony No. 3 (The Song of the Night); Stabat mater; Liturgy of the Virgin Mary

Jon Garrison (tenor), Elzbieta Szmytka (soprano), Florence Quivar (mezzo-soprano), John Connell (bass); City of Birmingham SO & Chorus/Simon Rattle

EMI CDC 5 55121 2 □ 56:04 mins □ 🎜🎜🎜

Szymanowski's Third Symphony sets verses by the 13th-century Persian mystical poet Rūmi for chorus and large orchestra as a glittering, bejewelled tapestry of sound. Sensuous, ecstatic, self-intoxicated, it marks the furthest stage in his music towards a nirvana of colour, oriental exoticism and saturated chromatic harmony. A heady brew indeed, and Rattle and his Birmingham forces stir it magnificently in sound that's absolutely demonstration class. This recording and performance provide a sumptuous feast of sonics. The *Stabat mater*, from Szymanowski's chaster, more folk-influenced final period, is comparatively austere, with echoes of old Polish church music, but possibly the greater work: a masterpiece of national religious fervour to set on a par with Janáček's *Glagolitic Mass*. The performance here is no less outstanding, and it's a valuable bonus to have the short but touching Litany, composed in much the same vein. This is one of Rattle's finest discs, a testament to Szymanowski's fastidious art in both its hedonism and mysticism. *CM*

TAVENER

Thunder Entered Her; Angels; The Annunciation; Lament of the Mother of God; Hymns of Paradise; God is With Us

Solveig Kringelborn (soprano); Winchester Cathedral Choir/David Hill

Virgin VC 5 45035 2 □ 62:40 mins □ 🎜🎜🎜

This Virgin release comprises a well-chosen group of short choral items, with two characteristic affirmations of faith in *Thunder Entered Her* for handbell, chorus and organ, and the 'Christmas proclamation' *God is With Us*. However, the *Hymns of Paradise*, premiere recordings along with *Angels* and *The Annunciation*, show the composer in more relaxed, humorous mood. The words are by St Ephrem the Syrian, the greatest poet of the patristic age. *Nicholas Williams*

TAVERNER/TYE/SHEPPARD

Western Wind Masses

Tallis Scholars/Peter Phillips

Gimell CDGIM 027 □ 79:40 mins □ 🎜🎜🎜

The *Western Wind* Masses are the English equivalent to the L'homme armé Mass tradition so popular in France during the 15th century. Both titles refer to the secular, indeed rather bawdy, songs used by composers as a basis for their Mass settings. But, whereas 'L'homme armé' is a rather irregular, bumpy tune, 'Western Wind' is beautifully melodic and graceful – qualities put to good use in these Masses.

In John Taverner's setting, the song's characteristic descending scale motifs are quite easily discernible, and around them he weaves relaxed, flowing counterpoint. The Tye and Sheppard settings use similar methods, though their works are by no means slavish copies of Taverner's original.

The Tallis Scholars perform in their usual precise, balanced manner. The natural flow of the music is followed, without allowing the underlying pulse to slacken. Sections for solo voices (so often the places where lesser choirs come unstuck) are well sung, and the wonderful uplifting effect as the full choir returns is not spoiled by too much clamour. As ever, the sound is glorious. *Edward Kershaw*

TCHAIKOVSKY

Songs

Elisabeth Söderström (soprano), Vladimir Ashkenazy (piano)

Decca 436 204-2 □ ADD/DDD □ 74:20 mins □ 🎜🎜

This treasury of Tchaikovsky romances discovers so much more than the melancholy and nostalgia that lie at the core of the composer's song output, though Söderström and Ashkenazy certainly handle those aspects with tender loving care. It's good to have some of Tchaikovsky's very early exercises in the genre, especially 'Zemfira's Song', to a text from a Pushkin verse-tale that inspired Mérimée to write the novella *Carmen*; Söderström cuts a dash as this particular freedom-loving gypsy and there are even a few spoken interjections from Ashkenazy, playing Zemfira's jealous lover Aleko.

It might have been better still to have had the composer's very last song as well as his earliest: 'Once Again, Alone', not included here, compounds the *Pathétique* legend of unhappiness and is splendidly captured by the dark, withdrawn tones of Olga Borodina on Philips. Borodina in her selection, however, cannot touch Söderström for subtlety: the famous 'None but the Lonely Heart' is so much more tinged with heartbreak, and 'Lullaby' has an exquisite lightness of touch. It would be unfair not to mention the young British soprano Joan Rodgers's astonishingly idiomatic Tchaikovsky programme on Hyperion; but the Söderström–Ashkenazy achievement here is surpassed only by their still more extensive Rachmaninov survey. *DN*

A Child of Our Time

Jill Gomez (soprano), Helen Watts (contralto), Kenneth Woollam (tenor), John Shirley-Quirk (baritone); BBC SO & Chorus/Gennady Rozhdestvensky

Carlton BBC Radio Classics BBCRD 9130 □ ADD □ 62:01 mins □ ⊘

Among the available versions of Tippett's wartime oratorio, the present recording, taken from a public concert at the Royal Festival Hall in 1980, achieves the greatest immediacy. The urgency of the composer's message is communicated primarily through powerful and expressive choral singing and a marvellous team of soloists. First and foremost, however, it's Rozhdestvensky's inspirational conducting that makes this performance so special, for he possesses an instinctive ability to pace the contrasting musical events with necessary flexibility of nuance and tempo. Those who normally fight shy of live recordings need not have any qualms about the quality of sound,

which is exemplary. Nor should they worry about extraneous noise, for, in a performance that is as compelling as this, the audience appears to be transfixed. An irresistible release, especially at bargain price, though newcomers to the work should be warned that Carlton's liner notes don't include the text. *EL*

Dona nobis pacem; Sancta civitas

Bryn Terfel (baritone), Yvonne Kenny (soprano), Philip Langridge (tenor); Choristers of St Paul's Cathedral, LSO & Chorus/Richard Hickox

EMI CDC 7 54788 2 □ 72:58 mins □ ⊘⊘⊘

Unbeatable, Vaughan Williams's two most profound choral-orchestral scores in first-class performances on a single disc. The oratorio *Sancta civitas* is one of his supreme masterpieces, setting the passages of the Book of Revelations relating to the fall of Babylon and the vision of the Holy City with unexampled mystical intensity. *Dona nobis pacem* is perhaps less convincing as a whole (the gifted Scottish composer Ronald Center composed a bitter parody of it – by no means a mere curiosity, worth looking out for on an Altarus CD). A product of the troubled Thirties, Vaughan Williams's cantata looks towards another imminent world war with anguish; its finest sections are inspired settings of Whitman, including the unforgettable 'Dirge for Two Veterans'. The work has never quite come off on disc: Hickox's reading gets nearest to the ideal. In *Sancta civitas*, Bryn Terfel as John of Patmos doesn't quite erase memories of John Shirley-Quirk in David Willcocks's marvellous reading with King's College Choir (not presently available), but in every other respect Hickox is the equal of that bench-mark performance's blazing intensity. EMI's studio sound is of the very best. *CM*

Vaughan Williams: On Wenlock Edge

Gurney: The Western Playland; Ludlow and Teme

Adrian Thompson (tenor), Stephen Varcoe (baritone), Iain Burnside (piano); Delmé String Quartet

Hyperion CDA 66385 □ 69:08 mins □ *➋➌➍*

The 'other' great *Shropshire Lad* song cycle, apart from George Butterworth's eponymous one, is his friend Vaughan Williams's collection of six songs, *On Wenlock Edge*. It's an early (1909) and slightly uncharacteristic work, with a melodramatic strain and touches of impressionism showing the effect of his recent studies with Ravel. The poet, who was unmusical but always allowed settings of his verse on the grounds that songs were his passport to immortality, was furious that Vaughan Williams truncated the text of 'Is My Team Ploughing?'. Yet the cycle remains a landmark in 20th-century English song, a uniquely passionate fusion of words and music.

Adrian Thompson's superb performance on this Hyperion disc is a clear first choice. An additional attraction is Ivor Gurney's two rarely heard Housman cycles, also with piano quintet – among the last important works he brought to completion before he was confined to a mental hospital after the First World War. Himself a poet, Gurney had a deep appreciation of Housman: his approach is more frankly lyrical than Vaughan Williams's, with a remarkable sensitivity to speech rhythm in the word-setting. In *The Western Playland*, Stephen Varcoe proves as intelligent and sympathetic an exponent as Thompson in the other two cycles. Excellent recording. *CM*

A Sea Symphony

Amanda Roocroft (soprano), Thomas Hampson (baritone); BBC SO & Chorus/Andrew Davis

Teldec British Line 4509-94550-2 □ 65:33 mins □ *➋➌➍*

Putting together an ideal recording of Vaughan Williams's first great symphonic essay is no easy task. The huge, burgeoning structures of the first and last movements test a conductor's formal grasp to the utmost, while the wide range of orchestral, choral and solo textures pose considerable engineering problems. Add to this the difficulty of assembling the right team of artists, and one begins to see why recordings have often failed the ultimate test.

The present issue comes as near as any to that expressive ideal, and a prime factor in its success is Davis's enthusiastic and commanding grasp of Vaughan Williams's richly proliferating forms. He draws from his BBC orchestral and choral forces the most elated singing and playing, and, with something like an ideal recorded sound, which yields a warm sonority without over-reverberance and blends textures while differentiating where necessary, Vaughan Williams's grand vision comes tinglingly alive. The soloists, too, are outstanding, Roocroft an incisive soprano, and Hampson among the finest baritones I've heard in the work. *Anthony Payne*

Serenade to Music
see **ORCHESTRAL**: VAUGHAN WILLIAMS: Symphonies Nos 1–9

Songs of Travel; Ten Blake Songs; Silent Noon; The Water-Mill; Linden Lea; Orpheus with his Lute
see **BUTTERWORTH**: A Shropshire Lad

Valiant for Truth
see **ORCHESTRAL**: Collection: Testimonies of War

L'Amfiparnaso; Il convito musicale (excerpts)

Ensemble Clément Janequin/Dominique Visse

Harmonia Mundi HMC 901461 □ 59:20 mins □ *➋➌➍*

Behind the refinement of high art lurks a seditious spirit. One of its musical outlets has been the *commedia dell'arte* figures, the old man Pantalone, Doctor Gratiano, Harlequin and Colombine. Orazio Vecchi's 'madrigal comedy' *L'Amfiparnaso* is one of the earliest manifestations of this earthy, vulgar wit – and it's hilarious. Six extraordinarily spirited voices sing the character roles, in madrigal fashion differentiated by register – five upper voices for the courtesan Hortensia; the topmost voice dropped and an additional lower one added for Pantalone, who is smitten by her charms.

To understand the words, you ideally need a total command of Italian and familiarity with 16th-century puns and vulgarities. For instance, it helps if you know that 'flo' means not only 'senile' but also the 'splashing of a chamber-pot', or that the name Zani puns in Venetian dialect as 'belly ache'. The excellent booklet is an effective substitute, the music heightening the jokes – Hortensia echoing her own name in grotesque parallel chords, Isabella reassuring Captain Cardon in a ludicrously nasal tone, that every part of her body is his.

Some moments are very beautiful too, like Lucio's lament at Isabella's apparent unfaithfulness. Vecchi creates a heartfelt poignancy all the more intense for being mere parody. *GP*

Requiem; Four Sacred Pieces

Elisabeth Schwarzkopf (soprano), Christa Ludwig, Janet Baker (mezzo-soprano), Nicolai Gedda (tenor), Nicolai Ghiaurov (bass); Philharmonia Chorus & Orchestra/Carlo Maria Giulini

EMI CDS 7 47257 8 □ ADD □ 127:38 mins (2 discs) □ ❂❂❂

Verdi's Requiem, composed to honour the memory of his idol, the novelist Alessandro Manzoni, is a Mass not for the dead but for the living. The agnostic composer set the sacred text using the art of the dramatist. The intensity and compassion of his tragic view of the human condition are positively Shakespearian in stature, and his Requiem, composed between *Aida* and *Otello*, speaks the musical language of those two great operas. Giulini penetrates to the heart of the work. His four soloists could hardly be bettered, and the Philharmonia Orchestra and Chorus are on top form. The Four Sacred Pieces, choral works written at various times over a period of nine years in Verdi's old age, are given performances of great dramatic intensity by Giulini and his forces. *CO*

Four Sacred Pieces – Te Deum
see also BERLIOZ: Grande messe des morts

Missa Trahe me, post te; Trahe me, post te; Alma redemptoris mater; Magnificat primi toni; Ave regina coelorum; Regina coeli; Salve regina

Choir of Westminster Cathedral/James O'Donnell

Hyperion CDA 66738 □ 67:32 mins □ ❂❂❂

Westminster Cathedral Choir's Victoria, heard as from the congregation, is crystal clear in its reverberant setting. The motet *Trahe me, post te*, a masterpiece of canonic ingenuity, is the basis for a parody mass, John IV of Portugal described Victoria's disposition as 'naturally sunny… he never stays downcast for long' – reflected here in a dancing triple-time Hosanna and a strong sense of major/minor key. Outstanding is the *Salve regina* for two choirs, one high, the other dark and low,

combining at climaxes in an all-enveloping stereo grandeur. *GP*

Vivaldi: Gloria in D, RV 589

Caldara: Stabat mater

Bach: Magnificat, BWV 243

Lynda Russell, Gillian Fisher (soprano), Alison Browner, Caroline Trevor (contralto), Ian Partridge (tenor), Michael George (bass); The Sixteen, Orchestra of The Sixteen/Harry Christophers

Collins 13202 □ 72:22 mins □ ❂❂❂

Vivaldi wrote the Gloria for the girls of the Ospedale della Pietà, an orphanage in Venice. The choral singing from The Sixteen is superbly controlled – I heard details that I'd never noticed before – from the crisp, opening Gloria to the final 'Quoniam' of almost Handelian proportions. Christophers has a fine team of soloists too. Lynda Russell, with oboist Sophia McKenna, sings an ecstatic 'Domine Deus' and is matched to perfection by Gillian Fisher in the 'Laudamus' duet; Alison Browner articulates the long runs of 'Qui sedes' quite effortlessly.

But the Pietà choir was of girls only, so why did Vivaldi write for mixed chorus? No one's sure, but Andrew Parrott (on Virgin) opts for female voices singing the tenor and bass parts an octave above their written pitch. It's a beguiling sound, though surprising when transposed 'tenors' soar, descanting, *above* sopranos in 'Domine fili' – perhaps only the bass-line should change. Meanwhile, Christophers offers a fine alternative to my recommended Bach Magnificat (Herreweghe) and the intriguing sound of two trombones enriching voices and strings in the less familiar *Stabat mater* by Caldara, another Venetian and contemporary of Vivaldi. *GP*

Gloria
see also PERGOLESI: Stabat mater

Belshazzar's Feast; In Honour of the City of London

David Wilson-Johnson (baritone); LSO & Chorus/Richard Hickox

EMI Eminence CD-EMX 2225 □ 53:16 mins □ ❂❂

Walton's Babylonian oratorio is nothing if not a great choral-orchestral showpiece, bloodthirsty and flamboyant Old Testament theatre in a sense that Handel would have understood, for all their differences in language. There have been many fine versions (an electrifying account under Solti is currently available on mid-price Decca; Previn has done it twice, superbly, on EMI and ASV; Walton's own richly rewarding 1959 recording is currently available only as part of EMI's four-disc Walton Edition). But this crackingly dramatic reading by Hickox must be the highest-voltage version currently available, and at mid-price too. David Wilson-Johnson, balefully sepulchral at the appearance of the Writing on the Wall, is perfect for the taxing solo baritone part, and the orchestral and choral contributions are consistently thrilling.

I choose this version also for its coupling. Walton's brilliant festal setting of William Dunbar's encomium of late-medieval London is seldom performed or recorded: a third the length of *Belshazzar's Feast*, it uses forces as large, and the choral writing is even more difficult. It's an intoxicating *tour de force* of wit, grandeur and sheer youthful exuberance, one of those rare occasional works that's also a major artistic achievement. It's good to have such a lusty performance of it here. *CM*

WALTON

Façade (complete)

Pamela Hunter (reciter); Melologos Ensemble/Silveer van den Broeck

Koch Discover International DICD 920125
□ 61:05 mins □ 🎵

Walton's youthful entertainment on Edith Sitwell's surreal-satirical verses went through several versions – some numbers dropping out, others going in – before becoming the 21-poem sequence so memorably recorded by, for example, Sitwell herself, Peter Pears, Constant Lambert, Hermione Gingold and others. Often described as the 'original version', this is best designated *Façade 1*, since late in life Walton published eight of the dropped numbers under the title *Façade 2*: the two sequences are very well done together by the composer's widow, Susana Walton, on Chandos, conducted by Richard Hickox. The classic Sitwell–Pears *Façade 1* is available at mid-price on Decca, while Peggy Ashcroft and Paul Scofield are conducted by Walton himself on a bargain-price Belart disc. But Pamela Hunter's version for Discover is unique, and just as inexpensive: only she offers every Sitwell setting that Walton made for the various early performances, forty in all. A few settings, in fact, are lost – in those cases she recites the text, using the same crisp, rhythmically stylised delivery as the extant

settings demand. She's a splendidly idiomatic soloist; the whole is beautifully played and recorded, and the unfamiliar numbers enhance the boldly experimental nature of Walton's enterprise. Sheer delight. *CM*

WARD
Madrigals and Fantasias; Psalms and Anthems
see Collection: Consort of Musicke

WARLOCK

The Curlew; Capriol Suite; Serenade for string orchestra; partsongs, songs, carols & Christmas songs

Janet Baker (mezzo-soprano), Ian Partridge, Robert Hammersley (tenor), Frederick Harvey (baritone), Robert Lloyd, Owen Brannigan (bass), Gerald Moore, Jennifer Partridge, Nina Walker, Ernest Lush (piano), Gavin Williams, Philip Ledger (organ); Music Group of London, Baccholian Singers of London; Guildford Cathedral Choir/Barry Rose, Westminster Abbey Choir/Douglas Guest, Choir of King's College, Cambridge/David Willcocks, English Sinfonia/Neville Dilkes, Bournemouth Sinfonietta/Norman Del Mar

EMI CDM 5 65101 2 □ ADD □ 69:46 mins □ 🎵🎵

The received image (still current in some circles) of Peter Warlock (*alter ego* of Philip Heseltine) as a mere arranger of folk-songs and bibulous producer of roistering ballads could never survive contact with his austere, disturbing, uniquely atmospheric masterpiece, the WB Yeats cycle *The Curlew*, one of the outstanding productions in British chamber music between the wars. It's doubtful if Ian Partridge's achingly expressive account with the Music Group of London has ever been bettered, and it's the outstanding item on this exceptionally well-planned mid-price conspectus of Warlock's vocal and instrumental output. The remarkable 'The Shrouding of the Duchess of Malfi', from Webster's drama, is similarly grave and intense; the collection of carols reveals a more familiar side of Warlock, and the solo songs include a judicious amount of rollicking, notably Owen Brannigan's irresistible 'Yarmouth Fair', recorded in 1960.

Fine performances of the perennially popular *Capriol Suite* on French dance tunes, and the lushly affectionate Serenade in celebration of Delius's 60th birthday, suitably balance the predominantly vocal contents of this eminently desirable compilation. Apart from some cavernousness in 'Bethlehem Down', recorded in Guildford Cathedral, the sound is highly acceptable throughout. *CM*

WEILL

Berlin im Licht

Rosemary Hardy (soprano), Ensemble Modern/HK Gruber

Largo 5114 □ 57:18 mins □ 𝕆𝕆𝕆

A most imaginative release of lesser-known compositions by Kurt Weill, devised with customary enterprise by David Drew and performed with tremendous rhythmic exhilaration by the Ensemble Modern under the incisive direction of composer HK Gruber. Gruber's rather gravelly voice also brings great immediacy to a number of the popular cabaret songs, including 'Berlin im Licht' and the 'Muschellied', and there are some fascinating extended instrumental suites derived from some of Weill's theatre scores.

The rest of the programme includes a number of early Romantic songs and the more substantial cycle *Frauentanz*, composed for soprano and a small chamber ensemble which offers an interesting stylistic parallel to some of Hindemith's early vocal cantatas. Rosemary Hardy, a much-experienced performer of 20th-century music, sings this work with considerable range of expression and sensitivity. A word of praise, too, for Largo for its exemplary recording and the extensive documentation, both of which serve to enhance one's appreciation of the music. *EL*

WEILL

Choral-Fantasie; Zu Potsdam unter den Eichen
see **ORCHESTRAL**: Collection: Testimonies of War

WEILL/BERG

Weill: The Seven Deadly Sins

Berg: Lulu Suite

Angelina Réaux (soprano); members of Hudson Shad, New York Philharmonic/Kurt Masur

Teldec 4509-95029-2 □ 67:41 mins □ 𝕆𝕆𝕆

Weill's ballet *The Seven Deadly Sins* has enjoyed almost unprecedented exposure in recent years, with many singers not normally associated with such repertoire vying to perform and record the role of Anna. Among recent celebrities, Brigitte Fassbaender and Anne Sofie von Otter have made notable contributions, though neither sounds wholly at ease with the idiom. The *chanteuse* Ute Lemper is less inhibited by the popular nature of Weill's writing, but her Decca recording is hampered by some lethargic conducting from John Mauceri. Unfortunately, the most gripping account of all, from Gisela May and the Leipzig Radio Orchestra under Herbert

Kegel, recorded in the Sixties, remains at present unavailable. This leaves us with Angelina Réaux, an American soprano who is equally adept at singing Mozart as well as Weill. Her performance may be less inflected than that of some of her illustrious competitors, but there's greater spontaneity, and the text is delivered without unwarranted mannerisms. Masur provides a superb accompaniment – there's a lightness of texture and rhythmic incisiveness rarely encountered in rival recordings. A similar clarity of texture illuminates the more emotionally torrid music of Berg, thus making this imaginative coupling of two almost contemporary works an irresistible proposition. *EL*

ROBERT WHITE

Tudor Church Music: Magnificat; Lamentations; Exaudiat te Dominus, etc

Tallis Scholars/Peter Phillips

Gimell CDGIM 030 □ 67:59 mins □ 𝕆𝕆𝕆

Peter Phillips's highly informative insert notes to this disc introduce composer Robert White (c1538–74) as 'arguably the leading figure in that lost generation of English composers which came to maturity between Tallis and Byrd, in the middle of the 16th century'. White's spaciously scored music (with the treble in an ethereally high register) offers an effective stylistic blend, whose poignantly expressive text setting is characterised by an inspiring architectural splendour.

On this recording, the Tallis Scholars' customary attentiveness to linear and harmonic detail produces compelling, appropriately uplifting performances that are appealingly distanced from the microphone. Try the beautifully eloquent account of White's vividly descriptive, exultant setting of the Magnificat, or the elegant portrayal of the composer's ingenious formal design in 'Portia mea'. In addition, the Scholars demonstrate White's remarkable compositional range, through subtle handling of diverse vocal combinations. They luxuriate in the satisfyingly rich sonorities of 'Regina caeli' (for men's voices only), and delight in the imaginatively varied vocal groupings of the two 'Christa qui lux es' settings, and delicious 'Exaudiat te Dominus'. *Nicholas Rast*

Italienisches Liederbuch

Felicity Lott (soprano), Peter Schreier (tenor), Graham Johnson (piano)

Hyperion CDA 66760 □ 79:20 mins □ ❷❷❷

Wolf considered his 46 settings of Paul Heyse's German translations of *rispetti* – short Italian poems – 'the most original and artistically consummate of all my works'. Lott, Schreier and Johnson, on this recording, give us an artistically consummate performance. These musicians bring an immediacy and intimacy to both text and music, which is thrilling. Here is longing, humour, love, pain – all intense observations on the complicated landscape of human emotion. Lott relishes her cameo characterisations from girlish spontaneity in 'Nein, junger Herr' to mature reflection in 'Wenn du, mein Liebster'. There is a glorious warmth and openness to her sound throughout. 'Wir haben beide lange Zeit geschwiegen' and 'Wohl kenn ich euren Stand' are particularly beautiful.

Schreier's radiant tenor sound ranges from full-throated intensity ('Dass doch gemallt') to haunting pianissimo tenderness ('Sterb' ich, hüllt in Blumen'). This is a visceral account. Schreier elongates vowel sounds and indulges in other vocal mischief-making during the more humorous songs. Some may consider this a little overdone, but it certainly adds to the colour and intensity. This is especially Johnson's shining hour. His remarkable instinct for Wolf's detail, while moulding his playing around the vocal lines and delivering the nuances of the piano writing, is brilliant. *Elise McDougall*

Mörike Lieder

Brigitte Fassbaender (mezzo-soprano), Jean-Yves Thibaudet (piano)

Decca 440 208-2 □ 66:36 mins □ ❷❷❷

This is the *Mörike Lieder* we have been waiting for. When Hugo Wolf turned to the poetry of Eduard Mörike in the 1880s, he worked with such total absorption that the 53 settings he eventually produced have a white-hot energy of response and a psychological depth unequalled in his output.

Fassbaender selects just 25, but encompasses their entire world. With Thibaudet's magnificent piano-playing she re-creates their meditations and their dramas with an intelligence and commitment that few singers, save Fischer-Dieskau, have found before her.

The harmonic breadth and freedom of vocal line which Wolf learned from Wagner enables the heart to wander far and wide; Fassbaender and Thibaudet find a truly Wagnerian ecstasy within the small scale of 'Auf eine Wanderung', and in the eye of the meteorological and emotional storm of 'Begegnung'.

Both the intimate mysticism and the ruddy-cheeked outdoor life of the poetry of Mörike, the Swabian pastor, are drawn out in Wolf's music and re-created with new intensity in these performances. What's more, the music seems to be in just the right vocal and spiritual register for Fassbaender at this stage in her career. *Hilary Finch*

Spanisches Liederbuch

Anne Sofie von Otter (mezzo-soprano), Olaf Bär (baritone), Geoffrey Parsons (piano)

EMI CDS 5 55325 2 □ 108:59 mins (2 discs) □ ❷❷❷

Fischer-Dieskau and Schwarzkopf's superb 1968 recording of this cycle may once have seemed peerless, but this account by Olaf Bär and Anne Sofie von Otter is a serious rival, for theirs is an ecstatic performance – supremely intelligent, exquisitely modulated and moving. The late Geoffrey Parsons's contribution is, as ever, far more than mere accompaniment: his playing is deft and searingly idiomatic in a way that stresses – though subtly – the sometimes elusive, yet intrinsic 'Spanish' quality of this work, with its seguidilla and fandango rhythms, its echoes of castanets and dance steps.

Bär has conceived an order for the 44 songs that runs contrary to Wolf's instructions, but that makes greater dramatic sense as a recital, forming, within their 'sacred' and 'profane' sections, delightful dialogues and their own coherent sub-cycles.

In some ways the soprano Elly Ameling's performance of 14 of these songs – three sacred, 11 secular, arranged in apparently random order, and coupled with seven settings of poems by Mörike on a rival Hyperion disc – is even more immediately beautiful. Her voice has an engagingly animated and luxuriant quality, but though she is beguiling to listen to (and Rudolf Jansen provides outstanding support), Ameling's interpretation lacks the edge, the depth even, that makes von Otter's contribution to the complete cycle so stunningly authentic. *Claire Wrathall*

WOLPE

Quintet with Voice
see **CHAMBER**: WOLPE: Suite im Hexachord

ZEMLINSKY

Lyrische Symphonie; Symphonische Gesänge

Alessandra Marc (soprano), Håkan Hagegård
(baritone), Willard White (bass); Royal
Concertgebouw Orchestra/Riccardo Chailly

**Decca Entartete Musik 443 569-2 □ 65:14 mins
□ ❷❷❷**

Like Mahler's *Das Lied von der Erde*,
Zemlinsky's *Lyric Symphony* is an extended
symphonic song cycle of magnificent opulence
which draws its inspiration from the orient, in
this case a sequence of love poems by the
Indian Rabindranath Tagore. It's the one work
in Decca's marvellous Entartete Musik series to
claim at least a toe-hold in the repertoire. For
many years Lorin Maazel's evocative account
for DG, with the Berlin PO and the husband-
and-wife team of Varady and Fischer-Dieskau,
remained the firm recommendation for this
wonderfully sensuous score. But Chailly and
the Royal Concertgebouw, aided by
impassioned singing from Alessandra Marc
and Håkan Hagegård, surpass their German
colleagues in projecting the physical
excitement and kaleidoscopic colours of the
music.

The coupling of the rarely heard
Symphonische Gesänge, another song cycle
composed in the late Twenties, based on Black
American texts, shows Zemlinsky responding
to the starker musical styles of his younger
colleagues, Weill and Krenek. Willard White
captures to perfection the work's powerful
images of oppression, isolation and
persecution, and the recorded sound is
outstanding. *EL*

COLLECTION: CITY OF STRANGERS

Songs by Sondheim, Prévert, Brodsky, Celan, Eisler, etc (arr. Fontaine)

Ute Lemper (chanteuse); orchestra/Bruno Fontaine

Decca 444 400-2 □ 74:02 mins □ ❷❷❷

A CD called *City of Strangers* subtitled 'Songs
by Sondheim, Prévert…' might give the
impression of being predominantly a
collection of songs by Stephen Sondheim. But
no. Only four of the fourteen tracks are
attributable to him (and of those, one is part
of a medley). But Sondheim fans should not
be deterred for Lemper's treatment of these
few classics is powerfully original.

Her version of 'Losing My Mind' starts
mezza voce, building gradually to a climax of

such abandon that it's plain that this is a song
about being, not going, mad, and all the more
powerful for it. Barbara Cook's elegiacally
sweet-suburban and Liza Minelli's disco-
frenetic versions – both outstanding in their
way – pale by comparison. Augmented by
Bruno Fontaine's searing arrangement of
supper-club piano and sawing strings,
Lemper's interpretation of what has become a
standard is a harrowing experience. Her
version of 'Being Alive', however, is much
more straightforwardly epic, and would not
sound out of place on Broadway. And 'Another
Hundred People', sandwiched between 'La
belle saison' and 'Chasse à l'enfant', is
transformed into a shattering discourse on
urban alienation. Only 'Ladies Who Lunch'
seems overblown, grotesque even, in its
attempt to satirise its subject.

The rest of the disc covers more familiar
Lemper territory – words and music by
Jacques Prévert, Joseph Brodsky, Paul Celan
and others – mostly in the classic cabaret
tradition, but the collection as a whole works
brilliantly and proves just what a challenging
and accomplished musician, impressive
linguist and astonishing actress Lemper is.
Anything but easy listening. *Claire Wrathall*

COLLECTION: CONSORT OF MUSICKE

The Monteverdi Circle: Cor mio, deh non languire (settings from Guarini by Grabbe, Ward, A Scarlatti, Caccini, Banchieri, etc)

Consort of Musicke/Anthony Rooley

Musica Oscura 070989 □ 71:26 mins □ ❷❷❷

The Orpheus Circle: The Mad Lover (Blow, Lawes, Boyce, Eccles, etc)

Evelyn Tubb (soprano), Frances Kelly (triple harp)

Musica Oscura 070987 □ 66:58 mins □ ❷❷❷

The Orpheus Circle: Arie antiche (Caccini, Strozzi, Carissimi, Lawes, Blow, Purcell, etc)

Emma Kirkby (soprano), Anthony Rooley (lute)

Musica Oscura 070988 □ 63:32 mins □ ❷❷❷

The Purcell Circle: The Mistress (poems by Abraham Cowley, set by Purcell, Blow, Reggio, King, Turner, etc)

Consort of Musicke/Anthony Rooley

Musica Oscura 070986 □ 77:19 mins □ ❷❷❷

Musica Oscura, Rooley's own label, allows him
to unveil some exquisite music. The riches of
the ongoing series The Monteverdi Circle
include 21 settings of a single poem, Guarini's
lament 'Cor mio, deh non languire'. Far from
a daunting expression of unrelieved

melancholy, these reveal remarkably inventive madrigals and solo songs, notably by a German, Johann Grabbe, an Englishman, John Ward, and by Alessandro Scarlatti, writing in a consciously anachronistic style a hundred years later than the earliest setting.

The Purcell Circle is similarly confined to one 17th-century best-selling poet, Abraham Cowley, in 23 delightfully varied guises.

The Orpheus Circle, though, is free-standing: Emma Kirkby selects 11 of her favourite songs, from the familiar – Caccini's 'Amarilli mia bella' – to the unknown – John Weldon's enchanting love-song 'Nature Framed Thee', in which Venus wins her Paris. Kirkby's deft and agile vocalising creates a wonderful sense of spontaneity, while Evelyn Tubb focuses on the 17th-century fashion for 'The Mad Lover' with manic gasps and wide-eyed naivety in *sotto voce* reflections. *GP*

COLLECTION: CONSORT OF MUSICKE

D'India: Il primo libro de madrigali a cinque voci, 1607 (The Monteverdi Circle)

Consort of Musicke/Anthony Rooley

Musica Oscura 070985 □ **51:18 mins** □ ⊘⊘⊘

Notari: Prime musiche nuove, 1613 (The Monteverdi Circle)

Consort of Musicke/Anthony Rooley

Musica Oscura 070983 □ **52:10 mins** □ ⊘⊘⊘

Stradella: L'anime del Purgatorio (Favola in Musica)

Emma Kirkby, Evelyn Tubb (soprano), David Thomas, Richard Wistreich (bass); Consort of Musicke/Anthony Rooley

Musica Oscura 070984 □ **65:22 mins** □ ⊘⊘⊘

Ward: Madrigals and Fantasias (The Fanshawe Circle)

Consort of Musicke/Anthony Rooley

Musica Oscura 070981 □ **51:54 mins** □ ⊘⊘⊘

Ward: Psalms and Anthems (The Fanshawe Circle)

Consort of Musicke/Anthony Rooley

Musica Oscura 070982 □ **78:46 mins** □ ⊘⊘⊘

The Monteverdi Circle, an ongoing series to which these first two discs contribute, does not question the composer's stature, but reveals contemporaries no less great. D'India admitted delighting in 'unusual intervals, moving with the greatest possible novelty from one chord to another...', dramatically demonstrated in 'Crud'Amarilli', dissonance resolving to dissonance with intensity beating even

Monteverdi's famously lawless setting. It momentarily beats the Consort too. Elsewhere, they are admirably anchored.

Notari lived in London, though not before he had absorbed Monteverdi's new instrumentally accompanied madrigal style. This 1613 collection of exquisite solo and duet settings calls for some extraordinary agility – and a staggering falsetto excursion by David Thomas. He is also a vicious, sneering Lucifer in Stradella's *Souls in Purgatory*, retrieved from the archives of West German Radio. Powerfully dramatic, it has moments of deep poignancy.

John Ward, too, created some striking mannerist colours in anthems and madrigals. The six-part fantasias, lacking words to spur the imagination, are harmonically rather predictable and less interesting.

In a radio interview, Rooley explained that in performance his artists direct themselves. The singing here reflects this, committed and individual, yet unselfishly integrated throughout. All five discs expand our horizons. *GP*

COLLECTION: ECCO LA PRIMAVERA

Works by Landini, Magister Piero, Giovanni da Firenze, Lorenzo da Firenze & Jacopo da Bologna

Early Music Consort of London/David Munrow

Decca 436 219-2 □ **ADD** □ **50:02 mins** □ ⊘⊘

A welcome reissue of another of David Munrow's pioneering collections of early music, this 1970 recording focuses on Florentine music of the 14th century. Francesco Landini is the chief composer featured, his gentle, amorous *ballate* comprising over half of the vocal tracks, which also include madrigals and *caccia* (hunt) songs. A sprinkling of keyboard solos and sprightly dances fills out the set, the whole performed with the Consort's peerless blend of skill and vivacity. *Graham Lock*

COLLECTION: ELIZABETHAN AND JACOBEAN CONSORT MUSIC

Works by Morley, Byrd, Lupo, Campion, etc

Catherine Bott (soprano), Michael George (bass); New London Consort/Philip Pickett

Linn CKD 011 □ **58:28 mins** □ ⊘⊘⊘

In early 17th-century English music, the forces required were often vague – 'for one Voyce alone, or to the Lute, the Basse Viole or both if you please', as one preface put it. The response has often been merely pretty performances of songs, balletts and 'Fal-las'. This delightful disc demonstrates how Pickett's imagination and scholarship transform and refresh often familiar music. I've never enjoyed more 'Now is the Month of Maying', first on a 'broken consort' of violin, recorder, plucked strings and viol, then with soprano and bass voices, creating a wonderfully transparent ensemble.

The singers Catherine Bott and Michael George, while full of character, are beautifully focused and vibrato-free. Their tuning is spine-tingling, their words impeccable – put aside the booklet, sit back and enjoy a catalogue of bird-songs, two dialogues between nymphs and shepherds, and a very naughty song about Mother Watkins's ale.

Pickett takes a bold approach to 'divisions', decorating music which looks rather bleak on paper. The ornamentation here was improvised in the recording sessions, creating a sparkling sense of spontaneity. The dance is never far away either, with springy rhythms and shapely phrasing. An exceptional recording, not to be missed. *GP*

COLLECTION: THE ETON CHOIRBOOK

Vol. 1: The Rose and the Ostrich Feather
Vol. 2: The Crown of Thorns
Vol. 3: The Pillars of Eternity
Vol. 4: The Flower of All Virginity

The Sixteen/Harry Christophers

Collins 13142, 13162, 13422, 13952 □ 62:34 mins, 64:35 mins, 61:09 mins, 62:52 mins □ 🎵🎵🎵

Not since the early Seventies has there been an attempt to record complete this magnificent collection of music from the late 15th and early 16th centuries. This version surpasses all others, and there are musical wonders on each disc. Vol. 1, after a slightly over-insistent stab at Turges's *From Stormy Windes*, resolves into grand tranquillity with Cornysh's *Salve regina*. Vol. 3 has the most variety: Davy's *O Domine* shows clearly what a blend of male and female voices can achieve in this repertory, and Wylkynson's bizarre 13-part canon forced from me a grin of disbelief. Vol. 4 opens (like the choirbook itself) with Kellyk's memorable *Gaude flore virginali*, sung here with slightly less flexibility than it needs. But the prize goes to Vol. 2, which gives us a finely-paced and ravishing performance of John Browne's masterpiece, *Stabat mater*. This is music that quietly overwhelms. *AP*

COLLECTION: THE ETON CHOIRBOOK

Vol. 5: Voices of Angels

The Sixteen/Harry Christophers

Collins 14622 □ 62:10 mins □ 🎵🎵🎵

The earliest works on this disc are two pieces by John Plummer, glorious souvenirs of an earlier and specially English tradition where lower voices hover in long melismatic parallel lines, doubly sweet at honeyed Burgundian cadences. Two *Salve reginas*, one by Walter Lambe, one by Richard Davy, testify to the extraordinary vocal skills of English Renaissance choirs, boys as well as men. The chosen pitch is high (to accommodate the total compass of the music) and sopranos float effortlessly up to top A. Lambe's setting, written in duple time, encourages a strong metrical pulse and from it a powerful sense of purpose. There's a wonderfully uplifting harmonic twist, too, at cadences, where Lambe suddenly shifts unexpectedly to the major mode. Davy discovers colours which characterise a later age; three dark lower voices contrast with three transparent trebles and then all combine in a remarkably rich sonority. Foreigners were astonished at the quality of English choirs. Theirs were 'the voices of angels', a tribute which The Sixteen deserve no less today. *GP*

COLLECTION: THE FEAST OF FOOLS

New London Consort/Philip Pickett

L'Oiseau-Lyre 433 194-2 □ 75:19 mins □ 🎵🎵🎵

This disc will give enormous pleasure to the listener whether familiar or not with the wiles of medieval music. Philip Pickett has, with remarkable skill, selected from various manuscripts some of the most captivating examples of music associated with the medieval Feast of Fools. The feast was a celebration held some time between Christmas and Epiphany, but particularly on New Year's Day, the Feast of the Circumcision. The feast provided the clergy with an excuse to let their hair down, with a show of mock disrespect to the Church: singing lascivious songs, dressing up as women, eating sausage at the altar, and generally behaving in a totally unacceptable manner.

In 75 minutes of music, Pickett and his superb ensemble of singers and performers of assorted medieval instruments magnificently catch the high jinks and vitality of this medieval ritual, demonstrating – particularly in the outrageous *Mass of the Asses, Drunkards and Gamblers*, where mercy is solemnly sought from an ass (with appropriate braying…) – why the Church repeatedly tried to curtail this feast. The care and dedication put into the performance are handsomely rewarded with excellent recorded sound. *Annette Morreau*

COLLECTION: FRENCH SONG

Ravel: Shéhérazade; Berlioz: Les nuits d'été; Debussy: Chansons de Bilitis; Poulenc: 7 Mélodies

Régine Crespin (mezzo-soprano), John Wustman (piano); Suisse Romande Orchestra/Ernest Ansermet

Decca 417 813-2 □ ADD □ 68:22 mins □ 🎵🎵

Forget the sour oboe tone at the beginning of *Shéhérazade*, for this is one of the most sensuous performances of Ravel's cycle ever committed to disc. Crespin is in radiant voice throughout the three songs, and after an unpromising start Ansermet draws some quite ravishing playing from his orchestra.

I'm less convinced by the Berlioz, since Crespin's voice seems at times to sound too full-blooded for music of such gentle intimacy. Nonetheless, this too is a compelling performance, and again Ansermet provides sensitive accompaniments.

The other two items, recorded in the late Sixties, are also memorable. Few performers rival Crespin in delineating the voluptuous colours of Debussy's *Chansons de Bilitis*, while singer and pianist seem ideally attuned to Poulenc's seductive mixture of gaiety and sadness. *EL*

COLLECTION: GERUSALEMME LIBERATA

Settings from Tasso

Consort of Musicke/Anthony Rooley

Musica Oscura 070990 □ 60:22 mins □ 🎵🎵🎵

Musica Oscura, Rooley's own label, allows him to unveil some exquisite music. The riches of the ongoing series The Monteverdi Circle include these settings of poems from Tasso's *Gerusalemme liberata*, full of drama and passion, myth and history from the First Crusade. Outstanding are Giaches de Wert's extended account of Armida seducing Rinaldo with her magic and, in Monteverdi's own version, her crazed outburst at his desertion, her weeping evoked by poignant, unashamed glissandi.

The programme is cleverly structured. For instance, four settings of one text, as madrigals and solo songs, reveal the sharp divide between Renaissance polyphony and the new thinking which heralded the Baroque. The notes, by

Tim Carter, help to bring alive the context of these intensely personal and sensuous settings.

Throughout, the Consort of Musicke is highly polished, exquisite intonation flexing, as it must, in the ongoing polyphony, and settling on the sweetest of velvety cadences. The recordings have clearly been in store for some time, made in 1985 for Westdeutscher Rundfunk Köln: they richly deserve to see the light of day again. *GP*

COLLECTION: THE LILY AND THE LAMB

Chant and polyphony from medieval England

Anonymous 4

Harmonia Mundi HMU 907125 □ 66:45 mins □ 🎵🎵🎵

This beautiful meditation on the Virgin Mary and her Son is gently constructed from medieval songs, both sacred and secular. First we sense the wonderful variety of singing here: the bell-like echoes of 'O mors', the twangy Middle English vowels of 'Stond wel, moder' and the oily purity of 'Ave Maria gracia plena'. Secondly, we are drawn to the constancy of atmosphere. These acclaimed female singers do not always please the purists, but here they are breathing air from another planet. *AP*

COLLECTION: MAD SONGS

Songs by Purcell, Eccles, Blow & Finger

Catherine Bott (soprano), David Roblou (harpsichord), Mark Levy (viola da gamba), Anthony Pleeth (cello), Paula Chateauneuf (vihuela), Tom Finucane (lute)

L'Oiseau-Lyre 433 187-2 □ 71:44 mins □ 🎵🎵🎵

This disc reflects imagination and a knowledge of the repertoire, and if the state of madness has been represented in this way before (maybe it has), the quality of the performances and music makes it very attractive. The paradox is, of course, that composers portray disordered minds prettily, just as they give operatic villains fine tunes to sing.

Catherine Bott offers both tonal beauty and an imaginative range of delivery (including speech in the second Eccles song), so that each song displays its own world. The composers (including two anonymous ones) are all Baroque British, but there's ample variety here and no less imagination in the diverse accompaniments provided by David Roblou and his colleagues.

With so much that is pleasing, it's hard to single out specific songs, but the seven by John Eccles show what a splendid composer he was. Indeed, the whole disc offers fine singing and style, while the recording has a fine balance and natural fullness. *Christopher Headington*

Scarlatti: Stabat mater; Cavalli: Salve regina; Gesualdo: Ave, dulcissima Maria; Clemens Non Papa: O Maria, vernans rosa

Soloists; Monteverdi Choir, English Baroque Soloists/John Eliot Gardiner

Erato 4509-99717-2 □ 46:43 mins □ 🎵🎵

The opening impact of this disc – Domenico Scarlatti's contemplation of Mary at the foot of the cross – is an extraordinarily retrospective monument of counterpoint. It grows majestically from a single voice to a total of ten independent parts yet, for all its self-consciously archaic texture, it is richly melodic, and its harmonic language belongs clearly to the 18th century. The contrasts between soloists and choir look back to the Venice of 100 years earlier, represented in fact by Cavalli's four-part *Salve regina*. The disc continues to retrace the Marian theme through the harmonic iconoclasm of Gesualdo to a magically still reflection on Mary, *Vernans rosa* (Blossoming Rose), by the mid-16th-century Clemens. The accompanying booklet comments on the pieces chronologically, and I recommend listening in this order, reserving the grandeur of Scarlatti as a final climax.

The Monteverdi Choir of 1984 was a finely honed ensemble. A pity only that we have a mean 46 minutes of them here, and no words, let alone translations, in the skimpy booklet – surely not a necessary economy of reissuing at mid-price. Packaging apart, this disc is a wonderfully imaginative overview of two centuries of music honouring the Virgin. *GP*

Extracts from the Mass Propers for Epiphany and the Dedication; Pérotin: Organa; Machaut: Motets

Choir of the Benedictine Abbey of Münsterschwarzach/Godehard Joppich; Early Music Consort of London/David Munrow

DG 439 424-2 □ ADD □ 72:34 mins □ 🎵🎵

Informative booklet notes and thoughtfully expressive interpretations contribute to an enjoyable programme. The Münsterschwarzach choir reveal the timeless beauty of the elaborately melismatic, single-voiced Gregorian chant. David Munrow and his Early Music Consort are characteristically authoritative in the organa by Pérotin, in which chant is embellished by additional

voices, and the dense harmonic polyphony of 14th-century motets, sacred and secular, by Machaut. The recordings are vividly atmospheric. *Nicholas Rast*

Odes by Clarke, Hall & Blow; works by Finger & Morgan

Ruth Holton (soprano), Rogers Covey-Crump, Charles Daniels (tenor), Simon Birchall (bass): The Parley of Instruments Baroque Orchestra & Choir/Roy Goodman, Peter Holman

Hyperion CDA 66578 □ 63:29 mins □ 🎵🎵🎵

Purcell's death in 1695 produced an unprecedented outpouring of grief from poets and musicians alike. Of more than a dozen poems, at least five were set to music. Don't be afraid that this will be an hour of unremitting gloom – far from it. Clarke's anonymous poem 'Come, come along' begins with a jolly scene of pastoral merrymaking by shepherds on holiday before a messenger arrives to break the news of Purcell's death – astonishingly similar to the announcement of Eurydice's death in Monteverdi's *Orfeo*. Formal songs and dances give way to passionate fragmented music in an amazing dramatic outburst as Ruth Holton 'croaks the dreadful voice of doom'.

Blow's 'Mark how the lark and linnet sing' is music of which Purcell himself would have been proud, with its extraordinarily daring approach to dissonances. Covey-Crump and Daniels duet passionately, a pair of recorders joining in the imitations whether the harmony permits it or not.

This disc of inventive and moving music, performed with great affection, demonstrates very clearly what this English Orpheus series is designed to show – that English music didn't simply die out, swamped by foreign imports, after the death of Purcell. *GP*

Music for the Courts of Avignon and Rome

Orlando Consort

Metronome MET CD 1008 □ 70:50 mins □ 🎵🎵🎵

The old papal palace at Avignon is now empty and lifeless, but here is a rare chance to hear its defiant music again. Some of it is brilliant: in the anonymous *Pictagores/O terra/Rosa* the individual lines collide to quite dazzling effect; and in Tapissier's *Eya dulcis* the music swarms about our ears still imploring us, after all this time, to 'end the Schism'. Occasionally the English choral background of the singers produces an inappropriately subdued hue (as in the brightly Italianate *Già per gran nobelta*), but in general this is a powerful presentation. There are two real gems – a virtuosic account of the daring textures of Ciconia's *O Petre*, and the best-ever recording of Dufay's wonderful *Ecclesia militantis*. Who said the Middle Ages were the Dark Ages? *AP*

<hr>

COLLECTION: RUSSIAN SONG

Shostakovich: From Jewish Folk Poetry; Ippolitov-Ivanov: Four Poems of Rabindranath Tagore; Shaporin: 5 Songs; Kabalevsky: Six Joyful Songs

Zara Dolukhanova (mezzo-soprano), Nina Dorliak (soprano), Alexei Maslennikov (tenor), Eduard Grach (violin), Dmitri Shostakovich, Berta Kozel, Nina Svetlanov (piano)

Russian Disc RD CD 15 015 □ ADD mono/stereo □ 57:33 mins □ 🎵🎵

If I had to choose a single performance of a Russian song, it would have to be the incomparable Zara Dolukhanova's heart-breakingly controlled partnership with Shostakovich the pianist in the tragic Lullaby of his remarkable cycle *From Jewish Folk Poetry*: the effect this track has on anyone who hears it seems quite extraordinary. There are other gems here, of course, although the progress of an oppressed people from suffering to collective-farm happiness and faith in a brighter future – necessary if the songs were to reach any kind of public, and entrenched Soviet anti-Semitism made sure they were heard as little as possible – inevitably rings a little false. Admittedly, even the lightest numbers – sprucely done by Nina Dorliak (Mrs Sviatoslav Richter) and tenor Alexei Maslennikov – seem like great music when set alongside some of the old-fashioned romances by Shaporin and Kabalevsky; though even these help to flesh out western appreciation for Dolukhanova – a famous mezzo in her own land, but all too little known outside it. *DN*

<hr>

COLLECTION: SONGS OF DESIRE

Songs by Rimsky-Korsakov, Borodin, Mussorgsky, Balakirev & Cui

Olga Borodina (mezzo-soprano), Larissa Gergieva (piano)

Philips 442 780-2 □ 54:10 mins □ 🎵🎵🎵

Tchaikovsky's *romansi* may be well known in the West, but those of his peers, especially the so-called Mighty Handful (Balakirev, Borodin, Cui, Mussorgsky and Rimsky-Korsakov), have remained neglected; an oversight partially redressed by the issue of this splendid

collection of 25 of the 500-odd songs written by the Five.

Olga Borodina, perhaps the most dazzling of the outstanding singers to have emerged from the Mariinsky, has a mezzo of glorious richness, infinite expressiveness and profound beauty. And it's a voice that's still developing, for compared with her excellent Tchaikovsky recital released in 1994, she now sounds less innately Russian: her vowels are more open, her upper register more robust, her style more colourful.

She could not ask for a better collaborator than Larissa Gergieva, a pianist of impeccable artistry and sensitivity, whose ability to conjure atmosphere is remarkable.

Though performances and sound cannot be faulted, Philips should be ashamed of the booklet – at full price, a CD demands more than the sloppy translations provided. Without the text (and even a transliterated one is better than nothing), how can the listener ever fully appreciate the nuances of language, phrasing and rhyming scheme these evocative lyrics involve? *Claire Wrathall*

<hr>

COLLECTION: THE STUDY OF LOVE

French songs and motets of the 14th century

Gothic Voices/Christopher Page

Hyperion CDA 66619 □ 60:10 mins □ 🎵🎵🎵

The Study of Love is the last in Gothic Voices' trilogy of recordings exploring chansons and motets from 14th-century France. As the title suggests, virtually all the pieces here are settings of courtly love poems, and no such collection would be complete without the finest of medieval poet-composers, Guillaume de Machaut. Here he's represented by five works, including two beautiful monophonic *virelais* – intricate solo songs, evocatively delivered by Rogers Covey-Crump and Margaret Philpot.

While Machaut's skill at wielding a quill is well known, less familiar is the vast number of works by the ubiquitous Anon. Much of the fascination of this disc lies in the many unattributed pieces which have been realised here for the first time in recent years. In most cases, Christopher Page has decided that only one voice should present the text, while the others sing the French vowel 'u'. How they managed to do so without laughing I'll never know, but the results are surprisingly successful. Mention should also be made of the extraordinary Gloria setting by Pycard – never mind if it seems rather out of place here – and of the harp solos, sensitively played by Andrew Lawrence-King. These are subtle, intelligent performances reflecting the refined art of 14th-century French music. *Kate Bolton*

COLLECTION: THE SWEET LOOK AND THE LOVING MANNER

Trobairitz Love Lyrics and Chansons de Femme from medieval France

Sinfonye/Stevie Wishart

Hyperion CDA 66625 □ **69:45 mins** □ 🎵🎵🎵

Life for women in 12th- and 13th-century Provence was, it would seem, little different from the lot of women today. Many of the texts by these trobairitz (female troubadours) feature wife-beating, lesbianism, even an agony aunt ('shall I marry a man of our acquaintance, or shall I stay a virgin?'), as well as the better-known medieval preoccupations of unrequited love, infidelity and love cut short by death.

The impassioned aspirations of Sinfonye's performing style are in stark contrast to the idealised refinements of the perhaps more immediately lovable Gothic Voices. Listen to the instrumental introduction to the first song, 'Lady Carenza': there's nothing 'sweet' or 'loving' about the juxtaposition of unrelated sonorities – screams from the fiddle, a manic flourish from the lute and a crazy riff from the drums. I'm not sure what medieval ears would have made of it, but there's no denying Sinfonye's capacity for alerting us to a small but distinctive repertoire from an age and mentality essentially no different from our own. *Antony Bye*

COLLECTION: THE SYPRES CURTEN OF THE NIGHT

Elizabethan and Jacobean lute-songs by Campion, Holborne, Dowland, Ford, Danyel, Rosseter & Anon.

Michael Chance (countertenor), Christopher Wilson (lute)

Chandos Chaconne CHAN 0538 □ **65:09 mins** □ 🎵🎵🎵

Thomas Campion's evocative line 'The Sypres Curten of the Night' is an apt title for this collection: a sypres was a black crêpe cloth used at funerals, and the mournful quality of Campion's ayre reflects the nature of so much of this repertoire. The lute-song is one of the finer aspects of the English musical heritage, but the genre blossomed and withered within a remarkably short period, all the printed collections appearing between 1597 and 1622.

Several of the ayres included here may well be familiar to listeners – Campion's 'Never weather-beaten saile' (better known in its adaptation as an anthem) and Dowland's

jewels, 'I saw my Lady weepe' and 'Sorrow, stay – but for those seeking something more esoteric the collection has plenty to offer. The programme has been thoughtfully arranged, with lute solos by Anthony Holborne serving to lighten the mood between the song groups.

Michael Chance, choosing modern rather than 17th-century pronunciation, communicates the texts with sensitivity and understanding, and he has an ideal partner in Christopher Wilson. The recorded balance has been well judged, and each piece has a commendable sense of shape and direction. *Kate Bolton*

COLLECTION: A TUDOR COLLECTION

Works by Cornysh, Taverner, Tallis & Byrd

Tallis Scholars

Gimell CDGIMB 450 □ **299:37 mins (4 discs)** □ 🎵🎵

What a prize: some of the Tallis Scholars' best recordings of the past dozen years or so, in a boxed set of four composers spanning the entire Tudor period.

It is fascinating to trace the religious affiliations of each Tudor monarch through the music: under Henrys VII and VIII, the essentially English florid style, described by John Milsom in his excellent accompanying essay, of Cornysh (disc one) and Taverner (disc two, also issued separately, CDGIM 995); for Edward VI's Protestant reformers, Tallis's simple English anthems and, under Mary, his joyful return to Catholic opulence (disc three). Finally we enter the world of the Elizabethan Catholics' clandestine country house Masses for which Byrd so fervently wrote (disc four), of necessity paring down the lavish early-Tudor style to a crafted Classicism.

Flexible and finely balanced performances, with richly resonant sound. *Janet Banks*

COLLECTION: THE UNICORN

Myth and Miracle in Medieval France, 1200–1300 (Thibault de Champagne, Gauthier de Coincy, Marie de France, Monoit de Paris, Philippe de Thaon & Anon.)

Anne Azéma (soprano), Cheryl Ann Fulton (harp), Shira Kammen (vielle, rebec, harp), Jesse Lepkoff (flute)

Erato 4509-94830-2 □ **56:53 mins** □ 🎵🎵🎵

Here, medieval songs and literary texts are gathered delicately together into rapturous themes – The Bestiary of Love, Miracles and Wonders, and The Abbey of Love. Azéma's voice is clear and warm and at its best in the mid-range, unrhythmicised pieces such as

Thibault's 'Aussi comme unicorne sui'. The soft-focus atmosphere is maintained throughout this unusual and striking collection. This does mean that some of the drama is lost in Marie de France's 'D'un gupil', but the dancing rhythms of 'Je chevauchoie l'autrier' at the end are light and fantastic. This is a disc for those who like the dream-time approach to history. *AP*

COLLECTION: VENETIAN VESPERS

Music by Monteverdi, Rigatti, Grandi, Cavalli, Finetti, Marini, Banchieri, G Gabrieli & Fasolo

Gabrieli Consort & Players/Paul McCreesh

Archiv 437 552-2 □ 95:35 mins (2 discs) □ 𝄞𝄞𝄞

It's a delightful and apt idea to present this vital, colourful music, functioning in its religious context, as a living musical event complete with ambient noise, rather than a collection of pieces for the archives. The voices characterise superbly – as distant monks chanting plainsong with thin Continental vowels; singing sensuous love-songs to the Virgin; combining with rasping martial brass in the psalmist's violent imagery of war. The scale, 20 voices and 15 instruments, calculated from descriptions in contemporary letters, perfectly balances clarity with, at times, magnificently weighty sonorities.

Outstanding are two high falsettists – one scaling soprano G. No less ravishing are the duetting sopranos in two Monteverdi psalm settings – though occasionally, in 'Laetatus sum', for instance, speed favours virtuosity at the expense of dancing lilt.

Among some less-familiar composers, Giovanni Antonio Rigatti is a revelation, a contemporary of Monteverdi and almost his match – and otherwise totally unrepresented on record.

Put on headphones, turn out the light, and there you are in St Mark's, from the distant tinkling of the sacristy bell, through intensely expressive Marian motets bordering on the erotic in both text and music, to the luxuriant grandeur of double choirs and instruments echoing under those golden cupolas. *GP*

COLLECTION: VENICE PRESERVED

Vocal and instrumental music by Bassano, A & G Gabrieli & Monteverdi

Gentlemen of the Chappell, His Majesties Sagbutts and Cornetts/Peter Bassano

ASV Gaudeamus CD GAU 122 □ 61:57 mins □ 𝄞𝄞𝄞

The wealth, political power and pride of the 'Serene Republic' was nowhere more strongly focused than in San Marco, principal church of the state and private chapel of the doge. Its architecture, familiar to tourists today, invited the use of spatially separated groups, singing and playing antiphonally, uniting at the musical climaxes. In the gloriously spacious acoustic of the basilica, cornetti and trombones, strings, lavish continuo, solo voices and choir created some of the most opulent music western Europe has ever known.

Preserved here are motets and instrumental music by Giovanni Gabrieli, including the innovative *Sonata pian' e forte*, the contrasting dynamics bathed in resonance. Monteverdi is represented by two fine psalm settings from 1640, by now contrasting solo voices with choir and instruments. Three members of the Bassano family confirm the distinction of the director's ancestors – though they rather monopolise the text of an eye-straining booklet!

His Majesties Sagbutts and Cornetts, augmented by strings, organ and chitarrone and the Gentlemen of the Chappell (including four ladies), match the forces of the San Marco choir of the 1590s. All are so cleanly focused that they generate a rich sonority, recorded in a thrillingly wide wrap-around stereo. *GP*

Instrumental

ALBENIZ

Suite Iberia; Navarra (compl. de Sevérac); Suite Española, Op. 47

Alicia de Larrocha (piano)

Decca 417 887-2 ☐ 120:06 mins (2 discs) ☐ 𝄞𝄞𝄞

It's hardly news that Alicia de Larrocha plays this music as to the manner born. The pity is that she's been able to corner the market quite so completely. Time was, in the first half of this century, when a goodly number of great pianists, Artur Rubinstein prominent among them, championed the Spanish school. Not so in the latter half. There are just as many pianists today who *could* do wonders in this again-neglected repertoire, but no one of Larrocha's stature seems interested. Never mind. As long as these performances are current, Albéniz's cause will not be lost – and who knows what talent may be out there now, just waiting to be discovered by some enterprising record company. Larrocha's playing here may lack some of the crackling electricity and finger-numbing virtuosity which she so often brings to her public recitals, but here, nevertheless, are all the dramatic, stark contrasts (the snow and blistering sun of the Spanish landscape), the seductive sensuality and the fierce seriousness of Spanish art, mustered in a manner that simply rivets the attention. Superb. *JS*

ALKAN

Concerto for solo piano (Études dans les tons mineurs, Op. 39/8–10)

Marc-André Hamelin (piano)

Music & Arts CD-724 ☐ 49:58 mins ☐ 𝄞𝄞𝄞

The reclusive French virtuoso Charles-Valentin Alkan, friend of Chopin and rival of Liszt, has been described, justly, as 'the Berlioz of the piano'. His Concerto (the piano takes the role, with contrasted playing styles, of both soloist and orchestra) is one of the greatest piano

works of the Romantic era, and comprises merely three of his phenomenal 1857 set of Études in all the minor keys (others make up a four-movement symphony and an overture: the entire set is recorded by Jack Gibbons on ASV). The first movement alone is nearly thirty minutes long, the largest sonata structure in 19th-century piano literature, and probably the most taxing.

Alkan's music – aristocratic, powerfully rhythmic, endlessly inventive, building with severe logic on Beethoven and prophetic of such later figures as Mahler – attracts only the greatest pianists, and few enough of them. Busoni, Petri and Arrau were exponents of the Concerto, and it was finely recorded on LP by Ronald Smith and John Ogdon. Marc-André Hamelin's studio-based CD is in somewhat thin sound compared to his more recent and equally prodigious Alkan recordings for Hyperion. But this is the most assured version of the Concerto yet to be put on disc, and represents the summit of Alkan's alchemical art. *CM*

ALKAN

Trois Grandes Études, Op. 76
see Collection: Marc-André Hamelin Live at Wigmore Hall

CPE BACH

Sonatas in A minor, Wq 49/1, in E minor, Wq 59/1 & in G minor, Wq 65/17; 12 Variations on Folie d'Espagne; Fantasies in C, Wq 61/6 & in F sharp minor, Wq 67; Rondo in C minor, Wq 59/4

Andreas Staier (harpsichord, fortepiano)

Deutsche Harmonia Mundi RD 77025 ☐ 70:00 mins ☐ 𝄞𝄞𝄞

CPE Bach, eldest son of JS's second marriage, enjoyed in his own time a fame far exceeding that of his father. He remains among the more important composers in the history of keyboard music, and was perhaps the first great pioneer of the then newfangled piano (just as his brother JC, the youngest son, was the first to perform on it in public.) Haydn and Mozart were both greatly indebted to him, but today it's his chamber, orchestral and choral work rather than his keyboard pieces which largely keep his name alive. His most original music was written for players rather than audiences, and Staier, among the most lively and imaginative of scholarly virtuosi, has made a judicious and intriguing selection of Bach's private and more public styles, clearly relishing every note, every startling change of mood, texture and tempo, every felicity of keyboard technique. Two centuries on, Bach's emotional frames of reference have lost much of their immediacy, and modern listeners may have difficulty in loving this music, but in performances such as these its vitality, its ruminative introspection and its seemingly inexhaustible fund of ideas are abundantly clear and enjoyable. *JS*

BACH

Chaconne in D minor (transcr. Busoni, etc)
see Collection: Cathedrals in Sound

BACH

English Suites, BWV 806–11

Glenn Gould (piano)

Sony SM2K 52606 □ ADD □ 111:45 mins (2 discs) □ 🌑🌑

Gould's individuality (to put it mildly) doesn't endear him to everyone, and one can hardly quarrel with those who find him too mannered and idiosyncratic by half – these things are inevitably very personal – but how anyone can listen to these performances and not agree that of all keyboard instruments the piano is the ideal vehicle for Bachian polyphony is more than I can understand. Of course, Gould's piano was almost as unique as his way of playing it (he tinkered with it endlessly), but the combination, for this listener at least, is uniquely satisfying, eccentricities and all. No other version has revealed more to me about the music (and about the experience of music generally) or induced in me a more seraphic state of mind. The fact is that even in our obsessively objective age music belongs ultimately to the world of magic, and its deepest workings remain implacably and blessedly mysterious. Anyway, if you want a less quirky piano version, you can turn to the ultra-pianistic András Schiff on Decca, whose set has its own enchantments. Far removed from both of these, and not only because she plays the harpsichord, is the admirable Huguette

Dreyfus on DG, whose version is unmannered, restrained and stylistically faithful, combining scholarship and instinct to very pleasing effect. *JS*

BACH

The Great Fantasias, Preludes and Fugues

Christopher Herrick (organ)

Hyperion CDA 66791/2 □ 150:03 mins (2 discs) □ 🌑🌑🌑

Organs are notoriously difficult to record. They require an elusive balance between clarity of an often very complex sound and a bare, resonant acoustical background. Hyperion's team has got it absolutely right. Shut your eyes and you're there, in the nave of the Jesuitenkirche in Lucerne, below a magnificent new organ by Metzler. Herrick has been presenting a different instrument from this fine builder in each of his Bach recordings to date, and every one is a revelation.

The two discs contain the large-scale fantasias and preludes, with their respective fugues. (Toccatas come on another disc, also highly recommended.) Herrick immediately asserts his authority in the grand gestures of the G minor Fantasia, BWV 542, binding together its disparate elements – free fantasia, rolling sequences and pithy counterpoint. His clarity is immaculate, every note telling despite the reverberation – final chords linger for five seconds or so. For me, the late C major Prelude and Fugue, BWV 547, is a particular delight, the prelude dancing unaffectedly over very slow harmonies, the fugue a masterpiece of technical wizardry, culminating in a long-delayed, gigantic pedal entry. Herrick's musical inspiration, matched by his technique, does full justice to this pinnacle of the organ repertoire. *GP*

BACH

French Suites, BWV 812–17

Ton Koopman (harpsichord)

Erato 4509-94805-2 □ 70:26 mins □ 🌑🌑🌑

Happily, most of the current CD versions have a great deal to recommend them. Leonhardt on RCA, Hogwood on L'Oiseau-Lyre, the admirable Davitt Moroney on Virgin, Kenneth Gilbert on Harmonia Mundi and Huguette Dreyfus on DG are all thoughtful, well informed and masterly, and their versions should please all but the most opinionated die-hards. The harpsichordist who most consistently appeals to my own temperament here, however, is the exuberant Koopman, whose beautiful copy of a Ruckers instrument is one of the finest harpsichords ever recorded. The wonder here, as so often with this artist, is that he can be so supple and flexible on so implacably mechanistic an instrument, and with so little in the way of obvious rubato. A real joy, this. Those, like myself, who actually believe that the *piano* is the ideal vehicle for Bachian polyphony can turn with confidence to Schiff on Decca, whose blend of knowledge, imagination and pianistic mastery is wellnigh irresistible. Some, though, may find the pianism altogether *too* pianistic. For them, Glenn Gould should fill the bill. Replete with the usual baggage of idiosyncracies, most of them exhilarating, this is unquestionably the most compellingly fresh and engaging version ever to reach CD. *JS*

<hr>

BACH

Goldberg Variations

Glenn Gould (piano)

Sony SMK 52594 □ ADD □ 46:00 mins □ 𝄢𝄢

No player has ever been more closely identified with this monumental work than Gould, who came closer than anyone else, before or since, to making it a household name, beginning with this 1955 release, recorded when he was 23. Near the end of his tragically curtailed life (he died at fifty) he made a second studio recording, since when other tapes of concert performances have found their way on to CD. He was never a man to play safe, and in each of his performances he lived dangerously, revealing different things about the music and about himself. In 1955 he had few rivals in this work. Today we have an embarrassment of riches, including remarkable and penetrating versions from the pianists Schiff, Rosen, Tureck, Nikolayeva (wonderful, if a little Romantic for some tastes, on Hyperion), Chen Pi-Hsien (fleet, stylish and often entrancing on Naxos) and Daniel Barenboim, whose concert performance on Erato, taking all the repeats and one hour twenty minutes, is one of the most impressive and beautiful ever set down. Among the most distinguished of the historically orientated harpsichord versions, the ones that have given the greatest pleasure and nourishment to me are those of Pinnock on DG, Dreyfus on Denon and, most fruitfully of all, Gustav Leonhardt on Harmonia Mundi (an extraordinarily supple and subtle performance, not to be confused with his earlier and less rewarding version on Teldec). But when all is said and done, it's to

Gould's debut disc that I return most often, and from which I still derive the most illuminating insights. *JS*

<hr>

BACH

Italian Concerto; Chromatic Fantasy and Fugue in D minor, BWV 903; Capriccio on the Departure of a Beloved Brother, BMV 992; Toccata in C minor, BWV 911; Fantasia in C minor, BWV 906 (authenticity doubtful); French Suite No. 6 in E, BWV 817

Joseph Banowetz, Monique Duphil (piano)

Naxos 8.550066 □ 66:02 mins □ 𝄢

This is an immensely attractive recital, and its division between two players, neither of them big names, only serves to heighten the emphasis put throughout on the music itself. Banowetz has identified himself mostly with the Romantic repertoire, but his affinity with that music in no way impinges on his approach to Bach, which is of the most admirable purity, grace and style. His account of the *Italian Concerto* is as lovely and rewarding as any I've heard – wholly lacking in idiosyncrasy or poetic self-indulgence, and he brings the same qualities to everything he plays here. He's not out to prove anything, much less to put his stamp on the music. Sensitive, intelligent and with a masterly command of the keyboard, he trusts his composer and never attempts to encumber him with interpretative 'insights' or to telegraph his analytical acumen to the listener. The playing has a pervasive naturalness, and the twin elements of song and dance are kept in perfect balance. Nor is Monique Duphil any less winning. Her French Suite is as captivating and fluent as any on record. *JS*

<hr>

BACH
Die Kunst der Fuge; Clavier-übung, Part 2
see **CHAMBER**: BACH: Die Kunst der Fuge

<hr>

BACH

'Leipzig' Chorales, BWV 651–68; Six Schübler Chorales

Martin Souter (organ)

Isis CD 007, CD 008 □ 73:25 mins, 75:31 mins □ 𝄢𝄢𝄢

Souter discovered the 1696 Arp Schnitger organ in the Dutch village of Noordbroek. Where wealthier congregations have rebuilt their instruments, this has been sensitively enlarged without compromising the original. Souter explains that he 'gave up searching for different sounds, letting the organ choose registrations and guide me for tempo, style and articulation'. Registration is not simply listed but explained in a text bubbling with enthusiasm and profound affection for the instrument.

The result is outstanding. We are in the nave, with a gentle ambient sound throughout. The organ's colours are glorious. 'Schmücke dich' is tenderly moving, helped by the gentle tremulant vibrating not on one manual alone but within the lungs of the whole instrument. Occasionally, emotion gets the better of rhythmic stability, though the G major Prelude and Fugue, a bonus on the second disc, has a springing pulse to match its concerto spirit. There's a fine sense of musical integrity – many tracks must surely be of single, unedited 'takes', with Souter wholly engrossed in the total musical structure. *GP*

BACH

Partitas, BWV 825–30; Preludes, Fughettas & Fugues

Glenn Gould (piano)

Sony SM2K 52597 □ ADD □ 148:00 mins (2 discs) □ ⚫⚫

No player of modern times has achieved such a reputation for eccentricity as Gould, yet his cycle of the partitas, with one great and not shining exception, is perhaps the least idiosyncratic and most simply conceived of all the piano versions currently on offer. I know of no other account of the partitas as a whole which is more contagiously joyful. In later life Gould scorned his early Bach recordings, saying that they sounded like Chopin nocturnes. It's hard to agree. For the most part this is playing of an expressive subtlety rarely achieved and never surpassed, though the pianism itself is on the ascetic side. A more obviously 'beautiful' piano version is András Schiff's excellent if sometimes mannered account on Decca – this, not Gould, is Bach as Chopin might have played it. Among the harpsichordists, Christophe Rousset gives in many ways the most straightforward account, in which a Classical sense of proportion prevails, free of all exaggeration and idiosyncrasy. Due precisely to its simplicity of utterance and its deep but unobtrusive musicality, this is an ideal set for listeners just discovering this wonderful music. My personal favourite of all harpsichord versions, however, is undoubtedly Staier – a scholar and virtuoso who combines great learning with an infectiously exuberant imagination and a capacity for the most rapt contemplation. His vitality fairly leaps through the speakers,

though for some his high-voltage double-dotted rhythms and surfing scales may well be too sprung with nervous energy for comfort. It seems unlikely, though, that any more sheerly exciting playing of this music will ever be entrusted to the harpsichord. *JS*

BACH

Sonatas & Partitas, BWV 1001–6

Sigiswald Kuijken (violin)

Deutsche Harmonia Mundi GD 77043 □ ADD □ 128:22 mins (2 discs) □ ⚫⚫

Bach himself transcribed movements from these six works for organ with and without orchestral accompaniment, and for harpsichord. Others have arranged them for lute, guitar, piano (left hand and two hands), with piano accompaniment (Schumann and Mendelssohn, no less) – there's even a recording for marimba. The sheer scale of the pieces invites transcription: how can a four-part fugue fit on a violin? Yet return to the instrument for which they were first conceived, and Bach's judgement is magically vindicated.

Kuijken plays an Italian violin restored to its original design and strung with gut. His bow, from the same era, springs lightly off the strings, creating a fresh, open articulation. No less important is the acoustic of a room in a villa in Italy, resonant enough to build up towers of harmony from the notes of a single line (the 'double' of Partita No. 1's Sarabande) or to weld together the broken counterpoint of the epic fugues – 354 bars in Sonata No. 3. Technique is wonderfully assured, intonation true and dance rhythms secure yet flexible.

If, though, you prefer the smooth grandeur of a modern violin, Arthur Grumiaux (on the Philips mid-price Duo label, recorded in 1960–61) remains very persuasive indeed. *GP*

BACH

Suites for Solo Cello, BWV 1007–12

Anner Bylsma (cello)

RCA Victor Red Seal RD 70950 □ ADD □ 125:40 mins (2 discs) □ ⚫⚫⚫

These pinnacles of the cello repertoire were regarded as mere exercises or 'encores' until Casals first recorded them in the Thirties. Now there are a score or more recordings available. Bylsma's was the first on a 'period' instrument – gut-strung, without supporting spike and, most important, with a Baroque bow to lift as freely *off* the string as to draw sound *on* it. The resulting structural clarity of the preludes which open each suite, the light-footedness of the dances, have been a revelation. Rhythmically most testing of all is the final Allemande, so slow that it has almost lost touch with its dance heritage. Bylsma sustains its steady heartbeat so that a ballet dancer could still portray above it a poignant, stylised allemande.

Bylsma recorded the suites again in 1992, with a modern bow (Sony). The sound is smoother, more reassuring, but doesn't match his totally compelling sense of discovery in 1979. Then tone quality was drier, far from the comforting warmth of a Romantic instrument – for that, Fournier on DG is superb. But Bylsma's preludes have a wonderful sense of improvisatory freedom, while it's impossible to keep still as you listen to the dances. *GP*

Toccata and Fugue in D minor, BWV 565; Prelude and Fugue in G, BWV 541; Pastorale in F, BWV 590; Passacaglia and Fugue in C minor, BWV 582; Four Chorale Preludes; Two Fugues

Peter Hurford (organ)

EMI Eminence CD-EMX 2218 □ 73:30 mins □ *@@*

The subtitle describes Hurford 'playing organs of Bach's time'. The organ of the Martinikerk, Groningen, dates from 1481, but was rebuilt, restored or added to about half a dozen times. So only part is, *en passant*, 'of Bach's time'. It's a magnificent instrument, though, recorded spaciously, cleanly, and at a realistic distance.

I've heard Hurford advocate using a single stop when practising large-scale Bach. Such discretion characterises his whole approach, the opening D minor Toccata and Fugue – so often a grandiose affair from an overblown 'king of instruments' – gleamingly transparent, without losing its majesty. The 'Gigue' Fugue is unmuddied by a 16-foot pedal, an uplifting dance not by virtue of registration alone but through precise and positive articulation.

A particular treat is the less familiar pastorale, its third movement illustrating Bach at his most ornamentally melodious. The great C minor Passacaglia is imaginatively structured, from a *pleno* opening through graded rather than violently contrasting variations.

The instrument's specification is given, with stops dated. If they had been numbered, too, Hurford's choices of registration could have been listed – perhaps revealing that he does indeed play an organ of Bach's time. Whatever the case, Bach is superbly represented on this generous disc. *GP*

Trio Sonatas

Christopher Herrick (organ)

Hyperion CDA 66390 □ 72:00 mins □ *@@@*

Bach himself described his unique set of six pieces as 'sonatas', and they are indeed like keyboard reductions of trio sonatas for two upper instruments and continuo – as, incidentally, the Palladian Ensemble (Linn Records) play them very successfully. They owe much to other influences too: the G major Sonata starts with a powerful recurring theme and violinistic figurations of a Vivaldian concerto; the last movement is a fugue. Other movements adopt da capo or binary form, or are lyrical aria duets. But all are magnificent examples of Bach's utterly logical and inevitable counterpoint.

They are also extremely hard to play – probably intended as practice pieces for Bach's eldest son, Wilhelm Friedemann. Organists who have struggled with the three independent lines will marvel at Herrick's fluency – he even 'unsimplifies' Bach's pedal version of the G major fugue subject, restoring the foot-knotting version which the hands have just played. But he's no mere technician. While fast movements have a splendid rhythmic drive and impeccably articulated lines, slow movements are exquisitely shaped and flow effortlessly.

Recording quality is superb, the recently built Metzler organ of St Nikolaus, Bremgarten, in Switzerland, a delight to the ear, and the documentation exemplary. Outstanding. *GP*

Das wohltemperirte Clavier, Bks 1 & 2

Edwin Fischer (piano)

EMI Références CHS 7 63188 2 □ ADD mono □ 236:41 mins (3 discs) □ *@@*

For consistent musicianship at the highest level, piano-playing of unsurpassable beauty and a profound spirituality beyond compare, Fischer's famous recording from the mid-Thirties is likely to remain unique. On three mid-price CDs, it should be in every music lover's library, and deserves a place somewhere near the Bible. After Fischer, I've derived perhaps the greatest stimulation, joy and insight from Gould on Sony, but he's far too idiosyncratic and inconsistent to recommend as a first choice, unless you've already got a more conventional version. The most unapologetically pianistic of the several first-rate versions currently available is undoubtedly Schiff on Decca. Far removed from Gouldian harpsichord-emulation and closer in outlook to Fischer, his playing is a feast of pianistic sophistication, of stylishness transcending the merely stylistic, of polyphonic and rhythmic enlightenment, and penetrating imagination. Deeply personal without being idiosyncratic, it has something to offer to any serious music lover, of whatever persuasion. Among the excellent harpsichord versions, two have made the deepest impression on me, and they come from opposite ends of the spectrum. Landowska on RCA (1949–54) sounds very 'concert grand' by today's standards, but, my, what imagination, immediacy and musicianship! Almost a Trappist by comparison, Kenneth Gilbert on Archiv is a highly persuasive advocate of the 'less is more' approach. His is perhaps the ideal starting-point. *JS*

BALAKIREV/MUSSORGSKY

Balakirev: Islamey

Mussorgsky: Pictures at an Exhibition

Jenő Jandó (piano)

Naxos □ 8.550044 □ 55:37 mins □ ⦿

Balakirev's oriental fantasy *Islamey* is a prodigiously taxing composition, calling for insight and physical stamina if it is to register as it should. Jandó's account is vivid, imaginative and technically impressive, and this splendid interpretation provides an ideal foil to an epic performance of Mussorgsky's musical gallery visit, *Pictures at an Exhibition*. One could, of course, cite numerous releases devoted to this work; many cost well over twice as much as Jandó's Naxos offering, yet very few can offer comparable musical rewards. These are altogether fabulous performances, and recorded sound, though very occasionally constricted at major climaxes, is more than acceptable, and certainly unmissable at this price. Stupendous piano-playing, at the service of aristocratic, sensitive and highly compelling realisations of these works. Highly recommended. *MJ*

BARTOK

Dance Suite
see Collection: The Hungarian Anthology

BARTOK

Fifteen Hungarian Peasant Songs; Suite, Op. 14; Allegro barbaro; Three Rondos on Folk Tunes; Ten Easy Pieces; Three Burlesques; Romanian Folk Dances; Two Romanian Dances, Op. 8a

Peter Frankl (piano)

ASV CD DCA 687 □ 74:39 mins □ ⦿⦿⦿

Bartók was unquestionably one of the greatest piano composers of the first half of the 20th century. Yet the current catalogues boast surprisingly few alternative recordings of his voluminous output for the instrument. Setting aside for the moment the indispensable comprehensive survey from Zoltán Kocsis for Philips, the most attractive single-disc compilation surely comes from Peter Frankl. His programme encompasses a number of crucial works, of which the dynamic Suite of 1916, the *Allegro barbaro* and the *Three Rondos on Folk Tunes* are especially significant. At the same time it's regrettable that the disc doesn't include the equally important *Out of Doors* suite and Sonata. Nonetheless, Frankl more than makes up for these omissions with truly outstanding playing, and the engineering, too, is of the highest quality. *EL*

BARTOK

Sonata for Solo Violin
see **CHAMBER**: ENESCU: Violin Sonata No. 3

BEETHOVEN

Piano Sonatas in F minor, Op. 2/1, in A, Op. 2/2 & in C, Op. 2/3

Murray Perahia (piano)

Sony SK 64397 □ 67:47 mins □ ⦿⦿⦿

As ever, refinement and sophistication, multi-hued pianism and a complete lack of distracting idiosyncrasies are the chief hallmarks of Perahia's playing here. Those who like their Beethoven fists to the fore may sometimes find him a little over-fastidious, yet in no way does he obscure or smooth over the darker, turbulent, more acerbic side of Beethoven's character. Nor does he ever go to the opposite extreme and exaggerate the music's violence (as in the finale of Op. 2/1). What he does is to convey with the greatest immediacy its white-hot integrity and honesty – and its humour (the opening of the Second Sonata, for instance, or the finale of the Third). Nowhere is there a phrase that doesn't make its point, a gesture that fails to connect, a build that doesn't cohere. Nor, despite its keen analytical insights into the music's structure, is the playing remotely didactic. It's his extraordinary combination of vision, impulse, rhetoric and thought which finally makes Perahia so unostentatiously inimitable. Artistry of this kind will always be a rarity. But you get hardly less of it from Tatiana Nikolayeva on Olympia, whose 'live' recital is enjoyable, illuminating and invigorating in equal measure. *JS*

BEETHOVEN

Piano Sonatas in D, Op. 10/3, in C minor, Op. 13 (Pathétique), in E, Op. 14/1 & in G, Op. 14/2; Piano Sonatas in B flat, Op. 22, in A flat, Op. 26, in E flat, Op. 27/1 & in C sharp minor, Op. 27/2 (Moonlight)

Tatiana Nikolayeva (piano)

Olympia OCD 563, OCD 564 □ ADD □ 73:52 mins, 76:26 mins □ 🎵🎵

Despite an occasionally grating stridency of tone and some technical fluffs that suggest a case of nerves, this is some of the most musicianly playing you're ever likely to hear. Anyway, better a rough diamond than a glossy rhinestone. And a lot of this isn't rough at all. The polyphonic clarity, the range of colour, articulation and rhythmic movement, the large-scale 'breathing' of the phrasing – all these combine with still other virtues to produce a mixture of spontaneity and deep reflection which is the very essence of great playing. As one might expect of a great Bach player (and the dedicatee of Shostakovich's Preludes and Fugues), the melodic layering is not merely immaculate but richly characterised and continuously developmental. Again and again, details of the music's inner weave are illuminated with an almost orchestral range of hues and textures, and the dramatic pacing would put many an opera director to shame.

I'd recommend anyone to go out and buy these discs and not relinquish them for love or money. *JS*

BEETHOVEN

Piano Sonatas in C sharp minor, Op. 27/2 (Moonlight), in C, Op. 53 (Waldstein) & in F minor, Op. 57 (Appassionata)

Mikhail Pletnev (piano)

Virgin VC 5 45131 2 □ 67:11 mins □ 🎵🎵🎵

What a superb pianist Pletnev is. Occasionally quirky (as in his revelatory Scarlatti recording), he has the power to rivet the attention, even in works as familiar as this. The pianism itself is pretty stunning, though this isn't, of course, what one looks for first in a Beethoven player. But all the other requisite qualities are here too: a commanding grasp of large-scale structure with no sacrifice of foreground detail, a wide-ranging tonal palette never indulged for its own sake, a muscular approach to rhythm which nevertheless avoids anything divisive or stodgy and a convincing blend of poetry and heroism. A winner in every way. *JS*

BEETHOVEN

Piano Sonatas in G, Op. 31/1, in D minor, Op. 31/2 (Tempest) & in E flat, Op. 31/3

Richard Goode (piano)

Nonesuch 7559-79212-2 □ 67:42 mins □ 🎵🎵🎵

If you want all three Op. 31 sonatas on a single disc, you won't find anything better than this. Even more than in his traversal of Op. 10 (now inexplicably deleted), this demonstrates the sheer range of Goode's approach to Beethoven, each performance being perfectly tailored to the demands of the particular music at hand. The wit and élan of the sadly neglected G major Sonata are delicious, the moodiness and unique colouration of the *Tempest* Sonata are wonderfully conveyed, and the unbuttoned Sonata in E flat is an exhilarating explosion of Beethovenian virtuosity and high spirits. If, on the other hand, you're not particular about completeness here, you'll not find anything superior to Perahia on Sony, who leaves out the first of the triptych but gives us the wonderful *Les adieux*, Op. 81a, instead – a performance unsurpassed in its combination of elegance, poetry, jubilation, colour and a continuous sense of movement. Unmissable, really. And then there's the wonderful Nikolayeva on Olympia, whose 'live' Moscow recital leaves out Op. 31/3 but includes a marvellously vital and imaginative account of the *Pastoral* Sonata, Op. 28. Rich pickings. *JS*

BEETHOVEN

Piano Sonatas in E minor, Op. 90, in A, Op. 101, in B flat, Op. 106 (Hammerklavier), in E, Op. 109, in A flat, Op. 110 & in C minor, Op. 111

Alfred Brendel (piano)

Philips Duo 438 374-2 □ ADD □ 148:26 mins (2 discs) □ 🎵🎵

The listener is extraordinarily well served when it comes to these greatest of all Beethoven's sonatas, with absolutely first-rate accounts from such diverse pianists as Goode, Pollini, Ashkenazy, Barenboim (on EMI and DG), Serkin (on Sony; his DG account, made in his late old age, is bitterly disappointing), Kempff (two versions) and Solomon. At the time of writing, Kovacevich, on EMI, has yet to do Opp. 106 and 109, but his recordings of Opp. 90, 101, 110 and 111 are of superlative quality, probing, pianistically all-encompassing and beautifully recorded. Goode's account is immensely impressive but lacks something of the incandescence that so often characterises his concert performances. Pollini is commanding to the nth degree but sometimes lacks a certain suppleness and continuity of line, and Barenboim, in both his versions (early on EMI, recent on DG) combines searching intelligence and pianistic authority. Brendel is now recording his third complete cycle (and on present evidence his greatest), but these performances (from his second) are quite great enough to be getting on with before he completes his latest traversal. Despite occasional whiffs of didacticism, they leave no stone unturned in their search for the music's essence, and combine finesse of detail, richness of pianistic resource and a magisterial overview that makes no sacrifice of incidental beauties (and jokes) along the way. A superb achievement at every level. *JS*

BEETHOVEN

Variations and Fugue in E flat, Op. 35 (Eroica); 32 Variations in C minor, WoO 80; Six Variations in F, Op. 34; Six Variations on 'Nel cor più non mi sento' by Paisiello, WoO 70

Jenö Jandó (piano)

Naxos 8.550676 □ 53:52 mins □ 𝄞

Any performance of the so-called *Eroica* Variations which can match the magisterial Gilels on DG, the towering, implacable Richter on Olympia, the almost Mozartily elegant Lortie on Chandos and the profoundly searching Brendel on Philips must be pretty good. Jandó is as prolific a recording artist as we've seen for some time, but his output has been remarkably variable. At his best, however, he's to be counted among the great pianists, and this disc finds him very nearly at his peak. The sonority isn't as multi-dimensional as Gilels's, perhaps, nor is there quite the sense of life-or-death concentration that you get with Richter, but who's to complain? This is A1 stuff, giving you the music, the whole music and nothing but the music. Free of idiosyncrasy and narcissistic didacticism, but deftly balancing the nobility, lyricism, toughness and arrogance that add up to Beethoven, this is one of the best, and best recorded, discs in the burgeoning Naxos catalogue. At bargain price, it's a must. *JS*

BEETHOVEN

33 Variations on a Waltz of Diabelli, Op. 120

Michael Oelbaum (piano)

Bridge BCD 9010 □ ADD □ 57:04 mins □ 𝄞𝄞𝄞

Only Bach's *Goldberg* Variations challenge the Diabelli's status as the greatest set of variations ever written. Unlike the *Goldberg* Variations, however, they can be as formidably difficult to listen to as to play. No one performance of such a work can possibly embrace all its possibilities. When we listen to Schnabel, or Serkin, or Brendel, or Kovacevich, or Horszowski (whose astonishingly profound and virtuosic performance on Pearl was recorded when he was ninety – and still had a decade of performing ahead of him), we're eavesdropping on an act of sustained concentration and meditation such as few works can elicit. We owe them all our attention and deep respect. The idea of 'best' becomes a nonsense. All of the pianists mentioned offer genuinely great performances, and each enjoys world fame. Yet none has taught me more about the piece than the otherwise wholly obscure American Oelbaum, of whom the record catalogues of two decades mysteriously reveal no other trace. It's not perhaps the most 'beautiful' performance (is the work itself?), but it goes deeper than most. Seek it out. *JS*

BERG

Piano Sonata
see Collection: The Glenn Gould Edition

BLACHER

Sonatina No. 2
see **ORCHESTRAL**: Collection: Testimonies of War

BRAHMS

Intermezzi, Op. 117; Piano Pieces, Opp. 118 & 119; Rhapsodies, Op. 79

Radu Lupu (piano)

Decca 417 599-2 □ ADD □ 70:56 mins □ 𝄞𝄞𝄞

Lupu's recording of these almost impermissibly touching, autumnal works (I exclude the rhapsodies from this description) is currently unchallenged by any single disc in the catalogues – though Katchen's, available at present only in a high-calorie six-pack, also from Decca, is likewise deeply satisfying, and Kovacevich on Philips is unlikely to disappoint. But while he leaves one in no doubt as to why Brahms poignantly referred to some of these late pieces as 'the cradle songs of my sorrows', Lupu is no 'mere' lyricist. True, his lyrical playing is of unsurpassed beauty and refinement, but he's equally true to the impassioned, the skittish and the rhetorical side of Brahms's nature. And can anyone sustain the charge that Brahms's textures are thick and heavy in the face of evidence like this? Rather, Lupu continually bears out Schnabel's unexpected description of Brahms as 'the first impressionist'. This is playing of the utmost sophistication, perfectly recorded and almost painfully immediate. *JS*

BRAHMS

Piano Pieces, Op. 76; Ballades, Op. 10; Scherzo, Op. 4; Piano Concertos Nos 1 in D minor & 2 in B flat

Stephen Kovacevich (piano); LSO/Colin Davis

Philips Duo 442 109-2 □ ADD □ 156:36 mins (2 discs) □ 𝄞𝄞

All the recordings of Brahms's Op. 76 that mean most to me are embedded in larger collections, of which Julius Katchen's on Decca (six discs) is the largest and best of all the solo sets. Kovacevich's, on the other hand, comes in an extraordinarily bounteous double pack which is a veritable feast of first-rate Brahms playing. Powerful, intense, passionate but never sentimental, his playing here combines a penetrating intelligence with a formidable technical and musical grasp of the pieces' inner logic. They unfold and develop with a deeply organic sense of Brahms's creative genius, and a poignant insight into the vulnerability behind the music's emotional forthrightness. Altogether a distinguished issue. *JS*

BRAHMS

Piano Sonata No. 3 in F minor; Intermezzo in E, Op. 116/6; Romance in F, Op. 118/5; Ballades, Op. 10

Artur Rubinstein (piano)

RCA Victor Gold Seal 09026 61862 2 □ ADD □ 62:50 mins □ 𝄞𝄞

Perahia's account of Brahms's F minor Sonata on Sony is widely admired and comes at the top of many people's lists. Just why it doesn't top my own is difficult to say, since by every objective criterion it's unassailable (in textural clarity, suppleness of line, structural grasp, etc it's unsurpassed). One feels that there isn't a bar that hasn't been deeply considered – but perhaps that's just it. It has everything but spontaneity. That and a certain rich, velvet, brown-bear sonority that seems to me essential to Brahms's particular sound-world. This is a cool, feline Brahms, and perhaps my own vision of Brahms is simply too canine. The performance that's made the deepest impression on me is Rubinstein's (not least in its ebullient warmth and its continuous forward thrust). Strange to say, in some ways it's not as sophisticated as Perahia, or at least not as conspicuously so – but therein may lie part of its virtue. There's no sense of a magnifying glass or a microscope here.

Rubinstein grabs the piece whole, embraces it wholeheartedly and puts one immediately in touch with the spirit of its composer. And the same holds for the other pieces here. Of similar cast and quality, and at budget price, is Idil Biret on Naxos – a powerfully impressive performance, also with the Ballades as filler. *JS*

BRAHMS

Variations and Fugue on a Theme of Handel, Op. 24; Piano Pieces, Op. 118; Rhapsodies, Op. 79

Emanuel Ax (piano)

Sony SK 48046 □ 67:41 mins □ 𝄞𝄞𝄞

Ax's disc is a winner – a superbly commanding and consistently penetrating account, but one in which the intellect is never allowed to take precedence over spiritual warmth, or clarity of texture over tonal beauty. While not perhaps as supremely elegant as Solomon (APR, Testament) and the sadly deleted Bolet on Decca, this is at once a powerfully integrated and a kaleidoscopic performance, revelling in every degree of light and shade and moving naturally from crystalline brilliance to tender introspection, from heroic rhetoric to an almost lacy delicacy. The cumulative effect of these finely crafted variations has seldom been so shrewdly moulded. The mounting excitement (and virtuosity) of the approach to the fugue is thrilling, and the fugue itself is a model of combined monumentality and grace. As in the variations, Ax's approach to Op. 118 is essentially Classical in outlook, beautifully proportioned, clean in line, never glutinous, and alive at all times to the almost unbearable immediacy and tenderness of this music. Nor do the Rhapsodies disappoint. This is a great pianist playing greatly. *JS*

BRAHMS

Variations and Fugue on a Theme of Handel
see also SCHUMANN: Fantasiestücke

BRAHMS

Variations on a Theme by Paganini, Bks 1 & 2; Ballades, Op. 10

Earl Wild (piano)

Vanguard 08 4034 71 □ ADD □ 49:15 mins □ 𝄞𝄞

The trouble with Brahms's notoriously difficult Paganini Variations is that pianists tend to mistake them for a kind of super-Czerny, chopping up the more obviously study-like ones with a chugga-chugga, four-square phrasing that wholly obscures the fact that these are at least as much studies in pianistic sonorities as in prestidigitation. Wild never falls into that trap, and it's a tribute to his innate musicianship that one hardly notices the astonishing feats of virtuosity which he dispenses at almost every turn. He's one of those rare pianists who make these wonderful variations beautiful from start to finish. Not that he lacks bravura or rhetorical flair. Far from it. But he continually focuses our attention on the extraordinary subtlety and (yes) lightness of Brahms's writing with a keen understanding that the essence of a truly Brahmsian sonority is polyphonic not chordal. The suppleness and spring of his rhythm are matched by the exemplary clarity of his articulation, and his lyricism is worthy of the finest singers. Of current versions his is matched, in my view, only by Katchen's more fruitily robust performance on Decca, but that's available, at present, only in a six-disc set. *JS*

BRITTEN
Cello Suites Nos 1 & 2
see **CHAMBER**: BRITTEN: Cello Sonata

BRITTEN
Elegy for Solo Viola
see **CHAMBER**: Collection: English Music for Viola

BUSONI
Fantasia Contrappuntistica; Fantasia nach JS Bach; Toccata

John Ogdon (piano)

Continuum CCD 1006 □ ADD □ 59:56 mins □ ✪✪✪

The *Fantasia contrappuntistica*, Busoni's most monumental piano work, combines his creative completion of the unfinished fugue from Bach's *Kunst der Fuge* in a seamless continuum with his latest discoveries in contemporary harmony, polyphony and post-Lisztian transcendental virtuosity. There are several versions, including one for organ and a final one for two pianos (superbly interpreted by Ronald Stevenson and Joseph Banowetz on Altarus). The 'edizione definitiva' for solo piano is, however, one of Busoni's cardinal achievements, and a standing challenge to the greatest pianists of any age.

John Ogdon's towering advocacy, majestic in architecture and demonic in dynamism, projects this visionary and philosophical work more eloquently than any other recorded version. And his incandescently spiritual presentation of the *Fantasia nach JS Bach* – not a 'Bach–Busoni' arrangement but Busoni's profoundly affecting elegy, incorporating Bach material, on the death of his father – is quite possibly the greatest performance of anything

that Ogdon committed to disc. These recordings (originally by Altarus), from the last years of Ogdon's career, illustrate the heights of wisdom to which his playing finally attained. The extraordinary account of Busoni's Faustian Toccata, thrown off almost impromptu at the end of a session, is utterly compelling despite fistfuls of wrong notes. *CM*

BUSONI
Sonatina No. 6
see Collection: Marc-André Hamelin Live at Wigmore Hall

BUXTEHUDE/SWEELINCK
Organ Works

Piet Kee (organ)

Chandos Chaconne CHAN 0514 □ 64:40 mins
□ ✪✪✪

Two of the most influential composers of Baroque organ music are represented here on an organ, in the Grote Kerk, Alkmaar, which uniquely suits both of them. The organ was built shortly after Sweelinck's death, and rebuilt by the legendary Schnitger, making it no less ideal for interpreting Buxtehude. For organ buffs, a lot of information is given – not only the specification of the present organ, recently restored, but the registration of each section of each piece. Variations by both composers invite Kee to explore some extraordinary colours, some unique to this instrument.

Recorded sound is excellent – distant enough to provide a deep perspective, bathed in resonance yet, thanks to Kee's open-textured articulation, fresh and transparent. Close your eyes, and you will sense the Gothic grandeur of this fine Dutch church, a unique organ, and music from two profoundly influential composers of the Baroque. *GP*

CARTER
Changes; Gra; Riconoscenza per Goffredo Petrassi; Scrivo in vento
see **CHAMBER**: CARTER: Eight Compositions (1948–93)

CHAMINADE
Piano Works

Peter Jacobs (piano)

Hyperion CDA 66584 □ 71:20 mins □ ✪✪✪

Cécile Chaminade (1857–1944) was one of the most successful women composers in history. At one time her pieces were found on almost every drawing-room piano. Anti-populist snobbery, and the fact that hardly anybody has pianos in the drawing-room any more, effectively killed off her music for many decades, but as the selections recorded by Peter Jacobs (and also Eric Parkin on Chandos) show, she was not only technically assured but highly gifted within her chosen modest compass. She belongs as definitely to the history of French piano music as Fauré, Chabrier or Saint-Saëns. Her most famous piece is the sub-Lisztian concert étude *Automne*, grandly expounded here, but the 16 other items show that she spanned a wide range, from delightfully mock-Baroque nods at the style of the *clavecinistes* (eg in *Autrefois*) to the dark and haunting barcarolle of *Pêcheurs de nuit*. Jacobs treats the music with affection, but also respect; he's served by an excellent recording. This is the first of three Chaminade discs he has made. *CM*

CHOPIN

Ballades Nos 1–4; Waltzes in E flat, Op. 18 & in A flat, Op. 42; Nocturne in F, Op. 15/1; Mazurkas in F minor, Op. 7/3, in A minor, Op. 17/4 & in D, Op. 33/2; Études in E, Op. 10/3 & in C sharp minor, Op. 10/4

Murray Perahia (piano)

Sony SK 64399 □ 60:41 mins □ 𝟈𝟈𝟈

In the degree of its refinement and sophistication, the range of its pianism, as in its complete lack of distracting idiosyncrasies, this may well take us as close to Chopin's own playing as we'll ever get. For some listeners, brought up, perhaps, on the muscular, robust lyricism of Artur Rubinstein, Perahia may seem at times a little over-fastidious (in itself a highly Chopinesque characteristic), but this is by no means pretty-pretty Chopin. In no way does it obscure or cosmetically smooth over the darker, turbulent, more acerbic side of Chopin's highly complex character. Nor does it go to the opposite extreme and exaggerate the music's violence. What it does do is to convey with almost painful immediacy the profound, almost pathological sadness that haunted Chopin's brief life, yet nowhere does it approach sentimentality.

Among the most remarkable facets of Perahia's playing is the degree to which he integrates passion and control, grief and discipline, anger and resignation, just as Chopin did. It's this extraordinary combination of vision and impulse which finally makes the playing quite inimitable. *JS*

CHOPIN

Études, Opp. 10 & 25; Trois Nouvelles Études

Louis Lortie (piano)

Chandos CHAN 8482 □ 67:21 mins □ 𝟈𝟈𝟈

The standard of current recordings here is mind-boggling. No sooner do you get your breath back after Pollini's astonishing playing on DG than along comes Lortie, combining a dazzling and resourceful technique with quite exceptional poetic insight and pianism of untrammelled beauty. Just as you conclude that Ashkenazy's traversal on Decca must be unbeatable, you discover the younger Ashkenazy on Saga. Strangely, neither Rubinstein nor Horowitz ever recorded the Études entire, but Cortot did, and what he misses in notes he makes up for in a depth of musical vision and pianistic sophistication which has never been excelled. No performance has given me more food for thought, or more abiding inspiration. At present it comes only as part of an invaluable six-disc set from EMI, and of course having been set down in 1942 it's not exactly the latest in hi-fi, though the transfers have been excellently done. In any case it's required listening for anyone who takes Chopin seriously. Of more recent recordings, however, I've heard nothing to surpass Lortie, who consistently manifests Chopin's famous exhortation to his pupils, 'Souplesse avant tout!' (Suppleness before everything), and employs a colouristic range matched only by Cortot. *JS*

CHOPIN

Mazurkas Nos 1–51

Artur Rubinstein (piano)

RCA Victor Red Seal RD 85171 □ ADD □ 140:08 mins (2 discs) □ 𝟈𝟈𝟈

Chopin's mazurkas are perhaps the most elusive branch of his output, easily made to sound banal when in fact they contain much of his most complex, subtle and revolutionary music. Rubinstein recorded them twice, and both are outstanding sets, whose robustness and inimitable rhythmic inflections (probably impossible for anyone not raised in the Polish tongue) are complemented by a pervasive underlying melancholy which may surprise those who think of this pianist only in terms of extroversion and irrepressible *bonhomie*. The earlier, EMI set, made in the Thirties, before thoughts of posterity added caution to his studio armoury, has a degree of spontaneity, at times even an exhilarating sense of danger, which isn't always so evident here, but the gains in accumulated wisdom outweigh the losses, and this version can be recommended without hesitation. The earlier set is still available, however, in a three-disc box from EMI which includes as well the complete polonaises and scherzos. And if the mazurkas are unfamiliar to you, I recommend as a taster Evgeny Kissin's 1993 Carnegie Hall recording (also RCA). He plays 11 of them, and if this doesn't get you nothing will. In any case, you also get a superlative account of the B minor Sonata. *JS*

CHOPIN
Mazurkas, Études, Waltzes, etc
see also SCHUMANN: Kreisleriana

CHOPIN
Nocturnes (complete)

Vladimir Ashkenazy (piano)

Decca 414 564-2 □ ADD/DDD □ **111:32 mins** (2 discs) □ ❷❷❷

Eloquent, unfailingly beautiful in tone and free of mannerism, Ashkenazy combines in almost perfect balance the simplicity of utterance required of all great Chopin playing and the inner tension, even turmoil, that so often lies behind it. But we're faced here with an embarrassment of riches: Katin's cycle on Olympia is profoundly poetic, consistently integrating subtlety and strength with complete naturalness, and an unerring sense of proportion which equally informs his accompanying account of the Impromptus. If he lacks anything, it's that final underlying shaft of violence that finally confirms Chopin as a tragic composer. Biret on Naxos, too, is richly rewarding. At every level her playing is blessedly curvaceous, communicating the 'singing' ideal which lies behind most of Chopin's music. This is a bargain in every sense. Rubinstein's 1965 readings for RCA are unequivocally virile, leaving one positively agape at Field's quip that Chopin was 'a sick-room talent'. His big, singing legato soars like an eagle over the supplest of accompaniments, and his rhythm is continuously on the move. Arrau on Philips is perhaps too idiosyncratic for a first choice, but this is nevertheless one of the noblest and most profound Chopin recordings ever made. *JS*

CHOPIN
Nocturne in C minor, Op. 48/1; Prelude in C minor, Op. 28/20
see Collection: Cathedrals in Sound

CHOPIN
Piano Sonata Nos 2 in B flat minor, Op. 35 & 3 in B minor, Op. 58; Ballades Nos 1–4; Nocturne in E flat, Op. 9/2

Alfred Cortot (piano)

Biddulph LHW 001 □ ADD mono □ **77:16 mins** □ ❷❷

1928 is a long time ago. But I haven't heard any performances of the Chopin sonatas which have told me more about the composer or about the works themselves than these, of which the B flat minor Sonata came first, the B minor following on three years later in 1931. I've chosen this disc for a simple reason. People will buy the wonderful recordings of Perahia, Pollini, Rubinstein, Horowitz anyway. They recommend themselves. And they *are* great. But who other than confirmed antiquarian pianophiles will think of buying this old crock of hiss and crackle and (occasional) missed notes? It's time the secret was out – to the big record-buying public: Cortot was one of the greatest giants in the history of musical performance. Even through all the gunge of seventy years' wear and tear you can hear what a wizard he was as a colourist, how incomparably he could shape a melodic line, and spin it out further than a champion angler on a good day. But most of all how he understood this *music*. You won't find better Chopin-playing anywhere. And talk about value for money! Both sonatas *and* the four Ballades *and* a nocturne (and in the best possible transfers)? Unbeatable and unmissable. *JS*

CHOPIN
Polonaises (complete); Andante spianato and Grande Polonaise; Funeral March, Op. 72/2

Cyprien Katsaris (piano)

Sony S2K 53967 □ **138:11 mins** (2 discs) □ ❷❷❷

Katsaris is a Chopin player of exceptional elegance. Fingers capable of meeting any challenge are complemented by footwork of great variety and resource (Chopin was the first genuinely great pioneer of the pedals, an aspect of his music which can hardly be over-estimated). From the very opening of this recital he shows a lovely suppleness of line. His use of rubato, too, is of an aristocratic restraint that Chopin himself would almost certainly have applauded. Equally impressive is his use of silence as an agent of rhythmic energy. And in the whole of this recital there's nary a bang to be heard. The sound is always beautifully rounded – often powerful but never strident.

It's entirely consistent with his beautifully idiomatic understanding of Chopin's sound-world that Katsaris avoids exaggeration of all kinds, and draws many of his most telling effects from the lower end of the dynamic spectrum. He has, too, a keen ear for Chopin's undercover polyphony, inner voices being enhanced with both subtlety and eloquence (especially striking, perhaps, in the easily ponderous C minor Polonaise and in the great and elusive Polonaise-Fantasy). *JS*

CHOPIN

Preludes (complete); Barcarolle, Op. 60; Polonaise in A flat, Op. 53; Scherzo No. 2 in B flat minor, Op. 31

Martha Argerich (piano)

DG Galleria 415 836-2 □ ADD □ 62:00 mins □ 🎵🎵

No great Chopin player has neglected any of these works, but in the case of the Preludes there may be only one who has surpassed this performance, and that's Alfred Cortot, whose now very elderly recording is available only in a large boxed set from EMI (something no serious lover of Chopin should be without). The age of the recording, however, and the occasional finger-slips, may put it out of court as a first choice, but once your basic library is established you should make a bee-line for it. Argerich's pianism is second to none. Nor is her innate musicianship or her compelling intensity exceeded by any living player. Her performance of the Op. 28 Preludes is something of a miracle, binding together these comprehensively disparate and wide-ranging miniatures with a sense of organic development which defies analysis. It must be said, however, that her playing throughout this magnificent recital may strike some listeners as excessively individual. These may well find themselves happier with the hardly less impressive Pollini on DG. Nor should connoisseurs, or even would-be connoisseurs, fail to consider Ivan Moravec on Supraphon, whose white-hot re-creation of the Preludes makes his relative neglect by record companies impossible to understand. *JS*

CHOPIN/SCHUMANN

Chopin: Scherzos Nos 1–4

Schumann: Bunte Blätter, Op. 99

Sviatoslav Richter (piano)

Olympia OCD 338 □ ADD □ 75:24 mins □ 🎵🎵

Few pianists have ever captured and sustained the tragic elements in Chopin so unnervingly

and masterfully as Richter does here. Spurning melodramatic gestures (and how the composer would have approved!), he balances his harmonies and angles his rhythms in the B minor Scherzo first to amplify the pain of its opening plunge, then to emphasise the sweet but doomed solace of its almost childlike middle section so that the unexpected, interruptive return of the opening chord, portending the triumph of tragedy, fairly sears the soul. At the same time, especially in the Second and Fourth Scherzos, he equally captures the happiness and self-confidence that help to render Chopin's tragedy quite so grippingly poignant. Along the way he does some of the most fabulous piano-playing you're likely to hear, but so perfectly and exclusively is it tailored to the music that it almost goes unnoticed. A highly Chopinesque aspect of its peculiar beauty is the simple and rare fact of its never being too loud. Would that more pianists followed suit. A further bonus is the inclusion here of Schumann's miscellaneous *Bunte Blätter*, seldom played but containing some real gems. *JS*

CHOPIN

Waltzes Nos 1–14; Barcarolle, Op. 60; Mazurka in C sharp minor, Op. 50/3; Nocturne in D flat, Op. 27/2

Dinu Lipatti (piano)

EMI CDH 7 69802 2 □ ADD mono □ 65:00 mins □ 🎵🎵

'Here,' wrote Chopin disparagingly from Vienna in 1830, 'they actually call waltzes "works"!' So, before long, did he – the first composer after Schubert to lift them repeatedly into the realm of highest art. These are emphatically not waltzes to be danced to, and yet the spirit of dance must permeate them or they lose their point. Lipatti's 1950 studio recording (greatly preferable to that of his tragic but transcendent final recital two months later) has never been bettered, and the transfers have been excellently done. This is playing of almost Mozartian purity and elegance, its virtuosity put wholly at the service of the music. Some, however, may be disconcerted by Lipatti's reordering of his material. The remaining works on this treasurable disc are likewise among the greatest Chopin recordings ever made. If you want completeness and thoroughly modern sound, as well as artistic merit, you could do a lot worse than to turn to Ashkenazy on Decca, whose buoyant, fleet and stylish renderings are full of life and sparkle and very well recorded.

Less well recorded but no less well played is Biret on Naxos, and at a bargain price too. *JS*

Works for Solo Piano (complete)

Leo Smit (piano)

Sony SM2K 66345 □ ADD/DDD □ 117:35 mins (2 discs) □ 𝄞𝄞

Although primarily regarded as a composer of orchestral music, Copland remained devoted to the piano throughout his career. He left at least three major works for the instrument, the tough and gritty Piano Variations (1930), the more lyrical Piano Sonata (1939–41), and the intellectually challenging Piano Fantasy (1957), which, like much of Copland's later work, explores serial technique, but in a manner that is far removed from the overwrought emotionalism of Schoenberg. Apart from these masterpieces, Copland's piano output encompasses less ambitious projects, but even here one can find some real gems, such as the simple and delightfully unpretentious *Down a Country Lane*. Over the years the American pianist Leo Smit regularly collaborated with Copland, and his performances must be regarded as definitive. *EL*

Pièces de clavecin, Bk 2 – Ordres 6, 8 & 11

Alan Cuckston (harpsichord)

Naxos 8.550460 □ 76:57 mins □ 𝄞

Couperin gathered together his harpsichord pieces into four books arranged in *ordres*, or suites. They range from miniatures, often with descriptive titles – 'The Gnat', 'The Gossip' – to programmatic sequences such as one selected here describing a street riot ending with 'Confusion and Rout… caused by the Drunkards, the Monkeys and the Bears', where Cuckston demonstrates that the harpsichord can make a truly horrid noise! At the other extreme are 'Les baricades mistérieuses', with its haunting, blurred harmonies, and 'Les bergeries', a gracious *rondeau* which Bach so liked that he copied it into the notebook he compiled for his wife, Anna Magdalena.

This disc contains three complete *ordres*, 6, 11 and 8, the last a conventional French suite of prelude and a series of dances. Cuckston's playing is flexible without ever losing that sense of a dance pulse essential in most French music. There's a spontaneity about his playing too – perhaps because the whole disc was recorded in a single day. The documentation offers nothing about pitch, temperament or

harpsichord (I discovered it's French, by David Way), but there's no more representative selection of the daunting total of 230 *pièces* better played than this – and at budget price it's unbeatable. *GP*

Harpsichord Works (complete)

Davitt Moroney (harpsichord)

Harmonia Mundi HMA 1901124/27 □ ADD □ 314:41 mins (4 discs) □ 𝄞𝄞

Louis Couperin, uncle of François Couperin ('Le Grand') was a musical phenomenon. He was invited to Paris, aged 25, to be taught by Chambonnières, founder of the French school of harpsichordists; by his death ten years later he had composed over 200 pieces. They're extraordinarily inventive, not least the 132 harpsichord movements that Moroney has assembled here into suites. Each begins with an improvisatory prelude, written in unmeasured notes and without time signature. So the player is responsible for deciding how to build up and release harmonies, extract melodies, and shape the pace of the string of bare semibreves and the slurs that sweep above them.

No one understands the problems or solves them more convincingly than Moroney. His programme notes – on the preludes, dance movements, tuning and temperament, and that most crucial ingredient of French music, ornamentation – are fascinating. He varies the colours of the 22 suites by using three magnificent original instruments, one of grand tonal proportions, another tending to dryness, the third warm and sweet.

Five hours of Louis Couperin may seem a lot. Dipped into as they were intended, the suites are a wonderfully varied *divertissement* as well as a precious archive. *GP*

Études

Mitsuko Uchida (piano)

Philips 422 412-2 □ 47:12 mins □ 𝄞𝄞𝄞

On paper, 47 minutes of music at full price represents poor value for money, but Uchida is simply peerless in this particular repertoire. What impresses me most about her playing is her ability to encapsulate the shifting moods of each study with razor-sharp precision, and her amazing clarity of articulation which makes light work of the terribly demanding running passagework in 'Pour les huit doigts'. Elsewhere, Uchida surpasses all rivals in terms of pianism – the pawkish humour of the opening study, the delicacy of 'Pour les arpèges composés' and the thrusting energy of the concluding 'Pour les accords' have never sounded more convincing than here. *EL*

DEBUSSY
Préludes, Bks 1 & 2

Krystian Zimerman (piano)

DG 435 773-2 □ 84:04 mins (2 discs) □ 🔾🔾🔾

Krystian Zimerman's recording of the two books of *Préludes* is remarkable for adopting an extremely precise approach to Debussy's markings without sacrificing any element of mystery or atmosphere. Occasionally, as in 'La fille aux cheveux de lin' and 'Bruyères', the playing may seem cool in comparison with some earlier performers. But elsewhere Zimerman's absolute control of voicing pays ample dividends, bringing just the right degree of malicious humour to 'La sérénade interrompue' and monumentality to 'La cathédrale engloutie'. Moreover, the clarity of fingerwork in 'Ce qu'a vu le vent d'ouest' and 'Feux d'artifice' is simply dazzling. *EL*

DEBUSSY
Prélude 'La cathédrale engloutie'
see Collection: Cathedrals in Sound

DEBUSSY
Suite bergamasque; Children's Corner; Images, Bks 1 & 2; Deux Arabesques; Préludes, Bk 1; Pour le piano; Estampes; L'isle joyeuse

Pascal Rogé (piano)

Decca Ovation 443 021-2 □ ADD □ 149:46 mins (2 discs) □ 🔾🔾

Rogé is an outstanding performer of French piano music, and this generous compilation of some of the major landmarks in Debussy's output, recorded mainly during the early Eighties, amounts to a tremendous bargain, notwithstanding the obvious claims of Michelangeli on DG in the *Images* and *Children's Corner*. Special highlights include a dazzling Toccata in *Pour le piano*, an ecstatic *L'isle joyeuse*, and a wonderfully fluid 'Soirée dans Grenade'. But Rogé is also adept at making the unpretentious salon pieces such as the 'Two Arabesques' sound more substantial than one might have imagined. Needless to say, Decca's state-of-the-art engineering surpasses many a recent disc of piano music. *EL*

DEBUSSY
En blanc et noir
see **CHAMBER**: BARTOK: Sonata for Two Pianos and Percussion

DOHNÁNYI
Gavotte and Musette
see Collection: The Hungarian Anthology

EMMANUEL
Sonatines Nos 1–6

Peter Jacobs (piano)

Continuum CCD 1048 □ ADD □ 59:43 mins □ 🔾🔾🔾

Close friend of Debussy, teacher of Messiaen, Maurice Emmanuel was France's leading authority on oriental, ancient Greek and modal music. Few of his own compositions gained much celebrity, but the six Sonatines for piano occupy a special niche in French music, deftly exploring his multifarious musical interests with wit, individual character and superb technique.

The best known, and most unusual, is No. 4 (1920), based on Hindu rāgās, but No. 1 (from 1893, on Burgundian folk-music) and No. 2 (the *Pastorale*, 1897, a neo-Baroque set of bird-song pieces) are equally delightful; while No. 5, *Alla Francese* (1926), is one of the masterpieces of French piano writing, worthy to set beside Ravel's *Le tombeau de Couperin*. This is the only recorded version, but Peter Jacobs's sympathy and ebullience make it a bench-mark for any future competitor. *CM*

FAURE
Piano Works

Pascal Rogé (piano)

Decca 425 606-2 □ 72:11 mins □ 🔾🔾🔾

Piano music and song stand at the very centre of Fauré's achievement. In each genre the French composer effected a gentle revolution, advancing from the salon-inspired style of his early years to much more daring harmonic pastures in old age. You can follow the early stages of this fascinating journey in Pascal Rogé's imaginatively designed and beautifully performed recital.

Central to his programme are the first five nocturnes, each one moving progressively further away from the models of Schumann and Chopin. Equally captivating are the Second and Third Impromptus, and the First, Second and Fourth Barcarolles, the last-named work, with its interesting rhythmic ambiguities, almost suggesting an unlikely parallel with Brahms. Finally, Rogé offers us the more conventionally extrovert side of the composer in the dashing, almost urbane *Valse-Caprice*. Having savoured the delights of early to middle Fauré, you shouldn't hesitate to move on and explore his later work, especially the overwhelmingly beautiful final nocturnes. *EL*

FRANCK

Organ Works: Chorales Nos 1-3; Fantaisie in A; Cantabile in B; Pièce héroïque in B minor; Fantaisie in C, Op. 16; Grande pièce symphonique, Op. 17; Prélude, Fugue et Variation, Op. 18; Pastorale, Op. 19; Prière in C sharp minor, Op. 20; Final in B flat, Op. 21

Michael Murray (organ)

Telarc CD-80234 □ 109:00 mins (2 discs) □ ❷❷❷

Hero of this triumphantly audacious two-disc survey of César Franck's grandest organ compositions is the Cavaillé-Coll instrument at St Sernin's Basilica in Toulouse. Installed in 1889, this venerable king among instruments has shown its age on more than one insensitively produced recording in the past. If this great organ is here in fine fettle, then so is celebrated American organist Michael Murray, who has, over the years, made this repertoire very much his own. Franck's reverence for the contrapuntal and polyphonic genius of JS Bach emerges time and again throughout these works; the three Chorales resound magnificently in this great church, and Murray's accounts of the *Pièce héroïque* and *Grand pièce symphonique* bear the unmistakable hallmarks of integrity and authentic distinction. The Toulouse instrument, of course, is virtually identical to that in St Clotilde's, Paris – the organ that Franck himself played for many years, and which first breathed life into much of the music heard in this outstanding two-disc set. The Telarc recording, it need hardly be said, is spectacular. *MJ*

FRANCK

Pièce héroïque; Chorale No. 2; Cantabile in B; Prélude, Choral et Fugue
see **CHAMBER**: FRANCK: Violin Sonata in A

FRANCK

Prélude, Choral et Fugue
see also **ORCHESTRAL**: FRANCK: Les Djinns

·FRESCOBALDI

Keyboard Works

Christopher Hogwood (harpsichords, virginal)

L'Oiseau-Lyre 436 197-2 □ 93:59 mins (2 discs) □ ❷❷❷

Frescobaldi was immensely popular as a performer, even if the account of 30,000 people attending his inaugural recital at St Peter's, Rome, must be an exaggeration. He was also fastidious about other people's performance of his music, as Hogwood's helpful notes explain, quoting the instructions in the preface to the first book of toccatas: not too rigid a beat... arpeggiation of slow opening passages... the speed of trills... principles determining different kinds of articulation... even the programming of the pieces. So you can judge for yourself the stylishness of Hogwood's playing.

He has selected the programme (rather short by today's expectations) with a lot of variety – the exuberant violence of the *Capriccio sopra la battaglia*, the battle depicting with rolling left-hand chords, bugle calls, galloping horses and dramatic silences; chromatically colourful variations on the shapely 'Ruggiero' bass; five well-sprung galliards. He varies the tone colours, too, using three distinctively different Italian harpsichords and a charming, if rattly virginal, all from the German National Museum at Nuremberg. The recording is excellent, close and intimate, but mercifully avoiding the all-too-common sensation of having one's head under the instrument's lid. *GP*

GERHARD

Fantasia
see Collection: Homage to Segovia

GRAINGER

'Dished up for Piano', Vol. 3: Folk-song Arrangements

Martin Jones (piano)

Nimbus NI 5244 □ 68:26 mins □ ❷❷❷

Among virtuoso composer-pianists, Percy Grainger must have been unique in claiming to loathe the piano. But if his most important and characteristic inspirations are rather for small orchestras and chamber ensembles, he couldn't avoid the convenience of his instrument as a medium for arrangements and transcriptions as well as original ideas; and as Martin Jones's five-disc survey shows, his catalogue of piano music is extensive and amazingly varied.

If Grainger's essential genius was as an interpreter and vivifier of folk-song, this collection of 27 English, Scottish, Irish, Danish, Faroese and American folk-song arrangements is the most vital volume to acquire. 'Country Gardens' is here, and 'Molly on the Shore', and 'Irish Tune from County Derry', 'Shepherd's Hey', 'The Sussex Mummers' Christmas Carol', 'Scotch Strathspey and Reel' and other favourites –

but also many fascinating and little-known settings, all 'dished up' with considerable art. Jones expounds it all with infectious verve, and for once Nimbus's typically over-reverberant but entirely natural piano sound is absolutely appropriate to the music. Irresistible stuff. *CM*

<hr>

GRIEG

Lyric Pieces (complete)

Balázs Szokolay (piano)

Naxos 8.553387, 8.550577, 8.550650
□ **68:16 mins, 63:38 mins, 51:13 mins** □ ❷

There are excellent collections of the *Lyric Pieces* by Emil Gilels on DG (a superb recording), Leif Ove Andsnes on Virgin (a close runner-up) and the outstanding Cyprien Katsaris on Teldec (a bonus here is the delicious *Holberg* Suite, in its original, pianistic dress, delightfully played), but if you want the lot, then Szokolay's your man – and not just because he's recorded them all (so have Gerhard Oppitz on RCA, Eva Knardahl on BIS and Peter Katin on Olympia – all of whom offer much to admire), nor because he comes at a bargain price, but because he brings to his playing of them an imaginative range greater than many of his better-known colleagues, a sophisticated but unobtrusive pianism which does exceptional justice to Grieg's highly idiomatic flair for the instrument (though not, admittedly, quite matching the extraordinary pianistic resourcefulness of Gilels), and an indefinable sense of nobility which makes one forget that these are 'mere' miniatures. *JS*

<hr>

JANACEK

On an Overgrown Path; In the Mists; Piano Sonata 1.x.1905; Theme and Variations

Rudolf Firkušný (piano)

DG 20th Century Classics 429 857-2 □ **ADD**
□ **78:48 mins** □ ❷ ❷

Janáček's relatively slender piano output may appear insubstantial in comparison with his operas, orchestral pieces or chamber music. But the originality of musical thought is just as striking here as in the rest of Janáček's mature work. For example, no one could fail to be moved by the powerful two-movement Piano Sonata, inspired by the brutal murder of a humble peasant who was stabbed to death while taking part in a political demonstration in Brno. A more concentrated exploration of emotions is found in the cycle of miniatures entitled *On an Overgrown Path*,

where images of childhood and imitations of native speech are often combined with acute sensitivity. A number of pianists have made outstanding recordings of these works. Among recent contenders, Leif Ove Andsnes (on Virgin) provides some extremely searching interpretations and can be recommended with confidence. But pride of place must still be awarded to the late Rudolf Firkušný. As a disciple of the composer, Firkušný understood better than many others the true nature of Janáček's musical inflections, and interprets each work with total commitment. The 1972 recording, though lacking the depth of Andsnes's version, is perfectly acceptable. *EL*

<hr>

KODALY

Sonata for Solo Cello
see **CHAMBER**: Kodály: Duo for Violin and Cello

<hr>

KODALY

Seven Pieces, Op. 11
see Collection: The Hungarian Anthology

<hr>

KRENEK

Piano Sonata No. 3
see Collection: The Glenn Gould Edition

<hr>

KUHNAU

The Biblical Sonatas

John Butt (harpsichord, clavichord, organ)

Harmonia Mundi HMU 907133 □ **72:23 mins**
□ ❷ ❷ ❷

Butt plays the extraordinarily vivid programme music of Kuhnau (1660–1722) – Old Testament high drama, violent, salacious, mournful – with no holds barred. He divides the six sonatas between three instruments, superbly recorded at their natural dynamic levels; though I've seldom heard such a wild clavichord touch, depicting rage. The chamber organ is exquisite, tremulant reflecting trembling Israelites, zimbelstern depicting joy, and two chorale settings anachronistically presenting pre-Christian drama to a Lutheran audience. Definitely not to be missed. *GP*

<hr>

KURTAG

Plays and Games
see Collection: The Hungarian Anthology

<hr>

LISZT

Csárdás macabre
see Collection: The Hungarian Anthology

<hr>

LISZT

Dante Sonata
see **ORCHESTRAL**: LISZT: Dante Symphony

LISZT

Fantasia and Fugue on 'Ad nos, ad salutarem undam'; Variations on 'Weinen, Klagen, Sorgen, Zagen'; Evocation à la Chapelle Sixtine; Prelude and Fugue on BACH

Thomas Trotter (organ)

Decca 440 283-2 □ 72:14 mins □ 🕘🕘🕘

Thomas Trotter gives an outstanding Liszt recital on an organ that the composer himself knew intimately, in Merseburg, near Leipzig in eastern Germany. Trotter has recorded the BACH Prelude and Fugue previously for Decca, but now plays the original version, premiered on the same organ by one of Liszt's pupils. For an example of Trotter's whiplash virtuosity and sense of devilry, sample the fugue from 'Ad nos…'. Sparkling playing. *Stephen Haylett*

LISZT

Piano Sonata in B minor; Three Petrarch Sonnets; Two Legends

Artur Pizarro (piano)

Collins 13572 □ 75:42 mins □ 🕘🕘🕘

Almost every great virtuoso pianist has recorded the Liszt B minor Sonata, so the task of choosing a definitive recording is by no means straightforward. For individualism and insight, there's little to match Richter (on Philips), while Brendel (also on Philips) offers the most intellectually satisfying conception without sacrificing any sense of bravado. But the performance that has impressed me above all is that of the young Artur Pizarro. No pianist, not even Brendel, manages to convey the epic sweep of the work with such a breathtaking sense of inevitability. Similar qualities abound in the *Two Legends*, both forward-looking studies in impressionism which are delivered here with brilliance and an unusually sensitive feel for colour. *EL*

LISZT
Die Weihnachtsbaum (excerpts)
see Collection: Cathedrals in Sound

LUTOSLAWSKI
Variations on a Theme of Paganini
see **CHAMBER**: BARTOK: Sonata for Two Pianos and Percussion

MACDOWELL
In Deep Woods
see Collection: Cathedrals in Sound

MAREK
Triptyque
see Collection: Cathedrals in Sound

MEDTNER
Danza festiva
see Collection: Marc-André Hamelin Live at Wigmore Hall

MEDTNER

Dithyramb in E flat, Op. 10/2; Sonata elegia, Op. 11/2; Skazka in B flat minor, Op. 20/1; Sonata reminiscenza, Op. 38/1; Canzona serenata in F minor, Op. 38/6; Canzona matinata, Op. 39/4; Sonata tragica, Op. 39/5; Theme and Variations in C sharp minor, Op. 55

Nikolai Demidenko (piano)

Hyperion CDA 66636 □ 71:11 mins □ 🕘🕘🕘

The refined, complex, aristocratic art of the pianist-composer Nikolai Medtner is finally coming into its own, as pianists discover a Russian master as consummate and varied in keyboard virtuosity as his close friend Rachmaninov, and at least as profound in his musical thought. The number of recital discs is ever-expanding, but few can touch this stunning Demidenko programme, excellently recorded and featuring playing of the highest order.

The items make a nicely balanced selection, juxtaposing some of Medtner's gentler, lyrical pieces against three of his piano sonatas. Medtner's sonatas are mainly concise, single-movement works, almost extended ballades, were it not for the intricate organicism of their developments. But they cover an enormous expressive range, as shown here by Demidenko's stupendous performance of the driven, passionate *Sonata tragica* and his rapt, almost dreamlike rendering of the serene *Sonata reminiscenza*, one of Medtner's most beautiful and affecting works. Subtle programming shows up the sonatas' interrelation with shorter works: these two were included in Medtner's collections of *Forgotten Melodies*, and the *Tragica* is here preceded by *Canzona matinata* from the same collection (as Medtner directed), while the *Reminiscenza*, which concludes the disc, opens with the same touching, unforgettable theme as the *Canzona serenata*, which begins it. *CM*

MEDTNER
Two Pieces, Op. 58
see RACHMANINOV: Suite No. 2

MENDELSSOHN
Andante and Rondo Capriccioso; Prelude and Fugue in E minor; Variations sérieuses
see **ORCHESTRAL**: MENDELSSOHN: Piano Concertos Nos 1 & 2

Songs without Words (complete); Albumblatt, Op. 117; Gondellied; Kinderstücke, Op. 72; Zwei Klavierstücke

Daniel Barenboim (piano)

DG Galleria 437 470-2 □ ADD □ 120:13 mins (2 discs) □ 🌓🌓

Once among the most familiar pieces ever written, Mendelssohn's *Songs without Words* later fell into a long period of relative obscurity. They owe much of their erstwhile popularity and their recent neglect to little more than snobbery. Their 20th-century reputation as the apotheosis of Victorian insipidity isn't entirely without foundation, but a lot here is first rate of its kind, and its current representation in the catalogue suggests that justice is at last being done. Complete sets are now available from Martin Jones on Nimbus (fine, but very inappropriately recorded, with all the cavernous bloom of an empty hall), Annie d'Arco on Erato (excellent throughout, and commendably unsentimental) and the unfailingly artistic and pianistically refined Livia Rév on Hyperion. Pride of place, though, must go to the infuriatingly prodigious Barenboim, whose 1974 version is not only superbly recorded but the most searching and wide-ranging of them all. The most beautiful, imaginative, penetrating and pianistically resourceful performances of Mendelssohn's *Songs without Words* ever recorded, however (though there are only nine of them), were set down in 1930 by Ignaz Friedman and come in an invaluable box from Pearl containing the complete solo recordings of this unique artist. *JS*

Organ Works (complete)

Gillian Weir (organ)

Collins 70312 □ 418:28 mins (7 discs for the price of 5) □ 🌓🌓🌓

What makes a first-rate interpreter of Messiaen's organ works? Certainly a player with a complete mastery of technique, but, moreover, a technique that enables the player to see beyond the printed page and actually interpret the music. Also a player with the imagination and feeling for musical colour that will lend potency to the rich religious symbolism that abounds there.

Gillian Weir displays all these prerequisites in abundance on this seven-disc complete cycle, recorded on the four-manual Frobenius organ in Aarhus Cathedral, Denmark. If you like to test both the water and the dynamic threshold of your speakers with toccatas from Messiaen's earlier cycles, sample the overwhelming impact of 'Transports de joie' from *L'ascension* or 'Dieu parmi nous' from *La nativité du Seigneur*. The reeds, French in origin, are among the most vividly recorded I have heard (the 32-foot pedal reed is surprisingly round and well focused) and Weir's sparkling dexterity is aided by a clear and distinct acoustic.

What impresses me most throughout these recordings is the innate coherence and imagination that Gillian Weir imparts to the various facets of Messiaen's art. In the cycle *Les corps glorieux*, there is an almost percussive rhythmic élan to 'Joie et clarté des corps glorieux', and there is a palpable tightening of the knot in 'Combat de la mort'.

The Frobenius organ has an array of distinctive mutation stops, used to fine effect in several movements of the *Livre d'orgue*. Listen to the opening 'Reprises par intervention' for a marvellous juxtaposition of mutations and growling pedal reeds.

There is a penetrating depth to the sound of the organ that has been captured well by the engineers, nowhere heard more awesomely than in the 'Apparition de l'église éternelle'.

This is a Messiaen cycle that should now enter the collection of every devotee of his music as a preferred version. *Stephen Haylett*

Vingt regards sur l'enfant Jésus

Peter Hill (piano)

Unicorn-Kanchana DKP(CD) 9122/23 □ 142:19 mins (2 discs) □ 🌓🌓🌓

Vingt regards is a landmark not only in Messiaen's output but also within the entire literature of French piano music. A work of visionary power, it makes tremendous demands of the performer, who must be able to master extremes of expression without compromise. Few indeed boast the requisite technical armoury to bring sufficient light and shade to the exceedingly taxing passagework, neither do many performers possess the necessary musical concentration to sustain and voice the melodic lines at the formidably slow speeds requested by Messiaen.

Of the current front-runners, Michel Béroff's pioneering mid-price version for EMI still looks an attractive proposition, especially with the generous inclusion of the composer's earlier *Préludes* on the second disc. Yet I find Hill's performance even more convincing, for the British pianist manages to bring a powerful intellectual rigour to his interpretation, but without in any way undermining the colour and imagination of Messiaen's poetic language. *EL*

MESSIAEN

Visions de l'Amen; Petites esquisses d'oiseaux; Fantaisie burlesque; Pièce pour le tombeau de Paul Dukas; Rondeau

Peter Hill, Benjamin Frith (piano)

Unicorn-Kanchana DKP(CD) 9144 □ 79:04 mins
□ 🌑🌑🌑

This disc ends Peter Hill's acclaimed complete anthology of Messiaen's piano music. As such, there is a sense of tying up loose ends, coupling some of his lesser-known early pieces with the two-piano *Visions*. Indeed, the first three pieces were recorded as long ago as 1984–5 and include the fascinating 1932 *Fantaisie burlesque*, a combination of ecstatic diminished seventh harmonies and Les Six-like jazz.

The mark of Hill's Messiaen has always been the skill with which he manages to conjure a seemingly endless range of sonorities from the piano, bringing to life the bird-song works with a particular veracity. The six 'little bird sketches' here, full of colour and life, are no exception. For the heavyweight work on this disc, the *Visions de l'Amen*, Hill is joined by Benjamin Frith. Between them they make a powerful sound. This is Messiaen in his transcendental mode, creating abstract sounds to express the mythical sense of his religious beliefs. Massed chordal progressions, plainchant allusions and ecstatic chorales often seem to defy the mechanical limitations of the piano, but Hill and Frith rise admirably to the challenge, and are helped by a generous but unobtrusive recording environment.
Matthew Rye

MILHAUD
Chorale for Piano
see **ORCHESTRAL**: Collection: Testimonies of War

MOMPOU
Suite compostelana
see Collection: Homage to Segovia

MOZART
Andante with Five Variations, K501
see **CHAMBER**: BARTOK: Sonata for Two Pianos and Percussion

MOZART

Piano (Duet) Sonatas in C, K19d, in D, K381, in B flat, K358, in F, K497 & in C, K521; Andante and Variations in G, K501; Sonata in D for Two Pianos, K448; Adagio and Allegro in F minor, K594; Fantasia in F minor, K608

Christoph Eschenbach, Justus Frantz (piano)

DG 435 042-2 □ ADD □ 151:11 mins (2 discs)
□ 🌑🌑

Piano duets are generally more rewarding to play than to listen to – not because they are innately inferior to any other kind of music but because one very seldom gets the opportunity to hear piano duos of the front rank, much less at a single keyboard. It's happened, of course: the Schnabels (father and son, but that's going back donkey's years), Badura-Skoda and Demus at their best, Lupu and Perahia (probably unsurpassable), Tal and Groethuysen... but already the list becomes hard to extend much further. Here, however, we have a duo of quite exceptional skill and insight in music that remains far less familiar than it ought to be. The later works in particular are on a par with the great symphonies and concertos. Only an intermittently glimpsed Achilles' heel (a certain squareness of metrical inflection) prevents this beautiful collection from being numbered among the genuinely great recordings. But the glimpses are so few, and the virtues so many (the vitality and overall grace, the emotional range, the combination of restraint and intensity, the abiding sense of proportion and dramatic pacing, to name only a few) that it seems churlish to cavil. Ideally, this should have a place in every serious record collection. *JS*

MOZART

Piano Sonatas (complete); Fantasia in C minor, K475

Mitsuko Uchida (piano)

Philips Complete Mozart Edition 422 517-2
□ 325:00 mins (5 discs) □ 🌑🌑

Prior to the imminent reissue of Walter Klien's definitive Mozart cycle on Carlton/Turnabout – and with an intimate knowledge of those by Barenboim (impressive but uneven on EMI), Ciccolini, Eschenbach (compelling on DG), Gieseking, Gould (unspeakable on Sony), Jand, Katin, Kraus, Pires, Pludermacher and Schiff (all of them beautiful) – I'd tip Uchida on Philips for the top spot. And for those who prize a historically informed approach on piano, she is peerless. Uchida doesn't do anything so simple-minded as imitating the fortepiano, but she approaches the instrument, as it were, through fortepianistic glasses. No one is more meticulous, more probingly thoughtful, or more pianistically sophisticated in this music than she, even though some may find in her finely crafted readings a degree of detachment which puts a certain distance between listener and composer. *JS*

MOZART/SCHUBERT

Mozart: Sonata in D for Two Pianos, K448; Andante and Variations in G, K501

Schubert: Fantasia in F minor, D940

Louis Lortie, Hélène Mercier (piano)

Chandos CHAN 9162 □ 50:24 mins □ ⚄⚄⚄

No performances of these inexpressibly wonderful works – including the Schnabels' and the justly celebrated recording by Lupu and Perahia on Sony – have given me greater or more lasting pleasure than these. Bowing to no one in elegance, pianistic refinement, meticulous attention to detail and sheer, joyous vitality (even in the Schubert, whose haunting, sweet melancholy they also catch to perfection), Lortie and Mercier demonstrate the kind of mutual empathy normally associated with identical twins. Breathing as one – and they do almost convince one that the piano itself does indeed breathe – they seem to have searched every corner of this music and to have distilled its very essence in every bar. Enough said. Run out and buy this right now. *JS*

MUSSORGSKY/TCHAIKOVSKY

Mussorgsky: Pictures at an Exhibition

Tchaikovsky (arr. Pletnev): The Sleeping Beauty (excerpts)

Mikhail Pletnev (piano)

Virgin VC 7 59611 2 □ 63:51 mins □ ⚄⚄⚄

With pianism like this, who needs an orchestra? Pletnev may be over-dependent on the sustaining pedal to create washes of sound, but his formidably controlled thunder becomes indispensable as the composer stretches the boundaries of the possible in his last two pictures. While the clangour of an Ashkenazy tends to become repetitive, Pletnev constantly opens up fresh perspectives – re-creating that sense of inspired wonder at the heart of Mussorgsky's memorial to his friend, the painter and architect Victor Hartmann. There's plenty of delicate fantasy here, too, for

such numbers as the 'Ballet of the Chicks in Their Shells', and the connections between pictures and promenades are strikingly made with a dash of this pianist's celebrated eccentricity. Pletnev's far from orthodox selection and transcription of numbers from Tchaikovsky's *Sleeping Beauty* is equally wonderful: the elaborate composite of his introductory narrative shows how well he knows the complete ballet, while the treatment of the final great *pas de deux* once again reveals an orchestral scope beyond the abilities of most pianists.

Ashkenazy's Decca *Pictures* has a special validity, since the piano version here is followed by Ashkenazy's own orchestration – so very different from Ravel's and especially valid as an interesting realisation of the instruments the pianist hears in his head when he plays. And Vladimir Horowitz's 1951 Carnegie Hall performance on RCA cries out to be heard: virtually a transcription of Mussorgsky's original with virtuosic elaboration, though surprisingly the quieter moments are the most spellbinding. *DN*

MUSSORGSKY

Pictures at an Exhibition
see also BALAKIREV: Islamey

NIELSEN

Chaconne; Suite 'Den Luciferiske'; Three Piano Pieces; Five Piano Pieces; Humoresque-bagateller

Leif Ove Andsnes (piano)

Virgin VC 5 45129 2 □ 54:20 mins □ ⚄⚄⚄

Nielsen's piano music has never had much currency in the concert hall, despite its individuality of musical and harmonic 'voice'. It well deserves this excellent recording. From the very opening of the Chaconne, inspired by Bach's D minor Chaconne from the Second Partita for solo violin, it is clear that this is music of a serious, uncompromising nature; as the piece progresses, its contrapuntal intricacy, beautifully voiced by Andsnes, increases, as does its originality.

Probably the most striking work on the disc is the 'Lucifer' suite – not, apparently, Lucifer the devil, but the Lucifer of Greek mythology, the bringer of light in the form of the morning star (though there is some distinctly devilish piano writing within its six movements).

The strength of personality evident in both music and performance will reward repeated listening and despite my terms 'strong' and 'uncompromising', these works are in no way unappealing. A recording, complete with top-class sound quality, to chew over and benefit from. *Jessica Duchen*

OHANA

Tiento
see Collection: Homage to Segovia

PAGANINI

Caprices for Solo Violin

Salvatore Accardo (violin)

DG Galleria 429 714-2 □ ADD □ 74:36 mins □ 🔊🔊

Alongside the unaccompanied partitas and sonatas of Bach, the 24 Caprices for Solo Violin by Nicolò Paganini represent an incomparable vade-mecum of violin art. They encompass every imaginable technical device available to the violinist, and demand outstanding virtuosity, dexterity and agility from executants. Indeed, it was long thought that no violinist, save Paganini himself (who never played the Caprices in public), was equipped to perform the entire set! Composed in around 1805, and published as Paganini's Op. 1 by Ricordi in 1820, the Caprices were intended as studies, taking as their model Pietro Locatelli's *L'arte del violino* of 1733. But, as with Chopin's études, pedagogical content was eclipsed by musical and melodic concerns, and the Caprices have continued to fascinate composers of every subsequent generation; Schumann and Liszt arranged many for piano, while the diabolical 24th Caprice in A minor inspired works from figures as diverse as Rachmaninov, Brahms, Lutosławski and Blacher. Salvatore Accardo recorded the set in 1977 during his distinguished recorded survey of Paganiniana, including memorable versions of the concertos with Charles Dutoit; digital remastering ensures superb transparency and presence, while Accardo's hair-raising performances have sensational authority and abandon. In summary, a galvanic traversal of music which never ceases to stun the listener into disbelief! *MJ*

PROKOFIEV

Piano Sonatas Nos 1–9; Toccata, Op. 11; Pieces from the ballet Cinderella, Opp. 95 & 102

Vladimir Ovchinikov (piano)

EMI CDS 5 55127 2 □ 220:26 mins (3 discs) □ 🔊🔊🔊

EMI has a roster of fine Prokofiev interpreters among its pianists – not least Peter Donohoe, whose powerful disc of the so-called *War* Sonatas (Nos 6–8) might have prompted a sequel – but the choice of Ovchinikov for a complete sonata cycle is richly vindicated in these riveting performances. Trained in the Russian school of orchestral pianism, he uses his phenomenal technique and full, well-weighted sonority only as a starting-point. No two sonatas sound the same; just one example is the way in which Ovchinikov reinforces the young Prokofiev's transition from Rachmaninov-style rhapsody in the First Sonata to his own, more angular lyricism in the Second by careful observation of the *non legato* marking in No. 2.

The *War* trilogy cries out to be heard in a single sitting: between the hair-raising whirlwinds of the Sixth and the Eighth, every note resonantly in place, the outer movements of the Seventh are treated more lightly, if no less dazzlingly. Here, it's the central Andante caloroso which plumbs the depths, generalised booklet notes hardly prepare newcomers for the crushing disintegration of the nostalgic theme, or the numb, keening aftermath so mesmerisingly sustained by Ovchinikov. He knows how to be simple, too, in the *Cinderella* transcriptions, the hypnotic slow movement of the Fourth Sonata and the luminously sad Ninth Sonata always close to tears. No rival cycle touches this one, though three surpassingly charismatic interpretations of the three greatest sonatas (in each case sharing a disc with works by other composers) have to be mentioned, all on DG: Pogorelich's haunting, often withdrawn Sixth, Pollini's shattering Seventh and Richter's magisterial Eighth – the Prokofiev performance you must have if limited to only one sonata. *DN*

PROKOFIEV

Visions fugitives
see SCRIABIN: Piano Sonatas Nos 2 & 9

RACHMANINOV

Piano Works (complete)

Howard Shelley (piano)

Hyperion CDS 44041/8 □ ADD/DDD □ 448:00 mins (8 discs) □ 🔊🔊

Rachmaninov was one of the greatest pianists of his age, and thus his piano music was written with great technical insight. The present issue of the complete solo piano music (also available on separate discs) brings together recordings made between 1978 and 1991.

The cellular construction of the Preludes, Op. 23, makes them effective either as individuals or as a unified set, and hearing them complete offers an unusual opportunity to reassess this music. For the Preludes, Op. 32, Rachmaninov resisted overtly Romantic melody in favour of more elaborate passagework and sudden, unpredictable flights of fancy. Some of the most eloquent examples of this stylistic change can be found in the spectacularly played *Études-tableaux*, Opp. 33 and 39.

Aside from fine performances of the two sets of variations to themes by Chopin (Op. 22) and Corelli (Op. 42), this collection is also valuable for its inclusion of the shorter early pieces, works in both their original and revised forms, such as the Piano Sonata, Op. 36, and the *Mélodie* from the *Morceaux de fantaisie*, Op. 3, and the transcriptions of works by composers such as Bach, Schubert and Mendelssohn, which provide a particularly interesting footnote.

The result is a fine achievement from pianist Howard Shelley and Hyperion alike. These superbly recorded, idiomatic readings demonstrate Shelley's virtuoso pianism and affinity for this music in performances of the highest calibre. *Nicholas Rast*

RACHMANINOV

Études-tableaux, Op. 33/5, 6 & 9; Op. 39/1–4, 7 & 9; Preludes, Op. 23/1, 2, 4, 5, 7 & 8; Op. 32/1, 2, 6, 7, 9, 10 & 12

Sviatoslav Richter (piano)

Olympia OCD 337 □ DDD/ADD □ 74:30 mins □ 🍎🍎

Richter's recorded legacy has not so far left us with complete sets of the *Études-tableaux* or the preludes, but since his dynamic and expressive range is second to none, this cross-section remains the one truly indispensable Rachmaninov recital disc. The sequence tends to the dark, obsessive side of the composer's character – there is little sun to pierce the clouds until the D major Prelude in track 12 – but within those self-imposed limits the sheer variety of Richter's fabulous palette can still surprise, ranging from even, transcendental velocity to the space he commands around massive, brooding chords. It is above all in the Seventh of the Op. 39 *Études-tableaux* that desolation takes on a majestic quality, objectively but not dispassionately viewed and capped by a pealing of Russian bells that always astonishes me no matter how often I return to this performance. Both recordings provide interesting challenges to the Richter sonority. The Bavarian studio surroundings for the *Études-tableaux* are truthful but dry, leaving the pianist to provide his own warmth and richness, while the earlier Salzburg recording subjects the instrument to such close scrutiny that a lesser artist would come across

as clattery and coarse; it is a measure of Richter's careful weightiness that the sound remains sumptuous and glowing at climaxes. *DN*

RACHMANINOV

Suites Nos 1 (Fantaisie-tableaux) & 2; Symphonic Dances

Martha Argerich, Alexandre Rabinovitch (piano)

Teldec 9031-74717-2 □ 77:48 mins □ 🍎🍎🍎

RACHMANINOV/MEDTNER

Rachmaninov: Suite No. 2; Russian Rhapsody; Symphonic Dances

Medtner: Two Pieces, Op. 58

Dmitri Alexeev, Nikolai Demidenko (piano)

Hyperion CDA 66654 □ 78:53 mins □ 🍎🍎🍎

Cheating a little, I include both these phenomenal displays of two-piano synchronicity by virtue of their different hors d'oeuvre, which tend to set the respective tones. Medtner was Rachmaninov's junior by only seven years but tends to a more robust cast of thought; the two Op. 58 pieces here are inventories of fleeting melodies, rhythmic variety and sheer virtuosity. Alexeev and Demidenko begin as they mean to continue, with a whirlwind intelligence that sometimes moves faster than you can read the printed notes (no wonder one of the page turners for the Wigmore Hall recital in which this disc has its origins found herself hopelessly lost at times).

Fire and air to Argerich's and Rabinovitch's earth and water – established with equal finesse in the early Rachmaninov mood-pictures – the Hyperion duo just have the edge in sleight of hand for the extrovert fun and games of Rachmaninov's coruscating Second Suite but rather skim the surface of the troubled Symphonic Dances. In this last, complex masterpiece of Rachmaninov's American years, the Teldec team employs more in the way of magisterial rubato to explore the darker corners; Alexeev and Demidenko bewitch only in their introspective handling of the very Russian melody at the heart of the first dance. My final observation has to be more or less the same as Ateş Orga's in his very original note for the Hyperion disc: not only did RCA turn down Rachmaninov's last chance to shine as the outstanding conductor that he was in the orchestral version of the Symphonic Dances, but the company even refused his suggestion of teaming up with

Horowitz for the two-piano version and the Second Suite. These transcendental offerings will have to serve as some kind of posthumous consolation. *DN*

RACHMANINOV

Suite No. 2
see also **CHAMBER**: BARTOK: Sonata for Two Pianos and Percussion

RAMEAU

Pièces de clavecin

Gilbert Rowland (harpsichord)

Naxos 8.553047 □ **74:28 mins** □ *☺*

Though Rameau was primarily a composer of opera and an influential theorist – his treatise on harmony is relevant to this day – his keyboard music is tuneful and charming. Rowland plays the single Suite in A minor/major (Rameau mixes modes freely) of the first book of *Pièces*, 1706, and the two suites of the second collection from 1724. He takes some liberties with the ordering of the movements – effectively and probably justifiably: the printed order leaves some limp ends to the suites, and I suspect was not intended to be inflexible.

Many movements are genre pieces, vividly descriptive – 'Le rappel des oiseaux', a delightful catalogue of bird-song, and 'Les tourbillons', a swirling sound picture of whirlwinds. The rest are dances, though some of these, too, are evocative, like the nasal bagpipe drone of a 'Gigue en rondeau'. Rameau's slow movements are particularly distinctive as he spreads chords across the hands to generate a rich sonority, helped by the fruity bass of this instrument (unidentified in the notes, alas!). Rowland's playing is first rate – meticulous in Rameau's precisely marked ornaments yet spontaneous and animated. *GP*

RAVEL

Gaspard de la nuit; Valses nobles et sentimentales; Miroirs; Sonatine; Le tombeau de Couperin; Ma mère l'oye; Jeux d'eau

Pascal Rogé, Denise-Françoise Rogé (piano)

Decca 440 836-2 □ **ADD** □ **141:34 mins (2 discs)** □ *☺☺*

We are pretty well spoiled for choice in this repertoire. For example, I cannot imagine many contesting Ivo Pogorelich's brilliant mastery of *Gaspard* (DG) or the limpid pianism of Anne Queffélec (on Erato). Also worthy of note are Louis Lortie on Chandos, whose *La valse* is a staggering *tour de force* of

virtuosity, while Boris Berezovsky (Teldec) provides unparalleled timbral excitement and musical sensitivity. But some of the most satisfying playing of all comes in this mid-price Decca reissue of analogue recordings made during the mid-Seventies. The clarity of Decca's engineering can stand worthy comparison with the latest digital sound, but, more important, Rogé encompasses a greater breadth of emotions than most of his rivals. His *Gaspard* operates on a high-voltage level, but he is equally persuasive in the more understated music of the Sonatine and *Le tombeau* or the flamboyant charm of *Valses nobles*. *EL*

RAVEL

Gaspard de la nuit
see also **ORCHESTRAL**: PROKOFIEV: Piano Concerto No. 3

RAVEL

La valse
see **CHAMBER**: BARTOK: Sonata for Two Pianos and Percussion
and (transcr. Gould) Collection: The Glenn Gould Edition

SCARLATTI

14 Sonatas

Glen Wilson (harpsichord)

Teldec 2292-46419-2 □ **60:14 mins** □ *☺☺☺*

'Reader, music lover or professional, whichever you may be, do not expect to find any deep musical thoughts in these compositions, but rather a joyful, imaginative execution of the art, intended to impart security and freedom on the harpsichord.' These disarming words were written by Domenico Scarlatti about his keyboard sonatas, of which more than 500 exist. Composed in the first half of the 18th century, they are remarkable for their harmonic language and exuberant rhythmic vitality, which was much influenced by the flamenco guitar accompaniments of Spanish popular music.

The American harpsichordist Glen Wilson gives marvellously vibrant, cleanly articulated performances of 14 sonatas, taking in the grave B minor Sonata, K87, the brilliant F minor, K463, and the wayward 'Cat's Fugue', so called because the theme is supposed to sound like a cat walking on a keyboard. Scarlatti, himself a formidable virtuoso, demands an awesome technique to manage the wide leaps, crossed hands and rushing scales. Wilson, performing on a copy, made by John Barnes in 1985, of an Aelpido 1726 instrument, makes light of the task.

Consider, too, Maggie Cole (on Amon Ra) playing no less fluently 12 *different* sonatas (happy chance – careful planning?) on contrasting English and Dutch instruments. *Annette Morreau/GP*

SCARLATTI

18 Sonatas

Vladimir Horowitz (piano)

Sony SK 53460 □ ADD □ 72:01 mins □ 🕭🕭🕭

Many great pianists have played Scarlatti, many of them greatly – Lipatti, Haskil, Hess, Michelangeli, Gilels and Perahia spring to mind at once – but none has made the composer quite so much his own as Horowitz. The piano-playing alone is breathtaking: the clarity and finesse of articulation at the most unimaginable speeds, the tone-painting (from the most strummingly and fiercely flamencan to the *n*th degree of pianissimo shadings), the ornamentation (rivalled in beauty, exhilaration and variety only by Gould at his best) – it's all quite fantastic. If Horowitz had a fatal flaw (like his counterpart in jazz, Art Tatum, and like Gould too) it was his propensity to show off. And no wonder. If *you* could do what he did, wouldn't *you* be tempted? It's to his eternal artistic credit, however, that he resists the impulse here. This is virtuosity combined with a rare degree of musicianship and emotional penetration, and no serious collector of piano music should give it a miss. Unfortunately, it dates from Columbia's worst period of piano recording, the tinny, clangorous mid-Sixties, and the transfixing Horowitzian sonorities have to do all they can to make it through the microphone. *JS*

SCHOENBERG

Piano Pieces, Opp. 11, 23 & 33; Six Little Pieces, Op. 19; Suite, Op. 25

Maurizio Pollini (piano)

DG 423 249-2 □ ADD □ 50:01 mins □ 🕭🕭

Schoenberg's piano music spans the most important years of his musical development. From the first tentative probing of a totally chromatic harmonic world in Op. 11 (not so tentative at all, once we get to the vertiginous self-inventing third piece) to the almost Brahmsian breadth of the matured 12-note technique in Op. 33, these works are both deeply expressive and sonically adventurous. In between come the tiny expressionist aphorisms of Op. 19, the iridescent proto-serial impressionism of Op. 23, ending with its 12-note waltz, and the spiky neo-classicism of the Op. 25 Suite, the first wholly 12-note work Schoenberg composed.

Pollini's fastidious, aristocratic readings, recorded in 1974, may be just *too* smooth for some tastes, but there's plenty of aggression where the music calls for it, and the DG sound is superb. There are rougher edges and occasionally irritating mannerisms in Glenn Gould's pioneering recording for Sony, but his versions still retain considerable validity. *CM*

SCHUBERT/SCHUMANN

Schubert: Fantasia in C, D760 (Wanderer)

Schumann: Fantasia in C, Op. 17

Murray Perahia (piano)

Sony Masterworks MK 42124 □ 52:00 mins □ 🕭🕭

Outstanding versions of the *Wanderer* Fantasia feature in the catalogue, including magnificent accounts by Ashkenazy (coupled with a superb reading of the great B flat Sonata, D960), Brendel, Pollini, Richter (one of the genuinely great recordings) and Rubinstein. Less familiar, though no less distinguished, is the almost criminally underrated Anton Kuerti on IMP Masters – a performance of rare vision and unsurpassed pianistic mastery, though perhaps a little too individual for a first choice. No one, however, finds more in the music than Perahia, or so comprehensively combines delicacy and power, long-spanned lyricism and breathtaking excitement, orchestral scope and the ultimate in pianistic refinement. Nor is the Schumann any less compelling. The only drawback is the quality of the recording itself, which suggests a more limited tonal palette than one usually gets from this infinitely resourceful pianist. *JS*

SCHUBERT

Fantasia in F minor for Piano Duet
see MOZART: Sonata in D for Two Pianos

SCHUBERT

Impromptus, D899 & D935

Radu Lupu (piano)

Decca 411 711-2 □ 66:35 mins □ 🕭🕭🕭

If there is a more consistently beautiful, searching and touching account of these wonderful works, then it's not to be found in this world. Lupu's identification with Schubert is so complete that one might be forgiven for suspecting that it was the composer himself on the other side of the microphone. The tenderness is almost excessive in its immediacy, yet there's never a hint of sentimentality or manipulation about it, the suppleness of line and subtlety of harmonic inflection are beyond compare, and the finesse of technical control is beyond the dreams of most pianists. If there's one thing lacking in Lupu's Schubert, it's perhaps a sense of the demonic. For some, his view may seem to lack an element of toughness, to achieve pathos at the expense of drama. These listeners may be happier with Brendel's approach, in any of his three recordings, and, for those who want something midway between the two, Perahia on Sony can be recommended without reservation. I looked to great things from Zimerman on DG, too, but in this case found his superb musicianship compromised by an excess of interpretative gesturing. *JS*

SCHUBERT

Lebensstürme, D947; Deux marches caractéristiques, D886; Divertissement à la hongroise, D818

Jenö Jandó, Ilona Prunyi (piano)

Naxos 8.550555 □ 55:12 mins □ ⊘

This is a thundering good record, which almost makes up for the inexplicable deletion of Pires and Sermet on Erato. But the energy, discipline, sonority, flexibility and conspicuous enjoyment brought by Jandó and Prunyi to their programme here are a joy from start to finish. They may not always match the suppleness and extreme sophistication you get from Lupu and Perahia, but for some that may in fact be a bonus. This is invigoratingly robust and often very exciting playing indeed, its drive and panache matched by its stylishness and infectious good humour. A wonderful treat – and very well recorded too. *JS*

SCHUBERT

Piano Sonata in C minor, D958; Moments musicaux, D780

Radu Lupu (piano)

Decca Ovation 417 785-2 □ 60:12 mins □ ⊘⊘

Lupu's performance of this magnificent sonata is as beautiful as any you're ever likely to hear. The refinement and variety of his tonal palette, the suppleness of his rhythm, the impeccable integrity of his view at every level and the immense sophistication of his phrasing (never once marred by mannerism of any kind) make this a recording to treasure – especially as it includes a comparably beautiful account of the *Moments musicaux*. It may be argued, however, that beauty *per se* is not what this sonata is all about, that it requires a mite more iron in the soul and steel in the wrists than the supremely cosmopolitan Lupu cares

to unleash; that it gives us, indeed, Schubert at his most Beethovenian and tough. If that's your view, then any of Brendel's recordings should more than fill the bill. My own preference is for the earliest one, on Vanguard, made before he had acquired the 'great man' status that he has enjoyed virtually from the start of his partnership with Philips. The earlier performance is as exciting and spontaneous as anyone could wish for, but without the didactic undertones that occasionally mar his later version. And the rhythmic energy, the far-reaching structural grasp and the razor-sharp articulation are achieved at no cost to the lyricism and emotional refinement of the work. As the other works on offer receive performances of equal stature, this is an altogether outstanding release. *JS*

SCHUBERT/SCHUMANN

Schubert: Piano Sonata in A, D959

Schumann: Piano Sonata No. 2 in G minor

Murray Perahia (piano)

Sony Masterworks MK 44569 □ 54:15 mins □ ⊘⊘

There are those – excellent musicians and pianists among them – who will tell you that Perahia over-prettifies this music, that he indulges nuance at the expense of symphonic integrity, that he lacks the ruthlessness required if the lyricism isn't to smooth over the rough edges, indeed the near-hysteria that occasionally threatens to break this extraordinary work apart at the seams (the central episode of the slow movement, for instance). Well, it takes all sorts. There are still those who will affirm that the world is flat and that the moon is made of green cheese. My own view is that while the present performance may indeed be matched in quality by other, very different views, it's unlikely ever to be surpassed. The range of emotions unleashed in Schubert's penultimate sonata is of bewildering variety and complexity and their successful integration is one of the major challenges of the entire piano repertoire. Perahia seems to me to manage this with extraordinary skill, giving full rein to the tenderness, even rapture of the music while never underplaying the drama. Nor is he any less persuasive in the Schumann. Listeners wanting a tougher line, however, may be happier with Pollini on DG. *JS*

SCHUBERT

Piano Sonatas in B flat, D960 & in A, D664

Radu Lupu (piano)

Decca 440 295-2 □ 59:11 mins □ ⊘⊘⊘

Piano Sonatas in E flat, D568 & in C minor, D958

András Schiff (piano)

Decca 440 308-2 □ 60:46 mins □ ⊘⊘⊘

Radu Lupu's Schubert recordings for Decca have been appearing sporadically ever since the early Seventies. His account of the last sonata has been worth waiting for; it is a splendidly sustained performance and one that never fails to allow the music to speak eloquently for itself. The subtle way Lupu handles the much-discussed first-time bars in the opening movement would in itself be sufficient justification for the long repeat.

The first work in Schubert's final triptych of sonatas is a far more intense affair – a dramatic essay in an overtly Beethovenian C minor. András Schiff gives an altogether compelling account of it, with every note strongly characterised, and the whole work shaped with a real sense of purpose. Perhaps there is room for a broader view of the slow movement (as in Radu Lupu's fine recording), but Schiff's is certainly convincing in its own terms. Above all, this is unmistakably a real performance, not a piece of studio patchwork.

Of the companion pieces, Schiff offers one of the most attractive among Schubert's lesser-known earlier sonatas, while Lupu has the genial and popular A major Sonata, D664. *Misha Donat*

SCHUMANN

Bunte Blätter, Op. 99
see CHOPIN: Scherzos Nos 1–4

SCHUMANN

Carnaval; Études symphoniques; Piano Trio No. 1 in D minor

Alfred Cortot (piano), Jacques Thibaud (violin), Pablo Casals (cello)

Biddulph LHW 004 □ ADD mono □ 77:00 mins □ ⊘⊘

Is it possible, with the millennium almost upon us, that the most dazzling recording ever made of Schumann's *Carnaval* was set down in 1929 by a lugubrious-looking composer who looked on piano-playing as a sideline? Most *pianists*, I think, would say so. And I'd hazard a guess that a similar poll conducted one hundred years hence would produce exactly the same answer. As a combination of

staggering pianism and creative interpretation at the highest level of imagination, Rachmaninov's famous recording (RCA) is one of the few artefacts which actually justify that much-abused phrase '... of all time'. That said, I wouldn't recommend it to anyone as a first choice, if only because it would entirely warp one's judgement of all other performances. So start out with a blueprint – one of those good 20th-century exercises in fidelity to the printed page, superbly brought off (artistic, virtuosic, exciting, the lot): something like Jenö Jandó's outstanding performance on Naxos (see p177). Then, understanding that you're embarking on a kind of space odyssey, sample the unsurpassed interpretative genius of Cortot, whose performance remains my own favourite. *Then*, and *only* then, move on to Rachmaninov and go on a mind-blowing adventure of musical re-creation. But then, if you're like me, you'll want to come back to earth – to find Cortot waiting for you.

Outstanding, even superlative performances of the *Symphonic Studies* abound, today more than ever. Unforgettable accounts by Perahia, Richter, Brendel and Rubinstein are all in the catalogue, and deserve to remain there for ever. So does the superb performance by the young Austrian Stefan Vladar on Naxos (and don't overlook Percy Grainger's on Biddulph). Cortot's, however, recorded in 1929, remains unsurpassed and seldom equalled. The piano-playing alone is staggering and ravishing by turns, the integration of Schumann's often bewildering range of moods (not to mention the five 'posthumous' variations, which Cortot scatters about among those of the original edition) is a psychological as well as an artistic marvel. Despite the excellent transfers by Ward Marston, there is inevitably the constant presence of surface hiss and crackle, but you soon get used to it, and to listening *through* it (one of the unsung virtues of old 78s: they force you to concentrate).

With an equally wonderful account of the D minor Trio (what a performance!), this disc is a runaway winner. If you're absolutely set on a modern version of the Études, however, I can heartily recommend Perahia on Sony. *JS*

SCHUMANN

Davidsbündlertänze; Piano Sonata No. 2 in G minor; Toccata in C, Op. 7

Boris Berezovsky (piano)

Teldec 9031-77476-2 □ 62:00 mins □ ⊘⊘⊘

For reasons beyond my ken, Murray Perahia's matchless record pairing the

Davidsbündlertänze and the Op. 12 *Fantasiestücke* has been deleted. Should it reappear, drop everything and go grab it before they decide to take it away again. Until then, you should find plenty to enjoy, admire and occasionally even marvel at in Berezovsky's really splendid account of the *Davidsbündlertänze*, which runs Perahia's a close second, *and* gives you a terrific tour of the G minor Sonata before going on to the Toccata in C which even calls to mind the legendary Richter performance. But let me also very warmly recommend Andreas Haefliger on Sony, whose account of the *Davidsbündlertänze*, the *Waldszenen* and the late, Op. 111 set of *Fantasiestücke* is of very high quality indeed. *JS*

SCHUMANN

Fantasia in C, Op. 17

see also SCHUBERT: Fantasia in C (Wanderer)

SCHUMANN/BRAHMS

Schumann: Fantasiestücke, Op. 12; Fantasia in C, Op. 17

Brahms: Variations and Fugue on a Theme of Handel, Op. 24

Benno Moiseiwitsch (piano)

Testament SBT 1023 □ ADD mono □ 78:00 mins
□ 🎧🎧

If state-of-the-art sonics are a prime consideration, forget it. The sound wasn't fabulous to begin with and the transfers here are OK at best. But the playing? Does anyone play the piano better (and I mean much more than right notes)? Or Schumann better? For some strange reason, Moiseiwitsch was never really given his due by a number of critics. By musicians and pianists, yes: and by the likes of Rachmaninov, Hoffmann and Bolet, no less. OK, so he messes up now and again – so did Cortot, Rubinstein, Schnabel, Paderewski... and as for Beethoven! But who cared? Who should care now? Not, mind you, that there's *much* messing up here. Just a smidgeon, in such places as the coda to the Fantasy's second movement, where almost everybody comes to grief anyway. And it's always in a good cause. Remember Schnabel's jubilant motto 'Safety last'. This record should go to the top of the classical pops. It won't, but it should. *JS*

SCHUMANN

Kinderszenen; Kreisleriana

Martha Argerich (piano)

DG 410 653-2 □ 52:00 mins □ 🎧🎧🎧

Schumann's *Kinderszenen* (Scenes from Childhood) are character pieces of the utmost delicacy and precision engineering, combining an infinitely affecting innocence with an impulsive, almost fierce element of fantasy that renders them among the most elusive of all his works. Yet many great pianists have captured them with memorable conviction and extraordinarily varying results (contrast Horowitz's quirky but entrancing playing on Sony, for instance, with the inexpressible simplicity of the nonagenarian Horszowski on Nonesuch). Barenboim, Brendel, Haskil, Jandó (a special bargain on Naxos) and Kempff have all done wonderful things with them, too, but for me the most immediate, subtle, spontaneous and affecting version now available is Argerich's quite bewitching re-creation. As usual with this incomparable artist, the sheer power of her personality may prove too much for some, but was there ever a more artless demonstration of artfulness? Nor is she any less persuasive in the prodigious *Kreisleriana*. Indeed, it would be hard to think of any player better suited to its fantastical extremes, let alone equipped with more fantastic fingers. *JS*

SCHUMANN/CHOPIN

Schumann: Kreisleriana; Variations on a Theme by Clara Wieck, Op. 14

Chopin: 7 Mazurkas; 6 Études; 2 Waltzes; 2 Polonaises; 2 Preludes; Introduction and Rondo, Op. 16

Vladimir Horowitz (piano)

Sony S2K 53468 □ ADD □ 112:54 mins (2 discs)
□ 🎧🎧🎧

Kreisleriana was written at white heat in the space of three days, and any really successful performance must reflect that in some way. Many a sober, upstanding musician has killed it with respect. Others, too wildly impulsive, have dismembered it with random passion. Getting the balance right isn't easy. Martha Argerich is ideally suited to this music, and her sizzling re-creation on DG is worth anybody's time. Its volcanic energy and improvisatory caprice are as electrifying as the pianism, and she captures the tenderness, the rapture and the peculiar vulnerability of Schumann's Romanticism with extraordinary vividness. Precisely because of its exhilarating sense of danger and its wild daring, however, it's not a performance to live with, but to be experienced and remembered. It thumbs its nose at the unnatural permanence of a recording. Of all recorded versions, Horowitz's first account (he returned to it later for DG) seems to me to succeed best on most levels. The virtuosity is electrifying, the poetry is eloquent but never overstated, and the magic of the moment coexists with a breadth of vision that gives the entire cycle a remarkable sense of unity and integration. The rest of the recital is similarly distinguished. *JS*

SCHUMANN

Papillons; Kinderszenen; Carnaval

Jenő Jandó (piano)

Naxos 8.550784 □ 61:06 mins □ 𝄞

The erratic Jandó is in excellent form here, striking a beautifully judged balance between Schumannesque capriciousness (*à la* Cortot) and excessive 20th-century literalism in the *Papillons*. The tone-painting is lovely, the rhythms have a beautiful, inviting lilt to them, and the quicksilver mood changes are handled with wonderful insight. The *Kinderszenen*, too, are very nicely done, and the performance of *Carnaval*, as mentioned on p175, is superb – quite as good as any other 'modern' performance in the catalogue. The recorded sound, too (often a problem with Naxos), is admirably judged. *JS*

SCHUMANN

Piano Sonata No. 2 in G minor
see SCHUBERT: Piano Sonata in A, D959

SCRIABIN

Études (complete)

Piers Lane (piano)

Hyperion CDA 66607 □ 55:46 mins □ 𝄞𝄞𝄞

More than his sonatas, which are heavily weighted towards his final period, Scriabin's études span his whole career. A complete collection of the latter thus makes for a fascinating survey of his gradually metamorphosing style, from the Chopin/Tchaikovsky rapture of Op. 2/1, written at the age of 15 in 1887, to the typically orgiastic and harmonically daring final three, completed in 1912, three years before his death.

Not surprisingly, they ask a great deal of the pianist (though one at least, Op. 8/8, was written for a less than virtuosic girlfriend). Piers Lane is easily up to tackling the volatile figures that abound in Scriabin's piano music. Indeed, his technical bravura is often breathtaking. The scurrying parallel ninths – which would have been out of Scriabin's own reach – in the first Étude of Op. 65, cause him no problems.

An hour of mere technical showmanship would ultimately be boring. Thankfully, Lane never lets us forget that the virtuosic and poetic exist in equal measure, encompassing in his playing the full technical and emotional range of these qualities in the often very brief movements. The melancholy penultimate study of Op. 8, for example, has a marvellously veiled quality, in contrast to its highly extrovert successor.

The close but ambient recorded sound is ideal, though one or two of the edits momentarily jar. *Matthew Rye*

SCRIABIN

Piano Sonatas Nos 1–10; Fantaisie, Op. 28; Sonate-Fantaisie in G sharp minor

Marc-André Hamelin (piano)

Hyperion CDA 67131/2 □ 145:40 mins (2 discs) □ 𝄞𝄞𝄞

Along with Robert Szidon on mid-price DG, Marc-André Hamelin's complete Scriabin sonata collection is the most complete available, though it inexplicably places the early *Sonate-Fantaisie* at the very end of an otherwise chronological survey. Yet Scriabin's ten sonatas, despite their modest length individually, are hardly a cycle of works to listen to from beginning to end, with their intense exploration of heightened emotion and their other-worldly theosophical associations.

Marc-André Hamelin rises to the challenges of this music with complete mastery. But his is more than a purely technical triumph (though the effortlessness of his playing has to be heard to be believed). Whether in the almost Brahmsian writing of Sonata No. 1, the heroicism of Nos 4 and 5, or in the visionary sound-world of No. 10, Hamelin draws the listener in through his acute shaping of every phrase and by achieving that almost impossible balance between languid, static ecstasy and momentous energy that characterises Scriabin's mature music. *Matthew Rye*

SCRIABIN/PROKOFIEV

Scriabin: Piano Sonatas Nos 2 & 9; Études, Op. 8/2, 4 & 5; Op. 42/3, 4 & 7; Four Pieces, Op. 51; Vers la flamme

Prokofiev: Visions fugitives

Nikolai Demidenko (piano)

Conifer 75605 51204 2 □ 73:13 mins □ 𝄞𝄞𝄞

This was Nikolai Demidenko's debut recording, and in many ways it remains one of his most formidable achievements. The Russian pianist certainly has the measure of the impulsive and mystical sides of Scriabin's personality, and the performances of the whirlwind Presto movement of the Second Sonata and the apocalyptic *Vers la flamme* have rarely been surpassed. The pairing of Scriabin and Prokofiev is also imaginative, reminding us that despite his desire to break free from the shackles of the Russian piano tradition, the younger composer learned a great deal from his erstwhile contemporary. Indeed, one could argue that the extremes of emotion explored by Prokofiev in his *Visions fugitives* represent a further extension of Scriabin's late exploratory style. Whether or not this is actually the case, Demidenko imbues Prokofiev's work with a staggering range of colours and articulations, and his interpretation teems with vivid interest. *EL*

SHOSTAKOVICH

24 Preludes and Fugues, Op. 87

Tatiana Nikolayeva (piano)

Hyperion CDA 66441/3 □ 165:53 mins (3 discs)
□ ❷❷❷

It says a great deal for the integrity of this great Russian pianist that she tried wherever possible to follow the composer's wishes by playing all 24 preludes and fugues in recital (usually on two separate evenings). The long-term result was this magnificent set courageously undertaken by Hyperion, a timely document of an interpretation fashioned from Nikolayeva's close collaboration with the composer at the time of composition (1950–51).

Nikolayeva's rather sober presentation takes some getting used to: she lacks the tonal palette of Sviatoslav Richter and the radiant intimacy of the composer's handful of performances (neither Richter nor Shostakovich recorded the complete cycle). But she does compel attention with tremendous inner strength and calm (touching on the transcendental in the F sharp major Prelude, the contemplative heart of the series) as well as some impressively big-boned playing when necessary. Above all, her Bachian experience, which is what prompted Shostakovich to write his own *Well-Tempered Clavier* in the first place, allows her to bring out with unhurried vividness each of the voices in the composer's rich and varied fugues. *DN*

SHOSTAKOVICH

Three Fantastic Dances; Preludes and Fugues from Op. 87
see ORCHESTRAL: SHOSTAKOVICH: Piano Concertos Nos 1 & 2

SMETANA

Czech Dances; Bagatelles and Impromptu

Radoslav Kvapil (piano)

Unicorn-Kanchana DKP(CD) 9130 □ 73:13 mins
□ ❷❷❷

Piano music makes up by far the greater part of Smetana's instrumental works. He was a piano virtuoso, and much of his music for the instrument reflects this. The present anthology, the second in a series of Czech piano music from Unicorn-Kanchana, focuses on the beginning and end of Smetana's career. The Bagatelles and Impromptus of 1844 have more than the occasional echo of Chopin and Mendelssohn, but there is a great deal which looks forward to the questing originality of Smetana's maturity.

Fascinating as they are, these relatively innocent jottings barely compare to the two sets of Czech Dances from the late 1870s: an anthology of national dance-types – the first four are examples of the composer's beloved polka – these dances are more consciously Czech than Dvořák's pan-Slavic Slavonic Dances of similar vintage. They are also more inward-looking, at times even disturbing. When writing these dances, Smetana was deaf and suffering increasingly from the depredations of syphilis. Any performance needs not only energy and virtuosity, but also insight. Radoslav Kvapil brings all these qualities to bear in performances which continually capture and hold the ear. While not ideal, the piano sound is appreciably better than on the first volume in the series.
Jan Smaczny

SORABJI

Gulistān

Charles Hopkins (piano)

Altarus AIR-CD-9035 □ 35:26 mins □ ❷❷

The music of Kaikhosru Sorabji (half Persian, half Spanish-Sicilian, British-domiciled throughout his long life) is assuredly not for everyone. Yet it represents an astonishing *ne plus ultra* of two seemingly exclusive styles: languorous, iridescent arabesque-nocturnes that go far beyond Liszt, Debussy, Scriabin and Szymanowski in complexity and improvisatory fantasy, and stark, uncompromising structures of architectonic polyphony which literally dwarf everything else in the Bach–Busoni tradition. Sorabji's works include probably the longest and most difficult (in terms of technique and stamina) ever composed for piano. But for many years his entire output remained unheard until the composer was convinced that certain selected players could do it justice.

In the ensuing two decades his reputation has flowered, thanks to a few dedicated exponents and to the CD medium, in which Altarus has shown itself the most committed to recording these fantastic blooms of keyboard imagination. Their most signal release remains John Ogdon's four-disc set of Sorabji's enormous *Opus clavicembalisticum* – at nearly five hours by no means his longest piano work, but the longest yet recorded. An easier entrée to this unexampled composer, however, is this voluptuously intricate, bejewelled fantasy-nocturne (1940), inspired by *The Rose Garden* of the 13th-century Persian poet Sa'adi. (Another would be Yonty Solomon's equally fine reading of the earlier *Le jardin parfumé*, also on Altarus.) Sorabji himself considered *Gulistān* one of his best works. Charles Hopkins, an Ogdon pupil, is entirely at ease with its transcendental demands, its proliferating filigree and fioritura: he also contributes an astonishingly detailed multicultural essay in the booklet notes. At a mere 35-odd minutes *Gulistān* is a 'short' work in Sorabjian terms, but effortlessly establishes its own time-scale. This is music for contemplation and abandonment of self. *CM*

SORABJI

Fantasiettina sul nome illustre dell'egregio poeta Christopher Grieve ossia Hugh MacDiarmid
see Collection: Cathedrals in Sound

STEVENSON

Heroic Song for Hugh MacDiarmid
see Collection: Cathedrals in Sound

STEVENSON

Passacaglia on DSCH; Prelude, Fugue and Fantasy on Themes from Busoni's 'Doktor Faust'; Recitative and Air

Ronald Stevenson (piano)

Altarus AIR-CD-9091 □ ADD □ 115:22 mins (2 discs) □ *❷❷❷*

With its pibroch variation, polonaise, fandango and Russian march, its evocation of African tribal drumming directly on the strings, its pulverising triple fugue using B–A–C–H and the Dies Irae, Ronald Stevenson's Passacaglia (1962) is an astonishing feat, eighty minutes of bravura pianism on a bass derived from Shostakovich's musical monogram. And there's not a dull or

miscalculated moment. It stands in a select company of 20th-century piano marathons (compare Busoni, Sorabji) that combine supreme contrapuntal mastery with transcendental keyboard technique (and hark back to Bach's *The Art of Fugue* and Beethoven's Diabelli Variations). It was championed by John Ogdon, who made a notable LP version for EMI.

If you want only the Passacaglia, and on a single CD, there's a more than dependable account by Raymond Clarke (Marco Polo). But the composer's own performance possesses unique authority and poetry, a spacious lyricism, plus a vein of improvisatory fantasy that comes naturally to a pianist in the Liszt–Paderewski–Busoni tradition. The coupling is a substantial operatic fantasy on themes from Busoni's opera (this also exists as a piano concerto, performed by Murray McLachlan on Olympia) and a starkly elegiac *Recitative and Air*, using DSCH in an entirely different way. Wonderfully natural piano sound. *CM*

SWEELINCK

Organ Works

James David Christie (organ)

Naxos 8.550904 □ 64:20 mins □ *❷*

Christie plays on a superb neo-classical organ at Houghton Chapel, Wellesley College, Massachusetts. It is pictured majestically on the booklet, though neither its specification nor any further information is offered (surely not a sacrifice needed to meet the Naxos budget price). It is delightfully colourful, from the sweetest of flutes to some fizzing, nasal reeds, ideal for the contrasting variations of the evocative *Mein junges Leben hat ein End*. Here, and in five more sets of variations, Christie's pacing within and between the sections generates a strong sense of organic growth. There's a charming *Echo Fantasia*, too, playing wittily with contrasting registers – up an octave and down again – as well as contrasts between manuals. Though two toccatas, intended as teaching materials, are of more interest to the student player developing finger technique than to the passive listener, this is a cleverly chosen programme, including examples of all the keyboard genres to which this remarkably prolific composer of the early Dutch Baroque turned his hand. *GP*

SWEELINCK

Variations; Echo Fantasia
see BUXTEHUDE: Organ Works

SZOLLOSY

Paesaggio con morti
see Collection: The Hungarian Anthology

TCHAIKOVSKY

Piano Works (complete)

Victoria Postnikova, Gennadi Rozhdestvensky (piano)

Erato 2292-45969-2 □ 533:00 mins (7 discs) □ 🌑🌑

A mighty achievement, yet dealing mostly with a miniature scale: that makes this a difficult set to market, though both pianist and company deserve well. Carefully poetic with even the slightest trifle, Postnikova holds no truck with the fashionable opinion that 'piano pieces', in Tchaikovsky's case at least, means 'salon music', with all the disparaging overtones that label entails. True, Tchaikovsky makes no pianistic steps forward – he was not himself a virtuoso – but he has much in Russian vein to add to his models in the field, Schumann and Liszt. The discs of the earlier piano music cast up frequent gems that Stravinsky was to 'treat' and adapt in his ballet *The Fairy's Kiss*, and the occasional testament (such as the Op. 9 *Rêverie*) to Postnikova's subtler virtues: instinctive use of rubato, real shaping of melody and a feel for the intuitive mood behind softer dynamics.

Later fascinations include the curious romp, shared with her husband Gennadi Rozhdestvensky, through the Russian folk-song book compiled in the late 1860s. The finest specimens, though, are the 12 miniature masterpieces of *The Seasons* and the aristocratic summing-up of the Op. 72 set the composer was working on up to his sudden death. Should Erato finally decide on separate release, the final volume is the one to choose; as for *The Seasons*, I prefer Pletnev's equally eccentric, rather more fanciful account on Virgin. *DN*

TIPPETT

Piano Sonatas Nos 1 & 2
see ORCHESTRAL: TIPPETT: Concerto for Double String Orchestra

TORROBA

Sonatina
see Collection: Homage to Segovia

TURINA

Fandanguillo; Sevillana
see Collection: Homage to Segovia

VERESS

Sonata for Solo Violin
see CHAMBER: KODALY: Duo for Violin and Cello

VILLA-LOBOS

Études; Preludes
see ORCHESTRAL: VILLA-LOBOS: Guitar Concerto

WEBERN

Variations, Op. 27
see Collection: The Glenn Gould Edition

WEINER

Three Hungarian Rural Dances
see Collection: The Hungarian Anthology

WIDOR

Organ Symphony No. 9 (Symphonie gothique); Symphonies Nos 5 (Adagio & Toccata), 6 (Allegro) & 7 (Moderato cantabile & Allegro); Trois Nouvelles Pièces

Thomas Trotter (organ)

Argo 433 152-2 □ 74:05 mins □ 🌑🌑🌑

A triumph on every count. Trotter performs on the 1879 Cavaillé-Coll organ in St-François-de-Sales in Lyon on which the composer apparently initiated his son in the art of organ-playing. But although authenticity of instrument is no guarantee of a successful performance and recording, its distinctive and rather biting sonority certainly suits this repertoire. It's good to report that the instrument itself seems in excellent working order despite the clatter of the action, which could be deemed distracting in some of the quieter passages.

Enthusiasts for French organ music may well object to Trotter's programme on the grounds that it presents only the *Symphonie gothique* in its entirety. But such an arrangement seems admirable for giving the best possible overview of Widor's art. The performances, too, are quite stunning, the highlights being brilliant renditions of the Allegro from the Sixth Symphony and the ubiquitous Toccata from the Fifth Symphony. *EL*

YSAYE

Solo Violin Sonatas, Op. 27/3 & 6
see CHAMBER: ENESCU: Violin Sonata No. 3

COLLECTION: CATHEDRALS IN SOUND

Works by Liszt, Chopin, Debussy, Marek, MacDowell, Stevenson, Sorabji & Bach–Busoni–Stokowski–Stevenson

Ronald Stevenson (piano)

Altarus AIR-CD-9043 □ 67:43 mins □ 🌑🌑🌑

This fascinatingly programmed recital contains one of the most stupendous and magisterially searching recordings of Busoni's great transcription of Bach's D minor Chaconne ever put on disc. And this version is unique, for Stevenson (composer-pianist, transcriber and Busoni scholar) adds his own transcription of the quiet coda that Leopold Stokowski gave Bach's Chaconne in *his* orchestral arrangement. Stevenson is a living reincarnation of the Godowsky/Paderewski Romantic piano tradition of expressive rubato, subtly improvisatory re-invention of the repertoire, and kaleidoscopic keyboard colour. This last quality is displayed to perfection in quite the most 'orchestral' realisation of Debussy's 'La cathédrale engloutie' I've ever heard. Among the other items, one should single out the Sorabji *Fantasiettina* – this time in cackling epigrammatic mode, and dedicated, like Stevenson's own piece with its sonorous horn and echo effects, to the Scottish poet Hugh MacDiarmid. But the most substantial piece here is an extreme rarity by Czeslaw Marek, a Polish disciple of Busoni long domiciled in Switzerland: his *Triptyque*, a cycle of three contrasted fugues prefaced, respectively, by a prelude, fantasia and chorale, is a noble essay in polyphonic mastery in the spirit of Bach and Busoni. Astonishing pianism, compelling advocacy, magniloquent Bösendorfer sound beautifully caught. What more could one ask? *CM*

COLLECTION: THE GLENN GOULD EDITION, VOL. 7

Berg: Piano Sonata, Op. 1; Křenek: Piano Sonata No. 3; Webern: Variations, Op. 27; Concerto for Nine Players, Op. 24; Debussy: Première rapsodie; Ravel (transcr. Gould): La valse

Glenn Gould (piano), James Campbell (clarinet); ensemble/Boris Brott

Sony SMK 52661 □ ADD mono/stereo □ 66:10 mins □ 𝄞𝄞

This fascinating collection of 'undiscovered Glenn Gould', largely from radio and TV broadcasts, finds the Canadian keyboard guru in some unfamiliar repertoire. It opens with the most passionate and powerful reading of Alban Berg's youthful Piano Sonata I've heard, and continues with a performance of Ernst Krenek's concise and pungent Third Sonata (from the same 1958 studio sessions in New York) which makes as forceful a case for its chameleon-like composer as any I can think of. The steel gossamer of Webern's Variations is deftly riveted in place in a 1964 radio broadcast (the only stereo item here): Gould, remember, helped propel the modern revolution in Soviet and Russian music by daring to perform this dangerous 'formalist' score in concert in Moscow in the Fifties. A rare opportunity to hear him as a chamber-music player comes in the elegantly cubist account of Webern's Concerto (a 1977 television performance). He accompanied the Debussy Clarinet Rhapsody in 1973 on sufferance, but you can't tell. The most dumbfounding item here, however, is Gould's own brilliant transcription of Ravel's *La valse* – an incredible *tour de force*, thrown off with sovereign assurance. Unmissable: the sound is variable, of course, but never less than acceptable. *CM*

COLLECTION: MARC-ANDRE HAMELIN LIVE AT WIGMORE HALL

Beethoven (transcr. Alkan): Piano Concerto No. 3 (first movement); Chopin (transcr. Balakirev): Piano Concerto No. 1 (Romanza); Alkan: Trois Grandes Études, Op. 76; Busoni: Sonatina No. 6; Medtner: Danza festiva, Op. 38/3

Marc-André Hamelin (piano)

Hyperion CDA 66765 □ 71:56 mins □ 𝄞𝄞𝄞

The young Canadian, recorded in a 1994 recital of 'Virtuoso Romantics', here produces some of the most astonishing playing of the decade, and all at the service of a repertoire that usually goes unheard and unrepresented, precisely because this is the kind of playing it requires. Alkan's titanic études for left hand, right hand and both together sit on a lonely pinnacle of transcendental virtuosity combined with profound musical expressiveness, but even they're surpassed, on both counts, by the same composer's solo piano transcription of the first movement of Beethoven's C minor Concerto, complete with Alkan's own electrifying cadenza (which quotes Beethoven's Fifth Symphony).

After these prestidigitational prodigies, Balakirev's charming adaptation of a Chopin concerto movement comes as welcome lyric filigree, preparing for quite the wittiest and most mercurial recorded account of Busoni's wonderful 'chamber fantasy' on themes from Bizet's *Carmen*. And as encore a totally effervescent reading of a bounding miniature by Medtner which audibly and rightly brings the house down. *CM*

COLLECTION: HOMAGE TO SEGOVIA

Turina: Fandanguillo; Sevillana; Mompou: Suite compostelana; Torroba: Sonatina; Gerhard: Fantasia; Falla: Homenaje pour le tombeau de Claude Debussy; Three Dances from The Three-Cornered Hat; Ohana: Tiento

Julian Bream (guitar)

RCA Victor Gold Seal 09026 61353 2 □ 57:55 mins □ 𝄞𝄞

Of the many fine guitar records Julian Bream has made, this is one of the finest, displaying not only his extraordinary command of the instrument but also musicianship of the

highest level. The subtlety and tonal variety of the playing in these 20th-century pieces is quite extraordinary, and Bream is recorded with superb realism. Presented as a celebration of the work of Andrés Segovia, this is one master guitarist's tribute to another.
David Michaels

COLLECTION: THE HUNGARIAN ANTHOLOGY

Liszt: Csárdás macabre; Dohnányi: Gavotte and Musette; Kodály: Seven Pieces, Op. 11; Bartók: Dance Suite; Weiner: Three Hungarian Rural Dances; Kurtág: Plays and Games, Vol. 3 (excerpts); Szöllösy: Paesaggio con morti

Peter Frankl (piano)

ASV CD DCA 860 □ 77:52 mins □ *❸❸❸*

A fascinating compilation that demonstrates the richness of Hungarian piano music beyond established masters such as Bartók, Liszt and Kodály. Of particular interest is the inclusion of excerpts from György Kurtág's *Plays and Games*, a collection of exquisite studies in piano texture which can be regarded as a kind of latter-day *Mikrokosmos*. Kurtág's older contemporary, András Szöllösy, is represented by a compelling work of almost Lisztian bravura which provides a dramatic contrast to the less intellectually demanding dance pieces of Weiner and Dohnányi. It's good, too, to hear Liszt's aggressive *Csárdás macabre* in tandem with Bartók's own inventive piano arrangement of his *Dance Suite*. But perhaps most memorable of all are Kodály's wonderfully atmospheric Seven Piano Pieces – a cycle that hardly deserves its current obscurity. Needless to say, Peter Frankl is perfectly equipped to deal with the differing demands of this repertoire, and he is supported by outstanding recorded sound. *EL*

Opera

ADAMS

Nixon in China

Sanford Sylvan, James Maddalena, Thomas Hammons, John Duykers, Carolann Page, Trudy Ellen Craney; Chorus & Orchestra of St Luke's/Edo de Waart

Nonesuch 7559-79177-2 □ 144:00 mins (3 discs) □ 😊😊😊

On the face of it, a chronicle that details the 1972 seven-day visit of US President Nixon to China seems less than promising material for a full-length three-act opera. Yet such is the poetic beauty of Alice Goodman's libretto, and the evocative nature of John Adams's music, that the listener inevitably gets drawn into the dramatic argument. The score abounds in moments of breathtaking power – one remembers in particular the mounting sense of anticipation that presages the American plane's landing at Peking airport, the rhythmic verve of the banquet music in Act II, and the more introspective character studies that dominate the final scene. In all these passages Adams offers the most convincing proof that minimalist techniques can be harnessed effectively and imaginatively over a relatively long time-span. The cast, drawn from the original stage production in Houston, sing with conviction and commitment throughout, and chorus and orchestra follow suit with outstanding contributions all round. *EL*

BARTOK

Duke Bluebeard's Castle

Siegmund Nimsgern, Tatiana Troyanos; BBC SO/Pierre Boulez

Sony SMK 64110 □ ADD □ 61:14 mins □ 😊😊

Bartók's compelling psychological drama doesn't require visual props to make its full impact, and as such it is almost ideally suited to studio recording. It's not surprising that the current catalogue boasts a number of strong performances, from Adam Fischer and the Hungarian State Opera Orchestra on

Sony and István Kertész and the LSO for Decca, and earlier versions from Antal Dorati and János Ferencsik deserve serious consideration. In comparison, Pierre Boulez may not offer such an idiomatic approach. Certainly, his interpretation is a good deal more measured than that of his Hungarian counterparts. Yet despite a broader overall conception, there is no loss of dramatic impetus, and the clarity of orchestral texture – one of Boulez's special gifts – is always illuminating. Furthermore, in Tatiana Troyanos Boulez has arguably the most convincing Judith on disc, her powerful singing proving to be an effective foil for the dark-hued voice of Siegmund Nimsgern. *EL*

BEETHOVEN

Fidelio

Christa Ludwig, Jon Vickers, Gottlob Frick, Walter Berry, Gerhard Unger, Ingeborg Hallstein, Franz Crass; Philharmonia Chorus & Orchestra/Otto Klemperer

EMI CDS 5 55170 2 □ ADD □ 128:03 mins (2 discs) □ 😊😊😊

Though there have been several fine recordings of *Fidelio* since this set was issued more than thirty years ago, Klemperer's magisterial account of Beethoven's only opera has never been surpassed. He conducts a most moving performance of Beethoven's marvellous score, and has the advantage of an almost uniformly excellent cast, all of whose members are fully in accord with his approach to the work. The warmth of Christa Ludwig's voice is well suited to the role of Leonore, whose character she brings vividly to life, delivering the dialogue with as much conviction as the music. Jon Vickers is an eloquent Florestan, Gottlob Frick conveys successfully Rocco's ambiguous personality, and the young couple, whose lives are so very nearly disrupted by Leonore's heroism, are appealingly sung by Ingeborg Hallstein and Gerhard Unger. *CO*

BELLINI

Beatrice di Tenda

Mariana Nicolesco, Piero Cappuccilli, Stefania Toczyska, Vincenzo La Scola, Iorio Zennaro; Prague Philharmonic Choir, Monte Carlo National Opera Orchestra/Alberto Zedda

Sony SM3K 64539 □ 163:13 mins (3 discs) □ 𝄞𝄞

Bellini's penultimate opera was received unenthusiastically at its premiere in 1833, and has never attained the popularity of *Norma*. Yet it's a dramatically vigorous and well-constructed work contains some of Bellini's finest and most characteristic melodies, among them a ravishingly beautiful trio, 'Angiol di pace'.

Zedda conducts an ardent performance, sung by a first-rate cast. As Orombello, La Scola sings throughout with pure tone and a fine appreciation of Bellini's long phrases. The experienced Cappuccilli is the vengeful Duke, heard at his best in 'Qui m'accolse', the aria in which he hesitates before signing the warrant for his wife's execution, and the Romanian soprano Mariana Nicolesco brings a vibrant and flexible voice and a forceful personality to the role of Beatrice. Highly recommended to all who know and love Bellini's more frequently performed operas. *CO*

BELLINI

Norma

Maria Callas, Christa Ludwig, Franco Corelli, Nicola Zaccaria; Chorus & Orchestra of La Scala, Milan/Tullio Serafin

EMI CMS 7 63000 2 □ ADD □ 161:27 mins (3 discs) □ 𝄞𝄞

Norma was surely Callas's greatest role, one in which her occasional vocal imperfections, a hardness in her top notes and a by no means ideally steady vocal line, are spectacularly outweighed by the dramatic fervour of her portrayal of the wronged Druid priestess. Christa Ludwig makes a most sympathetic Adalgisa, her duet scenes with Callas both moving and exciting, and Franco Corelli is a suitably stentorian Pollione. The conductor is Callas's great mentor, Tullio Serafin, who keeps the opera moving at a brisk pace while sacrificing none of its drama. He makes the usual theatre cuts. Those wishing to hear Bellini's complete score may prefer to invest in a rival Decca recording conducted by Richard Bonynge and featuring Joan Sutherland and Marilyn Horne, but Callas's fierce intensity finally wins the day. *CO*

BELLINI

La sonnambula

Joan Sutherland, Luciano Pavarotti, Della Jones, Nicolai Ghiaurov, Isobel Buchanan; London Opera Chorus, National PO/Richard Bonynge

Decca 417 424-2 □ ADD □ 141:58 mins (2 discs) □ 𝄞𝄞𝄞

Twenty years after her first recording of *La sonnambula*, Joan Sutherland returned to Bellini's most delightful opera, singing the title role even more impressively than before, and presenting an entirely convincing characterisation of the innocent country maid. From Amina's beguiling entrance aria, 'Come per me sereno', to the opera's final scene and the exhilarating fioriture of 'Sovra il sen', Sutherland is in her finest and most youthful voice, spinning out Bellini's languorous melodies with a fine legato line and sailing through the decorated cabalettas with apparently the greatest of ease. Pavarotti, too, is in rich voice, and gives one of his most engaging performances on disc. Nicolai Ghiaurov brings an air of elegance to the role of the Count; the smaller roles are all well taken; and Richard Bonynge, completely at home in the bel canto repertoire, conducts most stylishly. *CO*

BERG

Lulu

Teresa Stratas, Yvonne Minton, Hanna Schwarz, Franz Mazura, Kenneth Riegel, Toni Blankenheim, Robert Tear, Helmut Pampuch; Paris Opera Orchestra/Pierre Boulez

DG 415 489-2 □ ADD □ 171:18 mins (3 discs) □ 𝄞𝄞𝄞

Berg's opera about the sexually provocative femme-fatale who becomes wife and mistress to several different men, but ends her days as a prostitute at the hands of Jack the Ripper, is compulsive music-theatre from beginning to end. As the first fully extended opera to have been composed in the 12-note system, its musical language and dramatic structure are extremely sophisticated. Yet the technical sophistication that underlines the score by no means inhibits one's involvement in the drama.

It seems incredible that owing to the refusal of Berg's widow to allow anyone to prepare a fully orchestrated version of the third act, *Lulu* was performed for forty years in a totally unsatisfactory abridged version. However, thanks to the masterly reconstruction by the Austrian composer Friedrich Cerha in the Seventies, we now have the opportunity to hear every note Berg wrote. The present recording, utilising the same all-star cast that participated in the 1979 Parisian premiere of the complete work, conveys all the excitement of discovering a fully-fledged masterpiece for the first time, but also benefits from Boulez's exceptional ability to give clarity to Berg's complex textures without sacrificing any element of passion. *EL*

Berg: Wozzeck

Schoenberg: Erwartung

Eberhard Waechter, Anja Silja, Hermann Winkler, Horst Laubenthal, Heinz Zednik, Alexander Malta, Gertrude Jahn; Vienna State Opera Chorus, Vienna PO/Christoph von Dohnányi

Decca 417 348-2 □ 122:42 mins (2 discs) □ ❷❸❸

The current state of play with regard to recordings of Berg's masterpiece reveals no absolute clear winner. Although Claudio Abbado's highly praised 1988 live recording with the Vienna Philharmonic boasts a strong cast and a superbly incisive account of the orchestral part, DG's engineering is fatally flawed in favouring the orchestra very much at the expense of the singers. This Decca release, recorded in studio conditions, offers a far more satisfactory balance, but without sacrificing DG's clarity of orchestral detail. Dohnányi pays greater attention to the lyrical aspects of the score than Abbado does, yet the moments of catastrophe are equally overwhelming. It's a pity, therefore, that the normally excellent Eberhard Waechter makes such a limp impression as Wozzeck, but the rest of the soloists are excellent. A further incentive to buy this version is the generous inclusion of Schoenberg's monodrama *Erwartung*, which here receives a performance of devastating urgency. *EL*

Benvenuto Cellini

Nicolai Gedda, Christiane Eda-Pierre, Jules Bastin, Robert Massard; Chorus of the Royal Opera House, Covent Garden, BBC SO/Colin Davis

Philips 416 955-2 □ ADD □ 160:33 mins (3 discs) □ ❷❸❸

Its libretto very loosely adapted from the 15th-century Florentine sculptor's memoirs, *Benvenuto Cellini* oddly juxtaposes Romantic and farcical genres but contrives, nevertheless, to present a portrait of Cellini himself which gives him heroic stature. Some of the opera's individual numbers represent Berlioz at his most resourceful in terms of rhythmic complexity and orchestral colouring. The climactic point comes in Cellini's aria, 'Sur les monts les plus sauvages', in which he sings of his longing to exchange the cares of the artist for the simple life of a shepherd. The role of Cellini virtually belonged to Nicolai Gedda for many years, and he is here at the peak of his powers. There is not a weak performance among the supporting cast, and Davis conducts magisterially. *CO*

Les troyens

Jon Vickers, Josephine Veasey, Berit Lindholm, Peter Glossop, Heather Begg, Roger Soyer; Wandsworth School Boys Choir, Chorus & Orchestra of the Royal Opera House, Covent Garden/Colin Davis

Philips 416 432-2 □ ADD □ 239:56 mins (4 discs) □ ❷❸❸

Though this vast two-part opera, usually performed over two evenings, lacks dramatic cohesion and veers uneasily in style between a Gluckian Classicism and the inflated grand opera style of Meyerbeer, it is nevertheless full of musical felicities. Davis's magisterial account of the work is based on the Royal Opera House revival which he conducted in 1969, and much of the excitement of those performances survives on this recording. Davis takes Berlioz's score at a brisk pace, but allows time for the lyrical scenes to make their proper effect. In Part One Berit Lindholm is an effective Cassandra, and as Dido, in Part Two, Josephine Veasey gives her finest recorded performance, singing throughout in firm and commanding voice, with Jon Vickers, her partner on the Covent Garden stage, as a splendidly heroic Aeneas. The large supporting cast includes some of the Royal Opera's most reliable performers at that time, among them Elizabeth Bainbridge, Ryland Davies and Heather Begg, and the quality of the recorded sound is superb. *CO*

On the Town

Frederica von Stade, Thomas Hampson, Samuel Ramey, Cleo Laine, David Garrison, Kurt Ollmann, Evelyn Lear, Marie McLaughlin, Tyne Daly; LSO/Michael Tilson Thomas

DG 437 516-2 □ 74:33 mins □ ❷❸❸

Bernstein's musical about the adventures of three sailors who enjoy a day out on the tiles in New York City is a marvellously entertaining romp, full of good tunes, humour and insight.

Each of the protagonists is brilliantly drawn, from the sleazy night-club singer (Cleo Laine) to the upright Pitkin (Samuel Ramey).

A star-studded cast, recorded live at the Barbican in London, pulls out all the stops, milking each number for all it's worth. Among the highlights I would single out Tyne Daly's no-holds-barred delivery of 'I can cook too' and Thomas Hampson's affecting 'Lonely Town'. But perhaps the most impressive aspect of this whole enterprise is the superb playing of the LSO, which, under Michael Tilson Thomas's alert direction, negotiates Bernstein's jazzy syncopations with bristling energy. *EL*

BERNSTEIN

West Side Story

Natalie Wood, Richard Beymer, Russ Tamblyn, Rita Moreno, George Chakiris; orchestra/Johnny Green

Sony SMK 48211 □ ADD □ 77:30 mins □ 😊😊

It may seem perverse to recommend the original soundtrack film version of Bernstein's *West Side Story* over and above the composer's much-vaunted recording for DG. But in spite of persuasive claims as to this particular musical's operatic credentials, I believe DG's casting of Kiri Te Kanawa and José Carreras, in the title roles of Maria and Tony, to be flawed. In comparison, the principal singers on the soundtrack seem far less self-conscious, delivering Sondheim's lyrics with greater naturalness. DG's studio engineering may offer a superior balance between voices and orchestra, but in some ways the brittleness of Sony's recording, coupled with some exceptionally dynamic conducting from Johnny Green, appears more appropriate to the harsh sonorities favoured by Bernstein. *EL*

BIZET

Carmen

Maria Callas, Nicolai Gedda, Andréa Guiot, Robert Massard; René Duclos Choir, Jean Pesneaud Children's Choir, Orchestre du Théâtre National de l'Opéra, Paris/Georges Prêtre

EMI CDS 7 54368 2 □ AAD □ 146:24 mins (2 discs) □ 😊😊😊

Carmen is one of the most popular of all operas, and there have been at least two very fine exponents of the title role in recordings more recent than this one. For example, Julia Migenes is a delightfully earthy gypsy girl on Erato, while Teresa Berganza presents a more up-market heroine for DG. But the major flaw with both recordings is Plácido Domingo, who fails to find the correct style on either

occasion. For an altogether more rounded performance one should turn to Callas, who, as one would expect, is a powerfully magnetic Carmen. Although she never sang the role on stage, Callas is completely convincing, and sings the vocal part with consummate ease. Intensely dramatic in the Card Scene in Act II, she is splendidly seductive in the Habanera. Her impassioned José is Nicolai Gedda, whose fine acting is matched by a superb assimilation of the French style. Of the supporting roles, Andréa Guiot's individual French timbre helps to make Micaëla a very positive character, while Robert Massard brings Gallic flair, and again the right timbre, to the tricky role of Escamillo, successfully negotiating the awkward tessitura of the Toreador's Song. The smaller roles are capably handled by experienced French performers, and Georges Prêtre conducts with great flair. *CO*

BIZET

Les pêcheurs de perles

Barbara Hendricks, John Aler, Gino Quilico, Jean-Philippe Courtis; Toulouse Capitole Chorus & Orchestra/Michel Plasson

EMI CDS 7 49837 2 □ 126:57 mins (2 discs) □ 😊😊😊

Despite the superb performances of Nicolai Gedda and Ernest Blanc as the two friends Nadir and Zurga in an earlier EMI recording (which was conducted in masterly style by Pierre Dervaux), that version must yield pride of place to Michel Plasson's account of the opera, which uses the Choudens 1975 edition of the score, restoring, as far as possible, Bizet's original intentions. Plasson allows Bizet's sensuous melodies to speak for themselves, in leisurely tempi which seem to have a natural sense of flow. Barbara Hendricks is a sweet-voiced priestess, John Aler's high tenor, heard at its best in 'Je crois entendre encore', is well suited to the role of Nadir, and Gino Quilico makes an ideal Zurga. *CO*

BLOW

Venus and Adonis

Catherine Bott, Michael George, Libby Crabtree; Choristers of Westminster Abbey Choir, New London Consort/Philip Pickett

L'Oiseau-Lyre 440 220-2 □ 57:06 mins □ 😊😊😊

Venus and Adonis has too often been seen as no more than a weak, if well-meant, precursor of Purcell's *Dido*. It is no such thing, as this welcome recording clearly shows. For all its satire on court life in Restoration England,

and all its moments of light humour, its tragic climax is deeply moving. Within an hour the artificial characters of a masque have become people wrestling with deep emotions: Venus does not, as does Dido, escape tragedy in death.

Catherine Bott excels as Venus, and Michael George contributes a dark if somewhat aged Adonis. But the star is undoubtedly the Cupid of newcomer Libby Crabtree, whose mixture of sexual candour and childlike purity makes for a deeply disturbing cocktail. *Antony Bye*

BOITO
Mefistofele

Cesare Siepi, Mario del Monaco, Renata Tebaldi; Chorus & Orchestra of the Academy of Santa Cecilia/Tullio Serafin

Decca 440 054-2 □ ADD □ 140:54 mins (2 discs) □ 🎵🎵

Arrigo Boito's only completed opera is arguably the most ambitious written by an Italian composer between *William Tell* (1829) and Verdi's *Otello* (1887). Certainly, with its courageous assaults on some of Goethe's most theatrically demanding scenes from *Faust* (Parts One and Two) it aspires to, and occasionally matches, the visionary poetic ideals of the original poem. In a performance such as this – the finest, I contend, ever recorded – the work seems far more impressive than its critics generally allow.

Its success depends, however, on a conductor who really believes in it, such as the magnificent, still wickedly underrated Serafin, who, bar Toscanini and Bernstein in the versions of the Prologue only, has no peer in this music. Not only does he inspire the provincial Santa Cecilia forces to surpass themselves in the discipline and delicacy of their playing, but the three leading soloists (Tebaldi, del Monaco and Siepi) also seem to be under the spell of the maestro. Did del Monaco ever sing more musically for Decca than in this recording? Tebaldi, who could be somewhat indomitable even in pathetic roles, ravishes the ear and touches the heart as Margherita. Like his colleagues, Siepi is the most idiomatic interpreter of the title role in any complete recording, capturing the sinister and ironic qualities of the part to perfection. *Hugh Canning*

BOITO
Mefistofele – Prologue
see **CHORAL & SONG**: BERLIOZ: Grand messe des morts

BORODIN
Prince Igor

Mikhail Kit, Galina Gorchakova, Gegam Grigorian, Vladimir Ognovenko, Bulat Mingelkiev, Olga Borodina, Georgy Selezniev, Konstantin Pluzhnikov; Kirov Opera Chorus & Orchestra/Valery Gergiev

Philips 442 537-2 □ 209:01 mins (3 discs) □ 🎵🎵🎵

A cautionary tale of Kievan (12th-century) Rus and its submission to the lure and power of the exotic eastern Polovtsians, *Prince Igor* occupied Borodin throughout the last 18 years of his life. Nonetheless, without the hard work and brilliant orchestrations of Rimsky-Korsakov and Glazunov, it would never have seen the light of day; the Kirov's new performing edition, masterminded by Gergiev and heard for the first time here, adds some new music, thereby altering the structure of their already solid edifice.

For anyone coming fresh to this colourful culture-clash, the new discoveries will matter less than Gergiev's vivid response to every mood in the opera – be it the heavy brooding of the captive Igor (lugubriously, if a little stolidly, sung by Mikhail Kit), the supple exoticism of his Polovtsian hosts, or the vivid clash of honest and disreputable Slavs back in Igor's home town. One of the brightest stars in Gergiev's Kirov company is Olga Borodina; here, as a sinuous Konchakovna, she and Gegam Grigorian, as a prince radiantly under her spell, fare better than the fitfully brilliant Galina Gorchakova as Igor's resilient wife, Yaroslavna. Still, it's the ensemble work that counts, and as long as you can acclimatise to the purposefully unsensational Mariinsky acoustic, the gripping story should hold you in its thrall. *DN*

BOUGHTON
The Immortal Hour

Anne Dawson, Maldwyn Davies, David Wilson-Johnson, Roderick Kennedy; Geoffrey Mitchell Choir, English CO/Alan Melville

Hyperion CDA 66101/2 □ 124:36 mins (2 discs) □ 🎵🎵🎵

Based on a play by Fiona MacLeod about an Irish king who marries a princess of the fairy folk, to his ultimate doom, *The Immortal Hour* (1914) was the centrepiece of Boughton's famous Glastonbury Festival, a brave attempt to set up a British Bayreuth in a village hall. Transferred to London, the work took the artistic world by storm, although by the Fifties it was consigned to the deepest pit of unfashionability. So this superb complete recording was a salutary shock: the opera is a kind of masterpiece, bleak, passionate and inspired, superbly written for voices, and making astonishingly resourceful use of the chorus as participants in the drama. Boughton's scoring, often of the sparest, is magically atmospheric, his leitmotivic technique subtle and strong. His melodic writing encompasses utmost simplicity, and passages such as Midir's narration in Act II are also startlingly modern for their time. Anne Dawson is an alluring, vulnerable Etain, with Roderick Kennedy an impressive Lord of Shadow. As the doomed king Eochaidh, David Wilson-Johnson finds one of his finest roles, and Maldwyn Davies is chillingly alien as the ever-young fairy king. Enthusiastically recommended. *CM*

BRITTEN

Billy Budd; Holy Sonnets of John Donne; Songs and Proverbs of William Blake

Peter Glossop, Peter Pears, Michael Langdon, Owen Brannigan, Robert Tear, Dietrich Fischer-Dieskau; Wandsworth School Boys Choir, Ambrosian Opera Chorus, LSO/Benjamin Britten (piano)

Decca 417 428-2 □ ADD □ 204:56 mins (3 discs) □ 🎵🎵🎵

Despite its occasionally embarrassingly coy libretto drawn from Herman Melville's novel by EM Forster and Eric Crozier, *Billy Budd* is one of Britten's most exciting operas. It tells the story of a naive, handsome young sailor, pressed into service in the British navy in 1797, whose one defect – a stammer – proves to be fatal when he is unable to articulate his reply to a false accusation of treachery, striking out at his accuser and thus killing him. Peter Glossop is an open and honest Billy, with Michael Langdon giving a masterly portrayal of the evil and repressed Claggart. Peter Pears, in the role he created on stage, is perfect as the equally repressed Captain Vere, who fails to save Billy from a sentence of death. The smaller roles are all well sung and firmly characterised, and the composer himself conducts impressively. The album also includes Britten's *Holy Sonnets of John Donne* (sung by Peter Pears) and *Songs and Proverbs of William Blake* (Dietrich Fischer-Dieskau), both accompanied by the composer. *CO*

BRITTEN

Death in Venice

Peter Pears, James Bowman, John Shirley-Quirk; English Opera Group Chorus, English CO/Steuart Bedford

Decca London 425 669-2 □ ADD □ 145:19 mins (2 discs) □ 🎵🎵🎵

This recording of Britten's last opera is conducted by Steuart Bedford, who took over the work's premiere in 1973 when its composer was too ill to conduct. But Britten attended the subsequent recording sessions, and his guiding hand seems to be evident throughout. The opera is one that grows on one with repeated hearings, for Britten's masterly achievement in re-creating Thomas Mann's novella for the lyric stage is subtle in that it does not wear its heart on its sleeve. Peter Pears created the role of Aschenbach, the Apollonian novelist forced to come to terms with the dionysiac elements in his nature after watching an attractive youth on the Lido. Pears is found here in remarkable voice for a tenor then in his mid-sixties, and brings consummate artistry and penetrating intelligence to his portrayal of an extremely taxing role. The cameo roles of a traveller, an elderly fop, a gondolier, a hotel manager, a barber, the leader of a troupe of players, and the voice of the god Dionysus are all written to be performed by the same singer, and here John Shirley-Quirk brings each one convincingly to life. *CO*

BRITTEN

Gloriana

Josephine Barstow, Philip Langridge, Della Jones, Jonathan Summers, Yvonne Kenny, Richard Van Allan, Willard White, Bryn Terfel; Welsh National Opera Chorus & Orchestra/Charles Mackerras

Argo 440 213-2 □ 148:13 mins (2 discs) □ 🎵🎵🎵

Any feeling that Britten, by petitioning for royal patronage, was toadying to an establishment from which he felt alienated was rapidly quashed when the result of his diplomacy, the 1953 coronation opera *Gloriana*, finally saw the light of day. Instead of the expected Elizabethan pageant celebrating the legacy of a golden age and mirroring in anticipation the doubtless equally glorious achievements of the new Elizabeth, Britten painted a rather more veristic picture. Indeed the warts-and-all picture of Elizabeth I herself, all too humanly vulnerable, was viewed by the predominantly jewel-bedecked audience who inhabited the corridors of power as a positive insult, an act of downright treachery even. The ensuing controversy did nothing for the opera's future beyond ensuring its reputation as Britten's one major failure and its glaring absence from the record catalogues.

A highly successful production by English National Opera in the Eighties (available on video from Virgin) signalled an upward turn

in *Gloriana*'s fortunes, confirming its distinctive position in Britten's operatic canon. This first recording, with a strong cast, is more than ample testimony to its very special qualities. It captures vividly and movingly the unique blend of public ceremony, as exemplified by the many fanfares, marches and dances, and private confessional, encapsulated in the intimate encounters between Elizabeth and Essex. Josephine Barstow's Elizabeth is a commanding figure, at her best in moments of self-doubt and self-examination, and she's well partnered by Philip Langridge's Essex, a sympathetic portrayal of a figure driven by a volatile mixture of naivety and ardour. Jonathan Summers, Della Jones and Richard Van Allan offer equally strong contributions, and the whole set is crowned by the magnificent playing and singing of the WNO Orchestra and Chorus under Charles Mackerras's committed direction.
Antony Bye

BRITTEN
A Midsummer Night's Dream

James Bowman, Lillian Watson, Norman Bailey, Penelope Walker, Jill Gomez, John Graham Hall, Henry Herford, Della Jones; Trinity Boys Choir, City of London Sinfonia/Richard Hickox

Virgin VCD 7 59305 2 □ 154:26 mins (2 discs) □ ❷❸❹

The *Midsummer Night's Dream* from Virgin faces strong competition from Britten's own classic account (Decca London 425 663-2) and, while not superseding it, offers a viable alternative – further proof that Britten's operas are well able to sustain themselves outside his own favoured circle of interpreters. Britten, perhaps, finds greater Romantic breadth, especially in the expansive string tune that heralds the arrival of Theseus and Hippolyta, and he's better at pointing the humour of the ensuing Pyramus and Thisbe routine, a delicious parody of Italian opera conventions. But Hickox is not far behind: his depiction of the sleeping wood is richly atmospheric, his fairies are a vigorous, raucous bunch and his quartet of lovers convincingly young; John Graham Hall's fresh-voiced Lysander is certainly more appealing than the elderly-sounding Peter Pears, for all the latter's detailed verbal inflections. *Antony Bye*

BRITTEN
Peter Grimes

Peter Pears, Claire Watson, James Pease, Jean Watson; Chorus & Orchestra of the Royal Opera House, Covent Garden/Benjamin Britten

Decca 414 577-2 □ ADD □ 144:00 mins (3 discs) □ ❷❸❹

Of the four complete recordings of *Peter Grimes*, the earliest, conducted by the composer, is easily the best. Not all composers are their own best interpreters, but Britten was an exemplary conductor of other men's music as well as his own, and almost without exception the authoritative recordings of his operas and song cycles which he made in collaboration with Peter Pears, for whom Britten's leading tenor roles were conceived, are the versions to be preferred. Pears was an intensely moving Grimes on stage, and the essence of his interpretation is captured on these discs. The American soprano Claire Watson sings most beautifully the role of Ellen Orford, and James Pease, another American, makes a forthright and sympathetic Captain Balstrode. The opera's smaller character roles are handled by such reliable British singers as John Lanigan, Owen Brannigan, Geraint Evans, John Dobson and David Kelly, and Decca's recording is marvellously atmospheric. *CO*

BRITTEN
The Rape of Lucretia; Phaedra

Peter Pears, Heather Harper, Janet Baker, John Shirley-Quirk, Benjamin Luxon; English CO/Benjamin Britten, Steuart Bedford

Decca London 425 666-2 □ ADD □ 124:00 mins (2 discs) □ ❷❸❹

Ronald Duncan's libretto suffers from stilted diction and its unsatisfactory device of a Male and Female Chorus (two solo singers) framing the action in pre-Christian Rome of the rape of Lucretia by her husband's colleague Tarquinius, and commenting on it from a deliberately anachronistic Christian viewpoint. The opera's comparative lack of popularity among Britten's stage works is probably due to Duncan's text, for its score, written for a small chamber orchestra, is masterly. Janet Baker's portrayal of Lucretia, who, overcome by an irrational shame, commits suicide, is not only dramatically convincing but also very beautifully sung. Benjamin Luxon brings Tarquinius vividly to life, and the comments on the action by the Male and Female Chorus are clearly articulated by Heather Harper and

Peter Pears. The album also finds room for Janet Baker's superb recording of Britten's dramatic *scena*, *Phaedra*. **CO**

BRITTEN

The Turn of the Screw

Felicity Lott, Philip Langridge, Nadine Secunde, Phyllis Cannan, Eileen Hulse, Sam Pay; Aldeburgh Festival Ensemble/Steuart Bedford

Collins 70302 □ **106:20 mins (2 discs)** □ *𝄞𝄞𝄞*

Following the *Peter Grimes* from Bernard Haitink, the third generation of Britten opera recordings is now well into its stride. This later work is already available in two other versions: in Britten's own (Decca), and one from Colin Davis (Philips).

The cast of this *Turn of the Screw* could hardly be bettered; Felicity Lott is an involving Governess and Philip Langridge mesmerising as the ghostly Quint. The instrumentalists of the Aldeburgh Festival Ensemble are atmospherically recorded, and the whole enterprise, conducted by Britten's former assistant Steuart Bedford, is a worthy counterpart to the composer's own. The set is capped by an illuminating booklet article by Donald Mitchell. *Matthew Rye*

BUSONI

Arlecchino; Turandot

Theo Richter, Thomas Mohr, Stefan Dahlberg, Susanne Mentzer, Mechthild Gessendorf, Franz-Josef Selig, Markus Schäfer; Lyon Opera Chorus & Orchestra/Kent Nagano

Virgin VCD 7 59313 2 □ **137:11 mins (2 discs)** □ *𝄞𝄞𝄞*

Busoni's two theatrical caprices, attempts towards a *nuova commedia dell'arte*, were presented as a double bill, as here, at their 1917 Zürich premiere. Deftly tuneful, ironic, fantastical scores, they're the perfect embodiments of his ideal of 'rejuvenated classicality'. These sparkling performances, well sung, crisply recorded and sensitively directed, are a perfect introduction to Busoni at his wittiest and most playful.

Arlecchino, in which Harlequin cuckolds a gullible tailor, embodies an action as artificial as its puppet-play origins. Busoni joyously shuffles, parodies and re-polishes operatic clichés to create an acid comedy that hints at an altogether darker mockery of a world at war. His *Turandot*, more closely based on Gozzi's Venetian fable than Puccini's later one, shares something of the puppet-play stylisation and uncanny atmosphere, along with a scintillating mock-oriental flavour (broad enough in its references to include a rendition of 'Greensleeves').

Theo Richter shines in the virtuoso spoken role of Arlecchino, with Thomas Mohr an amusing tailor. Stefan Dahlberg, the very picture of a ridiculous operatic tenor in *Arlecchino* as the knight Leandro, makes the transition to ardent Romantic lead as Kalaf in *Turandot*, while Mechthild Gessendorf brings cool refinement to the icy eponymous princess. **CM**

BUSONI

Doktor Faust

Dietrich Fischer-Dieskau, Karl Christian Kohn, William Cochran, Anton de Ridder, Hildegard Hillebrecht; Bavarian Radio Chorus & SO/Ferdinand Leitner

DG 20th Century Classics 427 413-2 □ **ADD** □ **155:38 mins (3 discs)** □ *𝄞𝄞*

Busoni worked on his *magnum opus* for many years, but didn't live to complete it; the somewhat leaden conclusion is by his pupil Philipp Jarnach. Nevertheless, it's one of the most literally magical operas of all time, reaching back beyond Goethe to the 16th-century chapbooks to re-interpret the legend of the magus who signs away his soul for hidden knowledge and worldly success. There are none of the sentimental or Gothic elements of other treatments: all is clarity, wit, pain and spiritual fire. It is Busoni's greatest and most magnetic music, and its lithe classicality, phosphorescent colours and brilliant yet unified diversity justify the multifarious stylistic contrasts of the rest of his output.

Astonishingly, this is the only version; but if Fischer-Dieskau was born to incarnate just one operatic role, it was this Faust. He is incomparable in the role of the proud, troubled, disillusioned yet still idealistic sage. William Cochran's Mephistopheles is the perfect foil, brilliantly charismatic from his first terrifying entry (terrifying for listeners and singer alike in its inhumanly high tessitura) in the great spirit-conjuring scene of the Prologue. The other roles are efficiently done, apart perhaps from Hillebrecht's wobbly Duchess of Parma. Leitner directs with real ardour. There are many small cuts, but the disc deserves classic status. **CM**

CAVALLI
La Calisto

Ugo Trama, Peter Gottlieb, Ileana Cotrubas, James Bowman, Janet Baker, Hugues Cuenod, Owen Brannigan, Teresa Kubiak; Glyndebourne Festival Chorus, LPO/Raymond Leppard

Decca 436 216-2 □ ADD □ 119:50 mins (2 discs)
□ *◐◐*

Cavalli's prodigious, if neglected, output – he wrote more than forty operas between 1639 and 1666 – owes much to the fact that he notated only the vocal line and bass, adding indications of sinfonias and orchestration rather than writing out the full score. This excellent recording, made at Glyndebourne in 1972, therefore owes much to Raymond Leppard, whose recomposition it uses. As conductor, he also extracts compelling performances from his stellar cast. Janet Baker is a glorious and majestic Diana, James Bowman a sublime Endymion and Ileana Cotrubas a mellifluous Calisto. There are enchanting cameos from the veteran Swiss tenor Hugues Cuenod (then aged seventy) in the drag role of the crude and crotchety nymph Linfea, Teresa Kubiak as a soaring and tormented Juno, and Janet Hughes deliciously ardent and earthy as the young satyr.
Claire Wrathall

CHARPENTIER
Le malade imaginaire

Soloists; Les Arts Florissants/William Christie

Harmonia Mundi HMC 901336 □ 78:56 mins
□ *◐◐◐*

These are the musical interludes from a 'comédie-ballet' by Molière who, after years of collaboration with Lully, teamed up with Charpentier. However, Lully, ever a power-hungry schemer, solicited from Louis XIV 'closed-shop' restrictions, forcing endless revision to Charpentier's original plans.

This recording celebrates a reconstruction of the original music – and it's hilarious. In the first 'Intermède', for example, Polichinelle, a figure from the 16th-century *commedia dell'arte*, sings a serenade, swears at the violins which interrupt him, and is arrested by the night watch, who tweak his nose and beat him until he buys them off – all this in a mix of hysterical speech and witty music.

A 'Little Impromptu Opera' has two lovers openly expressing their passion, but in the guise of stage characters. Only at the end does the girl's father discover that they had improvised the words as they sang. A public

examination, in macaronic Latin, of a medical graduand makes a rowdy ending.

Christie enters wholeheartedly into the spirit of fun – a welcome glimpse of an aspect of French entertainment previously obscured by the loftier drama of Lully's tragedies. *GP*

DALLAPICCOLA
Il prigioniero; Canti di prigionia

Phyllis Bryn-Julson, Jorma Hynninen, Howard Haskin; Eric Ericson Chamber Choir, Swedish RSO & Choir/Esa-Pekka Salonen

Sony SK 68323 □ 69:19 mins □ *◐◐◐*

To present Dallapiccola's theatrical masterpiece *Il prigioniero* alongside his *Canti di prigionia* is an apt pairing, not only because both are anti-fascist works of protest, but because a quotation from the *Canti* lends bitter irony to the opera's closing scene, as the prisoner, making his bid for freedom, emerges into a starlit garden, only to fall into the arms of the Grand Inquisitor himself.

The main literary source for *Il prigioniero* is one of the *Contes cruels* by Villiers de L'Isle-Adam. The prisoner, having undergone every form of physical torture, is now subjected to the most cruel torment of them all – hope. Encouraged by his jailer, he is led to believe that he can escape; and as he makes his way through the underground vaults of Saragossa, Dallapiccola unfolds a series of ricercars whose contrapuntal web symbolises the maze through which he stumbles.

Esa-Pekka Salonen, aided by a fine cast, conducts a gripping performance of this great work, though his account of the *Canti di prigionia* is not quite in the same class: the slow outer panels of the triptych are hurried, and Salonen's instrumentalists cannot quite match their French colleagues on an Erato disc. But no one remotely interested in 20th-century opera should miss this. *Misha Donat*

MAXWELL DAVIES
The Lighthouse

Ian Comboy, Christopher Keyte, Neil Mackie; BBC Philharmonic/Peter Maxwell Davies

Collins 14152 □ 72:24 mins □ *◐◐◐*

First performed at the 1980 Edinburgh Festival, Peter Maxwell Davies's opera *The Lighthouse* must rank as one of the composer's most successful stage works, having enjoyed over eighty productions worldwide since its premiere. The opera deals with the unexpected disappearance at the turn of the century of three lighthouse keepers in the Outer Hebrides and reconstructs a possible scenario to explain the sequence of events that led to their mysterious vanishing. It opens with a court of inquiry in which officers of the ship's crew give evidence after discovering the empty lighthouse. At this point the mood is distinctly uneasy, but the claustrophobic tension of the drama is further heightened through a series of flashbacks in which the lighthouse keepers themselves re-create the nightmarish visions that drove them into the sea.

With its eerie orchestration, which makes distinctive use of a honky-tonk piano, Maxwell Davies's music commands the listener's attention throughout, and this live recording featuring the admirable BBC Philharmonic has tremendous atmosphere. *EL*

DEBUSSY

Pelléas et Mélisande

Maria Ewing, François Le Roux, José van Dam, Christa Ludwig, Jean-Philippe Courtis, Patrizia Pace; Vienna State Opera Chorus, Vienna PO/ Claudio Abbado

DG 435 344-2 □ 147:56 mins (2 discs) □ ⊘⊘⊘

The mysterious half-lit world of *Pelléas* can prove elusive to interpreters who feel that Debussy's music warrants a more extrovert theatrical approach. Yet erring too much on the side of understatement can also pose the danger that the listener becomes too detached from the action on stage. Fortunately, Abbado seems to strike an ideal halfway house between these two extremes. Aided by exceptionally supple playing from the Vienna Philharmonic, he paces the ebb and flow of the drama with unfailing instinct, and DG's glorious engineering allows one to appreciate the full subtlety of Debussy's orchestral textures. Because the recording was made in conjunction with a staged performance at the Vienna State Opera, there is an unusual sense of immediacy to the dialogue. Of the main characters, Maria Ewing is an inspired choice for the fragile Mélisande, while François Le Roux sings Pelléas with great ardour, particularly in the love scene in Act IV. Throughout the years there have been some outstanding recorded performances of *Pelléas* from Désormière, Ansermet and, more recently, Armin Jordan, but Abbado's version, economically presented on only two discs, is a clear winner. *EL*

DELIBES

Lakmé

Joan Sutherland, Alain Vanzo, Gabriel Bacquier, Jane Berbié, Claude Calès; Monte Carlo Opera Chorus & Orchestra/Richard Bonynge

Decca 425 485-2 □ ADD □ 138:00 mins (2 discs) □ ⊘⊘

Lakmé used to be known mainly for its so-called Bell Song, 'Où va la jeune Hindoue?', a favourite with coloratura sopranos, and sung in the opera by its eponymous heroine, a Brahmin priestess who falls in love with a young British army officer in 19th-century India. A British Airways advertisement on TV has made the Flower Duet popular as well. Delibes's charming piece of pastiche oriental confectionery is not often encountered in the theatre, so this recording is doubly welcome. Richard Bonynge conducts the sweetly scented score impeccably, and Joan Sutherland tosses off the fiendish coloratura of Lakmé's Bell Song with careless ease. Her French colleagues all give fine performances, especially Alain Vanzo, ideal as Gerald, the young British soldier, and Gabriel Bacquier as the heroine's High Priest father, while Monica Sinclair presents a vivid portrayal of Miss Bentson, the governess of two young English ladies. *CO*

DELIUS

A Village Romeo and Juliet

Helen Field, Alan Davies, Thomas Hampson; Arnold Schönberg Choir, ORF SO/Charles Mackerras

Argo 430 275-2 □ 111:21 mins (2 discs) □ ⊘⊘⊘

Delius was dedicated in his attempts to succeed as an operatic composer – he wrote six in all – but it seems generally agreed that the expressive profile of his music is essentially undramatic, best adapted to providing a continuum of mood and emotion. His operas are perhaps more successful on disc, in some ideal theatre of the mind, than they could ever be on stage. *A Village Romeo and Juliet* is not only the one Delius opera which has made its way into the stage repertoire, but undoubtedly contains some of his greatest music in any medium. (Indeed, the justly famous *Walk to the Paradise Garden* has found its true home in the orchestral repertoire.) Memorably recorded in 1948 by Beecham (now on mid-price EMI), and more recently by Charles Groves, it's nevertheless this most recent account by Mackerras that captures the work's expressive essence through dedicated and affectionate performances by all members of the strong cast, broad and well-judged tempi controlling the plastic ebb and flow of scene and mood, and a spacious recording that gives the off-stage events their full impact. Helen Field is a fresh, affecting Sali and Thomas Hampson appropriately enigmatic as the Dark Fiddler. *CM*

DONIZETTI

Anna Bolena

Edita Gruberová, Delores Ziegler, Stefano Palatchi, José Bros; Hungarian Radio Chorus & Orchestra/Elio Boncompagni

Nightingale NC 070565-2 □ 167:52 mins (3 discs) □ 😊😊😊

It was with this, one of the earliest of his 'English history' operas, that Donizetti's position was confirmed as the leading Italian composer of the day. The role of the unfortunate Anne Boleyn has in recent decades proved a superb vehicle for the talents of Maria Callas, Leyla Gencer, Beverly Sills, Renata Scotto and Joan Sutherland. Here, Edita Gruberová proves a worthy successor to those distinguished sopranos, investing Anna's plangent Act I cavatina with an affecting simplicity, dealing fearlessly with the coloratura of its imaginative cabaletta, and offering a persuasive interpretation throughout the opera, culminating in the brilliant solo finale in which Anna goes to her execution.

Delores Ziegler makes the most of her opportunities as Anna's rival, Giovanna, and Helene Schneiderman is convincing as Smeton, the page who is in love with Anna. The male roles are well handled, with José Bros bringing an attractive timbre to the tenor role of Lord Riccardo Percy, and Stefan Palatchi dominating as Henry VIII. Elio Boncompagni conducts authoritatively, keeping the action flowing with brisk tempi, and obtaining fine performances from a chorus and orchestra to whom Donizettian style is hardly first nature. *CO*

DONIZETTI

Don Pasquale

Renato Bruson, Eva Mei, Frank Lopardo, Thomas Allen; Bavarian Radio Chorus, Munich RO/Roberto Abbado

RCA Victor Red Seal 09026 61924 2 □ 120:00 mins (2 discs) □ 😊😊😊

One of the rivals to this recording was made in 1932, and it is still worth hearing for the delightful performance of the great Tito Schipa as Ernesto. Schipa's colleagues, however, are not in his league, and the soprano is decidedly shrill. There are more recent versions of the opera, each containing one or two highly satisfactory performances, but Roberto Abbado's is the cast that works best as a team, with Renato Bruson singing the title role of the crusty old bachelor more accurately than many of his rivals, Eva Mei lively as Norina who outwits him, Thomas Allen a vivid Malatesta and the American Frank Lopardo a charming Ernesto. *CO*

DONIZETTI

L'elisir d'amore

Mariella Devia, Roberto Alagna, Pietro Spagnoli, Bruno Praticò; Tallis Chamber Choir, English CO/Marcello Viotti

Erato 4509-91701-2 □ 129:30 mins (2 discs) □ 😊😊😊

There are a number of highly enjoyable recordings of this engaging comedy which, from the first high-spirited bars of its prelude to the end of its equally happy finale, is crammed with rich melody. The story of the village nobody (as his name, Nemorino, suggests), who resorts to what the quack doctor Dulcamara assures him is an elixir (actually, cheap claret) to win the love of the disdainful, wealthy Adina, is conveyed in a masterly blend of sparkling gaiety and warm sentiment.

The work does not lack recommendable recordings, among them a Decca version by Richard Bonynge with Joan Sutherland sailing impressively through the role of Adina, and Luciano Pavarotti an appealing Nemorino. There's also a fine Philips recording with Katia Ricciarelli a sympathetic Adina and José Carreras a touching Nemorino. But first place must go to Erato's recent account of the opera, with Mariella Devia an adorable Adina, and opera's new young tenor hero, Roberto Alagna, not only singing the role of Nemorino beautifully but also presenting a vivid characterisation as the love-sick peasant. Bruno Praticò is an excellent Dulcamara, and the conductor, Marcello Viotti, brings out all the charm and vivacity of Donizetti's irresistible score. *CO*

DONIZETTI

Lucia di Lammermoor

Joan Sutherland, Luciano Pavarotti, Sherrill Milnes, Nicolai Ghiaurov; Chorus & Orchestra of the Royal Opera House, Covent Garden/Richard Bonynge

Decca 410 193-2 □ ADD □ 140:00 mins (3 discs) □ 😊😊😊

There is strong competition here, the two principal rivals being Maria Callas and Joan Sutherland, both famous for their portrayals of the title role in the theatre. Callas recorded her Lucia twice in the studio, but she is to be found at her most exciting on a live recording (EMI) of a Berlin performance conducted by Herbert von Karajan. Fans of Callas will want to have this, but my own preference is for Sutherland, who realises the drama of the role as forcibly as Callas, though by vastly different means, and who sings it more beautifully and with greater vocal security and style. Sutherland also recorded Lucia twice in the studio, and it is her second recording that is to be preferred. Her range and agility, and again the sheer beauty of her tone, made her Lucia not only viscerally exciting but also intensely moving. Sutherland's duet with the excellent Enrico of Sherrill Milnes, sung a tone higher than usual – as it is found in Donizetti's autograph, though not in any score – makes a thrilling effect, as does her Mad Scene. Pavarotti is likewise eloquent as Edgardo, and Richard Bonynge conducts a fast-moving account of the score with great panache. *CO*

DVORAK

Rusalka

Eduard Haken, Milada Šubrtová, Marie Ovčačíková, Ivo Žídek; Prague National Theatre Chorus & Orchestra/Zdeněk Chalabala

Supraphon SU 0013-2 □ **AAD** □ **148:51 mins (2 discs)** □ *♦♦♦*

Dvořák's treatment of the story of *The Little Mermaid* transposed to the Bohemian forest needs no special pleading, but Chalabala's version goes well beyond the merely creditable; it is a superb realisation of the score, and for sheer emotional impact could hardly be bettered. For my money it is far superior to Václav Neumann's excellent set, and Milada Šubrtová for Chalabala is a much more believable Rusalka than Gabriela Beňačková, for all her beauty of tone. Her exchanges with the Water Goblin, sung by Eduard Haken, another National Theatre legend, are extraordinarily touching, and her performance at the denouement of the tragedy is deeply moving. For some the only hitch in this distinguished performance will be Ivo Žídek's Prince. I rather enjoy his youthful ardour; others may find the tone hard and ungraceful. But this is a small price to pay for Chalabala's conducting; superbly flexible, he had a magical touch with Dvořák's

glorious orchestration and never lost sight of the theatrical dimension. There is a slight hiss perceptible on the recording, but for the early Sixties the sound is surprisingly good. *Jan Smaczny*

ENESCU

Oedipe

José van Dam, Gabriel Bacquier, Marcel Vanaud, Gino Quilico, Brigitte Fassbaender, Marjana Lipovšek, Barbara Hendricks; Orféon Donostiarra, Monte Carlo PO/Lawrence Foster

EMI CDS 7 54011 2 □ **156:37 mins (2 discs)** □ *♦♦♦*

Enescu's only opera, worked on for over twenty years (1910–31) is his *summa*. The myth of Oedipus, from birth to death, brings together all the Romanian master's varied qualities and astonishing expertise. His folkloric side is to the fore in the choral dances celebrating Oedipus's birth; his modernism and deep individuality in the central action, with the hero's murder of his father, his confrontation with the Sphinx (one of the most chillingly alien creations in opera) and his self-rejection as the source of the plague decimating Thebes. In the final act, based on Sophocles's *Oedipus at Colonus*, the scapegoat achieves radiant transformation in music of idealistic ardour which, with its elaborate and inspiring choruses, proclaims *Oedipe* to be the true successor of that other yearningly serene 'Greek' masterwork, Fauré's *Pénélope*. Caviare for the general, perhaps: its other spiritual kin are Busoni's *Faust* and Szymanowski's *King Roger*, operas short on love interest but filled with wonder and mystery. And Enescu's orchestration produces a glinting, jewelled tapestry of sound like no other score.

The major role for the chorus indicates the work's cantata-like nature; apart from Oedipus, few of the many characters have substantial parts to sing. Nevertheless, the star-studded cast of this lovingly prepared production projects every protagonist for all he or she is worth. José van Dam heroically embodies Oedipus with tremendous presence and sincerity. Fassbaender is an affecting Jocasta, Lipovšek a blood-chilling Sphinx. Altogether a triumphant presentation of one of the rarest and greatest 20th-century operas. *CM*

FAURE

Pénélope

Jessye Norman, Jocelyne Taillon, Alain Vanzo, José van Dam; Ensemble Vocale Jean Laforge, Monte Carlo PO/Charles Dutoit

Erato Libretto 2292-45405-2 □ ADD □ 124:00 mins (2 discs) □ 🎵🎵

Fauré's only opera, based on the story of the homecoming of Ulysses, is statuesque, undramatic, musically austere, with an inferior libretto. It's also a timeless masterpiece – first-rate late-period Fauré through and through, raised to a plane of epic simplicity: perhaps the most piercingly intense musical vision that any composer has achieved of the lost paradise of classical antiquity. Gravely joyful, alternately sombre and drenched in Aegean sunlight, it breathes an atmosphere of mysterious serenity and inhabits a unique, frieze-like (but not two-dimensional) landscape of the mind.

Ulysses's wife Penelope, still faithfully fending off importunate suitors after twenty years, is the still yet passionate centre of the work. In this fine Erato recording, Jessye Norman has all the vocal power and *gravitas* that the role requires. Alain Vanzo is a vibrant Ulysses, and the rest of the cast are faultless. Beautiful orchestral playing, and Dutoit's sure handling of the light and shade of Fauré's original and utterly characteristic scoring, do this 'unstageworthy' opera – almost as great a piece as Debussy's *Pelléas* – entire justice. *CM*

GERSHWIN

Porgy and Bess

Willard White, Cynthia Haymon, Damon Evans, Cynthia Clarey, Bruce Hubbard, Marietta Simpson, Gregg Baker, Harolyn Blackwell; Glyndebourne Chorus, LPO/Simon Rattle

EMI CDS 7 49568 2 □ 189:00 mins (3 discs) □ 🎵🎵🎵

This release, based on the much-acclaimed 1986 Glyndebourne Festival stage production, is a triumph from start to finish. Soloists, chorus and orchestra work with unstinting energy to re-create the dramatic immediacy of Gershwin's opera. The three major protagonists all make a powerful impression – Willard White proves to be a sympathetic Porgy, Cynthia Haymon's Bess is exceptionally alluring, while Damon Evans fully exploits Sporting Life's banter. Simon Rattle shows an instinctive understanding of Gershwin's musical style. His comprehensive experience of conducting the work in the theatre is exemplified through an unerring sense of pacing and the flexibility with which he shapes the melodic line. The urgency of the whole enterprise makes one wonder how on earth Gershwin's opera could have enjoyed such a mixed press during its first years of existence. *EL*

GIORDANO

Andrea Chénier

Renata Scotto, Plácido Domingo, Sherrill Milnes; John Alldis Choir, National PO/James Levine

RCA Victor Gold Seal GD 82046 □ ADD □ 114:17 mins (2 discs) □ 🎵🎵

A 1941 EMI recording with Beniamino Gigli in the title role is worth seeking out, but Giordano's red-blooded verismo account of love, intrigue and heroic sacrifice at the time of the French Revolution has been well served in more recent recordings as well. Renata Tebaldi and Mario del Monaco (Decca) are exciting, while Montserrat Caballé and Pavarotti, on a later Decca recording, are perhaps the more mellifluous pair. The best of modern recordings, however, is that conducted with dramatic urgency by James Levine, with Renata Scotto an eloquent Maddalena, Plácido Domingo probably the best Chénier since Gigli, and Sherrill Milnes a strongly characterised Gérard. The smaller roles are all strongly cast, and the recording is strikingly bright and vivid. *CO*

GLASS

Einstein on the Beach

Philip Glass Ensemble/Michael Riesman

Elektra Nonesuch 7559-79323-2 □ 200:40 mins (3 discs) □ 🎵🎵🎵

Those of us who grew up, Minimally speaking, on the LP boxed set of *Einstein* always knew that, while our four discs of this post-operatic extravaganza added up to two and three-quarter hours, the original production in the theatre was famous for lasting almost twice that, without a break. This recording – made with the cast (a few of them the same as on the 1978 LPs) which toured the work in 1992 to just about everywhere except Britain – is some 35 minutes longer.

Philip Glass's *Einstein*, with libretto by Robert Wilson, is one of the masterpieces of modern music theatre, and its score – with only numbers or *solfège* syllables for sung text – is among the most joyous, and disturbing, of our time: hard-edged and without sentimentality. The CDs offer not only sharper performances (Gregory Fulkerson is a particularly fine Einstein, portrayed not by a singer but by a violinist), sometimes suitably faster speeds, more repetitions (not quite always a blessing outside the theatre) and a generally much better recording, but also – as in the Building Scene in the last act – a new expressivity coupled with a slower interpretation. A pity the booklet notes on such a complex work aren't clearer. But a must. *Keith Potter*

GLUCK

Orfeo ed Euridice

Janet Baker, Elizabeth Gale, Elisabeth Speiser; Glyndebourne Chorus, LPO/Raymond Leppard

Erato Libretto 2292-45864-2 □ **120:07 mins (2 discs)** □ ✸✸

Given the current vogue for male Orfeos (Jochen Kowalski on Capriccio, Michael Chance on Sony) and Amores, this entirely female cast may stretch dramatic credibility, but in every other way it is a superb performance matched by an excellent recording.

Janet Baker, in her last operatic role (this is a recording of Peter Hall's celebrated Glyndebourne production dating from 1982), produces a sound of such glorious richness, depth and beauty that its inherent femininity does nothing to disconcert. In the supporting roles, Elizabeth Gale is a sweet and affectingly uncomprehending Euridice, and Elisabeth Speiser an attractive, though somewhat mature-sounding Amore.

Raymond Leppard uses the 1859 Berlioz version of the score, but retains the Italian text. He also includes the final, celebratory ballet, which is usually omitted. Under his masterly direction, the London Philharmonic Orchestra gives a marvellously vivid performance, urgent and atmospheric, but slower-paced and markedly less frenzied than is often the case. The Glyndebourne Chorus, directed by Jane Glover, is also on outstanding form: the Furies convincingly malign and the Heroes and Heroines noble. *Claire Wrathall*

GOLDSCHMIDT

Der gewaltige Hahnrei; Mediterranean Songs

Roberta Alexander, Robert Wörle, Michael Kraus, Claudio Otelli, Helen Lawrence, John Mark Ainsley; Berlin Radio Choir, Deutsches SO, Berlin, Leipzig Gewandhaus Orchestra/Lothar Zagrosek

Decca Entartete Musik 440 850-2 □ **125:14 mins (2 discs)** □ ✸✸✸

Decca's invaluable series Entartete Musik (Degenerate Music) is specifically concerned with bringing back to life 'important works lost, destroyed or banned by the political disruptions of the 20th century, most conspicuously the music suppressed by the Third Reich'. *Der gewaltige Hahnrei* (The Magnificent Cuckold), completed in 1930, was rapturously received at its first performance in Mannheim in 1932 and immediately scheduled for a further production under Carl Ebert the following year in Berlin. But neither Goldschmidt nor Ebert was to remain in Germany. Both were removed, Ebert for political reasons and Goldschmidt because of his race. Goldschmidt's career was shattered by the Nazis and only now, with the composer in his nineties and living in London (he emigrated to England in 1935), does it seem probable that his stature will once again be recognised. Stylistically, his music occupies territory neighbouring Berg and Weill, although the richness and tenderness of Goldschmidt's love music is in a class of its own. Roberta Alexander, Robert Wörle, Michael Kraus and the Deutsches SO of Berlin under Lothar Zagrosek are persuasive advocates for these works. *Annette Morreau*

GOUNOD

Faust

Jerry Hadley, Cecilia Gasdia, Samuel Ramey, Alexandru Agache, Susanne Mentzer; Welsh National Opera Chorus & Orchestra/Carlo Rizzi

Teldec 4509-90872-2 □ **211:40 mins (3 discs)** □ ✸✸✸

Gounod's profusely tuneful, sentimental (per)version of Goethe's *Faust* was neglected for many years, but in our present melodically starved era it has come back into favour. Among recent recordings, the best are those conducted by Michel Plasson on EMI, and by Carlo Rizzi on Teldec. My preference is marginally for the Teldec set, sung most elegantly by Jerry Hadley as Faust, Cecilia Gasdia as Marguerite and Samuel Ramey as Mephistopheles. Plasson's cast, led by the Americans Richard Leech, Cheryl Studer and Thomas Hampson, is equally adept at producing an authentic French style, but the balance is tipped by Rizzi, who conducts Gounod's score lovingly, and who uses an edition that restores passages cut before the opera's premiere. *CO*

HANDEL

Ariodante

Lorraine Hunt, Juliana Gondek, Lisa Saffer, Jennifer Lane, Nicolas Cavallier, Rufus Müller; Wilhelmshaven Vocal Ensemble, Freiburg Baroque Orchestra/Nicholas McGegan

Harmonia Mundi HMU 907146/48 □ 201:59 mins (3 discs) □ ❷❷❷

Handel's *Ariodante* has, in addition to the usual dependable succession of wonderful arias, at least two absolute showstoppers for the singer of the title role: 'Scherza infida' and 'Dopo notte'. Lorraine Hunt brings off an unforgettably poignant performance of the former, the orchestra providing a ravishingly dark-hued accompaniment with melancholy bassoons. In 'Dopo notte', however, she is audibly taxed by the aria's pyrotechnics (the part was written for the great castrato Carestini). She is also up against competition from one of the greatest Handelians of our time: Janet Baker, in her prime in the 1979 Philips recording with Raymond Leppard. Nor does Hunt quite convey Baker's blazing anger in 'Tu preparati a morire', though it is still, in general, a very fine account of the role. Juliana Gondek is excellent as Ginevra, and Lisa Saffer as Dalinda. In fact, the only weak link in the Harmonia Mundi cast is the unstylish bass Nicolas Cavallier. McGegan's tempi are fleeter than Leppard's (some arias are a minute or more faster) and he imparts a more dramatic sweep to the action. The orchestral playing is superb. *Barry Millington*

HANDEL

Giulio Cesare

Jennifer Larmore, Barbara Schlick, Bernarda Fink, Marianne Rørholm, Derek Lee Ragin, Furio Zanasi; Concerto Köln/René Jacobs

Harmonia Mundi HMC 901385/87 □ 243:21 mins (4 discs) □ ❷❷❷

Less than a decade ago Winton Dean had to protest that 'it is still exceptional to find Handel's operas accepted as serious works of art'. Now, we are almost spoiled for choice in recordings, though the opera houses remain shamefully neglectful.

Of Handel's 'heroic' operas, *Julius Caesar* has proved by far the most popular – and deservedly. Its plot is relatively simple, compared with the convolutions of many; written for an all-star cast, it stimulated some of Handel's best music; the orchestration is lavishly colourful. Above all, characters are painted with exceptional depth and subtlety.

Larmore is a magnificently heroic Caesar, taking the role designed originally for the great castrato Senesino. Her almost instrumental virtuosity for 'Al lampo dell' armi' is breathtaking, her duet with horn, 'Va tacito', stately enough for some stirring ornaments. Schlick is a seductive, scheming Cleopatra, outstanding in her famous *scena* with on-stage orchestra, 'V'adoro, pupille'. They are matched by a heart-rending Cornelia (Fink) and as vicious a Ptolemy, murderer and rapist, as you are ever likely to meet in Derek Lee Ragin.

This is an impressive starting-point for heroic Handel on record. Follow it with *Radamisto* (McGegan, on Harmonia Mundi) and *Tamerlano* (Gardiner, on Erato). *GP*

HANDEL

Orlando

James Bowman, Arleen Auger, Catherine Robbin, Emma Kirkby, David Thomas; Academy of Ancient Music/Christopher Hogwood

L'Oiseau-Lyre 430 845-2 □ 157:57 mins (3 discs) □ ❷❷❷

The plot, from the epic poem *Orlando furioso*, tells of the hero's frenzy engendered by frustrated love. London audiences, accustomed to the almost inevitable alternation of recitative and formal aria, must have been amazed at the Mad Scene, where drama conquers convention. Orlando holds the stage alone for nearly ten minutes, fluctuating wildly between calm and delirium in an awe-inspiring representation of schizophrenia.

This recording followed a live performance at a BBC Prom concert. Although not staged as opera, it included considerable movement and gesture – and the sense of real theatre remains. Among the major soloists, Bowman is superb as Orlando, a part written for the great castrato Senesino; Auger is an appealing Angelica, while Thomas is majestic as the benevolent magician Zoroastro.

The visual impact is lost in recording, of course, as it is in concert performance. It's intended to be specially vivid here, with magical transformations, gushing fountains appearing at the wave of a wand, chariots flying through the air – the devices that amazed and delighted 18th-century audiences. But the music is so strong that it evokes very clearly the theatre of Handel's own mind in this, the most powerful of his 'magic' operas. *GP*

HANDEL

Teseo

Eirian James, Della Jones, Julia Gooding, Derek Lee Ragin, Catherine Napoli, Jeffrey Gall; Les Musiciens du Louvre/Marc Minkowski

Erato 2292-45806-2 □ **148:00 mins (2 discs)**
□ *🟡🟡🟡*

In *Teseo*, Handel, a thoroughly Italianate German living in England, turned for the only time in his operatic career to France, using an adaptation of Quinault's libretto for Lully's *Thésée* from forty years earlier. So the five-act structure is unique to Handel, with colourful orchestration influenced by Parisian conventions. Yet the drama is more taut than in any of his previous operas.

Colour and drama are in plentiful supply in this excellent recording of the work from Minkowski and Les Musiciens du Louvre. Minkowski's lively pacing and taut rhythms move the action forward at a good lick, yet allow phrases time to breathe. Of the soloists, Della Jones is outstanding as the 'amorous sorceress' Medea, not least in the spluttering rage of her jealousy aria.

This, the first *Teseo* recorded on disc, has everything you could ask of a Handel opera in terms of dramatic pace, passion and virtuosity, exquisite singing – and not a moment of weak musical invention. *GP*

HENZE

The Bassarids

Kenneth Riegel, Andreas Schmidt, Michael Burt, Robert Tear, Karan Armstrong, Celia Lindsley, Ortrun Wenkel; RIAS Chamber Choir, Südfunk Choir, Berlin RSO/Gerd Albrecht

Koch Schwann 314006 □ **119:57 mins (2 discs)**
□ *🟡🟡🟡*

In the time-honoured tradition of *opera seria*, *The Bassarids* is based on Greek tragedy, in this case Euripides's drama *The Bacchae*, which is brilliantly adapted for the modern stage by Auden and Kallman. It's a play about the conflict between freedom and repression, sanity and madness, asceticism and sensuality. Henze responds to these familiar themes in a compelling manner. The legacy of Wagner can be perceived, not so much in the actual style of Henze's music as in his preoccupation with the psychoanalytical aspects of the drama, and in the consciously symphonic structure, which divides the opera into four large-scale movements that are performed without a break. This recording, released in honour of the composer's 65th birthday, is notable for the outstanding singing of Andreas Schmidt in the major role of Pentheus, and for the impassioned contribution from the chorus, who really set the pulses racing with their thrilling delivery of the Hunt Scene. As always, Gerd Albrecht marshals the huge vocal and orchestral resources with exemplary authority. *EL*

HENZE

Der junge Lord

Barry McDaniel, Loren Driscoll, Vera Little, Manfred Röhrl, Patricia Johnson, Edith Mathis, Bella Jasper, Donald Grobe; Schöneberg Boys Choir, Chorus & Orchestra of the Deutsche Oper, Berlin/Christoph von Dohnányi

DG 449 875-2 □ **ADD** □ **138:36 mins (2 discs)**
□ *🟡🟡*

Hans Werner Henze's dark comedy *The Young Lord*, to a well-crafted libretto by his one-time partner Ingeborg Bachmann, was premiered in Berlin in 1965 and has since received numerous stagings. This 1967 recording captures the original cast in good though dryish sound.

The arrival of the mysterious Sir Edgar and his strange retinue in a provincial German town produces curiosity among local society that turns to resentment when the aristocrat cold-shoulders the town's leading figures. He executes a poetically apt yet disturbing revenge… Henze sets this discomfiting satire in neo-classical style, following the precepts of *opera buffa* in a manner similar to Stravinsky in *The Rake's Progress*. His music shows a mastery of means, and a neat combination of lyricism and sharpness, but slides intermittently into anonymity.

The performance is precisely controlled by Christoph von Dohnányi. Donald Grobe deploys a fresh lyric tenor as Wilhelm, a young man of sensibility, and Edith Mathis is eminently sweet-toned as Luise, the object of his affections. Patricia Johnson is effective as Baroness Grünwiesel, the snobbish and spiteful social arbiter of Hülsdorf-Gotha, while Barry McDaniel combines the sinister side of Sir Edgar's secretary with an appropriately *de haut en bas* manner. *George Hall*

HINDEMITH

Mathis der Maler

Dietrich Fischer-Dieskau, James King, Urszula Koszut, Rose Wagemann, William Cochran, Peter Meven; Bavarian Radio Chorus & SO/Rafael Kubelík

EMI CDS 5 55237 2 □ **ADD** □ **182:54 mins (3 discs)**
□ *🟡🟡🟡*

It has taken nearly sixty years for Hindemith's opera to reach the British stage, though the work has secured a formidable reputation in Germany. Composed during the troubled Thirties, when Hindemith became *persona non grata* with the Nazi regime, *Mathis der Maler* – a portrayal of the life and times of the famous 17th-century painter Matthias Grünewald – wrestles with complex issues concerning the creative artist's role in a repressive society. It's clearly a major work whose overriding lyricism marks a departure from the iconoclastic Hindemith of the Twenties. Some may feel that the opera overstays its welcome, but with Fischer-Dieskau's insightful portrayal of Mathis, and Kubelík's persuasive conducting, such doubts are banished. The EMI production is suitably lavish, but a recording of this age should ideally retail at mid-price. *EL*

HUMPERDINCK

Hänsel und Gretel

Franz Grundheber, Gwyneth Jones, Ann Murray, Edita Gruberová, Christa Ludwig, Barbara Bonney; Dresden Opera Women's Chorus & Children's Chorus, Dresden Staatskapelle/Colin Davis

Philips 438 013-2 □ 103:23 mins (2 discs) □ ❷❷❷

Ever since Karajan's Fifties mono recording, Humperdinck's fairy-tale opera has been lucky on disc. Davis's reading of this perennial favourite comes up both against that much-admired interpretation as well as a quartet from Solti (a somewhat over-'Wagnerised' account on Decca), John Pritchard (Sony), Jeffrey Tate (EMI) and Donald Runnicles (Teldec).

Davis's greatest attribute is the Dresden Staatskapelle. The orchestra has admittedly been given too restricted a recorded perspective for my taste, but one is unlikely to hear this gloriously inventive music more beautifully and lovingly played and, under Davis's inspired and detailed direction, one can revel in the aural delights of the orchestra's woodwind, the silkiness of its strings and the wonderfully open sound of the horns.

The cast of singers is fine too. As Hansel and Gretel, Ann Murray and Edita Gruberová often pare their voices down to express an ideal childlike innocence, while Gwyneth Jones is unusally steady of voice as the mother and, where we might perhaps have expected her larger-than-life voice to be particularly appropriate – in the role of the witch – we have instead a witty romp from veteran Christa Ludwig. Also worth a mention is the warm-hearted singing of Franz Grundheber as the father, and delightful cameos from Barbara Bonney and Christiane Oelze as the Sandman and Dew Fairy respectively. *Matthew Rye*

JANACEK

The Cunning Little Vixen; plus orchestral suite (arr. Talich)

Lucia Popp, Dalibor Jedlička, Eva Randová, Richard Novák, Vladimir Krejčík, Václav Zítek; Vienna State Opera Chorus, Vienna PO/Charles Mackerras

Decca 417 129-2 □ 108:49 mins (2 discs) □ ❷❷❷

With his roots in Romanticism, his radical innovations in the setting of a text and the possibilities of orchestral colour, and his keen eye for subject-matter that still seems astonishingly modern or pertinent to us today, Janáček remains both the strangest and most immediate operatic composer of the 20th century. If his time has truly come, then it is largely thanks to Charles Mackerras, a tireless champion both in the opera house and on a pioneering series of recordings. It is hard to say which is the more impressive: the white-heat drive of Mackerras's conducting or the results of his painstaking concern to restore all the perilous orchestral lines smoothed out in decades of play-safe Czech performances. For the first time, on this CD reissue, Decca allows us to compare and contrast by following up *The Cunning Little Vixen* with the subdued colours of Václav Talich's orchestral suite.

The opera itself is the most easily lovable of all Janáček's late-flowering masterpieces, and no easy option, crowned as it is by an epilogue of searing musical and human wisdom which bears out the composer's fervent belief in the meaning of life's natural cycle. The interpretation, too, seems unlikely to be surpassed: warm and sensuous but also red in tooth and claw when it needs to be, infinitely keener on the dramatic uptake than Neumann's hazy Supraphon recording or Rattle's earthbound EMI recording (with a fine cast singing in English). *DN*

JANACEK

From the House of the Dead; Mládí; Říkadla

Jiří Zahradníček, Ivo Žídek, Václav Zítek, Dalibor Jedlička; Vienna State Opera Chorus, Vienna PO/Charles Mackerras; London Sinfonietta & Chorus/David Atherton

Decca 430 375-2 □ DDD/ADD □ 123:19 mins (2 discs) □ ❷❷❷

Here are some of the most vivid moments ever to be captured in a recording studio. We know what kind of prison-camp drama to expect as soon as we hear the great brass manifestos of freedom leaping out in the prelude – evidence that Janáček shared the faith of his autobiographical source, Dostoevsky's *From the House of the Dead*, that 'in every human being there is a spark of God'. We also hear the untrammelled brutality never far from the surface in the Vienna PO's astonishing handling of the Act I curtain. But Mackerras is definitely not after sensation: he makes quite sure not to let the music match the ultimate cruelty in the last of a string of confession narratives (all the opera boasts in the way of a structure or a plot-line, but it works), and he lets the enigma remain both here and in the rapid end of the opera as Janáček conceived it, neither bleak nor uplifting.

Vocally, the achievement falls slightly short of the rest of Decca's Janáček series. The leading monologuists in the (virtually) all-male cast rush headlong into the brute force of their characterisations without attending to that crucial 'spark of God'; again, Mackerras makes ample amends. The bonuses are full of character, with the woodwind cries towards the end of *Mládí* craning forwards to the world of the opera and some much-needed epigrammatic wit in the idiomatic-sounding delivery of the *Nursery Rhymes*. *DN*

JANACEK

Jenůfa; Jealousy Overture (Žárlivost)

Elisabeth Söderström, Eva Randová, Wiesław Ochman, Petr Dvorský, Lucia Popp; Vienna State Opera Chorus, Vienna PO/Charles Mackerras

Decca 414 483-2 □ **130:22 mins (2 discs)** □ **⦿⦿⦿**

If the issues of infanticide and forgiveness against all odds strike the right emotional chords in you, and the sharp-edged Romanticism suits, then there is no more powerful and – ultimately – more exhilarating opera in the entire repertoire than *Jenůfa*. Janáček's first masterpiece, it is also his most often recorded opera – but not, until recently, in its raw and uncompromising original orchestration. As in the recording of *The Cunning Little Vixen*, Mackerras shows us what we might have missed in the smoothed-out re-orchestration (in this case of the blazing final scene, added as an appendix and followed by the authentically febrile *Jealousy* Overture, intended for the opera but never performed with it).

Elisabeth Söderström matches Mackerras's characteristic fervour, though not always his orchestra's tonal beauty. It is a questionable

piece of casting: Lucia Popp, making an all-too-brief appearance in Act III as Karolka, might have been a more apt choice for the village girl dignified by suffering, and Gabriela Beňačková on Supraphon is certainly more youthful of voice if less vivid a communicator. The intensity of dramatic delivery on the Decca set, however, is never in doubt, and Söderström is powerfully complemented by the driving force of Wiesław Ochman's restless Laca and Eva Randová's raw but exciting Kostelnička; her exit as she goes to meet her accusers, forgiven by her foster-daughter for her desperate act in drowning the girl's baby, is realised by a blinding magnesium flare in the orchestra – another of those moments that make the Mackerras Janáček series one of the greatest glories in recorded history. *DN*

JANACEK

Katya Kabanova; Capriccio; Concertino

Elisabeth Söderström, Petr Dvorský, Naděžda Kniplová, Libuše Márová; Vienna State Opera Chorus, Vienna PO/Charles Mackerras; Paul Crossley (piano), London Sinfonietta/David Atherton

Decca 421 852-2 □ **ADD** □ **139:52 mins (2 discs)** □ **⦿⦿⦿**

Poor Katya, heroine of Russian playwright Ostrovsky's *The Storm*, which is the basis for Russophile Janáček's opera, cannot live with the guilt of an adulterous liaison. In that respect the bleak, abrupt end of the opera sets it apart from its companions in the Janáček canon, all of them reaching out beyond the chaos and tragedy of life to something greater. Even so, Mackerras and Söderström between them find much beauty along the way in Katya's brief blossoming; the intelligence of Söderström's portrayal makes Katya's death seem only the more pointless. The grotesques among the supporting cast, Katya's one-dimensional dragon of a stepmother and her ridiculous suitor Dikoj, are nicely rounded out by two distinguished veterans of the Czech operatic scene, Naděžda Kniplová and Dalibor Jedlička.

This was the first release in Decca's Janáček series, and it set the standard for recordings to come: the often stratospheric string writing, harsh brass or woodwind edges and unmixed colours are never compromised for a moment by the stupendous, judiciously balanced engineering. The two additional works for piano and chamber ensemble, taken from a three-LP set of Janáček's chamber works, are no mere fillers, and are vividly characterised by Crossley and London Sinfonietta soloists. *DN*

JANACEK

The Makropulos Case; Lachian Dances

Elisabeth Söderström, Petr Dvorský, Václav Zítek,
Beno Blachut; Vienna State Opera Chorus, Vienna
PO/Charles Mackerras; LPO/François Huybrechts

**Decca 430 372-2 □ ADD □ 117:52 mins (2 discs)
□ 𝄞𝄞𝄞**

Janáček's most elusive opera needs a diva to
play a diva, though Söderström has never been
a soprano of the more self-serving variety. Her
multifaceted characterisation of the 337-year-
old Emilia Marty, *aka* Elina Makropulos,
coldly toying with human suffering before she
philosophically refuses to renew her option on
eternal life, is a minutely observed study that
repays repeated listening. The coldness of the
burned-out tricentenarian, the almost
caricatured humour of her all-knowing
indifference, and finally the human warmth
she allows to surface in admitting the
pointlessness of a life prolonged beyond its
natural span are all ideally judged. Mackerras,
too, captures the icy chill that sometimes
settles on the score before releasing the tidal
wave of feeling towards the end of the opera.

Janáček's unique attention to the melody
inherent in human speech – his art of so-called
speech song – is stretched to its limits in an
opera which packs its detective-story
information into a remarkably short span; and
so the idiomatic Czech supporting cast is more
than usually welcome. Whether you will want
to return to the set for more than the last
scene, however, is another matter. *DN*

LEONCAVALLO/MASCAGNI

Leoncavallo: Pagliacci

Mascagni: Cavalleria rusticana

Maria Callas, Giuseppe di Stefano, Tito Gobbi,
Rolando Panerai; Chorus & Orchestra of La Scala,
Milan/Tullio Serafin

**EMI CDS 7 47981 8 □ ADD □ 150:59 mins (3 discs)
□ 𝄞𝄞𝄞**

In this coupling of the two masterpieces of
verismo, which are usually performed together
in the theatre, Maria Callas gives wonderfully
dramatic performances in both operas. The
vocal shortcomings which marred so many of
her portrayals of bel canto heroines are
distinctly less damaging in the music of
Leoncavallo and Mascagni, and in *Pagliacci* she
finds more depth in the role of Nedda than do
any of her rivals. Di Stefano is on top vocal
form, acting and singing with a blazing
intensity as Canio, and Tito Gobbi gives a
characteristically full-blooded portrayal of

Tonio. *Cavalleria rusticana* finds Callas in her
best voice; di Stefano and Gobbi are again
vivid interpreters, and Tullio Serafin conducts
powerfully. The recording, though more than
forty years old, is perfectly acceptable. *CO*

LULLY

Armide

Guillemette Laurens, Howard Crook, Véronique Gens,
Noémi Rime, Bernard Deletré, Gilles Ragon; Choir &
Orchestra of the Collegium Vocale and La Chapelle
Royale/Philippe Herreweghe

**Harmonia Mundi HMC 901456/57 □ 156:03 mins
(2 discs) □ 𝄞𝄞𝄞**

The music historian Charles Burney wrote of
Lully's operas: 'The airs, choruses and dances
are so easy and natural, that it is hardly
possible for a lover of Music… to hear them
frequently performed, without remembering
them.' Yet only one opera was available
complete on record before this fine
performance of *Armide*, arguably Lully's best.

The singers are first rate. Guillemette
Laurens is a subtle Armide, not merely evil-
minded, but arousing pity as the victim of false
love created through her own sorcery. Howard
Crook (Renaud) is equally convincing as
valiant knight and lyrical spellbound lover. But
the overriding impression is of the rhythmic
vitality which Herreweghe generates, not only
in airs, choruses and dances, but throughout
the measured *récit*, the 'speaking in music'
which the French treated so sensitively
compared with perfunctory Italian recitative.
And the orchestral playing of the splendidly
colourful score is crisp and springy. You're
swept along through the dances and accompanied songs by the lilting dotted rhythms.

On disc, of course, the spectacle – of
entrancing scenery, dancing, acting, costume –
is lost. Yet the French have always had a gift
for creating magical atmosphere, and here the
music alone is enough to suspend both belief
and time. *GP*

LULLY

Phaëton

Howard Crook, Rachel Yakar, Jennifer Smith,
Véronique Gens, Gérard Thervel, Jean-Paul
Fouchécourt, Philippe Huttenlocher, Laurent Naouri,
Virginie Pochon; Ensemble Vocal Sagittarius, Les
Musiciens du Louvre/Marc Minkowski

**Erato MusiFrance □ 4509-91737-2 □ 144:00 mins
(2 discs) □ 𝄞𝄞𝄞**

Phaëton, written at the height of Lully's career,
richly merits this revival. The plot inhabits the
mystical, exotic area between earthly characters

and deities: in his search for glory, Phaëton persuades his father, the Sun, to lend him his fiery chariot. Struck by Jupiter's thunderbolt, the joyrider finally crashes to his doom.

Lully and his librettist, Quinault, so integrate music with action and spectacle – stage sets and machinery, costume, dancing – that something is inevitably lost in a concert recording. But Minkowski's pace and drive compensate for much that is missing. The fluid musical speech of French *récit*, sung so rhythmically, slips almost imperceptibly into charming, measured *air* and back again, creating a fine sense of dramatic continuity. Although there are no independent *divertissements*, there are two extended passages of delightful music, as dance and celebration are woven into the drama. At times Minkowski is frenetic: as Phaëton's impending crash threatens to set fire to the whole universe, choir and orchestra engage in astonishing feats of virtuosity.

Among the soloists, Howard Crook is superb as the posturing Phaëton; Rachel Yakar, intensely expressive as his ambitious mother, sometimes allows passion to affect pitch; while Jean-Paul Fouchécourt's vocal fluency is outstanding. *GP*

MARTINU

Julietta

Maria Tauberová, Ivo Žídek, Antonín Zlesák, Zdeněk Bednár, Vera Soukupová; Prague National Theatre Chorus & Orchestra/Jaroslav Krombholc

Supraphon 10 8176-2 □ ADD □ **144:45 mins (3 discs)** □ 𝄞𝄞𝄞

The opera's subtitle, 'A Dream Book', tells us a great deal about the nature of Martinů's subject-matter, for the scenario, based on a play by Georges Neveux, explores the borderline between reality and fantasy, truth and falsehood, remembrance and forgetfulness, and ultimately between sanity and madness. Events take place in an unknown country village, where a young man searches in vain for Julietta, a girl he thinks he had met before. When he eventually finds her, it isn't clear whether or not she recognises him. He then loses her and returns to the real world. Continuing his quest to find her again, he surrenders all semblance of reality and becomes insane.

Composed in the late Thirties, just before the composer's emigration to the United States, *Julietta* contains some of Martinů's most hauntingly inspired music. Indeed, some of the opera's principal thematic ideas were to cast a spell over subsequent compositions, most notably the Sixth Symphony.

A seminal work in Martinů's output, the current neglect of *Julietta* outside the Czech Republic seems incomprehensible, but this recording, though made as long ago as 1964, presents the best possible case for its reappraisal. *EL*

MASCAGNI
Cavalleria rusticana
see LEONCAVALLO: Pagliacci

MASSENET

Manon

Ileana Cotrubas, Alfredo Kraus, Gino Quilico, José van Dam; Toulouse Capitole Chorus & Orchestra/ Michel Plasson

EMI CDS 7 49610 2 □ **153:50 mins (3 discs)** □ 𝄞𝄞𝄞

Massenet's *Manon* comes closer to the spirit of the Abbé Prévost's novel than Puccini's *Manon Lescaut* and also reveals its composer's mastery of a number of musical styles, the elegant 18th-century pastiche of the Cours-la-Reine Scene contrasting vividly with the dramatic concerted finale of Act IV and the passionately Romantic music for Manon and Des Grieux. A famous EMI recording dating from 1955 is still worth hearing, if only for the irresistible Manon of the young Victoria de los Angeles, and the idiomatic conducting of the veteran Pierre Monteux. But Henri Legay is a pallid Des Grieux, and the recording now shows its age. My recommendation is for this later EMI version, with Ileana Cotrubas as a most touching, vulnerable Manon, and Alfredo Kraus a stylish, sweet-toned Des Grieux. The other principal roles are well taken, with Gino Quilico a lively Lescaut and José van Dam superb as the elder Des Grieux. Michel Plasson conducts a loving account of this charming work. *CO*

MASSENET

Werther

Georges Thill, Ninon Vallin, Germaine Feraldy, Marcel Roque, Armand Narçon, Louis Guenot, Henri Niel; Théâtre National de l'Opéra-Comique Chorus & Orchestra/Elie Cohen

EMI Références CHS 7 63195 2 □ ADD mono □ **121:06 mins (2 discs)** □ 𝄞𝄞

Each time I hear Georges Thill sing 'Je ne sais si je veille, ou si je rêve encore' in this classic account of *Werther*, a shiver of excitement goes down my back. The dark, baritonal, Wagnerian timbre, the perfect marriage of the French text and Massenet's music: these are qualities unheard of in a *Werther* of the postwar period. Indeed, the entire performance by the two most famous French singers of their generation, and an Opéra-Comique ensemble under Elie Cohen, remains a paragon of a now virtually extinct French style of music-making. Cohen acknowledges Massenet's debt to Wagner without overburdening the French delicacy of the score, and it is a delight to hear evenly produced voices singing such idiomatic French. In the great set pieces, Werther's 'Invocation' and 'Pourquoi me réveiller?', Charlotte's 'Air des lettres' and 'Ah, mon courage m'abandonne!', Thill and Vallin give object-lessons, unsurpassed by any of their successors in complete recordings (though de los Angeles and Gedda, also on EMI, come close).

The drawbacks for modern listeners are obvious: the recording, made in 1931, is not kind to the orchestra and there are uncomfortable transitions between the side-breaks on the original 78s. But those prepared to tolerate 'historic' sound will discover a performance which seems to grow in stature with the passing years. *Hugh Canning*

MERIKANTO

Juha

Matti Lehtinen, Raili Kostia, Hendrik Krumm, Taru Valjakka, Maiju Kuusoja; Finnish National Opera Chorus & Orchestra/Ulf Söderblom

Finlandia 1576-51105-2 □ AAD □ 106:33 mins (2 discs) □ 🎵🎵

Aarre Merikanto (1893–1958) was perhaps the most gifted Finnish composer of the post-Sibelius generation, and the most courageous in striking out on a path that owed as little as possible to that overwhelming figure. Yet his distinctive and sophisticated art, developing into an intensely felt, dissonant, almost expressionist idiom, was shunned by the musical establishment, and in later years he radically simplified his style, destroying and mutilating his earlier scores in despair and depression. His *Juha* was rejected for performance while he was alive; first staged five years after his death, it is now generally considered *the* great Finnish national opera.

A dark tragedy of love and jealousy among farming people in the remote sub-Arctic backwoods, *Juha* is nevertheless a powerful,

inspiring and magically atmospheric theatrical experience. The score brims with bright, glittering colour and warmth of emotion. It has sometimes been compared with *Jenůfa*, and indeed there is something Janáček-like in Merikanto's sure handling of folk-material and naturalistic speech rhythm in a highly individual idiom. Though slightly elderly now, this pioneering recording blazes with conviction. Matti Lehtinen's *Juha* is a towering figure, Raili Kostia almost unbearably touching as his young wife, and the orchestral playing is very fine. *CM*

MEYERBEER

Les Huguenots

Joan Sutherland, Anastasios Vrenios, Gabriel Bacquier, Martina Arroyo, Huguette Tourangeau, Dominic Cossa, Nicola Ghiuselev; Ambrosian Opera Chorus, New Philharmonia Orchestra/Richard Bonynge

Decca 430 549-2 □ ADD □ 217:12 mins (4 discs) □ 🎵🎵

Meyerbeer's operatic version of events leading up to the slaughter of Protestants by Catholics in 16th-century France is one of those large-scale French grand operas of the 19th century which are difficult to revive successfully on stage today. The finest music in *Les Huguenots* is in Act IV, with its scene of the Consecration of the Swords and the impassioned love duet which follows for the Catholic Valentine and the Huguenot Raoul. Seven first-rate artists are needed for the opera's leading roles, and an impressive array of singers has been assembled here. Joan Sutherland is a forceful Queen Marguerite and Martina Arroyo a passionate Valentine, while the other roles are all more than competently filled. The conductor, Richard Bonynge, holds the performance together most impressively, and Meyerbeer's score is given absolutely complete. *CO*

MONTEVERDI

L'incoronazione di Poppea

Danielle Borst, Guillemette Laurens, Jennifer Larmore, Axel Köhler, Michael Schopper, Lena Lootens, Dominique Visse, Christoph Homberger; Concerto Vocale/René Jacobs

Harmonia Mundi HMC 901330/32 □ 197:18 mins (3 discs) □ 🎵🎵🎵

Monteverdi's later operas are not the easiest fare for the listener, shorn as they are on disc of spectacle and movement. Furthermore, they are exceptionally dependent on the invention and interpretation of performers. A great deal is missing: instrumental sinfonias and ritornellos, added instrumental parts that probably enriched the bare vocal lines, indications of tempo, how to realise the continuo and so forth. On this recording, Jacobs matches scholarship with invention, imposing a common pulse on potentially fragmented music, and thus creating a rare sense of rhythmic continuity and direction. Moreover, his cast is superb. Borst is a seductive Poppea, manipulating Nero (Laurens), petulant in anger, delirious in love. Schopper provides a finely focused Seneca with a magnificent bottom C, while Larmore is a tragic Ottavia.

The best tunes are given to the servant characters, and no holds are barred in their comic interludes where the page ridicules Seneca's yawn with a sinuous vocal slide, while the nurse revels in her imagined power, when her charge is made queen. *GP*

MONTEVERDI
L'Orfeo

John Mark Ainsley, Catherine Bott, Tessa Bonner, Julia Gooding, Christopher Robson; New London Consort/Philip Pickett

L'Oiseau-Lyre 433 545-2 □ **107:51 mins (2 discs)** □ 🎵🎵🎵

Pickett's extensive programme notes for *L'Orfeo* reveal not only the remarkable thoroughness of his preparatory researches but also how imaginatively he applies them. Finding that *L'Orfeo* was conceived as if within a *galleria* in the ducal palace, Pickett makes inspired deductions about the number and positioning of performers, and there is a wonderful sense of the space in which they play and sing. Thoughtful pacing holds together potentially fragmented music, while contrasting sections are often united by a common pulse. Recitative is propelled along by 'keeping the continuo active'.

The courtly extravagance of Monteverdi's conception is revealed in a kaleidoscope of colours, from rasping, muted trumpets in the opening Toccata to *pochettes* (miniature violins tuned an octave higher), suggesting bird-song in a pastoral ritornello.

The cast is excellent. It is led by John Mark Ainsley so vocally secure that all his artistry can focus on the fate of the central character in this, one of the greatest love stories of all time. In short, Pickett's recording of *L'Orfeo* represents an outstanding marriage of scholarship and practice, creating a definitive and absorbing performance. *GP*

MONTEVERDI
Il ritorno d'Ulisse in patria

Christoph Prégardien, Bernarda Fink, Christina Högman, Martyn Hill; Concerto Vocale/René Jacobs

Harmonia Mundi HMC 901427/29 □ **177:55 mins (3 discs)** □ 🎵🎵🎵

As with his *L'incoronazione di Poppea*, Jacobs has enriched the repertoire by re-creating a coherent and effective drama from the very incomplete manuscript sources. Again he meets the challenge of binding together music of many contrasting fragments by some sprightly rhythms. This recording is based upon a previous stage production in France and Japan, and its vocal scale is for a modern stage. Jacobs's direction is full of colour and energy, and his casting is first rate, above all of Bernarda Fink as the faithful Penelope. The result is another major Monteverdi recording. *GP*

MOZART
La clemenza di Tito

Philip Langridge, Lucia Popp, Ruth Ziesak, Ann Murray, Delores Ziegler, László Polgár; Zürich Opera Chorus & Orchestra/Nikolaus Harnoncourt

Teldec 4509-90857-2 □ **128:43 mins (2 discs)** □ 🎵🎵

Despite its late acceptance into the canon of Mozart's operatic masterworks, *Tito* has not fared badly on disc. Versions by Davis, Böhm and Gardiner can all be recommended, even if none presents the *recitativo semplice* (probably composed by Mozart's pupil Süssmayr) in its entirety. Harnoncourt also cuts much of the recitative, and the reprise of the Act I March.

Emperor Leopold II, whom the opera glorifies (it was first performed at one of his coronations in the last years of Mozart's life), might have been alarmed by the impetuousness, even brutishness, with which Harnoncourt tackles some of the numbers; but apart from muffing the arresting elision between Vitellia's show-stopping 'Non più di fiori vaghe catene' and the Act II finale, and a slightly *laissez-faire* attitude to the finales (no sense of catastrophe at the end of Act I, nor the necessary joyous intoxication at the end of the opera), his is a model reading, with tempi beautifully judged and textures wonderfully transparent.

He's blessed, too, with probably the best all-round cast so far, led by Lucia Popp's eloquent Vitellia (her last recording), Philip Langridge's intense Tito and Ann Murray's commanding Sesto. *Antony Bye*

MOZART

Così fan tutte

Elisabeth Schwarzkopf, Christa Ludwig, Hanny Steffek, Alfredo Kraus, Giuseppe Taddei, Walter Berry; Philharmonia Chorus & Orchestra/Karl Böhm

EMI CMS 7 69330 2 □ ADD □ 165:03 mins (3 discs) □ ⊘⊘

Several excellent recordings of Mozart's enchanting comedy are available on CD, but none of them outclasses the version produced by Walter Legge well over thirty years ago, with his wife Elisabeth Schwarzkopf as Fiordiligi, and Christa Ludwig as her sister Dorabella. Schwarzkopf and Ludwig, who often sang these roles together on the stage in Vienna and Salzburg, are a delightful pair of sisters, singing beautifully and characterising their roles most vividly. Hanny Steffek is a lively Despina, and the three male roles are equally strongly cast. Alfredo Kraus's silken tones make the most of Ferrando's music, while Giuseppe Taddei is an ebullient, Italianate Guglielmo, and Walter Berry is in his element as the cynical and manipulative Don Alfonso. Karl Böhm, one of the finest Mozart conductors of his day, always chooses the right tempi and keeps the action moving naturally and spontaneously. There are some cuts, but they are not damaging ones. For those who must have the score absolutely complete, there is a highly recommendable performance on Archiv, played on period instruments and conducted by John Eliot Gardiner. *CO*

MOZART

Don Giovanni

Andreas Schmidt, Alastair Miles, Amanda Halgrimson, Lynne Dawson, John Mark Ainsley, Gregory Yurisich, Nancy Argenta, Gerald Finley; Schütz Choir of London, London Classical Players/Roger Norrington

EMI CDS 7 54859 2 □ 201:10 mins (3 discs) □ ⊘⊘⊘

Don Giovanni is the most Romantic of all Mozart's operas, but it loses nothing through an imaginative period-instrument performance such as this one. Indeed, the leaner, fitter sonorities serve only to heighten its intensity. Roger Norrington's is a natural, unforced account, relying on purely musical means to project the drama and maintaining tension through an apt choice of tempi and a deft, conversational handling of recitative. Happily, too, he resists the temptation to make 'revelatory' musicological points through

extremes of tempo or textural oddities. There is certainly no lack of gravity (listen to the overture, properly awe-inspiring with a sense of impending catastrophe) and no lack of urgency. Only occasionally, as in the Commendatore's jaunty death agony and a pedestrian Champagne Aria, does Norrington miscalculate.

He's well complemented by a fresh, young team of singers led by Andreas Schmidt's suave Giovanni and Gregory Yurisich's benevolent Leporello. They may not offer such richly rounded characterisations as the notable exponents of yore, but their singing is unfailingly stylish and perfectly matched with Norrington's essentially non-interventionist approach. An added attraction of this fine set is a facility for programming in either version – the original Prague or the slightly later Vienna – sanctioned by Mozart without having to jump CDs. *Antony Bye*

MOZART

Die Entführung aus dem Serail

Hans-Peter Minetti, Stanford Olsen, Luba Orgonasova, Cyndia Sieden, Uwe Peper, Cornelius Hauptmann; Monteverdi Choir, English Baroque Soloists/John Eliot Gardiner

Archiv 435 857-2 □ 132:37 mins (2 discs) □ ⊘⊘⊘

Like Harnoncourt and Hogwood, Gardiner restores many of the cuts (probably made by Mozart himself) in the very elaborate arias of the composer's first mature German *Singspiel.* He also includes the recently discovered March first recorded by Hogwood, but otherwise these rival period-instrument sets have little in common. Hogwood is swift and light in his pacing of the music, and delightful enough in the outer sections of the overture and the comic arias, but Gardiner is altogether more dramatic and expressive. Preference will depend, I suspect, on whether one regards the *Seraglio* as a comic opera with serious elements, or vice versa.

Gardiner opts for the latter approach, with wonderfully expressive playing in the great emotional numbers – Konstanze's 'Traurigkeit', the sublime duet – and he moves the 'action' ensembles – the Act I Trio, the great Quartet – with a propulsive theatrical momentum which I find more exhilarating than Hogwood's version. The two casts are fairly evenly balanced: Hogwood's Blondchen is more of a charmer than Gardiner's accurate but brittle Sieden, but Olsen's Belmonte, velvet-toned like Beecham's Simoneau, is a superior stylist to his Decca

counterpart. Pepe r is the best Pedrillo since the peerless Gerhard Unger (also Beecham) and Hauptmann's light lyric bass, only just making his low notes at Classical pitch, is a welcome change from the black-voiced Wagnerians who have dominated this role on disc. The clincher, though, is Orgonasova's fearless Konstanze: 'Martern aller Arten' holds no terrors for her, thanks to her fabulous technique and rich-toned soprano. She establishes an unusually erotic rapport with Minetti's noble yet menacing Pasha, the most complete vocal portrait of the spoken role on disc. Ravishing wind-playing, discreet fortepiano continuo, and superb choral singing set the seal on an enthralling issue.
Hugh Canning

MOZART

Idomeneo

Anthony Rolfe Johnson, Anne Sofie von Otter, Sylvia McNair, Hillevi Martinpelto; Monteverdi Choir, English Baroque Soloists/John Eliot Gardiner

Archiv 431 674-2 □ 210:33 mins (3 discs) □ ❶❷❸

Based on live performances given at the Queen Elizabeth Hall in London, this is a thrilling account of Mozart's greatest *opera seria*. The conductor's intention, to approach as closely as possible the kind of performance that might have been given in Mozart's time, is successfully realised with the superb specialist forces of his chorus and orchestra. Anthony Rolfe Johnson brings a fine technique and a lively dramatic imagination to Idomeneo, with Sylvia McNair singing the role of Ilia beautifully. Hillevi Martinpelto is a suitably ferocious Elettra, and Anne Sofie von Otter is perfectly cast as Idamante. The three discs include, in appendices which take up the whole of the third disc and part of the second, all the variants to the score which Mozart provided for different performances.
CO

MOZART

Le nozze di Figaro

Rodney Gilfry, Hillevi Martinpelto, Alison Hagley, Bryn Terfel, Pamela Helen Stephen, Susan McCulloch, Carlos Feller, Francis Egerton; Monteverdi Choir, English Baroque Soloists/John Eliot Gardiner

Archiv 439 871-2 □ 178:40 mins (3 discs) □ ❶❷❸

Mozart's operas are so all-embracing in their concerns that no single conductor is able, it seems, to do equal justice to each. I found John Eliot Gardiner's *Così* rather bland and uninspired. This *Figaro* – a more ambivalent,

indeed more cynical work in so many ways – is on a higher level altogether, an enlightening period performance galvanised by a palpably sure sense of dramatic wherewithal.

In common with others these days, and with good musicological reasons, Gardiner re-jigs the ordering of Act III, positioning 'Dove sono' somewhat earlier than usual. He departs more radically from tradition by offering, in addition, a reordered version of Act IV. This is convincing as scholarship as well as drama – two qualities which inform the whole of this sparkling yet searching performance, a team effort which nonetheless permits plenty of sharply etched characterisation, as well as some exceptionally fine singing.

Indeed, the casting can hardly be faulted: a dark, even menacing Figaro (Bryn Terfel), a vixenish, knowing Susanna (Alison Hagley), a suave yet incisive Count (Rodney Gilfry), a radiant but far from droopy Countess (Hillevi Martinpelto) and an ardent, hyper-sexed Cherubino (Pamela Helen Stephen). Excellent cameo support too. Perhaps this is the near-perfect *Figaro* we've all been waiting for...
Antony Bye

MOZART

Die Zauberflöte

Gundula Janowitz, Nicolai Gedda, Lucia Popp, Walter Berry, Gottlob Frick; Philharmonia Chorus & Orchestra/Otto Klemperer

EMI CDS 5 55173 2 □ ADD □ 134:02 mins (2 discs) □ ❶❷❸

Otto Klemperer's conducting could at times be magisterially heavy, and his tempi accordingly slow, but he gauges the conflicting moods of Mozart's pantomime-opera perfectly, giving the quasi-Masonic ritual aspects their due solemnity but investing the lighter Papageno scenes with a perhaps unexpected lightness. EMI's producer, Peter Andry, assembled a cast that contained some of the finest Mozart interpreters of the time. Gundula Janowitz is a forthright Pamina, Nicolai Gedda an absolutely exemplary Tamino – in my view the finest on disc – and the young Lucia Popp copes brilliantly with the Queen of Night's fierce coloratura. Walter Berry is a lovable Viennese Papageno, Gottlob Frick the weightiest of Sarastros, and Elisabeth Schwarzkopf, Christa Ludwig and Marga Höffgen are lavishly cast as the Queen of Night's Ladies. The dialogue is not included. Nor is it on my alternative choice, the historical 1937 Berlin performance conducted by Thomas Beecham, with Gerhard

Hüsch's incomparable Papageno, Tiana Lemnitz an exquisite Pamina, and Erna Berger a perfect Queen of Night (reissued on CD by Nimbus). *CO*

MUSSORGSKY

Boris Godunov

Anatoly Kotcherga, Samuel Ramey, Sergei Larin, Marjana Lipovšek, Philip Langridge, Sergei Leiferkus, Gleb Nikolsky, Elena Zaremba, Liliana Nichiteanu, Valentina Valente, Evgenia Gorochovskaya; Slovak Philharmonic Chorus, Berlin Radio Chorus, Tölz Boys Choir, Berlin PO/Claudio Abbado

Sony S3K 58977 □ **200:42 mins (3 discs)** □ *♪♪♪*

It has often been said that the protagonist of *Boris Godunov* is the chorus – which rings less true, incidentally, when you consider that the first of Mussorgsky's two own versions ended with the death of Boris, not the chaotic Kromy Forest crowd scene – but the stars of this show are undeniably Abbado and his orchestra. As always, Abbado knows exactly when and how to quicken or slow the pulse according to the psychology of the drama, and he vindicates Mussorgsky's orchestration as a thing not just of unorthodox wildness but also of incomparably chaste beauty (notable in the Chudov Monastery scene).

Kotcherga's Boris, though good in guilty self-communing, is hardly the toweringly charismatic figure the great histrionic basses, from Chaliapin through to Evgeny Nesterenko, have made of him, and only three members of the cast (Lipovšek, Langridge and Larin) prove ideally sensitive to the text. What counts is the fluency with which Abbado, vividly assisted both by the sound and the sound-effects department, lights the way for the 1874 version, with the bonus of the magnificent scene from 1869 where the tsar comes face to face with the simpleton and the starving Russian people. *DN*

MUSSORGSKY

Khovanshchina

Aage Haugland, Vladimir Atlantov, Vladimir Popov, Anatoly Kotcherga, Paata Burchuladze, Marjana Lipovšek, Joanna Borowska, Heinz Zednik; Slovak Philharmonic Chorus, Vienna Boys Choir, Vienna State Opera Chorus & Orchestra/Claudio Abbado

DG 429 758-2 □ **170:32 mins (3 discs)** □ *♪♪♪*

Mussorgsky's uncompromising view of events leading up to Peter the Great's emergence as the first Russian emperor – a work left unfinished and largely unscored at the time of the alcoholic composer's early death in 1881 – raises even more questions

over a viable performing edition than *Boris Godunov*. By welding together the better part of Shostakovich's 1958 orchestration and Stravinsky's final chorus for Diaghilev's 1913 production, Abbado suggests that the composer's sympathies lay, if anywhere, not with the concept of Peter as progress personified, but with the long-suffering, martyrdom-bound Old Believers. He is supported to the hilt by a richly sonorous orchestra, dedicated choirs and one singer, Marjana Lipovšek as Marfa who, above all others, joins intelligent forces with her orchestral counterparts and conjures a rare calm in this still-youthful Old Believer's meditative moments. Abbado's final scene builds on that spiritual dimension, and makes a much clearer goal than the abrupt Rimsky-Korsakov ending favoured by Gergiev on his equally fine, if less vividly recorded Kirov Opera version (Philips). *DN*

OFFENBACH

Les contes d'Hoffmann

Plácido Domingo, Joan Sutherland, Gabriel Bacquier, Hugues Cuénod, Huguette Tourangeau; Lausanne Pro Arte Choir, Brassus Chorale, Suisse Romande Chorus & Orchestra/Richard Bonynge

Decca 417 363-2 □ **ADD** □ **142:26 mins (2 discs)** □ *♪♪♪*

Offenbach's Romantic fantasy remains a popular favourite for its wealth of melody and for the splendid opportunities it offers its singers, notably the soprano, who is required to range from the coloratura virtuosity of the doll Olympia, through the lyrical style of the consumptive Antonia to the more dramatic requirements of the courtesan Giulietta. The four incarnations of the evil genius who frustrates Hoffmann are also intended to be portrayed by one singer, and the role of Hoffmann is especially demanding, calling for a dramatic tenor with both style and stamina.

Plácido Domingo is a splendidly ardent Hoffmann, and Joan Sutherland, in superb voice, is fully equal to the vocal demands of all three heroines and of the opera singer, Stella, as well. Gabriel Bacquier sings and characterises all the villains superbly, while the veteran Hugues Cuénod demonstrates his versatility in the four roles for character tenor. Richard Bonynge conducts with aplomb an excellent edition of the opera which he has himself put together from the various choices available. *CO*

OFFENBACH

Orphée aux enfers

Mady Mesplé, Jane Rhodes, Jane Berbié, Michel Sénéchal, Charles Burles, Michel Trempont; Toulouse Capitole Chorus & Orchestra/Michel Plasson

EMI CDS 7 49647 2 □ ADD □ 140:07 mins (2 discs) □ 𝄞𝄞𝄞

The Offenbach operettas really do need French actor-singers who are steeped in the genre, and this performance has them in abundance. The score is one of the composer's wittiest, with exuberant and occasionally tender melodies shared among the principal characters, and, of course, there is the famous cancan. Michel Sénéchal is a delightful Orpheus, Mady Mesplé brings great flair to the role of Euridice, and Jane Rhodes clearly enjoys herself as Public Opinion. Michel Plasson and his Toulouse forces perform with elegance and vigour. *CO*

PFITZNER

Palestrina

Peter Schreier, Siegfried Lorenz, Ekkehard Wlaschiha, Fritz Hübner; Berlin State Opera Chorus, Berlin Staatskapelle/Otmar Suitner

Berlin Classics 0310 001 □ 202:37 mins (3 discs) □ 𝄞𝄞

Like his contemporary Wilhelm Furtwängler, Hans Pfitzner's relationship with the Nazis was, to say the least, ambivalent. While never an active party member, his upholding of traditional German artistic values was enough in some eyes to brand him as a Nazi sympathiser, if not outright supporter, and this, coupled with his somewhat austere brand of post-Wagnerian musical Romanticism (at least in comparison with the glitzier confections of Richard Strauss), led to his marginalisation both in the history books and in the hearts and minds of music lovers. It's hardly surprising that he identified strongly with Palestrina, or at least the mythical Palestrina who at the last minute rescued polyphony for the Catholic Church, thereby affirming the value of high art over the superficial, trite and merely functional.

These adjectives are certainly inappropriate when describing this deeply serious and intensely moving opera. Its didactic nature is plain, and if the music, particularly during the long first act, tends to veer towards the devotional (sometimes even dull) rather than the galvanisingly dramatic, the whole is definitely greater than the sum of the parts. Peter Schreier's finely nuanced Palestrina

surpasses even that of Nicolai Gedda on the rival DG recording, tipping the balance in this version's favour. *Antony Bye*

PONCHIELLI

La Gioconda

Maria Callas, Pier Miranda Ferraro, Fiorenza Cossotto, Piero Cappuccilli; Chorus & Orchestra of La Scala, Milan/Antonino Votto

EMI CDS 7 49518 2 □ ADD □ 166:39 mins (3 discs) □ 𝄞𝄞𝄞

Though it is hardly ever performed in Britain, this splendid old melodrama by the leading Italian composer of the generation between Verdi and Puccini remains popular in Italy, and deservedly so. Its plot is preposterous, and most of its characters are distinctly unpleasant, but Ponchielli's opera is redeemed by the warmth of its passionate melodies and by its effective orchestration. The tenor 'Cielo e mar' is one of the most popular arias in the repertoire, and 'Suicidio!' is a gift to any dramatic soprano. But the music best known outside the context of the opera is that of the ballet, the Dance of the Hours. La Gioconda was the role of Maria Callas's Italian debut, and her full-blooded performance here is one of her finest on disc. The rest of the cast are worthy of her. *CO*

POULENC

Les dialogues des Carmélites

Catherine Dubosc, Rita Gorr, Rachel Yakar, José van Dam, Brigitte Fournier, Michel Sénéchal; Lyon Opera Chorus & Orchestra/Kent Nagano

Virgin VCD 7 59227 2 □ 151:08 mins (2 discs) □ 𝄞𝄞𝄞

Throughout his life Poulenc harboured serious doubts about his ability to compose a serious opera. But when he encountered Georges Bernanos's play about life in a nunnery during the period of the French Revolution he was so captivated that he immediately set to work on a full-length score. The work cost him a great deal in physical and mental effort, but it eventually enjoyed a successful premiere in Milan and Paris during 1957. The old EMI recording, featuring some of the main singers of the Paris production and bearing the composer's own seal of approval, still remains the yardstick by which all other versions must be judged. Fortunately, Kent Nagano and the Lyon Opera rise to the challenge magnificently, and if Catherine Dubosc doesn't quite eclipse memories of the irreplaceable Denise Duval in the role of Blanche, the rest of the cast are superb, and the immeasurably better-balanced recording allows one to appreciate more of the inner subtleties of Poulenc's deeply affecting score. *EL*

PROKOFIEV

The Fiery Angel

Galina Gorchakova, Sergei Leiferkus, Konstantin Pluzhnikov; Kirov Opera Chorus & Orchestra/Valery Gergiev

Philips 446 078-2 □ 118:57 mins (2 discs) □ 𝄢𝄢𝄢

Conjuring a strange medieval world where the human capacity for good and evil is trammelled on the one hand by necromancy real or imagined and on the other by the looming shadow of the Inquisition, these hair-raising operatic tableaux based on Bryusov's symbolist novel can seem haphazard at first hearing. Make no mistake, though: Prokofiev's infernal machinery is finely tuned, and it takes the impeccable timing of Valery Gergiev in the equally vital context of a live performance to show us how this unrelenting study in ambiguous obsession so carefully packs its punches. The fraught counterpoint of thrashing orchestral climaxes, when the demons that plague heroine Renata have their high noon, is expansively negotiated; blistering Kirov brass help to twist the screw that failed to turn in Neeme Järvi's DG studio recording. Gorchakova's lustrous portrayal of the tormented Renata is her finest recorded hour so far. She lacks the last degree of hysterical edge and some of the middle-range beauties discovered by Järvi's Nadine Secunde; but her unbeatable upper-register strengths make her a more companionable hysteric. Leiferkus plays her long-suffering knight straight, with blunt humour; his strange meetings with supernatural traffickers – among them Pluzhnikov's frighteningly coarse Mephistopheles – have all the vividness of scenes from Mussorgsky. That, of course, was part of Prokofiev's point, and in this magnificent piece of Petersburg teamwork his most disturbing masterpiece returns decisively to the Russian tradition it so singularly follows. *DN*

PROKOFIEV

The Love for Three Oranges

Gabriel Bacquier, Jean-Luc Viala, Georges Gautier, Catherine Dubosc, Michèle Lagrange, Vincent Le Texier; Lyon Opera Chorus & Orchestra/Kent Nagano

Virgin VCD 7 59566 2 □ 101:52 mins (2 discs) □ 𝄢𝄢𝄢

This is very much *L'amour des trois oranges* – as indeed it was performed at its Chicago premiere – rather than the *Lyubov k trem apelsinam* of Prokofiev's native Russian, and accordingly a performance of gallic deftness and fluency. There are times when a Russian blatancy of emphasis would come in useful, but Kent Nagano's quicksilver pacing holds the supernatural and lyrical elements of the score in perfect balance. Such skilful dovetailing helps to banish any suspicions that the fantastical orchestration of Prokofiev's satirical fairy-tale (based on a *divertimento* by the 18th-century Italian author Gozzi, of *Turandot* fame) needs to be complemented visually by a series of crazy stage images, as it so strikingly was in Richard Jones's unsurpassable Opera North/English National Opera production.

Vividly characterised performances from the largely French cast, with a true sense of ensemble, help to ensure that this is never less than a fizzing theatrical experience; they include outstanding cameos from the veteran baritone Gabriel Bacquier and the Belgian bass Jules Bastin. Prokofiev always insisted that *The Love for Three Oranges* had no other purpose than to amuse and entertain. When the presentation is as witty and sophisticated as this, who could ask for anything more? *DN*

PROKOFIEV

War and Peace

Galina Vishnevskaya, Lajos Miller, Wiesław Ochman, Nicolai Gedda, Nicola Ghiuselev, Stefania Toczyska, Eduard Tumagian; French Radio Chorus, French National Orchestra/Mstislav Rostropovich

Erato 2292-45331-2 □ 240:05 mins (4 discs) □ 𝄢𝄢

Like the opera itself, which Prokofiev worked so painstakingly to perfect throughout the last 12 years of his life but never lived to see staged in its entirety, this recording is both a generous labour of love and generously flawed. Too much has been made of the ageing Galina Vishnevskaya's return to the role she created in 1958, as the lovable, impulsive Natasha; there's no concealing frayed, spreading tones in the rapture of the opening scene, but, as soon as Natasha's doubts begin, Vishnevskaya commands the listener's involvement.

In any case, Natasha is absent from seven of Prokofiev's sensitively selected thirteen scenes from Tolstoy, and there the strengths both of the magnificent male casting, including the Bulgarian bass Nicola Ghiuselev rising to the challenge of General Kutuzov's profoundly moving aria, and the passionate commitment to Rostropovich of the French forces depicting for the most part (irony of ironies) their opponents of 1812. Valery Gergiev's recent Kirov contender (Philips) is bedevilled on disc by an unusually distracting audience shuffle and stage noise, not to mention weaker vocal characterisations in several key roles, though it does cry out for complementary viewing on video or laser disc, particularly for the heart-breaking Natasha of the remarkable young singing actress, Elena Prokina. *DN*

PUCCINI

La bohème

Renata Tebaldi, Gianna D'Angelo, Carlo Bergonzi, Ettore Bastianini, Renata Cesari, Cesare Siepi; Chorus & Orchestra of the Academy of Santa Cecilia/Tullio Serafin

Decca 425 534-2 □ ADD □ 111:54 mins (2 discs) □ 𝄞𝄞

La bohème is the ideal work for anyone coming new to the art of opera. Some may find Puccini's score too cloyingly sentimental, but most will surrender completely to its magical evocation of early 19th-century Paris and to its string of memorable melodies. There are a number of fine recordings, the earliest of which is that conducted by Thomas Beecham on EMI, with Victoria de los Angeles and Jussi Björling as the young lovers Mimì and Rodolfo. Herbert von Karajan, on Decca, with Mirella Freni and the young Pavarotti, almost as fine, is somewhat more recent. But an earlier Decca release, recorded more than 35 years ago, with Tullio Serafin conducting a relaxed and loving account of the opera, gets my vote. The Rome studio recording marvellously captures the atmosphere of a stage performance, and there can rarely have been a more beautiful-sounding Mimì than Renata Tebaldi. That great stylist Carlo Bergonzi is an exemplary Rodolfo, and Ettore Bastianini, a baritone who died young and who is still sorely missed, makes a strong Marcello. *CO*

PUCCINI

La fanciulla del West

Carol Neblett, Plácido Domingo, Sherrill Milnes, Francis Egerton, Robert Lloyd, Jonathan Summers; Chorus & Orchestra of the Royal Opera House, Covent Garden/Zubin Mehta

DG 419 640-2 □ ADD □ 129:36 (2 discs) □ 𝄞𝄞𝄞

Puccini's 'wild west' opera, set in the Sierra Nevada mountains of California during the gold-rush days of 1849, and derived from a play by the American David Belasco, is a work that grows on one's affections with repeated hearings. It wastes little time on lyrical expansion, but its subtly orchestrated score moves briskly, serving the libretto faithfully. This recording, lovingly and excitingly conducted by Zubin Mehta, benefits from being based on a Royal Opera production with the same conductor and many of the same cast. As she did in the opera house, Carol Neblett brings her rich, eloquent timbre to the role of Minnie, the saloon owner, and Plácido Domingo, in sturdy voice, is convincing as the bandit who wins her heart. Sherrill Milnes is well cast as the sheriff, and a large company of Covent Garden regulars is, without exception, superb. *CO*

PUCCINI

Madama Butterfly

Leontyne Price, Richard Tucker, Rosalind Elias, Philip Maero; RCA Italiana Opera Chorus & Orchestra/Erich Leinsdorf

RCA Victor Red Seal RD 86160 □ ADD □ 128:40 mins (2 discs) □ 𝄞𝄞𝄞

There are several recordings of Puccini's popular opera which contain one or more superb performances, and at least three of them are on EMI. Victoria de los Angeles may not be the ideal Butterfly, but her vocal timbre is glorious, and Jussi Björling brings his suave tone and stylish approach to the role of Pinkerton. Renata Scotto, a more traditional Butterfly, is partnered with the elegant Carlo Bergonzi, somewhat erratically conducted by John Barbirolli. Maria Callas is an over-emphatic Butterfly, but her Pinkerton, Nicolai Gedda, is one of the finest on disc, and Herbert von Karajan conducts impeccably. However, the best all-round performance, strongly and briskly conducted by Erich Leinsdorf, has Leontyne Price as a sympathetic and moving Butterfly, with Richard Tucker appropriately cast as Pinkerton, and a very strong, predominantly Italian supporting cast. *CO*

PUCCINI

Manon Lescaut

Mirella Freni, Luciano Pavarotti, Dwayne Croft, Giuseppe Taddei; Metropolitan Opera Chorus & Orchestra/James Levine

Decca 440 200-2 □ 120:07 mins (2 discs) □ 𝄞𝄞𝄞

Puccini's earliest real success was with *Manon Lescaut*, a not surprisingly more full-blooded, Italianate operatic version of the Abbé

Prévost's novel than Massenet's *Manon*. Mirella Freni's tone may not sound youthful enough for the teenage Manon, but she brings such passion and sensuality to the role that she contrives to be more convincing than any of her rivals on disc, even Maria Callas. Recording the role of Des Grieux for the first time when in his late fifties, Pavarotti is even more impressive, singing with forward tone, clear Italian diction, beautiful legato phrasing and dramatic intelligence. Giuseppe Taddei makes a welcome appearance as the elderly Geronte, and James Levine, conducting, offers an account of the score that combines vitality and Romantic ardour. The best alternative version comes from EMI, with Callas and Giuseppe di Stefano, conducted authoritatively by Tullio Serafin. *CO*

PUCCINI

Tosca

Maria Callas, Giuseppe di Stefano, Tito Gobbi; Chorus & Orchestra of La Scala, Milan/Victor de Sabata

EMI CMS 7 69974 2 □ ADD mono □ 112:05 mins (2 discs) □ 😊😊

Herbert von Karajan's version, dating from the Sixties, of Puccini's almost singer-proof melodrama is magnificent, with Leontyne Price in glorious voice as Tosca, Giuseppe di Stefano clearly in his element as Cavaradossi, and Giuseppe Taddei a suavely menacing Scarpia. But by far the most desirable recording of *Tosca* is that conducted by Victor de Sabata more than forty years ago, which projects the drama with even greater force and conviction than Karajan. Giuseppe di Stefano, in younger and fresher voice than for Karajan, is again an exciting Cavaradossi, and the *comprimario* roles are strongly cast.

The two chief glories of this version are the totally convincing Tosca of Maria Callas and the Scarpia of the incomparable Tito Gobbi. Gobbi's vocal inflections bring the character of the evil chief of police to life with extraordinary vividness, while Callas, in a role not as demanding as many others she undertook, is able to involve herself completely in the dramatic situation with little fear of vocal problems arising. This is one of the controversial prima donna's finest achievements on disc. *CO*

PUCCINI

Il trittico

Tito Gobbi, Victoria de los Angeles; Rome Opera Chorus & Orchestra/Vincenzo Bellezza, Tullio Serafin, Gabriele Santini

EMI CMS 7 64165 2 □ ADD □ 160:35 mins (3 discs) □ 😊😊

Puccini's comic masterpiece *Gianni Schicchi* may still lay claim to a place in the popular repertoire, but otherwise his 'triptych' of one-act operas is unfairly neglected by opera houses and has hitherto been disappointingly served on CD. This EMI set, recorded in the late Fifties but admirably remastered, offers Tito Gobbi and Victoria de los Angeles at the height of their considerable powers.

The impassioned and highly charged Grand Guignol of *Il tabarro* may be short on subtlety, but Vincenzo Bellezza plays down its inherent melodrama and, despite the wonderfully indulgent and lyrical score, manages to keep a grip on the reality of the opera's low-life setting, making the final scene all the more horrifying. Gobbi's performance as the cuckolded Michele is exemplary: sinister and cruel as well as melancholic and misunderstood.

If *Il tabarro* is inclined to melodrama, then *Suor Angelica*, with its all-female cast and quasi-mystical convent setting, verges on cloying sentimentality. Here, though, Victoria de los Angeles's portrayal of the eponymous nun is so utterly moving and serene that the piece is lifted from mawkishness. Her sweetness is all the more affecting when compared with Fedora Barbieri's formidable and imperious Zia Principessa.

Inevitably, perhaps, *Gianni Schicchi* is the highlight of the set, with Gobbi brilliantly compelling and wittily manipulative in the title role, and de los Angeles appealingly girlish and bright as Lauretta. *Claire Wrathall*

PUCCINI

Turandot

Eva Marton, José Carreras, Katia Ricciarelli, John-Paul Bogart; Vienna Boys Choir, Vienna State Opera Chorus & Orchestra/Lorin Maazel

Sony M2K 39160 □ ADD □ 126:34 mins (2 discs) □ 😊😊

Puccini's last opera, though left unfinished at his death in 1924, is probably its composer's greatest. It is also, without a doubt, the most recent Italian opera to have achieved worldwide popularity, even if one discounts the present notoriety of its Act III tenor aria

'Nessun dorma', which has proved so useful to TV commercials and to football.

For EMI, Birgit Nilsson is a predictably sturdy exponent of the title role, with Franco Corelli a more than acceptable Calaf. Joan Sutherland, on Decca, conducted by Zubin Mehta, is, perhaps surprisingly, a highly effective Turandot, her voice riding with ease over the orchestra in her great aria, 'In questa reggia'. But the best all-round performance on CD is a more recent one, recorded live at the Vienna State Opera in 1983, during the conductor Lorin Maazel's short-lived directorship of that prestigious institution. Eva Marton is the most exciting Turandot on disc, José Carreras is in fine, youthful voice as Calaf, and Katia Ricciarelli is an affecting Liù. The Vienna chorus and orchestra, under Maazel, are in thrilling form, and the atmosphere in the opera house, with a highly enthusiastic audience, is well caught. *CO*

PURCELL

Dido and Aeneas

Catherine Bott, Emma Kirkby, John Mark Ainsley, David Thomas; Academy of Ancient Music & Chorus/Christopher Hogwood

L'Oiseau-Lyre 436 992-2 □ 52:28 mins □ 𝄞𝄞𝄞

The recent re-dating of Purcell's only full opera has had profound implications for its performance. Once it is accepted as an adult entertainment for the court, rather than a decorous presentation by the girls of a genteel Chelsea boarding-school, the selection of voices, the size and constitution of chorus and orchestra, and the theatrical effects are all open to re-interpretation. Hogwood has a bass Sorceress, a countertenor Spirit, and a boy sailor. The chorus includes high tenors to make sense of the low 'alto' line, and the orchestra matches the King's Band, with the absence of 16-foot bass noticeably lightening the texture.

The recording reflects a strong sense of theatre – Aeneas enters from a distance, and the witches echo spatially. The Drottningholm Court Theatre in Sweden provides authentic thunder- and wind-machines to truly terrifying effect.

The performance matches the concept and the resources. David Thomas is a horrid Sorceress, though he and his witches never descend to mere farce. Catherine Bott sings the tragic queen's lament with great pathos, understated and yet evoking a deeply touching sense of despair. *GP*

PURCELL

The Fairy Queen

Susan Bickley, Lorraine Hunt, Catherine Pierard, Howard Crook, Mark Padmore, Richard Wistreich; Schütz Choir of London, London Classical Players/Roger Norrington

EMI CDS 5 55234 2 □ 122:06 mins (2 discs) □ 𝄞𝄞𝄞

This recording derives from a semi-staged revival of the 1692 adaptation of *A Midsummer Night's Dream*, complete with Purcell's overture and five masques, one to be inserted into each act of the play. The music here, undiluted by the play, is a rich diet bordering on the indigestible, as short, charming airs and dances follow each other at breakneck speed. Yet additional CDs of bowdlerised Shakespeare, still lacking the spectacle of the original staging, with machinery, costumes, dance and stage action, are clearly impractical.

The performance is superb, resonating with the wider dramatic context in which it was conceived. The rustic love scene between Coridon and Mopsa is hilarious, Padmore's high tenor slipping into a falsetto giggle at the end. The stillness of Wistreich's 'Sleep' is breathtaking as Titania is lulled into 'sweet repose'. The upper voices contrast – Hunt colourful, Pierard and Bickley more artless – yet they blend perfectly in duets.

The orchestral sound, striking for its (authentic) absence of 16-foot bass, creates a translucent texture matched by the 19-voice choir. The recorded sound is comfortably close, warmed by a gentle ambient resonance. *GP*

PURCELL

The Indian Queen

Tessa Bonner, Catherine Bott, Rogers Covey-Crump, Peter Harvey; The Purcell Simfony, The Purcell Simfony Voices/Catherine Mackintosh

Linn CKD 035 □ 60:20 mins □ 𝄞𝄞𝄞

Purcell's widow Frances thought this contribution to a play which almost failed his 'last and best Performance in Musick'. Following an industrial dispute, the stage designer and most of the cast stormed out, to be replaced at short notice with young, inexperienced actors and singers. This information, and more, is in the authoritative programme note by Andrew Pinnock. But there the booklet abruptly ends, with no further information regarding the plot and libretto, or any indication of the dramatic context of the songs, which characters sing what…

Fortunately, the performance is stunning. Seven voices (four soloists and three more to provide a tiny chorus), one-to-a-part strings, with wind and a simple harpsichord continuo, create a remarkable range of textures. Clever engineering makes the ensemble sound larger than it is, but the crystal clarity remains.

Bonner and Covey-Crump are finely matched yet distinctive in ensembles together, and Bott's 'I attempt from love's sickness' is simply ravishing. Songs swing jauntily as they should, but the recitative moves as well, sensitively structured over a purposeful pulse. I can't imagine a finer tribute to Purcell's last composition before his untimely death. *GP*

PURCELL

King Arthur

Jennifer Smith, Gillian Fisher, Elizabeth Priday, Gill Ross, Ashley Stafford, Paul Elliott, Stephen Varcoe; Monteverdi Choir, English Baroque Soloists/John Eliot Gardiner

Erato 4509-96552-2 □ 90:00 mins (2 discs) □ 🎵🎵

King Arthur is the only semi-opera that was designed as such from the start by both its librettist, Dryden, and its composer, Purcell. Music and spoken drama are therefore particularly interdependent and integrated, and a great deal is lost by recording the music alone. For this reason it's a pity the booklet doesn't describe more fully the dramatic context and stage sets. One recent recording (Christie, also on Erato) followed a fully staged production, but only a few disconcerting crowd noises – and some choral 'a-tish-oos' from the Cold People – are transferred to disc.

Gardiner's conception, from 1983, has worn very well. The instrumental sound is bright, unweighted by 16-foot string bass. The artlessness of the tenor, Paul Elliott, is particularly appealing, matched by Gillian Fisher and Jennifer Smith as two risqué shepherdesses (their duet was censored in an 1897 performance). 'How happy the lover' from Act IV shows Purcell at his most ingenious: an instrumental ritornello, a solo, chorus, duo and trios, unfolding successively over 59 repetitions of a descending ground bass to match the great operatic chaconnes of Lully. *GP*

RAMEAU

Castor et Pollux

Howard Crook, Jérôme Corréas, Agnès Mellon, Véronique Gens, René Schirrer, Sandrine Piau, Mark Padmore, Claire Brua; Les Arts Florissants/William Christie

Harmonia Mundi HMC 901435/37 □ 173:00 mins (3 discs) □ 🎵🎵🎵

Rameau's reputation as one of the greatest French composers of the late Baroque rests chiefly on his operas, with their colourful orchestrations, dramatic choruses and subtle blends of aria and expressive recitative. These attributes are already to the fore in *Castor et Pollux*, his second completed *tragédie en musique*, which was first staged in 1737.

Though Rameau prepared a shorter, much-revised, version in 1754, it is the original that is performed here, complete with its enchanting allegorical Prologue and leisurely procession of dances, airs and set-piece spectacles.

William Christie and Les Arts Florissants are outstanding exponents of this repertoire. The playing is superb and the singing, from principals through to chorus, is magnificent. *Castor et Pollux* may not be Rameau's most compelling opera but it couldn't receive a more brilliant or persuasive account. *Graham Lock*

RAMEAU

Hippolyte et Aricie

Véronique Gens, Jean-Paul Fouchécourt, Bernarda Fink, Thérèse Feighan; Ensemble Vocal Sagittarius, Les Musiciens du Louvre/Marc Minkowski

Archiv 445 853-2 □ 167:25 mins (3 discs) □ 🎵🎵🎵

To my mind, successful performances of French Baroque opera need two qualities. One is a feeling for the drama, a readiness to exaggerate contrasts in mood, and therefore in tone, timbre, pace and dynamic, for all they're worth. The other is an intuitive elegance that enables lines to breathe naturally, harmonic progressions to flow with Gallic suaveness, charm and shape. Both elements are usually present in William Christie's offerings of French music, but for Marc Minkowski in his much-heralded debut for the Archiv label, a live recording made at the lovely little Theatre Royal in Versailles, the drama counts for everything.

Since this is such a dramatic piece, with underworld confrontations and overtones of incestuous love expressed in arresting, vividly coloured music, Minkowski just about gets away with it. But often moments of poignancy

sound either a little anxious or a touch
wooden.

The singers' character portrayals are
excellent. Jean-Paul Fouchécourt and
Véronique Gens are both good in the title
roles, though Russell Smythe's Thésée –
wonderfully assertive and rich-toned – and
Bernarda Fink's unscrupulous Phèdre almost
steal the show for the parents.

Minkowski's chosen text is a hybrid based
mainly on the first version of 1733, but with
bits added and subtracted here and there.
However, he chooses the 1757 version for the
opening two scenes of Act II, when Thésée
ventures to the underworld, a wildly colourful
torrent of sound that hasn't been heard since
Rameau's day. All these decisions are fully
documented in the excellently produced
booklet. *Stephen Pettitt*

RAVEL

L'enfant et les sortilèges

Françoise Ogéas, Jeannine Collard, Jane Berbié,
Sylvaine Gilma, Colette Herzog, Heinz Rehfuss,
Camille Maurane, Michel Sénéchal; RTF Chorus &
Orchestra/Lorin Maazel

DG 423 718-2 □ ADD □ **42:56 mins** □ 🎵🎵🎵

Colette's story of the ill-tempered child who
abuses his toys, pets and furniture to the
extent that they come to life and wreak their
own revenge upon him inspired Ravel to
write some of his most enchanting and
imaginative music. Composed during the
Twenties, *L'enfant and les sortilèges* responds
effectively to the contemporary craze for jazz
in the deliciously exuberant 'china-cup
foxtrot', but later the luxuriant sound-world
of the forest scene from *Daphnis et Chloé* is
recalled.

Although it's over thirty years old, this DG
recording of Ravel's enchanting opera still
sounds remarkably vibrant. A youthful Lorin
Maazel galvanises soloists, choir and orchestra
to performances of urgency, humour and
tenderness which surpass all subsequent
versions in extracting the maximum impact
from each episode. For those who feel that 42
minutes of music is a little ungenerous for a
CD, Charles Dutoit's recent Decca recording
runs it a pretty close second, and offers the
benefit of an exquisitely sung *Shéhérazade* into
the bargain. *EL*

RIMSKY-KORSAKOV

Sadko

Vladimir Galusin, Valentina Tsidipova, Marianna
Trassaova, Larissa Diadkova, Bulat Minjelkiev,
Gegam Grigorian, Alexander Gergalov; Kirov Opera
Chorus & Orchestra/Valery Gergiev

Philips 442 138-2 □ **172:53 mins (3 discs)** □ 🎵🎵🎵

If you asked Russians who knew and loved
their Rimsky-Korsakov operas to choose a
favourite, *Sadko* would probably not come to
the very top of the poll. But since earlier,
classic Russian opera recordings have appeared
only fitfully on CD, and since Gergiev is still,
at the time of writing, waiting to re-record the
jewel in his Rimsky festival series, *The Invisible
City of Kitezh*, this saga of a minstrel-
merchant's fortunes fills the bill very happily.
Gergiev's supple conducting helps the
deliberate illusion of a charmingly naive
meander through Russian fairy-tale territory,
but symphonic mastery is at work beneath the
surface, contrasting and ultimately fusing the
free flow of unusual folk-song metres and the
supernatural watery world into which Sadko is
drawn – a magical half-way house between
Wagner and Debussy.

The Kirov star names are found in the vital
smaller roles. Even so, it's good to hear the
young tenor Vladimir Galusin finding his feet
as a heroic Sadko, while the silvery tones of
Valentina Tsidipova are perfect for the liquid
rhapsodies of the Sea King's daughter. Both
she and the chorus are rather disadvantaged by
the cowled acoustics of a live Kirov recording,
but once you adjust to the lack of artificial
studio brilliance, the natural presence of the
sound is an aid to the easy enjoyment of this
gourmet feast. *DN*

ROSSINI

Il barbiere di Siviglia

Jennifer Larmore, Raúl Giménez, Håkan Hagegård,
Alessandro Corbelli, Samuel Ramey; Chorus of the
Grand Theatre, Geneva, Lausanne CO/Jesús López-
Cobos

Teldec 9031-74885-2 □ **151:03 mins (2 discs)**
□ 🎵🎵🎵

Rossini's comic masterpiece is one of the most
enjoyable of operas, full of delightful and apt
melodic invention, and bubbling over with
gaiety and high spirits. Verdi once told a critic
that Rossini's *Barbiere*, 'with its abundance of
real musical ideas, its comic verve, and its
truthful declamation, is the most beautiful
opera buffa in existence'. It is an opinion with
which few would disagree.

Among a number of excellent recordings, the most desirable is one of the most recent, conducted with elegance and flair by Jesús López-Cobos. Håkan Hagegård is a near-ideal Figaro, with plenty of vocal personality and charm, and Jennifer Larmore brings a warm and alluring mezzo-soprano timbre to Rosina. Raúl Giménez copes easily with Almaviva's music, even the lengthy and usually omitted 'Cessa di più resistere', with its demanding cabaletta, and the two bass roles are cast from strength, with Samuel Ramey an impressive Basilio and Alessandro Corbelli a marvellously funny Bartolo. EMI's 1959 version with Callas and Gobbi is, however, a splendid alternative. *CO*

ROSSINI

La Cenerentola

Jennifer Larmore, Raúl Giménez, Gino Quilico, Alessandro Corbelli, Adelina Scarabelli, Laura Polverelli; Chorus & Orchestra of the Royal Opera House, Covent Garden/Carlo Rizzi

Teldec 4509-94553-2 □ **154:21 mins (2 discs)** □ 😊😊😊

Rossini's 1817 version of the familiar fairy-tale of Cinderella, though not quite the equal of his *Barbiere* of the previous year, is nevertheless a highly entertaining work, with splendid opportunities for the performers of the comic bass roles of Don Magnifico and Dandini, and richly expressive music for Cinderella and her Prince Charming. Three of the singers from the preferred recording of *Il barbiere di Siviglia* reappear in this delightful account of *La Cenerentola*, with a different conductor, Carlo Rizzi, who proves a superb Rossinian. Jennifer Larmore's warm and sympathetic timbre is ideally suited to the title role, which she sings with great elegance and, in her final aria, 'Non più mesta', astonishing agility. Raúl Giménez has no difficulties with the Prince's music, and Alessandro Corbelli demonstrates once again that he is the leading Italian *basso buffo* of the day. Gino Quilico is an engaging Dandini, and the comic stepsisters, Scarabelli and Polverelli, are hugely entertaining. *CO*

ROSSINI

Le Comte Ory

Sumi Jo, John Aler, Diana Montague, Gilles Cachemaille, Gino Quilico; Lyon Opera Chorus & Orchestra/John Eliot Gardiner

Philips 422 406-2 □ **131:49 mins (2 discs)** □ 😊😊😊

This is one of Rossini's most enjoyable comic operas, not in the ebullient Italian manner of

Il barbiere di Siviglia but in a style which might be said to have initiated the genre of French operetta. The story of the licentious Count Ory, who disguises himself as the mother superior of a group of nuns (his own men in disguise) in order to gain entrance to a castle where a beautiful young countess has taken refuge, clearly appealed to Rossini's temperament, inspiring him to produce one of his most delightful scores. Based on a stage production at the Lyon Opera, this recording has great theatrical presence, is conducted most stylishly by John Eliot Gardiner, and is gloriously sung by its entire cast. The Korean soprano Sumi Jo copes with Rossini's agile vocal writing with consummate ease, while John Aler, in the even more demanding high-lying title role, is equally impressive. Diana Montague as Isolier, the Count's page, and Gino Quilico as his colleague Raimbaud could not be bettered. The only other recording, on EMI – based on Glyndebourne performances in the Fifties, with Sari Barabas and Juan Oncina and conducted by Vittorio Gui – is a perfectly acceptable alternative. *CO*

ROSSINI

Guillaume Tell

Gabriel Bacquier, Montserrat Caballé, Nicolai Gedda, Mady Mesplé, Louis Hendrikx, Gwynne Howell; Ambrosian Opera Chorus, RPO/Lamberto Gardelli

EMI CMS 7 69951 2 □ **ADD** □ **237:42 mins (4 discs)** □ 😊😊

Rossini's final opera, its subject the 13th-century Swiss patriot (who, like Robin Hood, may or may not have existed), is immensely long and, given its subject, curiously leisurely in pace. Nevertheless, it contains some glorious music, especially in Act II. EMI's 1972 performance is to date the first and only absolutely complete recording of the original French version of the work, and fortunately it is superb. Gabriel Bacquier brings a warm voice and a convincing interpretation to the role of William Tell, while Montserrat Caballé, exquisite in her melancholy aria 'Sombre forêt', is also brilliant in Mathilde's coloratura flights, her voice never losing its tonal beauty under pressure. In the fiendishly high-lying tenor role of Arnold, Nicolai Gedda is not only a model of elegant French style but also encompasses mellifluously and with apparent ease the character's 19 high Cs and two C sharps. Lamberto Gardelli draws rich and expressive playing from the orchestra, and the opera's beautiful choruses are sung magnificently by the Ambrosians. *CO*

ROSSINI

L'italiana in Algeri

Teresa Berganza, Luigi Alva, Rolando Panerai, Fernando Corena; Chorus & Orchestra of the Maggio Musicale, Florence/Silvio Varviso

Decca 417 828-2 □ ADD □ 129:39 mins (2 discs)
□ 🟢🟢

There are at least two other splendid recordings of Rossini's sparkling comedy, one from Erato, with Marilyn Horne as the Italian woman who finds herself unexpectedly reunited with her missing lover when she is shipwrecked near the court of the lecherous Bey of Algiers, and one from Sony, with Lucia Valentini Terrani as the resourceful heroine. But even more enjoyable is Decca's 1963 version, stylishly conducted by Silvio Varviso, with Teresa Berganza a most elegant Isabella, and three of the finest Italian Rossini singers of the day as the men in her life. *CO*

ROSSINI

Semiramide

Cheryl Studer, Samuel Ramey, Jennifer Larmore, Frank Lopardo; Ambrosian Opera Chorus, LSO/Ion Marin

DG 437 797-2 □ 207:22 mins (3 discs) □ 🟢🟢🟢

Semiramide, Queen of Babylon, has the misfortune to fall in love with Arsace, the young commander of the Assyrian army, who turns out to be her son. A huge success when it was first staged in 1823, Rossini's tragic opera, with its masterly ensembles, arias and duets, had, by the end of the century, fallen into neglect. A production with Joan Sutherland and Giulietta Simionato at La Scala in 1962 gave it a new lease of life, and since then other artists have emerged who are able to cope with the heavy demands Rossini places on his singers. The four leading roles in this 1992 recording are taken by Americans, all of whom are first rate. Cheryl Studer dispatches her great aria 'Bel raggio lusinghier' with consummate ease, and, as Arsace, Jennifer Larmore blends her warm mezzo-soprano voice exquisitely with Studer's dazzling soprano in their duets. Samuel Ramey gives a characteristically forthright account of the evil Assur, and Frank Lopardo, in the tenor role of Idreno, sounds entirely at ease in his difficult arias. The score is performed complete, and is competently conducted by Ion Marin. In an older Decca recording, also highly recommended but performed with a few cuts, Joan Sutherland and Marilyn Horne are Semiramide and Arsace. *CO*

ROSSINI

Tancredi

Ernesto Palacio, Marilyn Horne, Nicola Zaccaria, Lella Cuberli, Bernadette Manca di Nissa, Patricia Schumann; Teatro La Fenice Chorus & Orchestra/Ralf Weikert

Sony S3K 39073 □ 169:06 mins (3 discs) □ 🟢🟢🟢

Tancredi, its libretto derived in part from Voltaire's tragedy, is the earliest serious Rossini opera of any consequence. (It was preceded mainly by comic pieces, many of them in one act.) Though uneven, it contains some of Rossini's finest music and was highly acclaimed by its first audiences in Venice in 1813: one of its arias, 'Di tanti palpiti', became so popular that it was hummed and whistled in the streets and alleyways. This live recording, made in 1983 at the Teatro La Fenice, where the opera had its premiere, does full justice to the work, with Lella Cuberli an expressive and vocally exciting heroine (Amenaide), and Marilyn Horne in splendid form as the eponymous hero who sings the opera's pop tune. Ernesto Palacio's agile tenor makes light of the difficult role of Argirio, the heroine's father. Ralf Weikert conducts efficiently, using Rossini's second (and preferable) version of the finale, which has Tancredi dying on stage instead of living happily ever after with Amenaide. *CO*

SAINT-SAENS

Samson et Dalila

Plácido Domingo, Waltraud Meier, Alain Fondary, Jean-Philippe Courtis, Samuel Ramey; Chorus & Orchestra of the Bastille Opera/Myung-Whun Chung

EMI CDS 7 54470 2 □ 123:31 mins (2 discs)
□ 🟢🟢🟢

The only opera by Saint-Saëns to have survived in the international repertoire, albeit perilously, *Samson et Dalila* works well on stage. The almost Bach-like choruses in Acts I and III are a reminder that the work was originally conceived as an oratorio, but Delilah's arias are suitably seductive, and the great duet in Act III (often recorded as a solo, 'Softly awakes my heart') is undeniably erotic. Myung-Whun Chung's masterly account of the score has no currently available serious rivals. Domingo makes a splendidly heroic Samson, exciting in the first two acts, and moving in Act III. Waltraud Meier succeeds with Delilah more by virtue of her intelligence and style than by voluptuousness of voice. Though one can think easily of other mezzos more suited to the role vocally, Meier is nonetheless dramatically convincing. Fondary is a magnificent High Priest, and Samuel Ramey brings firm characterisation to the small but telling role of the Old Hebrew. *CO*

SCHOECK

Penthesilea

Helga Dernesch, Jane Marsh, Mechthild Gessendorf, Marjana Lipovšek, Theo Adam; ORF Chorus & SO/Gerd Albrecht

Orfeo C 364 942 □ ADD □ 79:59 mins □ ☺☺☺

Although championed by no less a figure than Fritz Busch, Othmar Schoeck's *Penthesilea* failed to make much impact when it was premiered at the Dresden Opera during the heady days of the Weimar Republic. Sixty years later, however, a concert performance of the Swiss composer's neglected masterpiece at the 1982 Salzburg Festival drew a standing ovation and resulted in the work being staged in several opera houses. The present recording, culled from Austrian radio tapes made at that historic concert, confirms this positive impression. It's a truly electrifying experience, exemplifying Schoeck's innate gift for theatrical representation, and, in its graphic exploitation of violence, must be counted a worthy successor to Strauss's *Elektra*. A star-studded cast makes the most of the score's fast-moving dialogue, while Gerd Albrecht effects an impressive command over the technically challenging orchestral writing. An urgent recommendation to all those wishing to make the acquaintance of a major 20th-century opera. *EL*

SCHOENBERG

Erwartung; Variations for Orchestra; Chamber Symphony No. 1

Phyllis Bryn-Julson; Birmingham Contemporary Music Group, City of Birmingham SO/Simon Rattle

EMI CDC 5 55212 2 □ 75:02 mins □ ☺☺☺

Schoenberg's monodrama, a cardinal, imaginative feat of musical modernism, opens up a miasmic world of nightmare (he called it an *Angsttraum*). Its sole protagonist, searching at night for her lover and finding his body, is perhaps demented and may even be the murderer. There are several fine recordings, but this one is lyrical and iridescent to a previously unguessable degree, and infused not just with horror but with an unexpected quality of tenderness.

Bryn-Julson really enters the character of the anguished sleep-walker: the most accurate account yet of the fiendish solo part, largely

observing (and demonstrating the naturalness of) its intricate speech rhythms. Rattle seems to have thought about and placed every detail in this score of a thousand luminous, tremulous details in relation to the whole. The CBSO responds magnificently, in a superb recorded balance, and as the work progresses we realise how much of it is actually great love music, an expressionist Liebestod.

Rattle's account of the Orchestral Variations, one of the most impressive masterworks of Schoenberg's 12-note period, is similarly preferable to all others in balance, tempi and large-scale articulation, by turns granitic and beguiling, with notable textural clarity and rhythmic pointing. By contrast the Chamber Symphony performance is rather routine, but for the other two works this is an essential buy. *CM*

SCHOENBERG

Erwartung
see also BERG: Wozzeck
and **CHORAL & SONG**: SCHOENBERG: Pierrot lunaire

SCHOENBERG

Moses und Aron; Chamber Symphony No. 2

Günter Reich, Richard Cassilly, Felicity Palmer, John Winfield; BBC Singers, Orpheus Boys Choir, BBC SO, Ensemble InterContemporain/Pierre Boulez

Sony SM2K 48456 □ ADD □ 121:07 mins (2 discs) □ ☺☺

Most operas are about love or politics; or they're epics, or satires, or magical fantasies. Only Schoenberg would attempt one about the incommunicability of God. That's *Moses und Aron*'s philosophical core: but in portraying Moses's struggle to bring his people out of Egypt, and his struggle with his golden-tongued brother Aaron whose words cheapen the religious ideal at every turn, Schoenberg wrote his most truly dramatic work, one that always 'communicates' to listeners with astonishing power. It's the summit of his mature music, based on a single 12-note row from which he conjures Moses's painful Sprechstimme, Aaron's airy *arioso*, huge choral-orchestral tableaux and the visceral, orgiastic dances around the Golden Calf. Though Schoenberg never wrote the music for the projected third act, Moses's soliloquy at the end of the second, one of the most moving passages of our century, is a true finale.

There have been several distinguished versions (no team attempts this daunting work without courage, artistry and long preparation). Solti's Chicago-based recording on Decca is certainly worth consideration for his grand opera approach to this monument of modernism. But Boulez's radiant and statuesque account, with BBC forces, gets closest to the opera's heart. Günter Reich is an impressively tragic Moses, Richard Cassilly a supple, vigorous Aaron; Felicity Palmer injects far more character than we normally hear into the small role of the Young Girl. The orchestra plays as if possessed; the recording is warm, bright, fully equal to Schoenberg's tremendous colouristic gamut; the strings have a welcome bloom on their passionate melodic lines. The (curious) coupling is an impressive account of Schoenberg's neglected Second Chamber Symphony, worked on over thirty years, one of his most refined explorations of late-tonal harmony. *CM*

SCHREKER

Die Gezeichneten

Heinz Kruse, Elizabeth Connell, Monte Pederson, Alfred Muff, László Polgár; Berlin Radio Chorus, Deutsches SO, Berlin/Lothar Zagrosek

Decca Entartete Musik 444 442-2 □ 170:42 mins (3 discs) □ *☻☻☻*

As a self-confessed musical eroticist, it is unsurprising that – his Jewishness apart – Franz Schreker was labelled as a 'degenerate' by the Nazi cultural purists. *Die Gezeichneten* (The Marked Ones) has been recorded before, for Marco Polo, and has been staged recently in Zürich and Düsseldorf, so is not as completely forgotten as other works in Decca's Entartete Musik series. Its composition came about when Schreker was asked by his friend Zemlinsky to write a libretto on the subject of 'the tragedy of the ugly man', which Schreker then decided to set himself between 1911 and 1915.

The music is typical of its period. Anyone already hooked on Korngold or Zemlinsky will warm to its heady, yearning melodies and harmonies, its lush orchestration and its sordid psychological drama about a deformed Genoese nobleman's tragic love for a local beauty, set against the ultimate in natural beauty he has created in an island park (scene for an orgy in the last act).

Instantly eclipsing the Marco Polo recording, this new one could hardly be bettered, with Elizabeth Connell a touchingly vulnerable and passionate Carlotta and Heinz Kruse and Monte Pederson an ardent pair of rivals for her love. The playing of the Deutsches SO is both sublime and dramatic, and Zagrosek has full command of this complex score. *Matthew Rye*

SHOSTAKOVICH

Lady Macbeth of Mtsensk

Aage Haugland, Philip Langridge, Maria Ewing, Sergei Larin, Kristine Ciesinski; Chorus & Orchestra of the Bastille Opera/Myung-Whun Chung

DG 437 511-2 □ 155:46 mins (2 discs) □ *☻☻☻*

This is only the second recording of the original version of Shostakovich's self-termed 'tragedy satire'. The first, conducted by Rostropovich on EMI, never brought the same degree of excitement and involvement one gets from seeing the work live on stage, despite its role in reviving interest in the work, and a marvellous portrayal of Katerina from Galina Vishnevskaya. In DG's recording, derived from a production staged at the Bastille Opera in Paris in 1991, on the other hand, the opera is brought vividly to life, from its lurid depiction of sex, sadistic violence and murder, through merciless, grotesque satire to its inevitably tragic conclusion.

Maria Ewing always tends to overact with her voice and in any other context her whining and swooping would be out of place, but she puts her dramatic range to good use, aptly conveying Katerina's obsessive destruction of all obstacles in her path to fulfilment, if not fully grasping the tragedy when she realises the true character of the man for whom she has been acting. Aage Haugland is a sonorous Boris, playing the lecherous tyrant for all he is worth, while Philip Langridge is effective as the spineless husband, Zinovi, and Sergei Larin passionately involved as her usurper, Sergei. There is strong casting, too, in even the smallest of roles, from Kurt Moll's Old Convict to Heinz Zednik's Shabby Peasant. Under Chung's intelligent and sympathetic direction the intensity never lets up, with the superb chorus and orchestra caught in an often overwhelming way by the flattering recording. The whole enterprise leaves one in no doubt, if any remains, that this is one of the great operas of the 20th century. *Matthew Rye*

SMETANA

The Bartered Bride

Gabriela Beňačková, Peter Dvorský, Richard Novák, Miroslav Kopp; Czech PO & Chorus/Zdeněk Košler

Supraphon 10 3511-2 □ 136:52 mins (3 discs) □ *☻☻*

This is by far the most popular of Czech operas. The vivacious overture, which gallops along at a sparkling pace, has long been a favourite concert piece. But the opera itself, with its lively choruses, its sentimental arias for the young lovers, and its irresistible comic duet for Jeník, the young hero, and Kečal, the marriage-broker, is similarly a work of immense charm – a folk-opera in the best sense of the term. Supraphon's 1981 version, recorded in Prague with some of the finest Czech singers of the time, is an authentic and highly enjoyable account of the opera. Peter Dvorský is in his element as Jeník, the youth who loves Mařenka, here most appealingly sung by Gabriela Beňačková. The entire cast sounds thoroughly at home in this delightful work, and the Czech PO is on top form. *CO*

JOHANN STRAUSS

Die Fledermaus

Julia Varady, Lucia Popp, Hermann Prey, Ivan Rebroff, René Kollo, Bernd Weikl; Bavarian State Opera Chorus & Orchestra/Carlos Kleiber

DG 415 646-2 □ ADD □ 106:38 mins (2 discs)
□ *🌑🌑*

Johann Strauss's masterpiece is Viennese gaiety incarnate. The most brilliant and tuneful of operettas, it is full of delightful numbers, especially in Act II, which contains the maid Adele's high-spirited Laughing Song ('Mein Herr Marquis'), Rosalinde's spirited csárdás, an elegant duet for Eisenstein and Rosalinde in which he attempts unwittingly to seduce his own wife, and the magnificent finale, launched with Falke's tipsily sentimental 'Brüderlein und Schwesterlein'.

Carlos Kleiber conducts superbly, with real Viennese feeling, and has the benefit of a cast which, with one exception, it would be difficult to improve upon. Eisenstein was written by Strauss as a tenor role, but its tessitura is not high, and the baritone Hermann Prey sails through it with stylish aplomb. Julia Varady as Rosalinde, and Lucia Popp as a vivacious Adele, are both entrancing. Bernd Weikl is likewise a delightful Falke, and René Kollo proves convincing as the amorous opera-singer Alfredo. The role of the bored Russian prince, Orlovsky, at whose mansion the Act II party takes place, should be sung by a mezzo-soprano. Here it is entrusted to a male falsettist, Ivan Rebroff, who emits entirely the wrong kind of sound.

There are two fine alternative versions, but they both date from the Fifties. Herbert von Karajan on EMI has the exemplary Viennese operetta duo of Elisabeth Schwarzkopf and Nicolai Gedda as the Eisensteins, while on Decca a historic performance with Clemens Krauss conducting the Vienna PO, and an *echt Wienerisch* cast headed by Julius Patzak and Hilde Gueden, is sheer delight. *CO*

JOHANN STRAUSS

Der Zigeunerbaron

Herbert Lippert, Pamela Coburn, Rudolf Schasching, Julia Hamari; Arnold Schönberg Choir, Vienna SO/Nikolaus Harnoncourt

Teldec 4509-94555-2 □ 150:04 mins (2 discs)
□ *🌑🌑🌑*

The Gypsy Baron tells the story of a young man who returns from exile to Hungary hoping to claim his ancestral lands, only to find them occupied by gypsies, with one of whom he falls in love. This is Johann Strauss's most serious and ambitious operetta, an exhilarating work full of exotic and highly flavoured music. This recording with Viennese forces conducted by Nikolaus Harnoncourt may not vocally surpass EMI's version from the Fifties, which was headed by Schwarzkopf and Gedda, both in radiant voice, but there are several very strong reasons for acquiring it.

Those reasons are the numbers excised from the score before the operetta's premiere in Vienna in 1885 and now restored by Harnoncourt. Most of this music has not been played until now, and all of it is well worth hearing: the Act II finale, for example, here performed at its full length of twenty minutes. Herbert Lippert brings an *echt Wienerisch* timbre and style to the title role, blending delightfully with the American soprano Pamela Coburn in their lilting duet, 'Wer uns getraut'. The rest of the mainly Austrian cast give excellent and authentic performances, and Harnoncourt conducts impeccably.

The old EMI recording referred to above, conducted by Otto Ackermann, is still a highly attractive alternative, and so is the (formerly Decca) version with the Vienna PO under Clemens Krauss, and a cast headed by Julius Patzak and Hilde Zadek, which has re-surfaced recently on Phonographe/Nuova Era. *CO*

STRAUSS

Arabella

Lisa Della Casa, Dietrich Fischer-Dieskau, Anneliese Rothenberger, Georg Paskuda, Karl Christian Kohn; Bavarian State Opera Chorus & Orchestra/Joseph Keilberth

DG 437 700-2 □ ADD □ 159:27 mins (3 discs)
□ *🌑🌑*

This was recorded live at the 1963 Munich Opera Festival, when Lisa Della Casa, who remains unsurpassed as Arabella, was at the height of her form, as was Dietrich Fischer-Dieskau, who was surely created by an opera-loving God to portray Mandryka. After *Der Rosenkavalier*, this is Strauss's most charming, nostalgically Viennese opera. The score may not represent the composer at his most sustained peak of inspiration, but Arabella's solos and her duets with Zdenka and with Mandryka, all of which incorporate Croatian folk-tunes, are a sheer delight. *Arabella* is an opera which comes to life in the theatre, and anyone who was fortunate enough to see Della Casa as the impoverished Viennese beauty, and Fischer-Dieskau as her rich Croatian admirer will almost certainly want to have this version. Anneliese Rothenberger is ideally cast as Zdenka, and the supporting roles are similarly strong. *CO*

STRAUSS

Ariadne auf Naxos

Gundula Janowitz, Teresa Zylis-Gara, James King, Sylvia Geszty, Theo Adam, Peter Schreier; Dresden State Opera Orchestra/Rudolf Kempe

EMI CMS 7 64159 2 □ ADD □ 118:21 mins (2 discs)
□ 🎵🎵

The reissue of this 1968 EMI recording is a cause for loud cheering: this is one of the best of all Strauss opera recordings, and one of the elect among opera recordings of any kind.

The work – an elaborate, richly wrought backstage comedy-drama with a disquisition on the nature of art at its centre – can seem one of the delights of the medium, or else a slightly arch, ponderous operatic conceit. The deciding factor is always the conductor; and here Rudolf Kempe, one of the century's supreme Straussians, renders the piece whole, natural in balance (a tricky business given Strauss's opulent scoring for chamber forces), fluently dramatic through all of its sections, and radiant of sound and substance in every bar. He has the inestimable bonus of the Dresden players, who are natives to this music, but the unfussed style of the performance – apparently so effortless, actually so hard to achieve – is the conductor's hallmark.

Kempe also has the benefit of one of the best-balanced *Ariadne* casts on record. One might argue that individual contributions have been equalled or even surpassed elsewhere: it is the apt matching and idiomatic rightness of the ensemble that one admires here.

Gundula Janowitz, an eloquently steady, refined, inward-turned *opera seria* heroine, lacks only the final degree of expansiveness in the highest-lying phrases; Teresa Zylis-Gara, a

touch cool with some of the composer's most memorable utterances, sings with parallel refinement of tone; Sylvia Geszty is the wittiest and most exuberantly colourful of Zerbinettas.

The antics of the *commedia dell'arte* quartet give unalloyed pleasure (by no means always the case): each of Strauss's marvellous small parts registers its exact point and purpose. Only James King's Bacchus, loud and callow, counts as a weak point. *Max Loppert*

STRAUSS

Capriccio

Elisabeth Schwarzkopf, Christa Ludwig, Nicolai Gedda, Dietrich Fischer-Dieskau, Eberhard Waechter, Hans Hotter; Philharmonia Orchestra/Wolfgang Sawallisch

EMI CDS 7 49014 8 □ ADD □ 134:58 mins (2 discs)
□ 🎵🎵🎵

In a château near Paris, in the 18th century at the time of Gluck's operatic reforms, a young Countess and her guests discuss whether words or music are more important in opera. During the course of the evening, the Countess is also called on to decide which of two suitors she prefers: the poet Olivier or the composer Flamand. In a final solo scene, the Countess addresses the question without arriving at a definite answer.

Improbable though it may seem from that bald synopsis, Strauss's final opera, which he and his librettist Clemens Krauss called a 'conversation piece', is a work of mellow beauty. There is a very fine account of the work on DG, conducted by that great Straussian, Karl Böhm, but EMI's 1957 version is so close to ideal that it is the one to be preferred. Elisabeth Schwarzkopf, all artifice and style until that final impassioned solo, is in her mannered element as the Countess; Gedda and Fischer-Dieskau are unsurpassable as her ardent suitors; and Hans Hotter vividly characterises the theatre director, La Roche. The conductor, Wolfgang Sawallisch, presents Strauss's score with clarity and wit. *CO*

STRAUSS

Capriccio – Final Scene
see **CHORAL & SONG**: STRAUSS: Four Last Songs

STRAUSS

Daphne

Hilde Gueden, Vera Little, James King, Fritz Wunderlich, Paul Schöffler; Vienna State Opera Chorus, Vienna SO/Karl Böhm

DG 445 322-2 □ ADD □ 94:21 mins (2 discs) □ 🎵🎵

Strauss's bucolic tragedy brings to life most movingly the ancient Greek myth of the young woman transformed into a tree by the god Apollo. A lyrical tone poem in the reflective style which the composer adopted as he grew older, the delicate texture of its large orchestra beautifully conjures up the magic of the approaching night in Daphne's first aria, while the quiet ecstasy of its final scene, in which Daphne sings a greeting to her brother and sister trees as she feels the earth rise within her, brings the work to a serene, poetic conclusion. *Daphne* is among the most rewarding of Strauss's later works, and this performance, recorded live on the occasion of the opera's first Viennese performance in 1964 at the Theater an der Wien, is magnificent. Karl Böhm conducts, as he did at *Daphne*'s 1938 Dresden premiere. Hilde Gueden's silvery, individual timbre is ideal for the eponymous heroine, and a first-rate cast of popular Viennese regulars of the Sixties presents the work to its best possible advantage. *CO*

STRAUSS

Elektra

Birgit Nilsson, Marie Collier, Regina Resnik, Gerhard Stolze, Tom Krause; Vienna PO/Georg Solti

Decca 417 345-2 □ ADD □ 107:50 mins (2 discs) □ 🔊🔊

By comparison with the colourful glittering savagery of *Salome*, the opera that immediately preceded it, the Strauss–Hofmannsthal version of Sophocles's tragedy sounds both more harshly violent and more single-minded in its relentless thrust, battering at its hearers' senses with a vehemence surely not unlike that with which classical Greek tragedy assaulted its first audiences. The role of its obsessed heroine provides magnificent, though taxing opportunities for a dramatic soprano, but it is finally Strauss's huge orchestra that plays the leading role in *Elektra*. The Vienna PO is always at its incomparable best in Strauss, and so is the conductor Georg Solti. They, together with Birgit Nilsson, whose firm and powerful soprano voice makes her an ideal Elektra, are the stars of this exciting performance, recorded complete without any of the usual theatre cuts. Marie Collier is a vivid Chrysothemis and Regina Resnik a frighteningly convincing Clytemnestra. *CO*

(A superbly controlled reading under Barenboim, with Deborah Polaski commanding in the title role, was issued by Teldec as this book went to press. *Eds*)

STRAUSS

Die Frau ohne Schatten

Birgit Nilsson, Leonie Rysanek, Ruth Hesse, James King, Walter Berry; Vienna State Opera Chorus & Orchestra/Karl Böhm

DG 445 325-2 □ 195:28 mins (3 discs) □ 🔊🔊

A synopsis of the plot of *Die Frau ohne Schatten* tends to make it sound more than somewhat pretentiously obscure. The opera is set in the mythical past, and its action takes place on three levels of existence: the spirit world, the world of mankind, and an in-between state in which the Emperor and Empress live, hovering between the earthly and the spiritual. The Empress must acquire a shadow, which she can do only by robbing the Dyer's Wife of her ability to bear chidren. Her acquisition not of a shadow but of humanity is the real point and meaning of the work. Hofmannsthal never wrote a more fascinating and complex libretto, nor Strauss a more lavish or exciting score, one which abounds in typical Straussian melody and which has remarkably few *longueurs*. For many years Leonie Rysanek virtually owned the role of the Empress, as did Walter Berry that of Barak, the Dyer, and here they are caught at the peak of their form. Birgit Nilsson, perhaps a surprising choice for the Dyer's Wife, gives the character Wagnerian stature, and James King is a poetic Emperor. The conductor, Karl Böhm, had no equals in this opera, and the orchestra plays gloriously for him. *CO*

STRAUSS

Der Rosenkavalier

Maria Reining, Sena Jurinac, Hilde Gueden, Ludwig Weber, Anton Dermota; Vienna State Opera Chorus, Vienna PO/Erich Kleiber

Decca 425 950-2 □ ADD mono □ 197:06 mins (3 discs) □ 🔊🔊

The essentially Viennese blend of high spirits and nostalgic melancholy in Strauss's most popular opera is irresistible. The Marschallin, one of the most lovable of all operatic characters, dominates the entire action of the work, even though she appears only in Acts I and III. Erich Kleiber's 1954 performance with the Vienna PO and a cast of the finest Vienna State Opera-based singers of the day has not yet been surpassed. Kleiber's way with the score is both lighter and more delicate than that of the conductors of most rival versions, with the action flowing swiftly along, even though the work is performed without cuts. Sena Jurinac's warmth of timbre and sympathetic personality make her an ideal Octavian, and Hilde Gueden is a delightful Viennese Sophie. Ludwig Weber was the finest and ripest Baron Ochs of his time, Anton Dermota sings the Italian Singer's aria beautifully, and the smaller roles are all vividly characterised. Maria Reining's musicianship and complete understanding of the Marschallin more than compensate for the fact that her interpretation has been caught somewhat late in her career. Of course, no lover of *Der Rosenkavalier* should be without the famous Viennese abridged recording of 1933 with Elisabeth Schumann as Sophie, Richard Mayr as Ochs, and the greatest of Marschallins, Lotte Lehmann. *CO*

<hr>

STRAUSS

Salome

Catherine Malfitano, Bryn Terfel, Hanna Schwarz, Kenneth Riegel; Vienna PO/Christoph von Dohnányi

Decca 444 178-2 □ 100:04 mins (2 discs) □ 😊😊😊

Although recorded in conjunction with staged performances at the 1994 Salzburg Festival, the major strengths of this recording are musical rather than theatrical. Indeed, Dohnányi treats *Salome* neither as an orchestral showpiece (though, as one might expect, the Vienna PO plays quite magnificently) nor as a medium for bizarre vocal extravagance, but as a beautiful, symphonically propelled tone poem with voices.

Dohnányi's symphonic intentions are clear from the start: the textures are diaphanous, the counterpoint crystal clear and the voices, though not unduly recessed, are but one strand in the fabric. Dohnányi's sense of symphonic proportion means, too, that climaxes are not gratuitous indulgences but stages in a logically unfolding musical argument. Thus, Salome's final monologue provides just the right degree of resolution and peroration without being denied any of its weight and voluptuousness.

His singers provide the perfect complement to this approach. Catherine Malfitano, appropriately, is a more subtle Salome than most, almost withdrawn in places and rarely prone to histrionic excess. Sterling musical qualities also underline Bryn Terfel's sturdy and dignified Jokanaan, while the supporting roles of Herod and Herodias from Hanna Schwarz and Kenneth Riegel are delivered with great finesse. *Antony Bye*

<hr>

STRAVINSKY

The Rake's Progress

Jayne West, Jon Garrison, Arthur Woodley, John Cheek, Shirley Love, Wendy White, Melvin Lowery, Jeffrey Johnson; Gregg Smith Singers, Orchestra of St Luke's/Robert Craft

MusicMasters 01612-67131-2 □ 128:00 mins (2 discs) □ 😊😊😊

Stravinsky's opera, set in 18th-century England, was to be the last of his so-called neo-classical works. Completed in 1950 with a masterly libretto by WH Auden and Chester Kallman, it triumphantly demonstrates the Russian composer's ability to make an effective setting of the English language, a process that was to be continued in subsequent vocal works, such as the Cantata. Furthermore, Stravinsky's score manifests a brilliant but entirely individual assimilation of the stylistic gestures of Classical *opera buffa*.

Each of the four recordings of the opera which have been issued on CD (from the composer, on Sony, Riccardo Chailly, on Decca, Kent Nagano, on Erato, and Robert Craft) have positive virtues, but Craft's version, recorded in 1993, has special authority, since the conductor worked intensively with Stravinsky during the gestation of the score. To be fair, Alexander Young in the role of Tom Rakewell on Stravinsky's own recording brings a unique three-dimensional conception to the character, something that eludes Jon Garrison for Craft. But in most other respects Craft has the edge, with a more natural balance between singers and orchestra, as well as superbly incisive playing from the Orchestra of St Luke's. *EL*

<hr>

SULLIVAN

The Mikado

Owen Brannigan, Richard Lewis, Geraint Evans, Ian Wallace, John Cameron, Elsie Morison, Monica Sinclair; Glyndebourne Festival Chorus, Pro Arte Orchestra/Malcolm Sargent

EMI CMS 7 64403 2 □ ADD □ 90:48 mins (2 discs) □ 😊😊

The Mikado proved the most successful of the Gilbert and Sullivan operettas when it was first presented at the Savoy Theatre, London, in 1885, achieving a run of more than 600 performances, and it has retained its popularity to this day. Performed without dialogue, but with its score given absolutely complete, EMI's version from the mid-Fifties, conducted with élan by Malcolm Sargent, includes some of the finest British singers of the day in its stylish cast. Richard Lewis is a most mellifluous Nanki-Poo, the delightful Geraint Evans a strongly characterised Ko-Ko, and Elsie Morison the most charming of Yum-Yums. Monica Sinclair booms away most engagingly as the elderly Katisha, and the recording, as remastered, sounds remarkably vivid. *CO*

SULLIVAN

The Pirates of Penzance

Marilyn Hill Smith, Susan Gorton, Philip Creasy, Eric Roberts, Malcolm Rivers, Simon Masterston-Smith; D'Oyly Carte Opera Chorus & Orchestra/John Pryce-Jones

TER CD TER 2 1177 □ 85:24 mins (2 discs) □ *② ②*

The D'Oyly Carte company has not always been at its best in recent years, but here it is caught on top form in one of the most engaging of the G&S operettas with Gilbert's wit and Sullivan's tunefulness and genius for musical parody well to the fore. Marilyn Hill Smith is a charming Mabel, and the remainder of the cast gives richly characterised and well-sung performances, especially Eric Roberts as the endearingly eccentric Major-General Stanley. There is no dialogue. An earlier D'Oyly Carte performance dating from the late Sixties, on Decca, which includes the dialogue and has a fine Mabel in Valerie Masterson, is a reasonable alternative. *CO*

SULLIVAN

The Yeomen of the Guard

Sylvia McNair, Jean Rigby, Kurt Streit, Thomas Allen, Robert Lloyd; Academy of St Martin in the Fields & Chorus/Neville Marriner

Philips 438 138-2 □ 115:09 mins (2 discs) □ *② ② ②*

The use of leading opera singers doesn't automatically guarantee the success of G&S. To my mind Charles Mackerras's star-laden *Mikado* (Telarc) was over-mannered in phrasing and tempi, and occasionally obscured Gilbert.

However, no faults beset Neville Marriner's splendid *Yeomen*. Gilbert is especially well treated since the dialogue (in abbreviated form) is included – as in no previous recording of this work, to my knowledge. The gain in dramatic continuity is heightened by allowing the beginning of a musical number occasionally to overlap dialogue, and by the bold insertion of a few chords to link 'Rapture, rapture' to the second finale.

Kurt Streit (Fairfax) and Sylvia McNair (Elsie), two Americans in this uniformly

excellent cast, sing as good 'British English' as the rest, and Thomas Allen calls on his native Durham accent to characterise Jack Point in song as well as in speech. The vocal and orchestral sound is excellent. Here is G&S as fresh, appealing and as musical as it should be, and Sullivan at his very best. *Arthur Jacobs*

TCHAIKOVSKY

Eugene Onegin

Galina Vishnevskaya, Evgeny Belov, Sergei Lemeshev, Ivan Petrov, Larissa Avdeyeva, Evgenia Verbitskaya, Valentina Petrova; Bolshoi Theatre Chorus & Orchestra/Boris Khaikin

BMG Melodiya 74321 17090 2 □ ADD □ 140:07 mins (2 discs) □ *② ② ②*

Tchaikovsky was so concerned to put his self-styled 'lyrical scenes' after Pushkin's exquisite verse-novel into the right youthful hands that he entrusted the premiere to music students. Most recent studio *Onegins* have given us a distorted, grand opera view, but this classic recording finds exactly the right sincerity and truth in this lovable hybrid. Galina Vishnevskaya's vulnerable Tatyana epitomises these qualities. In 1956 hers was a bright young voice, sometimes a little unsupported and thin-toned, yet dramatically she is the passionately candid teenager of Tchaikovsky's and Pushkin's dreams incarnate.

Belov's sometimes bland Onegin has an easy way with the setting of the text that can be undervalued; and even though the great Lemeshev takes an idolised tenor's liberties with ill-fated poet Lensky's music, he sounds so ideally sweet and fresh of tone that you would never guess he was in his fifties in his second recording of the role. Khaikin's conducting represents the end of an era at the Bolshoi, when every phrase was lived and breathed to Classical perfection, with nothing in excess and with plenty of inner feeling. The sound is much cleaner than on many more recent Melodiya recordings, but the current presentation, unfortunately, is slipshod in style and virtually threadbare of essential information. *DN*

TCHAIKOVSKY

The Queen of Spades

Gegam Grigorian, Maria Guleghina, Vladimir Chernov, Nikolai Putilin, Irina Arkhipova; Kirov Opera Chorus & Orchestra/Valery Gergiev

Philips 438 141-2 □ 166:16 mins (3 discs) □ *② ② ②*

The quest of Hermann, Pushkin's obsessive outsider-hero, for the secret of three cards suffers a few diversions in Tchaikovsky's operatic setting. Valery Gergiev and his young, vital star tenor at the Mariinsky, Gegam Grigorian, rivet our attention through to a tension-laden denouement. Tchaikovsky's masterpiece of horror, the scene where Hermann visits the mysterious Countess in her bedchamber to learn her recipe for gambling success and frightens the speechless old woman to death, has never been more daringly stretched on the rack to make the flesh creep. Here you'll find some of the most intensive pianissimos ever recorded, and the Philips engineers have learned how to bring out presence and colours in the bizarre woodwind writing – the composer's most significant contribution to the forward march of orchestration.

Elsewhere, Gergiev keeps the action on the move. Even the prolix Ball Scene, where Tchaikovsky takes a diversion to pay tribute to idols Catherine the Great and Mozart, blazes grandly, capped by a predictably heart-on-sleeve Kirov chorus. Soloists are indulged in their tendency to hang on to high notes – Grigorian deservedly, since he always remains in character; Maria Guleghina, the dark-hued but powerful Lisa, less so. Vladimir Chernov, phrasing smoothly in Yeletsky's aria, makes up for the disappointingly under-focused Tomsky of Nikolai Putilin. Otherwise, as usual with this company, there are no weak links in the smaller roles and a true ensemble spirit. *DN*

TIPPETT

The Midsummer Marriage

Alberto Remedios, Joan Carlyle, Raimund Herincx, Elizabeth Harwood, Stuart Burrows, Helen Watts; Chorus & Orchestra of the Royal Opera House, Covent Garden/Colin Davis

Lyrita SRCD 2217 □ ADD □ 153:34 mins (2 discs)
□ *❂❂❂*

Colin Davis's recording of Tippett's first and finest opera was originally made for Philips in 1970, following a run of staged performances at Covent Garden. It is unquestionably the most stunning of Davis's many recordings of Tippett's music, revealing this magical, profound work to be one of the masterpieces of British opera. The cast is led by the radiant tenor of Alberto Remedios, who sings Mark's Act I apostrophe to love with unalloyed lyricism. Raimund Herincx is a powerful bully of a King Fisher, deserving all he gets from his daughter Jenifer (the admirable Joan Carlyle); the 'Papageno/Papagena' roles of Jack and Bella are engagingly taken by Stuart Burrows

and Elizabeth Harwood; and Helen Watts is a sonorous Madame Sosostris. But even more remarkable than the singing in terms of artistic prowess is the playing of the Covent Garden orchestra, which has surely never sounded so fine on disc. Strings and woodwind glisten, brass has force and bite.

For those yet to make its acquaintance, this classic recording should win over anyone who hears it in this superbly transferred CD reissue. Tippett enthusiasts will also want David Atherton's distinguished Decca recording of *King Priam*, reissued on Chandos.
Matthew Rye

ULLMANN

Der Kaiser von Atlantis; Hölderlin Lieder

Michael Kraus, Franz Mazura, Martin Petzold, Christiane Oelze, Walter Berry, Herbert Lippert, Iris Vermillion, Jonathan Alder (piano); Leipzig Gewandhaus Orchestra/Lothar Zagrosek

Decca Entartete Musik 440 854-2 □ 67:55 mins
□ *❂❂❂*

The extent to which creative energies seem to have flowed under the macabre and evil canopy of Terezín is truly remarkable – almost as if the menace of death liberated invention. Such a phenomenon extended to art, to performance and to composing, all of which were conceived with a kind of unearthly intensity that somehow overcame the unimaginable living conditions that were endured by inmates of this concentration camp. It would seem inconceivable not to remain aware of these circumstances while listening to any surviving music from this period. Yet one of the many strengths of Viktor Ullmann's opera *Der Kaiser von Atlantis* lies in the fact that it manages to transcend this background, and deal with universal issues that are relevant to us all.

The opera is a bold allegory on the nature of fascism and the low value that such a political system places on human life. Among its main protagonists are thinly veiled portrayals of Hitler (the Emperor Overall) and Goebbels (the Drummer Boy). But despite the undeniable cynicism of Peter Kien's libretto, Ullmann's score is more wide-ranging in mood, encompassing tenderness and passion in the moving love duet of Scene 3, as well as a stoic acceptance of death in the final number. In many ways the very limitations placed upon Ullmann in terms of available instrumentation at Terezín, as well as the necessity to communicate his message direct to his audience, enriched his musical idiom. The score contains powerful allusions to other music: the Lutheran chorale theme 'Ein' feste Burg', heard at the end of the opera. Mahler's *Das Lied von der Erde*, the all-pervasive Angel of Death motif from Suk's *Asrael* Symphony, and the grotesque distortion of the German national anthem, a passage which undoubtedly offended official sensibilities and prevented the work from reaching performance in Terezín.

This long-awaited first recording boasts extraordinarily vivid engineering in which chilling use is made of loudspeaker recordings of some of Hitler's speeches. More important, however, the combination of an outstanding team of soloists and committed playing from the Leipzig Gewandhaus Orchestra under Lothar Zagrosek serves to maximise the dramatic impact of Ullmann's music. *EL*

VAUGHAN WILLIAMS

Hugh the Drover

Bonaventure Bottone, Rebecca Evans, Alan Opie, Richard Van Allan, Sarah Walker; New London Children's Choir, Corydon Singers & Orchestra/Matthew Best

Hyperion CDA 66901/2 □ 102:00 mins (2 discs) □ 🟊🟊🟊

Vaughan Williams wrote *Hugh the Drover*, the most successful of his five operas, between 1910 and 1914, at about the same time as *A London Symphony*. Set during the Napoleonic Wars in a Cotswold village, it tells the story of an itinerant cattle-dealer, Hugh, who saves a young woman, Mary, from a loveless marriage. Vaughan Williams's intention was to write an English 'rustic comedy', a romantic ballad opera', as an English counterpart to the likes of *The Bartered Bride*.

A recording of excerpts was made with members of the original 1924 Sadler's Wells cast under Malcolm Sargent (now on a Pearl CD: GEMMCD 9468), but the first complete recording, by Charles Groves, was made as recently as 1978. Despite some beautiful singing and playing, Groves's direction of this performance, well received in its day, now seems dramatically uninvolving. Bottone and Evans, on Best's 1994 recording, are more believable as characters; both give particularly clear articulation to words and notes and achieve a remarkable restraint in the pianissimo opening to Act II.

Subsidiary and cameo roles, none of them especially finely drawn by librettist Harold Child, are excellent. A strong sense of theatricality emerges at the opening of Best's recording, where the tempo honours the

marked Allegro vivacissimo and the fairground bustle is vividly drawn. Here also, the folk-songs and ballads evolve successfully out of the general musical flow.

The diction and ensemble of Best's Corydon Singers are wellnigh perfect, and the brief contributions of the New London Children's Choir give a good impression of a bunch of village children. *Matthew Rye*

VERDI

Aida

Zinka Milanov, Fedora Barbieri, Jussi Björling, Leonard Warren, Boris Christoff; Rome Opera Chorus & Orchestra/Jonel Perlea

RCA Victor Gold Seal GD 86652 □ ADD □ 147:13 mins (3 discs) □ 🟊🟊

Aida, written for Cairo and first performed there in 1871, is not only Verdi's most spectacular opera but also, paradoxically, one of his most intimate. The story centres around the conflict between Amneris, the Pharaoh's daughter, and her Ethiopian slave, Aida, both rivals for the love of Radames, the leader of the Egyptian army. There have been several fine recordings, featuring singers of the calibre of Leontyne Price, Jon Vickers, Renata Tebaldi, Giulietta Simionato, Carol Bergonzi, Luciano Pavarotti, and conductors such as Solti, Karajan and Maazel, on various Decca versions, not to mention a 1955 EMI performance with Maria Callas, Richard Tucker and Tito Gobbi, conducted by Tullio Serafin. However, my first choice is another 1955 recording, with Zinka Milanov – one of the great Verdi sopranos of the century – as Aida, Fedora Barbieri a formidable Amneris, and the incomparable Jussi Björling as Radames. Jonel Perlea conducts impressively, and Richard Mohr's production has real theatrical presence. *CO*

VERDI

Un ballo in maschera

Leontyne Price, Carlo Bergonzi, Robert Merrill, Shirley Verrett, Reri Grist; RCA Italiana Opera Chorus & Orchestra/Erich Leinsdorf

RCA Victor Gold Seal GD 86645 □ ADD □ 128:19 mins (2 discs) □ 🟊🟊

Though Verdi had set out to write an opera about the assassination of the historical King Gustav III of Sweden, censorship difficulties led to the characters being fictionalised and the locale moved to colonial Boston, which hardly matters, as the original librettist's portrait of Gustav was ridiculously inaccurate.

The opera is one of Verdi's middle-period masterpieces, a work whose melodies combine warmth and vigour with the lightness and elegance which had entered the composer's operas with *La traviata* a few years earlier. Erich Leinsdorf's excitingly conducted performance has two of the finest Verdi singers of the last half-century in the principal roles of Amelia and Riccardo: namely, Leontyne Price, in her creamiest, richest voice, and Carlo Bergonzi, the peerless Verdi stylist. The rest of the cast is similarly strong, with Reri Grist delightful as Oscar, the page. *CO*

VERDI

Don Carlo

Michael Sylvester, Aprile Millo, Dolora Zajick, Vladimir Chernov, Ferruccio Furlanetto, Samuel Ramey; Metropolitan Opera Chorus & Orchestra/James Levine

Sony S3K 52500 □ 203:00 mins (3 discs) □ ❷❷❷

James Levine's performance of the five-act Italian *Don Carlo* (plus the opening chorus from the original French score) supersedes all other versions, not only because he conducts Verdi's spacious score with such masterly skill and meticulous attention to detail, and has so magnificent an orchestra at his command, but also because his cast of Metropolitan Opera regulars is arguably the finest that could be assembled today for this opera.

Aprile Millo brings sumptuous tone to the role of Elisabetta, Dolora Zajick (Eboli) proves herself a real Verdi mezzo, and Kathleen Battle is lavishly cast as the Voice from Heaven. Vladimir Chernov's beautifully sung Rodrigo is especially impressive, and Michael Sylvester is a more than acceptable Carlo. I only wish that Ferruccio Furlanetto (Philip II) and Samuel Ramey (the Grand Inquisitor) had exchanged roles, for Ramey is the more interesting artist of the two. *CO*

VERDI

Ernani

Carlo Bergonzi, Leontyne Price, Mario Sereni, Ezio Flagello; RCA Italiana Opera Chorus & Orchestra/Thomas Schippers

RCA Victor Gold Seal GD 86503 □ ADD □ 130:07 mins (2 discs) □ ❷❷

A tale of passion set in 16th-century Spain, *Ernani* contains a wealth of beautiful and gloriously singable tunes, and characters who are painted in strong musical colours. This is the opera, written by Verdi at the age of thirty, which spread his fame throughout Europe.

Thomas Schippers conducts this 1967 performance with a fine sense of drama, and those great Verdians, Leontyne Price and Carlo Bergonzi, are superb as Elvira and the bandit, Ernani, with whom she is in love. Mario Sereni is effective as Don Carlo, King of Spain, and Ezio Flagello is particularly fine as the elderly Silva, to whom Elvira is unhappily betrothed. EMI's recording with Mirella Freni and Plácido Domingo, conducted by Riccardo Muti, is a worthy alternative. *CO*

VERDI

Falstaff

Rolando Panerai, Marilyn Horne, Sharon Sweet, Alan Titus, Frank Lopardo, Piero de Palma, Ulrich Ress, Francesco Ellero d'Artegna, Julie Kaufmann, Susan Quittmeyer; Bavarian Radio Chorus & SO/Colin Davis

RCA Victor Red Seal 09026 60705 2 □ 117:36 mins (2 discs) □ ❷❷❷

What a marvellous opera *Falstaff* is: a joyous work in which the nearly eighty-year-old Verdi scatters tunes about with such prodigality that you would think he was trying to give them away. It has been for the most part fortunate in its many recordings, among them Toscanini's glorious 1950 broadcast performance and Tito Gobbi's unsurpassed assumption of the title role for Karajan in 1956.

Though this new version will probably not replace either of those in anyone's affections, it is nevertheless immensely enjoyable. A generally excellent cast is welded into a perfect ensemble by Colin Davis, who conducts Verdi's golden score with a briskness that does not disguise his very evident love of this opera.

All four women are American; Falstaff himself is that engaging baritone Rolando Panerai. His voice has darkened somewhat over the years, but he is still a fine singer and a convincing actor who declaims Boito's delightful text most eloquently. Ford is strongly characterised by Alan Titus, and Sharon Sweet makes the most of Alice Ford's soaring vocal line in the concerted passages. Marilyn Horne is a formidable Mistress Quickly. Frank Lopardo and Julie Kaufmann are well matched as the young lovers, and it's good to encounter the veteran comprimario tenor, Piero de Palma, as Dr Caius.

The recording's natural balance between voices and orchestra allows the words to come across clearly, especially important in this enchanting comedy – a much finer work of art than the Shakespeare potboiler on which it is based. *CO*

La forza del destino

Leontyne Price, Richard Tucker, Robert Merrill, Shirley Verrett, Giorgio Tozzi; RCA Italiana Opera Chorus & Orchestra/Thomas Schippers

RCA Victor Gold Seal GD 87971 □ ADD
□ 175:45 mins (3 discs) □ *♪♪*

Verdi's stirring tale of abduction, inadvertent homicide and relentless revenge is a magnificent, sprawling, complex work, containing glorious arias, duets, choruses and, at the end, an incomparable trio. The opera has been fortunate in the quality of its recorded performances, with an EMI version conducted by Tullio Serafin, starring Maria Callas and Richard Tucker; a later EMI recording with Martina Arroyo, Carlo Bergonzi and Piero Cappuccilli; and an RCA set with Leontyne Price and Plácido Domingo. Pride of place, however, goes to an earlier RCA Victor recording, made in the company's Rome studios, with Leontyne Price stylistically superb and in beautiful voice as Leonora, Richard Tucker in one of his best roles as her lover, Don Alvaro, and Robert Merrill, impressive as Leonora's avenging brother. *CO*

Luisa Miller

Montserrat Caballé, Luciano Pavarotti, Sherrill Milnes; London Opera Chorus, National PO/Peter Maag

Decca 417 420-2 □ ADD □ 144:00 mins (2 discs)
□ *♪♪♪*

In addition to being an affecting and highly enjoyable opera, *Luisa Miller*, based on a play by Schiller, is an important transitional work, marking both the end of Verdi's first period and the beginning of his second, with *Rigoletto*, *Il trovatore* and *La traviata* just around the corner. Its first two acts still inhabit the world of Bellini and Donizetti, while Act III anticipates the musical style of *La traviata*. The domestic nature of the story calls for a more intimate kind of vocal writing than was required by the larger-scale melodramas of Verdi's earlier years, and the composer's response is completely successful. Montserrat Caballé is ideally cast as the gentle Luisa, and Pavarotti does full justice to the work's most famous aria, the elegantly nostalgic 'Quando le sere al placido'. Sherrill Milnes is convincing as Luisa's father, and Peter Maag conducts strongly. *CO*

Macbeth

Leonie Rysanek, Leonard Warren, Carlo Bergonzi, Jerome Hines; Metropolitan Opera Chorus & Orchestra/Erich Leinsdorf

RCA Victor Gold Seal GD 84516 □ ADD
□ 130:16 mins (2 discs) □ *♪♪*

There have been several fine recordings of Verdi's earliest Shakespeare opera. A live 1952 performance from La Scala, Milan, captures Maria Callas in her only assumption of the role of Lady Macbeth, which she otherwise never recorded. She is, predictably, superb. Enzo Mascherini is the excellent Macbeth, and Victor de Sabata conducts thrillingly. However, the sound ranges from poor to acceptable. A 1976 DG version with Piero Cappuccilli and Shirley Verrett (and Domingo as Macduff) has its admirers, and Riccardo Muti, on EMI, conducts a taut performance with Fiorenza Cossotto and Sherrill Milnes in fine voice. However, my allegiance remains with RCA Victor's 1959 recording in which the great Viennese soprano Leonie Rysanek, better known for her Strauss and Wagner roles, is a magnificent Lady Macbeth, with Leonard Warren fully her equal in the title role, and the stylish Carlo Bergonzi as Macduff. Moreover, Erich Leinsdorf conducts a brisk, strongly dramatic account of Verdi's marvellous score. *CO*

Nabucco

Tito Gobbi, Elena Suliotis, Bruno Prevedi, Carlo Cava; Vienna State Opera Chorus & Orchestra/Lamberto Gardelli

Decca 417 407-2 □ ADD □ 120:36 mins (2 discs)
□ *♪♪*

Nabucco, Verdi's third opera and first great success, is his earliest work still to hold its place in the repertoire today. Its biblical story of the plight of the captive Jews in ancient Egypt is told in music of great emotional intensity, reaching its climax in the moving chorus 'Va, pensiero', in which the Jews yearn for their homeland, a chorus to which Verdi's Milanese audience in 1842, under the yoke of Austria, responded with patriotic fervour. Tito Gobbi's vocal and dramatic gifts made him an ideal Nabucco, and Elena Suliotis, a young soprano who far too soon wore herself out vocally, is caught here near the beginning of her career as a vivid Abigaille, a character who is clearly an ancestor of Verdi's Lady Macbeth of five years later.

Lamberto Gardelli conducts his Viennese forces authoritatively. *CO*

Otello

Jon Vickers, Leonie Rysanek, Tito Gobbi, Florindo Andreolli, Myriam Pirazzini; Rome Opera Chorus & Orchestra/Tullio Serafin

RCA Victor Gold Seal GD 81969 □ ADD □ 150:31 mins (2 discs) □ 🅐🅑

No recording of the greatest of Verdi's Shakespeare operas is a complete failure, but neither is any one of them a complete success. One performance boasts a superb Otello, another an incomparable Desdemona, while a third has the best of all possibly Iagos. Many lovers of the opera will not part with their old Toscanini recording; others, myself included, find him too unyielding a conductor. All things considered, I would choose, as my preferred version to date, Tullio Serafin's loving approach to the work for RCA Victor. Jon Vickers is an affecting Otello (though not preferable to James McCracken, whose EMI recording suffers from its Desdemona and its conductor). Leonie Rysanek's Desdemona is sympathetic, though vocally uneven, but the glory of the performance is Tito Gobbi's incomparable Iago, perhaps the most magnificently acted of all his recorded Verdi roles. *CO*

Rigoletto

Tito Gobbi, Maria Callas, Giuseppe di Stefano, Nicola Zaccaria, Adriana Lazzarini; Chorus & Orchestra of La Scala, Milan/Tullio Serafin

EMI CDS 7 47469 8 □ ADD □ 117:59 mins (2 discs) □ 🅐🅑🅒

One of the most popular of all operas, *Rigoletto* is currently represented in the catalogues by at least 15 different recordings, none of which is entirely without merit. Some highly desirable versions include a 1972 Decca release with Joan Sutherland a heavenly Gilda; Nicolai Gedda as a most musicianly Duke of Mantua for EMI in 1967; and Robert Merrill a fiercely dramatic Rigoletto for RCA Victor in 1957, with Jussi Björling an exemplary Duke. Most memorable of all, however, is EMI's 1955 recording, conducted lovingly and masterfully by Tullio Serafin. Tito Gobbi's Rigoletto, a most powerful and moving performance, has not yet been surpassed. While in the theatre Gobbi was a great actor, on disc, through his voice alone he

conveys the anguish of the father whose daughter has been raped by the cynical Duke, Rigoletto's employer. Though her voice is not ideally suited to the role of Gilda, Maria Callas gives one of her most intelligent dramatic performances, and Giuseppe di Stefano is an exciting Duke even if it is regrettable that he is deprived of his Act II cabaletta. *CO*

Simon Boccanegra

Piero Cappuccilli, Mirella Freni, José Carreras, Nicolai Ghiaurov, José van Dam; Chorus & Orchestra of La Scala, Milan/Claudio Abbado

DG 415 692-2 □ ADD □ 136:16 mins (2 discs) □ 🅐🅑🅒

Verdi's lifelong concern with father–daughter relationships is well to the fore in *Simon Boccanegra*, an opera which, formally something of a mess in its first version of 1857, was fused remarkably into a successful and homogeneous whole by Verdi and his new librettist Arrigo Boito some 24 years later. A 1957 EMI recording that has become a classic was given a superb cast, with Tito Gobbi richly eloquent as Boccanegra, the pirate who becomes Doge of Genoa, Victoria de los Angeles in her most beautiful voice as his long-long daughter Amelia, and Boris Christoff dramatically vivid as the vengeful Fiesco. Marginally preferable, however, is DG's version of twenty years later, conducted with intensity by Claudio Abbado, and with a remarkable cast headed by Piero Cappuccilli, masterly in the title role, Mirella Freni a youthful-sounding Amelia, José Carreras credible as her lover, Gabriele Adorno, and Nicolai Ghiaurov fully the equal of Christoff as Fiesco. *CO*

La traviata

Angela Gheorghiu, Frank Lopardo, Leo Nucci; Chorus & Orchestra of the Royal Opera House, Covent Garden/Georg Solti

Decca 448 119-2 □ 127:21 mins (2 discs) □ 🅐🅑🅒

The only unsatisfactory element in the 1994 Royal Opera production of *La traviata*, produced by Richard Eyre and conducted by Georg Solti, was the décor. With no scenic problems, these CDs recorded live at the ROH are a sheer delight. Conducting his first *Traviata*, Solti wisely elects to perform the whole of the score (cabalettas and 'Addio del passato' in full) and nothing but the score (no variants, no E flat for Violetta at the end of Act I or top C for Alfredo in Act II). The orchestra plays Verdi's glorious score for Solti with delicacy and precision.

Nucci's Germont succeeds in conveying the parent's concern for his son as well as his harshness towards Violetta, and Lopardo's Alfredo, sometimes disconcertingly gauche in the theatre, comes across here as ardent, tender and vocally elegant. Most important of all, the young Romanian soprano Angela Gheorghiu portrays a credible and indeed moving Violetta, simply by virtue of singing the role so accurately, with a pure legato line and a voice of rich dark beauty. This *Traviata* will take some beating. *CO*

VERDI

Il trovatore

Vladimir Chernov, Aprile Millo, Dolora Zajick, Plácido Domingo, James Morris; Metropolitan Opera Chorus & Orchestra/James Levine

Sony S2K 48070 □ 129:04 mins (2 discs) □ 🎵🎵🎵

What a superb work this is: the quintessential Italian opera, with its absurd melodramatic plot and its wealth of glorious melody. It receives a fine, full-bloodedly Italianate performance from James Levine and his Metropolitan Opera forces, despite the fact that the international cast contains no Italians. As Manrico, Plácido Domingo compensates in musicianship, intelligence and attractive vocal quality for what he lacks in sheer visceral excitement, a quality which the other principals exhibit in abundance. Aprile Millo's note-values may not always be exact, but she is a convincing Leonora, at her best in her Act IV scene with the villainous Di Luna, suavely characterised and sung by Vladimir Chernov.

Dolora Zajick brings the gypsy Azucena to fierce and vibrant life, and the lavish casting of James Morris in the secondary role of Ferrando is a bonus. A full score is performed without any of the usual theatre cuts, and James Levine shows himself fully cognisant of the opera's real stature. His orchestra is prominent, but not damagingly so. Indeed, a lot of orchestral detail is heard, allowing more of Verdi's felicitous scoring to be noticed than is often the case. There are other fine performances of *Il trovatore*, but this one is better than most. *CO*

VERDI

I vespri Siciliani

Cheryl Studer, Chris Merritt, Giorgio Zancanaro, Ferruccio Furlanetto; Chorus & Orchestra of La Scala, Milan/Riccardo Muti

EMI CDS 7 54043 2 □ 199:05 mins (3 discs) □ 🎵🎵🎵

This is an Italian translation of the opera that Verdi composed to a French text. A fictional plot involving the love of Hélène (Elena), a Sicilian patriot, for Henri (Arrigo) who, unknown to her, is the son of the French governor of Sicily, is set against the historical events of 1282, when the Sicilians rose against the French in an act of wholesale slaughter known as the Sicilian Vespers. Though this recording comes from a live performance at La Scala, Riccardo Muti plays the score (a lengthy one for Verdi) absolutely complete, with none of the usual theatre cuts. He conducts with imagination and flexibility, and is rewarded with glorious playing from the Scala orchestra. Cheryl Studer is a fiercely dramatic Elena, and Giorgio Zancanaro an impeccably stylish Monforte. Chris Merritt's high tenor makes him an acceptable Arrigo, but one could have wished for a stronger bass in the important role of Procida, a character who is given one of the opera's best numbers, 'O tu, Palermo'. *CO*

WAGNER

Der fliegende Holländer

Robert Hale, Hildegard Behrens, Josef Protschka, Kurt Rydl; Vienna State Opera Chorus, Vienna PO/Christoph von Dohnányi

Decca 436 418-2 □ 145:11 mins (2 discs) □ 🎵🎵🎵

Dohnányi brings a demonic intensity to the overture and the Dutchman's monologue – the 'crack of doom' resounds hair-raisingly in the latter – and idiosyncrasies of tempo (such as the distant effect created for the 'mist of times long ago' in the Act II duet) are always well motivated. Unusually for a recording, Dohnányi adopts the version in three separate acts: an unsatisfactory decision unless one interpolates one's own interval, since the material repeated in this version is twice heard back to back.

Robert Hale's Dutchman is by turns powerful and introspective, almost tender, but, like many of his rivals in the role, he lacks the character's diabolic aura and sense of desperation. Hildegard Behrens as Senta may be vocally less secure – even squally at times – but she is right inside the part. For the trembling fervour of her dedication to death, and the burning conviction with which every phrase is invested, one can readily forgive technical shortcomings. Josef Protschka shapes Erik's 'Mein Herz' with a delicacy worthy of a Lieder singer, and Kurt Rydl's Daland is strongly sung.

Other well-conducted accounts include those of Woldemar Nelsson on Philips and Pinchas Steinberg on Naxos. Simon Estes's Dutchman for Nelsson is under-characterised, however, as is Alfred Muff's for Steinberg, but the latter version is otherwise a very impressive and highly attractive budget-price alternative.
Barry Millington

<hr>

WAGNER

Lohengrin

Siegfried Jerusalem, Cheryl Studer, Kurt Moll, Hartmut Welker, Waltraud Meier; Vienna State Opera Chorus, Vienna PO/Claudio Abbado

DG 437 808-2 □ 211:19 mins (3 discs) □ 𝄞𝄞𝄞

Claudio Abbado thought long and hard about his first Wagner opera before committing it to disc. He conducted *Lohengrin* at La Scala in 1981 and returned to it a decade later at the Vienna State Opera; this studio recording was made in 1991–2 and bears all the hallmarks of Abbado's dedicated study of the score. From the opening Prelude he conjures magically the mystical realm of the Grail and always shows the greatest sensitivity for the work's vibrant lyricism. He is able, moreover, to take the passages of this nature at a daringly slow tempo without losing his grip on the overall structure. Indeed, it is his adroit integration of the spheres of private intimacy and public clamour that most impresses. The pacing of crucial scenes, such as that of Ortrud and Telramund in the second act, or Elsa and Lohengrin in the third, is also marvellously assured, and he makes none of the traditional, disfiguring cuts.

He has at his disposal the Vienna PO on top form (those balefully reedy Viennese oboes come into their own in Ortrud's music) and a choir that is equally admirable in rapt meditation or vigorous acclamation. Siegfried Jerusalem, in the title role, is similarly able to switch from mystical introspection to forthright expressions of loyalty, love or anger. Cheryl Studer's tender, passionate Elsa is as intelligently sung as any on record, while Waltraud Meier's blood-chilling Ortrud makes a formidable enemy. Fine contributions too from Hartmut Welker and Kurt Moll as Telramund and King Henry.

Rudolf Kempe's classic 1963 recording has until now remained unchallenged, but Abbado's account is a match for it interpretatively, while offering all the advantages of modern digital sound.
Barry Millington

<hr>

WAGNER

Die Meistersinger von Nürnberg

Bernd Weikl, Ben Heppner, Cheryl Studer, Siegfried Lorenz, Kurt Moll, Cornelia Kallisch, Deon van der Walt; Bavarian State Opera Chorus & Orchestra/Wolfgang Sawallisch

EMI CDS 5 55142 2 □ 264:37 mins (4 discs) □ 𝄞𝄞𝄞

Given the formidable difficulties of mounting a performance or recording of *Die Meistersinger*, and the fact that the work had not had a new studio recording since Solti's in 1976 – the two facts are not unrelated – this set was not surprisingly keenly awaited. Much about it is excellent, though one has to confess to disappointment on several counts.

The set's greatest asset is its Walther. The Canadian Ben Heppner emerged a few years ago as the Great White Hope and continues to fulfil his promise as the outstanding Heldentenor of his generation. His tone is ample, richly coloured and thrilling in the top register, yet flexible enough to deal sensitively with finer nuances. When he sings his big number to Sachs for the first time, it really sounds like a dream inspiration. His Eva, Cheryl Studer, brings her usual musical intelligence to the role, lightening her voice to produce an aptly girlish quality at times.

Bernd Weikl plays Hans Sachs as a man of the people: down to earth, weary of the Masters' pedantry, human in his dealings with Walther, Eva and his apprentice David (well sung by Deon van der Walt). But the voice lacks the weight and authority of the greatest Sachses, and his despairing cry 'Wahn! Wahn!' sounds like an outburst of tetchiness rather than the prelude to a profound observation on the foibles of human nature. Siegfried Lorenz follows the misguided modern trend of dignifying Beckmesser: Wagner specifically wanted this character to sound grotesque and ridiculous. Kurt Moll's Pogner fails to muster quite the gravity the role demands.

Wolfgang Sawallisch is an experienced Wagnerian: his recordings of *The Flying Dutchman* and *Lohengrin*, though made over thirty years ago, still stand up well to the competition. The strength of his *Meistersinger* is its coherence and its sense of conversational flow. Its weakness is its repeated failure to rise above the level of the mundane.

In the absence of a modern digital version that can be recommended without qualification, this is a very serviceable alternative to Kempe (EMI) and Jochum (DG). *Barry Millington*

Parsifal

Siegfried Jerusalem, Waltraud Meier, José van Dam, Matthias Hölle, Günter von Kannen, John Tomlinson; Berlin State Opera Chorus, Berlin PO/Daniel Barenboim

Teldec 9031-74448-2 □ 240:16 mins (4 discs)
□ ❶❷❸

Wagner's final opera is a work that provokes strong reactions. By most critics it is revered as the sacred festival stage play its composer considered it to be, while one recent Wagner commentator refers to it as a 'brooding nightmare of Aryan anxiety'. What is not in dispute is that its music is as powerful and compelling as anything Wagner ever composed.

Daniel Barenboim conducts a performance of great conviction, and the Berlin PO responds with playing of translucent beauty. Siegfried Jerusalem, the most musically sensitive and tonally attractive of current Wagner tenors, is an impressive Parsifal, and Waltraud Meier an almost terrifyingly vivid Kundry. José van Dam is a moving Amfortas, and Matthias Hölle an acceptable Gurnemanz. A 1991–2 Metropolitan Opera performance conducted by James Levine, with Plácido Domingo (Parsifal) and Jessye Norman (Kundry) is also well worth hearing. *CO*

Das Rheingold

John Tomlinson, Günter von Kannen, Helmut Pampuch, Graham Clark, Linda Finnie, Eva Johansson, Birgitta Svendén; Bayreuth Festival Orchestra/Daniel Barenboim

Teldec 4509-91185-2 □ 149:09 mins (2 discs)
□ ❶❷❸

Die Walküre

John Tomlinson, Anne Evans, Poul Elming, Nadine Secunde, Matthias Hölle, Linda Finnie; Bayreuth Festival Orchestra/Daniel Barenboim

Teldec 4509-91186-2 □ 233:08 mins (4 discs)
□ ❶❷❸

Daniel Barenboim's conducting of *The Ring* complemented Harry Kupfer's gripping, anti-heroic Bayreuth staging of the cycle (1988–92)

so well that I wondered how successfully it would transfer to disc. For the full musico-dramatic experience, the video or laser disc is necessary, but Barenboim's account is no mere accompaniment.

John Tomlinson's full-throated Wotan is inseparable from his prowling, morally shabby stage persona: not so much father of the gods as Godfather. James Morris's Wotan for both Haitink (EMI) and Levine (DG) is more beautifully, more evenly, sung, but it lacks the bite – indeed, the whole range of emotional expression – that Tomlinson brings to bear. Anne Evans's Brünnhilde is as perceptive and moving on disc as in the theatre, while Nadine Secunde and Poul Elming are among the top Sieglindes and Siegmunds to be heard today. Casting is strong generally, and the Bayreuth Festival Orchestra plays with its customary virtuosity for Barenboim.

The latter brings to bear an astute musical and theatrical intelligence that does justice to the transient emotions – joy, grief, passion, pain – while accommodating them to an over-arching sense of structure. *Barry Millington*

Rienzi

René Kollo, Siv Wennberg, Janis Martin, Theo Adam, Nikolaus Hillebrand, Siegfried Vogel, Peter Schreier, Gunther Leib, Ingeborg Springer; Leipzig Radio Chorus, Dresden State Opera Chorus, Dresden Staatskapelle/Heinrich Hollreiser

EMI CMS 7 63980 2 □ ADD □ 217:46 mins (3 discs)
□ ❶❷

Bulwer-Lytton's tragedy *Rienzi – Last of the Tribunes* provided the young Wagner with ample scope to display his already impressive capabilities when his five-act opera was first staged in Dresden in 1842. The composer himself supplied the libretto to a vast, sometimes lumberingly teutonic spectacle, in which political correctness wins the day irrespective of human cost. Bulwer-Lytton's tale is, at its worst, horribly convoluted, and one ventures to suggest that Wagner breathed much-needed new life into the unfolding drama with this opera. Countless glimpses of his full maturity emerge from its pages. It is good to find Heinrich Hollreiser's performance still leading the field; his Dresden choral and orchestral forces are matchlessly appropriate and expertly drilled throughout, but it is the solo team who consistently impress despite the impossible demands of each of the principal roles. Sonics are a little dated, though the potential drawbacks of the rather dry and unresonant acoustic and occasionally harsh treble are more than offset by a performance which somehow manages to sustain the listener's interest, even during the more routine passages of this apprentice work. *MJ*

WAGNER

Siegfried

Siegfried Jerusalem, Anne Evans, Graham Clark, John Tomlinson, Günter von Kannen; Bayreuth Festival Orchestra/Daniel Barenboim

Teldec 4509-94193-2 □ 240:09 mins (4 discs)
□ ❷❷❷

Götterdämmerung

Siegfried Jerusalem, Philip Kang, Bodo Brinkmann, Günter von Kannen, Anne Evans; Bayreuth Festival Chorus & Orchestra/Daniel Barenboim

Teldec 4509-94194-2 □ 267:03 mins (4 discs)
□ ❷❷❷

Barenboim is the hero of this *Ring* recorded live at Bayreuth, where he conducted Harry Kupfer's thought-provoking production from 1988 to 1992. I saw this in its second year when his Act I of *Siegfried* (with the cast recorded here) was the most thrillingly conducted, most beautifully sung I had ever heard in the theatre. Teldec's recordings of performances from the 1991–2 festivals largely bear out my initial impression. I am more than ever impressed by Barenboim's exciting, excitable conducting. His ability to integrate massive dramatic peaks within the 'symphonic' span of Wagner's long, action-packed acts, his evident love of Wagner's orchestration and his deeply felt response to Wagner's most profoundly moving utterances make this the most compelling of modern recorded *Rings*, worthy to stand by the readings of Furtwängler (EMI), Böhm (Philips) and Karajan (DG).

No recording of *The Ring* has an ideal cast. The big disappointment to me is Graham Clark's Mime, wonderfully sung in 1989 but by 1991 a whining, shrieking caricature. Evans's Brünnhilde awakens in breathy, unfocused voice but in *Götterdämmerung* she surpasses anything I have heard from her: her singing is glorious, radiant, supremely musical, unforgettably touching – one of the most individual and loveliest Brünnhildes ever recorded.

Nor is Jerusalem a typically heroic Siegfried – like Evans, he experiences moments of passing strain – but his lyric tenor delivers the most alluring account of this part on disc. Tomlinson's Wanderer has both nobility and wit – his encounters with the Nibelung brothers are avuncular, informal – and Günter von Kannen is an Alberich in the Neidlinger

tradition. Waltraud Meier is riveting in Waltraute's desperate plea to her sister; Kang's Fafner and Hagen are only adequate. But this is Barenboim's, Evans's and Jerusalem's *Ring*, a powerful document of the finest staging I have yet seen. *Hugh Canning*

WAGNER

Tannhäuser

René Kollo, Helga Dernesch, Christa Ludwig, Victor Braun, Hans Sotin; Vienna State Opera Chorus, Vienna PO/Georg Solti

Decca 414 581-2 □ ADD □ 187:39 mins (3 discs)
□ ❷❷

Tannhäuser is an uneven work, but with many thrilling moments and a final act of sustained inspiration. This recording of the opera's revised version, which Wagner made for Paris, is absolutely magnificent. René Kollo is an exemplary Tannhäuser, and Helga Dernesch a most affecting Elisabeth. As Venus, Christa Ludwig produces the most gloriously sensuous tone quality, and Victor Braun is a sympathetic Wolfram. The supporting roles are all well sung and characterised, and the Vienna PO produces playing of superlative quality for Solti. The only rival to this 25-year-old recording is an even older one, recorded at Bayreuth in 1962 and conducted by Wolfgang Sawallisch, with an equally fine cast headed by Wolfgang Windgassen, Anja Silja, Grace Bumbry and Eberhard Waechter. *CO*

WAGNER

Tristan und Isolde

Siegfried Jerusalem, Waltraud Meier, Matti Salminen, Falk Struckmann, Marjana Lipovšek; Berlin State Opera Chorus, Berlin PO/Daniel Barenboim

Teldec 4509-94568-2 □ 235:38 mins (4 discs)
□ ❷❷❷

This is a *Tristan* to put in the pantheon with the Böhm, Furtwängler and Goodall. Barenboim has been conducting the opera regularly at Bayreuth since 1981, and the cast for this recording derives largely from the latest staging there.

The two lead singers, although Wagnerian stalwarts, had only recently turned to these roles, bringing to them a human warmth that dispels any sense one sometimes gets of this work being an extended symphonic poem with voices. Meier is a near ideal Isolde, and Jerusalem sounds more youthful and believable as a character than any of his rivals on disc, emphasising the lyrical aspect of the role as much as the heroic.

Struckmann is sometimes a little too quavery as Kurwenal, but is at his best in the final act. Lipovšek is a sympathetic Brangäne, and the role of King Marke boasts the unsurpassed voice of Finnish bass Matti Salminen. Above everything is the guiding hand of Barenboim. His interpretation of the score is seamless and full of insight. Maybe the acoustic masks some of the orchestral detail in tuttis, but overall it is a sonic wallow.
Matthew Rye

WEBER

Der Freischütz

Elisabeth Grümmer, Rudolf Schock, Lisa Otto, Hermann Prey, Karl Christian Kohn, Gottlob Frick; Chorus of the Deutsche Oper, Berlin, Berlin PO/Joseph Keilberth

EMI CMS 7 69342 2 □ ADD □ 134:04 mins (2 discs) □ 🎵🎵

Weber's *Der Freischütz* is one of the early masterpieces of German Romantic opera, a warmly orchestrated work full of the most appealing arias and lively choruses. Its Wolf's Glen scene of the casting of the magic bullets, presided over by Samiel, the devil's emissary, comes across as powerfully as ever, given a little sympathetic suspension of disbelief. Though there have been one or two excellent recordings in more recent years, EMI's 1959 version is the one that catches the atmosphere of the work most successfully, with Elisabeth Grümmer a warm-voiced Agathe, Rudolf Schock a Romantic, almost Tauber-like Max, and some of the finest German singers of the day in supporting roles. Joseph Keilberth conducts with an affectionate authority. *CO*

WEILL

Die Dreigroschenoper

Ute Lemper, René Kollo, Mario Adorf, Helga Dernesch, Susanne Tremper, Rolf Boysen, Milva; RIAS Chamber Choir, RIAS Sinfonietta, Berlin/John Mauceri

Decca 430 075-2 □ 73:54 mins □ 🎵🎵🎵

The Brecht/Weill updating of John Gay's *Beggar's Opera* became one of the major theatrical successes of the Weimar Republic, and was guaranteed immortality through the hit song 'Mack the Knife'. It was first recorded commercially in 1930 with Lotte Lenya singing the roles of Jenny and Polly Peachum. Although the Nazis subsequently attempted to obliterate all memories of the work, it resurfaced after the war and enjoyed a resurgence of popularity largely through the efforts of Lenya, who again was featured prominently in the famous 1958 recording on Sony. It's scandalous that neither of these historically important discs is at present available. But Ute Lemper, supported by some strongly characterised singing from René Kollo and Helga Dernesch, carries off the Lenya mantle with aplomb, even though John Mauceri's conducting is a mite sluggish at times. *EL*

ZIMMERMANN

Die Soldaten

Nancy Shade, Milagro Vargas, Mark Munkittrick, William Cochran, Klaus Hirte, Urszula Koszut, Raymond Wolansky; Stuttgart Opera Chorus & Orchestra/Bernhard Kontarsky

Teldec 9031-72775-2 □ 107:07 mins (2 discs) □ 🎵🎵🎵

Proclaimed the most significant German opera since Berg's *Lulu*, Bernd Alois Zimmermann's *Die Soldaten* challenges both performer and listener with its complex scenario which sometimes involves three or four simultaneous levels of action, and its highly expressionist musical style. Berg's legacy is most evident in the technically exacting central role of Marie, but Zimmermann goes beyond the Austrian master in demanding a greater vocal capacity from his singers, sometimes moving freely from coloratura to Sprechgesang within a couple of bars. It's the kind of work that repays detailed study, and this performance, emanating from a staged production by the Stuttgart Opera, serves the music to its very best advantage. *EL*

Orchestral

ADAM

Giselle

Orchestra of the Royal Opera House, Covent Garden/Mark Ermler

Royal Opera House 74321 18308 2 □ 73:48 mins □ 𝄾𝄾𝄾

Mark Ermler, born in St Petersburg and engaged as a staff conductor at the Bolshoi Theatre upon graduation, has probably more experience in this repertoire than any other conductor active today. He directs the Covent Garden Orchestra in a prim, graciously choreographic account of Adolphe Adam's masterpiece for the ballet stage, *Giselle*, written between April and June 1841. The present recording is based upon Henri Büsser's reconstruction of the original orchestral material for Paris Opera productions in 1924, which resolved certain inconsistencies of scoring, and cumbersome key-changes added by various editors. The performance from the Royal Opera House Orchestra is superb; Ermler invests each of the twenty numbers of the revised score with fine dramatic pulse and swagger and, where appropriate, no lack of tear-jerking sentimentality; solo violist John Brearley is admirable in the finale. This joint ROH/Conifer disc was made in the fine acoustic of All Saints' Church, Petersham, in May 1993; production and engineering are top notch. *MJ*

ADAMS

Harmonielehre; The Chairman Dances; Tromba Lontana; Short Ride in a Fast Machine

City of Birmingham SO/Simon Rattle

EMI CDC 5 55051 2 □ 61:50 mins □ 𝄾𝄾𝄾

This is a real winner. Simon Rattle feels very close to the American composer John Adams, and how it shows. Adams is an unreconstructed tonal composer. This disc celebrates his sheer delight in the lushest of harmonies, the brightest of instrumental colours, the joy of rhythmic play and cross-play and, quite simply, the power that music has to express emotion. Adams's music openly embraces the past, filtering Wagner, Mahler, Ravel, Sibelius, Stravinsky and first-generation minimalists – Riley, Reich and Glass – into his own rich mix. The massive *Harmonielehre* (1981) erupts with an energy of total certainty. Pounding chords in the first movement depict a dream that Adams had of a huge tanker exploding like a rocket out of San Francisco Bay, while the second movement, entitled 'The Amfortas Wound', with all its Wagnerian references, winds melancholically and sensuously up to an agonising orchestral scream of truly Mahlerian proportions. Adams's uninhibited sense of joy and fun comes out in 'The Chairman Dances' from *Nixon in China* and *Short Ride in a Fast Machine* – reputedly the most popular orchestral piece by a living American composer. This disc is a showcase for the CBSO, amply rewarded by a thrilling recorded sound. *Annette Morreau*

ALBERT

Cello Concerto (Ma)
see BLOCH: Schelomo

ALBINONI

Oboe Concerto in D minor
see Collection: Baroque Music

ALBINONI

Trumpet Concerto
see Collection: Baroque Trumpet Music

ALBINONI/VIVALDI

Wind Concertos

Paul Goodwin, Lorraine Wood (oboe), Colin Lawson, Michael Harris (clarinet); The King's Consort/Robert King

Hyperion CDA 66383 □ 69:39 mins □ 𝄾𝄾𝄾

This delightful disc demonstrates vividly Albinoni's remarkable individuality and invention. Within a genre so common, his concertos are full of surprises: conjuring virtuoso violins out of the accompanying strings in what purports to be a concerto for two oboes; rich six-part textures in a slow movement; the dazzling colours, and virtuosity, of trumpet, three oboes, bassoon and continuo, surely intended for outdoors – which is where I listened to it.

Vivaldi, born seven years after Albinoni, also wrote for some rich and unusual sonorities, as well as the staggering 230 concertos for solo violin. Two here for two oboes (with Lorraine Wood) and two Baroque clarinets (Colin Lawson and Michael Harris) are particularly entrancing.

Performance and crisp, fairly close recording are excellent, and worthy support for this colourful repertoire. *GP*

ALWYN

Symphony No. 2; Overture to a Masque; The Magic Island – symphonic prelude; Derby Day Overture; Fanfare for a Joyful Occasion

LSO/Richard Hickox

Chandos CHAN 9093 □ 62:00 mins □ 𝄞𝄞𝄞

Symphonies Nos 1 & 4; Nos 2, 3 & 5 (Hydriotaphia)

LPO/William Alwyn

Lyrita SRCD 227, SRCD 228 □ ADD □ 77:00 mins, 77:00 mins □ 𝄞𝄞𝄞

These keenly responsive, impressively recorded performances from Chandos provide an ideal introduction to the music of William Alwyn, and should have particular appeal to those considering the purchase of the Lyrita CDs containing the composer's own interpretations of his symphonies, but who might not have been totally convinced by what little they've heard hitherto of this talented and significant British composer. The fact is that, with something in excess of sixty film scores to his credit, Alwyn (1905–85) came late to the symphony yet brought to the genre a hard-won technical facility and a responsive and refined creative intellect; his own recordings of Symphonies Nos 1–5, reissued on the Lyrita label, are obviously definitive documents, and the works themselves are masterfully crafted. Richard Hickox and the LSO offer slighter, perhaps more readily accessible fare on their Chandos disc, and performances of the *Derby Day* Overture and the splendid *Fanfare for a Joyful Occasion* are especially fine. Given their age and pre-digital origins the Lyrita issues sound remarkable, while the high level of technical excellence which is the norm with the Chandos label will certainly impress in its impact and transparency. All three of these important releases merit strong commendation. *MJ*

ARNOLD

Symphony No. 6; Fantasy on a Theme of John Field; Sweeney Todd – Concert Suite; Tam o'Shanter Overture

John Lill (piano); RPO/Vernon Handley

Conifer 74321 16847 2 □ 77:39 mins □ 𝄞𝄞𝄞

Bonhomous, expertly crafted, prolific: the music of Malcolm Arnold has won many friends in the last half-century, though it's only in the CD era that many works have become available on disc. Perhaps his essential genius lies in such evocative, insouciant and superbly tuneful miniatures as the two sets of *English Dances*; if so, look no further than the excellent Lyrita release, where the composer conducts them along with the later but entirely comparable sets of *Scottish*, *Irish* and *Cornish Dances*. If you seek a wider view of Arnold's talents, look elsewhere, especially in the catalogue of Conifer, most active in issuing more ambitious pieces, many under the able baton of Vernon Handley.

At the time of writing there are no fewer than three complete cycles of the symphonies in progress (Conifer, Chandos and Naxos). This varied programme makes an intriguing sampler. Arnold's symphonies, with their shades of Britten and Shostakovich, are not universally admired, but their seriousness of purpose is undeniable. No. 6 (1968) is a typically ambiguous and haunting work whose central slow movement juxtaposes lament and cakewalk. More impressive perhaps is the strange Fantasy on a Theme of John Field, a large-scale set of concertante variations for piano and orchestra which becomes a kind of battle royal for possession of Field's beautiful and delicate theme. *Sweeney Todd*, a very tongue-in-cheek score for the Royal Ballet, is represented by a suite devised by David Ellis. The graphic and uproarious *Tam o'Shanter* Overture (1955) is a real *tour de force*, illustrating Burns's famous ballad with an almost palpably Scottish accent. Performances and recording are alike first-rate. *CM*

AURIC

Ouverture
see Collection: French Orchestral Music

AVISON

Concerto Grosso in C after Scarlatti
see Collection: Baroque Music

BABBITT

Correspondences
see Collection: American Orchestral Music

CPE BACH

Four Orchestral Sinfonias; String Symphony No. 5 in B minor

Orchestra of the Age of Enlightenment/Gustav Leonhardt

Virgin VER 5 61182 2 □ 54:15 mins □ 🗗🗗

The four orchestral sinfonias must be counted among CPE Bach's finest works. Composed during the mid-1770s, they epitomise his bold musical style in which stark contrasts of ideas, textures and emotions are very much the order of the day. Although unequivocally rooted in the 18th century, the rhythmic dynamism and wild modulations that characterise these sinfonias also point forward inexorably towards Beethoven.

Leonhardt and the Orchestra of the Age of Enlightenment deliver forceful and emotionally satisfying performances throughout this disc, although they don't quite achieve the level of reckless abandon that made such a stunning achievement of an earlier LP version with modern-instrument Munich Bach Orchestra under Karl Richter. *EL*

CPE BACH

Hamburg Symphonies Nos 3–5; Harpsichord Concerto in C minor; Oboe Concerto in E flat

Hans-Peter Westermann (oboe), Andreas Staier (harpsichord); Freiburg Baroque Orchestra/Thomas Hengelbrock

Deutsche Harmonia Mundi RD 77187 □ 70:34 mins □ 🗗🗗🗗

Quirky, wayward, unpredictable – these are some of the adjectives that spring to mind when listening to the music of CPE Bach, a composer who seems to refute the notion that every 18th-century musician was primarily concerned with balanced phrase structures and perfection of form. Yet for all his individuality, CPE must not be regarded as a maverick. He was certainly capable of turning out elegant works from time to time, and the present disc offers one such example with the 1765 Oboe Concerto. The rest of the programme, however, is more characteristic. There's a superbly inventive keyboard concerto, performed with brilliant dynamism by the harpsichordist Andreas Staier. But even more striking are the three string symphonies, works that never cease to astonish with their sequence of daring effects. They are performed here with consummate virtuosity, the Freiburg Baroque Orchestra making light work of their phenomenal technical difficulties. *EL*

JC BACH

Sinfonias, Opp. 6, 9 & 18; La calamità Overture

Netherlands CO/David Zinman

Philips Duo 442 275-2 □ ADD □ 145:39 mins (2 discs) □ 🗗🗗

Johann Christian Bach, the youngest son of Johann Sebastian, is more often remembered nowadays for the powerful influence he exerted on the young Mozart than for the intrinsic value of his own compositions. But this verdict seems quite unjustified when faced with such inventive works as these three sets of sinfonias. Composed between 1765 and 1780, they offer fascinating testimony to Bach's melodic elegance and his refined orchestration. One might imagine that such music would sound more convincing when performed on period instruments, but in fact these wonderfully fleet-of-foot renditions from the Netherlands Chamber Orchestra, recorded in the mid-Seventies, outclass all modern competition. A marvellous bargain. *EL*

BACH

Brandenburg Concertos Nos 1–6

Amsterdam Baroque Orchestra/Ton Koopman

Erato Duo Bonsai 4509-91935-2 □ 99:00 mins (2 discs) □ 🗗🗗

It's a measure of the variety and unique challenge set by the six Brandenburg Concertos that no one recording quite meets the demands throughout. Pickett's provocative set (L'Oiseau-Lyre) achieves a superb balance between the unlikely partners of trumpet, recorder, oboe and violin in No. 2. Schreier's solo strings – modern instruments – articulate No. 3 with transparency unmatched elsewhere (Philips). Harnoncourt (Teldec) lifts the dark-coloured forces of No. 6 into a swirling dance (until an appalling edit leaves the ghostly courtiers in a tangled heap on the ballroom floor). Goodman on Hyperion balances with impeccable judgement but sometimes drives relentlessly. Kuijken (Harmonia Mundi) meets every challenge but one, substituting horn for the brilliance of trumpet in No. 2.

Period instruments are a must, not for doctrinaire reasons but to solve the particular problems of balance and timbral distinctiveness of the soloists – in Concertos Nos 1, 2 and 5 especially. Both Pinnock (The English Concert, on Archiv) and Koopman let Bach speak for himself. Similarities are extraordinary – timings often within a few seconds of each other, intonation crises at identical points. Pinnock's soloists are a touch more distinctive; Koopman's shaping marginally more mannered. So art yields to economy. Koopman's set at mid-price wins unless the addition of the orchestral suites – and decent notes – persuade you towards Pinnock. *GP*

BACH

Concertos for One, Two & Three Violins

Alison Bury, Pavlo Beznosiuk, Catherine Mackintosh (violin); Orchestra of the Age of Enlightenment/Elizabeth Wallfisch (violin)

Virgin Veritas VC 7 59319 2 □ 62:46 mins □ 🕐🕐🕐

Only three of Bach's violin concertos have survived, but it is known that he rewrote several as harpsichord concertos. It has been possible to use the scores of those which exist in both versions to reconstruct the violin originals. The Concerto in D for Three Violins is a case in point. Reconstructed from the C major work for three harpsichords, its performance here is a triumph, wholly convincing, not least because of the brilliance of the playing.

The other, more familiar concertos sound no less fine, since they are performed with a real sense of spontaneity and consistently convincing tempi. The lack of vibrato may not be to all tastes – modern-instrument performances would offer rather more emotional warmth in slow movements, for instance – but phrasing is always sensitive, while in the faster music the articulation is precise and unmannered. Elizabeth Wallfisch and Alison Bury achieve a true partnership of equals in the great Double Concerto in D minor, and the OAE plays throughout with the utmost taste and refinement. The recording quality matches the performances in its naturalness and clarity. *Terry Barfoot*

BACH

Keyboard Concertos, BWV 1044, 1055 & 1060–5; BWV 1052–4 & 1056–9

Ton Koopman, Tini Mathot, Patrizia Marisaldi, Elina Mustonen (harpsichord); Amsterdam Baroque Orchestra/Ton Koopman

Erato Duo Bonsai 4509-91929-2, 4509-91930-2 □ 118:00 mins, 107:00 mins (2 discs each) □ 🕐🕐

All bar one of these 15 works are arrangements of violin or wind concertos by Bach himself or others, to be played at the Leipzig Collegium Musicum evenings over which he presided. Some of the less known have been unjustly undervalued – they are far from mere makeshifts. Leaving the string

accompaniments almost unaltered, Bach adapted the solo parts to create the whole genre of keyboard concerto for the Classical era and beyond. ('Un-arranging' them has allowed others – Hogwood on L'Oiseau-Lyre – to reconstruct lost originals.)

Koopman's exuberant personality shines through these performances, in the orchestral energy as much as in his own vividly imaginative playing. Driving, fast movements have a fine directional focus: middle movements are lively and full of resourceful decoration.

Koopman's partners in the multiple concertos, for two to four harpsichords, are no less animated – and the uniquely rich, dense textures are thrilling. High spots for me are the fugue of the C major two-harpsichord concerto, perhaps originally a duet without orchestra, and the concerto rescued from Cantata 35, for which Koopman uses the organ.

For good measure, the package ends with the triple concerto BWV 1044 – four discs of outstanding music and value for money. *GP*

BACH

Ouvertüren (Suites), BWV 1066–9; Ouvertüre, BWV 1070

Musica Antiqua Köln/Reinhard Goebel

Archiv 415 671-2 □ 110:32 mins (2 discs) □ 🕐🕐🕐

Time was when the orchestral suites were uncontroversially for orchestra. No longer! Two American ensembles (directed by Malloch and Parrott respectively) use strings one to a part throughout, including the majestic Third and Fourth Suites with their three trumpets, timpani and woodwind. Others eschew solo strings altogether, even for the concerto-like episodes in the opening movement of BWV 1068. Goebel compromises – single strings balance the lone flute of BWV 1067, while the full ensemble plays in the large-scale suites. The two-disc set is quite generous, too, with all repeats of the *allegros* of the opening French overture movements (how can Koopman deny them to us – on Erato – once we're hypnotised by his dynamic pulse?) and the attractive but surely spurious BWV 1070.

The flute Suite, with William Hazelzet in superb buoyant form, was recorded in 1982. By 1985 Goebel's views about note-values had changed. It's all explained in a (to me) highly suspect argument in the booklet – but the sound survives the theorising, with a springy step and a sense of total ease in breathtaking *allegros*. Much is fast but nothing is hurried, while the familiar Air of Suite No. 3 and the slow dances are finely poised and stately. *GP*

BACH

Violin Concertos in G minor, BWV 1056 & D minor, BWV 1052; Concerto for Violin and Oboe in C minor, BWV 1060; Concerto for Oboe d'Amore in A, BWV 1055

Orchestra of the Age of Enlightenment/Elizabeth Wallfisch (violin), Anthony Robson (oboe, oboe d'amore)

Virgin Veritas VC 5 45095 2 □ 60:29 mins □ 𝄐𝄐𝄐

A word of warning. The violin concertos here are not the familiar pair in A minor and E. Bach composed a number of concertos for orchestral instruments and later transcribed them as keyboard concertos. Reversing Bach's procedure, Wilfried Fischer has taken the harpsichord versions and from them has reconstructed the originals. BWV 1056 is a transposed transcription of the Keyboard Concerto in F minor (though *New Grove* identifies the outer movements as being from a lost oboe concerto).

The D minor work is also usually heard in its keyboard adaptation. The Concerto in C minor for Two Harpsichords appears in its original instrumentation for violin and oboe, the soloists here being perfectly balanced for clarity of line. It was Tovey who suggested that the A major concerto may have been intended for the oboe d'amore, an instrument pitched between the oboe proper and the cor anglais.

These are period performances, lively and resonant, employing a supporting ensemble of 12 string players and a harpsichord. To allow for the pitch difference between Bach's day and our own, the whole programme sounds about a semitone lower than the stated keys. A disc well worth exploring. *Wadham Sutton*

BALAKIREV

Symphony No. 1 in C; Russia

Philharmonia Orchestra/Yevgeny Svetlanov

Hyperion CDA 66493 □ 59:22 mins □ 𝄐𝄐𝄐

No wonder the genesis of the true Russian symphony was so protracted when Balakirev, its chief advocate and loyal encourager of other composers' efforts in that direction, took over thirty years to complete his own First Symphony. It is an ambitious work with a surprising consistency and a flavour all its own. Wholesome nationalist ideas of the 1860s are wrapped in piquant orchestration of the 1890s; the instrumental ingenuities of Tchaikovsky, who had died five years before

the symphony's 1898 premiere, seem to have been well observed in the many woodwind ensembles and solos, winsomely taken here by the Philharmonia players.

Yevgeny Svetlanov, who claims to have run the entire Russian symphonic gamut as conductor of the USSR (now Russian) State Symphony Orchestra, here sets his seal on an ideally handsome-sounding British orchestra, with recording to match: brass-laden climaxes richly blaze, though the listener's natural concert-hall perspective of a mid-stalls seat can have one straining for clarity in quieter passages. He provides a fine challenge to great phrase-makers Beecham and Järvi (neither currently in the catalogues), especially in the Andante's sinuous oriental melody and the brace of exciting folk-song adaptations in the finale. *Russia*, a finely wrought fantasy, simply extends that pleasure, and anyone captivated should seek out the companion volume (the two discs are also available as a set). *DN*

BANTOCK

Pagan Symphony; Fifine at the Fair; Two Heroic Ballads

RPO/Vernon Handley

Hyperion CDA 66630 □ 79:38 mins □ 𝄐𝄐𝄐

For a composer who was once (ie pre-1914) reckoned second only to Elgar, Granville Bantock's music fared badly in the LP era. His vast output – hedonistically Romantic, brilliantly orchestrated, opulently colourful, but often short on substance or dressing up commonplace ideas – was drastically out of fashion. But CD has brought a revaluation, spurred by Vernon Handley's series for Hyperion, playing the music for all its Romanticism and colour are worth. This is the strongest of his discs, and the most generous in playing time. The *Pagan Symphony* is one of Bantock's most inspired works, his sybaritic Attic strain translating into a shimmering dream of the ancient world, with a wittily grotesque Scherzo. *Fifine at the Fair*, after Browning, is maybe the finest of his many symphonic poems (it was memorably recorded by Beecham in the dying days of 78rpm), with some extraordinary textural invention and extended solo roles for viola and clarinet. The second of the *Heroic Ballads* is recycled from the best passage in Bantock's *Hebridean Symphony*. Stunning recording and utterly convinced performances. *CM*

BARBER

Adagio for Strings; Essays for Orchestra Nos 1 & 2;
Medea's Meditation and Dance of Vengeance; The School
for Scandal Overture
see **CHORAL & SONG**: BARBER: Knoxville – Summer of
1915

BARBER

Adagio for Strings
see also **CHORAL & SONG**: COPLAND: Eight Poems of
Emily Dickinson

BARBER/KORNGOLD

Barber: Violin Concerto

Korngold: Violin Concerto in D; Much Ado About Nothing – Suite, Op. 11

Gil Shaham (violin); LSO/André Previn (piano)

DG 439 886-2 □ 70:59 mins □ *𝄢𝄢𝄢*

These two concertos have a good deal in common. Both stress the introverted side of the violin, with bravura display concentrated in the busy finales. Elsewhere lyricism predominates, an enigmatic melancholy suffusing the Samuel Barber piece, written in 1939 and revised nine years later, a glowing, late-Romantic haze adding glamour to the rich yet ambiguous melodies of the Erich Wolfgang Korngold work (1945), whose material derives largely from his Hollywood film scores of the Thirties.

The young American-Israeli violinist Gil Shaham brings sensitivity and imagination to both scores, accomplishing all their technical demands and evoking the spirit of the music with an attractively grainy tone and impeccable interpretative assurance. André Previn secures stylish and vivid playing from the LSO, although when trying to create a more intimate rapport with Shaham in the violin and piano version of Korngold's *Much Ado About Nothing* Suite of 1920 – Shakespeare re-created in terms of Viennese light music – he proves a curiously reticent accompanist.

The sound throughout is beautifully balanced, the carefully chosen orchestral colours of both composers vibrant and warm. *George Hall*

BARTÓK

Concerto for Orchestra; Dance Suite; Two Portraits; Mikrokosmos – Bourrée and From the Diary of a Fly (arr. Serly)

LSO, Philharmonia Hungarica/Antal Dorati

Mercury Living Presence 432 017-2 □ ADD □ 71:31 mins □ *𝄢𝄢*

Despite the availability of innumerable streamlined digital versions of Bartók's most popular orchestral works, the classic recordings made by those conductors most closely associated with the composer have not yet been superseded (see also below). Here Antal Dorati directs a high-octane performance of the Concerto for Orchestra with the LSO at the very height of its technical powers. The result is invariably thrilling, especially in the opening movement, though some may feel that Dorati sometimes over-accentuates the melodic phrasing.

While there may be nagging doubts about some sections of the Concerto, the performance of the *Dance Suite* is simply breathtaking – a riotous celebration of Hungarian folk-culture delivered with great panache and a wonderful sense of instrumental colouring. The other two items, although not top-drawer Bartók, are equally compelling, not least because Mercury's close recording seems ideally suited to the hot-blooded nature of the music-making. *EL*

BARTÓK

Concerto for Two Pianos, Percussion and Orchestra
see **CHAMBER**: BARTÓK: Sonata for Two Pianos and
Percussion

BARTÓK/KODÁLY

Bartók: Divertimento; Romanian Folk Dances

Kodály: Dances of Marosszék; Dances of Galánta

St Paul CO/Hugh Wolff

Teldec 9031-73134-2 □ 60:19 mins □ *𝄢𝄢*

The conventional definition of a divertimento as a work that is light-hearted and amusing in character can hardly be applied to Bartók's sole essay in this genre. Composed against the background of gathering political turmoil in the Central Europe of the late Thirties, this piece is charged with bitterness and uncertainty, its momentary flashes of humour appearing caustic rather than playful. Although the current catalogue boasts several fine recordings of the Divertimento from virtuoso string orchestras, none is more convincing than the present version. Hugh Wolff has a particular empathy for Bartók's music, and the performance is notable for its extremely wide emotional range, from the eerie, almost nightmarish chromatics of the Molto adagio to the high-voltage energy of the outer movements. The rest of the programme is equally enthralling, with the American orchestra managing to convey the rustic simplicity and exuberance of the Bartók and Kodály dances in a manner that appears quintessentially Hungarian in character.

A wonderful disc, especially now that it retails at mid-price. *EL*

BARTOK

Hungarian Sketches; Romanian Folk Dances
see Collection: Hungarian Connections

BARTOK/JANACEK

Bartók: The Miraculous Mandarin; Two Portraits

Janáček: Sinfonietta

Shlomo Mintz (violin); Ambrosian Singers, LSO, Berlin PO/Claudio Abbado

DG Masters 445 501-2 □ 66:00 mins □ 🎵🎵

Among the most satisfying recordings of Bartók's compelling ballet, I would certainly single out both Rattle and Boulez for their marvellous attention to inner detail, though Claudio Abbado leads the field in terms of sheer theatricality and the ability to pinpoint with utter conviction every contrasting aspect of this powerful score. Supported by absolutely stunning playing from the LSO, Abbado draws us into Bartók's lurid world from the very outset. His approach may appear less emotionally charged than others (the slightly recessed orchestral sound may exacerbate this impression), but in fact this distancing actually serves to enhance the cumulative impact of the whole so that the final pages, in which the mandarin eventually achieves redemption through death, sound particularly moving.

It's a great pity that the rest of the disc isn't quite on the same level. Although Shlomo Mintz delivers beautifully moulded performances of the early *Two Portraits*, Abbado's performance of Janáček's Sinfonietta with the Berlin Philharmonic is somewhat uninvolving and no match for Mackerras on Decca. *EL*

BARTOK

Music for Strings, Percussion and Celesta; Concerto for Orchestra; Hungarian Sketches

Chicago SO/Fritz Reiner

RCA Victor Living Stereo 09026 61504 2 □ ADD □ 76:05 mins □ 🎵🎵

Like Dorati, Fritz Reiner remained a staunch advocate of Bartók's music at a time when his reputation was much less secure than it is nowadays. Needless to say, his 1955 recording of the Concerto for Orchestra has also stood the test of time, and with RCA's superb remastering it now sounds absolutely magnificent. Reiner may not drive the music to the same degree of emphasis as Dorati (see

above), but both the 'Giuoco delle coppie' and finale benefit from the even greater rhythmic precision of his Chicago SO.

Direct comparison with more recent versions of the *Music for Strings* also show Reiner in the most favourable light. Few manage to phrase the opening fugue subject with the same degree of subtlety – a quality that somehow embraces both desolation and restlessness. And one still marvels at the power and punch of the Chicago strings in the driving rhythms of the ensuing movement. *EL*

BARTOK

Piano Concertos Nos 1–3

Zoltán Kocsis (piano); Budapest Festival Orchestra/Iván Fischer

Philips 446 366-2 □ 73:14 mins □ 🎵🎵🎵

Despite the admirable qualities of performances from Stephen Kovacevich (Philips Duo) and Peter Donohoe (EMI), Hungarian pianists still lead the field in recordings of these masterly concertos. Over the years the top recommendation has remained Géza Anda who, in partnership with the incomparable Ferenc Fricsay and the Berlin Radio Symphony Orchestra, delivers forthright performances that underline the percussive nature of Bartók's writing. Now restored to the catalogue at mid-price on the DG Originals label, these early Sixties recordings sound remarkably fresh and will not disappoint admirers of these great artists.

For those wanting more modern sound at bargain price, however, there's much to be said for Jenö Jandó's accounts on Naxos which generate a terrific impact in the First and Second Concertos but also allow space for greater reflection in the atmospheric slow movement of No. 2. Yet for the most consistently incisive and musically illuminating playing of all, I would turn to Kocsis and Fischer. Their performances certainly live on the edge when it comes to hair-raising movements like the finale to No. 1, but the risk-taking invariably comes off, and the energy generated by this partnership literally takes one's breath away. *EL*

BARTOK

Rhapsody for Piano and Orchestra; Scherzo for Piano and Orchestra
see DOHNANYI: Variations on a Nursery Song

BARTOK

Viola Concerto
see BLOCH: Schelomo

BARTOK
Violin Concertos Nos 1 & 2

Isaac Stern (violin); Philadelphia Orchestra/Eugene Ormandy, New York Philharmonic/Leonard Bernstein

Sony SMK 64502 □ ADD □ 58:15 mins □ 🍷🍷

Composed in the wake of an abortive love affair, Bartók's First Violin Concerto was published only 13 years after the composer's death. Isaac Stern was in fact one of the first major violinists to take up the work, and his 1961 recording still remains unsurpassed in terms of its technical fluency and its ability to breathe life into every melodic nuance.

Similar qualities abound in the much better-known Second Concerto, but here Stern faces formidable competition from a roster of supreme violinists, including Kyung-Wha Chung, Menuhin, Zukerman, Szeryng and Perlman. Even so, I find myself returning to Stern in preference to these other artists for exploiting deeper resonances in the music, not only passion and nostalgia but also bitterness, irony and on occasions humour. The partnership with Bernstein is certainly telling in this respect, the maestro responding with quicksilver impulse to every change of mood. While this tendency to live dangerously produces some speculative ensemble from the New York Philharmonic, the net result is always invigorating. The recordings are certainly not state of the art, but they have stood the test of time pretty adequately. *EL*

BAX
Symphonies Nos 1 in E flat & 7

LPO/Myer Fredman, Raymond Leppard

Lyrita SRCD 232 □ ADD □ 77:56 mins □ 🍷🍷🍷

Less structurally convincing than the best of his symphonic poems, Arnold Bax's seven symphonies rank less with those of Elgar, Vaughan Williams and Havergal Brian than with the early symphonies of Sibelius and with the Russians from Borodin to Rachmaninov, from which he drew such abundant colouristic inspiration. Even so, they're full of striking and enjoyable music. Lyrita issued a sporadic series of them on LP, but only No. 3, often said to be the best, achieved multiple versions (Barbirolli's mono account from 1944 is available from EMI; Edward Downes's RCA performance cries out for re-release). Chandos has recorded the entire cycle on CD under the dependable Bryden Thomson, but for representative Bax symphonism you could hardly better this Lyrita reissue. Symphony No. 1 is an angry, brooding work of surprising

power, with a magnificent slow movement; Fredman's advocacy is vivid and urgent. The more expansive Seventh, written for the 1939 New York World Fair, was once seen as a mere nostalgic epilogue to the cycle. But it emerges with a strong and noble profile in Leppard's account: the finale, a series of variations in passacaglia style, has something of the spirit of craggy valediction we find in Vaughan Williams's Symphony No. 9. Completely acceptable sound, and very generous measure. *CM*

BAX
Three Pieces for Orchestra
see Collection: The Banks of Green Willow

BAX
Tintagel; The Garden of Fand; November Woods; Mediterranean; Northern Ballad No. 1

LPO/Adrian Boult

Lyrita SRCD 231 □ ADD □ 62:14 mins □ 🍷🍷🍷

The three symphonic poems which Arnold Bax composed between 1913 and 1919 comprise some of his finest music, and *Tintagel*, a passionate and glittering seascape uniting the influences of impressionism and Wagner's *Tristan*, remains his most widely admired work. These scores display his mastery in handling a large late-Romantic orchestra. Riotous sea-music of another kind infuses the gorgeously coloured *Garden of Fand*, based, like many of his works, on Irish legend. Yet perhaps the most wonderful music here is the tragic, wintry landscape of *November Woods*, buffeted by wild winds: one of the greatest nature-impressions in British music.

There are more impassioned accounts of *Tintagel* (Barbirolli, EMI), more voluptuous ones of *Fand* (Beecham, EMI). But Boult's noble interpretations of all three are classics, and he has no rival in *November Woods*. The stern and dark-hued *Northern Ballad*, a later work from Bax's Scottish period, is a powerful bonus, with the little *Mediterranean* an elegant extra bon-bon. These Lyrita recordings were among the finest of their time (1968 and 1972) and remain perfectly acceptable. *CM*

BEETHOVEN
Piano Concertos Nos 1–5; Choral Fantasy

Maurizio Pollini (piano); Vienna State Opera Chorus, Vienna PO/Eugen Jochum (Nos 1 & 2), Karl Böhm (Nos 3–5), Claudio Abbado

DG 419 793-2 □ ADD/DDD □ 190:51 mins (3 discs) □ 🍷🍷🍷

With complete cycles (in some cases more than one each) from Arrau, Ashkenazy, Barenboim, Brendel, Fleisher, Kempff, Pollini, Rubinstein, Serkin and Zimerman, to name only a few of the first-rate sets available, you can basically throw them all into a hat, reach in and live happily after with whatever version you happen to come up with. Both Barenboim and Pollini have recorded the cycle twice, but with their first versions – Pollini as above with the Vienna PO and an array of distinguished conductors, Barenboim (EMI) with the New Philharmonia under Klemperer – you also get the wonderful *Choral Fantasy*. These are all artists and pianists of the highest order, and their thoughts on this music, even on an off-day, are worthy of the greatest possible respect. If you're selecting a first version for your collection, however, it would be wise to choose something not too idiosyncratic (not Gould, for instance, or even Arrau, Kempff or Zimerman/Bernstein). I find it hard to imagine that anyone but the most determined misanthrope could fail to derive lasting pleasure and insight from Perahia and Haitink, but their complete cycle is currently (and inexplicably) not available, and it must be said that there *are* those who find Perahia a little too self-consciously poetic, a little too Mozartian perhaps. Certainly no one surpasses him in elegance or beauty of tone, nor does anyone find a more consistent rapport with their conductor. Those wanting that little extra bit of ruggedness can confidently turn to Pollini's later DG cycle – recorded live in 1992–3 with Claudio Abbado and the Berlin Philharmonic (also available as separate discs) – or to the still underrated Leon Fleischer on Sony. And for sheer mental stimulation, Arrau, Brendel, Gould, Kempff and Zimerman remain incomparable, provoking enough thoughts to last the proverbial month of Sundays. So what comes out of *my* hat? Both of Pollini's sets are remarkable, but for me it's the *Choral Fantasy* that decides it. *JS*

BEETHOVEN

Piano Concerto No. 3 (transcr. Alkan)
see **INSTRUMENTAL**: Collection: Marc-André Hamelin
Live at Wigmore Hall

BEETHOVEN

Symphonies Nos 1–9

Edith Wiens (soprano), Hildegard Hartwig (contralto), Keith Lewis (tenor), Roland Hermann (bass); Hamburg State Opera Chorus; NDR Chorus & SO/Günter Wand

RCA 74321 20277 2 □ **356:00 mins (5 discs)**
□ 🙂🙂

As HC Robbins Landon affirmed, when reviewing this cycle for *BBC Music Magazine*, the octogenarian master conductor Günter Wand's traversal of the nine symphonies of Beethoven ranks as one of the finest ever undertaken. Not for him the gratuitous scene-stealing of many of today's young pretenders; Wand's Beethoven is monumentally assured, noble and, above all, eloquently and rationally conceived. This is Beethoven-conducting in the illustrious Germanic tradition, totally devoid of affectation, and born of an era (sadly long gone) when conductors would forge performances of heaven-storming philosophical legitimacy, planned, rehearsed and expedited much as a great general marshals his forces. Wand's old-world values and winning modesty are sterling virtues, as is his reliance on Urtext editions of these scores, and he is punctilious in the observance of repeats. Ever precise over stylistic and textual matters, Wand's Beethoven reflects the composer's own craggy, heroically idiosyncratic view of the symphonies as musical manifesto for a new, revolutionary epoch. One senses throughout these performances that for Wand himself the re-enactment of each of the nine symphonies is a personally symbolic enterprise, and (as Robbins Landon suggests) the listener feels somehow 'present at the creation' of this music. The playing of the North German RSO is consistently fine throughout this set of five CDs, recorded between 1985 and 1988, and the vocal contributions in the Ninth are admirable. After an hour or two in the company of Günter Wand, I doubt you'll feel much need to sample any other rival cycle on modern instruments, save perhaps Nikolaus Harnoncourt's illuminating Teldec series with the Chamber Orchestra of Europe, which in any case, lacks the strength and lustre of the North German RSO. Wand's is a Beethoven cycle of new discoveries and revelations, seemingly purpose-built for our age of post-modernist scepticism. What's more, Wand convinces us that *fin de siècle* Beethoven is alive and well. *MJ*

BEETHOVEN

Symphonies Nos 1–9; Egmont Overture; Coriolan Overture

Lynne Dawson (soprano), Jard van Nes (contralto), Anthony Rolfe Johnson (tenor), Eike Wilm Schulte (bass); Gulbenkian Choir, Lisbon, Orchestra of the 18th Century/Frans Brüggen

Philips 442 156-2 □ **357:32 mins (5 discs)** □ 🙂🙂🙂

'Correctness', writes Alfred Brendel, 'tells us: this is how it has to be!… Boldness presents us with a surprising and overwhelming realisation: what we had thought impossible becomes true!' Such principles inform Frans Brüggen's questing, iconoclastic and revelatory Beethoven cycle, recorded between 1984 and 1993. Brüggen seems less pedantic in matters of textual fidelity than either Gardiner or Norrington, yet more assertive than Hogwood, revealing affinities with Harnoncourt's heroic musical dramaturgy. Brüggen's players employ gut strings, period woodwind, natural brass and hide-headed timpani (and bass drum in No. 9) struck with hard sticks. Individual performances will astonish; each is propelled with a determination which ably reflects the ferocity of Beethoven's creative vision. Tempi are brisk, though seldom controversial, even in the Trio of Symphony No. 7. Having heard the Seventh, Weber thought Beethoven 'ripe for the madhouse', and in Brüggen's hands the work sounds fearfully modernistic. The *Eroica*, its inflammatory rhetoric more telling with divided violins and the rejection of Hans von Bülow's unseemly alterations to the trumpet parts, is superbly done. Brüggen's accounts of Nos 1 and 2 are as venturesome as the rule-breaking dominant seventh chord which launches the First Symphony. The Fourth, its nebulous chromatic introduction seemingly incapable of supporting any emotional upswing, demonstrates Brüggen's skill in maximising every dramatic contrast, as here, with the cathartic arrival of the vigorous Allegro vivace first subject. The Fifth, meanwhile, is forged and finally won amid consuming heroic fervour. This series is crowned by Brüggen's epic account of the *Choral* Symphony; finer and somehow more plausible than John Eliot Gardiner's version, and with a team of excellent soloists who share Brüggen's own cosmic vision of what this music stands for. *MJ*

BEETHOVEN

Symphonies Nos 1 in C & 2 in D

Cleveland Orchestra/Christoph von Dohnányi

Telarc CD-80187 □ **58:49 mins** □ *♪♪♪*

Beethoven asserted himself as a radical thinker, and gave notice of future iconoclastic tendencies, with the very first chord of his C major First Symphony, composed in 1800. In defiant contravention of every established principle, Beethoven begins his great saga of symphonies with a 'wrong' dominant seventh chord of F, first manifestation of his oblique

use of harmonic tension, which would impart both drama and disorder to the works that followed it. Even today, we can sympathise with Beethoven's contemporaries who, having been hidebound by Classical formalism, must surely have found the experience disturbing and disorientating. Yet the First Symphony is for the most part charmingly jubilant, and Christoph von Dohnányi's alertly calculated direction ensures that its 'unbuttoned' Beethovenian wit emerges abundantly. The Symphony in D major, written two years later, reveals nothing of the mental torment occasioned by the onset of deafness, or of the emotional anguish set out in Beethoven's 'Heiligenstadt Testament'. The work is on a grander scale than its predecessor; the brilliance and power of the opening movement (with what George Grove called its 'fiery flash of fiddles') and the first of Beethoven's true Scherzos declare a new breadth and purpose for the medium. The Cleveland Orchestra performs both works magnificently; Christoph von Dohnányi is a master Beethoven interpreter, and Telarc's incredible sonics have become a byword for cutting-edge audio engineering. A superlative issue. *MJ*

BEETHOVEN

Symphonies Nos 1 in C & 4 in B flat; Egmont Overture

Berlin PO/Herbert von Karajan

DG Galleria 419 048-2 □ **ADD** □ **64:00 mins** □ *♪♪*

Beethoven's Fourth Symphony has been unfairly treated over the years and has become known, through no fault of its own, as a relaxed and comparatively un-monumental foil to its immediate neighbours in Beethoven's symphonic canon. Yet the fact is that for all its comparative modesty the Fourth is no less remarkable, nor significant; consider its impenetrably chromatic slow introduction, and the rich pathos of its slow movement. Here is a performance of stature and reliability, well able to overturn any misinformed prejudices about the eminence and importance of the work, and argued with impressive authority by Karajan and the Berliners. Symphony No. 1 is a lavish, large-scale affair, less ideal from the point of view of current performance scholarship, but predictably well played and directed, and hugely enjoyable. This well-filled reissue (the performances come from Karajan's finest Beethoven cycle, taped during the Seventies) offers detailed and resonant digital transfers of the original analogue masters and provides rewarding interpretations of these works which few more expensive issues can eclipse easily. *MJ*

BEETHOVEN

Symphonies Nos 2 in D & 8 in F

London Classical Players/Roger Norrington

EMI Reflexe CDC 7 47698 2 □ 59:00 mins □ 🎵🎵🎵

Roger Norrington's Beethoven's performances are among the most distinctive and characterful of all authentic traversals of these works. There's never any reluctance on his part to explore new or unfamiliar orchestral sonorities, and his players react to his utterly idiosyncratic mannerisms with great panache. The London Classical Players use the by now familiar gut strings, period bows, authentic wind and brass instruments, and hide-headed timpani of the Beethoven era, and their performances are exceptionally alert and vivid. Norrington's view of the D major Second Symphony is Classically disposed; tempi are fast, and antiphonally seated first and second violins enable much inner detail to register with admirable clarity. In the Eighth, a grander, more motoric conception of the music (the opening has enormous thrust and impetus) impresses the listener; the first movement recapitulation is thrilling, though elsewhere the character and rhythmic severity are somewhat more relaxed, with some memorably rustic displays from the horns in the perilous high-lying passages of the Trio of the Scherzo. Norrington plays the finale for all it's worth, and the coda (another of Beethoven's traps for unwary listeners!) has exemplary weight and good humour. Period performances of distinction and élan, and probably the best I've heard from Roger Norrington in Beethoven. EMI's sonics are of demonstration quality. *MJ*

BEETHOVEN

Symphony No. 3 in E flat (Eroica); Egmont Overture

Dresden Staatskapelle/Colin Davis

Philips 434 120-2 □ 65:00 mins □ 🎵🎵🎵

Beethoven's *Eroica* bestrides his creations as a musical and philosophical colossus. With the two declamatory tonic chords that launched the symphony, Beethoven flung aside convention and decorum, granting the medium cosmic relevance. Despite his original intention to dedicate the symphony to Napoleon (on learning of Napoleon's imperialist aspirations, Beethoven excised his name from the title-page with such vitriol that

his pen perforated it!), the work has come to be known as the greatest musico-political manifesto of all time. Performances of the work, and fine ones at that, are understandably legion, though the prime virtue of Colin Davis's reading is that it is totally objective and, though passionately reasoned, it never becomes smug or self-regarding. This is a superb textbook *Eroica*, magnificently played by an orchestra which has this music in their collective bones, and who live and breathe it as an organic expression of irresistible power and urgency. Davis convinces us that the inflammatory rhetoric of Beethoven's vision is just as potent in our day as it was in his, and for good measure presents Beethoven's overture to Goethe's *Egmont* as an apt filler. The Philips recording is in every sense as impressive and assured as these stunning performances. *MJ*

BEETHOVEN

Symphony Nos 5 in C minor & 7 in A

Vienna PO/Carlos Kleiber

DG Originals 447 400-2 □ ADD □ 72:08 mins □ 🎵🎵

Taped some twenty years ago in Vienna's fabled Musikverein, these performances of Beethoven's Fifth and Seventh Symphonies, with Carlos Kleiber conducting the Vienna Philharmonic, have assumed legendary status in the annals of Beethoven interpretation. Previously released on two prohibitively expensive single discs, Kleiber's Beethoven has an indomitable urgency and electricity which prove spellbinding; his account of the Fifth enkindles the turbulent radicalism of Beethoven's heroic vision in exemplary detail. The arcane and emphatically severe approach that is the hallmark of Kleiber's style generates thrilling impetus in Symphony No. 7, though again the comparative dryness of the 1976 analogue recording has been preserved on this digitised transfer, helping to clarify textures and impart a lean, somewhat astringent quality to the sound, very much in keeping with the conductor's watchful, tight-reined manner. Kleiber's finale is studiously repressed until the last few pages, when the cumulative torrent of physical energy is released to crown this transcendently masterful account of this extraordinary symphony. Now reissued in the DG Originals series of great recordings from the yellow label, this is an essential acquisition for every collector. Kleiber's performances have already been deified, here and elsewhere, but the revitalised sound is no less sensational in its impact. *MJ*

Beethoven: Symphony No. 6 in F (Pastoral)

Schubert: Symphony No. 5 in B flat

Vienna PO/Karl Böhm

DG Originals 447 433-2 □ ADD □ 74:07 mins □ 🎵🎵

A bracingly crisp and appealingly picturesque account of Beethoven's *Pastoral* Symphony from Karl Böhm and the Vienna Philharmonic. Taped, almost unbelievably, some 35 years ago, this account presents the work in pleasingly objective terms, without affectation or unwelcome mannerism, yet with a degree of warmth and genuine affection which is sadly at a premium nowadays. I doubt that even the most hardened modernist could listen to this performance without being profoundly moved by the experience. 'Pleasant Feelings upon Arriving in the Countryside' are rarely invoked with such anticipation and zest, the bird-song fragments at the close of 'By the Brook' are lovingly presented, and the peasants dance with stomping Teutonic gruffness. As the great deluge subsides, there is about Böhm's enunciation of the 'Shepherds' Hymn of Thanksgiving' a truly remarkable cathartic benediction which becomes more enraptured as, at the close, Beethoven is reluctant to abandon this idyllic vision. Böhm's reading is sublime and authoritative, and the Vienna Philharmonic plays magnificently for him. The filler on this DG Originals reissue (sound is radiantly expansive throughout, and now miraculously clear, too, thanks to digital reprocessing) is Böhm's 1971 performance of Schubert's Symphony No. 5 – another classic recording from DG's golden age. *MJ*

Symphony No. 9 in D minor (Choral)

Luba Orgonasova (soprano), Anne Sofie von Otter (mezzo-soprano), Anthony Rolfe Johnson (tenor), Gilles Cachemaille (bass); Monteverdi Choir, Orchestre Révolutionnaire et Romantique/John Eliot Gardiner

Archiv 447 074-2 □ 59:43 mins □ 🎵🎵🎵

John Eliot Gardiner's acclaimed traversal of the nine symphonies of Beethoven is crowned by an account of the *Choral* which, however radical and uncompromising it may at first appear, is nothing less than revelatory. Gardiner's approach is at once scholarly yet massively assertive and, in the last analysis, heaven-stormingly convincing. Tempi are predictably brisk; even the very opening will prove disconcerting if you've never experienced the Ninth outside the received Furtwängler–

Toscanini–Klemperer traditions on which the overwhelming mass of contemporary interpretations continue to be founded. There is about this entire performance the expected missionary zeal which Gardiner infuses into everything he directs; yet here, in Beethoven's greatest humanistic document, his response to the music is forged in the white heat of heroic spiritual affirmation, and the cumulative effect of this reading is overwhelming. He has an ideally balanced quartet of soloists, and the Monteverdi Choir are superbly drilled throughout the choral finale. Playing on instruments of the period, Gardiner's Orchestre Révolutionnaire et Romantique responds magnificently to the severe demands placed on it (the Scherzo is furiously propelled, and the notoriously difficult solo horn interjections of the Adagio sound totally assured, notwithstanding the presumably recalcitrant natural horn used in the recording). This majestically iconoclastic reading will, in all probability, alter your perceptions of the Ninth once and for all: it is, quite simply, the most challenging and uplifting recording of Beethoven's *Choral* Symphony to have appeared in decades. DG's 4-D technology results in exceptional clarity and dynamic range in this production, taped at All Saints' Church, Tooting, in October 1992. An indispensable Ninth, whose qualities should impel you to investigate the remainder of the Gardiner Beethoven cycle. *MJ*

Beethoven: Triple Concerto in C for Violin, Cello and Piano

Brahms: Double Concerto in A minor for Violin and Cello

David Oistrakh (violin), Mstislav Rostropovich (cello), Sviatoslav Richter (piano); Berlin PO/Herbert von Karajan, Cleveland Orchestra/George Szell

EMI Studio Plus CDM 7 64744 2 □ ADD □ 69:54 mins □ 🎵🎵

The multiple-instrument concertos by Beethoven and Brahms form an ideal CD package, and these performances are unrivalled elsewhere in the catalogues. The Soviet triumvirate of Oistrakh, Rostropovich and Richter give a noble and charismatic reading of Beethoven's Triple Concerto in C, a work which has come in for more than its share of critical censure over the years – and not without good reason, since it is manifestly not the equal of the composer's other concertos. It is, however, a creation of impressive proportions, offering ample scope for display to each of the soloists, who are also heard as an integral chamber group within the wider orchestral panorama. Herbert von Karajan is keenly responsive to the potential weaknesses of this score; Beethoven's text only partially overcomes the balance problems of juxtaposing three solo instruments with orchestra, making the conductor's role a critical factor if the piece is to register adequately. Karajan's rapport with his soloists and judicious control of his orchestral forces is masterful, and this extraordinary Soviet trio play gloriously, asserting their individual personalities and acting as a miraculously integrated unit. CD transfers are stunning, though there is a slight lack of warmth and immediacy in the case of the Cleveland performance of the Brahms Double Concerto under George Szell. Yet any slight sonic drawbacks seem trifling, given the fabulous performance by Oistrakh and Rostropovich; the bravura and the refinement of their playing are outstanding, and Szell's eloquent support makes their partnership the more telling and memorable. An indispensable addition to any collection. *MJ*

BEETHOVEN

Violin Concerto in D; Romances for Violin and Orchestra, Nos 1 in G & 2 in F

Henryk Szeryng (violin); Amsterdam Concertgebouw Orchestra/Bernard Haitink

Philips Solo 442 398-2 □ ADD □ 63:34 mins □ ⊘⊘

Henryk Szeryng's lordly, patrician and serene account of the Beethoven Violin Concerto, one of the greatest musical monuments of the Philips catalogue, will be remembered with reverence and affection as one of a handful of truly great recordings of the work. Now digitally revitalised, it emerges with renewed vitality and depth, with the unhurried splendour of Szeryng's playing seemingly more beautiful than before, and imbued with a ferocity and spiritual ardour which bespeaks his lofty and arrestingly eloquent manner with this great work. A hallmark of Szeryng's Beethoven was his lifelong espousal of the cadenzas by Joseph Joachim, a welcome and eloquent alternative to the familiar Kreisler offerings, and Szeryng ensures that they emerge as part of the organic unity of the entire work rather than as mere opportunities for virtuoso display. Bernard Haitink and the Concertgebouw Orchestra provide detailed and totally symbiotic accompaniments, and the general effect is one of rapt spiritual dialogue between soloist and orchestra,

rendered all the more palpable by the warmth and intimacy of the recording venue, the historic Concertgebouw hall, birthplace of so many bench-mark recordings on the Philips label. This disc is an exceptional bargain at mid-price, made the more irresistibly alluring for the inclusion of the two Romances. *MJ*

BERG

Lulu Suite
see **CHORAL & SONG**: WEILL: The Seven Deadly Sins

BERG

Violin Concerto; Three Pieces for Orchestra, Op. 6; Three Pieces from the Lyric Suite

Henryk Szeryng (violin); Bavarian RSO/Rafael Kubelík, Berlin PO/Herbert von Karajan

DG Classikon 439 435-2 □ ADD □ 63:21 mins □ ⊘⊘

Undoubtedly, the jewel in the crown in this exceptional compilation of Berg's orchestral works must be Henryk Szeryng's poetic account of the Violin Concerto. On first hearing, Szeryng might seem cool in comparison with the more emotionally overwrought Kyung-Wha Chung or Anne-Sophie Mutter, but both he and Kubelík find greater light and shade in this highly Romantic score than most interpreters. It's a pity, too, that the 1971 recording has a somewhat limited dynamic range, yet DG's engineers still achieve a satisfactory balance between soloist and orchestra. They are perhaps less successful in dealing with the high density of texture featured in the apocalyptic passages of the March from the Three Orchestral Pieces. But this hardly seems to matter given the fervour of Karajan's interpretation. These performances of Op. 6 and the *Lyric Suite* pieces also form part of Karajan's three-disc set of the Second Viennese School (see p323). *EL*

BERG

Violin Concerto
see also SCHOENBERG: Piano Concerto

BERLIOZ

Benvenuto Cellini Overture; Love Scene from Roméo et Juliette; La Damnation de Faust – Minuet of the Will-o'-the-Wisps, Dance of the Sylphs, Rakoczy March; Le corsaire Overture; Les troyens – Trojan March, Royal Hunt and Storm; La Marseillaise

Sylvia McNair (soprano), Richard Leech (tenor); boys choirs of St Michael and All Angels & St David's Episcopal Churches, Baltimore; Baltimore SO & Chorus/David Zinman

Telarc CD-80164 □ 73:52 mins □ ⊘⊘⊘

A useful disc containing Berlioz's most grandiloquent piece of patriotic ceremonial, his setting of Rouget de Lisle's ode to democracy, written at the height of the ferment of rebellion in 1830, and ever since France's national anthem, *La marseillaise*. This spectacular recording, in which David Zinman conducts massed choral forces, soloists and the Baltimore SO, is the concluding item of a brilliantly engineered Telarc release. The disc also includes the *Benvenuto Cellini* and *Le corsaire* overtures, in sonorous, technicolor performances of galvanic impulse and dramatic force. The substantial orchestral interludes from *Roméo et Juliette* and *Les troyens* are particularly impressive. Zinman's amorously inflected delicacy in the great love scene from *Roméo* draws richly saturated playing from the Baltimore strings, while, from *Les troyens*, the pomp and pageantry of the triumphant March which accompanies the wooden horse incident, following the Greeks' flight from their besieged Trojan garrison, is stirring. The *Royal Hunt and Storm*, which occurs at the start of Act IV, became virtually a symphonic poem after Berlioz detailed its progress microscopically in stage directions for the opera; David Zinman brings its programmatic details into sharp focus here. A majestically recorded disc, offering playing and singing of high calibre, in another memorable sonic spectacular from Telarc. *MJ*

BERLIOZ

Rêverie et caprice
see LALO: Symphonie espagnole

BERLIOZ

Symphonie fantasique; Le carnaval romain Overture; Le corsaire Overture; Harold en Italie; Symphonie funèbre et triomphale

Nobuko Imai (viola); John Alldis Choir, LSO/Colin Davis

Philips Duo 442 290-2 □ ADD □ 150:23 mins (2 discs) □ 𝄐𝄐

These definitive performances are from Colin Davis's pioneering Berlioz cycle for Philips. They are inspirational recordings that did much to bring Berlioz's output to international attention, and in large measure the spectacular, indomitably committed interpretations have never been eclipsed. Davis has an intuitive flair for theatre, nowhere more evident than in this fine account of the *Symphonie fantastique*, Berlioz's undisputed masterpiece for orchestra, a work that looked far into the future of western music and yet was written just three years after the death of Beethoven. It is an

electrifying reading, although the first disc of this Philips Duo issue also contains arresting accounts of the overtures *Le carnaval romain* and *Le corsaire*, with the LSO at the height of its powers under Davis's exacting direction. Disc two includes Nobuko Imai's outstanding *Harold en Italie*, recorded in 1975 and still probably the finest version available, and Berlioz's stirring tribute to the fallen of the July 1830 Paris uprising, the little-known, appropriately gargantuan *Symphonie funèbre et triomphale*, for massed wind band and chorus, with the optional string parts included in this account – the sombre trombone obbligato is gravely intoned by Denis Wick. These are exceptionally fine performances, and this double-disc mid-price offering is mandatory listening. *MJ*

BERLIOZ

Symphonie fantastique

Orchestre Révolutionnaire et Romantique/John Eliot Gardiner

Philips 434 402-2 □ 53:19 mins □ 𝄐𝄐𝄐

As John Eliot Gardiner points out in a thought-provoking introductory essay supplied with this disc, the desire to recapture something of the shocking originality of Berlioz's greatest creation, the *Symphonie fantastique* of 1830, was the driving force behind this performance, taped in the dry yet intimate surroundings of the old hall of the original Paris Conservatoire, where the work was premiered on 5 December 1830. If you know the symphony at all well, then this startling account will be nothing less than revelatory. Not only do the members of Gardiner's Orchestre Révolutionnaire et Romantique play on instruments of the period, but they also employ performing styles and orchestral seating familiar to the composer himself, and exhaustively researched for this unique project. This reading features the six harps specified in the score for 'Un bal', and cornets, ophicleides and serpent, plus numerous antique percussion instruments elsewhere, rekindling the paroxysms of astonishment which have reverberated throughout western music ever since this ground-breaking work appeared. Disclosure of one textual surprise after another is but one feature of this performance; the playing is stunningly vivid and intense, and will keep you in breathless anticipation from beginning to end – hear it, and the *Symphonie fantastique* will never seem the same again. At 53:19

minutes in total, this is short measure, but it is an indispensable release. *MJ*

BERNSTEIN

Symphonies Nos 1 (Jeremiah), 2 (The Age of Anxiety) & 3 (Kaddish); Chichester Psalms; Serenade after Plato's Symposium; Prelude, Fugue and Riffs

Jennie Tourel (mezzo-soprano), John Bogart (alto), Felicia Montealegre (speaker), Benny Goodman (clarinet), Philippe Entremont (piano), Zino Francescatti (violin); Camerata Singers, Columbus Boys Choir, Columbia Jazz Combo, New York PO/Leonard Bernstein

Sony SM3K 47162 □ ADD □ 162:00 mins (3 discs) □ 𝄞𝄞

This is the essential Bernstein commemorative set, drawing together Lennie's matchless performances of his three symphonies and other works, spread across three discs. A word concerning sound quality at the outset: not all of the fizz and top-end harshness of the original CBS LP masters has been tamed in these digitised CD transfers, so be prepared to make the required allowances. That prime caveat aside, these are readings of legendary authority and pertinence, since no other conductor has yet made out a comparable case for the Bernstein symphonies, and these accounts from the New York Philharmonic under the direction of the composer must be regarded as indispensable. The *Chichester Psalms* are heard here in Bernstein's original 1965 recording, and while sound on several more modern versions is understandably superior, there is something of a sense of occasion about this performance which has never been equalled. In addition, the street-wise vulgarity Bernstein brings to his only recording of *Prelude, Fugue and Riffs* is electrifying, though Zino Francescatti is certainly not in his element in the Serenade for violin and orchestra; an unhappily flawed performance from a soloist who clearly wasn't in sympathy with the work. As for the rest, it's nowhere less than stunning. *MJ*

BERWALD

Symphonies Nos 1 in G minor (Sinfonie sérieuse), 2 in D (Sinfonie capricieuse), 3 in C (Sinfonie singulière) & 4 in E flat

Gothenburg SO/Neeme Järvi

DG Masters 445 581-2 □ 111:08 mins (2 discs) □ 𝄞𝄞𝄞

Franz Berwald, founding father of the Swedish symphonic tradition, was born the year before Schubert, 1796, and died in 1868, just a year before Berlioz. His four remarkably progressive yet still neglected symphonies find their equilibrium somewhere between the early German Romantic style of Schumann and Mendelssohn and the mingled passion and dark-hued grandeur brought to bear upon Scandinavian music by later generations of composers, culminating with Nielsen and Sibelius. A figure of multi-faceted resourcefulness, Berwald managed a brickworks, sawmill and glass factory in the 1850s, and though lacking in formal education he was active as a polemicist on a wide range of social issues; he also founded an orthopaedic institute in Berlin (where he met Mendelssohn, who commented on his arrogant personality), and enjoyed brief success as a composer in Vienna.

Berwald's symphonies possess a verve and appealing charisma knowing few, if any, direct parallels. The imposing *Singulière* of 1845 is best known through Sixten Ehrling's 1968 LSO recording, though Järvi's Gothenburg players respond ardently to this work, and DG provides excellent recorded sound in these performances, recorded in the Gothenburg Konserthus in May 1985. Berwald's *Sinfonie capricieuse* and the last of his symphonies, No. 4 in E flat, are richly melodic and fresh, and reveal Mendelssohn's influence. The enigmatic diatribe of the First Symphony (*Sérieuse*) presages uncompromisingly Sibelian statements of this century. Neeme Järvi's advocacy of these engrossing works is potent and committed, while the Gothenburg SO plays magnificently throughout this valuable two-disc set. Robert Layton's insert notes are similarly erudite and entertaining. *MJ*

BIBER

Sonatas 1 & 10; Duets
see Collection: Baroque Trumpet Music

BIRTWISTLE

Earth Dances

BBC SO/Peter Eötvös

Collins 20012 □ 37:21 mins □ 𝄞

This CD single immortalises – in excellent sound – a 1991 Prom performance of one of Birtwistle's finest works, and one of the most impressive British orchestral scores of the Eighties. *Earth Dances* (1986) belongs ultimately, perhaps, to a very English tradition of quasi-pantheistic dark pastoral, an evocation of the inner life of landscape. Yet Birtwistle's approach is a mimesis of geological deep structures and seismic motion. The shifting interrelationships of up to six separate layers, defined by different hierarchies of intervals and, especially, by register from high to low, divide the orchestral gamut into superimposed strata, like the overlaid rock deposits of the earth. A welter of precise and highly original instrumental detail keeps the foreground in continuous, glinting, dancing activity, while in the background (and low in the bass) there's a quite different sense of motion: slow, glacial, inevitable. The overall result is monumentally impressive.

This performance (orchestra and conductor had played *Earth Dances* several times before) seems immensely assured, all the complexities mastered. *CM*

BIRTWISTLE

The Triumph of Time; Gawain's Journey

Philharmonia/Elgar Howarth

Collins 13872 □ 54:36 mins □ *② ② ②*

The Triumph of Time was the orchestral work of the Seventies which first brought Birtwistle out of the avant-garde ghetto and put his name before the wider concert-going public. Twenty years on, it retains its grim power. A grindingly slow processional taking its title from a Bruegel engraving, it is the perfect introduction to Birtwistle's thinking, as the musical objects are rolled past like a frieze, constantly presenting new perspectives and conjunctions. Boulez made a dark, menacing recording of *The Triumph of Time* in 1975 which has never reappeared on CD. Howarth's performance is smoother and less apocalyptic, yet guides the listener lucidly through the work's intricacies.

Gawain's Journey is a different animal altogether. The music is from his opera *Gawain*, first staged at Covent Garden in 1991 (a live recording is now itself available on Collins). Vocal lines have been absorbed into the orchestral texture and the disjuncted extracts knitted into a seamless sequence. It is no substitute for the full opera but makes a colourful orchestral showpiece, full of vivid images and dramatic effects, showing just how Birtwistle's craft has evolved in the two decades since *The Triumph of Time. Andrew Clements*

BIZET

Symphony in C; Jeux d'enfants; Scènes bohémiennes from La jolie fille de Perth

New Zealand SO/Donald Johanos

Naxos 8.553027 □ 59:08 mins □ *②*

Carmen Suite; L'arlesienne Suite No. 1; Symphony in C

Cincinnati SO/Jesús López-Cobos

Telarc CD-80224 □ 67:35 mins □ *② ② ②*

Jesús López-Cobos and the Cincinnati SO give a superbly idiomatic reading of the suite from Bizet's *Carmen*; the hot-blooded, strutting pomp of the Toreadors' March, and sultry, seductive intrigue of the Aragonaise are expertly portrayed in this performance. But there's more here than simply a review of the licentious sexuality of the opera in microcosm, for the technical quality of the orchestra's playing is memorable in itself, and López-Cobos, who has this music in his veins, is never reluctant to flesh out the numerous structural details of these extracts. His account of the Symphony in C is also admirable, and Telarc's high-tech digital sound is impressive. At budget price Donald Johanos and the New Zealand SO find a welcome variation on the regular couplings for the symphony, in *Jeux d'enfants* and the rarely played *Scènes bohémiennes*. The New Zealanders turn in solid, well-drilled performances under Johanos, and if the Naxos sonics don't quite match the range and outstanding clarity of the Teldec issue, you'd find very little at fault here, even at twice the asking price. *MJ*

BLACHER

Alla marcia; Dance Scenes; Chiarina; Partita
see Collection: Testimonies of War

BLOCH/ALBERT/BARTOK

Bloch: Schelomo

Stephen Albert: Cello Concerto

Bartók: Viola Concerto

Yo-Yo Ma (cello); Baltimore SO/David Zinman

Sony SK 57961 □ 78:04 mins □ *② ② ②*

Don't be deterred by the rather repellent title of this disc, *Yo-Yo Ma – The New York Album*; sure enough, various images of the cellist silhouetted against the Manhattan skyline are emblazoned across the liner notes, though links between the city and the music are actually a little tenuous. Still, hype sells records, and this is an exceptional one. Ernest Bloch's Hebrew Rhapsody *Schelomo* is a stunning work, based upon King Solomon's writings in the Book of Ecclesiastes: 'Vanity of vanities... I have seen all the works which are done under the sun, and behold, all is vanity and vexation of spirit.' Ma's account is shatteringly eloquent; the impassioned, improvisatory musings of a troubled monarch confronting the emptiness of human experience is starkly poignant. Ma receives outstanding orchestral support from Zinman and the Baltimore SO – there is simply no better recorded version than this. Also included here is the Cello Concerto written for Yo-Yo Ma by the New York-born composer Stephen Albert, who tragically lost his life in a car accident in 1992. Its inclusion is a fitting tribute to an uncanny, frequently enigmatic and profoundly soul-searching contemporary concerto, written in an accessible modern idiom. Yo-Yo Ma's account of Bartók's Viola Concerto, in Tibor Serly's realisation, is perhaps less satisfactory; he plays the work on a vertically held alto violin, of less than ideal sonority and power, though Ma's facility and daring are phenomenal. Here's the finest modern *Schelomo*, and a major addition to contemporary literature in the shape of Stephen Albert's fine Cello Concerto, in crystal-clear twenty-bit digital sound of amazing depth and amplitude – a must for all cello devotees. *MJ*

BLOCH/SEREBRIER

Bloch: Violin Concerto; Baal Shem

Serebrier: Momento psicologico; Poema elegiaca

Michael Guttman (violin); RPO/José Serebrier

ASV CD DCA 785 □ 67:00 mins □ 🕢🕢🕢

Ernest Bloch's noble, passionate and intensely evocative Violin Concerto is one of the more neglected of the great 20th-century concertos for the instrument, and recordings are few and far between. Yehudi Menuhin's classic 1963 account with Paul Kletzki is currently available on mid-price EMI, coupled with his perhaps too warmly lyrical reading of the Berg Concerto. Guttman, however, gives the Bloch a most spirited performance, full of dash and colour, wholly alive to the piece's spirit of voluble rhapsody and rugged landscape. He's equally good in the orchestral version of the *Baal Shem* Suite, and it's most satisfying to have both works in splendid modern sound. Conductor José Serebrier, an able accompanist here, is represented by two of his own compositions, comparatively slight in content, perhaps, but full of telling orchestral colour. *CM*

BOCCHERINI

Symphonies, Op. 12 (G503–8)

Deutsches Kammerakademie Neuss/Johannes Goritzki

CPO 999 172-2, 999 173-2 □ 69:00 mins, 55:00 mins □ 🕢🕢🕢

Boccherini's symphonies provide attractively diverting listening, and if there's little here to challenge or stimulate the intellect, there's still much to enjoy in the fertility and freshness of invention in these lively and wholly unostentatious works. These performances come from the series dubbed the 'complete' symphonies of Luigi Boccherini – a rather dubious claim, since it is not known just how many symphonies he actually wrote, nor how many have been lost over the years. Still, these discs are quite superb in every respect, and the players of the Deutsches Kammerakademie give a very fine account of themselves under the watchful leadership of Johannes Goritzki. Ensemble playing is tightly controlled and especially spirited in the faster movements, and this group of 21 musicians play with grace and style, although they use modern instruments throughout. Goritzki is not entirely faithful to the texts in every instance, and is prone to omit exposition repeats from time to time; in Op. 12/5 he excises a very lengthy portion of the first movement recapitulation for no apparent reason. But textual concerns and performing styles apart, these are fine performances, and recorded sound is consistently oi high quality. *MJ*

BORODIN
In the Steppes of Central Asia; Polovtsian Dances from Prince Igor
see also RIMSKY-KORSAKOV: Russian Easter Festival Overture

BORODIN
Polovtsian Dances from Prince Igor
see also RIMSKY-KORSAKOV: Sheherazade

BORODIN

Symphony No. 2 in B minor; In the Steppes of Central Asia; Prince Igor – Overture, Polovtsian March, Dance of the Polovtsian Maidens, Polovtsian Dances

John Alldis Choir; National PO/Loris Tjeknavorian

RCA VD 60535 □ ADD □ 64:10 mins □ 🕢🕢

Always spectacular in execution and recorded sound, rarely subtle, Tjeknavorian's Borodin showcase definitely has its heart in the right, leonine place. The doughty opening bars of the Second Symphony – a glittering complement to the epic world of *Prince Igor* –

announce a string section as weighty as that of any Russian orchestra: this is the long-defunct National Philharmonic, the conglomerate London super-band of the late Seventies and early Eighties.

The Polovtsian Dances, despite passing clumsiness in tempo-manoeuvres, prove demonstration worthy; and while Tjeknavorian does not reveal the individuality of phrasing that sets so distinctive a stamp on the conducting of Järvi (DG – investigate the inspirations of the other symphonies in the two-CD format if this appeals) or Rozhdestvensky (Chandos), he can generate a white-heat excitement rare in the studio. This is especially true of those two *Prince Igor* numbers supposedly reconstructed from memory by Glazunov after Borodin's death, the overture – its central adventure-sequence exceptionally keen and vivid – and the Polovtsian March. Never mind an early entry here from one of the chorus members; their presence, especially welcome in the dances, is a bonus that not every alternative version can offer. *DN*

BORODIN
Symphony No. 2; Notturno
see RIMSKY-KORSAKOV: Symphony No. 2

BOULEZ
Livre pour cordes
see **CHORAL & SONG**: BOULEZ: Pli selon pli

BOYCE

Symphonies, Op. 2

Academy of Ancient Music/Christopher Hogwood

L'Oiseau-Lyre 436 761-2 □ 60:45 mins □ 🎵🎵🎵

One of the factors that led to the emergence of the Classical symphony was the public's enjoyment of concerted instrumental music in operas, most notably their extended overtures. This disc clearly demonstrates the public's good taste: seven of Boyce's 'symphonies' began in the theatre, in odes, operas and a serenata, and eminently deserve to have been rescued as concert music.

Hogwood and the Academy of Ancient Music communicate wholeheartedly the music's intention to entertain. Opening Italianate Allegros and, in Symphonies Nos 5–8, French overtures are sometimes serious stuff – the passionate pulsing beginning of No. 3 is a striking example. No. 5, with splendid trumpets and drums, starts with a grand martial fanfare in echo.

The other movements, though, are sometimes self-consciously character pieces (a delightfully coloured unison of violins, violas

and bassoons, again in No. 3), sometimes utterly charming, lilting dances, and some boisterous rustic ones, such as the absurd 'Jigg' which ends No. 7.

Above all, Boyce could write a good tune. These symphonies are the very best of 18th-century easy listening. *GP*

BRAHMS
Double Concerto in A minor for Violin and Cello
see BEETHOVEN: Triple Concerto in C for Violin, Cello and Piano

---

BRAHMS

Piano Concerto No. 1 in D minor; Two Songs, Op. 91

Stephen Kovacevich (piano), Ann Murray (mezzo-soprano), Nobuko Imai (viola); LPO/Wolfgang Sawallisch

EMI CDC 7 54578 2 □ 59:28 mins □ 🎵🎵🎵

The idea of combining Kovacevich's accounts of the two Brahms piano concertos with a selection of his songs as fillers is an inspired one. Both concertos are desirable options for any collector seeking reliable performances in fine digital sound, but it is Kovacevich's searchingly impassioned account of the D minor Concerto which proves the more rewarding. This gripping, tempestuous and movingly elegiac work, whose opening movement began life as a sonata for two pianos before being incorporated into abortive sketches for a projected early symphony, provided both a requiem for Robert Schumann (the slow movement) and means of venting confused emotional angst occasioned by the young Brahms's repressed infatuation for Schumann's wife Clara, always his closest advocate and confidante. That such volcanic forces are conveyed in all their solemnity and gaunt power to the listener with no loss of cumulative drama and tension is very much to the credit of conductor Wolfgang Sawallisch. Stephen Kovacevich is on top form here; it is a pity, though, that the piano's first entry lacks a little in subtlety, partially the result of the focus and proximity of the otherwise breathtaking EMI engineering. We hear more of Kovacevich beyond his phenomenal piano-playing, and the occasional grunt and intake of breath underscore his concentration and utter absorption in the music. The confessional mood of the slow movement (Brahms headed the score with the Latin text *Benedictus qui venit in nomine Domini* – Blessed is he that cometh in the name of the Lord) is eloquent without becoming stodgy, and Sawallisch ensures that orchestral support is ideally blended and sustained, with fine playing, especially from the LPO first horn. The finale, a strutting Hungarian-style rondo with a lyrical counter-theme and much effective contrapuntal writing for the orchestra, is incisive and exuberant. The filler, performances of the Two Songs with viola obbligato, Op. 91, are touchingly sung by Ann Murray, with Kovacevich and violist Nobuko Imai, a splendid foil to this robust and compelling account of the Concerto in D minor, and another strong incentive to purchase this exceptionally fine issue. *MJ*

BRAHMS

Piano Concerto No. 2 in B flat

Alfred Brendel (piano); Berlin PO/Claudio Abbado

Philips 432 975-2 □ 49:00 mins □ 🎵🎵🎵

That Alfred Brendel's Philips version of Brahms's Second Piano Concerto will evolve into a performance of stirring and elevated proportions is evident from its very opening bars; the dialogue between solo horn and piano at the start has the kind of noble authority and intimacy which are fundamental requirements in the case of this work. Claudio Abbado directs the players of the Berlin Philharmonic with characteristic urgency, striving for and attaining a level of textural leanness and focus which makes Brahms's massive orchestral tuttis sound anything other than corpulent. Such welcome lightness, of course, facilitates greater intimacy in the exchanges between soloist and orchestra; despite its titanic canvas, what is effectively a four-movement symphony for piano and orchestra offers much more opportunity for meditative repose than many rival performances might suggest, and Brendel is as compelling in drawing the listener into this aspect of the work as he is in addressing its heroic and public content. The volcanically eruptive second movement, Allegro appassionato, is a maelstrom of orchestral and soloistic activity. Brendel and Abbado cut a spirited dash in the faster sections, though the hushed, contemplative Andante is pure balm. The cello solo (surely the finest in the orchestral literature) anticipates Brahms's song 'Immer leiser wird mein Schlummer', Op. 105/2, and is beautifully played here; Brendel, of course, is no less rapturous or involving, and the effect of this colloquy is deeply moving. The Sonata-Rondo finale, an ingenious series of highly original ideas moulded into a cohesive and convincing whole, is magnificently played, and Alfred Brendel's account of this concerto, an ideal

technical and intellectual traversal of a mammoth work, has been superbly captured by the Philips engineers. Incidentally, collectors hoping to locate a high-quality performance at mid-price should seek out the DG Galleria reissue of Maurizio Pollini's 1977 Vienna performance, also with Abbado. This, too, is piano-playing of the highest order; the performance has exceptional authority and dignity, and DG's remastered sonics are admirable. *MJ*

BRAHMS

Piano Concertos Nos 1 & 2
see also **INSTRUMENTAL:** BRAHMS: Piano Pieces, Op. 76

BRAHMS

Serenades Nos 1 in D & 2 in A

Westdeutsche Sinfonia/Dirk Joeres

IMP PCD 2046 □ 79:00 mins □ 🎵

Although composed when Brahms was only in his twenties, these two serenades cannot be lightly dismissed as mere apprentice works. It's true that both are strongly indebted to earlier masters. The spirit of Beethoven certainly hovers over the rustic first movement of the D major, and it's possible to detect Schubert's influence in the tender lyricism of the minuet of the A major. But there's much too that's entirely characteristic, not least the deeply ruminative slow movements and the dashing gypsy rhythms of both finales.

Many conductors, including Kertész and Haitink, tend to view both works as putative symphonies, thereby inflating their emotional message way beyond Brahms's initial intentions. A more intimate approach is adopted by Dirk Joeres, and his musically sensitive interpretations serve to remind us that despite their orchestral scoring these works remain essentially chamber music. His orchestra responds magnificently to this approach, and the combination of a 1992 recording, generous playing time (even though I must admit to regretting that there's no room for the exposition repeat in the first movement of the D major) and bargain price makes this an irresistible release. *EL*

BRAHMS

Symphonies Nos 1–4; Variations on a Theme of Haydn (St Antoni Chorale); Tragic Overture; Academic Festival Overture

Chicago SO/Daniel Barenboim

Erato 4509-94817-2 □ 212:00 mins (4 discs) □ 🎵🎵🎵

The Chicagoans have recorded the complete Brahms symphonies previously for Decca, under Georg Solti, fine as it was, the cycle is now largely superseded by these outstanding recent accounts from Daniel Barenboim, who succeeded Solti as the orchestra's music director in September 1991. The new Erato discs are resplendently engineered, and the fizz and top-heavy brilliance of the Chicago sound of previous years has given way to something more discernibly European in character. The string-playing has opulence and charisma, and Barenboim draws plush, expansive sonorities from the exceptional woodwinds and brass of this world-beating band. He also gives emphatic notice of his attributes as a Brahmsian of high distinction. These are finely-honed and intuitive readings of the symphonies; Nos 1 and 4 emerge as massive, spectacular and powerfully confrontational, with the triumph of the C minor work sealed with memorable grandeur, and the E minor assuming proper tragic status. Barenboim is more relaxed and naturally expressive in the central pair of symphonies, though there is never any lack of weight or gravity when needed. Erato offers substantial benefits in the form of superb performances of the Haydn Variations and the two overtures. Should completeness be a required virtue in addition to playing and recording of exemplary finesse, don't hesitate to purchase this Erato boxed set. *MJ*

Brahms: Symphony No. 1 in C minor

Schumann: Symphony No. 1 in B flat (Spring)

Berlin PO/Herbert von Karajan

DG Originals 447 408-2 □ ADD □ 76:30 mins □ 🎵🎵

Brahms was 43 years of age when his First Symphony was premiered under Otto Dessoff in Karlsruhe. At long last, he had been able to lay aside feelings of pathological self-doubt occasioned by an enduring admiration for Beethoven ('You've no idea how it feels to hear the footsteps of that giant behind you,' he lamented to Clara Schumann), giving the world a worthy successor to the master's nine symphonies in the process. In truth, the popular description of Brahms's C minor Symphony as 'Beethoven's Tenth' has more than a grain of truth about it, for there is some similarity between the stirring Allegro theme of the finale and Beethoven's setting of Schiller's ode, the culmination of his *Choral* Symphony. Long in gestation, yet powerful and immediate in effect, Brahms's First was

aptly likened by Rosa Newmarch to 'strong wine left to lie upon the lees for many years'. Its epic spirit and Beethovenian symbolism remain undiminished, and Herbert von Karajan's 1964 Berlin recording is of exceptional quality. Karajan addressed this score wilfully; there's a lean austerity about his approach which makes the opening movement seem unusually forbidding. The slow movement is gorgeously phrased and projected, though the transformation from tragedy to triumph, as the horn announces the great chorale theme of the finale, is resplendently managed. This exceptional Berlin performance shrugs aside its considerable vintage (the coupling, an admirable reading of Schumann's *Spring* Symphony is more recent) in a remarkably vivid CD transfer in the DG Originals series, and this mid-price reissue confidently retains its place in the catalogue – don't miss it. *MJ*

Symphony No. 2 in D; Academic Festival Overture

New York Philharmonic/Kurt Masur

Teldec 9031-77291-2 □ 50:00 mins □ 🎵🎵🎵

Kurt Masur's watchful and devoted direction secures a radiant, fulsome and outstandingly well-played response from the New York Philharmonic, which sounds every inch a great ensemble in this superb recording. Indeed, string-playing of such warmth and grace would not be outshone in Vienna or Berlin, and with incisive brass and characterful woodwind contributions to match, Masur's is a Brahms Second well able to hold its own in illustrious company. Ever the articulate and thoroughgoing intellectual among composers, Masur brings out the sunny lyricism of this work (it is the least rhetorical and impassioned of the Brahms symphonies) with a rapture and jubilance which are in themselves strongly appealing attributes. But there is also rigour and resolve where needed; just listen to the tension mount, then dissipate in the development of the otherwise unclouded opening movement. And how gloriously the New York cellos announce the burgeoning main idea of the Adagio, as Masur demands the utmost refinement and sensitivity from his players. Yet however subtly nuanced and outwardly deliquescent the performance may seem, Masur invests the finale with superb dramatic thrust, and the final culmination is overwhelmingly triumphant. The filler, the *Academic Festival Overture*, is equally impressive; Masur treats this assemblage of student songs, which climaxes with a majestic orchestral setting of 'Gaudeamus igitur', with straightforward deliberateness, but there's no bombast or pomposity despite the splendours of the New York Philharmonic brass-playing. Teldec obtains first-class sound in the acoustically refurbished Avery Fisher Hall, and you'll search at length for finer, more accomplished readings than these. *MJ*

BRAHMS

Symphony No. 3 in F; Alto Rhapsody

Jard van Nes (contralto); Tanglewood Festival Chorus, Boston SO/Bernard Haitink

Philips 442 120-2 □ 53:32 mins □ *ⓐⓐⓐ*

Bernard Haitink's assured musicianship and fresh unambiguous approach to Brahms interpretation makes his recording of the Third Symphony an especially attractive proposition. Haitink is brisk, urgent and objective: valuable attributes, surely, in this most elusive and personal of the four Brahms symphonies, where ardent, virile emotionalism so often defers to enigmatic radiance. The soaring opening phrases following the heroically aspirant wind chords which begin the work find the Boston SO's massed violins in spectacular form. Haitink charts his course with easy grace, no lack of either warmth or eloquence, and complete lack of affectation. The motto theme (the composer's musical monogram 'Frei aber froh' – Free but joyful) is enshrined in the rising F–A flat–F motif which begins the symphony. The idea (an optimistic response to Joachim's motto 'Frei aber einsam' – Free but solitary) itself has true heraldic grandeur, and Haitink sees to it that, by the end of the work, its character has become autumnally submissive, while its architectural status seems inexpressibly enhanced. This is a Brahms Third of noble serenity and plausible spiritual affirmation, magnificently played by the Boston SO; the songful cellos and plangent solo horn in the Allegretto are particularly memorable. Haitink is as his finest in the finale, where his superbly paced and structured reading assuages the unresolved tensions of the work in a ravishingly beautiful coda. As a filler, Jard van Nes and the excellent Tanglewood chorus join the BSO in a strongly idiomatic and satisfying performance of the *Alto Rhapsody*. As ever, Haitink's selflessly unadorned and unfailingly attentive direction scores highly, and this splendid disc merits emphatic recommendation. Also worth considering is the DG issue from Abbado and the Berliners, who provide a somewhat more prosaic, bracing account of the symphony, less telling than Haitink's at climactic points, and slightly better value for money with two generous fillers, the *Tragic Overture* and *Song of Destiny*. *MJ*

BRAHMS

Symphony No. 4 in E minor

Vienna PO/Carlos Kleiber

DG 400 037-2 □ 39:34 mins □ *ⓐⓐⓐ*

Alongside Tchaikovsky's *Pathétique* and Mahler's Sixth, the E minor Fourth Symphony of Johannes Brahms is one of the greatest essays in symphonic tragedy. You'll find no better arbiter of the work than Carlos Kleiber, who directs the Vienna Philharmonic in this legendary 1981 performance, at once austere, uncompromising and thrilling in its urgency yet imbued with a touching degree of pathos and vulnerability. Brahms composed his last symphony during the summer of 1885; the work is curiously paradoxical, even Janus-like, in its portrayal of apparent opposites, juxtaposing massive affirmation and optimism with a vision of intractable fatalistic negation. That's the underlying message of the searching passacaglia which ends the symphony; Carlos Kleiber's inexhaustibly vehement treatment of these thirty variations over a repeated ground-bass displays an intellectual prodigality and dramatic cohesion that leaves the listener stunned by the close. The playing of the Vienna Philharmonic is beyond criticism; the slow movement is profoundly eloquent, and the life-asserting Scherzo, an attempt to rekindle a spirit of optimism and find some measure of assurance despite the implacable intervention of fate, has fine gusto and electricity. Normally, I'd resist fiercely the purchase of any full-priced CD offering just 39 minutes of music, but there is simply no better Brahms Fourth available, and this monolithic, overwhelmingly powerful performance is unlikely to be displaced. This is an essential modern classic, and one that demands to be heard. *MJ*

BRAHMS

Violin Concerto in D

Itzhak Perlman (violin); Berlin PO/Daniel Barenboim

EMI CDC 7 54580 2 □ 40:00 mins □ *ⓐⓐⓐ*

Itzhak Perlman's digital version of Brahms's Violin Concerto, recorded in Berlin in 1992, is a worthy successor to his justly celebrated

Chicago Symphony performance, taped in 1976 and still available on CD from EMI. While Perlman's view of the work, the finest and most popular of a lengthy series of compositions for the great violin virtuoso Joseph Joachim, has altered little during the intervening years, the new recording is impressively spacious and the dynamic range is vast, with none of the shrillness at fortissimo climaxes that was noticeable in the previous Chicago version. Daniel Barenboim's orchestral accompaniments are a degree less purposeful than Giulini's, whose unduly ponderous opening tempo made one wonder how the soloist would manage to sustain any protracted dialogue without the performance foundering disastrously. The fact that it didn't seems remarkable in retrospect, and such are its glories (Chicago oboist Ray Still's solo in the slow movement still lingers in the memory) that one can only criticise the earlier EMI performance on the grounds of its rather fierce sound. Yet this recent Berlin version has pretty well everything that one might wish for in any reading of the Brahms concerto. Perlman's playing is incomparably beautiful, and his entire performance has been marvellously thought out in every detail. The opening movement is broad and serene, the middle movement lyrically charged, and the exuberant Hungarian-style finale displays Perlman's fabulous virtuosity to great effect. Orchestral playing and recorded sound are also superb, and this is definitely not to be missed. *MJ*

BRIAN

Symphonies Nos 7 in C & 31; The Tinker's Wedding Overture

Royal Liverpool PO/Charles Mackerras

EMI CDM 7 64717 2 □ 63:12 mins □ ⊘⊘

The best-played and perhaps best-recorded collection of Havergal Brian's music yet available, this splendid EMI issue is largely devoted to Symphony No. 7 (1948), the last of Brian's really large-scale symphonies but already presaging the more elliptical techniques of his later ones. Inspired by Goethe's autobiography and the cathedral city of Strasbourg, Brian described it (to me) as 'an English symphony on a German subject, much as *Hamlet* is an English play on a Danish subject'; in fact this is one of the most immediately and attractively 'English' in accent of his mature works. With its plethora of fanfare and bells, brooding slow movement and heroic march-finale, it's a complex,

gripping and beautiful musical drama. The *Tinker's Wedding* Overture, after JM Synge, dates from the same year and makes a breezy, colourful opener to the disc. Symphony No. 31 – composed, incredibly, at the age of 92 – is a taut, elliptically inventive single-movement structure, like a polyphonic fantasy for orchestra. Mackerras expounds all three works with a sure sense of structure and atmosphere; the RLPO plays heroically, and the recording is very fine indeed. *CM*

BRIAN

Violin Concerto; Symphony No. 18; The Jolly Miller (Comedy Overture)

Marat Bisengaliev (violin); BBC Scottish SO/Lionel Friend

Marco Polo 8.223479 □ 54:39 mins □ ⊘⊘⊘

Havergal Brian's Violin Concerto, completed in 1935, is one of the most challenging in the repertoire. Rewritten from one composed (and then irretrievably lost) in the previous year, it's on a heroic, symphonic scale, with a powerful set of passacaglia variations for the slow movement. The virtuoso solo part makes phenomenal technical demands, pitted against a large orchestra in a polyphonic idiom that often deliberately threatens the violin. Struggle is endemic to the piece, which ends in a march from which the violin drops out entirely. Yet it's a thrilling work, extending Elgarian tradition, with some of Brian's most memorable themes, and whether 'for' or 'against' the violin it's written with a sovereign knowledge of the instrument's capabilities.

The young Khazakh Marat Bisengaliev believes totally in this concerto, and it shows. His stunningly assured performance is excellently partnered by the conducting of Lionel Friend, one of Brian's contemporary champions. Friend's advocacy benefits the tough and pithy 18th Symphony, which finds Brian conjuring a big sound from an almost Beethoven-sized orchestra; he is equally good in the delightfully capricious little overture, structured as a set of variations on a well-known folk-tune, which displays Brian's dangerously humorous tendencies. The recording is one of Marco Polo's best. *CM*

BRIDGE

Phantasm
see IRELAND: Piano Concerto

BRIDGE

There is a Willow Grows Aslant a Brook
see Collection: The Banks of Green Willow

Cello Symphony: Sinfonia da requiem; Cantata misericordium

Mstislav Rostropovich (cello), Peter Pears (tenor), Dietrich Fischer-Dieskau (baritone); English CO, New Philharmonia Orchestra, LSO & Chorus/Benjamin Britten

Decca London 425 100-2 □ ADD □ 74:36 mins □ 🕮🕮

This coupling of two of Britten's most important orchestral works in authoritative readings from the composer, recorded with marvellous clarity by Decca's engineers, would be difficult to surpass. Indeed, few conductors match Britten in sustaining emotional tension through the long paragraphs of the opening 'Lacrymosa' movement of the *Sinfonia da requiem*, and then unleashing such a torrent of anger in the central Dies irae section. Similarly, the premiere recording of the Cello Symphony, composed especially for Rostropovich, finds the great Russian cellist probing deep beneath the surface of this emotionally elusive music, the bleakness of much of the argument finding incisive support from the English CO. The *Cantata misericordium*, dating from the same period as the Cello Symphony and drawing its inspiration from the parable of the Good Samaritan, works on a lower musical plane, but its concluding plea for love and charity to overcome the ravages of disease and war still makes a poignant impact, particularly in this fine performance. *EL*

BRITTEN
Sinfonia da requiem
see also **CHORAL & SONG**: BRITTEN: War Requiem

BRITTEN

Variations on a Theme of Frank Bridge; Simple Symphony; Prelude and Fugue

Northern Sinfonia of England/Richard Hickox

ASV CD DCA 591 □ 50:25 mins □ 🕮🕮🕮

Although this disc offers somewhat short measure in comparison with a more generous and highly rated collection of Britten's string orchestral works from the Norwegian Chamber Orchestra on Virgin, few conductors generate the same degree of urgency and physical impact from the music as Richard Hickox. Admittedly, these characteristics may be somewhat exaggerated in ASV's rather cavernous recording, but it would be equally misleading to suggest that the performances don't manage to embrace repose where necessary. Indeed, not even the composer is

able to move the heart to the same degree as Hickox in the Funeral March and Chant of the Frank Bridge Variations. Elsewhere, I find myself relishing Hickox's bustling energy in the outer movements of the *Simple Symphony*, not to mention his capacity for making the 18-part Prelude and Fugue seem to be a more substantial statement than I had ever imagined. *EL*

The Young Person's Guide to the Orchestra; Suite on English Folk Tunes; Johnson over Jordan; Four Sea Interludes from Peter Grimes

Bournemouth SO/Richard Hickox

Chandos CHAN 9221 □ 66:54 mins □ 🕮🕮🕮

Once again Richard Hickox demonstrates his effectiveness as an interpreter of Britten's music. Throughout this disc, one experiences the feeling that each familiar phrase has been invented anew, the net result being a freshness of delivery that prevents the listener from ever taking the music for granted. As one might expect, this is particularly welcome in *The Young Person's Guide*, where the more brilliant variations and the concluding fugue are dispatched with youthful energy and enthusiasm by the Bournemouth SO. Energy, indeed, is a key word here, for nobody rivals Hickox for the sheer savagery of attack that he generates in the fourth of the *Sea Interludes* from *Peter Grimes*. The earlier movements in this masterpiece don't quite operate on the same level of intensity, and, of recent performances, Leonard Slatkin with the Philharmonia on RCA offers a more imaginative conception. But my allegiance to Hickox remains steadfast, particularly as Chandos's recording is truly outstanding, and the disc also includes a fascinating glimpse of a lesser-known aspect of Britten's work in the form of the suite of his incidental music to JB Priestley's 1939 play *Johnson over Jordan. EL*

Violin Concerto No. 1 in G minor; Scottish Fantasy

Cho-Liang Lin (violin); Chicago SO/Leonard Slatkin

Sony SK 42315 □ 53:00 mins □ 🕮🕮🕮

Bruch's First Violin Concerto is one of the perennials of the repertoire, and for good reason. It's passionate, declamatory character, virtuosic potential, and above all else its superabundant tunefulness (did Richard Strauss knowingly quote its slow movement in his *Alpine Symphony*?) have earned it a special place in the affections of all music lovers. While the endearing *Scottish Fantasy* was a work that Heifetz made very much his own (his radiantly moving account is available on RCA), it, too, has been unjustly marginalised by the G minor Violin Concerto. Cho-Liang Lin performs both works on this 1987 Sony disc with flawless virtuosity and sustained expressive warmth. Though his playing is always beautifully tender and affecting, there's no recourse to self-indulgent wallowing or excessive sentiment, and the concerto, in particular, adopts the heroic stance that its composer surely envisaged. Lin's performance of the *Scottish Fantasy* is exceptionally brilliant, yet imaginative and, where appropriate, pliantly introspective. These are readings of exceptional finesse and tonal refinement, very sensitively accompanied by Slatkin and the Chicago SO. The coupling is a welcome departure from the over-familiar Bruch/Mendelssohn pairing, and recorded sound is invitingly atmospheric. *MJ*

<hr>

BRUCH/GOLDMARK

Bruch: Violin Concerto No. 2 in D minor

Goldmark: Violin Concerto No. 1 in A minor

Nai-Yuan Hu (violin); Seattle Symphony/Gerard Schwarz

Delos DE 3156 □ 60:23 mins □ 🎵🎵🎵

Here are two fine Romantic violin concertos, in adroit, musically sophisticated readings and exceptional sound. The soloist here is the Taiwanese virtuoso Nai-Yuan Hu, who plays magnificently throughout this beautifully produced disc, devoted to two rarities of the repertoire. Max Bruch's Violin Concerto in D minor is an imposing affair, at once more resolute and severe than its predecessor. Its opening movement is grippingly intense, while the finale is quite as bracing and virile as that of its G minor sibling. Fine as it is, Perlman's EMI recording of the work offers the predictable *Scottish Fantasy* as a coupling; it is a splendid option, of course, though the alternative from Delos is of considerably greater interest.

Karl Goldmark, the self-made son of an impoverished Hungarian cantor, lived between 1830 and 1915 and brushed shoulders with many of the most influential musical personalities of his epoch. A quintessential Romanticist, Goldmark's delightful *Rustic Wedding* Symphony was a Beecham favourite, though you'll search long and hard to hear it in the concert hall today. Similarly, his superb Violin Concerto in A minor has long since

fallen foul of today's violin virtuosi though, as Nai-Yuan Hu's expert espousal demonstrates, for absolutely no clear reason. Hu's readings are polished and cultured, and above all else his fine musicianship is instantly compelling; one can only hope that issues of this stature will win increasing popularity for these colourful and brilliant concertos. The Seattle Symphony and Gerard Schwarz accompany magnificently, and sonics are of demonstration quality. *MJ*

<hr>

BRUCH

Scottish Fantasy; Violin Concerto No. 1
see also VIEUXTEMPS: Violin Concerto No. 5

<hr>

BRUCKNER

Symphonies Nos '0'–9

Amsterdam Concertgebouw Orchestra/Bernard Haitink

Philips 442 040-2 □ ADD □ 592:00 mins (9 discs) □ 🎵🎵

Bernard Haitink's Concertgebouw Bruckner cycle was an illustrious and compelling undertaking, recorded between 1966 and 1972. The performances themselves are as impressive as ever, older collectors will remember the best of them with affection, and even the more workaday accounts of the problematic early works never disappoint. The recent CD transfers have done much to improve the richness and focus of the admittedly creditable analogue LP sound, imparting added breadth and clarity to Bruckner's textures without sacrificing the celebrated resonance of the Concertgebouw hall in which these Philips recordings were made. The symphonies (including No. '0') are comfortably housed on nine CDs, and as a mid-price compendium of Anton Bruckner's symphonic *oeuvre* this set is very hard to equal in terms of value for money and not easy to eclipse on musical grounds. There's much to admire in Haitink's diligent advocacy of the early works, none of which enjoys the currency they truly deserve. Symphonies Nos 5, 6 and 7 are magnificently done, while the justly famed versions of the Eighth and Ninth will stand comparison with the finest rival versions available. If you have the chance to sample the set before purchasing it, try Haitink's performance of Symphony No. 4 (the *Romantic*); this is Bruckner interpretation that's as solidly based on common sense as one could wish, and the quality of the Concertgebouw playing is outstandingly good. Probably the finest moderately priced option for those seeking a comprehensive traversal of the Bruckner symphonies. Strongly recommended. *MJ*

Symphony No. 4 in E flat (Romantic)

San Francisco Symphony/Herbert Blomstedt

Decca 443 327-2 □ 67:30 mins □ 😊😊😊

Herbert Blomstedt's account of Bruckner's *Romantic* Symphony is masterfully characterised. At the outset, one does not so much witness a beginning as become aware (through a soft shimmer of violin tremolando and a misty invocation from the solo horn) that the music has started to evolve. The effect is breathtaking, and Blomstedt re-creates precisely the atmosphere that Bruckner intended us to experience. The title *Romantic* was Bruckner's own; this is the only named Bruckner symphony, and though poetic and fanciful notions of dewy forest dawns and proud knights riding forth to expedite deeds of chivalry and virtue might well have helped the work on its way, Bruckner's descriptive efforts were at best a rather glib attempt to ally himself with the progressive Wagnerian musical *Zeitgeist*. But the strength and vision of Blomstedt's reading renders programmatic pointers utterly superfluous. The broad tempo of the opening movement allows the music to unfold at its own natural pace; the mighty brass chorales resound impressively, and the warmth and pliancy of string textures is ideally idiomatic. The coda is arresting, not least for the majesty of the San Francisco horns at the close, and the succeeding Andante, a subdued cello-led oration, is deeply felt and affectingly nuanced. The Scherzo, one of Bruckner's characteristic 'hunting' excursions, typifies Blomstedt's approach to Bruckner; there is fire, but also iron resolve and purpose, attributes that pay clear dividends here. The finale, always difficult to project convincingly because Bruckner's sense of design is less reassuringly complete than elsewhere in the symphony, responds to alert, quick-witted and objective leadership, and Blomstedt is magnificent, sustaining the logic of a musical argument that's as diverse and eruptive as any in Bruckner's output, and reserving the greatest revelations for the coda. This outstanding performance has been exceptionally well recorded by Decca, and it serves as a summary reminder of Blomstedt's achievements in raising the San Francisco Symphony to international stature. Blomstedt in Bruckner, bywords for excellence. *MJ*

Symphony No. 5 in B flat; Te Deum

Karita Mattila (soprano), Susanne Mentzer (mezzo-soprano), Vinson Cole (tenor), Robert Holl (bass); Bavarian Radio Chorus, Vienna PO/Bernard Haitink

Philips 422 342-2 □ 101:11 mins (2 discs) □ 😊😊😊

Bruckner never heard a note of his mighty Fifth Symphony (1875–8) in orchestral performance. Already too ill to attend the premiere in Graz in April 1894, he experienced one of his greatest, most spiritually affirmative creations only once, when it was played privately in a two-piano reduction in Vienna in 1887. The canvas of the symphony is vast, its epic panorama embracing broad emotions and a striving after eternal truth which was very much Bruckner's musical *via crucis*. Its sound-world is unlike that of its fellows; each movement begins with a pizzicato tread in the bass, and the re-gathering of the symphony's main ideas at the start of the finale carries echoes of Beethoven's *Choral* Symphony, as the various ideas are explored then rejected. The D minor Adagio runs deep, exploring the profundity of belief in forces beyond our comprehension, while the mood of the Scherzo, in the same key, ranges from one of abject terror to archaic simplicity. Yet it is the finale which proves decisive, for it is an expression of the majesty of faith and the assurance derived from the Christian experience which suffuses Bruckner's entire output. Bernard Haitink's performance with the Vienna Philharmonic is the finest I've ever heard, either on disc or in the concert hall. His clarity of vision, intuitive management of long-term thematic and tempo-related issues, and above all else his monumental conviction give his traversal of this symphony elasticity and incomparable visionary power. The concluding paragraphs are unbelievably magnificent: the great chorale cross-member which finally clinches Bruckner's discourse resounds heavenwards. With an outstanding account of the Te Deum as a filler, one could scarcely ask for more. The Philips recording is vivid and naturally balanced and, in this world at least, I don't expect to encounter a more cogently directed, better played Bruckner Fifth. *MJ*

Symphony No. 7 in E

New York Philharmonic/Kurt Masur

Teldec 4509-97437-2 □ 63:28 mins □ 😊😊😊

This performance of Anton Bruckner's Seventh Symphony formed part of Kurt Masur's inaugural concert as music director of the New York Philharmonic on 13 September 1991. No stranger to the piece, Masur directs a reading of searching depth and rich atmosphere, and, while many of the thirty-odd recordings in the current catalogues have commendable qualities, there is about this version a palpable sense of occasion and anticipation which communicates itself readily to the listener. The live Avery Fisher Hall recording is unexpectedly good; audience noise is so minimal as to be insignificant, and the playing of the New York Philharmonic is of world class. Like most of Bruckner's symphonies, the Seventh is summoned into being through an expectant haze of tremolando violins, before cellos and horn announce the soaring, aspiring main idea of the opening movement. The pious, naïve, eternally self-critical Bruckner maintained that the theme came to him during a dream, and the sonority of the orchestra's playing is hugely impressive. Masur's easy progression towards the second subject group is effortlessly accomplished. The C sharp minor Adagio, an inconsolably elegiac funeral ode, an outpouring of Bruckner's grief upon contemplating the imminent death of Richard Wagner, brings a quartet of Wagner tubas into the orchestra for the first time in a Bruckner symphony; Masur's reading of the movement is deeply moving, and he wisely excises the ugly cymbal clash at the climax, added by a compliant Bruckner at Nikisch's suggestion though not found in the original manuscript. Following an electrifying Scherzo, Masur and the orchestra conclude with a mighty, tautly argued finale. Masur is never a conductor to play to the gallery; there is no scene-stealing or vulgar antics here, and his interpretative rhetoric impels this thoroughly reasoned and logical performance to a titanic and uplifting climax, as the 'dream' motif from the start blazes out across the texture during the coda. A magnificent Bruckner Seventh, admirably played and recorded, well able to stand beside any in the catalogues. *MJ*

BRUCKNER

Symphony No. 8 in C minor

NDR SO/Günter Wand

RCA Victor Red Seal 09026 68047 2 □ 87:52 mins (2 discs for the price of one) □ ❸❸❸

Bruckner's mighty Eighth Symphony has been remarkably well served on disc during recent

years, and there are good grounds for hearing rival accounts by Herbert von Karajan and Daniel Barenboim before electing to purchase one or possibly several of these recommendations. Günter Wand's live Hamburg performance is altogether exceptional, combining qualities of assured insight and maturity with a devotional and scholarly approach to the music. The RCA recording replaces Wand's previous Lübeck Cathedral recording, also with the North German RSO – impressive in its way (when has Wand failed to illuminate in Bruckner?) but impossibly reverberant. Then comes Karajan's 1988 recording with the Vienna PO (DG), his very last appearance before the microphones. This is a sound document of massive valedictory symbolism, majestically played and recorded, and a triumphant summation of a lifetime of achievement. Now these octogenarian master conductors are joined by Daniel Barenboim (Teldec); his approach is perhaps more arcane and urgent (that much is reflected in the fact that his performance fits on just one CD, and represents a substantial cost-saving over Wand or Karajan), yet masterfully clear-sighted and played with utmost distinction and finesse by the Berlin PO. All three conductors favour the Robert Haas edition of Bruckner's 1890 score. The rival Nówak version, with its unseemly cuts and amendments, can be confidently overlooked on these grounds alone. (Should you wish to sample it, the DG Masters two-disc reissue of Carlo Maria Giulini's 1985 Vienna account certainly won't disappoint.) If you see Bruckner's Eighth as a musical rite of spiritual re-affirmation, don't hesitate to obtain the Wand performance. It's masterfully conceived and executed, and the playing (it is, in fact, Günter Wand's third commercial recording of the work) is admirable, though fractionally less polished and distinctive than that of the Vienna PO under Karajan. His is a performance close to my heart, and for reasons other than just its posthumous associations. Karajan's marshalling of the symphony's main themes at the close of the work is wholly unrivalled, and the Vienna playing is incomparably radiant throughout. Barenboim is excellent too, and the impetus and confrontational drama that unfolds throughout the symphony is especially compelling, while the recording itself has superb clarity and vast dynamic range. Günter Wand's traversal should meet the needs of even the most demanding Bruckner enthusiast, and his version is, in the last analysis, the one I'd nominate as probably the finest, most completely satisfying of three strong contenders. *MJ*

Symphony No. 9 in D minor

Chicago SO/Georg Solti

Decca 417 295-2 □ 61:02 mins □ 𝄞𝄞𝄞

Gaunt and agonisingly pained, Bruckner's Ninth Symphony was the culmination of a spiritual journey tragically curtailed by the intervention of frailty and affliction. He began the work just two days after the completion of the first version of the Eighth Symphony, in August 1887, yet it remained unfinished (the seemingly random and disjunctive sketches for the finale have been reconstructed by William Carragan) and is generally played in its extant three-movement form. Gone are the thunderous spiritual assertions of its predecessors, to be replaced by formidable destructive power; the crippling dissonance at the climax of the Adagio brings us face to face with all the forces of negation and catastrophe which Bruckner's visionary faith had all but exorcised from his previous symphonies. Then consider the message behind the massive, utterly implacable opening movement, seared by a spiritual isolation which is the very nadir of all that has gone before, or the titanic Scherzo, which unleashes the forces of juggernaut-like inevitability. Georg Solti and the Chicago SO play the work with utmost commitment and authority, and their 1986 recording is technically beyond reproach. The angst of the opening movement is palpably conveyed, yet there are moments of serene realisation too, notably in the broad second episode, with radiant playing from the violins in their soaring, rapturous theme. Solti has kept volcanic forces in check for the coda, where the brass choir intone the principal ideas with awesome gravity. The Scherzo is enervated and motoric; its impact, however, is venomous. The searching E major Adagio moves towards optimism and restitution, but it is not to be; any surviving hope is engulfed in the tragic dissolution of the symphony, yet Solti ensures that the leave-taking is serene enough, even if unavoidable. A profoundly reasoned and unfailingly distinguished account of a symphony which never fails to shock and chasten in equal measure. *MJ*

Berceuse élégiaque
see WEILL: Symphonies Nos 1 & 2

Piano Concerto in C, Op. 39

Garrick Ohlsson (piano), Cleveland Orchestra & Chorus (men's voices)/Christoph von Dohnányi

Telarc Bravo CD-82012 □ 71:45 mins □ 𝄞𝄞

Busoni's five-movement epic, completed in 1904, is the final culmination, and deconstruction, of the Romantic piano concerto. Its expansive form and tonal language suggest a development from Brahms's B flat Concerto, via late Liszt, but there are two disruptive, Italianate scherzi, and in the finale the soloist's bravura recedes into the background, as male voices intone a Lisztian 'chorus mysticus'. Seldom attempted except by the greatest virtuosi, it received just one LP recording – an almost ideal interpretation by John Ogdon, for EMI.

While that version (like Peter Donohoe's, also on EMI) is currently unavailable, there's much to admire in this mid-price Telarc offering: notably Ohlsson's fearless virtuosity on an awesome Bösendorfer. Triumphantly surmounting the demands of Busoni's often highly complex writing, he produces some of the most exciting thunder and glitter I've ever heard in a concerto recording. While Dohnányi provides a vividly intelligent accompaniment, purists might argue that the recording highlights the soloist too much, when the piece is more of a symphony with obbligato piano. But this is a thrillingly extrovert view of a still-underestimated masterpiece. *CM*

The Banks of Green Willow; Two English Idylls
see Collection: The Banks of Green Willow

Atlas eclipticalis
see Collection: American Orchestral music

A Symphony of Three Orchestras
see VARESE: Déserts

Three Occasions; Violin Concerto; Concerto for Orchestra

Ole Böhn (violin); London Sinfonietta/Oliver Knussen

Virgin VC 7 59271 2 □ 63:13 mins □ 𝄞𝄞𝄞

One of the most invigorating presences in today's music, Elliott Carter's work commands ever-increasing attention and respect. The complexity of his music – its multi-layered activity, dynamic drive and sheer density of thought – can require several listenings to make complete sense, but the effort is well worth making.

The Concerto for Orchestra, written for the 125th anniversary of the New York Philharmonic and premiered by them in 1970 under Leonard Bernstein, has earned itself the status of a modern classic, and its intensity and subtlety are here purposefully conveyed.

The *Three Occasions* are brief but no less pithy, conceived for the 150th anniversary of the State of Texas, as a memorial for the new-music supporter Paul Fromm, and as a 50th wedding anniversary present for Carter's wife respectively. Each has a strong personality and enough content for a much longer piece. The Violin Concerto, written for the present soloist who gave the premiere in San Francisco in 1990, is altogether more spare, allowing the lyricism of the solo part (which requires a lot of stamina) to shine through.

These excellent performances combine control and clarity, making Carter's prodigality of invention as lucid as possible. *George Hall*

CARTER

Variations for Orchestra
see Collection: American Orchestral Music

CHAUSSON/IBERT

Chausson: Symphony in B flat

Ibert: Escales; Divertissement

Dallas SO/Eduardo Mata

Dorian DOR-90181 □ **61:50 mins** □ 🎵🎵🎵

Eduardo Mata, the Mexican-born conductor and former music director of the Dallas Symphony Orchestra, lost his life in a flying accident in January 1995; this recording provides eloquent testimony to both his skills as an orchestra builder, and to his vision in spearheading the drive to fund and build the Morton H. Meyerson Symphony Center, home of the DSO since 1989, and the source of a stunning series of new recordings. Indeed, the phenomenal acoustic of the Eugene McDermott concert hall, centrepiece of the Meyerson complex, has set new standards of sonic excellence, never better evidenced than in Mata's superb account of the Chausson symphony. Although following his teacher Franck's D minor Symphony as a model, Chausson's Symphony in B flat is wholly distinctive and original in concept. The orchestra gives a performance of unerring quality and total assurance. Mata's handling of this score is unfailingly eloquent, the opening movement being pressed home with maximum intensity. The central slow movement unfolds mysteriously, and I've not experienced its

potent and enigmatic solemnity displayed so magically on disc hitherto; the final cadence has revelatory grandeur and impact. Mata's finale is gripping and purposeful, and the coda is unexpectedly cathartic. The Ibert works, *Escales* (Ports of call) and that riotous exercise in orchestral farce, *Divertissement*, are again magnificently played, though one can't fail to respond to the amazing radiance and naturalness of the sound captured by the Dorian engineers in what is, without question, one of the world's greatest concert halls. Serious audiophiles should note that the Meyerson Center, like Symphony Hall, Birmingham (the acoustics for both were designed by Russell Johnson of the New York firm Artec Consultants), sets new standards of fidelity and clarity by which all recording locations will now be judged. A sensational issue. *MJ*

CHOPIN

Piano Concertos Nos 1 in E minor & 2 in F minor

Murray Perahia (piano); Israel PO/Zubin Mehta

Sony SK 44922 □ **67:16 mins** □ 🎵🎵🎵

Excellent versions of both Chopin concertos are remarkably thick on the ground, making any kind of definitive choice a virtual impossibility. Perahia's readings are unlikely to be surpassed, and it's a measure of his quality that this remains perhaps my favourite version despite the perfunctory contribution of Mehta, who accompanies with tact and skill but only after trudging through the orchestral tuttis. If Perahia had had the kind of sympathetic partnership achieved by the little-known Székely and Németh in their very fine (and budget-price) Naxos recording or Zimerman and Giulini on DG (a superb release), this would have been one of the greatest recordings of the century. Other deeply satisfying accounts are Demidenko and Heinrich Schiff on Hyperion and the seriously underrated Tamás Vásáry on ASV, unusually doubling as both soloist and conductor (rather more extrovert readings than his earlier but also excellent versions with the Berlin PO on DG). Nor should one be distracted by less modern recordings from the magisterial Rubinstein on RCA. *JS*

CHOPIN

Piano Concerto No. 1 (transcr. Balakirev)
see **INSTRUMENTAL**: Collection: Marc-André Hamelin
Live at Wigmore Hall

COPLAND

El salón México; Dance Symphony; Fanfare for the Common Man; Four Dance Episodes from Rodeo; Appalachian Spring

Detroit SO/Antal Dorati

Decca Ovation 430 705-2 □ 74:30 mins □ 🎵🎵

Although Bernstein and, latterly, Leonard Slatkin have provided some of the most exciting Copland performances on disc, I can think of no finer introduction to his music than this generous compilation. The programme is dominated by some of Copland's most accessible works, including the ubiquitous *Fanfare for the Common Man* and the three ballet scores composed in a deliberately popular folkish idiom during the late Thirties and early Forties. A welcome addition is the less familiar and earlier *Dance Symphony*, its three movements culled from the then-unperformed ballet score *Grohg* (now available on Argo conducted by Oliver Knussen). Inevitably, Stravinsky's influence is especially noticeable here, though Copland's authorship is proclaimed through the work's pulsating rhythms and transparent orchestration.

A seasoned conductor of ballet music, Antal Dorati delivers characteristically vivacious performances of this music, yet injects greater warmth into his conception of *Appalachian Spring* than in his earlier LSO version for Mercury. Superb orchestral playing, coupled with demonstration-quality engineering, make this a highly desirable release, especially at mid-price. *EL*

COPLAND

Quiet City
see **CHORAL & SONG**: COPLAND: Eight Poems of Emily Dickinson

COPLAND

Symphony No. 3; Music for a Great City

St Louis SO/Leonard Slatkin

RCA Victor Red Seal RD 60149 □ 67:14 mins □ 🎵🎵🎵

Two contrasting sides of Copland's musical personality are posed here. First, there's the so-called 'open prairie' diatonicism of the Third Symphony, an expansive and often lyrical work completed after the end of the Second World War which incorporates in its affirmative finale material from the ubiquitous *Fanfare for the Common Man*. After this comes the gritty *Music for a Great City*, a portrayal of New York derived from the film score *Something Wild*. Here Copland's uncompromisingly dissonant harmonic idiom, with its frequent intimations of jazz and Latin-American rhythms, follows the manner of the spiky Piano Variations.

Leonard Slatkin has an unfailing capacity to project each work to its best advantage. His performance of the Third Symphony is both brilliant and expressive, and he avoids any temptation towards either bombast or sentimentality. In *Music for a Great City*, Slatkin revels in the many opportunities for rhythmic aggression and secures superb orchestral playing from the St Louis SO. *EL*

CORELLI

Concerti Grossi, Op. 6

Ensemble 415/Chiara Banchini, Jesper Christensen

Harmonia Mundi HMC 901406/07 □ 146:42 mins (2 discs) □ 🎵🎵🎵

Corelli's 12 concertos, Op. 6, are among the most influential music of their time. Published in 1714, they were immensely popular, were reissued in dozens of editions (and instrumentations, including a trio of two recorders and continuo!) and were the model for Handel's concertos – also 12, and with the same opus number.

They also invite large-scale performance. Research among the household accounts of Cardinals Pamphili and Ottoboni, successively Corelli's employers in Rome, discloses an orchestra of thirty to forty players. Georg Muffat tells of similar forces in a description of a performance in the 1690s, and an expanded Ensemble 415 reproduces this scale, with a rich continuo group – up to five archlutes and chitarrone. It's a grand sound, emphasising all the more clearly the concertato contrast with the trio of soloists. Speeds have also been carefully researched and turn out to suit admirably the weighty but focused tutti strings.

There are some surprises, not least the bucolic pastorale of the familiar *Christmas* Concerto, No. 8, placed at the very end of the two discs as a delightful punchline. *GP*

CRAWFORD SEEGER

Andante for Strings
see IVES: Three Places in New England

CUI

Deux morceaux
see Collection: Russian Cello Music

Symphony No. 5, Chat Moss; Cross Lane Fair; Five Klee Pictures

Philharmonia Orchestra, BBC Philharmonic/Peter Maxwell Davies

Collins 14602 □ 57:02 mins □ 🎵🎵🎵

Maxwell Davies's Fifth Symphony, first performed to great acclaim at the 1994 Proms, is undoubtedly one of the composer's most accessible orchestral works. Conceived as a large-scale single movement, its fluid musical landscape recalls the later symphonies of Sibelius in its seemingly effortless transitions from ruminative lyricism to supercharged intensity. Some of the musical material of the symphony is derived from a short and haunting orchestral piece, *Chat Moss*, itself a musical portrait of a wet Lancashire marshland that lay to the south of the composer's childhood home. Images of childhood also surface in *Cross Lane Fair*, where Maxwell Davies recalls with some nostalgia how as a young boy he was entranced by the wonders of the fairground, with its steam organs, roundabouts and numerous rides. With prominent solos for Northumbrian pipes and Celtic drums, this light-hearted score is a worthy addition to Maxwell Davies's substantial catalogue of occasional orchestral works, as is the *Five Klee Pictures*, an earlier work originally conceived for performance by youth orchestras. As in all Collins recordings of Maxwell Davies, performances and recordings are admirable. Strongly recommended, particularly as an entrée to the output of one of our finest living composers. *EL*

Worldes Blis; Sir Charles His Pavan
see **CHORAL & SONG**: MAXWELL DAVIES: The Turn of the Tide

Le martyre de Saint Sébastien (symphonic fragments); Nocturnes
see **CHORAL & SONG**: DEBUSSY: La damoiselle élue

La mer; Three Nocturnes; Prélude à l'après-midi d'un faune

Chicago SO & Chorus/Georg Solti

Decca 436 468-2 □ 55:16 mins □ 🎵🎵🎵

Fine performances of the three Symphonic Sketches, *La mer*, Debussy's orchestral masterpiece, from the Chicago Symphony Orchestra under Solti. On his own admission, had he not followed that particular *via crucis* which is the lot of the composer, Debussy

would have relished the prospect of a life at sea (he 'loved the sea, and listened to it with the passionate respect it deserves'). The result, in effect a three-movement symphony (Debussy found that term too inflexible a description of the work), is the greatest maritime triptych ever painted for orchestra. The pictorialist element (after all, this is the ultimate in musical expressionism) is what engages the imagination so powerfully in Solti's account. Indeed, as the composer suggested in a letter written soon after the completion of *La mer*, 'Music has this over painting – that it can represent all the variations of light and colour in one go'. Solti's ever-precise, microscopic adherence to every textual detail and performance direction generates playing of finely honed, majestic power – the great climax of 'Dialogue du vent et de la mer' is enthrallingly brilliant, and playing is particularly alluring during the second section, 'Jeux de vagues'. Solti's vivid imagination draws on an equally kaleidoscopic tonal palette in his superb readings of the *Three Nocturnes* – the distant trumpets of 'Fêtes' herald the processional advance of Debussy's 'dazzling, fantastic vision', with 'Nuages' and 'Sirènes' seeming other-worldly and effectively atmospheric. This fine disc reaches an enigmatically languorous, disarmingly erotic conclusion with crystalline, limpidly beautiful playing from the Chicago SO principal flute in the *Prélude à l'après-midi d'un faune*. Outstanding performances in matchless top-drawer Decca sound. *MJ*

Coppélia

National PO/Richard Bonynge

Decca 414 502-2 □ 92:00 mins (2 discs) □ 🎵🎵🎵

Ninety or so minutes of delightful, undemanding music, played with a freshness and vitality calculated to make Delibes's charming score stand on its own feet without the customary visual interaction of live dancers on stage. But can this music really attain to much more than the sum of its parts – namely as just one component in a wider artistic genre? With Richard Bonynge at the helm, the answer to that question is an emphatic yes! In playing the music for all it's worth, Bonynge engenders a physical potency and excitement that are instantly compelling, and he plainly relishes the whole experience. The celebrated show-stoppers, including the Mazurka, the Act II Boléro, and the winsome 'Valse des heures', are brilliantly characterised. Bonynge achieves resplendent response from the hand-picked National Philharmonic Orchestra. 'Les chasseuresses', for instance, is alluringly played and a fine tribute to Bonynge's unerring skill at moulding and propelling this delicious score with all the élan, preparedness, and commitment one would normally expect in the concert hall. Decca's 1984 digital sound has thrilling presence, and major fortissimo climaxes have palpably impressive impact. *MJ*

DELIUS

North Country Sketches; The Walk to the Paradise Garden from A Village Romeo and Juliet; Dance Rhapsodies Nos 1 & 2; In a Summer Garden

Bournemouth SO/Richard Hickox

Chandos CHAN 9355 □ 76:40 mins □ 🎵🎵🎵

Another intelligent and imaginative Delius programme from these artists, following their critically acclaimed 1993 CD of *Sea Drift*, etc. Hickox reveals all the intensity of the young lovers longing for former happiness in a thoroughly convincing and moving reading of 'The Walk to the Paradise Garden'. It is good to have both *Dance Rhapsodies* together. The popular first, cast in variation form, is full of joy and vitality but with a lovely penultimate variation that moved Peter Warlock to tears. Appropriate to the more delicate and luminous textures of the second, Hickox takes a more relaxed view than Beecham (1960) to express all the glittering and enchanting qualities of this short work. The sultry, sensuous beauty and vibrant colour of *In a Summer Garden* are wonderfully evoked; you can almost smell the lilies. In contrast, you shiver at the chilly invocation of a Yorkshire autumn and winter in *North Country Sketches*, and rustling ostinati reveal an empty white landscape. *Ian Lace*

DOHNANYI/BARTOK

Dohnányi: Variations on a Nursery Song

Bartók: Rhapsody for Piano and Orchestra; Scherzo for Piano and Orchestra

Zoltán Kocsis (piano); Budapest Festival Orchestra/Iván Fischer

Philips 446 472-2 □ 76:42 mins □ 🎵🎵🎵

A time there was when Dohnányi's wonderfully effervescent Variations on a Nursery Song featured regularly in concert programmes, but in recent years its star has waned somewhat. Yet such neglect is hardly deserved, as the score shows this late-Romantic Hungarian composer at his most inventive, delighting in the many opportunities for stylistic parody (there are affectionate tributes to Brahms, Liszt and Debussy, among others), and for subverting the audience's expectations.

Kocsis revels in the music's wit and virtuosity, and delivers a characteristically brilliant account that would be difficult to surpass. The rest of the disc is made up of Bartók's earliest works for piano and orchestra – neither of them is a masterpiece, but they illustrate the degree to which the young composer had succumbed to the influences of Liszt and Richard Strauss in the early years of this century. Once again, Kocsis, supported by incisive orchestral playing from Fischer and the Budapest Festival Orchestra, pulls out all the stops to demonstrate these scores in the best possible light. *EL*

DOHNANYI

Variations on a Nursery Song
see also RACHMANINOV: Rhapsody on a Theme of Paganini

DUKAS

Symphony in C; Polyeucte Overture

BBC Philharmonic/Yan Pascal Tortelier

Chandos CHAN 9225 □ 56:08 mins □ 🎵🎵🎵

It's good to find Yan Pascal Tortelier and the BBC Philharmonic in scintillating form throughout their fine Chandos account of the rarely encountered symphony by Paul Dukas, for it is a fine and immediately attractive work, richly deserving the memorable advocacy it receives here. The performance is galvanically impulsive and tremendously compelling, though Tortelier's manner is occasionally rather effortful, most noticeably in the opening movement which just misses the chance to shine as it did so convincingly in the deleted analogue performance from Michel Plasson and the Toulouse Capitole Orchestra on EMI. That said, the Chandos sonics are altogether more resplendent and wide-ranging, and Tortelier lingers gloriously (and at greater length) over the serene Andante which lies at the heart of this work. The finale is magnificently handled, and Tortelier finds the right blend of heady ardour and cumulative drama required in a score that's just occasionally a little ungainly. The Overture *Polyeucte* was written five years before the Symphony, in 1891, and labours valiantly, if not always especially convincingly, under the weighty influence of Wagner. It, too, receives a sterling performance, and the Chandos sound is miraculously clear and naturally balanced throughout. Definitely worth hearing, so why not seize the opportunity to experience a fine French symphony which is long overdue for general reappraisal? *MJ*

Dutilleux: Cello Concerto 'Tout un monde lointain'

Lutosławski: Cello Concerto

Mstislav Rostropovich (cello); Orchestre de Paris/Serge Baudo, Witold Lutosławski

EMI CDC 7 49304 2 □ ADD □ 52:34 mins □ ⊘⊘⊘

It goes without saying that the great Russian cellist Mstislav Rostropovich has almost single-handedly transformed the range and quality of cello repertoire composed since the Second World War. His playing has inspired a plethora of major figures, from Prokofiev to Schnittke, to compose masterpieces for the instrument, and among these the two concertos presented here must rank extremely high. Both works were premiered in 1970, yet they explore utterly different realms of experience. Dutilleux, basing his conception on the poetry of Baudelaire, is concerned with communicating the beauty of sound. But although the orchestral textures are indeed ravishing in a manner that recalls Ravel, there is a clear sense of direction in the musical argument that compels attention throughout. Similarly, Lutosławski never loses his grip on the audience, but his concerto is a much more dramatic affair, pitting the solo instrument in direct and sometimes desperate conflict with the orchestra. As you'd expect, the performances are totally authoritative, even though the engineers have sacrificed some inner detail by placing Rostropovich too near the microphone. *EL*

Dvořák: Cello Concerto in B minor

Tchaikovsky: Variations on a Rococo Theme

Mstislav Rostropovich (cello); Berlin PO/Herbert von Karajan

DG Originals 447 413-2 □ ADD □ 60:21 mins □ ⊘⊘

Of the many fine recordings made over the years of this great cello concerto ('Had I known this were possible, I'd have written one myself long ago' was Brahms's reported reaction to the work), this one stands head and shoulders above all others. Rostropovich has recorded the work on many occasions, yet never has he eclipsed this transcendently masterful reading. From the outset, it is clear that this is going to be a monumental performance, the playing of soloist and orchestra has that flair and epic spirit that makes one feel that these artists are discovering the piece for the first time. Rostropovich, heard at the summit of his cellistic and interpretative powers, delivers the solo part with arresting virtuosity and spontaneously inspired eloquence. Karajan addresses his orchestra with wilful severity, securing grandiloquent, heroically authoritative response from the Berliners. The coupling, Tchaikovsky's delectably crafted Rococo Variations, finds both soloist and conductor making the required economies of scale and sonority; again, this account remains to all intents and purposes wholly unrivalled. The original LP sound from Berlin's Jesus Christus Kirche was always impressive; now re-processed with the latest image-mapping techniques, this mid-price reissue, on DG's Originals label, cannot be overlooked in any collection of great performances. In short, a stunning and magnificent achievement, instantly belying its age – unbelievably, this recording was made in 1966. *MJ*

In Nature's Realm; Carnival; My Home; Hussite Overture; Othello; The Water Goblin; The Noonday Witch; The Golden Spinning-Wheel; The Wood Dove; Symphonic Variations

Bavarian RSO/Rafael Kubelík

DG Galleria 435 074-2 □ ADD □ 157:00 mins (2 discs) □ ⊘⊘

Rafael Kubelík has Bohemian blood coursing through his veins and knows instinctively how to forge and project these highly idiomatic orchestral pendants to Dvořák's cycle of nine symphonies. Not all of this music is as familiar as it surely deserves to be; Dvořák's trio of thematically linked concert overtures, *In Nature's Realm*, *Carnival* and *Othello*, originally subtitled *Nature, Life and Love*, have been recorded frequently, though more often than not separately, as makeweights to the symphonies. This double-disc reissue affords the opportunity to hear these works in context, and these performances could scarcely be more impressive. Among the symphonic poems, *The Golden Spinning-Wheel* and *The Noonday Witch* stand alone as the most familiar of Dvořák's forays into the world of the programmatic orchestral tone poem as perfected by Liszt. These are captivating works, whose inventiveness and melodic vitality often seem at odds with the horrific matter debated by Dvořák's subjects, drawn from the world of Bohemian folklore. Kubelík presents each work with gripping, omni-dimensional clarity and descriptive realism, and the orchestral playing has maximum commitment and impetus. The Bavarian RSO was recorded in the ample surroundings of the Herkules-Saal, Munich, and re-processed CD sonics are reverberant and warmly atmospheric. Kubelík's performances are wholly definitive. Recommended to all who love Czech music. *MJ*

DVORAK

Serenade for Strings in E, Op. 22; Serenade for wind instruments, cello and double bass, in D minor, Op. 44

St Paul CO/Hugh Wolff

Teldec 4509-97446-2 □ 55:00 mins □ *Ø Ø*

Dvořák's two serenades in E and in D minor fit conveniently on to a single disc with room to spare, and you'll seldom hear either played with greater sensitivity and allure than on this excellently recorded Teldec offering from Minneapolis, in which Hugh Wolff conducts the St Paul Chamber Orchestra. There is, about the String Serenade in particular, a compelling narrative and vocalised quality in Wolff's expertly crafted reading, which results in an unusually moving listening experience. The Scherzo has just the right Bohemian zest and bounce, although the outpourings of the lovely slow movement draw a rapturous, ravishingly expressive response from the superbly drilled St Paul string players. The closing section, Dvořák's dewy-eyed review of themes from the previous movements, is affectingly nostalgic, and the cock-a-hoop coda displays the stunning virtuosity of this fine American ensemble. The Wind Serenade is made of altogether sterner stuff; this is a bracing account, full of dramatic incident, spaciously recorded and again wonderfully played. Devotees of the Academy of St Martin in the Fields shouldn't demur over Neville Marriner's Philips pairing of these works, though for a decent budget offering, creditably played and recorded, you won't go far wrong with Discover International's 1993 recording by the Virtuosi di Praga directed by Oldřich Vlček. As ever, this label provides a generously filled, serviceably performed and engineered disc at rock-bottom price, and a worthwhile filler in the four Miniatures for strings, Op. 74a. *MJ*

DVORAK

Slavonic Dances, Opp. 46 & 72

Cleveland Orchestra/George Szell

Sony Essential Classics SBK 48161 □ ADD □ 74:00 mins □ *Ø*

We owe it to the commercial vision of the wily Berlin music publisher Fritz Simrock, who had already scored considerable success with the Hungarian Dances of Brahms, that Dvořák turned to the *furiant, dumka* and *sousedska*, indigenous dance forms of his native Bohemia, as the source of his two sets of Slavonic Dances. The first series appeared in 1878, in versions for piano duet; although the initial printrun sold out in a matter of weeks, the Slavonic Dances proved, if anything, even more universally popular in their orchestral versions. The second set appeared eight years later, though the vigour, passion and local colouring were no less appealing than before. These performances by the Cleveland Orchestra under the great George Szell were recorded at the orchestra's home, Severance Hall in Cleveland, between January 1963 and January 1965. Szell plays the dances as Dvořák intended us to hear them, with all of the repeats observed; these accounts are as generous and alluring as one could imagine, and remastered sound is fabulous – gone is the astringency and edginess of the original CBS LPs which many will remember fondly from the Sixties. An invaluable reissue, worth twice the price and considerably more. *MJ*

DVORAK

Symphonic Variations; The Noonday Witch; Serenade for wind instruments, cello and double bass, in D minor, Op. 44; Hussite Overture

LSO/István Kertész

Decca Ovation 425 061-2 □ ADD □ 75:36 mins □ *Ø Ø*

István Kertész began his fabled bench-mark recordings of Dvořák's symphonies with the London SO in 1971. For years one of the legends of the Decca catalogues, the cycle was complemented by fine accounts of many of the shorter orchestral works. These miscellanea are of similar vintage and possess the same admirable qualities. Kertész imparts to the scores a compelling blend of verve and profound musical understanding, generating performances that are slick, thrusting, yet thoroughly considered. He reveals the structural artifice behind Dvořák's Symphonic Variations with a clarity that few conductors have matched in the recording studio, while performances of the *Hussite Overture* and the tone poem *The Noonday Witch* are more or less definitive, save for passing and inconsequential inaccuracies of intonation among the woodwinds. The Kingsway Hall sound is brilliant, though some shrillness is noticeable in violin lines above the stave, a problem not completely overcome by digital re-processing of these acclaimed analogue LP masters. Still, with playing of such allure and electricity, who cares? *MJ*

DVORAK

Symphonies Nos 1–9; In Nature's Realm Overture; Carnival Overture; My Home Overture; Scherzo capriccioso

LSO/István Kertész

Decca 430 046-2 □ ADD □ 431:00 mins (6 discs) □ 𝕬𝕬

Decca has reissued the fabled Kertész/LSO Dvořák cycle of symphonies, recorded some thirty years ago, on six mid-price discs. Older collectors will recall with affectionate nostalgia the fine vinyl issues in this set, each LP having its own distinctive Bruegel reproduction on the sleeve, and of course superb sound quality. Visually, the modern packaging is a little drab, though the playing is gripping and splendidly authoritative. The refurbished CD sonics are breathtaking, the detail and perspective of the orchestral image are startlingly vivid, and Decca has breathed new life into these extraordinary performances. István Kertész was the first conductor to bring Dvořák's early symphonies to the attention of record enthusiasts, and although his accounts are still largely unrivalled, the pity of it is that these audacious works are still unplayed in the concert hall. Kertész directs a particularly memorable account of the Wagner-inspired Fourth Symphony and includes the important exposition repeat in his superb performance of Symphony No. 6. The LSO plays magnificently throughout (the last three symphonies, and particularly No. 8, the first to be taped in this survey during February 1963, are particularly fine); CD transfers readily convey the bloom and radiance of the famous Kingsway Hall acoustic in which these matchless recordings were made. Tragically, István Kertész met his untimely death in 1973; this illustrious set provides ample testimony to his genius, and a potential which was largely unrealised. *MJ*

DVORAK

Symphonies Nos 7 in D minor, 8 in G & 9 in E minor (From the New World)

Amsterdam Concertgebouw Orchestra, LSO/Colin Davis

Philips Duo 438 347-2 □ ADD □ 139:08 mins (2 discs) □ 𝕬𝕬

Colin Davis is a distinguished and respected Dvořákian, whose credentials were sensationally apparent in his outstanding collaborations with the Concertgebouw Orchestra in the Seventh and Eighth Symphonies. Incredibly, these Philips LP recordings were made in 1975 and 1978 respectively, though one would never guess as much from the outstanding warmth and detail revealed in these remastered CD reissues. Orchestral playing is of the highest distinction throughout and, with the Concertgebouw hall contributing its own special part, these recordings have exceptional clarity and brilliance within an entirely natural acoustic ambience. The 1979 *New World* finds the LSO in slightly less responsive form, though this is an acceptable and often exciting performance. Such shortcomings as there are seem the more apparent when set alongside the greater idiomatic flair of the Amsterdam performances of the previous symphonies, which remain in a class of their own. This is another particularly pleasing mid-price edition from Philips, and Davis's Concertgebouw recordings have long since attained classic status. His readings of these symphonies are required listening, particularly at this price. *MJ*

DVORAK

Symphonies Nos 7 in D minor & 9 in E minor (From the New World)

LPO/Charles Mackerras

EMI Eminence CD-EMX 2202 □ 76:15 mins □ 𝕬𝕬

With eighty-odd *New Worlds* currently available, Dvořák's last symphony is well-trodden territory. If the prospect of yet another dispiriting border incursion is unappealing, let Mackerras and the London Philharmonic restore your faith in this oft-abused score. This is an imposing performance (even without Dvořák's first movement repeat), purposeful yet never self-regardingly grandiloquent. The playing throughout is courageous, not bombastic, and the great cor anglais theme of the Largo is radiantly expounded. Impetus is held in check during the Scherzo in readiness for an unusually exciting coda and a truly epic finale. If this is a *New World* of slimmer proportions than some, it is direct, refreshingly unaffected, and certainly never economical with the truth. There follows a leonine, muscular account of Dvořák's greatest symphony: the Seventh, quite as penetrating as any in the catalogues, and again wholly unmannered yet thrillingly spontaneous. Mackerras shows himself a force to be reckoned with in a rough-hewn, craggy Seventh and reliably calculated Ninth, both superbly engineered performances. *MJ*

DVORAK/SIBELIUS

Dvořák: Violin Concerto in A minor

Sibelius: Violin Concerto in D minor

Salvatore Accardo (violin); Amsterdam Concertgebouw Orchestra, LSO/Colin Davis

Philips Silver Line 420 895-2 □ **ADD** □ **67:41 mins** □ *ⓐⓐ*

Like his Piano Concerto, Dvořák's Violin Concerto has been unfairly marginalised by the overwhelming popularity of his concluding symphonic trilogy, and by the Cello Concerto; a pity, because this exuberant work merits a place in every virtuoso violinist's repertoire, yet all too few have taken it to their hearts. One who has is Salvatore Accardo; his 1979 Concertgebouw recording is the finest I've heard, and vastly preferable to Kyung-Wha Chung's 1989 account with Muti and the Philadelphia Orchestra. Their EMI recording seems leaden and poorly balanced alongside this top-class Philips production, now beautifully vivid and clear in it digitally remastered guise. Chung and Muti's 47-minute, full-price offering does at least feature Dvořák's affectingly nostalgic Romance in F minor as a filler, though the Philips disc includes Accardo's account of the Sibelius concerto, again with Colin Davis, here conducting the LSO. A memorably powerful reading, though the Dvořák Violin Concerto also has phenomenal authority and brilliance, and this remains the best version in the catalogue. At the time of writing, Ilya Kaler's Naxos performance has just been issued; the main coupling is the Violin Concerto by Glazunov, though Dvořák's gorgeous F minor Romance is also included, making this a genuine bargain. Still, I'd be happy to pay a little more to experience Accardo's formidable advocacy of this undervalued masterpiece. *MJ*

ELGAR

Cello Concerto in E minor; Sea Pictures

Jacqueline du Pré (cello), Janet Baker (mezzo-soprano); LSO/John Barbirolli

EMI CDC 7 47329 2 □ **ADD** □ **70:00 mins** □ *ⓐⓐⓐ*

Du Pré's posthumous repute hangs largely upon her unsurpassable interpretation of Elgar's Cello Concerto, for which she displayed an almost prophetic affinity; indeed, as one listens to this astonishing performance thirty years after it was recorded, it is difficult to dissociate the tragic message of this score with Du Pré's heroic struggle against the multiple sclerosis which finally claimed her, destroying one of the most prodigious cellistic talents of the century. Her playing of this concerto was masterful, and even if you (as, I must confess, I certainly do) find her emotionally saturated accounts of other works difficult to stomach, you can't fail to be very deeply moved by this account. Du Pré is magnificently supported by the LSO and Barbirolli, who ensures that every elegiac nuance of this score registers as it should, while solo playing rings with matchless, fearless eloquence and passion throughout. Equally memorable is Janet Baker's performance of a work she made just as much her own, Elgar's orchestral song cycle *Sea Pictures*. Once more, this account has a symbiotic inner flair and a compulsion which are unforgettable, and the 1965 recording, now transferred to CD, is burgeoning and spectacularly vivid in both works. This is already a classic. You'll have no desire to hear another recording of the Elgar Cello Concerto after this – Du Pré has left nothing unsaid. *MJ*

ELGAR

Cockaigne Overture; Introduction and Allegro; Serenade in E minor; Variations on an Original Theme (Enigma)

BBC SO/Andrew Davis

Teldec British Line 9031-73279-2 □ **74:03 mins** □ *ⓐⓐⓐ*

Elgar dedicated his *Enigma* Variations to his 'friends pictured within'. Andrew Davis paints each of these intimate musical cameos in minute detail and with no lack of wit and poignant nostalgia. The cryptic *Enigma* theme, heard at the start, ultimately crowns the work triumphantly, but the 13 individual portraits assume almost tangible personality and realism in this performance: note how the blustering country squire 'WMB' hurries out of the music-room after reading the day's arrangements, slamming the door loudly behind him, and 'Ysobel', an amateur violist, struggles with a simple string-crossing exercise. Meanwhile, the bulldog Dan (Variation 11 – 'GRS') plunges into the River Wye, as the serious and devoted Basil Nevinson ('BGN') plays his cello eloquently. Andrew Davis ensures, though, that it is the composer himself who emerges in the most powerful relief during the concluding variation, with Elgar's optional organ part resounding impressively in the final, brilliantly affirmative peroration. The remaining offerings here could scarcely be bettered. The BBC strings cover themselves in glory in the two string orchestra works, with particularly eloquent interplay with the fine solo quartet in the *Introduction and Allegro*, and a delightfully sprung and deeply felt account of the Serenade for Strings; playing of slighter proportions, but winningly inflected and lovingly characterised. Andrew Davis is heard to memorable advantage, too, in a splendid and affectionately moulded reading of Elgar's great musical tribute to the city of London, the *Cockaigne* Overture. With playing of this level of distinction, it's difficult to believe in anything other than 'hearts at peace under an English heaven'. And this sumptuous performance will bring a lump to the throat and a tear to the eye of every Anglophile. *MJ*

ELGAR

Introduction and Allegro; Serenade in E minor; Elegy; Sospiri

see VAUGHAN WILLIAMS: Fantasia on a Theme of Thomas Tallis

ELGAR

Sursum corda; Salut d'amour; Chanson de matin; Chanson de nuit; Dream Children; Elegy; Sospiri

see **CHORAL & SONG:** ELGAR: The Music Makers

ELGAR

Symphony No. 1 in A flat; Pomp and Circumstance Marches Nos 1 in D, 3 in C minor & 4 in G

BBC SO/Andrew Davis

Teldec British Line 9031-73278-2 □ **70:41 mins**
□ *❂❂❂*

Symphony No. 1 in A flat; In the South

LPO/Leonard Slatkin

RCA Victor Red Seal RD 60380 □ **73:36 mins**
□ *❂❂❂*

Here are two extraordinary readings of Elgar's First Symphony, each offering magnificent orchestral playing and fine sound quality. Andrew Davis and the BBC SO attracted the plaudits of both critics and collectors for their superb series of recordings of Elgar's orchestral works for Teldec. Davis is a naturally sympathetic Elgarian, and his account of this symphony can be unhesitatingly commended as one of the best currently available. Davis has the measure of the work, from the solemn timpani-led call to attention at the start, and one senses great things to come in the masterfully eloquent, truly *nobilmente* manner in which he allows the great processional melody that dominates the work to unfold immediately afterwards. No one who loves this symphony will be disappointed. The Adagio is lovingly presented, with sublime playing from the BBC SO, yet Davis crowns this performance with inspired grandeur as the processional theme re-gathers itself, at first tentatively amid fragmentary gestures from the last desks of strings as the finale begins, and later in all its glittering pageantry during the triumphant closing pages, as all lingering doubt is swept aside. Davis also offers strongly characterised performances of three of Elgar's *Pomp and Circumstance* Marches, played by an orchestra which has this music in its blood.

Leonard Slatkin has emerged as one of the finest living interpreters of Elgar's works, and his performance of the First Symphony is equally memorable and deeply felt. His superb RCA disc opens with an electrifying performance of *In the South*, and his empathetic treatment of the music might suggest that his youth was spent amid the tranquillity of the Malvern Hills rather than in Hollywood. This is a sensational reading, most brilliantly played by the LPO, and if Elgar's grandiloquent utterances seem a little at variance with today's world, then Slatkin might just be the conductor to restore our faith in 'great charity, and a massive hope for the future', the composer's professed musical agenda for this most glorious of English symphonies. Try to hear something of each before purchasing, since both are outstanding. *MJ*

ELGAR

Symphony No. 2 in E flat; In the South

BBC SO/Andrew Davis

Teldec British Line 9031-74888-2 □ **78:46 mins**
□ *❂❂❂*

I have no hesitation in hailing this as a triumph for Davis and the BBC SO: in short, there is no other recording in the catalogues which can even begin to outshine this bench-mark performance of Elgar's Second

Symphony. From a technical standpoint, this recording, made at St Augustine's Church, London, in 1992, is quite astonishing in its richness of detail and dynamic range, within a warm and sympathetic acoustic ambience. The playing of the BBC SO is world-class; here indeed is a performance in which Shelley's elusive 'Spirit of Delight', the sentiment at the emotional axis of the work, is really never far from the surface. Davis finds just the right leaping exuberance and surging energy at the start to launch his players on a course that frankly never falters, even momentarily, throughout the duration of the work. While the bounding, life-asserting spirit is there in abundance, so are the funereal presentiments of human mortality; the elegiac dignity of the processional cortège for a dead monarch (Elgar was profoundly affected by the death of King Edward VII, though he denied any explicit portrayal of the event in this symphony) has never been so movingly delivered on disc. And Davis, having led us to see all things as they come to pass in this score, brings the work to a glowing sunset conclusion. This is a reading of unique and personally involving qualities, which is without serious competition from any rival source. No less impressive is the account of *In the South*, with Davis securing galvanic response and emphatic commitment from an orchestra whose members are clearly at the edge of their seats – Teldec's sonics are, in a word, gorgeous. I should mention that what you'll read in Christopher Palmer's comprehensive and erudite notes for this, and the remaining issues in the series, is every bit as compelling as what you'll hear on the disc itself. *MJ*

ELGAR

Violin Concerto in B minor; Cockaigne Overture

Dong-Suk Kang (violin); Polish National RSO/Adrian Leaper

Naxos 8.550489 □ 61:00 mins □ ⊘

Korean-born Dong-Suk Kang's breathtaking performance of Elgar's Violin Concerto makes out a superb case in support of the assertion that great music truly recognises neither cultural nor geographical boundaries. This is an enraptured, sophisticated and totally sympathetic account of a concerto which can all too readily become overbearingly schmaltzy in the wrong hands. The score bears the incomplete Spanish epigram 'Aqui es encerada el alma de…'; the true identity of the soul enshrined within this great work has provided

another enigmatic strand to Elgarian scholarship yet, as Kang suggests, the soul is really that of Everyman, for who is there that can remain unaffected by music as profoundly touching as this? Dong-Suk Kang possesses the very considerable technical skills needed to surmount the massive violinistic hurdles of the text, yet his fervent virtuosity is ably counterpoised by an interpretative insight and expressive gravity tailored towards the introspective aspect of the piece. The Polish National RSO plays ravishingly under Adrian Leaper, and their account of that familiar staple of British orchestras (Elgar dedicated it to his friends, the members of England's orchestras), the *Cockaigne* Overture, should draw a sigh of patriotic nostalgia from even the most hardened sceptic. A gloriously played and expertly recorded disc, and another outstanding bargain from Naxos. In passing, I should perhaps add that nothing will deter my enthusiasm for Itzhak Perlman's DG version with the Chicago SO under Barenboim; this is in every regard superlative, but had I not owned that disc already, I feel certain that I'd have chosen Kang on Naxos. That I'd have saved some money and have been just as fulfilled by the musical experience goes without saying. Hear Kang on Naxos as a priority. *MJ*

ENESCU

Orchestral Suites Nos 2 & 3 (Villageoise); Andantino

Romanian National RO/Horia Andreescu

Olympia Explorer OCD 495 □ 62:21 mins □ ⊘⊘

The Romanian George Enescu took his country's music into the 20th century as single-handedly and decisively as did Bartók in Hungary, Janáček in Czechoslovakia and Szymanowski in Poland. Long neglected on record, a gratifying amount of his music is finally appearing on disc, displacing the potboiling *Romanian Rhapsodies* which used to be all that were ever played. If the most sumptuous recording to date is of the Romantic and monumental First and Second Symphonies under Lawrence Foster on EMI, this disc – the fifth volume in Olympia's ongoing survey of Enescu's complete orchestral music – contains even finer works. Suite No. 3 is a masterpiece, evoking the landscapes and character of Enescu's homeland with superb orchestral skill and highly original melodic and polyphonic writing. Its five-movement design resembles in some respects the Bartók Concerto for Orchestra, which it pre-dates. Suite No. 2 (1915) belongs to a neo-classical phase that aligns Enescu more with Reger and Busoni; the six movements are deftly turned, ending with a huge and infectious bourrée. The performances are authoritative, the sound wholly acceptable. *CM*

FALLA/RODRIGO

Falla: El amor brujo; Noches en los jardines de España

Rodrigo: Concierto de Aranjuez

Alicia de Larrocha (piano), Huguette Tourangeau (mezzo-soprano), Carlos Bonell (guitar); LPO/Rafael Frühbeck de Burgos, Montreal SO/Charles Dutoit

Decca Ovation 430 703-2 □ 71:40 mins □ 🟐🟐

Falla's colourful ballet score *El amor brujo* appears tailor-made for the talents of the Montreal SO and Charles Dutoit, whose performance, supported by the sultry-voiced Huguette Tourangeau, achieves plenty of atmosphere and dynamism. The 1983 recording, one of Decca's earlier digital efforts, has certainly stood the test of time and still sounds extraordinarily vivid. Larrocha's version of *Nights in the Gardens of Spain* was made two years earlier, and the orchestral balance seems less naturally focused, with some rather strange spotlighting from time to time. Nonetheless, with the possible exception of Rubinstein, Larrocha remains peerless in this repertoire, and Frühbeck consistently draws some fascinating textures from the orchestral accompaniment. An added bonus to this highly enjoyable disc of 20th-century Spanish music is a beautifully moulded performance of the ubiquitous guitar concerto by Rodrigo. *EL*

FAURE

Pelléas et Mélisande
see **CHORAL & SONG**: FAURE: Requiem

FETLER

Contrasts for Orchestra
see Collection: French Orchestral Music

FIRSOVA

Cassandra
see GUBAIDULINA: Pro et contra

FOULDS

Dynamic Triptych
see VAUGHAN WILLIAMS: Piano Concerto

FOULDS

Three Mantras; Le Cabaret Overture; Pasquinade Symphonique No. 2; April – England; Hellas, a Suite of Ancient Greece

LPO/Barry Wordsworth

Lyrita SRCD 212 □ 61:07 mins □ 🟐🟐🟐

One of the most stylistically liberated of 20th-century British composers, the multi-talented John Foulds was typecast in his lifetime as a purveyor of light music and theatre scores. He was long forgotten after he died in India in 1939, but revivals of his largely unpublished serious works have revealed a speculative and mystical figure of tremendous energy: it's difficult to withhold the term 'genius'. There are parallels with Holst, especially a keen interest in oriental music; but technically some of Foulds's music is more exploratory, while the personality is less austere – the more so as he continued to produce tuneful works for popular consumption 'on the side'.

This revelatory selection from Lyrita spans something of the man's vast range, from the breezy *Cabaret* Overture to the awesome *Mantras*, an orchestral triptych of the utmost brilliance and daring drawn from an uncompleted Sanskrit opera. *Hellas*, for strings and percussion, composed in the Greek modes, is a serenely statuesque masterpiece, *April – England* a riotous nature-impression. First-rate playing and recording; anyone who cares about British music should have this disc. *CM*

FRANCAIX

Concertino for Piano and Orchestra
see Collection: French Orchestral Music

FRANCK

Les Djinns; Symphonic Variations; Prélude, Choral et Fugue

Kerstin Aberg (piano); Gothenburg SO/Okko Kamu

BIS CD-137 □ ADD □ 52:15 mins □ 🟐🟐🟐

This is a particularly useful issue, featuring performances from Swedish pianist Kerstin Aberg who, while not an international keyboard celebrity, is nonetheless a fine and uncommonly sympathetic exponent of these works. The analogue recordings were made in 1979, yet remastered CD sound is well up to BIS's traditionally excellent standards, and this disc may be recommended without the least reservation, although there are other, outwardly more glamorous issues available should your sole interest here be Franck's Symphonic Variations for piano and orchestra. Aberg's account of this popular work is both creditable and enjoyable. She is an able pianist who plays with admirable technique and poetic eloquence. But her performance of *Les Djinns*, an orchestral tone poem with piano, written in 1884 and based on Victor Hugo's poem of the same name, is of particular account, if only because of the scarcity of recordings of this work. This disc also includes Franck's demanding *Prélude, Choral et Fugue*, for piano solo, of the same year. Elsewhere, Okko Kamu draws responsive playing from the Gothenburg SO, and the BIS sound is characterised by the warmth and resonance one normally expects of recordings made in the orchestra's home, the Gothenburg Konserthus. *MJ*

FRANCK
Les Éolides; Symphonic Variations; Symphony in D minor
see **CHAMBER**: FRANCK: Violin Sonata in A

FRANCK
Symphony in D minor; Psyché et Eros from Psyché

Berlin PO/Carlo Maria Giulini

DG Galleria 439 523-2 □ **54:12 mins** □ 🔊🔊

Giulini allows this great symphony, his chosen métier, to evolve at its own unforced yet monolithically inevitable pace. True, there are conductors (and plenty of them) who get through this score much faster (that's not to imply that Giulini adopts controversially slow tempi), yet very few among the small bastion of stellar maestros who bother to play the work these days (when did you last attend a public performance – if, indeed, you've ever done so?) present it to us in such awesome majesty. The symphony is episodic, and Franck uses cyclic form to ensure that its impressive architectural cross-beams are deployed at just the right critical points. Giulini is a master of the stealthy interpretative advance and of the grandiloquent moment of revelation: there's ample opportunity to sample both attributes in this performance. The filler, the fourth movement from Franck's extended tone poem *Psyché*, is an apt choice, and is similarly well played by the Berlin PO. The recording, from the Philharmonie, is of high quality, and this is unquestionably the finest digital version of the Franck Symphony available at mid-price. Should you wish to pay more, Decca's impressive Montreal recording with Charles Dutoit offers an imaginative coupling in the form of Vincent d'Indy's *Symphony on a French Mountain Song* for piano and orchestra, with Jean-Yves Thibaudet as soloist. If your interests are confined to the César Franck Symphony in D minor, then don't miss the chance to hear Giulini's sovereign eloquence at mid-price. *MJ*

GEMINIANI
Concerti Grossi in D minor (La folia) & G minor; Trio Sonatas in F, A minor & D minor; Violin Sonatas in E minor, Op. 1/3 & in A, Op. 4/12

Purcell Quartet, Purcell Band

Hyperion CDA 66264 □ **51:48 mins** □ 🔊🔊🔊

Charles Burney wrote: 'Geminiani… was so circumscribed in his invention that he was obliged to have recourse to all the arts of musical cookery, not to call it quackery, for materials to publish.' Sure enough, here are three trio sonatas which Geminiani arranged from his own solos, a solo sonata which underwent revision, and a concerto grosso arrangement of Corelli's Op. 5/2 Sonata, the set of 23 variations on the theme called *La folia*. The disc ends with an original sonata and concerto.

Geminiani's lack of originality matters less than the quality of the music, arranged or new. His expansion of the Corelli variations is very exhilarating, ending with the original broken bass chords rattling upwards into the whole orchestra. His own concertos also expand their Corellian models by adding a viola to the two solo violins and cello of the concertino group. The sonatas, variations and one concerto grosso are played with great spirit and technical assuredness.

An attractive alternative is a whole disc of concertos (on Deutsche Harmonia Mundi) by Sigiswald Kuijken and La Petite Bande, full of vitality if not with such sweetly managed intonation as the smaller forces of the Purcell Band. *GP*

GERHARD
Symphonies Nos 1 & 3 (Collages)

Tenerife SO/Víctor Pablo Pérez

Auvidis Valois V 4728 □ **58:59 mins** □ 🔊🔊🔊

In 1940 Roberto Gerhard, the greatest Spanish composer since Falla, emigrated from his native Spain, an exile from Franco's regime, to Great Britain where he spent his last thirty years. A pupil of Granados and Schoenberg, he spanned folkloric nationalism to pioneering avant-gardism; his rhythmic dynamism, and evolution of an individual serial technique, discloses affinities with Stravinsky and Varèse. Belatedly championed by the BBC in the Sixties, the music dropped out of the repertoire again until a new surge of interest in recent years; but still, in his centenary year, this marvellous composer is under-represented on disc. Rattle should record the *Don Quixote*

ballet he introduced at the 1991 Proms; Colin Davis's LP accounts of the Violin Concerto and Fourth Symphony, Del Mar's of the Concerto for Orchestra and the London Sinfonietta's of the late 'astrological' chamber works for Decca must surely reappear in due course. Meanwhile, here are two of Gerhard's finest scores. These, too, were recorded in the LP era: Symphony No. 1 by Dorati, No. 3 by Prausnitz (both EMI) – excellent performances, not quite banished from memory by Víctor Pablo Pérez, but this disc is still startlingly good. The Tenerife orchestra rises valiantly to the symphonies' virtuoso orchestral demands. No. 1 (1953) is a transitional work, full of the heat, dazzling light and black shadow of Spain, and hints of Spanish music too for all its 12-note basis. Its final fade-out into a 'white noise' of string harmonics, however, presages the elemental new sound-worlds of the craggy, visionary *Collages* (1960), the greatest combination of orchestra and electronic tape since Varèse's *Déserts*. The sound quality is very good indeed.
CM

GERSHWIN

Rhapsody in Blue; Concerto in F; An American in Paris; Variations on 'I got rhythm'

Earl Wild (piano); Boston Pops Orchestra/Arthur Fiedler

RCA Classical Navigator 74321 17906 2 □ ADD □ 70:06 mins □ 🎵

If you must have *Rhapsody in Blue* in its original version for piano and small jazz orchestra, Michael Tilson Thomas and the Los Angeles Philharmonic on Sony, following the composer's own propensity for power-driven tempi, offer much the best interpretation. But for the more familiar full orchestral score, you need look no further than this budget-price recording in which the American virtuoso Earl Wild achieves a wonderful synthesis between jazzy exuberance and Lisztian bravura. Fiedler and the Boston Pops Orchestra provide enthusiastic accompaniments both here and in the Concerto in F, and their version of *An American in Paris*, although not quite in the Bernstein league, is still hugely enjoyable.

The recordings were made as long ago as 1959 and 1961, and don't possess the clarity and brilliance of more recent offerings. But if you are prepared to put up with this, and RCA's almost non-existent liner notes, the present coupling will do very nicely indeed.
EL

GLAZUNOV
Two Pieces; Chant du ménéstrel
see Collection: Russian Cello Music

GLAZUNOV

The Seasons; Scènes de ballet (Symphonic Suite)

Minnesota Orchestra/Edo de Waart

Telarc CD-80347 □ 66:00 mins □ 🎵🎵🎵

Few recordings do justice to Glazunov's endlessly fertile ballet score *The Seasons*, and it is good to be able to offer an unqualified recommendation on behalf of this fine, richly eventful account from Edo de Waart and the Minnesota Orchestra. The work is seldom heard in its complete form, although truncated suites and isolated excerpts do occasionally feature as CD makeweights (the Bacchanal from Scene 4, 'Autumn', will normally evince a smile of recognition even from those who profess never to have heard the complete work). De Waart's recording is a worthy successor to the glorious 1967 version from Ernest Ansermet and the Suisse Romande Orchestra, and is presented in sound yet more refined and expansive than the generally creditable engineering accorded to Neeme Järvi and the RSNO on Chandos. The work is scored for large orchestra, and Glazunov's late-Romantic style is seldom better revealed, even in his symphonies. But Telarc's high-tech twenty-bit engineering for de Waart is in a class apart, and the playing of the Minnesota Orchestra is highly distinguished in every section. The coupling, Glazunov's *Scènes de ballet*, is again magnificently realised by de Waart and this fine orchestra, and their Telarc release eclipses every other recorded version in the catalogues, though bargain-hunters should track down the decently played budget account from Ondrej Lenard and the ČSR Symphony Orchestra, Bratislava, on Naxos.
MJ

GLAZUNOV / SIBELIUS / TCHAIKOVSKY

Glazunov: Violin Concerto in A minor

Sibelius: Violin Concerto in D minor

Tchaikovsky: Violin Concerto in D

Jascha Heifetz (violin); LSO/John Barbirolli, Thomas Beecham

EMI Références CDH 7 64030 2 □ ADD mono □ 79:32 mins □ 🎵🎵

Technical facility is only a starting-point for Heifetz as he weaves his free and easy way through the rhapsodies of the Tchaikovsky and Glazunov concertos. Both works need this sense of fantasy and improvisation to maintain long-term interest, though the first movement of the Tchaikovsky is certainly less of a problem than usual: there is a small cut in the orchestral share of the development (another, more traditional, occurs in the finale) and Heifetz makes us sit up and listen with startling new swaths of double-stopping approved by his teacher Leopold Auer, Tchaikovsky's original choice of dedicatee before the violinist cancelled the premiere.

The dedication to Auer still stands at the head of Glazunov's compact late-Romantic piece of pleasant note-spinning, further proof of Heifetz as lawful heir, while the Sibelius performance was the work's first published record release. If wanting in gritty extremes, and with few stops pulled out in comparison to a latter-day live wire like Nigel Kennedy (EMI), Heifetz's partnership with Beecham is typically fluid and intonation-perfect. The sound for the soloist, in these classic accounts from the mid-Thirties, is impeccable throughout, though if you really want a state-of-the-art recording of the Tchaikovsky, then Joshua Bell's astonishingly fresh re-creation on Decca can hardly fail to delight. *DN*

GLIERE

Symphony No. 3 (Ilya Muromets)

BBC Philharmonic/Edward Downes

Chandos CHAN 9041 □ 78:08 mins □ ⨀⨀⨀

Premiered in Moscow in 1912, this is arguably the most sumptuous and the most extravagant of all late-Romantic Russian symphonies. Glière's programme depicts the life and heroic deeds of the 12th-century figure Ilya of Murom against the historical background of the struggle between paganism and Christianity. Cast in the traditional four movements, the symphony encompasses an astonishingly diverse range of landscapes, including the forest, a princely court and a battlefield, and the musical influences are equally extensive, with frequent allusions to Liszt, Wagner, Rimsky-Korsakov and Scriabin. Yet if the music hardly strikes a truly individual voice, one cannot help but admire the extraordinary skill with which Glière fashions these diverse episodes into a convincing entity, and savour his fantastic aural imagination and mastery of orchestration. Glière's epic was much championed by Leopold Stokowski, though his recordings mercilessly cut the score to

almost half its original length. Nowadays, it's far preferable to hear the work in its entirety, and for this one should turn to Downes and the BBC Philharmonic, who together deliver an absolutely riveting performance supported by a demonstration-quality recording. *EL*

GLINKA

A Life for the Tsar – ballet music
see Collection: Russian Music

GOLDMARK

Violin Concerto No. 1 in A minor
see BRUCH: Violin Concerto No. 2

GRIEG/SCHUMANN

Grieg: Piano Concerto in A minor

Schumann: Piano Concerto in A minor

Radu Lupu (piano); LSO/André Previn

Decca Ovation 417 728-2 □ ADD □ 61:20 mins □ ⨀⨀

Jenő Jandó (piano); Budapest SO/András Ligeti

Naxos 8.550118 □ 57:17 mins □ ⨀

Radu Lupu's classic performances of the Grieg and Schumann concertos were recorded at London's Kingsway Hall, home of many legendary Decca issues, during 1973. He is accompanied by the LSO, then in its heyday under Previn, in performances of the highest distinction which have seldom been equalled and never bettered. Radu Lupu's account of the perennial Grieg concerto is intensely personal. Each emotionally charged phrase is lovingly inflected, and this patrician pianism displays astounding breadth, passion and lyric ardour. After a grandly theatrical opening movement, the lovely Adagio is both affectionate and heroic, memorably so in the lush reprise of the main idea, and Previn and the LSO accompany gloriously. Lupu is just as impressive in the finale; rhythms are tightly sprung and zestfully articulated, and the closing peroration is irresistibly triumphant.

The coupling is Schumann's Piano Concerto in A minor, again in a performance long upheld as a bench-mark of interpretative excellence. Sound quality of this mid-price reissue on Decca's Ovation label is stunning. The wide dynamic range and pin-sharp focus of the original LP was memorable, and in refurbished CD format these majestic performances can be enjoyed in demonstration-quality sound. Meanwhile, at budget price Jandó's Naxos performances of these concertos has primacy amid a growing array of bargain discs devoted to these repertoire war-houses. Sound is marginally recessed alongside Decca's glittering sonics, but

Jandó is a fine pianist who may be relied upon to deliver formidably played and eminently well-considered accounts of these works, most ably supported by the Budapest SO under András Ligeti. *MJ*

GRIEG

Norwegian Dances; Lyric Suite; Symphonic Dances

Gothenburg SO/Neeme Järvi

DG 419 431-2 □ 68:00 mins □ *●●●*

Among the Grieg orchestral works in this recording, only the charming Norwegian Dances figure with any regularity in the catalogues – a pity, because there is much to enjoy here, in music which might not merit expressions of greatness but is beautifully constructed and full of life and character. Grieg's style was, of course, by no means as progressive or innovative as that of some of his counterparts elsewhere, yet who could fail to be utterly captivated by that well-spring of untainted Nordic exuberance which is his Op. 35 set of Norwegian Dances? The Symphonic Dances are, as their title implies, made of sterner stuff yet, on re-hearing them today, their almost complete neglect in our concert halls seems a criminal oversight. Both sets were originally for piano duet and orchestrated at a later stage. Grieg's *Lyric Suite*, Op. 54, shows him as both true master of the introspective graceful musical *morceau* and as a fastidious craftsman capable of writing melodies of bewitching sensitivity and pathos. The playing of the Gothenburg SO is first class under Neeme Järvi's inspired direction, and the DG recording is balm to the ears. *MJ*

GUBAIDULINA/FIRSOVA

Gubaidulina: Pro et contra

Firsova: Cassandra

BBC National Orchestra of Wales/Tadaaki Otaka

BIS CD-668 □ 55:34 mins □ *●●●*

Sofia Gubaidulina and Elena Firsova, both of whom have come to prominence in the post-*glasnost* era, share a liking for sonic extremity and a dark, mystical vision. This disc shows the former achieving an impressive *tour de force*, unmistakably her own, while the imagination of the younger Firsova still strains towards a personal synthesis.

Gubaidulina's music can appear to dwell in a darkness whose purpose is altogether mysterious: not so here. *Pro et contra* is a revelation. Its form can be seen as a church triptych: two short outer movements frame a centrepiece whose heart is the Russian Orthodox *Alleluia* in all its sombre glory. Melodic wisps wind their way inexorably towards and away from this chorale. The final, fugue-like movement weaves together the far-flung sonorities with tremendous energy. Gubaidulina's experience of the medium shows in a score full of subtlety and ravishing beauty.

Firsova's *Cassandra* was written with the apprehension of contemporary Russians in mind. Ostensibly a lyrical cello concerto (with echoes of Shostakovich), it fractures into frenzied gestures. Thundering climaxes are driven by a bass drum, the brazen persistence of which seems unnecessary. Some further alchemy was needed here. Nevertheless, Otaka and the orchestra give riveting performances of both works. *Helen Wallace*

HANDEL

'Airs from Vauxhall Gardens'
see Collection: Baroque Trumpet Music

HANDEL

Arrival of the Queen of Sheba
see Collection: Baroque Music

HANDEL

Six Concerti Grossi, Op. 3

The English Concert/Trevor Pinnock

Archiv 423 149-2 □ 56:30 mins □ *●●●*

The title-page of the first edition of the Op. 3 concertos declared that their solo instruments were two violins and cello. In fact they are nothing of the kind. Handel's publisher, Walsh, may have been capitalising on the popularity of Corelli's concertos, which *were* for this trio of soloists. Handel's use a splendid mix of oboes and violins, with contributions from recorders, bassoons and cellos, in a delightfully unpredictable manner.

There are over a dozen recordings available. I pick Pinnock's for its wit, poise – many others are faster, some positively scampering through allegros – and some fine playing, especially from the late David Reichenberg. One senses that it was harder to keep an oboe in tune over a decade ago, as both collective technique and instrument/reed manufacture had some way to go. But his playing was wonderfully expressive – hear the Largo movements of the first two concertos – and fluent, for instance in the Third in G major, at times effectively a solo oboe concerto. *GP*

12 Concerti Grossi, Op. 6

Handel & Haydn Society/Christopher Hogwood

L'Oiseau-Lyre 436 845-2 □ 157:08 mins (3 discs) □ ⓐⓐⓐ

Handel composed these 12 concertos astonishingly quickly, from 29 September to 20 October 1739, and unlike his other sets (Op. 3 and the organ concertos) they reflect their unity. Each contrasts with the next in key; the scoring is constant throughout (though he later added optional oboe parts to four of them); they are remarkably equal in quality.

Hogwood's approach is refreshingly plain – no optional wind, few decorations and rests seldom filled up with solo cadenzas. The beginning of the First Concerto is a microcosm of the whole set – a proud opening, strongly articulated; the unexpected turn to the minor falling ever deeper into pathos; a vigorously bustling Allegro. Tempi are lively but not rushed – the Musette of the Sixth Concerto is haunting; No. 12, virtually a solo concerto, sparkles with life.

The three solo strings, with separate continuo harpsichord, are centrally placed, the sound expanding widely in the tuttis. Although this was not a public recording, it is spacious and, I suspect, needed relatively little editing. Even if at the price of occasional less than perfect intonation, the string tone is free and uninhibited – Handel is able to speak for himself. *GP*

Music for the Royal Fireworks; Four Coronation Anthems

The King's Consort, Choir of New College, Oxford/Robert King

Hyperion CDA 66350 □ 56:52 mins □ ⓐⓐⓐ

To celebrate the Treaty of Aix-la-Chapelle in 1748, an enormous fireworks display was given in London's Green Park – somewhat disastrously, as part of the wooden structure which supported it burned down. Handel's music, though, was immensely successful; even the rehearsal in Vauxhall Gardens drew a crowd of over 12,000 and grid-locked traffic on London Bridge for three hours.

This recording re-creates the scale of that original outdoor performance with 24 oboes ('foreman' Paul Goodwin), nine each of horns and trumpets, a dozen bassoons and a mighty percussion of four pairs of timpani, including a unique pair of extra-large 'double drums',

and four side drummers. The effect is shattering, the clearest justification for 'authenticity' in performance. This vast army of wind-players remains crisp in Allegros and takes them as fast as any smaller-scale band. The most surprisingly sensuous sonority comes in the quiet 'La paix'.

As a bonus come the four anthems Handel composed for the coronation of George II, sung with polish and precision which would have been welcomed at the first performance when the presiding archbishop noted 'the Anthem all in confusion: All irregular in the Music'. *GP*

Water Music

English Baroque Soloists/John Eliot Gardiner

Philips 434 122-2 □ 53:13 mins □ ⓐⓐⓐ

Though some of Handel's intentions are unclear – the order of movements, exact details of scoring – there's no doubt that the performance of the *Water Music* – which so pleased George I in 1717 – was given by up to fifty instrumentalists in a barge on the River Thames. This serves as a guide, at least, through the maze of available recordings, currently over forty of them.

The English Baroque Soloists' forces are not only large but bold too. Brazen, close-recorded horns balance the rest of the band – a magnificently stirring sound. Gardiner is inventive, though never merely quirky: in the F major Suite, bourrée and hornpipe are interlinked, with a constant and very springy pulse; the familiar Air is spry and sensitively decorated; the brief minor half-movement is strongly coloured by four bassoons.

If your courage fails you, try Pinnock's account with The English Concert on Archiv – indeed, his six-disc set of the *Water Music*, *Fireworks Music* and Concertos Opp. 3 and 6 will set you up for life. But for me, Gardiner best recaptures the spirit of this water-borne extravaganza. *GP*

Harris: Symphony No. 3

Schuman: Symphony No. 3

New York PO/Leonard Bernstein

DG 419 780-2 □ 51:12 mins □ ⓐⓐⓐ

These two classics of the American symphonic repertoire were premiered within two years of each other by Koussevitzky and the Boston SO. Roy Harris's one-movement Third

Symphony (1939) is almost routinely referred to as the greatest American symphony (though this is the only current recording), and it remains a powerful one. Its rugged, wide-open-spaces qualities seem to speak of the rolling plains of the Midwest. The influence of Sibelius, though palpable, is transformed into something utterly individual. William Schuman, a Harris pupil, produced a Third Symphony (1941) twice as long and ten times as sophisticated as his teacher's, all involved contrapuntal structures, big-city sounds and gleaming orchestration. It, too, packs a mighty punch. Bernstein recorded both pieces at least twice with the New York Philharmonic: this, his last version of the Harris, is slower and lacks some of the sense of reckless adventure in his 1966 LP version, not currently available. But the Schuman is thrillingly done and the recording is first class. Both composers were prolific symphonists: in fact they wrote more important ones – but there's no current version of either the Harris 7 or the Schuman 6, and the two Thirds are essential for any collector of American music. *CM*

HARTMANN/HINDEMITH

Hartmann: Concerto funebre

Hindemith: Violin Concerto; Cello Concerto

André Gertler (violin), Paul Tortelier (cello); Czech PO/Karel Ančerl

Supraphon 11 1955-2 □ AAD stereo/mono □ 75:32 mins □ ⊘⊘

Karl Amadeus Hartmann's anguished *Concerto funebre*, composed at the outbreak of the Second World War, provides an eloquent testimony of the composer's staunch opposition to the Nazis. Concurrently, Hindemith also fell foul of the regime, but his response in these two powerful works appears to have been more resigned than defiant. Stirring performances from Gertler and Ančerl, though the Cello Concerto, recorded in mono, suffers from a rather primitive balance between soloist and orchestra. *EL*

HARTMANN

Sinfonia tragica; Symphony No. 2 (Adagio); Gesangsszene

Siegmund Nimsgern (baritone); Bamberg SO/Karl Anton Rickenbacher

Koch Schwann 3-1295-2 □ 63:50 mins □ ⊘⊘⊘

Karl Amadeus Hartmann's music hasn't travelled much outside his native Bavaria: unfortunate, since he was a key figure in 20th-century music, probably the most important Austro-German symphonist since Mahler. He died with eight numbered symphonies to his credit. An equal number of lost or unpublished symphonic works, from his years of 'internal exile' during Hitler's Reich, has since emerged to enlarge the picture of a restless, troubled spirit grappling with problems of symphonic form and meaning in a hostile, self-destructive world.

The long-suppressed *Sinfonia tragica* (1940) is the most easily assimilable work on this impressive Koch release: its two movements balance a lamenting post-Mahlerian/Bergian Adagio against a spookily dionysiac *danse macabre*. The 'official' Symphony No. 2 (1945–6), a single, intense Adagio, extends the spirit of lament in a more kaleidoscopic orchestral style. The *Gesangsszene*, on words from Giraudoux's *Sodom and Gomorrah*, was Hartmann's last work, unfinished at his death from cancer in 1963: a sermon on human folly, atomic power, materialism and environmental destruction. Fischer-Dieskau recorded this beautiful and disturbing piece with Kubelík on Wergo, but Nimsgern, on top form here, is an equally eloquent protagonist. Rickenbacher leads performances of urgent commitment, confirming Hartmann's mastery of the large orchestra. *CM*

HAYDN

Cello Concertos Nos 1 in C & 2 in D

Truls Mørk (cello); Norwegian CO/Iona Brown

Virgin VC 5 45014 2 □ 49:38 mins □ ⊘⊘⊘

HAYDN/KRAFT

Haydn: Cello Concertos Nos 1 in C & 2 in D

Kraft: Cello Concerto in C, Op. 4

Anner Bylsma (cello); Tafelmusik/Jeanne Lamon

Deutsche Harmonia Mundi RD 77757 □ 66:34 mins □ ⊘⊘⊘

Haydn's cello concertos are the most familiar Classical concertos (notwithstanding those fine, though comparatively neglected works by CPE Bach, Boccherini, Stamitz and others) for an instrument that was in a state of flux and undergoing a radical reappraisal of its technical possibilities. Both are brilliant showpieces, demanding utmost precision, clarity of articulation, and real daring, if the élan and spontaneity of Haydn's prodigious invention is to register fully. In Truls Mørk, these works have a soloist of phenomenal accomplishments and a vivid sense of imagination; his playing is a model of clarity and sheer audacity, too, particularly in the final movement of the C major Concerto. High praise for the Norwegian CO under the direction of Iona Brown, as the fiendish upper string writing is infused with a deftness and effortless grace which belie the difficulty of achieving perfect unanimity of ensemble among the violins, in the taxing ritornello sections of both concertos. Mørk is an articulate and sensitive player (he favours Maurice Gendron's splendidly idiomatic cadenzas in the D major Concerto), and this finely engineered recording is a clear first option among modern-instrument performances.

As ever, revelations of timbre and texture come thick and fast in Anner Bylsma's authentic accounts with the stunning Canadian period band Tafelmusik, directed from the violin by Jeanne Lamon. Both recorded sound and performances are in a class apart. Bylsma's playing is unfailingly distinguished, his tone constantly alluring and his virtuosity dazzling. Of special renown is his performance of a concerto in C by Haydn's principal cellist at Eszterháza, Anton Kraft, one of the founding fathers of modern cello-playing. These are outstanding discs. Since each represents the ultimate within their fields, I'd strongly advise you to sample both. *MJ*

HAYDN

Keyboard Concertos in F, Hob. XVIII:3, in G, Hob. XVIII:4 & in D, Hob. XVIII:11

Franz Liszt CO/Emanuel Ax (piano)

Sony SK 48383 □ 58:41 mins □ 😊😊😊

Bracingly alert and crisply sculpted pianism from Emanuel Ax, who also directs the Franz Liszt Chamber Orchestra, Budapest, in infectiously high-spirited accounts of three of Haydn's keyboard concertos. The playing itself displays all the dash, élan and sheer polish that one could possibly crave in music of this kind, though it should be remembered that the modern piano and orchestral instruments heard on this disc have very little in common with the more limited sonority and leaner timbre of the fortepiano or clavier of the Classical era, and Haydn himself would have expected the accompanying orchestral forces to be far smaller than those employed here. That said, and allowing for obvious changes in perspective in matters of articulation, phrasing and ornamentation, Ax's readings leave very little to be desired; there is a freshness and spontaneity about the faster movements which is pure delight, while the Andante slow movements are warmly and affectionately

enunciated. The recording, made at the Italian Institute, Budapest, is exceptionally clear and wide-ranging, and the inescapable charm and magic of these readings makes the looming issues of Classical performance scholarship seem dry and pedantic – why not just sit back and enjoy the music in all its prodigal inventiveness? *MJ*

HAYDN

Keyboard Concerto in D, Hob. XVIII:11
see also Collection: Baroque Music

HAYDN

Sinfonia concertante in B flat for violin, cello, oboe & bassoon, Hob. I:105; Symphony No. 6 in D (Le matin); Cello Concerto No. 2 in D

Ralph Kirshbaum (cello), Gordon Hunt (oboe), Robin O'Neill (bassoon); English CO/Pinchas Zukerman (violin)

RCA Victor Red Seal 09026 62696 2 □ 68:09 mins □ 😊😊😊

Haydn's Sinfonia concertante, an adjunct to his *London* Symphonies, is a ceremonially expansive work, less often played than it surely deserves to be. It receives majestic and exuberant attention here, in a newly recorded performance of incomparable grandeur and idiomatic power. Pinchas Zukerman and Ralph Kirshbaum join ECO principals Gordon Hunt and Robin O'Neill in a large-scale reading that never falters or loses sight of the classically poised architecture of this work, sometimes catalogued as Haydn's Symphony No. 105. The term isn't inappropriate, given that Haydn wrote it with the violinist and impresario Johann Peter Salomon (prime mover in attracting Haydn to Great Britain in 1791) and several of his colleagues in view. This excellent disc also features a winningly articulate, vigorous and poised account of Haydn's Symphony No. 6 (*Le matin*), first in a trilogy of new works marking his arrival at Eszterháza in 1761, and Ralph Kirshbaum's cultured, clean-limbed performance of the Cello Concerto in D. This is a particularly valuable issue, given that there is no finer recording currently available of the gloriously inventive Sinfonia concertante, a work representing Haydn in the full flood of his genius. *MJ*

HAYDN

Symphonies Nos 26, 35, 38, 39, 41–52, 58, 59 & 65

The English Concert/Trevor Pinnock

Archiv 435 001-2 □ 370:23 mins (6 discs) □ 😊😊

Of all orchestras specialising in period performance, none gives more consistent value than The English Concert. Not from this orchestra will you find the sort of mannered stylistic 'calling-cards' that mar many otherwise excellent period performances. Nor will you have to tolerate the whining tonal anaemia that so often hides (though not well enough) behind the cloak of scholarship. Pinnock is acutely alive to the freshness and adventure of these invigorating if uneven works. Indeed, some may find him too lively by half in matters of tempo and sheer rhythmic momentum. Texturally, the performances are a revelation, bringing unsurpassed clarity to the part-writing and an almost chamber-musical quickness of reaction – and, more important, of consequence. There's nothing haphazard here, yet the sense of ceremony and formalised drama never preclude a feeling of spontaneity. The squeaky-clean precision of the playing is matched by superb recording, neither too close nor too spacious. Of so-called traditional performances, none has given me greater pleasure in Haydn than those of the Orpheus Chamber Orchestra on DG. *JS*

Symphonies Nos 82–87 (Paris)

Austro-Hungarian Haydn Orchestra/Adám Fischer

Nimbus NI 5419/20 □ 147:57 mins (2 discs) □ ❷❷❷

Recorded (perhaps a little over-resonantly) in the Haydnsaal at the Esterhazy Palace in Eisenstadt, which saw the birth of most of Haydn's masterpieces, these performances use modern instruments and playing styles but are in all other ways as authentic as you could wish – a delight from first note to last. The spirit of 'Papa' Haydn, long if simplistically known as 'the father of the symphony', emanates from every bar: the vitality, the humour, the occasional burst of turbulence, the tenderness and the apparently effortless craftsmanship and ingenuity all burst out here in a recording project which was quite audibly a labour of love (this box, whose contents are also available separately, is Vol. 6 of a complete cycle that can hold its own against all-comers). True, there are textural felicities and colouristic shades that emerge more clearly in the splendid Kuijken recordings of the same works on two Virgin CDs – period performances as distinguished and enjoyable as any yet recorded – but in overall balance, pregnant phrasing and instrumental excellence these

offer in compensation a degree of warmth and imagination which makes up for the loss of a few details here and there. A right and welcome feast. *JS*

London Symphonies, Vols 1 (Nos 95, 96, 98 & 102–4) & 2 (Nos 93, 94, 97 & 99–101)

Amsterdam Concertgebouw Orchestra/Colin Davis

Philips Duo 442 611-2, 442 614-2 □ ADD □ 151:27 mins, 152:03 mins (2 discs each) □ ❷❷

Despite the persuasive claims of Harnoncourt and Rattle with modern instruments, or for that matter the 'authentic' performance approaches of Norrington and Brüggen, these recordings of the *London* Symphonies, dating from the mid-Seventies and early Eighties, still reign supreme. Admittedly, this is big-band Haydn with an unequivocal nod towards Beethoven in movements such as the Vivace of No. 102. But there's such rhythmic vitality and rumbustious humour in Davis's conducting that any doubts about the size of the orchestra are swept aside. In any case, the Concertgebouw performs like chamber musicians with marvellously crisp and light articulation throughout. Tempi in slow movements may be more deliberate than in recent recordings, but Davis manages to effect a high level of expressivity and musical characterisation without ever sounding in the least bit stodgy. This is a wonderful set, and undoubtedly one of the highlights of Philips's invaluable Duo series. *EL*

Concerto a 8
see Collection: Concerti di flauti

Requiem

Ueli Wiget (piano), Håkan Hardenberger (trumpet); Ensemble Modern/Ingo Metzmacher

Sony SK 58972 □ 63:02 mins □ ❷❷❷

Though a requiem in name (and intention), with movement titles from the Requiem Mass, Henze declines to set the text of the Mass – there is no choir – preferring instead a wholly instrumental work. The piece is subtitled 'Nine Sacred Concertos', recalling 17th-century models, and is unusually scored for piano solo, trumpet concertante and a chamber orchestra of special timbres: saxophone, celesta, harp, alto flute, contrabass clarinet and Wagnerian brass instruments – bass trumpet and contrabass trombone – are added to the expected strings and wind.

Henze, an atheist, reinterprets the Mass so that his instrumental numbers 'tell of the fears and afflictions of people of our own time'. The 'Rex tremendae', which features Håkan Hardenberger's virtuosic solo trumpet in aggressive mood, evokes a recent brutality – Henze deplored US military tactics in the Gulf War – but also quotes the Badenweiler March, Hitler's favourite. This thundering section is movingly followed by a desolate Agnus Dei for strings and piano alone. The solo trumpet does speak lyrically in the 'Lacrimosa', but the real commentary comes from Ueli Wiget's eloquently portrayed piano line. The C major chord reverberating at the end affirms Henze's belief in 'the world that must not be destroyed'. *Deborah Calland*

HENZE

Symphony No. 7; Barcarola per Grande Orchestra

City of Birmingham SO/Simon Rattle
EMI CDC 7 54762 2 □ **59:52 mins** □ 🟢🟢🟢

In the Seventh Symphony, composed for the centenary of the Berlin Philharmonic in 1982, Henze deliberately set out to write a German symphony, casting his first movement in the manner of a sonata-form Allemande and following this with an elegiac slow movement and a Scherzo and finale inspired by one of Hölderlin's most desolate poems. It's a deeply impressive work, masterfully scored and cogently argued, unlike the composer's previous work in this genre. The *Barcarola* dates from 1979 and is dedicated to the memory of the composer Paul Dessau. Like the symphony, the *Barcarola* has strong extra-musical connotations, in this case a haunting vision of the ferryman Charon rowing the dead and dying across the River Styx. This imagery is projected in music of dark and threatening power, again demonstrating Henze's formidable aural imagination. The composer is well served by Rattle and the CBSO, recorded live in Symphony Hall, which delivers outstanding and committed performances of both works. Urgently recommended. *EL*

HINDEMITH

Cello Concerto
see HARTMANN: Concerto funebre
and SCHUMANN: Cello Concerto in A minor

HINDEMITH

Horn Concerto
see STRAUSS: Horn Concertos Nos 1 & 2

HINDEMITH

Kammermusiken Nos 1–7

Ueli Wiget (piano), Michael Stirling (cello), Peter Rundel (violin), Werner Dickel (viola), Wolfram Just (viola d'amore), Martin Lücker (organ); Ensemble Modern/Markus Stenz

RCA Victor Red Seal 09026 61730 2 □ **127:16 mins (2 discs)** □ 🟢🟢🟢

RCA's double set, celebrating the centenary of Hindemith's birth, tricksily resembles a birthday cake wrapped in brown paper. In fact it contains probably the best complete recording yet made of the seven *Kammermusiken*, perhaps his central achievement of the Twenties, which have good claim to be considered the 20th-century equivalent of Bach's Brandenburg Concertos. Stenz here directs the Ensemble Modern and its solo instrumentalists in crisp, fondly idiomatic accounts which for wit and technical command, as well as their tangy recorded sound, outdo the rival version from the Concertgebouw soloists under Chailly (on Decca).

All the performances are outstanding; the real triumphs are *Kammermusik* No. 4 (the Violin Concerto), which emerges as a work of considerable stature and eloquence, and No. 7, the Organ Concerto, whose balance problems are well solved in RCA's studio sound. *CM*

HINDEMITH

Mathis der Maler Symphony; Trauermusik; Symphonic Metamorphoses on Themes by Carl Maria von Weber

Geraldine Walther (viola); San Francisco Symphony/Herbert Blomstedt
Decca 421 523-2 □ **56:08 mins** □ 🟢🟢🟢

Nobilissima Visione; Konzertmusik for viola, Op. 48; Der Schwanendreher

Geraldine Walther (viola); San Francisco Symphony/Herbert Blomstedt
Decca 433 809-2 □ **66:57 mins** □ 🟢🟢🟢

The Hindemith centenary year (1995) inspired a number of major releases of the composer's most popular orchestral works, most notably from Sawallisch and Abbado. But despite the considerable distinctions of their recordings, my allegiance to Herbert Blomstedt's two discs from 1988 and 1992 remains steadfast.

Blomstedt is an outstanding Hindemith interpreter. At every point he challenges the popular conception of the composer as a dry academic with interpretations that burst with vigour and variety of colour. The *Mathis der Maler* Symphony is particularly powerful, weighty without ever suggesting ponderousness, emotionally committed yet controlled. He is supported by magnificent orchestral playing throughout, and Geraldine Walther proves an eloquent soloist in the two viola concertante works. Together the two discs serve to confirm Hindemith's status as one of the major figures in 20th-century music. *EL*

HINDEMITH

Symphonic Metamorphoses on Themes by Carl Maria von Weber

see also REGER: Variations and Fugue on a Theme by Mozart

HINDEMITH

Violin Concerto

see HARTMANN: Concerto funebre

HOLLOWAY

Violin Concerto; Horn Concerto

Ernst Kovacic (violin), Barry Tuckwell (horn); Scottish CO/Matthias Bamert

Collins 14392 □ **73:04 mins** □ *♪♪♪*

No contemporary British composer has thought more deeply about the issues involved in a wholehearted return to the once-forbidden fruits of tonality than Robin Holloway (b1943). He has composed a large number of effective and inventive concertos and concertante works: none is finer or more originally planned than his scintillating Violin Concerto of 1990. Nine 'windows', letting in light both textural and harmonic, turn the concerto's large single movement into a chain of Scherzos and Trios, revolving around a particularly luscious centre which proves to be an orchestration of Fauré's song 'Le parfum impérissable'. Ernst Kovacic, for whom it was written, rises seemingly effortlessly to the taxing demands of the solo part; the bejewelled orchestral writing is sensuous delight.

The expansive Horn Concerto (1980), more traditional in form and more Straussian in orientation, is nevertheless one of the finest contributions to its genre since Strauss's own, and one of the most difficult: Tuckwell (the dedicatee) expounds it with mastery and affection. Holloway's teeming Second Concerto for Orchestra on NMC is as important an achievement as the Violin Concerto, but this disc is much more generous in duration and gives a more detailed picture of the composer. *CM*

HOLMBOE

Symphonies Nos 1, 3 (Sinfonia rustica) & 10

Aarhus SO/Owain Arwel Hughes

BIS CD-605 □ **70:30 mins** □ *♪♪♪*

The senior Danish composer Vagn Holmboe (b1909) is without question his country's greatest symphonist since Nielsen, while his prolific achievements in the field of the string quartet far outrank his elder countryman (catch, if you can, three of Holmboe's earlier quartets excellently played by the Kontra Quartet on Marco Polo dacapo). Few of the symphonies – which enshrine Holmboe's personal principles of organic development through continual metamorphosis of melodic cells, owing as much to Bartók as to Nielsen or Sibelius – were recorded in the LP era, but BIS has now completed a CD cycle. The present disc, Vol. 3 of that cycle, perhaps offers the most varied introduction to this admirable composer, though in fact the standard of these works is remarkably consistent all through. The trim and lively First Symphony of 1935, 'for chamber orchestra' (Holmboe has since composed three chamber symphonies proper), shows something of the influence of Stravinsky and between-wars neo-classicism. No. 3 (1941) based on medieval singing games from Jutland, is on one level a pastoral comedy, on another a defiance of the Nazi invaders of Denmark. The much more recent No. 10, with its superscription from Walt Whitman, is a powerful expression of Holmboe's mature symphonic methods. Excellent performances from the Welsh conductor Owain Arwel Hughes – who has the composer's imprimatur as a trusted interpreter of his music – and a recording well up to BIS's highest standard. *CM*

HOLST/VAUGHAN WILLIAMS

Holst: The Planets

Vaughan Williams: Symphony No. 4 in F minor

LSO/Gustav Holst, BBC SO/Ralph Vaughan Williams

Koch Legacy 3-7018-2 □ **ADD mono** □ **69:17 mins** □ *♪♪*

Some will think this a perverse choice, especially for the Holst. With literally dozens of modern sonic spectaculars of *The Planets* cramming the shelves, why go back seventy years to the composer's own electrical recording of 1926? (You can sample his even earlier acoustic version on Pearl.) On the other hand, as Charles Ives so wisely said, what has music got to do with sound? Anyway, just hear the bouncing strings leap into your room at the very start of 'Mars'. The liveliness of the playing is amazing and puts some contemporary accounts to shame. The speeds are very fast by modern standards, which has nothing to do with the shortness of 78rpm sides but reflects the actual lighter, more flexible orchestral practice of the time – and also how Holst, an experienced conductor (and orchestral player) wanted the piece to go. 'Venus' loses its incipient sentimentality without surrendering an ounce of lyricism; 'Saturn' gains remorselessness and nobility. And hear the end of 'Uranus' for a glimpse into the mysterious heart of the void.

Dear reader, it's your right to demand a digital stereo soundfest if you so desire – what is *The Planets* if not one of the greatest orchestral showpieces ever composed? (Actually, a lot more than that.) There are many good ones: for instance, James Judd with the RPO on Denon; Andrew Davis on Teldec (coupled with a fine account of *Egdon Heath*); Adrian Boult, the work's first conductor, superb on EMI at bargain price; Vernon Handley at super-bargain price on Tring. John Eliot Gardiner (DG) gets brownie points for a stimulating coupling: Percy Grainger's 'imaginary ballet' *The Warriors*. But look at the coupling here!

Vaughan Williams's own 1937 recording of his Fourth Symphony is rightly legendary, unmatched for fierceness and focused violence. Speeds are again recklessly fast by today's standards, but the BBC SO, playing as if their lives depended on it, isn't fazed. The CD transfer has resulted in a slightly 'whiter', more congested sound than the LP version – in fact, *The Planets* has more natural perspective – but this blazing performance remains my first choice for this challenging symphony. To have both on one disc is luxury indeed. *CM*

HONEGGER/STRAVINSKY

Honegger: Symphonies Nos 2 & 3 (Liturgique)

Stravinsky: Concerto in D

Berlin PO/Herbert von Karajan

DG Originals 447 435-2 □ ADD □ 71:33 mins □ *♪♪*

These great symphonies date from the war years, the Second from the dark days when Honegger lived through the occupation of Paris, the Third from 1945. In No. 2, this Berlin performance features superlative playing, intensifying the conflicts which are only resolved in the closing bars.

The *Symphonie liturgique* also confronts images of hope and despair, culminating in a long postlude sounding 'the song of the bird'.

Again the performance is magnificent, and the expressive power is extraordinary, for in this repertoire Karajan remains without peer. Completed by a beautifully balanced Stravinsky Concerto in D, this is a very special disc. *Terry Barfoot*

HUMMEL

Piano Concertos in A minor, Op. 85 & in B minor, Op. 98

Stephen Hough (piano); English CO/Bryden Thomson

Chandos CHAN 8507 □ 60:06 mins □ *♪♪♪*

It's strange to think that there was a time when Hummel was incomparably more renowned than Schubert, and that Chopin, growing up in Warsaw, heard more of Hummel's music than of Beethoven's. Posterity has rather over-redressed the balance, so that Hummel now stands in need of championship. He's unlikely to find any more accomplished or persuasive an advocate than Stephen Hough – still an underrated pianist, though by no means unacknowledged. The reference to Chopin is not fortuitous. Hummel's music was one of the shaping forces of his own style, and the source of the debt is fascinatingly plain to hear in these sadly neglected concertos. Hough brings to his playing of them all the sparkling virtuosity, subtlety of shading and rhythmic flexibility more famously associated with Chopin, and he receives splendid support from Thomson and the English CO. Nor should the recording team be excluded from the praise. This is an outstanding disc in all respects. *JS*

IBERT

Escales; Flute Concerto; Hommage à Mozart; Paris (Suite symphonique); Bacchanale; Bostoniana; Louisville-concert

Timothy Hutchins (flute); Montreal SO/Charles Dutoit

Decca 440 332-2 □ 79:00 mins □ *♪♪♪*

Because Jacques Ibert's chief claim to fame remains the uproarious *Divertissement*, it is tempting to assume that all his other work is couched in a similar vein. That this is clearly not the case is emphasised here in a generously filled disc that offers a useful cross-section of his orchestral output. Beginning with the atmospheric *Escales* (Ports of Call), whose sensuous textures are worthy of comparison with either Debussy or Ravel, we move to the technically demanding Flute Concerto and a sequence of rhythmically dynamic orchestral works of almost Waltonian brilliance. Only *Paris*, an affectionate and witty portrayal of the composer's native city, recalls the satirical high jinks of the *Divertissement*. Throughout the 79 minutes of music, Dutoit and the Montreal SO seem to be enjoying themselves very much. Needless to say, they exploit every opportunity for virtuosity, and remain peerless in this particular repertoire. *EL*

IBERT

Escales: Divertissement
see CHAUSSON: Symphony in B flat

IPPOLITOV-IVANOV

Caucasian Sketches
see KHACHATURIAN: Gayaneh

IRELAND/BRIDGE/WALTON

Ireland: Piano Concerto in E flat

Bridge: Phantasm

Walton: Sinfonia concertante

Kathryn Stott (piano); RPO/Vernon Handley

Conifer74321 15007 2 □ 69:53 mins □ 𝄞𝄞𝄞

John Ireland's is among the best-loved of English piano concertos and one of his most representative works – one of his most sophisticated, too, showing a thorough assimilation of contemporary (1930) influences, from Ravel to Stravinsky. The first movement combines a vein of elegy and sublimated jazz style to produce a gentler yet richer expressive vein than Constant Lambert. The slow movement, darker and deeply felt, gives way to a playful, almost childlike finale that nevertheless makes an exciting conclusion. Kathryn Stott's finely attuned performance, sometimes almost improvisatory in feel, finds more in this score than any previous performer; she is ideally partnered by Handley's orchestral accompaniment in a lively and full-bodied acoustic.

The couplings are generous and enterprising: Frank Bridge's haunted, broodingly atmospheric single-movement *Phantasm* (1931) is one of his most substantial and imaginative late scores, and Walton's invigorating, jazzy Sinfonia concertante (1928) is recorded for the first time in its original version with large orchestra and more complex solo part, in which form it emerges with added punch and dynamism. A superb combination of three key British works for piano and orchestra. *CM*

IVES/VARESE

Ives: Symphony No. 4; The Unanswered Question

Varèse: Amériques

Cleveland Orchestra & Chorus/Christoph von Dohnányi

Decca 443 172-2 □ 60:52 mins □ 𝄞𝄞𝄞

The brief 'cosmic landscape' *The Unanswered Question* is probably Ives's best-known piece, and beautifully done here, the solo trumpet evocatively situated in the distance. Its tranced, ironic meditation on the mysteries of time, space and human life gets the full transcendental philosophic treatment in the epic Fourth Symphony: perhaps Ives's greatest work, and certainly the most essential. It unites the amazing extremes of his musical personality, from the homely and hymnic to the abrasively exploratory, with an utterly radical vision of the orchestra. It wasn't premiered complete until 1965, fifty years after it was written. Stokowski, the conductor on that occasion, went on to make a blazingly visceral recording (CBS/Sony, currently unavailable). If Dohnányi lacks Stokowski's sheer sense of musical history in the making, he keeps the spiritual *quietus* behind the riotous detail coolly in view, and Decca's recording is texturally much clearer – a great gain in the scarifying heterophony of the 'Comedy' movement.

Varèse's *Amériques* (another work Stokowski premiered) may be the closest its composer comes to Debussy, and to the Straussian symphonic poem. But this stunning performance stresses its essential 'New World' qualities. This first and biggest of Varèse's American works is revealed in all its jazz swing and turbine beat, its grandiose big-city sprawl, sirens and all. Balance, rhythmic tension and sheer excitement easily outclass Nagano on Erato, and the recording is in the demonstration class. *CM*

IVES/RUGGLES/SEEGER

Ives: Three Places in New England; Orchestral Set No. 2

Ruggles: Sun-Treader; Men and Mountains

Ruth Crawford Seeger: Andante for Strings

Cleveland Orchestra & Chorus/Christoph von Dohnányi

Decca 443 776-2 □ 62:15 mins □ 𝄞𝄞𝄞

Throughout his period as the Cleveland's music director Dohnányi has been at pains to conduct American composers as well as the works of the Central European tradition that are his mainstay, and this collection of early US masterpieces shows how potent a force he can be in such repertoire, especially with such an accomplished and forthright orchestra.

The Ives works are the most familiar here, both in superbly delineated and controlled performances, and the Crawford Seeger the most unexpected: the *Andante for Strings* is a transcription from her famous String Quartet of 1931, and a chance to sample the whole work's astonishing radicalism and sheer originality; it's no substitute for a brand-new recording of the original quartet, though, which is badly needed.

Most fascinating of all are the two pieces by Carl Ruggles. Dohnányi's version of *Sun-Treader* is the best so far on disc, a musical machine of uncompromising dissonance and dogged counterpoint that never loses its remorseless momentum for an instant. *Men and Mountains* was the starting-point for *Sun-Treader*. It is the lesser work, yet still full of those moments of unique vision that make Ruggles's tiny output so significant in the development of American music.
Andrew Clements

JANACEK
The Cunning Little Vixen Suite
see **OPERA**: JANACEK: The Cunning Little Vixen

JANACEK
Jealousy Overture (Žárlivost)
see **OPERA**: JANACEK: Jenůfa

JANACEK
Lachian Dances
see **OPERA**: JANACEK: The Makropulos Case

JANACEK/SHOSTAKOVICH

Janáček: Sinfonietta; Taras Bulba

Shostakovich: The Age of Gold Suite

Vienna PO/Charles Mackerras, LPO/Bernard Haitink

Decca 430 727-2 □ **66:15 mins** □ 🎵🎵

According to Charles Mackerras, no orchestra in the world plays Janáček's Sinfonietta quite like that of the composer's home city, Brno. This, surely, is the next best thing: a conductor who knows how this piece can sound, urging this most sophisticated of orchestras to capture an authentic roughness of timbre. The brass fanfares are blatant but thrilling – the last few bars as recorded here always send shivers down my spine – while the close recording is able to bring more fragile instruments into the limelight, including the solo viola d'amore which here stands in for the entire viola section in the third movement (this is one of several important textural restorations ensured by the diligent Mackerras).

In the earlier (1915) but still undeniably modern-sounding rhapsody on scenes from the life of Gogol's Ukrainian hero Taras Bulba, the balance between pagan jagged edges and Romantic tenderness – very Viennese, as one might expect from these strings – is once again perfect. Shostakovich's snook-cocking *Age of*

Gold Suite seems worlds away, although the complete ballet appeared only a few years after the Sinfonietta, and its provenance is different. Typical of Haitink's LPO Shostakovich series, the performance has polish, breadth and vivid sound, though it lacks the very last degree of audaciousness. *DN*

JANACEK
Sinfonietta
see also BARTOK: The Miraculous Mandarin

JANACEK
Suite for String Orchestra
see SUK: Serenade for String Orchestra

KABALEVSKY
The Comedians Suite
see Collection: Russian Music

KANCHELI

Symphonies Nos 1 & 7 (Epilogue); Mourned by the Wind (Liturgy for viola and orchestra)

Sviatoslav Belonogov (viola); Moscow State SO/Fedor Glushchenko

Olympia Explorer OCD 424 □ **78:14 mins** □ 🎵🎵

If you know and love the spiritual integrity of those two great loners under Soviet rule, Alfred Schnittke and the Estonian Arvo Pärt, then Georgian composer Giya Kancheli is for you. Like Pärt before his emigration to the West in 1981, and Schnittke throughout his career, Kancheli finds his still centre – be it heartfelt lamentation or an introspective sense of peace – only between bouts of furious conflict.

Kancheli creates a riveting tension between extremes; there's no way of predicting whether the last bars will be deeply disquieting (as in the doom-beats of the First Symphony), profoundly consoling or unequivocally tragic (the whispered response to the forced victory parade in the Seventh, boldly following the example of the finale in Shostakovich's Fourth Symphony). The sincerity of the performances, which swivel arrestingly between the taut and the atmospheric under the firm guidance of Glushchenko, is no more in doubt than Kancheli's own when he uses the simplest, strongest elements of musical vocabulary to state his case. The cross-section of works makes this disc the best Kancheli starting-point – a film-maker taking up the *Liturgy* could do for it what *Platoon* did for Barber's *Adagio* – though there has been a host of vivid newcomers since. If haunted, you may like to proceed to fellow-Georgian Jansug Kakhidze's championship on Sony or a very fine sequence of the symphonies conducted by James DePreist (Ondine). *DN*

KHACHATURIAN/IPPOLITOV-IVANOV

Khachaturian: Gayaneh – five dances; Spartacus Suite; Masquerade Suite

Ippolitov-Ivanov: Caucasian Sketches

Armenian PO/Loris Tjeknavorian

ASV CD DCA 773 □ 75:57 mins □ 𝄞𝄞𝄞

Armenians might well be unhappy to find the outside world confusing their national music with that of their neighbouring state. But since Armenia's musical hero Aram Khachaturian grew up in Georgia, absorbed the local folk-idiom and in his maturity fused it with a conventional western Romantic style, no one is going to mind the passionate Armenian artists on this disc slipping across the musical border for Russian composer Ippolitov-Ivanov's much earlier Georgian impressions. The range is, in any case, wide – hardly a whiff of trans-Caucasian exoticism in Khachaturian's straightforward *Masquerade* pastiches – and authentic Armenian exuberance swashbuckles its way through the *Gayaneh* excerpts. Tjeknavorian's bravura here is borne out by brilliant strings and brass as well as an alarmingly vivid national percussion section.

The hybrid *Spartacus tours de force* are no less brilliantly done, and the famous Adagio treads air after a rather dim oboe solo. Sparer in colouring, and capturing a surprising ethnic authenticity, the *Caucasian Sketches* expose weaknesses in intonation – more from *Gayaneh* would have been preferable – but offer a showcase for the Armenians' panache in the dashing 'Procession of the Sardar'. If a different companion-piece and a different selection from *Gayaneh* are what you want, then Khachaturian's vivid 1962 recording of the suites is followed by excerpts from Maazel's complete recording of Prokofiev's *Romeo and Juliet* on Decca. For an exhausting, often exhilarating hour's worth of *Spartacus*, turn to the indefatigable Neeme Järvi (Chandos). *DN*

KHACHATURIAN

Masquerade – Waltz & Galop
see Collection: Russian Music

KHACHATURIAN

Violin Concerto in D minor; Masquerade – Waltz, Nocturne & Mazurka; Gayaneh – excerpts

David Oistrakh (violin); Philharmonia Orchestra/Aram Khachaturian

EMI CDC 5 55035 2 □ ADD mono □ 78:31 mins □ 𝄞𝄞𝄞

There are more meaningful showcases for David Oistrakh's flawless musicianship than the Khachaturian Violin Concerto, a shambling monster with a sackful of good tunes. Since, however, it was composed very much with this violinist in mind, and since Khachaturian's conducting is spirited enough to paper over the cracks in his own musical construction, this very impressive piece of teamwork deserves to be heard whether or not you can stand the piece itself. The accuracy of Oistrakh's pitching even in the most fiendishly difficult runs is compounded by his masterly freedom of phrasing and distinctive dark timbre, for which Khachaturian caters so effectively (even if the argument is frequently left with nowhere to go).

The 1954 mono recording offers the soloist extraordinary presence, setting the orchestra a little further back – unhelpful when Oistrakh duets with the Philharmonia clarinet or collective woodwind. But even though composer-conductor and soloist repeated their partnership in subsequent years, it never caught the same brilliant spark. Khachaturian's extensive selection from *Gayaneh* is very much alive and kicking too: has anyone subsequently carried off the Sabre Dance at such an audacious speed? *DN*

KODALY

Háry János Suite
see Collection: Hungarian Connections

KODALY

Dances of Marosszék; Dances of Galánta
see BARTOK: Divertimento

KOECHLIN

The Jungle Book

Iris Vermillion (mezzo-soprano), Johan Botha (tenor), Ralf Lukas (bass); RIAS Chamber Choir, Berlin RSO/David Zinman

RCA Victor Red Seal 09026 61955 2 □ 89:53 mins (2 discs) □ 𝄞𝄞𝄞

Fabulously prolific, the French composer and pedagogue Charles Koechlin was one of the greatest masters of the orchestra of the 20th century. Neglected during his life and since, his music is gradually coming into its own. This first complete recording of one of his central achievements, *The Jungle Book* – a Kipling-inspired cycle of four symphonic poems and three orchestral songs, composed at intervals over forty years – is the best possible introduction to Koechlin's cornucopic variety, from the stern, sonorous monody of *La loi de la jungle* to the super-Ravelian lushness of the seal lullaby, *Berceuse phoque*. The monkey scherzo *Les bandar-log* brilliantly satirises tonality and neo-classicism, the passacaglia *La méditation de Purun-Baghat* evokes Himalayan grandeur, and the torrential *La course de printemps* is simply the greatest French orchestral score between Debussy's *La mer* and Messiaen's *Turangalîla*. This appropriately sumptuous recording catches Koechlin's most glowing colours, though the balance in the vocal items could be better. *CM*

KORNGOLD
Violin Concerto: Much Ado About Nothing Suite
see BARBER: Violin Concerto

KORNGOLD

Symphony in F sharp, Op. 40; Abschiedslieder

Linda Finnie (contralto); BBC Philharmonic/Edward Downes

Chandos CHAN 9171 □ 67:57 mins □ *⊘⊘⊘*

Pronounced a musical genius by Mahler at the tender age of ten, Korngold should have become one of this century's major composers. But by ploughing the furrow of Austro-German late Romanticism at a time when such a style had become virtually moribund, he was sidelined until his gifts were more fully realised in Hollywood. Here, as an exile from Nazi-occupied Europe, he wrote some of the most sumptuous film scores of all time. In recent years Korngold's reputation has been considerably enhanced by the increasing representation of his output on disc. Certainly this eloquently performed premiere recording of the orchestral version of the 1920 *Abschiedslieder* (Songs of Farewell) will prove irresistible to those who relish the autumnal colours of Strauss's *Four Last Songs*.

The symphony is a much tougher proposition. Written during the composer's final years in the United States, the work is imbued with an air of deep personal tragedy that comes to the fore in an extended slow movement of considerable emotional power. While failing to eclipse memories of Rudolf Kempe's pioneering Seventies interpretation (Varèse-Sarabande), Downes and the BBC Philharmonic give it a wholly committed performance which will surely attract many more converts to this fascinating composer. *EL*

KRAFT
Cello Concerto in C
see HAYDN: Cello Concertos

LACHENMANN
Tanzsuite mit Deutschlandlied
see CHAMBER: LACHENMANN: String Quartet No. 2

LALO
Cello Concerto in D minor
see SAINT-SAENS: Cello Concerto No. 1 in A minor

LALO/SAINT-SAENS/BERLIOZ

Lalo: Symphonie espagnole

Saint-Saëns: Violin Concerto No. 3 in B minor

Berlioz: Rêverie et caprice, Op. 8

Itzhak Perlman (violin); Orchestre de Paris/Daniel Barenboim

DG Masters 445 549-2 □ 68:39 mins □ *⊘⊘*

Perlman is at his dazzling best in this magnetic account of Lalo's sultry Mediterranean masterpiece, the *Symphonie espagnole*. The verve and élan of the solo playing (one need only hear Perlman's sizzling opening salvo to appreciate what's in store here!) is in a class of its own. Perlman's legendary virtuosity inflames and illuminates this score, by turns tempestuously virile and heroic and then disarmingly seductive in character, with thrilling intensity. There is simply no finer account available, and the recording itself has magnificent presence and bloom. There is some spotlighting of the soloist but, given the excellence of Perlman's playing, this is scarcely a disadvantage. The Third Violin Concerto, in B minor, was Saint-Saëns's greatest creation for the instrument, and was written for the Spanish virtuoso Pablo de Sarasate; it receives playing of heroic stature from Perlman, who is also heard to great advantage in the rarely performed *Rêverie et caprice* by Berlioz. The Paris Orchestra provides discreet and idiomatic support under Daniel Barenboim, and this mid-price reissue on DG's Masters label offers illustrious playing and high-quality sound at comparatively modest cost; I'd hate you to miss it! *MJ*

LAMBERT
Aubade héroïque
see CHORAL & SONG: LAMBERT: The Rio Grande

LANGGAARD

Symphonies Nos 4–6

Danish National RSO/Neeme Järvi

Chandos CHAN 9064 □ 62:55 mins □ *⊘⊘⊘*

The eccentric and highly prolific Danish composer Rued Langgaard (1893–1952) wrote 16 symphonies that span a stylistic gamut from reactionary Romanticism to prophetic modernism, sometimes in the same work. Symphonies Nos 4 and 6 are among his best. Indeed, No. 6 (1919–20), 'The Heaven-Rending', is perhaps his masterpiece, a cogent, dramatic and utterly individual score depicting the cosmic struggle of good and evil, full of memorable ideas. No. 4 (1916), 'Autumn', is more of a rhapsodic and episodic nature poem, but its material is both original and delightfully memorable. The musical language occasionally reminds us that these scores are contemporary with the mature symphonies of Nielsen (whom Langgaard loathed), but there's no mistaking the distinctiveness of Langgaard's musical personality. The Fifth Symphony, 'Nature of the Steppe', heard here in its second version of 1931, is considerably more recidivist, lapsing in the end into a kind of Nordic Mendelssohnian dance music; but even this has attractive ideas and, like the other two, it receives outstanding advocacy from Järvi and his orchestra. All Langgaard's symphonies are available on the Danacord label, conducted by Ilya Stupel; but this superior Chandos release constitutes the best possible sampler for a true original. *CM*

LECLAIR

Violin Concertos, Opp. 7/4 in F, 7/6 in A & 10/2 in A; Flute Concerto, Op. 7/3 in C

Rachel Brown (flute); Collegium Musicum 90/Simon Standage (violin)

Chandos Chaconne CHAN 0564 □ 65:23 mins □ ❷❷❷

The recent upsurge of interest in Leclair's music continues apace. This disc is Vol. 2 of Chandos's three-CD series of the 12 violin concertos. The music certainly deserves more exposure. The premier French violinist-composer of the Baroque era, Leclair was among the first to marry the technical brilliance of Italian virtuosi like Vivaldi with the more formal elegance of the French style. The result is a graceful, ebullient music spiced with bravura passages for the soloist, who is asked to negotiate multiple-stopping and similar hazards, often at dazzling speeds.

Simon Standage rises to the challenge with relish, displaying great élan in the feisty opening movements of Op. 7/4 and 7/6 and in the dramatic solo/tutti exchanges that run through Op. 10/2. But no less captivating is Op. 7/3, which Leclair wrote for violin *or* oboe *or* flute! The last option is taken here, with Rachel Brown's supple tones dancing gaily through the fast movements and bringing a plaintive beauty to the richly textured Adagio. A splendid release. *Graham Lock*

LIADOV

Kikimora; Baba-Yaga; The Enchanted Lake; A Musical Snuffbox
see Collection: Russian Music

LIGETI

Piano Concerto; Cello Concerto; Violin Concerto

Pierre-Laurent Aimard (piano), Jean-Guihen Queyras (cello), Saschko Gawriloff (violin); Ensemble InterContemporain/Pierre Boulez

DG 439 808-2 □ 67:10 mins □ ❷❷❷

For all its stark contrasts between hyperactivity and stasis, the overriding impression gleaned from Ligeti's music is one of dislocation, even disorientation. Nowhere is this more apparent than in the outer movements of both the Piano and Violin concertos, where the listener seems to be party to a kind of aural nightmare in which different musical layers seem to move spontaneously in and out of focus with incredible rapidity. Yet this notion of randomness is quite illusory, for Ligeti exerts absolute control in the balancing of texture. A simpler, sometimes folk-like idiom underlines the slow movements, though the use of alternative tuning and the presence of unusual instruments such as the ocarina serves to emphasise an element of desolation that in moments of greatest emotional intensity even recalls Berg. In the earlier Cello Concerto of 1966, the emotional subtext is less ambiguous, though the musical language is in many ways more advanced.

Both the Piano and Cello concertos receive equally fine advocacy from the Ensemble Modern and Peter Eötvös on Sony. But the present disc scores over its rival by offering the only recording of the Violin Concerto, undoubtedly one of the finest and most provocative works Ligeti has ever written, here played with staggering virtuosity by its dedicatee, Saschko Gawriloff. *EL*

LISZT

Ce qu'on entend sur la montagne; Tasso, lamento e trionfo; Les préludes; Orpheus; Prometheus; Mazeppa; Festklänge

LPO/Bernard Haitink

Philips Duo 438 751-2 □ ADD □ 126:59 mins (2 discs) □ ❷❷

During his years at Weimar (1848–61) Liszt is generally credited with having invented the descriptive, programmatic medium known as the symphonic (or tone) poem, and these fine discs include performances of seven of his series of 12 such compositions. Though *Les préludes* and *Orpheus* are occasionally heard in the concert hall, many of the remainder are less than ideally familiar. Bernard Haitink's performances are admirable. As ever, he keeps the music on a tight rein, and these accounts, though spirited and exciting, never become vulgar or bellicose. *Tasso, lamento e trionfo* began life as preface to Goethe's play, though Liszt maintained that Byron's poem on the same tragic subject was just as potent a stimulus. *Orpheus* and *Prometheus* take classical legend as their inspiration; *Mazeppa* recalls the horrific fate of the eponymous 17th-century Cossack, while *Festklänge* (Festival Sounds) has no specific programme. The set begins with the first of the tone poems, *Ce qu'on entend sur la montagne* (after Victor Hugo), and these impressive performances come on two excellent remastered Philips discs. *MJ*

LISZT

Dante Symphony; Après un lecture de Dante (Dante Sonata) from Années de pèlerinage, Deuxième année (Italy)

Berlin Radio Chorus (women's voices), Berlin PO/Daniel Barenboim (piano)

Teldec 9031-77340-2 □ 67:00 mins □ *❷❷❷*

Liszt's engagement with the writings of Dante found fullest musical outlet in the symphony which bears his name, and the extract from the Italian year of his *Années de pèlerinage*, which here forms an apposite coupling for the *Dante Symphony*, both works receive committed and expert performances from Daniel Barenboim, heard here as both conductor and pianist. The *Dante Symphony* is generally less successful, and certainly less familiar, than Liszt's finest orchestral work, the *Faust Symphony*; each shares a common fascination with things both apocalyptic and transcendent, and each deserves greater currency in the concert hall (there is no shortage of fine recordings of the latter). With the Berlin Philharmonic at his command, Barenboim is master of all he surveys in this elusive score; the narrative associations with the writings of Dante fall less instantly into sonic relief in this work than do the Mephistophelian machinations of its companion piece, yet Barenboim's pictorialist imagination and fine dramatic flair evince a performance of gripping intensity. Orchestral playing is wholly beyond criticism; the horrific impressionism of the 'Purgatorio' section (normally the most difficult to mould and project meaningfully) is chillingly eloquent, and the live recording, made at the Berlin Festspielhaus in February 1992, is realistically balanced and admirably detailed. The *Dante Sonata*, a studio performance, is nowhere less than totally engrossing, and Barenboim's all-encompassing technique confidently

surmounts every successive hurdle with complete aplomb. If you've enjoyed the *Faust Symphony*, I'd urge you to sample the Dante-inspired works as a follow-up – you'll find no finer performance than these. *MJ*

LISZT

De profundis; Piano Concerto in E flat; Totentanz

Steven Mayer (piano); LSO/Tamás Vásáry

ASV CD DCA 778 □ 66:32 mins □ *❷❷❷*

Seasoned Lisztians probably acquired these world premiere recordings first time around, but if you did happen to miss Steven Mayer's accomplished performances of three major additions to the Liszt discography, I'd urge you to seize the moment now! *De profundis*, a monumental ternary-form epic for piano and orchestra, and Liszt's diabolical showpiece, *Totentanz* (heard here in Busoni's little-known edition, based on the original 1849 text), frame Jay Rosenblatt's reconstruction of a recently exhumed (and modestly proportioned) adjunct to the familiar pair of Liszt concertos. Vivid recordings, and arresting pianism from Mayer – enthusiastically recommended. *MJ*

LISZT

A Faust Symphony

Peter Seiffert (tenor); Prague Philharmonic Choir (men's voices), Berlin PO/Simon Rattle

EMI CDC 5 55220 2 □ 68:49 mins □ *❷❷❷*

The *Faust Symphony* is Liszt's finest orchestral work. It comprises three large-scale cameos of the principal protagonists of Goethe's epic and conveys graphically the sinister undercurrents and explosive passions which culminate in Faust's ultimate redemption, through the unsullied love of the virginal Gretchen (or Marguerite in Gérard de Nerval's French edition, the basis of Berlioz's *La damnation de Faust*), Goethe's ideal of the Eternal Feminine. The first movement, much the longest, presents the character of Faust, variously as mystic, romantic, philosopher and hero, embarked on a perilous quest to discover the key of human existence at whatever cost. Gretchen is saintly, inviolate and innocent; she alone can grant Faust absolution from the pact he has enjoined with Mephistopheles, whose malevolent spirit of negation turns every worthy human aspiration to dust. Strong stuff, then, and Rattle's sensational live performance pulls no punches. The Berlin PO plays for him as men possessed, and the virtuosity and grandeur of orchestral response is unrivalled in any other performance. The concluding choral apotheosis is profoundly moving, as Peter Seiffert and the Prague chorus sing radiantly of Faust's absolution. A magnificent account, warmly and atmospherically recorded at Berlin's Philharmonie in April 1994. Miss it at your peril! *MJ*

LISZT

Mephisto Waltz No. 1; Hungarian Rhapsody No. 2
see Collection: Hungarian Connections

LISZT

Piano Concertos Nos 1 in E flat & 2 in A; Totentanz

Alfred Brendel (piano); LPO/Bernard Haitink

Philips Silver Line 426 637-2 □ ADD □ 55:46 mins
□ 𝄞𝄞

Philips seem to have something of a monopoly over the strongest recordings of these works, for apart from Brendel and Haitink their catalogue also boasts the marvellously impulsive performances of Sviatoslav Richter with the LSO under Kondrashin, which are now coupled with a mighty version of the B minor Sonata from the Russian maestro. Choosing between the thrills and spills of Richter and the more measured intellectual approach of Brendel is almost impossible. Suffice it to say that in the last resort I glean greater musical satisfaction from Brendel, who is more probing in the slower sections of the two concertos. Similarly, while Brendel never takes you by the scruff of the neck, he loses nothing to his colleague in terms of physical dynamism. Other advantages of the present version include a better-balanced recording and a highly charged version of the extraordinary *Totentanz*. If you prefer a more up-to-date recording of all these works, I would opt for Boris Berezovsky on Teldec, but at mid-price the present release still remains irresistible. *EL*

LLOYD

Symphony No. 7

BBC PO/George Lloyd

Albany TROY 057-2 □ 49:48 mins □ 𝄞𝄞𝄞

The Cornish-born symphonist George Lloyd, wounded in the navy, quit music for market gardening for some decades. In the Eighties he became something of a *cause célèbre*, his name brandished in the eternal hostilities between traditionalists and modernists in British music. Undeniably tuneful and scintillatingly scored,

innocent of any desire to shock, his works seem to appeal to a large audience hungry for modern music that sounds more or less like familiar Romantic masterpieces of earlier eras. Whether that makes him the equal of Tchaikovsky or more of an Eric Coates figure who doesn't quite know when to stop is the moot point, and his output is in fact very variable. The three-movement Seventh Symphony, however, is unquestionably Lloyd at his very best – a gripping work, inspired by the Greek myth of Proserpine, goddess of fertility and death, queen of the underworld. Lloyd's mainly dance-measures unleash a genuinely symphonic argument that sustains a vital stream of imaginative invention in the tradition of Bax and Walton. This is an authoritative performance (the composer is a fine conductor) outstandingly well recorded. *CM*

LOCATELLI

L'arte del violino, Op. 3

Elizabeth Wallfisch (violin); Raglan Baroque Players/Nicholas Kraemer

Hyperion CDA 66721/3 □ 213:06 mins (3 discs)
□ 𝄞𝄞𝄞

Pietro Locatelli, one of the Baroque era's most flamboyant virtuosi, would play his violin only standing up and refused to remove his coat even when performing for two or three hours. A contemporary reported that he played 'like a devil', his technical facility engendering speeds and intensity that seemed truly demonic at times.

Locatelli trained in Rome (possibly with Corelli) then later settled in Amsterdam, where *L'arte del violino* was published in 1733. At the time this set of 12 three-movement concertos extended the technical language of the violin to the limit, particularly in the lengthy solo Capriccios that he placed in each concerto. Here the violinist has to execute a host of difficult techniques – trills, double-stopping, slurs – often at high speed.

These displays of extreme virtuosity can be tremendously exciting, though they do tend to disrupt the flow of the concertos, which are otherwise charming but rather less dramatic affairs.

Elizabeth Wallfisch, as the violin soloist, meets Locatelli's formidable challenges with splendid brio. Helped by sensitive support from the period-instrument Raglan Baroque Players, she imparts a lilting gaiety to the music and negotiates the Capriccios with breathtaking finesse.

All lovers of Baroque violin will want this release, but its cache of bright, lively music and brilliant playing deserves the widest audience. *Graham Lock*

LUTOSLAWSKI

Cello Concerto
see DUTILLEUX: Cello Concerto

LUTOSLAWSKI

Concerto for Orchestra; Jeux vénitiens; Livre pour orchestre; Mi-parti

Polish Radio National SO/Witold Lutosławski

EMI Matrix CDM 5 65305 2 □ ADD □ 77:32 mins
□ 🏵🏵

Thanks to EMI's considerable foresight, the great Polish composer Witold Lutosławski made some notable recordings of his music for the company during the late Seventies. Newly restored to the catalogue on the enterprising Matrix label, the vast majority of these performances more than hold their own against some formidable competition. The present disc is particularly valuable for offering a bird's-eye view of Lutosławski's evolution from the post-Bartókian folk style (Concerto for Orchestra) to the sophisticated exploitation of orchestral texture that characterises *Mi-parti*. This journey includes some wonderful music, not least the perennially fascinating *Livre pour orchestre*. As one might expect, the performances are tremendously authoritative, although those wishing to acquire the most scintillating version of the popular Concerto for Orchestra will have to invest in a rather uneconomic two-disc RCA set, in which Marek Janowski and the French Radio Philharmonic Orchestra also perform Messiaen's *Un sourire* and *Turangalîla Symphony*. *EL*

MACCUNN

Land of the Mountain and the Flood; Jeanie Deans (excerpts); The Dowie Dens o' Yarrow; The Ship o' the Fiend; The Lay of the Last Minstrel

Janice Watson, Lisa Milne (soprano), Jamie MacDougall (tenor), Peter Sidhom, Stephen Gadd, Graeme Danby (bass); Scottish Opera Chorus, BBC Scottish SO/Martyn Brabbins

Hyperion CDA 66815 □ 70:04 mins □ 🏵🏵🏵

From the arresting opening, a real Scottish atmosphere is immediately established by the BBC Scottish SO's fine accented playing, Brabbins's firm rhythmic drive propels a really stirring reading of *Land of the Mountain and the Flood*, Hamish MacCunn's best-known

work. You can visualise granite crags, lochs and glens. Wagner echoes through the Highlands in *The Dowie Dens o' Yarrow*, which is great fun: bold, epic, heroic music of knightly gallantry and dastardly deeds. *The Ship o' the Fiend* carries the devil and the heroine, whom he has seduced away from her husband, to hell. This is exceptionally fine, graphic music – sensual, scary, darkly beautiful. It is amazing that MacCunn's opera *Jeanie Deans* has never been recorded. On this evidence, a complete recording is imperative. Among an outstanding cast, Lisa Milne is a splendid Effie, determinedly asserting her innocence in her baby's murder; so too is Peter Sidhom, her unforgiving, reproachful father. A glorious rendition of the lustily patriotic *The Lay of the Last Minstrel* by a commanding Stephen Gadd and the chorus rounds off another consistently, thoroughly enjoyable Hyperion disc of discovery. The sound is demonstration class with a floorboard-cracking bass end. *Ian Lace*

MCEWEN

A Solway Symphony; Hills o' Heather; Where the Wild Thyme Blows

Moray Welsh (cello); LPO/Alasdair Mitchell

Chandos CHAN 9345 □ 60:31 mins □ 🏵🏵🏵

John Blackwood McEwen was better known as principal of the Royal Academy of Music (where he succeeded another notable Scot, Alexander Mackenzie) than as a composer. Though he was prolific in the field of chamber music – it's surprising none of his many expertly crafted string quartets is available on disc – this recording testifies to a natural orchestral composer with an independent voice.

The stirring three-movement *Solway Symphony* (1909) is one of the outstanding British symphonies from before the Great War. Its wild sea-music, as opulent as Elgar, has an impressionistic slant which suggests McEwen knew his Debussy. The first British symphony ever to be recorded (by HMV), *Solway* had occasional performances after its 1922 premiere, but the other works were not played before Chandos's recording sessions, and were specially edited by the conductor. *Hills o' Heather* (1918) is a charming, indeed haunting intermezzo for cello and orchestra. But *Where the Wild Thyme Blows*, McEwen's last orchestral work (1936) is a real discovery – a melancholy and evocative symphonic poem with something of the sense of barren landscape found in Holst's *Egdon Heath*. The performances are nothing short of superb in their sympathy and insight, and the recording is to Chandos's highest standard. A must for collectors seeking jewels of the British musical renaissance. *CM*

Veni, veni, Emmanuel; …as others see us…; Three Dawn Rituals; After the Tryst; Untold

Evelyn Glennie (percussion), Ruth Crouch (violin), Peter Evans (piano); Scottish CO/James MacMillan, Jukka-Pekka Saraste

BMG Catalyst 09026 61916 2 □ 68:38 mins
□ ❶❷❸

The Scottish composer James MacMillan leaped to national prominence with the performance of his orchestral work *The Confession of Isobel Gowdie* at the 1990 Proms. Recorded by the BBC Scottish SO under Jerzy Maksymiuk on Koch Schwann, it's certainly an impressive work worth anyone's collection. But an even better introduction to MacMillan is this BMG Catalyst collection featuring his hugely virtuosic percussion concerto for Evelyn Glennie, *Veni, veni, Emmanuel*, an equally striking hit of the 1992 Prom season. Glennie's justly famed bravura is displayed to the full in this stimulating work based on the famous plainsong, which contrasts furious dance-like fast music with a central marimba meditation and a resplendent coda teeming with bells. The smaller, earlier chamber pieces reflect the spikier side of MacMillan, a pupil of Peter Maxwell Davies ('… *as others see us*' is a suite of satirical ensemble portraits of famous English people), but also his strong poetic gift, as in the little violin and piano piece *After the Tryst*. First-rate performances and sound throughout. *CM*

Symphonies Nos 1–9 & 10 (Adagio)

Amsterdam Concertgebouw Orchestra/Bernard Haitink

Philips 442 050-2 □ ADD □ 692:00 mins (10 discs)
□ ❶❷

Adapting Mahler's famous dictum that 'the symphony is like the world; it should contain everything', one might add that his own magnificent series can (and does) embrace every kind of performance and approach. For that reason alone, it might seem self-restricting for the listener to be limited to one conductor's view of the Mahlerian universe. A theatrical grand master like Bernstein may shoot too wide of the mark in the subtler

symphonies or movements, and the finest of interpreters may have moulded his overall vision across such a wide span of time – decades, very often – that inconsistencies between performances demolish the very notion of a 'cycle' (this is true of the often transcendental Abbado set, with its rather lightweight recent Symphonies Nos 2 and 8, and of Bernstein's second cycle for DG, filling in for the potentially splendid Eighth he never lived to record with an unacceptably engineered radio broadcast).

Understandably, perhaps, I have opted for a golden mean in Bernard Haitink's first thoughts from the Sixties and early Seventies. He has since gone on to take a more passionately expressive second and, in some cases, third look at the symphonies for the same record company. Here the avoidance of sharp, searing detail and the painful extremes of the Mahlerian temperament are sometimes sacrificed to the longer vision. But Haitink's slow movements – both supple and long of line – remain, after all this time, second to none; time and again Concertgebouw strings defy the recording's boxy close-quartering and keep their special radiance without the proper acoustic to support it.

Haitink is an excellent companion, too, for repeated listening, revealing the workings of such terrific and exhausting *tours de force* as the march finale of the Sixth and the lurid Rondo-Burleske of the Ninth. Curiously enough, the next best thing, a very recent surprise, also hails from the Concertgebouw and reveals a second Dutch orchestra, the Netherlands Radio Philharmonic, as a force to be reckoned with under its principal conductor Edo de Waart on RCA. These, too, are clear and sometimes careful performances, recorded live in a strikingly short period of time and crowned by quite the most intelligent Ninth to be found anywhere. No cycle as yet, incidentally, offers Deryck Cooke's crucial completion of the Tenth as the end of the line, only its first-movement Adagio. *DN*

Symphony No. 1; Lieder eines fahrenden Gesellen

Dietrich Fischer-Dieskau (baritone); Bavarian RSO/Rafael Kubelík

DG 439 410-2 □ ADD □ 66:28 mins □ ❷❷

Heavy emphasis and hand-wringing emotion are the keynotes of Mahler interpretation today, and up to a point both are called for by the music. In the process, though, it's a pity to have lost so much of that crystalline delicacy and light, witty phrasing that play so large a part in the Mahlerian cosmos-in-the-making of the First Symphony. So you could say they really don't play Mahler like this any more: the Bavarian RSO's grace and beauty as Kubelík eases it into the symphony's first expansive melody – based on the second song, 'As I walked this morning over the field', from the *Lieder eines fahrenden Gesellen* (Songs of a Wayfarer) – proves the point, with the flipside of storm and stress always firmly sculpted.

The fashion on many recent issues is to present the 'Blumine' movement discarded from the symphony as a bonus, but the companion piece here may be more precious – the set of *Wayfarer Songs* heard in what strikes me as the most movingly pointed of Fischer-Dieskau's several recordings. If you want a masculine viewpoint to complement Janet Baker's indispensable disc of the song cycles, you can do no better than this. *DN*

MAHLER

Symphony No. 2 (Resurrection)

Barbara Hendricks (soprano), Christa Ludwig (mezzo-soprano); Westminster Choir, New York PO/Leonard Bernstein

DG 423 395-2 □ 93:28 mins (2 discs) □ ❷❷❷

Blazing theatricality is essential in any performance of the younger Mahler's prolonged grand gesture, but Bernstein live offers something beyond even that: namely, the kind of extreme dramatic tension which makes you fearful for the outcome, however well you think you know the symphony. The opening funeral rites, all incisive lunges and graphic sobs with distant glimpses of the heaven to come, hang together well because although Bernstein takes Mahler's tempo-markings to his own idiosyncratic extremes, the playing is never less than perfectly balanced and focused.

Superbly coordinated New York Philharmonic brass carry their heads high throughout a massively atmospheric judgement day too – horns resounding, trumpets fanfaring dazzlingly – and the Westminster Choir outstrips all comparable choirs in its painstaking progress from murmured chorale to full-throated affirmation (would it manage quite the same for anyone else but Bernstein, one wonders?). Another bonus is the calm authority of Christa Ludwig at the still heart of the symphony; unlike some versions which offer an awkward break

between discs, DG has made sure that her solo follows the human vanity of the Scherzo, as Mahler intended. Only the cold-blooded will want something purer, though if you have a problem with Mahler's fledgling love of extremes, Herbert Blomstedt provides a more even-tempered, cleanly articulated reading in state-of-the-art Decca sound. *DN*

MAHLER

Symphony No. 3

Jessye Norman (soprano); Vienna State Opera Chorus, Vienna PO/Claudio Abbado

DG 410 715-2 □ 102:44 mins (2 discs) □ ❷❷❷

No movement in Mahler's symphonies is more clear-cut in its contrasts between extreme delicacy and brute force than the lengthy first part of the Third Symphony – its place in the composer's original programmatic 'summer morning's dream' was to chart the progress of Pan's awakening and summer's jubilant approach – and no performance realises this with more finesse than Abbado's. His masterly way with pianissimos conjures the discreet approach of the merry marchers with exquisite delicacy, while the thunderous inflexibility of primordial nature is tirelessly projected by the thrustful brass and graphically trilling woodwind.

The inner movements are illumined with all Abbado's unsurpassable concern for textural detail, and very much crowned by Jessye Norman's statuesque midnight muse. Then, as Mahler comes of age in the finale, his first great slow movement, the Vienna strings have all the time they need to shed their unique inner radiance: not for Abbado the sudden spurts or distorted phrasing of so many interpretations (including that of the great Jascha Horenstein on Unicorn – essential listening up to this point). The subdued timpani strokes in the closing bars come as a disappointing surprise, but by then the resplendent point has already been made. *DN*

MAHLER

Symphony No. 4

Frederica von Stade (mezzo-soprano); Vienna PO/Claudio Abbado

DG 413 454-2 □ ADD □ 57:58 mins □ ❷❷❷

The sleighbells at the start of Abbado's Mahler Four announce a journey into a fantastical and unusually frightening world. Customary distinctions between the symphony's two poles of all-embracing innocence and hostile experience are blurred simply because Abbado observes the plethora of dynamic markings (exceptionally detailed even by this composer's meticulous standards) and then compounds them in the first movement with an unusually volatile sequence of tempi. The results are disquieting but infinitely more interesting than those of other conductors who hold the reins tighter.

Nor has the child's vision of heaven, reached just before the finale, ever been harder won; as in Abbado's recording of the Third Symphony, the vocalising range of the Vienna Philharmonic strings leads us unerringly through a great slow movement and makes it extremely difficult to contemplate in the hands of any other orchestra. Mezzo von Stade colours the upper reaches of the deceptively simple-seeming final song more luminously than many a soprano – a suitably personable angel to meet at the end of a performance that yields even greater long-term riches than two other widely praised contenders deserving a mention. Both are on Sony: the classic Cleveland/Szell partnership and another VPO treasure, jewel of a generally underrated cycle from Lorin Maazel. *DN*

MAHLER

Symphony No. 5

Vienna PO/Leonard Bernstein

DG 423 608-2 □ 75:00 mins □ 🟢🟢🟢

A concert may be one thing and a recording quite another. Yet anyone who heard Leonard Bernstein's Mahler Five with the Vienna Philharmonic live in London or elsewhere still speaks of a concert-hall experience to eclipse all others (certainly the case for me). A CD can never quite recapture the magic, especially when the balances are as synthetic as here, but DG's Frankfurt-based document comes close. There is the same sense of absolute control allied to expressive certainty in every bar which prevents you from fully feeling the impact of the densely written first two movements, or the complementary chattering radiance of the finale, until the last note has died away.

The pivotal Scherzo, very much dancing into the light here, makes perfect sense, and the famous Adagietto is all the finer for Bernstein's avoidance of what many would label as Bernstein-like extravagance – compare Haitink's uncharacteristic self-indulgence with this movement in his recent Berlin Philharmonic recording (Philips) or Wyn

Morris (Carlton) sprinting through the dream to mar what is in every other respect a supreme achievement from an underrated Mahlerian. Reacquaintance with John Barbirolli's performance (EMI – a standard first choice) reveals an urgency less magisterial than Morris's, trailing loose ensembles and the occasional wrong entry. *DN*

MAHLER

Symphonies Nos 6 & 8 (Symphony of a Thousand)

Erna Spoorenberg, Gwyneth Jones, Gwenyth Annear (soprano), Anna Reynolds, Norma Procter (mezzo-soprano), John Mitchinson (tenor), Vladimir Ruzdjak (baritone), Donald McIntyre (bass); Leeds Festival Chorus, Orpington Junior Singers, Highgate School Choir, Finchley Children's Music Group, LSO & Chorus, New York PO/Leonard Bernstein

Sony SM3K 47581 □ ADD □ 157:26 mins (3 discs) □ 🟢🟢

A symphony which should embody a healthy if colossal struggle against the odds too often becomes Tragic with a capital 'T' at a conductor's hyper-Romantic whim, its conflicts so bludgeoning from the start that one rarely has the energy left to face the last, taxing half-hour. This is why I prefer to return to Leonard Bernstein's first thoughts on the Sixth from the Sixties.

Very much in the prime of life, as was Mahler when he wrote this energetic prophecy of disaster, Bernstein knew then how to make the first-movement march really *move* – admittedly at the expense of space and atmosphere around the mountain reverie at the heart of the movement, but it sets up an unremitting tension which holds right through to the huge finale. This is sheer heart-attack, the balance between strings and brass absolutely even, the playing as phenomenal as any in the history of recording (though now matched, between the second and unplayed third hammer-blows of fate, by the Vienna Philharmonic under Boulez on DG, lower in temperature elsewhere but the only recent contender to prefer an even crisper point of view). The old CBS set of records came with a fascinating talk on the symphony; the present packaging is unhelpful, with Bernstein's view on the Eighth Symphony nullified by poor recording, but not prohibitively expensive. *DN*

Symphony No. 7; Kindertotenlieder

Bryn Terfel (baritone); Philharmonia
Orchestra/Giuseppe Sinopoli

DG 437 851-2 □ 114:01 mins (2 discs) □ ❷❷❷

Too exposed in its forward-looking scoring to
let sloppy preparation pass muster, Mahler's
ambitious Seventh Symphony has had more
first-rate interpretations than any of the other
symphonies. Rattle, Abbado, Bernstein (twice),
Chailly, Haitink, Kubelík, Tennstedt, Solti and
Gielen all shed fascinating lights on this strange
meeting of past rituals and futuristic
nightmares. That so fitfully perceptive a
Mahler conductor as Sinopoli should have
most to say speaks volumes about the work's
maverick nature. One might have expected his
master balancing skills to keep weird orchestral
mixes in harness, but for once he does much
more than that. Every sound is graphically to
the point, from screaming high frequencies –
the Philharmonia woodwind and first trumpet
(John Wallace, I presume) are superlative – to
extreme rhythmic tension and clarity in the
bass-lines; and his pacing of the outer
movements is (again uncharacteristically) fine.

Some may balk at the controversially slow
speed for the second 'Nachtmusik', but that,
too, has its value in lengthening the night
shadows of this bitter-sweet serenade and
making it more significant a half-way house
between darkest night and the garish day of the
final ceremonials. The companion piece is no
reason for running to two discs if your budget
is limited to one (in which case Rattle on EMI
is excellent value). Terfel looked, on paper, to
be the star of the set, but his score-faithful
reading of the *Kindertotenlieder*, though
phrased with artistry, only springs off the
printed page in the last, hallowed bars. *DN*

Symphony No. 8 (Symphony of a Thousand)

Heather Harper, Lucia Popp, Arleen Auger (soprano),
Yvonne Minton, Helen Watts (mezzo-soprano), René
Kollo (tenor), John Shirley-Quirk (baritone), Martti
Talvela (bass); Vienna State Opera Chorus, Wiener
Singverein, Vienna Boys Choir, Chicago SO/Georg
Solti

Decca 448 293-2 □ ADD □ 79:34 mins □ ❷❷❷

Any new recording of Wagner's *Ring* cycle is
bound to find the biggest and best voices for
such a venture. The same should be true of
Mahler's Eighth Symphony, which would seem
to call for singers of comparable stature and
presence: however sweeping and fervent the

conducting, one weak link in the chain of
solos that lead us ever upwards from rocky
valley to heavenly heights in Part Two – the
text of which comes from the end of another
Part Two, that of Goethe's *Faust*, and deals
with the saving of the protagonist's soul –
weakens the impact of the whole.

Never before or (so far) since Solti's 1971
Vienna spectacular has a more remarkable
line-up of singers been assembled. The
performance is shot through with
characteristic Soltian theatrics, especially
appropriate for the drive of the first-movement
Hymnus where many conductors (most
puzzlingly of all, Abbado) hang fire. It was the
first recording of the work to manage the
massive forces (not quite a thousand, but who's
counting?) with successful artifice; it still
sounds strikingly handsome. *DN*

Symphony No. 9

Amsterdam Concertgebouw Orchestra/Leonard
Bernstein

DG 419 208-2 □ 89:02 mins (2 discs) □ ❷❷❷

Mahler's Ninth has had more long-term success
with the record industry than most of its
symphonic predecessors: Bruno Walter, who
gave the first performance a year after Mahler's
death in 1911, recorded it in 1938 and then,
on the eve of the Mahler explosion, in 1960.
Fascinating documents, both of high orchestral
standards, his interpretations sometimes lack
the volatility implied in the score and taken to
logical extremes by Leonard Bernstein in this,
his last recording of the work. Bernstein's
searing response to the respective elements of
the first movement's repeating cycle – struggle,
collapse and consolation – is achieved without
artificial gear-changes and with an ear for
perfect balances even in the most
overwhelming cataclysms (only compare
Karajan, who always seems to favour strings
over wind and brass and smooths over the
jagged fabrics of ensemble).

Scherzo and Rondo-Burleske bring none of
the usual lowering of temperatures – these are
enervating, rather than grotesquely funny,
encounters with vulgar adversaries – and
Bernstein's entrenched, protracted view of the
death-hymn finale brings little release, only a
long-term listeners some listeners will find hard
to bear (nor should this be bearable music).
The recording, as so often with DG's Mahler,
plays nasty up-front tricks, but even those are
worth tolerating for a live performance in a
thousand. *DN*

ORCHESTRAL

MAHLER/SCHOENBERG

Mahler: Symphony No. 10 (performing version by Deryck Cooke)
Schoenberg: Verklärte Nacht

Berlin RSO/Riccardo Chailly

Decca 444 872-2 □ 109:36 mins (2 discs) □ ◍◍

It can only be our loss that many conductors turn their backs on Deryck Cooke's performing version of the Tenth Symphony, so much of which the composer either scored or sketched with indications for scoring, especially when it sheds so radiant a light on the composer's farewell to life after the often unsettling mysteries of the Ninth's closing pages. The opening Adagio performed alone offers no solution. The finale, on the other hand, incorporating the dissonant screams of piled-up ninths from that first movement, answers them differently – with the return of a profoundly at-one-with-the-world melody, ultimately smoothed of most of its former harmonic doubts. That this epilogue can move the listener so profoundly in Chailly's performance is due to the miraculous refinement he draws from his unexpectedly fine Berlin RSO strings, and the way they negotiate the surprise last-minute leap, the defiant cry of an open heart; its effect here is literally stunning.

For that alone Chailly's rather more abstracted view of earlier stages in the symphonic story is worth following: less graphic than Rattle, a great champion of this symphony (EMI), but always bewitchingly textured. Schoenberg's earlier, more prolix transfiguration benefits from the same lithe textures and superb recorded presence in the bass-line. *DN*

MARCELLO

Flute Concerto in G
see Collection: Concerti di flauti

MARTIN

Concerto for Seven Wind Instruments, Timpani, Percussion and Strings; Ballades for flute, trombone, piano & alto saxophone

Jacques Zoon (flute), Christian Lindberg (trombone), Ronald Brautigam (piano), John Harle (saxophone); Royal Concertgebouw Orchestra/Riccardo Chailly

Decca 445 455-2 □ 65:32 mins □ ◍◍◍

It's regrettable that DG have deleted the Chamber Orchestra of Europe's masterly recordings of the Concerto for Seven Wind Instruments, *Polyptique* and string orchestral Études, for their disc offered probably the best introduction to the music of this fascinating

Swiss composer. Fortunately, there's a useful alternative version of the Concerto from Riccardo Chailly and the Concertgebouw which matches the tremendous rhythmic verve of the COE in the outer movements, but doesn't quite achieve the same degree of magical stillness in the central Adagietto. Chailly pairs the Concerto with a sequence of instrumental Ballades, composed between 1938 and 1940, that further illustrate the composer's capacity to balance refinement with emotional intensity.

If you become hooked on Martin as a result of listening to this disc, you should note that Chandos are at present engaged in recording the composer's major works under the resourceful baton of Matthias Bamert. *EL*

MARTINU

Double Concerto; Sinfonietta giacosa; Rhapsody-Concerto for Viola and Orchestra

Dennis Hennig (piano), Rivka Golani (viola); Brno State PO, Australian CO/Charles Mackerras; Bern SO/Peter Maag

Conifer 75605 51210 2 □ 73:13 mins □ ◍◍◍

This immensely enjoyable disc offers one of the best overviews of Martinů's concerto grosso style. First, there's the masterly Double Concerto of 1938, a work whose tragic intensity and bitter defiance represents a direct response to the impending German invasion of the composer's native country. In contrast, the *Sinfonietta giacosa*, completed two years later when Martinů was contemplating emigration to the United States, is a delightful and high-spirited composition that seems utterly divorced from the troubled political circumstances of the period. Finally, there's the lyrical Rhapsody Concerto, a work of haunting nostalgia composed seven years before Martinů's death. All the performances project the music with commitment and devotion, that of the Double Concerto in particular conveying the urgency of Martinů's writing with tremendous power. *EL*

MARTINU

Symphonies Nos 1 & 2; Nos 3 & 4; Nos 5 & 6 (Fantaisies symphoniques)

Bamberg SO/Neeme Järvi

BIS CD-362, CD-363, CD-402 □ 60:52 mins, 62:44 mins, 59:16 mins □ ◍◍◍

Like Brahms, Martinů came to the symphony relatively late in his career: his first work in this form was composed in 1942, when he was over fifty years of age. During this period Martinů

295

had emigrated to the United States as a refugee from German-occupied France, and it's hardly surprising that images of war, coupled with a profound sense of nostalgia for his Czech homeland, should pervade the musical argument of these works. Such images recur in the later Sixth Symphony, although here Martinů relinquishes his Classical poise for a more imaginary and exploratory sound-world.

Selecting the best recordings of these important works is hardly a straightforward process. Neumann and the Czech Philharmonic on Supraphon have the right sound for this repertoire, but the performances fail to generate the same level of involvement as some earlier recordings of selected symphonies with the same orchestra under Karel Ančerl. Unfortunately Ančerl is somewhat let down by antiquated sound that hardly does full justice to Martinů's luminous orchestration. Of more recent recordings, Neeme Järvi and the Bamberg SO are the most convincing. Järvi extracts the maximum degree of excitement from the music, and if the playing isn't perhaps as refined as that of the Czech orchestra, it is more than acceptable. *EL*

MAW

Odyssey

City of Birmingham SO/Simon Rattle

EMI CDS 7 54277 2 □ 95:29 mins (2 discs) □ 𝄞𝄞𝄞

Laboured over for 15 years, Nicholas Maw's *Odyssey* must be one of the longest continuous movements for orchestra ever written, and a landmark composition of the Eighties. A kind of epic poem expressive of an inner journey, it's best to think of it as a vast single-movement symphony, encompassing a series of five very broadly conceived movements. Like all the best such long works (Bruckner, for instance), it doesn't feel overlong because the pacing and manner of the musical invention – such as the vast cello melody at the start of the second section – imposes its own time-scale. The music is in fact very varied in tempo, character and texture, with some titanic climaxes and some of the lushest orchestral writing of which any contemporary composer is capable.

This disc originates in a live performance (the work's first complete one) and there are a few roughnesses that a studio recording might have smoothed out. Ideally, too, the work requires a string section of proportions as heroic as the music. But the sound is very

good and though *Odyssey*, as big as it is, is short measure for a full-price two-disc set, it's eminently worth acquiring. *CM*

MEDTNER

Piano Concertos Nos 2 in C minor & 3 in E minor (Ballade)

Geoffrey Tozer (piano); LPO/Neeme Järvi

Chandos CHAN 9038 □ 73:02 mins □ 𝄞𝄞𝄞

Medtner's piano concertos lack, on the whole, the big, soulful tunes that have made their close cousins, the Rachmaninov concertos, so popular. But they have everything else: the transcendental keyboard demands, the driving, dancing rhythms, the Russian melancholy and epic sweep. Considering that Medtner wrote nothing else with orchestra, they're also superbly scored – and the sheer onrush of their argument, brimming over with ideas continually in organic transformation, sometimes excels even Rachmaninov in sheer intoxicating invention. The pounding, toccata-like opening movement of the Second Concerto sets the blood racing; the Third Concerto, though more lyrical melodically, has no lack of bounce. (In fact, unlike the Second, which has a delicate Romanza, No. 3 has no real slow movement, just a brief prelude to the fast finale.)

Medtner's own magisterial version of these works, recorded in the late Forties with the Philharmonia under Issay Dobrowen, is now available on Testament – a document of the first importance. But for fine performances in modern sound it's hard to choose between Tozer, listed above, and Demidenko on Hyperion with the BBC Scottish SO under Maksymiuk. Tozer yields a shade – just a shade – to Demidenko on the fire and excitement of his playing, but has better orchestral support, and the Chandos recording is much superior to Hyperion in richness and perspective. Whether you choose Tozer, Demidenko or the composer himself, these are endlessly engrossing works which yield rich rewards on repeated listening. *CM*

MENDELSSOHN

A Midsummer Night's Dream – incidental music

Edith Wiens (soprano), Sarah Walker (mezzo-soprano); LPO & Choir/Andrew Litton

Classics for Pleasure CD-CFP 4593 □ 50:00 mins □ 𝄞𝄞

The 16-year-old Mendelssohn's overture to *A Midsummer Night's Dream* must rank as one of the most prodigious achievements of any young composer. Already revealing many of the attributes of mature genius, this overture invoked Shakespeare's plot in microcosm with remarkable flair and pictorialism: note, for example, the gruff, donkey-like snarlings and the reluctance to leave this dream-like world of the imagination at the close. The remaining numbers, which combine to form the complete incidental music to the play, were written at the request of the king of Prussia for a production of Ludwig Tieck's German edition, staged unsuccessfully in Potsdam in October 1843. Mendelssohn's score (there are more than a dozen pieces in all) has enjoyed a healthy, independent life ever since; the fairy world is sensuously evoked, in keenly detailed portraitures of Titania, Oberon, Nick Bottom and the rest, and you'll seldom hear a finer account of the complete score than Litton's. The London Philharmonic plays admirably for him, the solo horn is serene and majestic in the Nocturne, and the familiar Wedding March and mercurial Scherzo are skilfully characterised. Vocal contributions from Edith Wiens, Sarah Walker and the London Philharmonic Choir are highly distinguished, and the CFP recording is ample and resonant. *MJ*

MENDELSSOHN

Overtures – The Fair Melusina; A Midsummer Night's Dream; Calm Sea and Prosperous Voyage; Overture for Wind Instruments, Op. 24; 'Trumpet' Overture, Op. 101; Ruy Blas; The Hebrides (Fingal's Cave)

LSO/Claudio Abbado

DG 423 104-2 □ 73:54 mins □ ⊘⊘⊘

Abbado's lean, athletic manner and Romantically infused sensibilities serve him faithfully in Mendelssohn's most famous overtures, the seascapes *The Hebrides* and *Calm Sea and Prosperous Voyage*, the latter perhaps the finest of Mendelssohn's independent orchestral works. Other familiar overtures, *Ruy Blas* and *A Midsummer Night's Dream*, the latter composed during Mendelssohn's 17th year, sit beside less popular fare, including the impressive 'Trumpet' Overture, the Op. 24 Overture for Wind Instruments (both somewhat anomalous in character, but worth hearing occasionally, nonetheless), and the delightful *Fair Melusina* Overture. Abbado's readings are sheer delight; there's ample drama and momentum in the more rhetorical offerings, such as *Ruy Blas*, while the 16-year-old Mendelssohn's

Shakespearian prelude is played with quicksilver deftness and clarity, with the London SO on peak form throughout. Recorded sound is sonorous and resonant, and this fine disc is worth every penny of its full price. *MJ*

MENDELSSOHN

Piano Concertos Nos 1 in G minor & 2 in D minor; Prelude and Fugue in E minor, Op. 35/1; Variations sérieuses, Op. 54; Andante and Rondo Capriccioso, Op. 14

Murray Perahia (piano); Academy of St Martin in the Fields/Neville Marriner

Sony MK 42401 □ ADD/DDD □ 70:00 mins □ ⊘⊘

A difficult choice, actually. Four versions of the Mendelssohn piano concertos jostle each other for top place. It's almost inconceivable that Perahia's performances will ever be surpassed. They have all the dazzle and brilliance of Serkin's classic 1960 recording (the first really to establish these works as major virtuoso vehicles), but without that great pianist's sometimes almost manic tension. Combining bravura with a deep-rooted lyricism untainted by sentimentality, Perahia probably comes as close as anyone could to playing these wonderful works as Mendelssohn himself must have done, and he receives superb support from Marriner and the ASMF. With Serkin, on the other hand (and they're great performances by any standard, though the sound is rather brittle), you also get Stern in the Mendelssohn Violin Concerto. The best bargain by far is Benjamin Frith on Naxos. With him you get not only first-rate performances (making allowances only for the fact that the Slovak Philharmonic isn't quite the Philadelphia Orchestra) but two other substantial works, the *Capriccio brillant* and the *Rondo brillant*, both given renderings befitting the works' titles. Schiff on Decca is likewise a brilliant advocate, with superb recorded sound, but with him you get no fillers. *JS*

MENDELSSOHN

String Symphonies

London Festival Orchestra/Ross Pople

Hyperion CDA 66561 □ 203:00 mins (3 discs) □ ⊘⊘⊘

Mendelssohn's prodigal and prophetic series of 12 symphonies for string orchestra find a transcendently gifted composer, barely into his teens, flexing his muscles with the symphonic idiom, and all its latent expressive pathos, for the first time. Beethoven noted in one of his conversation books of the period that 'One Mendelssohn – twelve years old, promises much'. Such promise amazed and perplexed the boy's composition teacher Carl Friedrich Zelter, at whose bidding the earliest of these remarkable symphonies were written, ostensibly as mere technical studies. Ross Pople and his London Festival Orchestra recorded the cycle over some five years; their Hyperion discs are of memorably high calibre, alertly and capably played and beautifully recorded. One listens (as Zelter must have done) with mounting incredulity that one so young could have absorbed so deeply a vista spanning high-Baroque principles (Symphony No. 4 opens with an austere Handelian *Grave*), the fiery disposition of *Sturm und Drang* and the rigours of Viennese Classicism, all in a matter of months. Ross Pople directs wilfully and passionately; he evidently believes in the worth and stature of these youthful creations, and conveys their vigour and inventiveness with minute attentiveness. His players, too, share in his delight at exploring these works, and these three excellently engineered discs will more than repay careful and diligent listening. *MJ*

MENDELSSOHN

Symphonies Nos 3 in A minor (Scottish) & 4 in A (Italian)

San Francisco Symphony/Herbert Blomstedt

Decca 433 811-2 □ **66:59 mins** □ ⦿⦿⦿

Two deservedly popular early-Romantic symphonies, and two performances of quite exceptional brilliance and interpretative distinction. Herbert Blomstedt and his revitalised San Francisco Symphony have become a major force in American musical life during his tenure as music director; the orchestra plays superbly for him, and its series of recordings for Decca has earned universal praise. Their account of Mendelssohn's *Italian* Symphony opens with pulsating fervour and anticipation; the exposed violin line surges forward majestically and, since Blomstedt observes the exposition repeat, we get to hear it twice! Elsewhere, he holds the music powerfully on course, and the coda positively explodes with exuberance. The middle movements (the solemn processional Andante is suavely austere) progress admirably, while the concluding Saltarello bristles with nervous vitality. Blomstedt's performance of the *Scottish* Symphony is similarly impressive. The barren, Walter Scott-inspired opening canvas is

painted in epic orchestral greyness, suggesting the wind-swept desolation that so impressed the composer during his first Scottish tour in 1829. The outdoor, tramping Scherzo and serene Adagio are gloriously invoked, though Blomstedt's account culminates in glorious ceremonial after the combative main section of the finale, which Mendelssohn marked *guererro* or 'war-like'. Arresting performances from a great virtuoso ensemble kept at the edge of their seats, and a fabulously rich and detailed recording from San Francisco's acoustically endowed Davies Symphony Hall. You couldn't, in all fairness, expect much more. *MJ*

MENDELSSOHN

Violin Concertos in D minor & in E minor, Op. 64

Viktoria Mullova (violin); Academy of St Martin in the Fields/Neville Marriner

Philips 432 077-2 □ **49:36 mins** □ ⦿⦿⦿

Mendelssohn's Violin Concerto in E minor became a staple of the virtuoso repertory almost from the day of its premiere (13 March 1845 – the composer was already too ill to conduct, and so Niels Gade directed the Gewandhaus Orchestra, whose Konzertmeister, Ferdinand David, had been entrusted with the solo part). Its earlier D minor sibling (published, thanks to Yehudi Menuhin, as recently as 1952), written in 1822, the composer's 13th year, is still largely unknown. This three-movement work, for violin and strings alone, was a compositional exercise for Mendelssohn's teacher, Eduard Rietz; it displays remarkable assurance and passion, and Viktoria Mullova's account is a model of precision and grace. Her performance of the universally beloved E minor Concerto is both technically brilliant and heart-rendingly eloquent; the opening movement has tempestuous, thrusting energy, though one hears the bassoon-led transition into the central Andante absolutely in tune for once, with superb contributions from the ASMF wind-players. Mullova's incandescent tone and lucid phrasing are memorably beautiful, and she tosses off the mercurial finale with effortless élan. The ASMF supports her admirably under Marriner's watchful direction, and recorded sound is miraculously fresh and detailed. There are, of course, countless superlative recordings of the E minor work, but I'd be more than happy to call this a first among equals, and acquire the rare D minor Concerto into the bargain. *MJ*

MESSIAEN

Chronochromie; La ville d'en-haut; Et exspecto resurrectionem mortuorum

Cleveland Orchestra/Pierre Boulez

DG 445 827-2 □ 57:48 mins □ * **

In the Fifties and Sixties, while his younger contemporaries were busy trying to build a 'brave new world', Olivier Messiaen turned instead to nature. His *Chronochromie* not only presents us with numerous songs from his beloved birds but also depicts wind, rocks and gushing streams, fusing these natural phenomena together with 'colour-chords' and abstruse rhythmic procedures into a gritty and exhilarating masterpiece.

This is a stunning rendition from Boulez. It is not so much the remarkable accuracy from the Cleveland Orchestra in this often fiendish score which is so impressive as the fine shading of every textural nuance, thus allowing the music's latent poetry to shine through – a trait sadly lacking in most performances. In short, this is quite simply the best recording of *Chronochromie* ever made.

The immense *Et exspecto* is also awesome in Boulez's hands. Indeed, it seems almost churlish to say that the first movement should ideally be somewhat slower while the overwhelming tam-tam and gong rolls in the third movement could have had longer to die away. A magnificent account of the late monumental miniature (not a contradiction in terms, I assure you) *La ville d'en-haut* completes an epic programme. Strongly recommended. *Christopher Dingle*

MESSIAEN

Réveil des oiseaux; Trois petites liturgies de la Présence Divine

Yvonne Loriod (piano), Jeanne Loriod (ondes martenot), Luc Héry (violin), Michel Sendrez (celesta), Marie Griffet (soprano); Maîtrise de Radio France, French National Orchestra/Kent Nagano

Erato 0630-12702-2 □ 56:13 mins □ * **

Dating from 1944, the *Trois petites liturgies* is an unashamedly heady brew of intoxicating sensuality and religious devotion combining luxurious tonal and modal harmonies with Eastern influences. Provoking an outcry from the musical intelligentsia at its premiere, it has now entered the repertoire as one of Messiaen's most popular works.

Although the *Réveil des oiseaux* was composed just eight years later, its similar public emotionalism was by then untenable in the 'brave new world' of the Fifties. However, having shown his pupils the path to total serialism, Messiaen rejected abstraction and instead devoted a decade to the depiction of nature, particularly birdsong.

The performance of *Trois petites liturgies* is without parallel, while the equally outstanding account of *Réveil des oiseaux* – a work long overshadowed by its ornithological successor, *Oiseaux exotiques* – should win many new devotees for the piece. *Christopher Dingle*

MESSIAEN

Turangalîla Symphony

Yvonne Loriod (piano), Jeanne Loriod (ondes martenot); Orchestra of the Bastille Opera/Myung-Whun Chung

DG 431 781-2 □ 78:32 mins □ * **

In recent years there has been a tendency to understate the provocative aspects of Messiaen's *Turangalîla*, yet in the right hands the work still retains a capacity to shock. Myung-Whun Chung is one interpreter who achieves such an effect without recourse to sensationalism. The strength of his interpretation lies in the thrilling precision of the orchestral playing, the powerhouse solo playing of Yvonne Loriod, and Chung's infallible control of inner detail which effects a satisfying clarity of texture in those passages where the rhythmic interplay is at its most complex. Taken as a whole the performance is far more intense than the rival Chailly/Concertgebouw performance on Decca, though the orchestral playing here is equally stunning. And as an economic investment, it appears far more enticing than the two disc sets from Janowski (RCA) and Rattle (EMI). *EL*

MIASKOVSKY/TANEYEV

Miaskovsky: Cello Concerto

Taneyev: Suite de concert

Mstislav Rostropovich (cello), David Oistrakh (violin); Philharmonia Orchestra/Malcolm Sargent, Nicolai Malko

**EMI Matrix CDM 5 65419 2 □ ADD □ 70:45 mins □ ** **

Miaskovsky's Cello Concerto is one of his most lovable works, and a comparatively late one, written at the end of the Second World War. Perhaps no other score so perfectly embodies the vein of exquisite lyrical melancholy to which his music was prone, and which the cello, of all instruments, is most perfectly fitted to express. It's a finely balanced two movement structure: the second movement is fast and energetic, but continually lapses back into the introspective poetry of the first.

For long the only recording, this comparatively early example of Rostropovich's artistry (1956) remains the definitive one, despite some fuzzy sound and studio noise: he captures, sustains and refracts Miaskovsky's prevailing moods with sonorous sympathy and affection. The unusual coupling is Taneyev's seldom-heard Suite – an attractive rarity, much more virtuosic than the Miaskovsky and given an equally definitive reading by Oistrakh, and worth having for the soloist's superb displays of technical skill. *CM*

MIASKOVSKY

Symphony No. 6 in E flat minor

Yurlov Russian Choir, USSR SO/Kirill Kondrashin

Russian Disc RD CD 15 008 ☐ AAD mono ☐ 65:18 mins ☐ ⓐⓐⓐ

This is the largest, most dramatic and probably greatest of the 27 symphonies that made Miaskovsky the chief architect of the genre in the Soviet era. The turbulent and deeply emotional No. 6, written in the aftermath of the October Revolution and the ensuing civil war, was influenced as much by personal sorrows as the sensitive and deeply principled composer struggled to come to terms with events.

This was also the period when his musical language was at its most radical. The huge first movement suggests parallels with Mahler and Scriabin; the sinister, demonic Scherzo is a remarkably original invention; the slow movement is as eloquent and songful as Rachmaninov. The finale, beginning in carnival mood with French revolutionary songs, comes as a stylistic jolt, but before long the Dies Irae and a chorus singing a deeply moving Orthodox chant for the dead return to the prevailing mood of passionate tragedy. It's an astonishing piece. Neither of the two modern versions (on Olympia and Marco Polo) can touch this elderly (1959) but blazingly eloquent account by Kondrashin, one of his finest recordings. The sound shows its age but comes up vividly in the transfer. *CM*

MILHAUD
Le boeuf sur le toit
see Collection: French Orchestral Music

MOERAN
Lonely Waters; Whythorne's Shadow
see Collection: The Banks of Green Willow

MOZART

Clarinet Concerto in A, K622; Clarinet Quintet in A, K581

Thea King (basset clarinet); Gabrieli String Quartet, English CO/Jeffrey Tate

Hyperion CDA 66199 ☐ 64:00 mins ☐ ⓐⓐⓐ

Excellent accounts of both these masterworks have never been scarce but one would have to search long and hard to find any that surpassed these for sheer musicianship, both sophisticated and innate (if I myself had come up with one, you'd be reading about it now). In keeping with Mozart's intentions, Thea King uses a basset clarinet, with its extended lower range, and has attempted to restore both works to their original specifications (for many decades both have been adjusted to suit the modern clarinet). But it's her playing more than her scholarship or historical intentions that makes this such a treasurable release. Beautifully inflected, immaculately phrased, subtly coloured and impeccably responsive as well as eloquent, her performances here make one wonder how she has contrived to avoid a major international reputation, of the kind enjoyed for many years now by Richard Stoltzman (whose own recording of these works on RCA – with the ECO, this time directed by himself, and the superb Tokyo String Quartet – is likewise a model of refinement, sophistication and expressive felicity, though not all listeners will warm to his often rather lean and nasal tone). *JS*

MOZART

Divertimenti in E flat, K113, in D, K136, in B flat, K137, in F, K138, in D, K205, in F, K247, in D, K251, in B flat, K287 & in D, K334; Marches in F, K248, in D, K290 & in D, K445; Serenade in G, K525 (Eine kleine Nachtmusik); A Musical Joke, K522

Academy of St Martin in the Fields/Neville Marriner

Philips Complete Mozart Edition 422 504-2 ☐ 331:00 mins (5 discs) ☐ ⓐⓐ

Neville Marriner and the Academy of St Martin in the Fields made a significant contribution to the overall excellence of the Philips Complete Mozart Edition, issued in 1991, to mark the bicentenary of the composer's death. Here, they are heard to great advantage in this comprehensive traversal of the Divertimenti, in performances of exceptional finesse and clarity. That this undemanding music never cloys during some four and a half hours of listening time attests to the admirable zest and brilliance of the

ASMF's playing, and Marriner's alert, unmannered style, from which all fragile artifice and posturing (neither have any place in this music) are skilfully excluded. But these bravura works, typical of Mozart's matchlessly inventive ceremonial style, less weighty than the Serenades, and quite as captivating, often impose cruel demands upon the players. Upper string parts present virtuoso hurdles to a violin section, who are dangerously exposed in the small numbers for which the music was intended, and the problems of balance and ensemble are legion. The ASMF surmounts every technical difficulty, and Marriner invests the music with the relaxed, crisply articulated jubilance it requires. Another prime virtue of the Philips Mozart Edition (in addition to the uniform excellence of the performances) is the very high quality of the booklets adorning each volume of this leviathan among recording projects, lavishly illustrated and informatively detailed, and, at mid-price, this is irresistible! *MJ*

MOZART

Horn Concertos Nos 1–4; Rondo in E flat (ed. Tuckwell); Fragment in E, K.Anh.98a

Philharmonia Orchestra/Barry Tuckwell (horn)

Collins 11532 □ 71:20 mins □ ⊘⊘⊘

The most famous recording of the Mozart horn concertos – with Dennis Brain and the Philharmonia under Karajan – was made in 1954 and remains for many people unequalled, not least for Brain's wonderful, outdoorsy evocation of the hunting-horn. Tuckwell is no less accomplished, some will tell you, but he's too sophisticated by half, too polished, too 'indoorsy'. Take the present performances, re-record them in the prevailing conditions of 1954, remove from studio and sample. Can the claim still hold water? I wonder. This is Tuckwell's fourth recording of works he must have played hundreds of times, but they come up as fresh as new paint and have the benefit of first-rate engineering and a wonderfully rich and responsive contribution from the Philharmonia (any veterans from 1954 still in it?). Running it a very close second indeed, for my money, however, is the ASV version with Jonathan Williams and the Chamber Orchestra of Europe under Alexander Schneider – less dazzlingly virtuosic maybe, and orchestrally a little thinner, but what life and style! Listeners wanting period instruments can turn with complete confidence to Timothy Brown and the Orchestra of the Age of Enlightenment on

Virgin, which outshines even the excellent Hermann Baumann and Harnoncourt on Teldec. *JS*

MOZART

Piano Concertos Nos 11 in F, K413, 12 in A, K414 & 14 in E flat, K449

English CO/Murray Perahia (piano)

Sony SK 42243 □ ADD □ 70:23 mins □ ⊘⊘⊘

I suppose it's conceivable that these performances will be bettered one day, just as it's conceivable that there is intelligent life elsewhere in the universe – but you're not likely to encounter either in our lifetime. Perahia is a born Mozartian, but he brings to his playing far more than merely talent and intinct, however prodigious. At every turn there's a penetrating intelligence at work here, yet the performances are never remotely didactic or point-making. So convincing are these interpretations that they have about them a feeling of inevitability, yet they gleam with spontaneity. No pianist, and certainly no conductor, is more painstakingly attentive to details of phrasing, articulation, balance and pacing, but not once does Perahia sound fussy (at least not here). Poetic refinement is evident at every turn, but it's never self-conscious or ingratiating. It never sounds contrived. At the same time there's an edge to the playing that renders it occasionally unsettling, a sense of underlying urgency and of dark shadows beyond the glint of sunlight on the surface. There's an intensity in K449 which borders on the genuinely tragic. Why these works are not among the most popular of Mozart's concertos is beyond me. If all performances were like these, perhaps they would be. *JS*

MOZART

Piano Concertos Nos 12 in A, K414, 14 in E flat, K449 & 21 in C, K467

Jenő Jandó (piano); Concentus Hungaricus/András Ligeti

Naxos 8.550202 □ 71:07 mins □ ⊘

Though Mozart is one of the hardest of all composers to bring off greatly, the catalogue abounds in first-rate accounts of K467 (now sometimes and wholly unjustifiably nicknamed *Elvira Madigan*) – Barenboim, Brendel, Perahia, Schiff, Serkin and Uchida just for starters – yet none has given me more immediate pleasure than this one. Not perhaps as supremely polished and urbane as Perahia (Sony), or quite as individually incisive or as meticulously sculpted as Brendel and Uchida respectively (both on Philips), Jandó nevertheless catches the almost insolent vitality, lyrical ease and good humour of this endlessly thrilling work to a degree unsurpassed even by the ebullient and treasurable Serkin/Schneider performance on Sony (which it greatly resembles). And both he and Ligeti succeed admirably in conveying both the rapt poetry and the harmonic audacity of the famous and often sentimentalised slow movement (whose discordant clashes deeply shocked the composer's father). In the two other concertos they acquit themselves equally well, making this a bargain in far more than price. *JS*

MOZART

Piano Concertos Nos 16 in D, K451 & 25 in C, K503; Rondo in A, K386

Jenö Jandó (piano); Concentus Hungaricus/András Ligeti

Naxos 8.550207 □ **61:27 mins** □ ⊘

Naxos has now demonstrated time and again that the highest quality is by no means the exclusive preserve of the glamorous, the rich and the famous. Even today, with a discography that embraces the complete Beethoven, Mozart and (almost) Haydn sonatas, reams of Schubert, Bach and Schumann, and the complete Mozart piano concertos, Jenö Jandó's is not yet a name to bandy about alongside those of Brendel, Barenboim, Ashkenazy, Perahia, Pollini and so on. Yet his best playing is not inferior to theirs. Many of his Mozart concerto recordings can stand comparison with the best, and this one is no exception (nor should his excellent colleagues escape their own fair share of credit). While not eclipsing Fleisher's magisterial 1959 account of K503 with Szell, Jandó and Ligeti turn in an absolutely splendid account, musicianly to its figurative fingertips. In its way, this is very straightforward playing, never rhetorically glossy or self-indulgently poetic, but at no point is it remotely pedestrian or instrumentally lacklustre. As in their even finer reading of K451 (and why do we not hear this masterwork more often?), they convey with exceptional immediacy the sheer joy and robust good health of this wonderful music. *JS*

MOZART

Piano Concertos Nos 17 in G, K453 & 18 in B flat, K456

English CO/Murray Perahia (piano)

Sony SK 36686 □ **ADD** □ **59:07 mins** □ ⊘⊘⊘

Once again, Perahia demonstrates that he is a Mozartian without superior. In clarity of articulation, elegance of phrase, textural translucency and dramatic pacing, these performances are unsurpassed. Rhythmic and tonal nuances have a naturalness and subtlety of inflection more commonly associated with the human voice than with instruments of any kind, and the continuous interplay of ideas and emotional shadings is almost operatic in its immediacy – but only in the best and purest Mozartian sense. There's never the remotest hint of exaggeration here, not even of poetic sensibility, the only form of exaggeration to which Perahia is occasionally prone. At the same time, there's nothing bland or prettified. Mozart's concertos represent the apotheosis of musical Utopianism, and Perahia is acutely alive to every passing tension and its subsquent resolution and integration. A further bonus here is the combination of one of the most famous concertos, the G major, with one of the most mysteriously neglected, the wonderful K456, whose central movement is among the most profound and affecting things Mozart ever wrote. *JS*

MOZART

Piano Concertos Nos 20 in D minor, K466 & 27 in B flat, K595

English CO/Murray Perahia (piano)

Sony SK 42241 □ **61:31 mins** □ ⊘⊘⊘

With several truly exceptional versions in the catalogue, from the likes of Brendel, Curzon, Serkin (on Sony; steer clear of his DG version with Abbado), Gilels, Haskil, Horszowski, Kempff and others, a single choice can't help feeling a little invidious, but while affirming that you can't really go wrong with any of the aforementioned, let me go for Perahia, whose complete cycle with the ECO is one of the foremost jewels in the crown of 20th-century recording, and whose particular combination of finesse and drama, of simplicity and immense sophistication, of broad design and ravishing detail, and of spontaneity and unerring judgement adds up to a definitive recipe for great Mozart playing. Not the only way, by any means, but one that convinces you, while listening, that to ask for more would be asking for the moon. But then you hear Brendel or Haskil or Uchida and Barenboim at their best… or Serkin or Fischer or Schiff… or… *JS*

MOZART

Piano Concerto No. 21 in C, K467

see also SCHUMANN: Piano Concerto in A minor

MOZART

Piano Concertos Nos 24 in C minor, K491 & 25 in C, K503

Berlin PO/Daniel Barenboim (piano)

Teldec 9031-75715-2 □ 62:02 mins □ 𝄞𝄞𝄞

These performances appear to have been entirely unaffected by the epidemic of authenticitis which has spread over the globe in the last thirty years and are none the worse for it. Barenboim takes an unabashedly symphonic view of both works, most appropriately in K503, which is certainly the grandest and most ceremonial in the entire canon of Mozart's concertos, and the results are absolutely splendid – stylish, polished, sweeping in scope yet attentive to detail at every level, immaculately integrated and superbly recorded. This is a disc I really can't conceive of anyone *not* enjoying. If, however, you fancy something a little less big-city glossy, a trifle more incisive in rhythm perhaps (not that Barenboim is in any sense sluggish) and a bit leaner in texture, then I can unhesitatingly recommend Zoltán Kocsis and the Franz Liszt Chamber Orchestra on Harmonia Mundi, which gives you two other C major concertos, K246 and K415, and miles of youthful zest. On period instruments, Bilson and Gardiner on Archiv are exemplary in every way, but at the time of writing their performances are available only as part of the complete nine-disc set. *JS*

MOZART

Serenades in G, K525 (Eine kleine Nachtmusik), in D, K237, in D, K203, in D, K250 (Haffner), in D, K320 (Posthorn), in E flat, K375, in B flat for 13 wind instruments, K361 (Gran Partita), in C minor, K388 (Nacht Musique), in D, K215, in D, K204 & in D, K239 (Serenata notturna)

Thomas Zehetmair (violin), Peter Damm (posthorn); Concentus Musicus Wien, Dresden Staatskapelle, Wiener Mozart Bläser/Nikolaus Harnoncourt

Teldec 4509-95986-2 □ 339:47 mins (5 discs) □ 𝄞𝄞

This is an outstanding package of fine performances, felicitously crafted by that most exacting and prepossessing of authenticists, Nikolaus Harnoncourt. The grand, lavishly ceremonial works, K250 and K320 (the *Haffner* and *Posthorn* Serenades) are performed by the Dresden Staatskapelle, the former occupying the second of these five CDs. Harnoncourt secures playing of arresting élan and brilliance in each case; K250 is at once

imperious and majestic, and features Thomas Zehetmair as the agile and rich-toned soloist in the Menuetto and Rondo movements where, temporarily, the work becomes an adjunct to Mozart's series of concertos for the instrument (the majority of which also date from his Salzburg years). No less impressive is Harnoncourt's reading of K320, in which the posthorn obbligato is played by Peter Damm. These Dresden offerings are stunningly recorded, and orchestral playing is predictably magnificent. The strings of Concentus Musicus Wien, Harnoncourt's ground-breaking period band, are heard to compelling effect in the familiar *Eine kleine Nachtmusik*, K525, and the delectable *Serenata notturna*, K239. Polished and rigorous, these accounts have a freshness and panache often absent in most modern-instrument versions, and the performance of the Serenade in D, K203 (the March K237, forms its customary intrada, and it seems probable that Mozart intended the work to be heard in this form) is likewise superb. Harnoncourt directs the Wiener Mozart Bläser in K375, a chaste, sprightly affair, and the magnificent K361 and K388. The former, the Serenade for 13 Wind Instruments, is a sublimely beautiful seven-movement work, long upheld as the finest of its genre: this account is matchlessly realised, and the distinctive timbre of the Viennese wind-playing is a delight. These five discs offer exceptional performances of these works in outstanding digital recordings made variously between 1984 and 1993. As mid-price reissues, the discs have no serious competition, assuming, that is, that you do not require the works on individual discs. Teldec does not provide much in the way of insert notes; in every other regard, this is altogether superb. *MJ*

MOZART

Sinfonia concertante in E flat, K364; Concertone in C, K190

Cho-Liang Lin (violin), Jaime Laredo (viola), Neil Black (oboe), Charles Tunnell (cello); English CO/Raymond Leppard

Sony SK 47693 □ 60:00 mins □ 𝄞𝄞𝄞

A wicked choice here. Perlman, Zukerman and Mehta on DG are at their best, in the same programme, and the Orpheus Chamber Orchestra in K364 (also on DG, but with the earlier Sinfonia concertante, K297) is if anything more entrancing, but this Sony version keeps making its way to the top of my own list. Lin and Laredo bring an unsurpassed combination of brilliance and refinement to their playing, as elegant and eloquent as one could hope to hear, and Leppard is an exemplary colleague throughout, coaxing some of the best playing ever from the ECO. In sweetness of tone, richness of colour, clarity of texture and suppleness of phrase, all concerned need bow to no one – and the same can be said of the recording team. Nevertheless, there's one other performance of the Sinfonia that demands equal billing, even if it is almost half a century old: Stern, Primrose and Casals (also on Sony), recorded in 1951 and superbly remastered, bring naturalness, spontaneity and joy to their playing that leave one listener, at least, with a sense of extraordinary privilege. *JS*

MOZART

Symphonies Nos 25, 27–36 & 38–41

Capella Istropolitana/Barry Wordsworth

Naxos 8.505004 □ 322:10 mins (5 discs) □ *◯*

Nothing has surprised me more in my researches for the present volume than the quality of these recordings by a hitherto little-known orchestra and a British conductor who has never been among the jet-setting celebrities who grace the catalogues of the bigger record companies. The playing is perhaps not as streamlined as that of the Berlin Philharmonic under Karl Böhm (whose traversal of the Symphonies Nos 35–6 and 38–41, in its rather dated, chromium-plated way, is well worth anyone's time), but is far closer than most 'traditional' readings to the kinds of sounds that Mozart himself would have had in mind. Textures are impeccably clear, details of articulation are meticulously realised, but above all the sheer spirit of the music is brought delightfully to life. Without being in any way idiosyncratic, these performances have an exceptionally personal feel to them, like chamber music writ large (but not all that large). This is not to say, however, that Marriner on EMI is not equally rewarding in his rather sleeker way, and certainly does nothing to invalidate the wonderful old performances of Bruno Walter on Sony, which remain among the most cherishable of all Mozart recordings. A further bonus of this bargain-basement box from Naxos, incidentally, is that the five discs are also available separately. Listeners who want a period approach can turn with complete confidence to Trevor Pinnock and The English Concert on DG. *JS*

MOZART

Symphonies Nos 29 in A, 30 in D & 31 in D (Paris)

Amsterdam Concertgebouw Orchestra/Nikolaus Harnoncourt

Teldec 4509-91187-2 □ 75:18 mins □ *◯◯*

I've never heard performances of any of these works that have given me as much sheer, unfettered pleasure as these. The playing of the Concertgebouw is sensational in its accuracy, precision and verve, and Harnoncourt brings to his direction of a traditional orchestra the lessons of a lifetime spent in the study of historical performance practices. He's sparing but not austere when it comes to string vibrato, he allows the brass a tanginess and bite as exhilarating as the best champagne, his tempi on the whole are bracingly energetic, like his rhythms, and the general clarity of texture is like proverbial crystal. Barring a sometimes Glenn Gould-like partiality for accompanimental figures, he keeps mannerism and idiosyncrasy at bay, and lavishes on the music all the care and sophisticated enthusiasm of the true amateur (literally, one who *loves*). The only substantial criticism I can make of these performances is that they doom most others to sounding hopelessly lacklustre and tepid in comparison. And of the recorded sound I can make no criticism of any kind. *JS*

MOZART

Symphonies Nos 40 in G minor & 41 in C (Jupiter)

The English Concert/Trevor Pinnock

Archiv 447 048-2 □ 72:32 mins □ *◯◯◯*

Trevor Pinnock has always, and refreshingly, been among the least doctrinaire exponents of the period-instrument movement, and these outstanding performances are wonderfully free of mannerism, including that institutionalised whine which is so often the badge of the card-carrying authenticist. Like Mozart, he has always been an enemy of exaggeration, and his readings of these two great works contrive to be both supremely elegant and deeply moving without once falling prey either to stylised rhetoric or self-conscious 'profundity'. He has no axe to grind, no 'points' to make, other than those made by Mozart himself. He has the humility and the sense of true joy to trust the composer. Fortunately, he also has a splendidly vital and subtle sense of rhythm and proportion, and an ear for that unique blend of harmony and counterpoint which is Mozart's own. Too many 'period' performances remind me of Mark Twain's observation that 'Wagner's music is better than it sounds'. Here the music sounds just as good as it is. *JS*

Violin Concertos Nos 1–5; Adagio in E, K261; Rondos in C, K373 & in B flat, K269

Itzhak Perlman (violin); Vienna PO/James Levine

DG Masters 445 535-2 □ 137:02 mins (2 discs) □ ⊘⊘

Violin Concertos Nos 1–5

Arthur Grumiaux (violin); LSO/Colin Davis

Philips 422 938-2 □ ADD □ 110:50 mins (2 discs) □ ⊘⊘

Itzhak Perlman's ravishingly beautiful playing is a joy to experience. He proves himself an adept and scholarly Mozartian, in performances of effortless brilliance and enviable Classical poise and propriety. Perlman has staunch allies in the members of the Vienna Philharmonic and in the conductor James Levine, though it is the warmth and clarity of the Musikvereinsaal itself which imparts particular lustre to these outstanding examples of the sound engineer's artifice. Perlman plays with his customary energy and insight; slow movements are exquisitely crafted, affectionately lingering, though never vulgar, and the brisk, clean-limbed outer movements of the concertos are unfailingly stylish and brilliant. Cadenzas are by Perlman himself (and they are particularly fine), though the familiar ones by Sam Franko and Joachim, both almost as mandatory as Kreisler's in the Beethoven concerto, appear in K216 and K219. DG has also included the Adagio in E major, K261, and the Rondos, K373 and K269, at the close of the first disc.

No lover of the violin should overlook Arthur Grumiaux's celebrated accounts of these concertos, taped in the early Sixties with Davis and the LSO. Having grown up with Grumiaux's Mozart, I've never tired of the noble, illustrious grandeur and captivating eloquence that were prominent features of his playing. Philips has reissued these incomparably noble performances on a mid-price double-disc set and, Perlman notwithstanding, I shouldn't wish to be without it. *MJ*

Symphonies Nos 1–6

Gothenburg SO/Neeme Järvi

DG 437 507-2 □ 201:40 mins (3 discs, also available separately) □ ⊘⊘⊘

'The orchestra played absolutely brilliantly under my baton, and why? Because they wanted to, on account of old friendship and dedication.' Fifty years after Carl Nielsen penned that tribute to the Gothenburg SO, the dedication burns as strongly as ever. The strings are the heart and soul: whether negotiating the unpredictable thickets of notes which convey instability and uncertainty, or singing out a fine and noble melody like the theme that appears like a knight in shining armour at the crisis-point of the Fifth's first movement, their instinct for the nuances behind the notes is peerless.

As Nielsen's strenuous battle with negative forces gathers weight in the later works, Järvi finds plenty of human warmth and flexibility to offset his unerring storming of the heights, while in the first two symphonies the hushed reminders of all that the composer found 'idyllic and heavenly in nature' constantly surprise here. Preferable to the less loving San Francisco Symphony under Blomstedt (Decca), the authentic voice of the Gothenburg SO can also be heard on BIS, with the performances split between Järvi – the same Fourth and Sixth, by a freak of licensing – and the slightly less charismatic Myung-Whun Chung. That set also includes a bonus disc featuring the Flute and Clarinet concertos, vital final instalments in Nielsen's Twenties quest for new directions after the astonishing *Sinfonia semplice*. *DN*

Symphony No. 4 (Inextinguishable); Pan and Syrinx
see SIBELIUS: Symphony No. 5

Symphonies Nos 5 & 6 (Sinfonia semplice)

Royal Stockholm PO/Gennady Rozhdestvensky

Chandos CHAN 9367 □ 71:49 mins □ ⊘⊘⊘

Newcomers to Nielsen may be familiar with the name of the *Inextinguishable*, and perhaps also with the celebrated battle of two timpanists in its finale; it makes a stirring introduction to his music, especially in the company of Sibelius. Yet its successor, the Fifth Symphony, makes an even better starting-point, creating a stupendous tension on the way to a victory that is clinched only in the last few bars. Its tireless first-movement routing of a combative side-drum is capped by the most athletic finale in the symphonic repertoire. Rozhdestvensky paces it with unparalled breadth and evenness; steely energy wrenched to the surface by Bernstein and Järvi here stays very firmly between the lines.

Earlier, the Stockholm strings struggle to hold their ground against Nielsen's ambassadors of chaos, and Rozhdestvensky has some trouble making them vocalise their fiendishly difficult part in the life-and-death struggle that launches the ever-elusive *Sinfonia semplice* (anything but simple). Still, his characterising skills have the upper hand in its unhappy 'Humoreske' and the lurking anarchy of the final theme and variations: pointers forward to Shostakovich's Fourth and Fifteenth symphonies are inescapable in the hands of a conductor who understands both composers *in extremis. DN*

PACHELBEL

Canon and Gigue
see Collection: Baroque Music

PAGANINI/SAINT-SAËNS/WAXMAN

Paganini: Violin Concerto No. 1 in D

Saint-Saëns: Introduction and Rondo Capriccioso, Op. 28; Havanaise, Op. 83

Waxman: Carmen Fantasie

Maxim Vengerov (violin); Israel PO/Zubin Mehta

Teldec 9031-73266-2 □ 63:07 mins □ ⊘⊘⊘

Among the current young lions of the violin world, Maxim Vengerov remains pre-eminent; he is, by any reckoning, a legitimate phenomenon capable of incredible feats of execution, and endowed with rare insight and musical intelligence. His account of Paganini's devilishly difficult First Violin Concerto faces stern competition, with stunning recent versions from the likes of Sarah Chang and Gil Shaham, and celebrated recordings from Accardo, Perlman and the late Michael Rabin. From a textual viewpoint, Vengerov's performance scores significantly over several of its rivals, in that Mehta gives us the splendid orchestral ritornello of the opening movement complete, and the solo part is spared many of the insensitive excisions customary today. Vengerov also plays the hair-raising Cadenza by Emile Sauret; here, as throughout this performance, his bravura and virtuosity are palpably enthralling; the slow movement is deliciously exaggerated and the Rondo finale bounds along splendidly. The two Saint-Saëns works are again enthrallingly played; the concluding section of the *Rondo Capriccioso*

defies description – Vengerov's dazzling articulation even at break-neck speed is miraculous! The disc also includes Franz Waxman's Fantasy on themes from Bizet's opera *Carmen,* tailor-made for Jascha Heifetz; a welcome alternative to the regular Sarasate show-piece, particularly in Vengerov's consummately skilled hands. Recorded sound and orchestral support from Mehta and the Israel PO are likewise beyond criticism. *MJ*

PANUFNIK

Sinfonia sacra; Arbor cosmica

Royal Concertgebouw Orchestra, New York Chamber Symphony/Andrzej Panufnik

Nonesuch 7559-79228-2 □ 58:35 mins □ ⊘⊘⊘

The third of Panufnik's nine symphonies, the *Sinfonia sacra* of 1963 draws its musical inspiration from the old Polish hymn 'Bogurodzica', which was sung regularly both in church and on the battlefield and held a special emotional significance for a composer who had escaped relatively recently from the shackles of communism in his native country. Images of struggle are especially potent in the dramatic and militant third section of the symphony, but the work's resolution is one of powerful optimism, with the hymn resounding throughout the full orchestra supported by glorious brass fanfares in a manner that recalls the coda of Janáček's Sinfonietta. *Arbor cosmica,* a sequence of 12 contrasting movements, inspired according to the composer by the mysterious powers exuded by trees, was composed twenty years later and demonstrates remarkably resourceful writing for string orchestra, a quality Panufnik shared with his compatriot, Lutosławski. At only 58 minutes, the disc is rather stingy in terms of duration, but the definitive performances and excellent recording make this an attractive issue. *EL*

PARRY

Symphonic Variations; Overture to an Unwritten Tragedy; Lady Radnor's Suite; An English Suite; Bridal March from The Birds

LSO, LPO/Adrian Boult

Lyrita SRCD 220 □ ADD □ 63:09 mins □ ⊘⊘⊘

Parry's Variations of 1897, a sumptuous and memorable sequence that unfolds continuously while suggesting a concise four-movement symphonic plan, was overshadowed almost immediately in its genre by the success of Elgar's *Enigma* set. But for many decades it was his only orchestral work to maintain a toehold in the repertoire, usually on the specious reasoning that it was his 'best' (from critics who hadn't heard any of the others). Now that – thanks to CD – we know Parry the symphonist, the Variations still hold their place as a highly characteristic score and an early classic of the English musical renaissance to boot.

Adrian Boult, a Parry pupil, twice recorded the work. This, his earlier and finer account, has a thrusting dynamism that shapes the symphonic architecture more imposingly than his 1979 LPO performance for EMI. The vintage Lyrita recording ages well. The couplings, all worth having, include a searing account of the gorgeous Sarabande in Parry's late *An English Suite* for strings. A dependable modern version of the Symphonic Variations (LPO/Matthias Bamert) is available on Chandos coupled with different and on the whole more significant Parry works: the early, fiery *Concertstück*, the *Elegy for Brahms* written in the same year as the Variations, and the late, elegiac symphonic poem *From Death to Life*. *CM*

PETTERSSON

Symphony No. 9

Deutsches SO, Berlin/Alun Francis

CPO 999 231-2 □ 69:52 mins □ 😊😊😊

The raw, angst-ridden music of the Swedish symphonist Allan Pettersson, who died in 1980, arouses strong feelings. Some find it nihilistic, self-pitying, impossibly long drawn out. Certainly Pettersson, who rose from poverty-stricken slum childhood to be a noted orchestral violist, then spent his last decades imprisoned in his tiny flat by painful and crippling disease, had plenty to get depressed about. Yet no late 20th-century composer writes music so much as if his very existence depended on it, and none (not even Schnittke) has sought more viscerally to extend the tradition of symphonic protest from Mahler and Shostakovich. Pettersson's techniques of development are partly continuous metamorphosis, partly stream of consciousness, and he demands virtuoso playing from every member of the orchestra. Difficult, yes, cross-grained, but perseverance reveals him as intensely rewarding, even inspiring. Elegy, appeal, pain, outrage, anger: the music has all of these, but also wonderful islands of song, or of sheer aching serenity, the more blessed for being so rare. This is 'Seventh Seal' land, where death and despair are offset

by pale sunlight and the strength of human passion. Both CPO and BIS have each undertaken a cycle of Pettersson's 16 symphonies. Many of the composer's champions swear by the Seventh Symphony, which first established his name outside Sweden: if you want to sample it, it's well served on BIS by Leif Segerstam and the Nörrkoping SO, coupled with the shorter Eleventh. But I seem to have a personal blind-spot with No. 7, and offer instead this taut, bravura performance of the Ninth (1970), an echt-Petterssonian creation in an enormous single movement. If you warm to it, you'll manage the rest. Next, perhaps, go to Segerstam's BIS disc that couples Pettersson's Third, his only symphony in (apparently) conventional four-movement form, with the late, sardonically inventive Fifteenth. *CM*

PISTON

Symphony No. 4; Capriccio for Harp & String Orchestra; Serenata; Three New England Sketches

Theresa Elder Wunrow (harp); Seattle Symphony, New York Chamber Symphony of the 92nd Street Y/Gerard Schwarz

Delos DE 3106 □ 64:05 mins □ 😊😊😊

The Boston composer Walter Piston, a pupil of Nadia Boulanger, was perhaps American music's Haydn: the craftsmanship is impeccable, the personality genial, forms Classical, textures clean, tunes finely balanced, rhythms athletic. His music so determinedly eschews bombast and portentousness, and thus displays the virtues that made him an outstanding teacher, that one might miss the unassuming depth of thought, the serene gravity of spirit that underlies its blithe efficiency.

The core of Piston's output is the series of eight symphonies, and No. 4 (1950: once recorded on LP by Ormandy and the Philadelphia) is probably the finest, drama growing seamlessly out of serenely pastoral beginnings, with an invigorating, dancing-fiddling Scherzo and eloquently singing slow movement. The *Serenata* is like a lighter rerun of the symphony, the *Capriccio* a dapper display piece: but the *New England Sketches* (1960) is also a major work, whose craggy finale maps out the more dissonant territory Piston annexed towards the end of his career.

This is perhaps the best disc of Delos's Piston series. Gerard Schwarz, in the symphony, can't efface memories of Ormandy, but he runs a taut ship and the music is excellently served. *CM*

POULENC

Organ Concerto; Concert champêtre; Concerto for Two Pianos in D minor; Piano Concerto; Aubade

Marie-Claire Alain (organ), Ton Koopman (harpsichord), François-René Duchable, Jean-Philippe Collard (piano); Rotterdam PO/James Conlon

Erato Duo Bonsai 4509-95303-2 □ 105:00 mins (2 discs) □ ⊘⊘

Though the lack of any descriptive notes is reprehensible, this is an irresistible bargain: all five Poulenc concertos on two discs for the price you'd normally pay for a single full-price one – reissues of modern performances, wholly idiomatic and affectionate, in first-rate sound. Written at intervals over more than twenty years, Poulenc's concertos span the gamut of his musical language, from the *café-concert* urbanity of the Piano Concerto to the dark neo-Baroque rhetoric and rhythmic salacity of the Concerto for Organ, Strings and Timpani. This is one of the most striking pieces in the genre this century, and never better presented than in Alain's sovereign performance here. Poulenc's unfailing charm, his skill in parody and lifelong alliance with the theatre are suggested in the fractured mock-Classicism of the *Concert champêtre* and the 'choreographic concerto' *Aubade*, and in the gamelan-like tinkling and naughty *Folies Bergère* tunefulness of the Double Piano Concerto. If Ton Koopman does not banish fond memories of Aimée van de Wiele on the Columbia LP on which I first got to know the *Concert champêtre*, all the soloists are excellent and Conlon's orchestral support always delightfully pointed and idiomatic. Self-recommending sweetmeats. *CM*

PROKOFIEV

Chout (The Buffoon) – Suite; Romeo and Juliet – excerpts

LSO/Claudio Abbado

Decca 425 027-2 □ ADD □ 54:03 mins □ ⊘⊘

Romeo and Juliet Suites Nos 1–3

Scottish National Orchestra/Neeme Järvi

Chandos CHAN 8940 □ 78:27 mins □ ⊘⊘⊘

The Decca disc is a glittering testament to Abbado's racy younger days. He was right to have faith in the spangled fantastics of the earlier suite, drawn from Prokofiev's first successful score for Diaghilev. Never one to resuscitate old atmosphere, the impresario had found the barbarous poundings of *Ala and Lolly* – eventually salvaged as the *Scythian Suite* – too close to the recipe of the already successful *Rite of Spring*; *Chout* succeeded because it was something new – a Russian tale with absurdist overtones. The score reflects that canny balance, wrapping folk-like tunes in garish, sometimes brazen orchestration – one step on from *Petrushka* – and the LSO's razor-sharp performance is presented in suitably brilliant recorded sound.

Abbado's half-hour *Romeo and Juliet* selection favours the aggressive or extrovert sides of the score and delivers them with faultless panache; the rarely heard numbers with mandolins have never been better done. What's missing – perhaps wisely, given the time-limit – is any hint of the lovers' tragedy. For the heart of the matter, Järvi's expansive and highly atmospheric account of the three suites is unsurpassable if a little rough around the edges. A pity Chandos attempted no reordering of the numbers to follow approximately the course of the drama. Another excellent selection, this time wisely mixing Prokofiev's telescoped movements from the suites with numbers from the complete ballet, is Dutoit's (Decca). *DN*

PROKOFIEV

Cinderella

Cleveland Orchestra/Vladimir Ashkenazy

Decca 410 162-2 □ 107:36 mins (2 discs) □ ⊘⊘⊘

Generally leaner of texture and more elusive in character than *Romeo and Juliet*, Prokofiev's second full-length ballet needs a special helping hand. Ashkenazy, a nimble dance-master who can make even Brahms's Second Symphony sound like ballet music (and that's meant as a compliment), provides exactly that. The virtues of his sweepingly affectionate performance are all the more apparent when you listen to Mikhail Pletnev's chilly brand of elegant dancing on the inexplicably well-favoured new *Cinderella*. That recording is further weakened by DG's failure to close the gaps between numbers (especially the shorter movements), something to be taken for granted in the Decca presentation. Artful balances are a bonus, given Prokofiev's unorthodox combinations of instruments, and the Cleveland strings survive the close recording in singing melodies like that of the ardent *pas de deux* at the ball – an excellent track to compare with Pletnev if you need to confirm the greater warmth of Ashkenazy's poster-paint fairy-story. *DN*

PROKOFIEV

Lieutenant Kijé – Symphonic Suite; Andante for string orchestra; Autumn (Symphonic Sketch); The Stone Flower – Prologue and Wedding Suite

Scottish National Orchestra/Neeme Järvi

Chandos CHAN 8806 □ 67:00 mins □ ❷❷❷

Prokofiev's score for Alexander Faintsimmer's film about a non-existent lieutenant at the time of Tsar Paul I, fictional product of Russian bureaucracy, was his first major project on Soviet soil in the early Thirties and reflects his (self-formulated) belief in striking melodies simply adorned. Järvi's fascinating cross-section points up the wry leanness of *Lieutenant Kijé* by putting it in the company of *Autumn*, a youthful meandering into Scriabinesque territory; a full-string transcription of the searching final Andante of the First Quartet; and a rich selection from the last of Prokofiev's Soviet ballets. In *Autumn*, Järvi's sense of purpose allows us to register the orchestral hues without worrying about what's going to happen next; while the icy, staggered summons of *The Stone Flower*'s Mistress of the Copper Mountain is narrated in ringing tones from the SNO brass before a characterful string of set pieces cheerfully lowers dramatic temperatures. Acoustics could be drier for *Kijé*'s sharply focused satire, but cornet, saxophone and piccolo solos are wittily vocalised, and Järvi's relaxed tempi help to give the right amount of air around the dances. *DN*

PROKOFIEV

Piano Concertos Nos 1–5

Vladimir Ashkenazy (piano); LSO/André Previn

Decca 425 570-2 □ ADD □ 126:29 mins (2 discs) □ ❷❷

Ashkenazy and Previn provide a spirited, Puckish partnership to guide us through the gymnasium of the five Prokofiev piano concertos. Flawless dexterity can be taken for granted and never draws attention to itself, a virtue most noticeable in the best known of the five, No. 3, beautifully dovetailed and paced yet without charging self-regardingly at the racy codas of the outer movements (even Argerich's *tour de force* on DG can seem flashily brilliant by comparison). In careful collusion with Previn's orchestra, strings silkily to the fore, Ashkenazy also emphasises the role

introspective lyricism has to play even in the restless First Concerto. In these performances the slow movements of Nos 4 (for the left hand only, the most underrated of several works commissioned by Paul Wittgenstein) and 5 powerfully point the way forward to the new, striking melodies of the composer's fertile Soviet years.

Only the steel fist of the hair-raising Second Concerto is more than Ashkenazy can handle: though all the notes are in place, his tone in the massive first-movement cadenza is clangorous alongside the sonorities of a Russian heavyweight like Dmitri Alexeev (a shattering performance, not currently available). Even here, though, his teamwork with Previn spares us combat fatigue and clearly registers all the audacities of scoring even in the noisiest thrashes. *DN*

PROKOFIEV/RAVEL

Prokofiev: Piano Concerto No. 3

Ravel: Piano Concerto in G; Gaspard de la nuit

Martha Argerich (piano); Berlin PO/Claudio Abbado

DG Originals 447 438-2 □ ADD □ 70:50 mins □ ❷❷

Absolutely stunning. These legendary, award-winning Berlin performances, full of Latin fire and sensuality, capture Argerich at her most characteristically brilliant. Grippingly partnered by Abbado (in what was his DG debut), here is concerto playing of miraculous lyricism and whiplashing rhythmic panache, with a rapport between soloist and conductor that's consistently high-tensioned. The diamond-edged glitter and voluptuous sonorities of *Gaspard* (recorded later) show an equally fantastic imagination at work. Demonstration transfer. *Ates Orga*

PROKOFIEV

Scythian Suite
see **CHORAL & SONG**: PROKOFIEV: Alexander Nevsky

PROKOFIEV/TCHAIKOVSKY

Prokofiev: Symphony-Concerto for cello and orchestra

Tchaikovsky: Variations on a Rococo Theme; Andante cantabile (version for cello and orchestra)

Yo-Yo Ma (cello); Pittsburgh SO/Lorin Maazel

Sony SK 48382 □ 68:07 mins □ ❷❷❷

The Symphony-Concerto really belongs to Mstislav Rostropovich, who worked long and hard on its details with the ailing composer in the early Fifties. Since, however, the fate of his best performance (made in the Soviet Union with Rozhdestvensky) hangs in the balance, this is a suitably intense alternative version of a troubled masterpiece. Symphony-Concerto, not Sinfonia concertante, is the correct title, but this is without doubt a concertante performance, a meshing with the extraordinarily spare orchestration that seems to have required no engineering manipulation. Maazel's tempi – with which Ma was surely in agreement – stress the dark undertow with clear bass-lines and eerily characterful orchestral solos; the few occasions when Prokofiev unleashes the full orchestra make the hair stand on end.

Ma has the last word, though, spot on in ferocious articulation of the last, high-pitching gesture of defiance, while earlier cadenzas are shaded with a graphic concern for the spirit of combat, and the poignant Russian melody that surfaces in the central conflict has all the necessary introspection. In the Rococo Variations, a smiling relief from so much nervous tension, his flawless intonation is indispensable in making light of the technical difficulties Tchaikovsky lays thick over charming subject-matter; only purists who insist on the original version could ask for anything more. *DN*

PROKOFIEV

Symphonies Nos 1–7

Scottish National Orchestra/Neeme Järvi

Chandos CHAN 8931/4 □ 259:59 mins (4 discs) □ 🎵🎵

Separate issues: Symphony No. 2; Romeo and Juliet Suite No. 1 – CHAN 8368; Symphonies Nos 1 (Classical) & 4 (revised version) – CHAN 8400; Symphony No. 6; Three Waltzes from Waltz Suite – CHAN 8359; Symphony No. 7; Sinfonietta – CHAN 8442

The starting point for this revelatory cycle was a recording of the tragic Sixth Symphony which brought it out from the shadow of its more popular predecessor and awoke the listening public to the astonishing results Estonian Neeme Järvi was achieving as the Scottish National Orchestra's principal conductor. It is a performance which achieves poignant refinement in the score's more nostalgic moments but never shrinks from the acidic colours of Prokofiev's painful cries for help; Järvi characterises to chilling perfection the edgy orchestration of the powerful slow movement and the tell-tale warning signs below the finale's jolly surface which finally lead to unequivocal catastrophe. How refreshing, too, to find a performance of the Seventh Symphony that brings out the implicit pathos of this subtle, lovely symphonic swan-song; for too long conductors and critics alike have followed the Soviet line that it is a 'light and happy' work.

The SNO brass come in useful for the more exuberant thrash of the Second Symphony – written to please a Parisian audience newly enthralled by the *style méchanique* of Honegger's *Pacific 231* – and the flesh-creeping supernaturalism of the Third. Perhaps surprisingly, the tone of this Fifth veers more towards light irony than bludgeoning sarcasm. A special edge of this cycle over long-absent predecessors (including the comparably characterful Rozhdestvensky) comes in the shape of both Fourths. The original is a short, sharp repackaging of themes from the ballet *The Prodigal Son*, but in his Soviet-era version Prokofiev added so much new music – including a motto that turns into a grindingly ambivalent 'hail to Stalin' – that, as he pointed out, it was virtually a new symphony. Since Järvi seems happier with epic form than with neo-classical precision, the revision gets the better deal, and the spacious, sometimes diffuse Chandos open-hall sound is more suitable too. Except for a splashy if spirited *Classical* Symphony, the original Fourth and the Fifth, all the performances are top recommendations in their original single guises (with some startling bonuses not featured on the set). *DN*

PROKOFIEV

Symphony No. 1 (Classical)

see also Collection: Russian Music

PROKOFIEV

Violin Concertos Nos 1 & 2

Dmitry Sitkovetsky (violin); LSO/Colin Davis

Virgin VC 5 45108 2 □ 48:53 mins □ 🎵🎵🎵

Sitkovetsky prefers to point up the similarities rather than the differences between the fantastical offspring of Prokofiev's *enfant terrible* days and the Second Concerto's tough, quizzical acerbity. His dark, intensely serious manner brings the long opening melody of No. 1 lucidly into line with that of its successor – clear, songful, lovingly pointed. Much else in this First Concerto is made of tougher stuff, thanks to the violinist's keen teamwork with Davis and the LSO: a steadier-than-usual pace for the Scherzo allows grotesque detail to register with ruthless accuracy, while the outer movements build towards a rare menace, a landscape with lurking monsters, more commonly detected in the Second Concerto. And how chillingly it strikes there. The double-stopping dance of the finale lashes out ever more desperately on each return, brakes applied in vain as we head for the abyss; and it's intriguing to hear the solo line in the famous slow movement keeping deadpan faith with the ironic tocking accompaniment (Prokofiev has no *espressivo* marking for the violin here). There are many alternative viewpoints on each concerto – not least Maxim Vengerov's brilliant First on Sony – but Sitkovetsky makes the most compelling argument for hearing both at a single sitting, so forget about the short measure and enjoy. *DN*

PURCELL

Chacony in G minor
see Collection: Baroque Music
and **CHAMBER**: PURCELL: Fantasias

RACHMANINOV

Piano Concertos Nos 1–4; Rhapsody on a Theme of Paganini

Howard Shelley (piano); Scottish National Orchestra/Bryden Thomson

Chandos CHAN 8892/3 □ 153:47 mins (2 discs) □ 𝅘𝅥𝅘𝅥𝅘𝅥

Rachmaninov the pianist has to be the first point of reference for his concertos (see essay, p24), but Howard Shelley proves the worthiest of heirs in moving fluently and without false rhetoric to the heart of the matter. As light and dextrous in passages of transcendental fantasy as Vladimir Ashkenazy on two slightly overrated cycles, Shelley can call upon a tonal depth and weight which leave Ashkenazy sounding brittle at key moments: never more impressive than in the daunting first-movement cadenza of No. 1 or the epic build that launches the Second Concerto (worth sampling for starters if you're worried that a less than big name can't produce a big sound).

The refreshing thing about the set is that Shelley proves so scrupulous and selective in employing that grand manner. He is the only pianist to convince me that there is not a redundant note in the Third Concerto, moving the melodies along without sacrificing any essential soulfulness (this is my first recommendation for a single-disc version too). All the finales are thrilling – even the last variations of the Paganini Rhapsody, otherwise a surprisingly low-key affair by the standards of the set (though it's amazing it was accommodated at all on the first CD). Thomson and the orchestra, excitingly recorded on a level with the soloist, are very much equal partners; the horns at the start of Concerto No. 1 announce imposing things to come, and the clarinet in the slow movement of the Second phrases the famous melody with supreme artistry. *DN*

RACHMANINOV/TCHAIKOVSKY

Rachmaninov: Piano Concerto No. 2 in C minor

Tchaikovsky: Piano Concerto No. 1 in B flat minor

Sviatoslav Richter (piano); Warsaw PO/Stanisław Wisłocki, Vienna SO/Herbert von Karajan

DG 447 420-2 □ ADD □ 71:00 mins □ 𝅘𝅥𝅘𝅥𝅘𝅥

Grand Romantic gestures are few, but overwhelming, in Richter's awesome performances of these concertos. Nobly assisted by two conductors prepared to share his vision, he has all the weight necessary to pull off the two most majestic utterances, at the end of the Rachmaninov concerto and the beginning of the Tchaikovsky, and an unparalleled control in making the softer passages of both works uniquely searching and introspective. We see, perhaps for the one and only time, how Rachmaninov's inclination to morbid introspection loses him the right to lyrical consolation in the first movement's return journey; all the more reason for holding one's breath at the unexpected poise and calm of the Adagio.

Richter's Tchaikovsky richly deserves the right to self-assertion at the end of the opening movement, the real journey of a soul, before retreating into the world of dreams and only cautiously assuming the finale's extrovert character: a disappointment to those who want more in the way of Russian song and dance, but consistent with the philosophy of the performance as a whole. An old war-horse will never sound the same again. *DN*

RACHMANINOV/DOHNANYI

Rachmaninov: Rhapsody on a Theme of Paganini; Piano Concerto No. 2 in C minor

Dohnányi: Variations on a Nursery Song

Julius Katchen (piano); LPO/Adrian Boult, LSO/Georg Solti

Decca 448 604-2 □ ADD □ 78:31 mins □ 𝅘𝅥𝅘𝅥

This Rhapsody may be a misalliance, and a primitively recorded one at that, but I find it fascinating as Boult and his orchestra, firm of purpose, try to meet Katchen's fast and furious challenge. Better than a nearly garbled finale – double octaves delight Katchen more than mercurial lighter textures, a problem for most pianists – are the quicksilver of the fourth and fifth variations and the fine gait of the climb towards the plateau of the big tune (there's plenty of shadowy atmosphere along the way, and the release is very subtly done indeed). No nonsense but plenty of imagination make Katchen's Second Concerto a joy; his masterful, life-kindling sense of rubato is immediately apparent, his orchestra and conductor prove keener travelling-companions, and passages in the finale crackle with electricity.

Since, however, you must hear Richter in the concerto, this disc is still worth it for the Rhapsody (my favourite performance has not been available for some time and comes from a little-known pianist, Ilana Vered: an oddly balanced recording from the days of Decca's Phase Four stereo but the only one I know to catch all the diabolical flickerings of this *danse macabre*). Room has also been found for Dohnányi's Variations on a Nursery Song, with which this Paganini Rhapsody has traditionally been coupled. *DN*

RACHMANINOV

Symphonies Nos 1–3; The Isle of the Dead; Symphonic Dances; Vocalise; Aleko – Intermezzo & Women's Dance

LSO/André Previn

EMI CMS 7 64530 2 □ ADD □ **216:52 mins (3 discs)** □ 🎵🎵

Brilliant landmarks in restoring Rachmaninov's symphonic reputation when first issued in the Seventies, Previn's readings remain prime examples of how to keep the music on the move without losing out on lavishness or flexibility. Never again will there be any truck with the verdict of the old Pelican second volume on *The Symphony* that Symphonies Nos 2 and 3 simply don't count. If you prefer a more leisurely Romanticism (and all repeats) there's now Andrew Litton and the Royal Philharmonic Orchestra on Virgin to furnish a persuasive alternative, though they are less convincingly opulent in the fantasies of the Third Symphony and less trenchant in the craggy profiles of the Symphonic Dances (finely shaped here as a very powerful Fourth Symphony). Hothouse ambiences are avoided, though EMI's CD transfers are fierce, unacceptably so in the finale of the First Symphony (my LP copy sounds fine). At its best the recording helps out the LSO's macabre incandescence in the oozing tears of *The Isle of the Dead* and the sensuous-sombre waltz in the Symphonic Dances. *DN*

RACHMANINOV

Symphony No. 1 in D minor; The Isle of the Dead

RPO/Andrew Litton

Virgin VC 7 90830 2 □ **66:54 mins** □ 🎵🎵🎵

Symphony No. 2 in E minor; Vocalise

RPO/Andrew Litton

Virgin VC 7 90831 2 □ **70:05 mins** □ 🎵🎵🎵

Immersion in symphonic Rachmaninov can be like running round a hothouse pursued by little Russian devils, so it's a relief that Litton regulates the temperature – not that anything is coldly studied in these finely observed, lovingly prepared performances. If Litton's speeds are generally more expansive than Rachmaninov suggested – or would have contemplated as conductor – then the RPO fleshes out every detail with rich and focused playing.

Some listeners might like a little more obsession, hysteria even, in the morbid fragmentations of the First Symphony – Ashkenazy is an exciting alternative on mid-price Decca – but I found the individual players' shading of mood enough, and the steady dance towards the abyss in the terrifying finale is the more gut-wrenching as it careers to the brink with open eyes. Portamenti in the violins at the start of the Second Symphony suggest a Hollywood touch in store, but lush second subjects and a specially incandescent Adagio reveal muscle in the phrasing and forward detail from inner string parts. The recording helps by standing back to allow luminous perspectives on the many finely honed woodwind solos, and some subtly disturbing haloes around stopped horns and muted trombones. *DN*

RACHMANINOV

Symphony No. 3 in A minor; Symphonic Dances

St Petersburg PO/Mariss Jansons

EMI CDC 7 54877 2 □ **72:16 mins** □ 🎵🎵🎵

Made in the United States, but building powerfully on the Russian orchestral tradition, Rachmaninov's late masterpieces here return to their roots. Mariss Jansons makes amends for the St Petersburg Philharmonic's neglect of Rachmaninov during its (Leningrad) days under Mravinsky, drawing dark, well-blended colours in the truthful acoustic of the city's white-marble Philharmonic Hall.

It's a far cry from the hyper-sensuous Philadelphia sound magnificently controlled by Rachmaninov in a rare sample of his genius (the 1939 recording of the Third Symphony; see essay, p24); but as Dutoit's recent Philadelphia recordings of these works on Decca unhappily proved, surface glamour counts for nothing if Rachmaninov's frequent demands for a flexible *tempo rubato* meet only with stiff metronomic precision. Jansons is carefully free with the serpentine lyrical themes of the symphony – no need, though, for (unmarked) timpani to bolster swooning strings in the finale – and he digs surprisingly deep for the ache at the heart of the Symphonic Dances. Extrovert moments are keenly accented, rather light of tread for the third-movement battle of Alleluias and Dies irae. There, my first choices would be dedicatee Eugene Ormandy on Sony or the hyper-atmospheric Järvi (Chandos), who takes such thrilling liberties with the second-movement Valse triste. But the human, even-handed voice of the St Petersburg PO certainly offers a new perspective on Rachmaninov's orchestral mastery. *DN*

RAMEAU

Orchestral suites from Naïs & Le temple de la gloire

Philharmonia Baroque Orchestra/Nicholas McGegan

Harmonia Mundi HMU 907121 □ 71:08 mins
□ *♪♪♪*

These two suites are quite simply superb. Their blend of elegance and fiery imagination make them compulsive listening and provide still more evidence, if any were needed, that Rameau is quite worthy of comparison with Handel. The overture to *Naïs*, starting with nervous sequences, erupts into wild syncopation more characteristic of Slavonic nationalism than Parisian propriety. While the rest of the suite follows a more familiar pattern, none of the dances is less than ear-catching and some, notably the broad Chaconne are full of evocative detail.

The music from *Le temple de la gloire* – taken from an opera ballet commemorating the victory of Fontenoy – is more dignified but is richly rewarding. McGegan's interest in French music has deep roots. Interpretatively he does not put a foot wrong. His instinctive feel for tempi and unfailingly elegant sense of *inégalité* is shared by the band. The playing is not without blemish, but the sheer sense of fun and stylish commitment of these performances, and, not least, the music itself,

puts this CD into the top category.
Jan Smaczny

RAVEL

Boléro; Rapsodie espagnole; La valse; Valses nobles et sentimentales; Le tombeau de Couperin; Ma mère l'oye; Daphnis et Chloé Suite No. 2; Alborada del gracioso; Pavane pour une infante défunte; Menuet antique

Amsterdam Concertgebouw Orchestra/Bernard Haitink

Philips Duo 438 745-2 □ ADD □ 141:18 mins
(2 discs) □ *♪♪*

Bernard Haitink's classically clear and direct approach combines élan, elasticity and, where appropriate, tremendous rhythmic punch – his readings of *Boléro* and *La valse* are volatile yet thrillingly disciplined to the last. He brings a natural compulsion to the languorous eroticism of *Daphnis et Chloé* Suite No. 2, while his idiomatic handling of the earliest (and slightest) of these works, the *Menuet antique* and familiar *Pavane pour une infante défunte*, is equally beguiling. Haitink's painstaking attention to fine orchestral detail adds refined distinction to his *Valses nobles et sentimentales* and crystalline delicacy to both *Le tombeau de Couperin* and the more elusive *Ma mère l'oye*. There are few more vibrantly evocative or palpably exciting versions of the *Rapsodie espagnole* and *Alborada del gracioso*. Don't be in the least surprised, however, if the phenomenal sound quality prompts an incredulous second glance at the recording dates (1971–6) quoted in the booklet! *MJ*

RAVEL

Daphnis et Chloé

Montreal SO & Chorus/Charles Dutoit

Decca 400 055-2 □ 55:57 mins □ *♪♪♪*

The original, and still far and away the best digital *Daphnis*. This seductively beautiful disc created a furore during the early Eighties, and was widely cited as the finest exemplar of the multitudinous technical and aesthetic virtues of the revolutionary compact disc format when the new medium was introduced to the listening public. Now, as then, the transparency and vast dynamic range of this recording are exceptionally impressive, as is the sense of spatial positioning of instruments across the sound field. But Charles Dutoit's handling of this evocative and coercively erotic score is never less than masterly in its flexibility and subtlety; arguably no other great conductor of this century has come closer to exposing the mingled fragility and rapture of this work since it was first heard under Pierre Monteux in June 1912. It is also fair to say that, with the release of this CD, the Montreal SO came of age, taking its rightful place among the roster of great transatlantic orchestras. Its playing is astounding; this is an ensemble with character and distinction in every section, though special praise must go to principal flautist Timothy Hutchins, whose extended flute solo is mesmerically beguiling. The concluding Danse générale has exhilarating dynamism and pulse, and this is a performance to marvel at, wonderfully captured in incomparable digital sound. A sonic masterpiece. *MJ*

RAVEL

Piano Concerto in G; Piano Concerto for the Left Hand; Menuet antique; Une barque sur l'océan; Fanfare from L'Eventail de Jeanne

Pascal Roge (piano); Montreal SO/Charles Dutoit

Decca 410 230-2 □ 57:31 mins □ 𝄞𝄞𝄞

The Montreal Ravel series denoted another illustrious plateau of critical approbation in the history of the Decca catalogue. These performances of the two Ravel piano concertos and sundry orchestral transcriptions of piano works provided the bench-mark beside which all rival versions are inevitably assayed; the overwhelming majority, it has to be conceded, barely survive scrutiny, such is the exceptional quality of both performances and sound engineering here. In Pascal Rogé, we have the Ravel pianist *par excellence*; never deterred by the staggering technical demands of these scores, Rogé's crystalline lightness and pristine clarity imbue this music with compelling impetus and brilliance, nowhere more evident than in the bristlingly energetic, jazz-influenced outer movements of the Piano Concerto in G of 1931. The Adagio has heartfelt intensity and refinement, and Rogé's lustrously cultivated pianism is rapturously supported by Dutoit and the Montreal SO. The Piano Concerto for the Left Hand, dedicated to the pianist Paul Wittgenstein (who lost his right arm during the First World War), is more subdued, even tragic in character, demanding great expressive insight as well as exceptional dexterity. This performance is superb in every regard, and Pascal Rogé probes the introspective gravity of the score with rare facility. The disc also includes orchestrations of the piano pieces *Menuet antique* and *Une barque sur l'océan*, and the brief Fanfare from Ravel's 1927 score

for the ballet *L'éventail de Jeanne* (Jean's Fan). Recorded sound has exceptional warmth and fidelity, with the famed acoustic of the Church of St Eustache, Montreal, proving as radiantly atmospheric as the music itself. *MJ*

RAVEL

Piano Concerto in G
see also PROKOFIEV: Piano Concerto No. 3

RAWSTHORNE

Symphonies Nos 1–3

Tracey Chadwell (soprano); LPO/John Pritchard, Nicholas Braithwaite, BBC SO/Norman Del Mar

Lyrita SRCD 291 □ ADD/DDD □ 74:47 mins □ 𝄞𝄞𝄞

Sandwiched between reissues of the First and Third Symphonies is a 1993 recording of the Second, the *Pastoral* Symphony. It is a remarkable work: delicate flowerings and joy contrasted with tragedy and struggle in wild, empty landscapes. The final movement, reminiscent of Vaughan Williams's *A Pastoral Symphony*, tellingly employs a soprano (Tracey Chadwell, deeply affecting) expressing cold sorrow against summer warmth. All these are rich and powerful performances. The unsettling Walton-like First Symphony is strong and assertive with flashes of gritty humour and tough tenderness; the Third Symphony, with its dark, stately Sarabande, uses, not unattractively, contained atonality. Rewarding for the adventurous. *Ian Lace*

REGER

Variations and Fugue on a Theme by JA Hiller; Ballet Suite, Op. 130

Bavarian RSO/Colin Davis

Orfeo C 090 841 □ 59:12 mins □ 𝄞𝄞𝄞

Variations and Fugue on a Theme by JA Hiller; Four Tone Poems after Böcklin

Royal Concertgebouw Orchestra/Neeme Järvi

Chandos CHAN 8794 □ 66:50 mins □ 𝄞𝄞𝄞

Despite increased representation in the catalogues over recent years, Max Reger has yet to secure the level of admiration accorded to his great contemporary, Richard Strauss. All too often he has been tarred with the brush of academicism and long-windedness. But those coming to either of these discs with open minds may wonder why such labels had been so readily attached to him. True, his writing is elaborate and dense in texture – witness the concluding fugue of the Hiller Variations. But as in the case of composers like Schumann, his music requires a master conductor to clarify the part-writing and bring a lucid sense of direction to the musical argument.

The ideal introduction to Reger's orchestral output would probably be a coupling of the Mozart and Hiller Variations, his two most popular works. But in the event, no wholly recommendable disc offers such a programme. Davis provides the most satisfying account of the Mozart Variations (on Philips; see following entry) and his 1983 recording of the Hiller Variations, coupled with an affectionate account of the more lightweight Ballet Suite, is distinguished by subtle playing and delightful touches of humour.

Järvi, recorded in the luxuriant acoustic of the Concertgebouw in Amsterdam, is more spontaneous, encouraging the Dutch orchestra to project the music with greater variety and dramatic incident. Of the two, his version is the more striking, so it's disappointing that his imagination is less well focused in the Four Tone Pictures, where for example the opening movement depicting Böcklin's dour painting *The Hermit Playing the Violin* lacks atmosphere in comparison with a recent recording of the same work under Leif Segerstam on BIS. *EL*

REGER/HINDEMITH

Reger: Variations and Fugue on a Theme by Mozart

Hindemith: Symphonic Metamorphoses on Themes by Carl Maria von Weber

Bavarian RSO/Colin Davis

Philips 422 347-2 □ 55:16 mins □ 𝄞𝄞𝄞

Although by no means the most generous of couplings, especially at full price, this release is worthy of serious consideration for the exceptional quality of the Reger. The Mozart Variations remains this composer's most popular work, yet no version in my experience manages to convey its beauty and charm to the same extent as Davis. Where other interpreters tend to get stuck in a quagmire of mushy orchestration, Davis and his wonderful orchestra attain a breathtaking degree of clarity without ever sacrificing any Romantic warmth. The engineers, too, have worked miracles to effect such transparency of detail, making light work of the overblown textures that cap the concluding fugue. In the Hindemith, Davis may not match the chromium-plated brilliance of George Szell and the Cleveland Orchestra (Sony Essential Classics), but his gentler version is

distinguished for its sophistication and good humour. *EL*

RESPIGHI

Ancient Airs & Dances, Suites Nos 1–3; Aria; Berceuse

Sinfonia 21/Richard Hickox

Chandos CHAN 9415 □ 62:34 mins □ 𝄞𝄞𝄞

Ottorino Respighi wasn't simply a purveyor of grandiose technicolor scores for large orchestra. He also pioneered the rediscovery and presentation of early music to the audiences of his time in wonderfully effective arrangements for modern instruments. His three Suites of *Antiche danze ed arie* (No. 1 for chamber orchestra, No. 2 for full orchestra, No. 3 for strings alone) are skilful, loving adaptations and combinations of 16th- and 17th-century Italian songs and dances for the lute, melodically delightful and scored with a master touch.

There are many versions (including a classic Minneapolis/Antal Dorati recording on Mercury), but this stylish, elegant and irresistibly enjoyable rendition of all three suites, in beautiful sound, comes as near perfection as I can imagine, and is coupled with the first recordings of two early and gorgeous examples of Respighi's neo-Baroque vein. The disc is a jewel of Chandos's long-running Respighi series. *CM*

RESPIGHI

Concerto Gregoriano; Concerto all'antica

Andrea Cappelletti (violin); Philharmonia Orchestra/Matthias Bamert

Koch Schwann 3-1124-2 □ 63:21 mins □ 𝄞𝄞𝄞

The *Concerto Gregoriano*, its main themes based (rather distantly) on Gregorian chant and modes, is one of Respighi's finest works and one of the most gorgeous violin concertos in the repertoire. Yet there were few LP recordings; CD has brought a revaluation of the Italian master and a number of versions. Many may prefer the excellent Lydia Mordkovitch on Chandos, yet her performance somehow hangs fire, slaved to Edward Downes's rather leaden tempi and a recording that swathes Respighi's warm summer-night sonorities in too much dark velvet.

Andrea Cappelletti, less rich in tone and atmosphere, nevertheless gets the spirit of the piece, which flows better under Bamert's direction. The triumph of the finale is as intoxicating as one could wish for, and the recording is exceptionally vivid. The early, little-known *Concerto all'antica* (1908) is a delightful piece of mock-Baroque, like an updated Vivaldi concerto but written before anyone had started performing *The Four Seasons* again. This is a more generous coupling than Mordkovitch (who is ravishing, though, in Respighi's *Poema autunnale*), and well worth hearing. *CM*

<hr>

RESPIGHI

Pines of Rome; Roman Festivals; Fountains of Rome

Montreal SO/Charles Dutoit

Decca 430 729-2 □ 60:24 mins □ ⊘⊘

People in high places still tend to be snooty about Respighi. Yes, his music can be bombastic, even hollow at times, but the craftsmanship is impeccable and his slow movements in particular show he was capable of writing music of genuine substance and great subtlety. Dutoit, master of the Romantic-impressionist French repertoire (to which Respighi was undoubtedly indebted), brings this out in his typically refined reading of the evergreen Roman triptych. Goes nicely with the classic Toscanini account (RCA).
Antony Bye

<hr>

REVUELTAS

Homenaje a Federico García Lorca; Sensemayá; Ocho por radio; Toccata; Alcancías; Planos; La noche de los mayas

New Philharmonia Orchestra/Eduardo Mata; London Sinfonietta/David Atherton; Jalapa SO/Luis Herrera de la Fuente

BMG Catalyst 09026 62672 2 □ ADD □ 69:28 mins □ ⊘⊘⊘

Like Charles Ives, the Mexican composer Silvestre Revueltas (1899–1940) is one of music's great originals, a modernist whose fiercely independent musical language brooks no easy compromises. At its best, as in the compelling *Homage to García Lorca*, Revueltas conjures up a bizarre and disturbingly powerful world in which diametrically opposed emotions vie with each other for our attention. No less gripping is the short orchestral piece *Sensemayá* – a brutal study in rhythmic primitivism, described somewhat aptly in the liner notes as an intriguing cross between Stravinsky and Varèse. A number of chamber works contrasting austerity with an unexpected light-heartedness fill out the picture before the final extended item brings us a welcome sample of Revueltas's awesome

film music. Clearly this is not music for the faint-hearted, but the excellent performances and recordings combine to make one eager to find out more about this intriguing and undeservedly neglected composer. *EL*

<hr>

RIMSKY-KORSAKOV/TCHAIKOVSKY/BORODIN

Rimsky-Korsakov: Russian Easter Festival Overture; Capriccio Espagnol

Tchaikovsky: 1812 Overture; Marche Slave

Borodin: In the Steppes of Central Asia; Polovtsian Dances from Prince Igor

Gothenburg SO & Chorus/Neeme Järvi

DG 429 984-2 □ 76:10 mins □ ⊘⊘⊘

This Russian *tour de force* finds the performances of Rimsky's two most spectacular shorter orchestral works more marketable company than the composer's extremely variable three symphonies (with which they originally appeared in a two-disc set). Järvi makes sure that the Orthodox chants of the *Russian Easter Festival* Overture have just as much emphasis as the tolling or the glitter of Russian bells; and from the fandango onwards the *Capriccio espagnol* is a real roller-coaster of a performance. In this *1812* you have the optional mixed choir as well as bells and cannons – a predictably well-weighted showpiece to rout your neighbours – while earlier the conductor shows his hand in a vigorously etched battle and a helpful lift for the lyrical melody (reworked by Tchaikovsky from an unsuccessful early opera) at the overture's core.

Järvi's heart, though, is pinned on *Marche Slave* – seemingly shaped in one long breath, urgent without ever being hurried. Idiosyncratic tempi cause a few problems in the Borodin pieces; and woodwind rather than polite Swedish choir are the stars of these Polovtsian Dances, in which Järvi doesn't speed up to a truly exciting prestissimo at the end. But that's an exception on this disc. *DN*

<hr>

RIMSKY-KORSAKOV
Serenade, Op. 37
see Collection: Russian Cello Music

<hr>

RIMSKY-KORSAKOV/BORODIN

Rimsky-Korsakov: Sheherazade

Borodin: Polovtsian Dances from Prince Igor

Beecham Choral Society, RPO/Thomas Beecham

EMI CDC 7 47717 2 □ ADD □ 58:05 mins □ ⊘⊘⊘

No *Sheherazade* tells her tales of a thousand and one nights more personably than

Beecham's. The threats of the sultan and the undefined menace in the Kalendar Prince's Tale are real enough, but what lends the performance its special charm is the graceful individuality of the many chamber-music passages which surround or interrupt the main events; the reciting woodwind of the second movement characterise more beguilingly than on any other version and the clarinettist is a subtle delight throughout.

Vintage EMI recording captures the many instrumental voices in their natural environment, while the impact of the brass still excites after all those years: the sudden re-introduction of the sea and Sinbad's ship into the frantic final narrative proves thrilling. The hardly less imaginative Kletzki version, another classic, offers a bargain-price challenge on CFP and a more lustrous leader (Hugh Bean) to handle *Sheherazade*'s violin solos. Borodin's Polovtsian Dances provide another good reason for staying with Beecham, offering the same blend of barbarism and femininity; the chorus (in antiquated English, unfortunately, not Russian) 'strive to please thee', and they do. *DN*

RIMSKY-KORSAKOV

The Snow Maiden Suite; The Golden Cockerel Suite; Dubinushka
see Collection: Russian Music

RIMSKY-KORSAKOV/BORODIN

Rimsky-Korsakov: Symphony No. 2 (Antar)

Borodin: Symphony No. 2 in B minor; Notturno (Andante amoroso from String Quartet No. 2)

Gothenburg SO/Neeme Järvi

DG Masters 445 568-2 □ 71:03 mins □ *②②*

The composer always regarded *Antar*, like *Sheherazade*, as a symphonic suite, but its honorary title of Second Symphony makes it a rose between two thorns, the First being a self-conscious teenage ramble tailored by mature second thoughts and the Third a testament to the academic knowledge Rimsky belatedly acquired as professor of the St Petersburg Conservatoire. *Antar*, in the last of its polished revisions, is lucky to have been extracted from that dubious context on the original DG two-disc set and to share this disc with another work of comparable fantasy and epic breadth. Järvi draws the richest of oriental colours from his Gothenburg players: some irresistibly physical string-playing, an unusually strong profile for the languishing Antar's theme early on – shades of *Manfred* – and delicate pastels for the magical gazelle that turns into the

wish-granting fairy of the legend, woodwind players turning their arabesques with exquisite grace.

This performance of the Borodin Second is a serious evocation of 13th-century knights and bards, not a showy costume drama. It may encourage listeners to seek out Järvi's original Borodin cross-section (also two CDs) – a parade of far richer delights than the sometimes unsuitable cases for treatment on the Rimsky-Korsakov set. *DN*

ROCHBERG

Violin Concerto
see STRAVINSKY: Violin Concerto in D

RODRIGO

Concierto de Aranjuez
see FALLA: El amor brujo

ROSSINI

Overtures – La scala di seta; Il signor Bruschino; L'italiana in Algeri; Il barbiere di Siviglia; La gazza ladra; Semiramide; Guillaume Tell

London Classical Players/Roger Norrington

EMI Reflexe CDC 7 54091 2 □ 60:00 mins □ *②②②*

Roger Norrington and the London Classical Players give us an hour of zestful, eager music-making, which rests agreeably upon the ear. It should be stressed, of course, that there are numerous self-recommending issues devoted to compilations of Rossini overtures, including Neville Marriner's complete three-disc set from Philips, and the enthralling disc from the conductorless Orpheus Chamber Orchestra on DG, your choice will depend largely on the programme selected in each case and on personal taste. Assuming, though, that relatively few of us will need all 26 overtures, and that most will want *William Tell*, Marriner and the ASMF and the Orpheus CO issues may be overlooked, though both offer exemplary playing and sonics. Roger Norrington offers something engagingly different here; the London Classical Players employ period instruments and playing techniques, and these, when applied to this scintillating music, pay substantial dividends. Most of the familiar favourites are present: *William Tell* has splendid drive and energy, the celebrated galop being especially well done; *Semiramide* (the opening horn passage particularly characterful on early piston-valved instruments) is thrillingly done; and Norrington invests *La gazza ladra* with mock-heroic pomp and near-criminal high spirits. A fine compilation of overtures, and most alluringly played by this admirable period band. *MJ*

Symphony in E

Cincinnati Philharmonia Orchestra/Gerhard Samuel

Hyperion CDA 66366 □ **58:00 mins** □ *⊘⊘⊘*

Hans Rott, a friend and fellow student of Mahler in Vienna, went insane at the age of 22 in 1880 having composed only a few large-scale works. Mahler testified to Rott's influence on him, but it was only with the first performance of Rott's huge symphony, more than a century after he finished it, that the influence has become palpable. Though the piece has a few longueurs and miscalculations, it's without doubt a work of genius, and the pre-echoes – the Scherzo sounds like what Mahler was writing a quarter of a century later – are startling. The synthesis of Wagner, Bruckner, Brahms and Austrian folk influences was already taking place in Rott's work, far ahead of when the history textbooks say it was possible. But it's Rott's grasp of large-scale symphonic structure that is so impressive. The music is often very moving indeed, the work of a genuinely gifted composer whose premature demise was a tragedy for music in general. The performance is spacious and very committed (this is a student orchestra, but you'd never know it), and the recording, if not absolutely top notch, deals well enough with the often massive orchestral sound. *CM*

Symphonies Nos 1–4

Radio France PO/Marek Janowski

RCA Victor Red Seal 09026 62511 2 □ **119:11 mins (2 discs)** □ *⊘⊘⊘*

Roussel's last two symphonies are the best known: No. 3, with its ear-splitting energy (think of Walton's first), commissioned by Koussevitzky for the commemoration in 1930 of the Boston Symphony Orchestra's first half-century; and the equally inspired Fourth, which hit Paris five years later.

Anserme and Munch each recorded both, though it was André Cluytens's awesome EMI reading of No. 3 (still to be re-issued) which supplied my first tingling experience of this composer – by the end (Roussel died in 1937) he was Impressionist, Romantic and Modernist all rolled into one.

There is no need to question this superb Janowski offering on RCA, even though his over-brisk handling of the Third (paired with No. 1, like Dutoit on Erato) comes a bit too close to the strutting exit of No. 4, rather than

telegraphing the unnerving, subliminal sound-world into which the cocksure initial bars rapidly dissolve. (A key part of Roussel's skill is the way statements suddenly feel like questions, and vice versa.)

Janowski elicits superb playing from his Radio France players, with countless subtle touches throughout in all departments: wind, strings, trumpets, horns.

But buy this disc no less for the lush post-Wagnerian discoveries to be made in Symphony No. 1 (1906), a Scriabin-like canvas of sumptuous Impressionism – veritable 'forest music', as its subtitle ('Le poème de la forêt') denotes. The Lento, 'Soir d'été', armed with a melting (though uncredited) violin solo, is a reincarnated *Prélude à l'après-midi d'un faune.*

Lend an ear, too, to the three-movement No. 2: more of a curio, with an almost Ivesian mix of styles. It fell flat at its 1922 premiere, so should be nicely placed to convert to a Nineties hit. Whatever you make of it, this fine, articulate orchestra sails through with flying colours. Riches indeed. *Roderic Dunnett*

Symphony, Op. 6a; The Vintner's Daughter

New Zealand SO/James Sedares

Koch International 3-7244-2 □ **56:04 mins** □ *⊘⊘⊘*

Miklós Rózsa was one of the most successful film composers of all time, but like Korngold he began his career as a 'serious' composer, and remained one, continuing to compose concert works throughout his life. The huge symphony he wrote at the age of 23 impressed Pierre Monteux and Bruno Walter, but it wasn't actually played because of its length and difficulty; Rózsa kept the score in his drawer for over sixty years, occasionally revising. Somewhere along the way the Scherzo was lost, leaving a still-satisfying three-movement structure. This first recording, made in the last year of Rózsa's life, was also the world premiere, and something of a revelation. Anyone who loves the orchestral music of Kodály will adore this powerful, full-blooded work, big and bold, superbly written for orchestra, full of impulsive rhythm and heroic melodies. The performance seems utterly convinced, and the recording is one of Koch's best. If you agree this shows a composer of unusual promise, you should look for Heifetz's recording of the violin concerto Rózsa wrote for him. The *Vintner's Daughter* variations, based on a French folk-song and themselves orchestrated from a violin piece, are attractive too. *CM*

RUBBRA

Symphonies Nos 6 & 8 (Hommage à Teilhard de Chardin); Soliloquy for cello and orchestra

Rohan de Saram (cello); Philharmonia
Orchestra/Norman Del Mar, LSO/Vernon Handley

Lyrita SRCD 234 □ ADD □ 72:38 mins □ ⦿⦿⦿

Edmund Rubbra is one of the most impressive British symphonists, as much for the sincerity and spiritual *quietus* of his music as for its more dramatic designs. Drama in any case is less important than the organic flowering of his forms, and the later one-movement symphonies resemble vast polyphonic motets for orchestra.

A very recent Chandos issue conducted by Richard Hickox, offering the finest performance I've yet heard of the Fourth Symphony, along with satisfying ones of the chamber-orchestral No. 10 and No. 11 (its premiere recording), may be the best Rubbra disc so far. But the range of mood – they're all lyrical, meditative pieces – is narrower than on this excellent Lyrita disc, perhaps a better introduction. No. 6 (1954) is one of Rubbra's greatest inspirations, with a sensuous, Italianate slow movement, uproarious Scherzo and finale of basaltic grandeur. No. 8 (1968), more elusive, inspired by the philosophy of Teilhard de Chardin, contains some of his deepest thoughts. Del Mar's performances are exemplary; the eloquent *Soliloquy*, almost a one-movement cello concerto, is a welcome bonus. *CM*

RUDERS

Violin Concerto No. 2; Dramaphonia, for Piano and Chamber Ensemble

Rebecca Hirsch (violin), Poul Rosenbaum (piano);
Collegium Musicum Copenhagen/Michael
Schønwandt, Lontano/Odaline de la Martinez

dacapo DCCD 9308 □ 61:07 mins □ ⦿⦿⦿

With his symphony, written for the BBC Prom concerts and first performed there in 1989, the Danish-born, British-based composer Poul Ruders (born in 1949) achieved a compositional breakthrough – a work on a large scale, with appropriately large gestures made in a dramatically strong yet simple way. Neither of the offerings on this disc (on the dacapo label) seems quite so rounded an achievement; nevertheless, each explains and indeed justifies the international interest Ruders has aroused.

The earlier *Dramaphonia* (1987), for piano and ensemble, is the first of a Ruders triptych of theatre-inspired instrumental pieces. A steadily unfolding progression from slow to fast, low to high, frozen emotions to jagged ones, it establishes a relationship between quietly turbulent solo instrument and sostenuto accompaniment later frenziedly rescripted.

The concept is, again, boldly simple, though the louring, scratchy colour palette takes some getting used to; its eventual pay-off is excitingly brought off. By contrast, the second of Ruders's two violin concertos – a nature evocation in a bleak yet sometimes lyrically wide-spanning neo-Romantic idiom – seems at once more listener-friendly and more loose-limbed. In both cases, since the performances are expert and the musical sound-worlds wholly individual, the experience 'adds up'. *Max Loppert*

RUGGLES

Sun-Treader; Men and Mountains
see IVES: Three Places in New England

SÆVERUD

Peer Gynt Suites, Op. 28/1 & 2; Sinfonia dolorosa; Galdreslåtten; Kjempevise-slåtten

Stavanger SO/Alexander Dmitriev

BIS CD-762 □ 67:18 mins □ ⦿⦿⦿

For Norwegians, Harald Sæverud (1897–1992) is deemed the successor to Grieg as the national composer and is the country's most significant symphonist. His mature style is marked by a refined neo-classicism and a resolute adherence to tonality. It was this directness of language that made him the ideal composer to provide music for a production of Ibsen's *Peer Gynt* in 1948. Sæverud's brief was to counteract the over-Romanticised music of Grieg and to emphasise the psychology rather than the local colour.

Sæverud went into internal exile during the wartime Nazi occupation of Norway, but his music became a focus for the Resistance, particularly his best-known work, the *Ballad of Revolt* for piano, which here appears in its lengthened orchestral guise. The 12-minute *Sinfonia dolorosa*, the sixth of his nine symphonies, meanwhile, was written as a direct response to the execution of a friend in the Resistance movement.

The Stavanger SO's playing is fully alive to the vibrant colour and rhythmic vitality of Sæverud's music and the orchestra is recorded in the generous but clear acoustic of the Stavanger Konserthus. Warmly recommended. *Matthew Rye*

Saint-Saëns: Cello Concerto No. 1 in A minor

Lalo: Cello Concerto in D minor

Schumann: Cello Concerto in A minor

János Starker (cello); LSO/Stanisław Skrowaczewski, Antal Dorati

Mercury Living Presence 432 010-2 □ ADD □ 65:00 mins □ ⚪⚪

This is one of the great cello concerto discs of the century. János Starker, an artist of exceptional nobility and intellect, is heard in a sensationally vivid CD remastering of these Mercury masters, taped thirty years ago using revolutionary 35-millimetre film technology. Starker, who recorded on several occasions for the label during the Sixties, plays the first of Saint-Saëns's cello concertos with exceptional brilliance and resolve. His performance is outstanding for its concentration of expressive moods within a short, though structurally cohesive, expanded sonata form unit. Every nuance and detail is zealously observed. Starker's fearsome virtuosity produces staggering results, and he is deftly accompanied by the LSO under Antal Dorati. The accounts of the Lalo and Schumann cello concertos are likewise exemplary and arrestingly authoritative. Starker is rigorous and passionate in an engagingly athletic and sinewy reading of the Schumann concerto (he's recorded the work again for RCA – an even more imposing affair, the product of a lifetime's involvement with this elusive work; see p325), and his version of the Lalo has electrifying impact and gravity. The Mercury sound is, in a word, astonishing; though I shouldn't wish to exclude Pierre Fournier's memorably distinguished DG reissues of the Saint-Saëns and Lalo works, and notwithstanding my enduring admiration for Yo-Yo Ma's version of the former (part of his mid-price *Great Cello Concertos* package from Sony), János Starker's remarkable performances are still mandatory listening. *MJ*

Havanaise; Introduction and Rondo Capriccioso
see PAGANINI: Violin Concerto No. 1

Piano Concertos Nos 1–5

Aldo Ciccolini (piano); Orchestre de Paris/Serge Baudo

EMI Rouge et Noir CMS 7 69443 2 □ ADD □ 138:04 mins (2 discs) □ ⚪⚪

Piano Concertos Nos 2 in G minor & 4 in C minor

Jean-Philippe Collard (piano); RPO/André Previn

EMI CDC 7 47816 2 □ 50:00 mins □ ⚪⚪⚪

Of the five Saint-Saëns piano concertos, only the two minor key works have found an enduring niche in the Romantic concerto repertoire – which shouldn't blind us to the considerable qualities of their fellows. This music is, without exception, admirably constructed and compellingly melodic. Solo parts are in the heroic virtuoso mould of the post-Lisztian epoch, but there is a freshness, lightness and transparency in much of the writing which are instantly captivating. Jean-Philippe Collard is a superb advocate of the most popular pairing of the series, Concertos Nos 2 and 4. The G minor Concerto, written in barely three weeks, is built around its fleet-footed central Scherzo; the recurring string counter-melody is among the most warmly expansive and distinctive of all Saint-Saëns's themes. Collard plays with grace and fluency, and receives buoyant support from the RPO under Previn. The disc also includes a memorably imposing performance (also very well recorded) of the finest of the concertos, the C minor, Op. 44. This striking single-movement work (the customary three movements are nonetheless discernible within the overall structure) should be better known; the great chorale-like melody of the finale is introduced by the soloist, who plays it with just one finger initially, and with instant cathartic effect. Collard's performance is breathtaking, and the final peroration is tremendously uplifting. Adventurous collectors wishing to sample the remaining three concertos (No. 5, the so-called *Egyptian* Concerto, in effect a musical travelogue written in 1896, the composer's fiftieth year as a performer, is well worth hearing) won't regret purchasing Aldo Ciccolini's EMI France reissues, with the Paris Orchestra and Serge Baudo: capable and refined interpretations, and serviceable if occasionally over-bright CD transfers, the whole cycle fitting neatly on to two discs. *MJ*

Symphony No. 3 in C minor (Organ); Danse macabre; Bacchanale from Samson et Dalila; Trois rhapsodies sur des cantiques bretons

Hans Fagius (organ), Karl-Ove Mannberg (violin); Royal Stockholm PO/James DePreist

BIS CD-555 □ 68:08 mins □ ⚪⚪⚪

Like Richard Strauss's mighty *Also sprach Zarathustra*, Saint-Saëns's Third Symphony is archetypal hi-fi demonstration material, and as such it falls prey to the vagaries and dubious artifice which are the province of the modern, digitally endowed sound engineer. Here is a magnificent performance, which impresses as music-making, not knob-twiddling! That's not to infer that this is anything less than the product of state-of-the-art recording technology (indeed, one would expect nothing less from BIS), but the superb acoustic setting of the Stockholm Concert Hall, its fine 1981 Gronlund organ, and the city's excellent Philharmonic Orchestra are heard in a natural concert-hall setting, and the sonic results are enthralling. Equally impressive is the performance, expertly realised by James DePreist, with the organ part taken by Hans Fagius. The superb account of the symphony precedes a generous batch of Saint-Saëns miscellanea, including the tone poem *Danse macabre*, and the orgiastically cinematic Bacchanale from Saint-Saëns's Old Testament operatic epic *Samson et Dalila*. For good measure, BIS gives us the opportunity to hear another impressive Swedish organ, as Hans Fagius concludes this outstanding release with the *Trois rhapsodies sur des cantiques bretons*, Op. 7, played on the 1976 Marcussen instrument of St Jacob's Church, Stockholm. Altogether a highly distinguished offering. *MJ*

SAINT-SAENS/WIENIAWSKI

Saint-Saëns: Violin Concerto No. 3 in B minor

Wieniawski: Violin Concerto No. 2 in D minor

Julian Rachlin (violin); Israel PO/Zubin Mehta

Sony SK 48373 □ 51:53 mins □ *❷❸❸*

Julian Rachlin, born in the Lithuanian capital (birthplace, incidentally, of Jascha Heifetz) and not yet twenty when this recording was made, is a performer blessed with remarkable intelligence, maturity and technical facility. His account of Saint-Saëns's Third Violin Concerto, written for the great Spanish virtuoso Sarasate in 1881, and taped live at the Mann Auditorium, Tel Aviv, with Zubin Mehta and the Israel Philharmonic, is exceptionally fine. Rachlin plays with fine-spun tone and an intuitive feel for the structure and direction of the music. Moreover, he applies himself to the score totally, and his absorption and concentration are strongly communicative. Superfluous, scene-stealing gestures are avoided (in writing a grand Romantic/virtuoso concerto, Saint-

Saëns left ample opportunity for them!), and the work as a whole is elevated to a level of quality and purpose with which it is rarely associated. This distinguished and eloquent account of the Saint-Saëns prefaces a stirring reading of the Violin Concerto in D minor by Henryk Wieniawski, one of the great 19th-century violinist-composers to emerge after Paganini. This is an alarmingly taxing work; Rachlin makes light of its difficulties, and the *à la zingara* finale is a bravura display of volatile temperament and technical prowess, though the recording does not emanate from concert performances. Zubin Mehta conducts with authoritative panache, with the Israel PO sounding exceptionally well drilled and supportive. The recordings, too, are of demonstration quality. *MJ*

SAINT-SAENS

Violin Concerto No. 3 in B minor
see also LALO: Symphonie espagnole

SALLINEN

Symphonies Nos 4 & 5 (Washington Mosaics); Shadows

Malmö SO/James DePreist

BIS CD-607 □ 74:24 mins □ *❷❸❸*

Aulis Sallinen is one of Finland's most prolific and most internationally respected contemporary composers. He is especially celebrated for his operas, but he has produced numerous orchestral and chamber works. His music is immediately dramatic, essentially tonal and assimilable, distantly echoing Sibelius but with a much wider, more contemporary spectrum of instrumental colour. A Shostakovichian sense of irony makes it more alienated, too, despite the ease with which it imposes itself on the ear.

The Fourth Symphony (1979) contrasts dance-like outer movements with a funeral-march slow movement headed 'Dona nobis pacem' and ends with ambiguous pealing bells. The Fifth, written for the National Symphony Orchestra of Washington, DC, is darker and more fragmented, essentially exploring the same ideas in different ways throughout five movements: there is a Schnittke-like bleakness to the central one. Perhaps more impressive than either symphony is the highly atmospheric *Shadows*, an extremely economical and effective piece based on music from Sallinen's opera *The King Goes Forth to France*. Performances are dedicated, and this is one of BIS's finest recordings. *CM*

Quattro Pezzi (Ciascuno su una nota sola); Anahit; Uaxuctum

Carmen Fournier (violin); Orchestra & Chorus of Polish Radio & TV (Cracow)/Jürg Wyttenbach

Accord 200612 □ 49:40 mins □ 🌑🌑🌑

Pathologically shy, the aristocratic Giacinto Scelsi (1905–88) lived a hermit-like existence in Rome, evolving a startlingly original music which expressed his esoteric and mystical concerns. Since the 'discovery' of him in the last decade of his life, Scelsi's multifarious, often strangely titled pieces have become a genuine phenomenon of contemporary music, much recorded and widely performed. Most of his works from the Fifties onwards are essentially invention on a single note – with octave doublings, intricate ornamentation (often in quarter-tones) and kaleidoscopic changes of colour. That might seem impossibly restrictive; in fact the music comes across in performance with uncanny, visionary power.

The Four Orchestral Pieces (Each One on a Single Note), the landmark work that established this technique, exemplifies Scelsi's extraordinary powers of invention and shamanistic conjuring with sound, mating the apparently primitive and ritualistic with the highly sophisticated. The 'poème lyrique' *Anahit* (the title refers to the moon goddess Astarte) is a kind of violin concerto, full of voluble, fluttering passion. The awesome *Uaxuctum* (a legendary city of the Mayan people, built and then destroyed as a religious ritual) deploys choruses and large orchestra in an utterly stunning way: it's perhaps the only true successor to Varèse's *Ecuatorial*. Performances and recording are, as far as one can tell, first rate. Those intrigued could explore further into Scelsi's string quartets (recorded by the Arditti Quartet), and there are several discs of his inventive and percussive piano music. *CM*

Concertos Nos 2 & 3 for Four Recorders
see Collection: Concerti di flauti

Symphony No. 4; Variations on a Hussar's Song

London Philharmonic/Franz Welser-Möst

EMI CDC 5 55518 2 □ 69:59 mins □ 🌑🌑🌑

In Austria the music of Franz Schmidt (1874–1939) elicits the same degree of admiration as that of Bruckner, but elsewhere he remains scandalously neglected. Could this excellent release turn the tide in his favour elsewhere, I wonder? Certainly, the Fourth Symphony deserves a place in the repertoire. Composed in the mid-Thirties, it's a work haunted by personal tragedy, specifically the untimely death of his daughter, but the music, although couched in an unashamedly late-Romantic idiom which owes something to Bruckner, Strauss and Reger, is cogently argued in the grand symphonic manner. Zubin Mehta and the Vienna PO recorded a memorable account of the symphony for Decca (now available, alas, as a filler to a less than overwhelming performance of Mahler's *Resurrection* Symphony) yet Welser-Möst and the LPO are equally persuasive, and the performance as a whole demonstrates a level of commitment that is not always prevalent in this particular partnership. The *Hussar* Variations, composed a few years before, don't operate on the same level of musical urgency, though the Introduction, laden with mournful chromatic harmony, provides an eloquent foretaste of the deeply felt slow movement of the symphony. *EL*

Concerto Grosso No. 1; Quasi una Sonata; Moz-Art à la Haydn; À Paganini

Gidon Kremer, Tatiana Grindenko (violin), Yuri Smirnov (harpsichord, piano); CO of Europe/Heinrich Schiff, Gidon Kremer

DG Masters 445 520-2 □ 75:08 mins □ 🌑🌑

Schnittke's earliest foray into the Concerto grosso medium dates from 1977 and almost single-handedly brought the composer to wider attention than any of his previous works. It's a spectacular composition juxtaposing a bewilderingly wide range of musical styles, from neo-Baroque imitations to the most brutal dissonances of the avant-garde, with the kind of obsessiveness that somehow compels admiration. *Quasi una Sonata*, an orchestral adaptation of the earlier Second Violin Sonata, is more obviously anarchic and reflective of the tensions that arose from composing advanced music under the strictures of Soviet authoritarianism. Together with the playful *Moz-Art à la Haydn* and technical high-jinks of *À Paganini*, this disc presents a most satisfying introduction to Schnittke's individual world in performances of staggering virtuosity. *EL*

Concerto Grosso No. 3; Concerto Grosso No. 4/Symphony No. 5

Royal Concertgebouw Orchestra/Riccardo Chailly

Decca 430 698-2 □ 58:51 mins □ *❷❸❸*

Schnittke may well be regarded as one of the major composers of our time, but his output remains notoriously uneven. At his best, however, he plumbs depths of emotional intensity which are almost unrivalled by any other contemporary musician. The hybrid Fourth Concerto Grosso/Fifth Symphony is certainly one work which never fails to make an overwhelming impression. The familiar juxtapositions of startlingly varied musical styles are all present – allusions to Russian Orthodox chant, Baroque music, Mahler, Berg and Shostakovich – but the resulting melting-pot of ideas here sounds entirely convincing, revealing no hint of contrivance. Commissioned by the Concertgebouw Orchestra in 1988, the symphony receives brilliant advocacy, and the recording is of demonstration quality. *EL*

Accompaniment to a Cinematographic Scene; Five Pieces for Orchestra, Op. 16
see **CHORAL & SONG**: SCHOENBERG: A Survivor from Warsaw

Chamber Symphony No. 1; Variations for Orchestra
see **OPERA**: SCHOENBERG: Erwartung

Chamber Symphony No. 2
see WEILL: Symphonies Nos 1 & 2
and **OPERA**: SCHOENBERG: Moses und Aron

Schoenberg: Pelleas und Melisande; Variations for Orchestra, Op. 31; Verklärte Nacht

Berg: Three Orchestral Pieces, Op. 6; Three Pieces from the Lyric Suite

Webern: Passacaglia, Op. 1; Five Movements, Op. 5 (version for string orchestra); Six Pieces, Op. 6; Symphony, Op. 21

Berlin PO/Herbert von Karajan

DG 427 424-2 □ ADD □ 180:32 mins (3 discs) □ *❷❷*

Karajan's is the lushest, most hedonistically Romantic of all versions of Schoenberg's huge, texturally complex early symphonic poem *Pelleas und Melisande*. Yet Karajan shapes the whole work with rare intelligence, finding every beauty and chance for drama in its long expository first half before rising to ever-higher heights of passion, as the love scene and

succeeding music piles climax on climax. DG's recording, too, brilliantly clarifies the score's many instrumental layers and levels, revealing Schoenberg's shimmering orchestral apparatus in its true glory. There are other ways to read *Pelleas*, but it has never been more glamorously expounded than in this glorious Berlin Philharmonic performance.

In *Verklärte Nacht* the Berlin strings almost inevitably produce a sheen and a richness no other orchestra can top, and Karajan's account is a *ne plus ultra* of *fin de siècle* gorgeousness. Surprisingly, perhaps, the craggy serial Variations for Orchestra are also expounded with affection, understanding and iridescent orchestral colour. In fact, I used to consider this the best recorded version of Op. 31, but it's now surpassed by Rattle and the CBSO on EMI (coupled with a peerless *Erwartung* from Phyllis Bryn-Julson) and by Boulez and the Chicago SO on Erato (coupled with a very different, dark and gripping view of *Pelleas* which unfortunately loses conviction around the middle). Those more modern recordings boast only slight gain in sound over DG's vintage sonics for Karajan, however. The Berg pieces are to a similar standard (the Op. 6 Orchestral Pieces is a shattering reading) – and so, unexpectedly, is Karajan's pointed, characterful and passionate view of Webern, whose sculptural 12-note Symphony has never sounded more Romantic. *CM*

Schoenberg: Piano Concerto; Violin Concerto

Berg: Violin Concerto

Alfred Brendel (piano), Zvi Zeitlin, Henryk Szeryng (violin); Bavarian RSO/Rafael Kubelík

DG 431 740-2 □ ADD □ 77:29 mins □ *❷❷*

Recordings of Schoenberg's two solo concertos are strangely few, considering that the Violin Concerto is one of the most formidable challenges in its repertoire and the Piano Concerto one of the most approachable and tuneful of 12-note works: nothing in it could affright anyone who enjoys, say, the Bartók concertos. Emanuel Ax (Sony) quite sensibly couples it with the Liszt concertos, which are certainly part of its ancestry. In this work, however, Brendel remains supreme in understanding, *gemütlich* warmth and aristocratic poise. Zvi Zeitlin, a fine and fiery player, turns in a committed performance of the somewhat sterner Violin Concerto, but intelligently exploits its many opportunities for lyricism, especially in the serenely melodious slow movement. DG's recording, dating from 1972, is up to its best standards of the time, and the CD transfer further clarifies the orchestral textures. Szeryng's fine account of the much better-known Berg concerto, both passionate and tender, makes an attractive bonus to this well-programmed mid-price disc. *CM*

SCHOENBERG

Verklärte Nacht
see also MAHLER: Symphony No. 10
and WAGNER: Siegfried Idyll
and **CHAMBER**

SCHUBERT

Symphonies Nos 1–6, 8 & 9

Royal Concertgebouw Orchestra/Nikolaus Harnoncourt

Teldec 4509-91184-2 □ 264:21 mins (4 discs)
□ ❷❷❷

Harnoncourt is the most exacting and exploratory of authenticists, endowed with a rare facility for revealing a composer's intentions in ways that seem often radically different from the norm and are yet remarkably fulfilling and unquestionably authoritative. Note, however, that Teldec's packaging uses the revised (and correct) numberings of the New Schubert Edition and the Deutsch cataloguings, so that the *Unfinished* and *Great* C major are listed as Symphonies Nos 7 and 8; the fragmentary E major work, traditionally No. 7, D729, is excluded here.*

I've absolutely no hesitation in proclaiming this the finest available traversal of the Schubert symphonies on CD. Harnoncourt and the Concertgebouw work miracles with the earlier works. The B flat Symphony (No. 2, D125) positively overflows in its youthful jubilation, and it's good to find the Third Symphony in D delivered with the kind of rigorous authority needed to raise it to its true

---

*Calum MacDonald adds: It depends what you mean by 'correct' numberings: collectors who feel more at ease with the *Unfinished* as No. 8 and the *Great* C major as No. 9 should be reminded that there exist performing realisations of the fragmentary but highly characteristic No. 7 in E. Perhaps the finest is by the noted Schubert scholar Brian Newbould, who has also published a realisation of Schubert's Symphony No. 10 in D major, sketched in the last weeks of his life – uneven, but containing a profound slow movement and a startling Scherzo-finale of real genius. Both these 'extra' Schubert symphonies are recorded by Neville Marriner on Philips, unfortunately only as part of a perhaps prohibitively expensive six-disc set including all the others.

status. Harnoncourt's indomitable and severely applied interpretation of the C minor *Tragic* Symphony and his equally purposeful account of the *Unfinished* possess exceptional cohesive strength, their distinctive element of pathos somehow made the more palpable by his lithe, enervated style and keenly judged architectural flair. Symphonies Nos 5 and 6 are immediately more relaxed and unfettered in character, but, as ever with Schubert, darker premonitions, here made disturbingly public in Harnoncourt's hands, are never deeply concealed; these are superbly conceived performances. Yet it is appropriate that, regardless of their individual organic unity, each of these accounts anticipates the last and greatest of the series. Harnoncourt's olympian presentation of the *Great* C major has both imperious grandeur and, notably in the slow movement, a palpable distillation of the angst and apprehension of Schubert's perceived act of leave-taking within the medium which he at once feared yet loved profoundly (he did not, of course, write the work in 1828, but shortly after the *Unfinished*, two or perhaps three years earlier). Harnoncourt's performance of this work is a triumphant summation of a great and deeply considered traversal of Schubert's symphonies; recording quality is again exceptional. A major contribution to recent Schubert performance scholarship. Very highly recommended. *MJ*

SCHUBERT

Symphonies Nos 3 in D & 4 in C minor (Tragic)

CO of Europe/Claudio Abbado

DG 423 653-2 □ 58:00 mins □ ❷❷❷

These accounts of Schubert's Symphonies Nos 3 and 4 are taken from Abbado's award-winning integral survey of the symphonies with the Chamber Orchestra of Europe. Not only is the quality of interpretation, orchestral execution and sound engineering of unusually high order, but from textual and scholarly viewpoints this series (also available as a five-disc boxed set) is of unique interest. Detailed research has in some cases had a drastic effect on music we thought we knew well. But this is not solely a matter of pedantic cleansing and restitution, for Abbado's classically poised and objectively balanced interpretations are a joy to experience, and nowhere more so than in the graceful and athletic Third Symphony in D, here played with a honeyed charm which proves utterly beguiling. You are unlikely to encounter Schubert performances of greater commitment and polish than these, and if the experience prompts an investigation of the complete Abbado/COE survey, such questing won't go unrewarded. *MJ*

Symphony No. 5 in B flat
see BEETHOVEN: Symphony No. 6 in F

Symphonies Nos 8 in B minor (Unfinished) & 9 in C (Great C major)

Berlin PO/Günter Wand

RCA Victor Red Seal □ 09026 68314 2 □ 84:59 mins (2 discs for the price of one) □ ⊘⊘⊘

The octogenarian Günter Wand is a legend among today's great conductors. Eschewing the jet-setting, high-profile image of most media-hyped stellar maestros, Wand's public appearances are infrequent, though invariably great events. His is the genius of profound awareness of how music, and particularly its functional and architectural aesthetics, really operates.

These masterful performances, recorded live at Berlin's Philharmonie in March 1995, bear eloquent witness to his incomparable skill at allowing these scores to evolve at their own inevitably natural pace. Both symphonies emerge in a new and massively authoritative light, the Eighth now questing, challenging and almost Faustian in its intensity, and the Ninth a monument to the grand traditions of Viennese Classicism, now fearlessly propelled into the future.

Two minor caveats, neither of which diminishes my total admiration for these readings, still remain: Wand omits the first-movement exposition repeat in the *Great* C major Symphony, and some audience noise has inevitably found its way on to the CDs. But these accounts have an incomparable majesty and correctness which are deeply compelling. Incidentally, listeners seeking a fine budget Ninth shouldn't miss Michael Halász and the Budapest-based Failoni Orchestra on Naxos; this, too, comes very highly recommended. *MJ*

Spectra
see Collection: American Orchestral Music

Symphony No. 3
see HARRIS: Symphony No. 3

Schumann: Cello Concerto in A minor

Hindemith: Cello Concerto

János Starker (cello); Bamberg SO/Dennis Russell Davies

RCA Victor Red Seal 09026 68027 2 □ 51:36 mins □ ⊘⊘⊘

Of the numerous cellists who have recorded the elusive Schumann concerto, János Starker comes nearest, perhaps, to revealing the true spiritual virtues of the work without becoming entrenched in angst-ridden pity, for this concerto reflects the composer's tortured paranoia and mounting inner despair in graphic terms. János Starker's reading is technically dazzling, and this deceptively taxing work holds no terrors for him. He is thus enabled to probe the innermost psychological undertones of the piece in minute detail, yet this remains a performance in which poetry, introspection and fantasy come strongly to the fore. The soloist's opening presentation of the lyrical principal idea has heart-rending gravity, yet here, as elsewhere, there are moments of powerful, even declamatory heroism, demonstrating that the schizophrenic polarisation of Schumann's divided 'Florestan and Eusebius' personality is still at work in this concerto. The finale is stupendously dispatched, as Starker forges a degree of heroic restitution amid near catastrophe; he plays his own, highly idiomatic cadenza. The coupling, an acerbic, confrontational account of the undervalued Hindemith Cello Concerto of 1940, is both welcome and compelling. These are illustrious and noble performances, adroitly and urgently supported by Dennis Russell Davies and the Bamberg Symphony Orchestra. Recorded sound, from the orchestra's new home, the Joseph Keilberth Saal of the Sinfonie an der Regnitz, is beyond criticism. A magnificent issue. *MJ*

Cello Concerto in A minor
see also SAINT-SAENS: Cello Concerto No. 1

Schumann: Piano Concerto in A minor

Mozart: Piano Concerto No. 21 in C, K467

Dinu Lipatti (piano); Philharmonia Orchestra, Lucerne Festival Orchestra/Herbert von Karajan

EMI Références CDH 7 69792 2 □ ADD □ 58:53 mins □ ⊘⊘

Some performances date, and that's not necessarily a criticism, but others are timeless, dating only in terms of technology. These performances are among the classics of the age, and if there's any justice in the world should remain in the catalogue for ever. Lipatti had the rare knack of getting the balance exactly right in practically everything he played. Never too theatrical but never inhibited or dull, technically unsurpassed yet never succumbing to flashy bravura, stylistically apt but never didactic or too devout, lyrical but never self-consciously poetic, powerful but never gladiatorial, he brought to his playing a sense of such rightness that while listening to it one can scarcely conceive of the music going any other way. And what an effect he seems to have had on Karajan, who proves himself here an ideal concerto partner, bringing to his handling of the orchestra a born pianist's understanding of his soloist's needs. Sonically, the performances are inevitably showing their age, but with playing like this who could care less? If, however, modern sound is of paramount importance to you, you'll not find anything more polished, exciting or convincing than Perahia with Colin Davis on Sony (Schumann). *JS*

SCHUMANN

Piano Concerto in A minor
see also GRIEG: Piano Concerto in A minor

SCHUMANN

Symphonies Nos 1–4

LPO/Kurt Masur

Teldec 4509-95501-2 □ 121:34 mins (2 discs) □ ❷❷

Kurt Masur's dedicated and scholarly approach pays enormous dividends in this erudite, admirably recorded mid-price Schumann cycle from Teldec. These are outstanding interpretations, vibrantly recorded and most expertly played by the London Philharmonic, on this evidence truly a world-class ensemble. Kurt Masur senses keenly the structural majesty of the *Spring* Symphony, allowing the music to unfold at its own pace, though with admirable precision and clarity; the Scherzo and finale are particularly impressive. Symphony No. 2 contains a brilliant, yet virtuosically demanding Scherzo, which places cruel responsibilities upon the massed violins, particularly at Masur's brisk tempo. But the orchestra responds magnificently, and this account is crowned by a jubilant and triumphant finale, in which Schumann's aspiringly idealistic four-note ascending motto figure assumes heraldic prominence. Masur's reading of Schumann's symphonic holiday

journal, the *Rhenish* Symphony, is no less impressive; the great evocation of Cologne Cathedral has impressive gravity and power, while outer movements are aptly celebratory and direct. The D minor Fourth Symphony, arguably the most elusive and enigmatic of the cycle, completes the first disc and illustrates the considerable virtues of Masur's unadorned and clear-sighted approach. Always cultivated, efficient and hugely accomplished, he shepherds his players through a potent yet never vapidly theatrical reading of this complex score. Recording quality is of impressively high order throughout, and despite the absence of insert notes these Teldec discs offer unusually good value at mid-price. Recommended, though collectors seeking a thoroughgoing (and decently documented!) cycle, with only marginally less punch, may prefer Wolfgang Sawallisch's Dresden set, also including the Overture, Scherzo and Finale, on EMI Studio. *MJ*

SCHUMANN

Symphony No. 1 in B flat
see also BRAHMS: Symphony No. 1 in C minor

SCHUMANN

Symphonies Nos 3 in E flat (Rhenish) & 4 in D minor

Cleveland Orchestra/Christoph von Dohnányi

Decca 421 643-2 □ 58:43 mins □ ❷❷❷

While this disc is certainly expensive, providing somewhat less than a full hour of music at premium price, its musical worth is incalculable, and certainly beyond valid criticism. Christoph von Dohnányi is an expert and purposeful interpreter of these works, and he has at his command one of the world's great virtuoso ensembles, the Cleveland Orchestra, which plays with a warmth, flair and stylistic awareness which would in no wise disgrace the Vienna or Berlin Philharmonics which, unlike their American rivals, should have this repertoire in their blood. Dohnányi's account of the *Rhenish* Symphony, Schumann's most pictorial and therefore most popular symphony, is strikingly passionate and committed. Orchestral playing is magnificent; strings are warm and pliant in the central slow Intermezzo, and the imperious, majestic tread of processional brass in the Cologne Cathedral episode is monolithic in its grave seriousness. The enigmatic Fourth Symphony emerges in a fresh, wholly unambiguous light, which should have strong appeal to those as yet unconvinced by this work. Decca's recording, made in Cleveland's cavernous Masonic Auditorium in the late Eighties, is in the demonstration class; you'll rarely encounter Schumann's symphonies re-created with comparable insight or integrity. *MJ*

Piano Concerto; The Poem of Ecstasy; Prometheus

Vladimir Ashkenazy (piano); LPO, Cleveland Orchestra/Lorin Maazel

Decca 417 252-2 □ ADD □ 66:23 mins □ ⊘⊘⊘

Although recorded in the Seventies, these performances still represent the best available introduction to Scriabin's orchestral output. Ashkenazy is particularly eloquent in the rather Chopinesque Piano Concerto, offering playing of elegance and refinement, and the LPO accompanies with discretion and admirable restraint. Naturally, these qualities are abandoned in Maazel's suitably impulsive account of *The Poem of Ecstasy*, but the conductor succeeds more than most in steering a sure sense of direction through the work's innumerable climaxes. Finally, there's an incandescent performance of *Prometheus* in which solo piano and a huge orchestra, augmented by wordless choir, produce some of the most sensuous sounds in the entire orchestral repertoire. As in the rest of the programme, Decca's engineers cope brilliantly with Scriabin's heavily congested textures, and the recordings hardly show their age. Strongly recommended. *EL*

(CRAWFORD) SEEGER
Andante for Strings
see IVES: Three Places in New England

SEREBRIER
Momento psicologico; Poema elegiaca
see BLOCH: Violin Concerto

Symphonies Nos 6, 7 & 9

American Composers Orchestra/Dennis Russell Davies

Argo 444 519-2 □ 70:56 mins □ ⊘⊘⊘

Arnold Schoenberg, seldom effusive about the works of younger composers, or Americans generally, said of Roger Sessions: 'Now I know how Schumann must have felt when he first heard the music of Brahms.' The formidably gifted Sessions studied with Bloch, not Schoenberg, though he spent several years in Europe between the wars. His mature music uses a highly developed 12-note serial technique: musical ideas are in a constant state of metamorphosis, textures highly contrapuntal, rhythms very lively, orchestral colour kaleidoscopic, always changing. Complex, uncompromising, it demands utter attention. It's seldom been as well presented as in this disc of three late symphonies. Sessions associated Nos 6 and 7 with his feelings about the Vietnam War: most palpable in No. 7, his own favourite among his symphonies and perhaps the finest, with its tragic, militaristic overtones and deeply elegiac epilogue. No. 6 is more jagged and flinty, difficult to catch hold of; the Ninth, more expansive, evokes the contrast of the Tiger and the Lamb in William Blake's famous poem, but its language is just as highly developed as it is in the others. Works such as these yield up their secrets only gradually, but that makes them ideal for repeated listening on disc. Argo's recording is excellent, and clarifies the textural web nicely. *CM*

Fanfare for Those Who Will Not Return
see Collection: Testimonies of War

The Age of Gold

Royal Stockholm PO/Gennady Rozhdestvensky

Chandos CHAN 9251/2 □ 133:46 mins (2 discs) □ ⊘⊘⊘

Yet another splendid revelation of the Shostakovich of which we knew (almost) nothing! Here, for the first time on record, is the full-length ballet of 1930, *Zolotoy vek*, in 37 numbers of which only four were excerpted for the published suite. The alternative English translation, though literally correct, is misleading: this is not the paradisal 'golden age' of mythology but a 'gilded age' of extravagance and debauchery. The wicked capitalist forces of female seduction and crooked finance try their wiles on a visiting Soviet football team.

You might suppose a score so full of parodied western musical 'depravity' would quickly pall. On the contrary, the variety is such that it dazzles. A football whistle, accordion, flexatones and much glissando tromboning are absorbed by sheer musical impulse. A witty arrangement of 'Tea for Two' becomes an entr'acte.

The solo baritone (brass instrument) in No. 9 oddly fails to be prominent enough but the sound quality is otherwise vivid, and the whole score is driven by Rozhdestvensky's customary irresistible zest. *Arthur Jacobs*

The Age of Gold Suite
see JANACEK: Sinfonietta

SHOSTAKOVICH

The Bolt

Royal Stockholm PO/Gennady Rozhdestvensky

Chandos CHAN 9343/4 □ **146:38 mins (2 discs)**
□ ⊙⊙⊙

Less impudent and brazen than its amazing predecessor *The Age of Gold* (also complete on Chandos), *The Bolt* is better suited to the tempered steel of Rozhdestvensky's Stockholmers. The work itself may not be required listening, but this beautifully engineered performance has to be one of the most perfect Shostakovich recordings ever made.

Gone, for the most part, are the capitalists of *The Age of Gold*, their naughty musical vocabulary and (nearly) all that jazz, but *petit bourgeois* elements in the factory non-plot give Shostakovich a few opportunities in that line. What's new are the glittering orchestration and the clear-cut Soviet melodies, brilliantly characterised here; and there are plenty of lop-sided phrases and odd colours to delight the ear (full marks to the woodwind in their many Act II solos, and to the supremely artistic xylophonist). Only the endless banalities of the final Red Army sequence fail to send off the necessary rockets, but maybe Rozhdestvensky can't be bothered with Shostakovich in un-ironic mode. The many sly tributes to Tchaikovsky and Offenbach are treated with due sophistication, and the conductor handles with aplomb his megaphoned injunctions (in the factory exercise sequence). *DN*

SHOSTAKOVICH

Cello Concertos Nos 1 & 2

Natalia Gutman (cello); RPO/Yuri Temirkanov

RCA Victor Red Seal RD 87918 □ **65:41 mins**
□ ⊙⊙⊙

Serious struggles both, the two Shostakovich cello concertos heard together provide some fascinating contrasts: the First relatively extrovert even in its moments of deepest sorrow, the Second introspectively summoning voices from beyond the grave in one of the first manifestations of the composer's starkly emotional late style.

Mstislav Rostropovich is the dedicatee of the two works, so the ideal would be to have his interpretations together on a single disc.

Since, however, his most recent performance of the First (Erato) comes with a reading of the Prokofiev Symphony-Concerto less highly charged than it can be in his hands, and since his spine-tingling Second has companions (in two separate DG manifestations) that few listeners will want, another Russian cellist of distinction will fill the bill nicely. Natalia Gutman may not have Rostropovich's searing forward momentum under pressure, but her handling of the more inward moments has, if anything, even greater intensity. The weird final Rondo of the Second Concerto, perhaps the greatest music, also provides the finest example of her subtle collaboration with Temirkanov and the RPO (keener teamwork even than that of Heinrich Schiff and the composer's son on Philips); the other-worldly coda will haunt you for days. *DN*

SHOSTAKOVICH

Piano Concertos Nos 1 & 2; Three Fantastic Dances; Preludes and Fugues, Op. 87/1, 4, 5, 23 & 24

Dmitri Shostakovich (piano), Ludovic Vaillant (trumpet); Orchestre National de la RDF/André Cluytens

EMI CDC 7 54606 2 □ **ADD mono** □ **76:10 mins**
□ ⊙⊙⊙

Shostakovich was the soloist when his First Piano Concerto was premiered by the Leningrad Philharmonic under Fritz Stiedry in 1933. His son Maxim gave the premiere of the Second Concerto in 1957. The recordings of both concertos on this disc were made in Paris in the following year and are of course an invaluable record of the composer playing his own music. But they are also terrific performances in their own right. More than any other interpreter on disc, Shostakovich brings out the sheer fun to be found in both works, and he is second to none in quick-fire precision. Outer movements are taken at a cracking pace, ideas tumbling over each other in a headlong rush of nervous energy. In the slow movements he is elegiac and tender – the echo of Rachmaninov in the Romantic theme of Concerto No. 2 undisguised.

Cluytens and the French National Radio Orchestra match Shostakovich in high spirits, and the important trumpet part in the First Concerto is executed stylishly by Ludovic Vaillant (placed close to the piano, as the composer preferred).

An altogether different side of Shostakovich is shown in the five Preludes and Fugues from his Op. 87 set. As in the concertos, his playing is very direct; and it makes a fascinating contrast with the greater fantasy, and slower tempi, of Tatiana Nikolayeva in her complete set for Hyperion.

The disc was one of the first releases in EMI's Composers in Person series. Full price seems excessive for recordings which, in this case, are nearly forty years old, but with good, fairly modern sound, admirers of Shostakovich will find these exhilarating performances hard to resist. *David Michaels*

Festival Overture; October; Symphony No. 2 (To October); The Song of the Forests

Mikhail Kotliarov (tenor), Nikita Storojev (bass); Brighton Festival Chorus, New London Children's Choir, RPO/Vladimir Ashkenazy

Decca 436 762-2 □ **71:43 mins** □ *ⓐ ⓐ ⓐ*

Reaction to Ashkenazy's Shostakovich cycle has so far been mixed. Why, one might ask, is Decca doubling up on repertoire recorded so successfully by Bernard Haitink for the same label only a decade before? But when the result is this good, there is room for both. Apart from the exuberant *Festival Overture*, which really fizzes, these works represent Shostakovich in his agitprop, social realist mood, complete with such choral injunctions as 'Arise, people of the great Soviet land, and do great deeds!' in his eulogy to the Soviet postwar forestry industry, *The Song of the Forests*. The tone poem *October* has the stature of a symphonic first movement in the style of Symphony No. 10. The most intriguing work, however, is the Second Symphony, which packs a lot into its 17 minutes, with complex modernism leading, by way of a blast on the factory whistle, into a choral hymn to 'October, the Commune and Lenin'. All are performed with panache – the Royal Philharmonic hasn't sounded this uniformly good in ages, though the recordings date from 1989–92. *Matthew Rye*

Symphonies Nos 1–15

Evgenia Tselovalnik (soprano), Evgeny Nesterenko, Arthur Eisen (bass); Choirs of the Russian Republic, Moscow PO/Kirill Kondrashin

BMG Melodiya 74321 19952 2 □ **ADD** □ **539:33 mins (10 discs)** □ *ⓐ ⓐ*

Sound is of the essence in choosing a cycle of Shostakovich symphonies – not so much recorded sound as orchestral. If, for example, you value instrumental sophistication allied to a fair amount of commitment, then Haitink's stunningly engineered series on Decca – all performances now available on single, mid-price discs – will fill the bill. But if you feel, as I do, that Shostakovich is 'about' dark, full string tone, blistering brass and biting winds, then the experience has to be through the medium of a Russian orchestra. My first choice here would unquestionably have been the shattering cycle of Gennady Rozhdestvensky, formerly on Olympia before the licence ran out (some shops may still have copies). Kondrashin's Shostakovich offers generally more consistent Melodiya engineering – still crude, but less echo and fewer monster-miked woodwind solos – but rather more wayward, sometimes wilful conducting.

In the cases of several later symphonies there were more distinguished alternatives made in the Soviet Union at around the same time, not least the authentic Fourteenth conducted by Rostropovich and featuring Vishnevskaya (creator of the soprano role). But in the deliberately crude assaults, screams and laments of the Fourth and Eighth symphonies, the intensity is unmatched. Contributions of Russian choirs in the early revolutionary experiments (Nos 2 & 3) and *Babi Yar* (No. 13) are invaluable. A final caution: I should not wish to restrict myself to a single view on the Shostakovich symphonies, but these recordings made during the last decade of the composer's lifetime do offer a rare consistency. *DN*

Symphony No. 1
see also Collection: Russian Music

Symphony No. 4 in C minor

Scottish National Orchestra/Neeme Järvi

Chandos CHAN 8640 □ **61:20 mins** □ *ⓐ ⓐ ⓐ*

Baggy monster it may be, devouring and regurgitating the unheeded novelties of the astonishing early ballet *The Age of Gold*, but there are sounds and abysses in Shostakovich's Fourth Symphony which he never dared again (and little wonder the work was withdrawn in the wake of the 1936 scandal over *Lady Macbeth of Mtsensk*. Nothing in the composer's output is more breathtaking than the holocaust launched by strings in frantic, fuguing semiquavers at the heart of the first movement; and no performance blisters and skids quite like the SNO's under Järvi, ripping up the earth in an awesome display of elemental force.

In a Mahlerian finale of even more harrowing emotions – a reflection, surely, of the composer's suicidal thoughts at the time – Järvi's ruthless control of the structure keep us tense, anxious to know the outcome of the nervy central dance-sequence. The SNO brass then unleash the peroration with queasy force, and the desolate, faltering-heartbeat coda induced by this murderous display of strength is supremely atmospheric. This is a grimly sympathetic interpretation which leaves others – including the recent Rattle version, superbly prepared but less engaged – out in the cold. *DN*

SHOSTAKOVICH

Symphonies Nos 5 in D minor & 9 in E flat

Atlanta SO/Yoel Levi

Telarc CD-80215 ☐ 77:38 mins ☐ ♦♦♦

It may seem perverse to go to Atlanta, Georgia, for a recommended version of Shostakovich's most famous and most recorded symphony. But this is perhaps the outstanding disc in Yoel Levi's generally excellent Shostakovich series for Telarc. No. 5 is broadly shaped throughout, with an absolute certainty of direction from first bar to last that makes this a very impressive musical experience indeed. The clarity and tension of the opening Moderato are remarkable, and there's a Mahlerian intensity of feeling to the slow movement. The basic tempo for the finale is slower than most interpretations and gains thereby in balefulness, reminiscent of Karel Ančerl's great Sixties Supraphon performance. Telarc's sonics cope superbly with some awesome climaxes. The Ninth is equally impressive – a 'light' symphony with very serious purpose. If you prefer a Russian orchestra in these pieces, Rozhdestvensky on Olympia is just as good as you might imagine; there's an impressive Haitink version on Decca. An unexpectedly strong bargain contender comes from Naxos, with the Belgian Radio and TV Orchestra conducted by Alexander Rahbari. But if it's just a bargain Fifth you want, Previn's 1965 LSO recording (RCA, now interestingly coupled with Shostakovich's *Hamlet* music under José Serebrier) remains supreme. *CM*

SHOSTAKOVICH

Symphonies Nos 6 in B minor & 10 in E minor

Leningrad PO/Yevgeny Mravinsky

BMG Melodiya 74321 25198 2 ☐ ADD ☐ 77:34 mins ☐ ♦♦

Acknowledged in Elizabeth Wilson's fascinating *Shostakovich: A Life Remembered* (Faber) as 'the authentic interpreter of Shostakovich's symphonic music', Yevgeny Mravinsky has left a variable legacy of symphonic readings shaped by his detailed work with the composer. These two recordings reveal a perfectionist prepared to throw caution to the winds in quest of terror: the whirlwind Scherzo of the Tenth, supposedly (and plausibly) a portrait of Stalin composed in the euphoria following the Beloved Leader and Teacher's death in 1953, and the double-edged victory dance of the finale receive the most dangerous, biting performances I know.

The same goes for the second movement and riotous fairground finale of the Sixth, deliberately heavy and crude when necessary. But dynamic detail remains formidable, and Mravinsky's shaping force is clear in the big opening movements of both symphonies. The sound in both these live recordings is perfectly vivid, if marred by the occasional up-front blatancy (a grotesque bass clarinet in the Sixth, maybe apt) and the bronchial antics of a Russian audience in winter. If you seek a purer sheen in these works, try Mariss Jansons's meticulous, and far from faceless, Oslo Sixth and Philadelphia Tenth on EMI. *DN*

SHOSTAKOVICH

Symphony No. 7 (Leningrad)

Scottish National Orchestra/Neeme Järvi

Chandos CHAN 8623 ☐ 69:06 mins ☐ ♦♦♦

You can tell with Järvi that the Seventh Symphony is not just 'about' Soviets facing Germans, and it is certainly not an ultimate celebration of resistance rewarded. He creates something very personal out of the second movement, eloquently pleading with material that can sound second rate; here, strings and later clarinet cast a soft, sad glance back to the golden-age subject of the first movement before hopes are squashed flat. The brass are clearly the villains of the piece: pitilessly trampling scruples, peering eerily over the brow of the hill as the first-movement war-machine gets under way (though the recording seems unable to cope with the welter of snare-drum at the climax of this famously repetitive 'juggernaut of destruction', and Järvi's sudden spurt whips up the violence a little too crudely). Their presence at the end quells optimism – brilliant but undeniably menacing, with Järvi driving home the sarcasm of the 'Khachaturian touch' and the dissonances as only he knows how.

Preferences for a more lithely sprung and objective view of the *Leningrad* should be well served by Jansons (EMI) conducting the Leningrad players for whom the piece was made (well, maybe not literally); and don't overlook historic documents featuring Stokowski (Pearl) and Toscanini (RCA). *DN*

SHOSTAKOVICH

Symphony No. 8 in C minor

National SO of Washington, DC/Mstislav Rostropovich

Teldec 9031-74719-2 □ 63:31 mins □ 🎵🎵🎵

No performance can be too raw for Shostakovich's most uncompromising statement on the horrors and the pity of war, and it is a shame that Rozhdestvensky's Eighth, a bludgeoning brute in coarse Melodiya sound, is no longer in the catalogues. Next best thing is another interpretation from a Russian who realises the necessary pole-axing force of the work, and who encourages a formerly soft-grained American orchestra to help him. Few opening bars can tell you more about what kind of playing to expect, and the grim opening gauntlet of cellos and basses here is very impressive.

In the machine-like impassivity of the relentless third movement, violas cut ruthlessly against woodwind screams, and after a wryly 'pop' trumpeter in the central mass-produced galop, the brass go flat out for the returning toccata. Rostropovich stretches the passacaglia to rightly unbearable limits, though there is warmth elsewhere, especially from collective cellos in outer movements, and the suggestion that the finale is a kind of concerto for orchestra doesn't undercut the tension of a second storm ready to break. A suggestion that the engineers can't quite handle massive climaxes seems like a small price to pay for natural sound which gives space to Rostropovich's tough vision. *DN*

SHOSTAKOVICH

Symphony No. 11 (The Year 1905)

National SO of Washington, DC/Mstislav Rostropovich

Teldec 9031-76262-2 □ 68:56 mins □ 🎵🎵🎵

You might have expected Rostropovich to go straight for the jugular in Shostakovich's scenes of massacre and mass struggle. Instead, this is a spacious, thoughtful and always expressive argument for a difficult symphony of revolutionary songs, bringing out the extreme colours in the broad, Mussorgskian canvas as never before. Meticulously observed expectation and lament frame a slaughter of automatic, machine-like precision, anything but the usual bloody pageant in technicolour.

The expressionless shell-shock and heavy pacing (much slower than the score suggests) of violas in the fine socialist song 'Eternal Memory', and the way it slowly warms to life, are even finer, and the finale proves remarkable: a spring-heeled, determined Weillian procession outstripping even Järvi (Chandos) and the excellent James DePreist (Delos), capped by a bitter coda and the last warning of the echoing tocsin (parallels here with the equally ominous resonating tam-tam some conductors espouse at the end of Rachmaninov's Symphonic Dances). The recording holds departmental forces in fine, clean balance, though a little at bay in climaxes. A revelation of the Eleventh, then, as a greater symphony than we used to think. *DN*

SHOSTAKOVICH

Symphonies Nos 13 & 14
see also **CHORAL & SONG**

SHOSTAKOVICH/STRAVINSKY

Shostakovich: Symphony No. 15

Stravinsky: Agon

Leningrad PO/Yevgeny Mravinsky

BMG Melodiya 74321 25192 2 □ ADD □ 63:31 mins □ 🎵🎵

Full marks to BMG Melodiya for offering us so thought-provoking a Mravinsky double bill. Both works mix serial techniques, or adaptation of serial procedures, with tonal procedures; though while Shostakovich's wise distillation of his symphonic thinking sometimes exchanges its skeletal enigmas and quotations (from Rossini and Wagner) for unequivocal full-orchestral anguish, *Agon* usually sounds ice-cold in Stravinsky's calculated blends of ensemble. Not on this occasion: Mravinsky, a thorough rehearser capable of getting absolute precision from his Leningrad PO, manages to inform the ballet with a passion and ferocity that link it back to *The Rite of Spring*.

The Shostakovich performance was recorded a year after the composer's death, lending an even greater edge to the threat of the brass chorales and the near-silences in the funereal Adagio. Mravinsky's relentless logic powers the outer movements – the first, like a grotesquely speeded-up *adagio*, as keenly articulated as you will ever hear – and although regular coughs betoken a live performance, no applause follows (and none is necessary) after the final, chastening percussion whirring and clicks. *DN*

SHOSTAKOVICH

Violin Concertos Nos 1 & 2

Lydia Mordkovitch (violin); Scottish National Orchestra/Neeme Järvi

Chandos CHAN 8820 □ 69:22 mins □ *🎵🎵🎵*

Shostakovich's First Violin Concerto has everything that a player with intelligence and brilliant technique in equal measure could wish for, and there seems to have been no end of first-rate recordings, most recently from the young violinists Maxim Vengerov (Teldec, with Prokofiev One) and Vadim Repin (Erato, with Prokofiev Two.) If the companionship of the later concerto is less essential than in the case of the two cello concertos (see above) – and certainly not advisable for consecutive listening – it still makes for a compelling demonstration of how Shostakovich was able to ring the changes within a relatively narrow emotional frame of reference that also happens to be harrowing in the extreme.

Lydia Mordkovitch (pupil of David Oistrakh, to whom both concertos are dedicated) and Järvi's SNO negotiate the dance of death scherzos with frightening ferocity; I've never found the music more dangerous, or absolute precision less essential. As for the soloist's many moments of loneliness, be they stalked by orchestral bass-lines or alone in the most heroic cadenzas of the 20th-century violin concerto repertoire, Mordkovitch is simply phenomenal. Ensembles could be tighter than the reverberant recording allows, but she never once loses her edge. *DN*

SIBELIUS

Finlandia; Karelia Suite; Valse triste; Pohjola's Daughter; Lemminkäinen's Return

Hallé Orchestra/John Barbirolli

EMI CDM 7 69205 2 □ ADD □ 50:17 mins □ *🎵🎵*

Finlandia; Karelia Suite; Tapiola; En saga; Luonnotar

Elisabeth Söderström (soprano); Philharmonia Orchestra/Vladimir Ashkenazy

Decca Ovation 430 757-2 □ 72:30 mins □ *🎵🎵*

These two most vivid of Sibelius compilations offer suitable alternatives according to whether you prefer the brighter or the darker sides of the composer. True, *Valse triste* is the most

lugubrious of hits; but the keynote of Barbirolli's selection is shining heroism, whether ultimately defeated by the tall orders of Pohjola's daughter as she sits spinning on her rainbow or ultimately triumphant in the shape of Lemminkäinen homeward bound from his ordeals. Certainly, this seething performance of *Lemminkäinen's Return* and the no-holds-barred combativeness of the Hallé *Finlandia* stand alongside the EMI recording of Vaughan Williams's *A London Symphony* as epitomes of Barbirolli's bracing art. Ashkenazy, on the other hand, engages in mysteries which he has no intention of solving; but the superbly recorded sounds and landscapes of his Philharmonia *Tapiola* and *En saga* provide ample excitement along the way. If you find the *Lemminkäinen* finale especially exciting, then you might like to seek it out in the context of the three other tone poems which keep it company (the best known, and much more frequently extracted, being *The Swan of Tuonela*) in the early *Four Legends from the Kalevala*, bracingly performed by the veteran Eugene Ormandy and the Philadelphia Orchestra on EMI. *DN*

SIBELIUS

Symphonies Nos 1, 2, 4 & 5

Boston SO/Colin Davis

Philips 446 157-2 □ ADD □ 155:22 mins (2 discs) □ *🎵🎵*

Symphonies Nos 3, 6 & 7; Violin Concerto in D minor; Finlandia; Tapiola; The Swan of Tuonela

Salvatore Accardo (violin); Boston SO, LSO/Colin Davis

Philips 446 160-2 □ ADD □ 145:48 mins (2 discs) □ *🎵🎵*

Striking a perfect balance between lightness of touch and true grit, nature and nurture, in any Sibelius cycle is far from easy. Sometimes the orchestra lacks the weight necessary for taking wing in the early symphonies or the thrust that can effect a sudden cloudburst in later Sibelius; such are Järvi's Gothenburg SO on BIS (despite several interpretations that are wholly successful) and Jukka-Pekka Saraste's Finnish RSO (Finlandia). Other problems rest with an overemphatic conductor: some of the effects in Simon Rattle's cycle (EMI) or Colin Davis's second thoughts on RCA are simply too hard-hitting when they need to seem effortless. Davis's earlier cycle is a perfect meeting between a charismatic (not to mention highly vocal) interpreter and an orchestra of outstanding natural warmth.

All the readings are underpinned by firm bass-lines – reassuring or awesome, according to mood – and the most adaptable playing from the Boston strings, though woodwind are better in more withdrawn meditations than biting high profile, and the brass can be poorly coordinated. The insecure cornerstone trombone of the Seventh Symphony, however, hardly detracts from Davis's flawless pacing of a work which has eluded the grand mastery of Mravinsky or Karajan. At least a handful of tone poems should be essential in any survey of the seven symphonies: the brooding mystery of *Tapiola*, another outstandingly fluent performance, makes the most disturbing of epilogues to the symphonic sequence of the second two-CD set, where the interpretations of Symphonies Nos 3 and 7 stand as top individual recommendations. *DN*

SIBELIUS

Violin Concerto in D minor

see also DVORAK: Violin Concerto in A minor
and GLAZUNOV: Violin Concerto in A minor

SIBELIUS

Symphony No. 1 in E minor; The Oceanides

City of Birmingham SO/Simon Rattle

EMI CDM 7 64119 2 □ 52:11 mins □ 🏵🏵

For all its structural gaucheries, Sibelius's First Symphony bristles with a sense of adventure, and this live-wire performance is exactly what it needs. The sinewy splendour of the strings keeps the proportion of Tchaikovskian style to true Sibelius in the big themes lower than usual, though Rattle backs it up with a spaciousness not always apparent (or wished for) in his performances of the Second and Fifth Symphonies. The acoustic, at fault only in the timpani-dominated blur of the Scherzo's last spurt, helps to emphasise the scoring for lower instruments and to carry the sometimes aimless gestures of the last-movement fantasia; here, for once, Sibelius is perceived to be stretching out to new worlds of sound and frenzy, not flailing in the darkness of some late-Romantic crisis. How seamless the composer was later to make the transition from light to dark and back is perfectly exemplified by *The Oceanides*, no mere filler. In phrasing, Rattle equals Beecham; in achieving a greater richness of sound from his orchestra and in overall symphonic shaping of this impressionistic water-music, he is even finer. *DN*

SIBELIUS

Symphonies Nos 2 in D & 6 in D minor

LSO/Colin Davis

RCA Victor Red Seal 09026 68218 2 □ 72:53 mins □ 🏵🏵🏵

This second instalment of Davis's second Sibelius cycle is purest gold. Hardly a phrase in these performances passes without new light being shed on it, and yet there is a strong feeling of spontaneity throughout. Davis's readings are far from conventional; he often focuses on the darker sides of these symphonies, bringing out rarely heards depths in the Second and adding a fascinating new dimension to the Sixth. In both, he projects a strong sense of narrative and in the Second Symphony guides the argument towards the finale with overwhelming results – the appearance of the big tune gains immeasurably from a determined lack of sensationalism. Still more revealing is the finale of the Sixth: along with the expected 'pastoral' reflection he finds more than a hint of menace.

Davis is admirably served by the LSO. The strings respond to the detail of his interpretation with superb flexibility, and wind and brass groups are richly voiced. There is a wealth of magically observed orchestral detail, with the start of the slow movement of the Second Symphony – a polar-bear growl from the timpani and singing pizzicato – being especially memorable. These performances command attention and will satisfy listeners for many years to come.
Jan Smaczny

SIBELIUS

Symphonies Nos 2 in D & 7 in C

Philadelphia Orchestra/Eugene Ormandy

Sony Essential Classics SBK 53509 □ ADD □ 66:25 mins □ 🏵

I suppose orthodox Sibelians will find this an eccentric first choice for the Finnish master's Seventh Symphony, but at bargain price I consider it irresistible. Ormandy was a dedicated if uneven champion of Sibelius: few eminent conductors have made a poorer fist of the Sixth, and on the present disc his eminently recommendable account of No. 2, though full-blooded and colourful, is a fairly old-fashioned Romantic view. But his No. 7, recorded in 1960, is the most gripping I know.

Not everyone will approve the high-power sheen of the Philadelphia strings, the old-style CBS spotlighting of wind soloists; while the thrilling crescendo which Ormandy makes of the final bars is not exactly what Sibelius wrote. But he brings out magnificently the score's dark and turbulent undertow, articulating its monolithic single movement with impressive command of its subtle changes of mood and tempo. The great storm-like sequence has never sounded so baleful. If you want a modern version, Ashkenazy (Decca), Järvi (BIS) or Rattle (EMI) are entirely serviceable, but none – not even the much-revered Beecham, which I feel rather pale by comparison – has the majestic bloom I find here. The recording, of demonstration standard in its day, still retains tremendous presence. *CM*

SIBELIUS

Symphony No. 4 in A minor; Canzonetta; The Oceanides

Gothenburg SO/Neeme Järvi

BIS CD-263 □ 52:15 mins □ *0 0 0*

Most listeners might reasonably expect another Sibelius symphony to keep the Fourth company on CD. Yet this score of withering concision and brevity remains one of the towering symphonies of the century. And since I could easily spend a review twice this length happily examining the subtle means Sibelius employs in the slow movement alone to work his way painfully towards a brief tragic catharsis, a tentatively vocal progress uniquely realised in Järvi's finely nuanced interpretation, this disc needs no apology.

No other conductor sustains the spare first movement with a greater combination of brooding atmosphere and keen focus – Karajan's early DG recording sounds both stiff-jointed and occasionally blurred by comparison – and Järvi shapes with infinite care the many cries from the heart in what even the reticent Sibelius himself was willing to define as a 'psychological symphony'. The inward shades of the Gothenburg strings are fully equipped to meet every nuance; the solo cello-playing is especially fine. In the remaining short measure, we move through the less harrowing introspection of the short *Canzonetta* into the varied lights of *The Oceanides*, the tone poem which sparklingly celebrates the end of the composer's dark age. *DN*

Sibelius: Symphony No. 5 in E flat

Nielsen: Symphony No. 4 (Inextinguishable); Pan and Syrinx

Philharmonia Orchestra, City of Birmingham SO/Simon Rattle

EMI CDM 7 64737 2 □ 76:59 mins □ *0 0*

These two symphonies make a wonderful pairing. They both move from uncertainty to light, but the journey isn't a straight one, and unflagging concentration and commitment are needed from players and conductor to make the goal seem inevitable. They certainly receive both here. But although Rattle always has the end in sight, the detours never seem hurried or forced. The Sibelius is especially fine, better even than Rattle's 1992 versions with the CBSO. These are outstanding performances, captured in first-rate recordings. *Ivan Hewett*

SIBELIUS

Symphony No. 6 in D minor; Pelléas and Mélisande Suite

Gothenburg SO/Neeme Järvi

BIS CD-237 □ 56:27 mins □ *0 0 0*

Of all the Sibelius symphonies, the Sixth is the one that earns the most loving devotion from listener and conductor: a glass of pure spring water that needs the purest of approaches, though not without a certain drive for the strange turbulences that develop in the outer movements. It is interesting that Järvi, a conductor who can produce the most idiosyncratic results for better or worse, never over-interprets; no doubt the unforced, well-earthed sound of his Gothenburg SO was a decisive factor. The hymns and responses of the strings at the start and end of the symphony – two of the most simply moving passages in Sibelius, but easily overstressed in a performance like Rattle's – sound both fervent and natural, while woodwind hone to perfection the forest murmurs in the twilight zones of the middle movements.

After the contrasting heart of oak of 'At the Castle Gate', celebrated as the signature-tune to *The Sky at Night* and first of the incidental numbers Sibelius provided for Maeterlinck's *Pelléas and Mélisande*, Järvi establishes a darker, heavier mood for the mystery of the play's oppressive setting. Fortunately, orchestral nuances are too keen to create any impression of mere drabness. *DN*

The Tempest – incidental music (excerpts); Scènes historiques – Festivo (Set One), Set Two; Karelia Suite – Intermezzo & Alla marcia; Finlandia

RPO, BBC SO, LPO/Thomas Beecham

EMI CDM 7 63397 2 □ ADD mono □ **72:35 mins** □ 🎵🎵

Some composers seem born to write the music for certain plays: Mendelssohn's incidental music to *A Midsummer Night's Dream* and Grieg's complete score for *Peer Gynt* – now that we know it in the round, not just from the suites – prove the point. Increasing interest in resurrecting Sibelius's many numbers for *The Tempest* and relating them to their Shakespearian context now reveals the work to be a third great example.

Even in Beecham's selection of short movements from the suites you can glean a sense of how special a case this is. And it is for the conductor's ineffable grace and charm in Sibelius's music of the spheres, rather than for the rather careful handling of the more grotesque elements of the storm itself, that this mono recording proves treasurable. I can think of no more exquisite one-minute orchestral piece than the Second Song (first heard in the play as the setting for Ariel's 'Where the Bee Sucks'), exquisitely turned by Beecham's RPO clarinettist, and nicely dovetailed into its dreamier companion pieces. The other items of special interest on this disc are the selectively scored *Scènes historiques*, full of Beechamesque character, though an outstanding RCA recording conducted by Jukka-Pekka Saraste, currently not available, is even finer. *DN*

Symphonies Nos 2 & 4

Bournemouth SO/Vernon Handley

Hyperion CDA 66505 □ **74:50 mins** □ 🎵🎵🎵

Robert Simpson's 11 symphonies represent, in sum, one of the most powerful contributions that any composer has made to the genre in the second half of this century. Dynamic, hard-headed, cogent in their tonal thinking, blending aspects of Beethoven, Bruckner and Nielsen in the crucible of a fearlessly independent musical mind, they impressively and organically extend symphonic tradition without being in any sense backward-looking.

Hyperion's nearly complete series of the symphonies under Vernon Handley is thus immensely valuable, providing exemplary performances in superb sound. For sheer power the towering, monolithic one-movement Ninth might be many listeners' first choice, but this disc of Symphonies Nos 2 and 4 is perhaps easier of access, both works among Simpson's finest yet comparatively Classical in design and showing him at his most approachable. No. 2 has a very expressive palindromic set of variations for slow movement. The masterly No. 4 features a thrilling Scherzo (which makes delicious play with a quotation of a Haydn symphony) and a beautiful slow movement which is among the most deeply affecting things Simpson has written. *CM*

Má vlast (My Fatherland)

Royal Liverpool PO/Libor Pešek

Virgin Ultraviolet CUV 5 61223 2 □ **76:29 mins** □ 🎵

Libor Pešek's authoritative and affectionate reading of Smetana's nationalistic tone poems, collectively entitled *Má vlast*, marked the zenith of a series of Czech works recorded for Virgin with the Royal Liverpool PO. Pešek, of course, has the true measure of this epic score well within his grasp, and communicates his every wish to a highly responsive and alert orchestra, which has never sounded so distinguished or polished on disc. No mean achievement, when one considers the virtuoso demands placed upon every section of the orchestra throughout this vast composition. *Má vlast* is the most ambitious and eloquent musical testimony to the Bohemian landscape and spirit ever attempted, and marked the climax of the great revival of Czech culture, within which Smetana's personal contribution was deeply significant. *Vyšehrad*, an ancient citadel overlooking the city of Prague, and last resting-place for many of the heroes of Bohemia's turbulent past, opens the cycle; Pešek evinces with eloquent nostalgia its glorious, chivalrous heritage, its figures of renown, and its frequent scenes of conflict. The bard Libuše sings, to the accompaniment of a harp, of freedom and glory for his homeland. *Vltava* (or *Moldau*), the most popular of the six tone poems, follows the course of the great river of Bohemia from its two sources, to scenes of majestic grandeur, as its waters flow serenely past the fortifications of Prague, intoning again the lay of the bard himself. *Šárka*, a blood-curdling portrait of the vengeful warrior maiden of the title, sworn to take vengeance upon the entire male population because of previous infidelity, is masterfully played here, and Pešek's orchestra responds intuitively to the pastoral evocation of Bohemia's heartland in the fourth of the six episodes of *Má vlast*. The concluding sections, *Blánik* and *Tábor*, are again thematically linked, invoking the patriotic Hussite hymn 'Ye who are God's Warriors'. This unfaltering, mightily distinguished performance ends triumphantly, and represents an incomparable mid-price offering meriting a place in every collection. *MJ*

STANLEY

Six Concertos in Seven Parts, Op. 2

The Parley of Instruments/Roy Goodman

Hyperion CDA 66338 □ 58:12 mins □ ⨀⨀⨀

This was the very first of Hyperion's English Orpheus series, a major contribution – approaching forty discs now – to our view of English music between the 16th and 19th centuries.

This was a well-judged starter. The six concertos, by a composer hitherto known mainly for his organ voluntaries, were very popular in their day. Originally for the standard Corellian ensemble – two solo violins, cello and harpsichord set against a ripieno of strings and separate continuo –they were also arranged as harpsichord or organ concertos, always popular since Handel had invented the genre. Two are so performed here, Paul Nicholson playing a sparklingly 'chiffy' four-rank chamber organ.

But there's plenty of variety even within the original string scoring. In the Second Concerto, one movement is virtually a cello solo, another alternates fast and slow in no fewer than seven nervously brief sections, a fugal Allegro matches anything Handel has to offer, and a final dance will haunt your memory for days.

The hopes and challenges of the English Orpheus series seem to have inspired The Parley of Instruments. The players are technically superb, but also play with a grace and lightness which are wholly uplifting. *GP*

STENHAMMAR

Symphonies Nos 1 & 2; Excelsior! Symphonic Overture; Serenade in F

Gothenburg SO/Neeme Järvi

DG 445 857-2 □ 138:37 mins (2 discs) □ ⨀⨀⨀

The Swedish composer Wilhelm Stenhammar (1871–1927) has suffered in comparison with his more popular Scandinavian contemporaries, Sibelius and Nielsen. A less innovative figure than either of these composers, he nonetheless ploughed an individual furrow and in his two symphonies can be regarded almost as a kind of Nordic Bruckner. The Serenade is a rather different composition, a brilliant orchestral showpiece drawing its inspiration from the sunnier climes of the Mediterranean.

Järvi has recorded these works before with the same orchestra for the BIS label, and his earlier recordings have the advantage of including the discarded 'Reverenza' movement from the Serenade. However, the DG set enjoys the same high standards of performance and recording, but Järvi's interpretations, particularly that of the fine Second Symphony, have greater breadth and intensity of expression. This is especially crucial in the ambitious double fugal finale of the Second Symphony, where Järvi paces the musical argument with greater conviction than on his first recording. *EL*

STEVENS

Violin Concerto; Symphony No. 2

Ernst Kovacic (violin); BBC Philharmonic/Edward Downes

Meridian CDE 84174 □ 62:50 mins □ ⨀⨀⨀

More celebrated in his lifetime as a notable teacher of composition, the late Bernard Stevens's own works have been coming into their own in the past decade through a series of fine recordings: his is one of the most impressive British composers of his generation, trenchant in utterance, endlessly inventive and a superb contrapuntist. The Violin Concerto is a comparatively early work, written during army service in the Second World War for Max Rostal (whose own performance of it is preserved on a fascinating two-disc set of archive recordings from Symposium Records). It's an expansive, passionate work, worthy to stand with its near contemporaries, the Shostakovich and Bloch concertos. The slow movement is particularly profound, and the 12-note theme at the outset shows Stevens's interest in using serial principles within a strong tonal framework, an idea he took up much more rigorously in the Second Symphony, a strong, subtle and invigorating piece that's had far fewer performances than it deserves. Ernst Kovacic's heroic account of the concerto's solo part is stunning; orchestra and recording are very good. There's more Stevens orchestral music to be explored on Meridian and Marco Polo, and his masterly string quartets on Unicorn-Kanchana. *CM*

STRADELLA
Sonata for Strings and Trumpet
see Collection: Baroque Trumpet Music

STRAUSS (FAMILY)
see Collection: Ein Straussfest II

STRAUSS

An Alpine Symphony

Berlin PO/Herbert von Karajan

DG 439 017-2 □ 51:02 mins □ 🔊🔊🔊

Karajan always said that he lived for the epilogues of Strauss's operas and tone poems. That seems abundantly clear in this glowing sunset rhapsody; but the last of the *Alpine Symphony's* 24 hours in the mountains are by no means typical. The radiance drains away, the music steers itself round into a sombre minor key and, in the very last bars, the once-confident theme of the mountaineers' bold ascent dies on the violins. Bearing in mind the compositional finishing date of 1915, it is tempting to see this as Strauss's first war requiem – the second, of course, being *Metamorphosen* – and Karajan's Berlin strings disquietingly bear that out in their final glissando.

Certainly the darker, more elemental side of the work is well served throughout, notably in a piercing climax to the 'Vision' sequence, and in Karajan's hands the comparison with Bruckner occasionally seems apt; but there's also plenty to enjoy in the glittering parade of orchestral effects during the ascent. The remixing process of the Karajan Gold series has in effect saved what was a nastily synthetic recording from sabotaging a great performance, as it did when the issue was first released in 1980. This is now a demonstration-worthy disc, though reflecting an undeniably fierce orchestral sound at times in Strauss's thickest scoring. *DN*

STRAUSS

Also sprach Zarathustra; Don Juan; Till Eulenspiegels lustige Streiche; Tod und Verklärung; Ein Heldenleben; Der Rosenkavalier – First Waltz Suite

Amsterdam Concertgebouw Orchestra/Bernard Haitink, Eugen Jochum

Philips 442 281-2 □ ADD □ 148:23 mins (2 discs) □ 🔊🔊

Broadly paced and spaciously recorded, Haitink's Strauss gives pause for serious thought: welcome when the composer's more philosophical aspirations need a luminous hand, less apt when there ought to be under-lying ironic intent (the *Hero's Life*, effective on its own grand terms, is surely more portentous than Strauss intended). That puts this *Zarathustra* right at the top of a distinguished list, though when the composer sheds seriousness and sends his Nietzschean superman dancing into the light the playing brims with chamber-musical humour. Haitink excels throughout in revealing the full incandescent richness of the string writing; inner parts are duly highlighted without losing their mystery, and the voids between the major actions of the piece reveal bewitching perspectives.

Those larger-than-life adventurers Till and Juan are splendidly characterised, Eulenspiegel a sharp-witted by warmly limned protagonist unequal to the frightening world beyond his prankstering, Don Juan brilliant, richly detailed and broadly heroic at the zenith. As in so many performances of *Tod und Verklärung*, the supernatural seems more present in sick-room gloom than in the transfiguration itself, though that must be ascribed partly to the composer. Previn, on EMI, is one of the few to make it transcendently powerful. Stocked to the brim, this set should serve as a compact reference-point for Straussians as well as a handsome introduction. *DN*

STRAUSS

Divertimento; Der Bürger als Edelmann

Orpheus CO

DG 435 871-2 □ 68:24 mins □ 🔊🔊🔊

By the standards of his times, if not of our own authentically high-toned age, Strauss set about past masters with tact and discretion. He paid a celebrated homage to the French 17th-century composer Lully as a service to librettist Hofmannsthal's 'little Molière project' (*Le bourgeois gentilhomme*, first resting-ground for that pretty hybrid *Ariadne auf Naxos*), but we're much less familiar with his penchant for Couperin, as displayed in two Viennese fancy-dress ballets.

The conductorless Orpheus ensemble turns to the later of the two harpsichord-piece arrangements, the Op. 86 Divertimento, restoring an other-worldly purity of intent which isn't always to the point. I prefer the sweet tooth of the Strauss disciple Clemens Krauss in 'Le tic-toc choc' in a 1954 radio broadcast. But these nimble New Yorkers do help to reinforce the delicacy of the scoring, and when in *Le bourgeois gentilhomme* Strauss makes his own artful presence felt, there's always a point of view. It may be speedy – the expert violinist in the Dance of the Tailors has no trouble with that – but it invariably smiles. Although DG's presentation leaves the Orpheus personnel nameless, all the soloists deserve a credit, from the songbird clarinettist to fencing trombone and trumpet. Not quite in the Kempe or Beecham league, but classy all the same. *DN*

STRAUSS

Don Quixote

Mstislav Rostropovich (cello), Ulrich Koch (viola); Berlin PO/Herbert von Karajan

EMI CDC 7 49308 2 □ ADD □ 43:50 mins □ ⊘⊘⊘

Strauss's orchestral masterpiece in terms of blending story-line and musical substance, *Don Quixote* needs a cellist and a conductor prepared to share in the lofty ideals of its protagonist. Here the real world of mendicants, sheep and windmills only briefly stands in the way. All the great moments of this wonderful tribute to Cervantes – for Rostropovich the central vigil and a death-bed scene of unparalleled nobility, for Karajan the 'castles-in-the-air' sermon of Variation Three and a hair-raisingly tragic home-coming – have an aristocratic breadth and sheen matched by no rival version. Inevitably in a score so often of such labyrinthine complexity, not every orchestral strand has a chance to register, and the recorded balancing-act can be selective. But in an interpretation which has the gift to be simple when the work most needs it, those drawbacks are less significant than they might otherwise be.

For more vivid humour and scene-painting, try Tortelier and Kempe (EMI); for a woeful-countenanced knight raging against the dying of the light, go for the surprises of Karajan's third and most dangerous recording (DG). The present measure is, of course, short – but just think of how many notes you're getting for your money! *DN*

STRAUSS/HINDEMITH

Strauss: Horn Concertos Nos 1 & 2

Hindemith: Horn Concerto

Dennis Brain (horn); Philharmonia Orchestra/ Wolfgang Sawallisch, Paul Hindemith

EMI CDC 7 47834 2 □ ADD □ 53:21 mins □ ⊘⊘⊘

Between full-voiced fanfares and brazen summons, Strauss shows the horn as chameleon, and no one has ever brought out the mercurial *Till Eulenspiegel* moods of the two concertos quite as distinctly as Dennis Brain. Even the early Concerto No. 1, tailored

to please Strauss's horn-playing father, has its share of daring, the smoking-jacketed roué throwing off his guise to cock a decisive final snook; and the *grazioso* element of the Indian Summer Second has Brain vying with characterful Philharmonia woodwind for grace-noted suavity.

There's plenty of smooth singing, too, in the slow movements, that dark-woods Romanticism which Hindemith exploited with a sharp-edged difference in his tribute to this player's artistry. The recordings are paragons of their kind, fairly close and detailed in the Strauss concertos to serve the hard-working textures Sawallisch draws from his orchestra. A likeable new contender has recently appeared on the scene featuring the horn-player David Pyatt (EMI Eminence) and offering a beguiling companion piece in the Duet Concertino, another late delight based on a dialogue between a clarinet Beauty and a Beast of a bassoon who turns into a handsome prince (of course) in the finale's happy-ever-after burblings. *DN*

STRAUSS

Metamorphosen
see WAGNER: Siegfried Idyll

STRAUSS

Orchestral music from Intermezzo, Capriccio, Die schweigsame Frau, Guntram & Die Frau ohne Schatten

Rotterdam PO/Jeffrey Tate

EMI CDC 7 54581 2 □ 75:00 mins □ ⊘⊘⊘

Had it been marketed unashamedly as featuring 'the most beautiful melodies from the Strauss operas', this marvellous disc might have achieved wider recognition at the time of its release. As it is, any playing to the gallery is nicely balanced by a fair amount of investigative spirit. 'Dream by the Fireside', third of the four symphonic interludes from *Intermezzo*, is Strauss's warmest, most profound tribute to the beautiful soul of his complex wife Pauline. Tate lets it evolve at leisure with painstaking tenderness as the great, occasionally disturbing love-song that it is. The Rotterdam strings, no muscle-rippling athletes, have intimacy on their side; lines expressively doubled with woodwind sound much more luminous when the burden is shared.

This is a chamber-musical Strauss in the Dresden ensemble tradition. It goes on to serve Tate admirably in the gaily conspiratorial Potpourri-Overture to *Die schweigsame Frau* and to illustrate neatly where Strauss parts company from his Wagnerian model in the prelude to his first opera, *Guntram*. It was a mistake to espouse the composer's half-hearted Fantasia on themes from *Die Frau ohne Schatten*; to have ended instead with the concert finale from the comedy *Feuersnot* would have given unbounded pleasure, but at least there's an unbroken hour of detachable delight before the mêlée. *DN*

STRAUSS

Orchestral Works (three volumes)

Dresden Staatskapelle/Rudolf Kempe

EMI CMS 7 64342 2, CMS 7 64346 2, CMS 7 64350 2 □ ADD □ **223:37 mins, 223:14 mins, 207:39 mins (3 discs each)** □ 🎵🎵

Ein Heldenleben; Also sprach Zarathustra; Till Eulenspiegels lustige Streiche; Tod und Verklärung; Don Juan; Dance of the Seven Veils from Salome; Der Rosenkavalier – Waltzes

Dresden Staatskapelle/Rudolf Kempe

EMI Rouge et Noir CZS 5 68110 2 □ ADD □ **156:56 mins (2 discs)** □ 🎵

Like Strauss himself as a conductor, Kempe was a natural: easy in his sense of movement, with never a rigid tempo in earshot (try the voluptuous first lady of *Don Juan* for flexibility) and certainly no seeker after extreme sensation. That might seem odd in music such as this, and there are some stretches of the tone poems where one momentarily longs for an over-the-top bravura beyond the ken of the Dresden orchestra. But that Kempe manages to keep in sight the shapely proportions of the organised Romantic's Classical structures while relishing the idiosyncrasies of the Straussian picture gallery seems, most of the time, exactly right. His *Till Eulenspiegel* is all things to all men, flipping from rage to insouciance at the tap of a shoulder, while *Don Quixote* – another multi-faceted performance, borne out by Tortelier's larger-than-life solo role – flies through the air at every sally.

In the three-volume format, rarities are distributed with a canniness that lovers of only first-rate Strauss might find distressing: on the first set, you have to wade your way through three oddities for piano and orchestra as well as the delightful Indian Summer concertos from a number of mellow Dresden soloists (no problem) before reaching the first three tone poems. An alternative Rouge et Noir two-CD bargain featuring the same recordings, on the other hand, provides the best possible Straussian cross-section and would be my top recommendation for *Ein Heldenleben* alone: Kempe, of all conductors, is the one to realise its mock-epic exuberance and not to take the heroics at solemn face value. The highly synthetic sound-packaging is warm and helpful at best (especially for a surprisingly genial *Also sprach Zarathustra*), at worst brutally up-front (hectoring strings in *Metamorphosen*). For the most part, Kempe and company come smiling through. *DN*

STRAUSS

Symphonia domestica; Till Eulenspiegels lustige Streiche; Zueignung; Die heiligen drei Könige

Felicity Lott (soprano); Scottish National Orchestra/Neeme Järvi

Chandos CHAN 8572 □ **65:51 mins** □ 🎵🎵🎵

Tolstoy might have reconsidered his verdict on the similarities of all happy families had he heard this one. No domestic ensemble can ever quite have resembled Papa, Mama and Bubi Strauss as transformed through symphonic metamorphoses of dazzling virtuosity – least of all in Järvi's half-tender, half-grotesque labour of love. He's not afraid to go flat out in quest of the final ridiculous exuberance of the protracted happy ending. Only Strauss the conductor, in a poorly recorded but astonishing 1944 Vienna performance (DG), takes the horn-whooping last rites at a similarly dangerous speed; the care of even the greats like Kempe, Clemens Krauss and Reiner at this point marks them down as lesser beings. The strings vocalise their often operatic phrases; despite diffuse acoustics, the woodwind detail is exemplary in the dewy-eyed lovely Scherzo sequence (shades of Mahler Four). A light and airy *Till Eulenspiegel* and two songs from the radiant Lott/Järvi partnership gild the measure: 'Die heiligen drei Könige' comes complete with another crying infant worthy to be worshipped in an orchestral postlude less rambunctious than Bubi's but no less warm-hearted. *DN*

STRAUSS

Tod und Verklärung
see also **CHORAL & SONG**: STRAUSS: Four Last Songs

STRAVINSKY

Agon
see also SHOSTAKOVICH: Symphony No. 15

Ballets, Vol. 1: The Firebird; Petrushka; The Rite of Spring; Les noces; Renard; The Soldier's Tale; Scherzo à la russe; Scherzo fantastique; Fireworks

Soloists; American Concert Choir, Columbia Percussion Ensemble, Columbia SO, CBC SO/Igor Stravinsky

Sony SM3K 46291 □ ADD □ 193:45 mins (3 discs) □ 𝄞𝄞

Ballets, Vol. 2: Apollo; Agon; Jeu de cartes; Scènes de ballet; Bluebird Pas de deux; Pulcinella; Orpheus

Irene Jordan (soprano), George Shirley (tenor), Donald Gramm (bass); Columbia SO, Los Angeles Festival SO, Cleveland Orchestra, Chicago SO/Igor Stravinsky

Sony SM3K 46292 □ ADD □ 202:03 mins (3 discs) □ 𝄞𝄞

The old adage that the composer invariably proves to be the best interpreter of his own music can be challenged in many instances, though not so much with Stravinsky, whose own recordings often provide the bench-mark by which other performances should be judged. Admittedly these discs, extracted from Sony's complete Stravinsky Edition, were made when the composer was well into his eighties. But the performances betray precious little sign of their conductor's venerable age, for they are characterised by tremendous rhythmic drive and an acute ear for instrumental detail.

Unfortunately, not everything here represents the last word in interpretations of this repertoire. For example, Les noces, sung in English, is a bitter disappointment, with some distinctly flabby piano-playing from the four composer pianists Copland, Barber, Sessions and Foss. The performance of Pulcinella is also let down by some poor singing. But in the three early ballets, and in Agon and Orpheus, Stravinsky is almost peerless; and while Rattle's Apollo remains first choice for this particular work, Stravinsky's own interpretation achieves great sublimity, especially in the closing pages. While the orchestral playing is not always as polished as on some more recent recordings, these two volumes remain indispensable. *EL*

Concerto in D
see HONEGGER: Symphonies Nos 2 & 3

The Fairy's Kiss Divertimento; Suites Nos 1 & 2; Octet; The Soldier's Tale – Suite

London Sinfonietta/Riccardo Chailly

Decca Enterprise 433 079-2 □ 75:42 mins □ 𝄞𝄞

This is a terrific disc that serves to remind one of the brilliance of the London Sinfonietta, whose championship of 20th-century music has so enriched the British musical scene. Under the incisive direction of Riccardo Chailly, the orchestra presents tremendously vibrant accounts of the Tchaikovsky-inspired Divertimento, the neo-classical Octet and the suite from L'histoire du soldat, the last-named performance if anything even more exciting than the composer's own recording for Sony. The two suites (drawn mainly from Satie-esque miniatures originally composed for piano duet) may be of lesser musical consequence than these particular works, but Chailly extracts the maximum degree of character from each movement, and the players revel in the many opportunities for ironic humour. With over 75 minutes of music at mid-price, this is a must for all Stravinsky enthusiasts. *EL*

Stravinsky: Dumbarton Oaks; Agon; Circus Polka; Greeting Prelude; Eight Instrumental Miniatures; Scherzo à la Russe; Scènes de ballet

Bach (arr. Stravinsky): Chorale Variations on 'Vom Himmel Hoch'

Gregg Smith Singers, Orchestra of St Luke's/Robert Craft

MusicMasters 01612-67113-2 □ 74:38 mins □ 𝄞𝄞𝄞

Subtitled 'American Stravinsky', the fourth volume of Robert Craft's masterly exploration of the composer's works offers the most invigorating performance of the late ballet Agon since Stravinsky's own pioneering 1957 version on Sony. The approach is characterised by sharp-edged rhythmic urgency, an impeccable ensemble and a wonderful transparency of texture. As in many of the other discs in this series, Craft favours swift tempi in order to maximise the physical impact of the music. This serves to enhance one's impression of the Scènes de ballet, previously regarded as one of Stravinsky's less distinctive scores. Dumbarton Oaks is equally riveting, and here Craft manages to convey the charm of the music without sacrificing its motoric energy. Those wishing to explore the nooks and crannies of the master's voluminous output are rewarded by some precious nuggets, in particular the original jazz-band version of the *Scherzo à la russe* with its jaunty echoes of the fairground scenes from *Petrushka*. *EL*

STRAVINSKY

Petrushka (1947 version); Pulcinella

Anna Caterina Antonacci (soprano), Pietro Ballo (tenor), William Shimell (bass); Royal Concertgebouw Orchestra/Riccardo Chailly

Decca 443 774-2 □ 73:06 mins □ 🍊🍊🍊

Over the years there have been several outstanding recordings of *Petrushka*, but choosing a top recommendation is by no means a straightforward process. For one thing, listeners need to decide whether they prefer the original and more opulently scored 1911 version of the work to the later and much leaner 1947 revision. And even then, some conductors muddy the waters by performing a compromise mixture of both scores.

My decision to choose Chailly in preference to others is determined not by a personal bias towards the 1947 version, but rather more by the brilliance of his interpretation, which abounds in fascinating detail and incisive characterisation of every internal detail in the score. It's a truly breathtaking experience, supported by outstanding orchestral playing. It's possible that Chailly's account is almost too febrile to allow for the more fragile and human aspects of the score. In this respect Claudio Abbado with the LSO, performing the 1911 version on a mid-price DG release, achieve greater poetry while maintaining a similar level of incisiveness. But DG's rather brash Eighties digital recording is no match for Chailly. If you still harbour doubts about this *Petrushka*, there's little need to hesitate over the *Pulcinella* – another *tour de force* of orchestral playing supported by expressive soloists and punctuated by moments of uproarious humour, not least in the solo trombone and double-bass antics of the famous Vivo movement. *EL*

STRAVINSKY

The Rite of Spring; Apollo

City of Birmingham SO/Simon Rattle

EMI CDC 7 49636 2 □ 65:10 mins □ 🍊🍊🍊

The Rite of Spring; Fireworks; Circus Polka; Greeting Prelude

LPO/Charles Mackerras

EMI Eminence CD-EMX 2188 □ 42:00 mins □ 🍊🍊

Since it came to be regarded as the archetypal virtuoso orchestral showpiece, conductors from all over the world have seemed only too eager to set down their interpretation of Stravinsky's *Rite*. Yet although the current catalogues boast a veritable feast of brilliantly executed recordings of this work, only a few really set the pulses racing. Among these, Stravinsky's own recording remains peerless, as does Igor Markevitch's blazing Fifties performance with the Philharmonia (on EMI). More recently, Bernard Haitink delivered a strong and deliberately unbombastic account with the LPO (on Philips Insignia) that still more than holds its own against some more glamorously recorded rivals.

Mackerras's dogged and often ferocious version follows very much in the Haitink mould. The conductor obeys Stravinsky's precise instructions to the letter, never subjecting the music to interpretative gimmicks. Given an excellent digital recording, this release is certainly worth serious attention, although the disc's other offerings are somewhat insubstantial.

For an entirely different, more thought-provoking version, I would turn to Rattle. A good starting-point is the 'Danse sacrale' in Part Two which is much more deliberately paced than normal. But it would be mistaken to infer from this that Rattle's interpretation lacks fire, for the performance concentrates more on achieving cumulative growth of tension. As such, it actually generates greater power than interpretations that are more overtly theatrical in nature. The coupling of *Apollo* is also highly imaginative, presenting side by side the two diametrically opposed sides of Stravinsky's musical personality. It's a performance of noble elegance and a marvellous testament to Rattle's outstanding achievements in Birmingham. *EL*

STRAVINSKY

Symphony in C; Symphony in Three Movements; Symphonies of Wind Instruments; Scherzo fantastique

Suisse Romande Orchestra, Montreal SO/Charles Dutoit

Decca Ovation 434 474-2 □ 71:11 mins □ 🍊🍊

Dutoit's Eighties recording of the two orchestral symphonies received an enthusiastic welcome in the early days of CD. Now reissued at mid-price, alongside the original version of the *Symphonies of Wind Instruments* and the early *Scherzo fantastique*, the performances have withstood the test of time and sound as fresh and exciting as ever.

Of course the Suisse Romande Orchestra possesses a particular affinity for Stravinsky's music, having recorded much of his orchestral output under their founder-conductor Ernest Ansermet. But in all honesty it was never a world-class ensemble, and some of the orchestral playing on Ansermet's recordings left much to be desired. Fortunately, no such criticism can be levelled against this particular disc, for it seems that Dutoit has inspired the same levels of clarity and precision of ensemble that he has achieved successfully with the Montreal SO. Furthermore, Dutoit more than matches the athleticism and energy of the composer's own accounts on Sony, but enjoys the added benefits of superior engineering and better disciplined orchestral playing. *EL*

STRAVINSKY
Symphony in C; Symphony in Three Movements
see also **CHORAL & SONG**: STRAVINSKY: Symphony of Psalms

STRAVINSKY
Symphonies of Wind Instruments
see also **CHORAL & SONG**: STRAVINSKY: Perséphone

STRAVINSKY/ROCHBERG

Stravinsky: Violin Concerto in D

Rochberg: Violin Concerto

Isaac Stern (violin); Columbia SO/Igor Stravinsky, Pittsburgh SO/André Previn

Sony SMK 64505 □ ADD □ 59:01 mins □ 🎵🎵

Stravinsky's Violin Concerto in D is regarded generally as one of the more percusive works in the 20th-century violin repertoire. Yet as this definitive recording shows, the spikiness of Stravinsky's writing represents only one aspect of the work. For instance, an examination of the two inner movements, both entitled Aria, illustrates not only Stravinsky's conscious attempt to emulate Bach but also a degree of emotional warmth not normally associated with the composer's neo-classical period. This element is certainly brought to the fore by Stern, who manages to sculpt the melodic line with greater subtlety than any of his rivals. In the outer movements, too, Stern, supported by an incisive orchestral accompaniment and an appropriately dry recording ambience, plays with absolute technical wizardry and, where appropriate, makes the most of the music's

satirical humour and its obvious allusions to *The Soldier's Tale*.

The coupling of George Rochberg's Violin Concerto may appear unappealing to those who would prefer Stravinsky to be paired with more mainstream items from the repertoire. But the music, dating from a period when this American composer was turning his back on the avant-garde style of his earlier period, is heartfelt and is certainly worth further exploration. *EL*

STRAVINSKY
Violin Concerto in D
see also SZYMANOWSKI: Violin Concertos Nos 1 & 2

SUK

Asrael Symphony

Bavarian RSO/Rafael Kubelík

Panton 81 1101-2 □ AAD □ 64:15 mins □ 🎵🎵🎵

The composition of the *Asrael* Symphony was inspired by two tragic experiences. In 1904 Dvořák died, and Suk, overcome by sadness, wished to honour his teacher and father-in-law through the writing of a grand symphony. But halfway through writing the work Suk's wife, Otylka, Dvořák's daughter, also died. Suk never recovered from this blow, but sublimated his grief through the completion of the symphony which was dedicated to the 'sublime memory of Dvořák and Otylka'.

The five-movement symphony was Suk's most ambitious composition, and its sustained level of emotional intensity and chromatic late-Romantic harmonic idiom invite obvious parallels with Mahler. It remains one of the towering masterpieces of the Czech orchestral repertoire.

Most of the currently available recordings of the work deserve commendation, not least the historical Talich/Czech Philharmonic (Supraphon) and Bělohlávek with the same orchestra (Chandos). One of the clear front-runners, however, comes from Libor Pešek and the Royal Liverpool Philharmonic (Virgin) recorded in 1990 – a magnificent performance full of interpretative insight and distinguished by outstanding engineering. It would have been my unequivocal first choice had it not been for the release of this overwhelming Bavarian Radio broadcast from 1981 in which the legendary Rafael Kubelík extracts even more passion and fervour from the music than any of his colleagues. *EL*

SUK/JANACEK

Suk: Serenade for String Orchestra; Meditation on an Old Czech Hymn 'St Wenceslas'

Janáček: Suite for String Orchestra

Virtuosi di Praga/Oldřich Vlček

Koch Discover International DICD 920234
□ 51:39 mins □ 🎵

Suk's String Serenade dates from 1892 when the composer was the star pupil of Dvořák. It's an effortlessly melodious work that is worthy of comparison with his master's equally attractive E major Serenade. In contrast, the Meditation, composed at the outbreak of the First World War, is much darker and emotionally intense, recalling the manner of Suk's orchestral masterpiece, the *Asrael* Symphony. These two works prove an attractive foil for the early Janáček Suite for String Orchestra, an appealing composition, though one that barely hints at the startling originalities of his later output. Fine performances from these outstanding Czech players, coupled with clear if somewhat bright sound, make this an enticing issue which should not be missed at such a give-away price. *EL*

SZYMANOWSKI/STRAVINSKY

Szymanowski: Violin Concertos Nos 1 & 2

Stravinsky: Violin Concerto in D

Chantal Juillet (violin); Montreal SO/Charles Dutoit

Decca 436 837-2 □ 69:43 mins □ 🎵🎵🎵

Szymanowski's two violin concertos are an ideal way of getting to know this sensual late-Romantic composer. By any standards this is a fine recording, beautifully engineered, with violin and orchestra well balanced. The Montreal players produce a sumptuous, full-blooded sound, with clear detail from solo wind and muted brass. Chantal Juillet is a characterful soloist, well on top of the tricky cadenzas Szymanowski cooked up with his friend, the virtuoso Pavel Kochanski.

I have some doubts, though. The First Concerto, like Szymanowski's songs of the period, is shot through with subtle orientalism, while the Second is soaked in Polish folk tradition. One waits in vain for those extremes – exotic delicacy, or real gut-raspiness. Instead of magic fireflies and quick flashes of lightning, you keep hearing John Williams-like themes bursting from the woodwork.

Szymanowski, one suspects, would still prefer Rowicki's rickety old Olympia recording with Wanda Wilkomirska. I would buy this

disc for the relaxed Stravinsky concerto that precedes, with the Szymanowski as a bonus. The pairing is a good one: and if Stravinsky's quirkiness gets lost, the Bach-like underlay doesn't. It offers a cosy way into a still curiously little-known Stravinsky work. *Roderic Dunnett*

SZYMANOWSKI

Mandragora
see **CHORAL & SONG**: SZYMANOWSKI: Harnasie

TAKEMITSU

Dreamtime; Nostalghia; Vers, l'arc-en-ciel, Palma; Far Calls, Coming, Far!; A Flock Descends into the Pentagonal Garden

Michael Duath (violin), Norio Satoh (guitar), Jeffrey Crellin (oboe d'amore); Melbourne SO/Hiroyuki Iwaki

ABC 8.770006 □ 59:27 mins □ 🎵🎵🎵

Toru Takemitsu became by far the best known of Japanese composers in the West, partly through his film music for Akira Kurosawa but mostly because his work, for all its 'oriental' character of meditation and calligraphic precision, relates so closely to European traditions and thus falls easily on the western ear. Takemitsu's fascination with Debussian impressionism is patent in these exquisitely colourful pieces, and *Dreamtime* could almost be a John Williams-type score for a Steven Spielberg interstellar epic were it not for the post-Messiaen ecstasy of some of the harmonic writing. Though he's sometimes ranked as an avant-gardist, most of Takemitsu's works sweetly beguile. *Nostalghia* for violin and strings, written for Yehudi Menuhin and dedicated to the memory of the Russian film director Andrei Tarkovsky, will faze nobody who warms to the gentler passages of the Berg concerto; while *Vers l'arc-en-ciel, Palma*, a kind of concerto for guitar and oboe d'amore, refers lyrically to Catalan folk-song and Spanish guitar style. This well-played, excellently recorded anthology of Takemitsu's music includes one of his best-known pieces, the hypnotic, MC Escher-inspired *A Flock Descends into the Pentagonal Garden*. This is definitely modern music without tears, but also a glimpse into a unique imaginative world. *CM*

TANEYEV

Suite de concert
see MIASKOVSKY: Cello Concerto

TCHAIKOVSKY

Andante cantabile
see PROKOFIEV: Symphony-Concerto

1812 Overture; Marche Slave
see RIMSKY-KORSAKOV: Russian Easter Festival
Overture

Francesca da Rimini; Serenade for Strings; Marche Slave

USSR Ministry of Culture SO/Gennady
Rozhdestvensky

Erato 2292-45629-2 □ **67:50 mins** □ 🎵🎵🎵

Here, on a single disc, are the two extremes of
Tchaikovsky's musical personality. Both the
light of the Serenade for Strings, straight from
the heart as the composer declared, and the
darkness of *Francesca da Rimini*, a narrative of
doomed love pursued by hellfire with the usual
element of searing autobiography concealed
within, receive big-hearted, expansive
performances. Some listeners may feel that
inappropriate in the case of the Serenade;
exposed regularly to the chamber-orchestra
point of view, we sometimes miss the nimble
spring in the heel (in which case there are
plenty of sunny alternatives, with Marriner's
Academy of St Martin in the Fields top of the
list). Rozhdestvensky simply adapts to the
grand symphonic string sound of his Russian
players, something that Tchaikovsky himself
must have envisaged; sonority, especially in the
violas and cellos, is never less than gorgeous.

About the Dantean tragedy *Francesca* there
can be no doubt. Rozhdestvensky realises the
fiery inferno and the central sorrowing, a love
scene to surpass that of *Romeo and Juliet*, with
magisterial breadth and sense of atmosphere.
Vivid recording spectacularly supports the odd
extra percussive touch, exciting rather than
overdone. Don't overlook the old Stokowski
roller-coaster, putting the hair-raising point
across despite coarse sound (Dell'Arte, with
the curiously selective *Hamlet* Fantasia). *DN*

Manfred Symphony; Romeo and Juliet

NBC SO/Arturo Toscanini

RCA Victor Gold Seal GD 60298 □ **ADD mono**
□ **66:40 mins** □ 🎵🎵

Why put up with a *Manfred* shamelessly re-
touched in the orchestration of its first
movement and extensively cut in its finale
(though not re-composed, as many conductors
today prefer it, to avoid the ghastly bathos of
its weakest point, the ultimate apotheosis)?
Because this is Toscanini, and no subsequent
version has been more even-handed in
reaching to the heart of the work's dark

passions without losing absolute clarity in
textures, rhythm and an overall sense of
direction.

The opening bars – a tribute, apparently, to
the fateful shipboard meeting of Wagner's
Tristan and Isolde – seize the listener by the
throat, and not even the occasional distortions
of the 1949 recording can momentarily release
us from Toscanini's spell. He wrests an
astonishing virtuosity from his American
orchestra in one of the most treacherously
difficult and at the same time scintillatingly
scored scherzos in the repertoire (the model
here is Berlioz's 'Queen Mab' Scherzo from
Romeo and Juliet) and even the fustian curtain
to the work, so alien to Tchaikovsky's nature,
falls painlessly. The narrative of Tchaikovsky's
own *Romeo and Juliet* moves, as one might
expect, with unparalleled speed and vividness;
less predictably, there's an aching tenderness in
the love music. *DN*

The Nutcracker

Ambrosian Singers, LSO/André Previn

Classics for Pleasure CD-CFPD 4706 □ **ADD**
□ **86:04 mins (2 discs)** □ 🎵

There have been numerous recordings of the
complete *Nutcracker* since Previn launched his
Tchaikovsky ballets series with the LSO in
1972 – not least another from the same
conductor for the same record company,
surplus to need and not so good – but none
more richly coated or exotically spiced. As
master of the long symphonic paragraph, he
takes us into seventh heaven for the after-
midnight developments of Act I – two great
scenes which, like the sumptuous *pas de deux*,
show us Tchaikovsky extracting real magic
from something as basic as portions of the
rising, or falling, scale. On the simpler but no
less intricately wrought level of dancing
entertainment, Previn finds all the necessary
exuberance in the Act II *divertissement*, making
us wonder more than ever why rumbustious
Mother Gigogne never found her way into
Tchaikovsky's own seven-movement suite (or
for that matter certain choreographed
versions).

Opulently recorded in vintage EMI sound,
this is now one of the best bargains in the
catalogue; there seems no reason why anyone
need look elsewhere. Excerpts feature on a
single CD (EMI Studio Plus – apt because this
is the familiar ballet suites 'plus') with
imaginatively selected plums from the other
two ballets in performances of an almost hectic

---

brilliance: still the best ballet highlights disc in an overcrowded market. If you want even more, there are two CDs-worth of excerpts on EMI Rouge et Noir, but why not just settle for all three ballets in their tirelessly inventive entirety. *DN*

TCHAIKOVSKY

Piano Concerto No. 1 in B flat minor
see RACHMANINOV: Piano Concerto No. 2

TCHAIKOVSKY

Piano Concertos Nos 2 in G & 3 in E flat

Peter Donohoe (piano); Bournemouth SO/Rudolf Barshai

EMI CDC 7 49940 2 □ 63:13 mins □ 🎵🎵🎵

Epic high spirits and generous invention abound in the second, and by no means the weaker, of Tchaikovsky's two full-scale piano concertos. What it needs is an unashamedly big-boned approach – Donohoe is merely the latest in a long line of extrovert, thundering giants – as well as faith in the original broad canvas. There this recording made special headway; it had been Russian performing tradition to adhere to the 'edition' of Tchaikovsky's pupil, Alexander Siloti, which so drastically reduces the 'triple concerto' dimensions of the second movement. EMI fanfared its support for the composer's expansive first thoughts by engaging two other outstanding British-born soloists of the younger generation; the resulting teamwork is aristocratic. The one-movement Third Concerto, based on themes for a symphony Tchaikovsky discarded in favour of the *Pathétique*, is rather short on striking ideas and piquant orchestration – both abounding in the scintillating *Concert Fantasy*, featured in Donohoe's Vol. 1 – but it does give us another chance to hear the pianist's heavyweight bravura in a huge piano cadenza. *DN*

TCHAIKOVSKY

The Sleeping Beauty

Orchestra of the Royal Opera House, Covent Garden/Mark Ermler

Royal Opera House 74321 16075 2 □ 172:39 mins (3 discs) □ 🎵🎵🎵

Stravinsky rated the complete, three-hour score of *The Sleeping Beauty* as Tchaikovsky's finest achievement, and listening to Ermler's opulent labour of love it's hard to disagree. The conductor takes advantage of studio circumstances to pull himself out from under the dancers' more or less tyrannical feet and to aim for an expansively symphonic

interpretation which pulls all the stops out for the big moments. None is more riveting than the prince's breaking of the spell in Act II and the spellbinding tone poem of Aurora's sleep that precedes it (against a significant hundred-bar high C tremolo from muted violins – pure genius!) For that alone, a touchstone of Tchaikovsky's inspiration never excerpted in any of the concert-hall suites, I would want this set.

Ermler is also thoroughly delightful in the dances and variations of the fairies at Aurora's christening and the fairy-tale characters at her wedding, well prepared to go for high velocity in several presto codas. Gergiev on Philips is more consistently nimble, less willing to overwhelm and tends to keep his brass more in check; the Kirov sound is both drier and less exaggerated than the Conifer spectacular. For the real magic and the true *frisson*, however, Ermler has to come first. *DN*

TCHAIKOVSKY

The Sleeping Beauty (excerpts, arr. Pletnev)
see **INSTRUMENTAL**: MUSSORGSKY: Pictures at an Exhibition

TCHAIKOVSKY

Swan Lake

Russian State SO/Yevgeny Svetlanov

BMG Melodiya 74321 17082 2 □ 153:36 mins (3 discs) □ 🎵🎵

In the absence of Rozhdestvensky's dark and dashing Melodiya recording, another Russian *Swan Lake* fills the authentic bill well enough. Svetlanov's team – formerly the USSR State Symphony Orchestra – knows its mind, and when Soviet engineering could be bothered to work in its favour (as here) the results can at times be electrifying. Stocked with ingenious melodies, some of the first successful symphonic narrative in ballet (before the lakeside *divertissement* of Act II) and a string of inventive waltzes, *Swan Lake* sometimes lacks the orchestral variety of its balletic successors, and it takes a conductor of sweeping energy to spare us a certain fatigue (all that brass and percussion!). Svetlanov breezes through the scenes and variations with panache, saving his idiosyncrasies – apart from a whirling princess or two at the Act III ball – for the final tragedy, where blaring trumpets may not be to all tastes.

The Russian rawness of it all would hardly do for *The Sleeping Beauty* or *The Nutcracker*, but it works here. Sawallisch and the Philadelphia Orchestra, in rich and spacious EMI sound, tell a more sophisticated story – if that's what you want – and manage to include (on two full-to-the-brim CDs) the supplementary *pas de deux* mostly orchestrated by Vissarion Shebalin, which can't be accommodated here on three discs (admittedly at a cheaper price). *DN*

Symphonies Nos 1–6; Romeo and Juliet

Philharmonia Orchestra, New Philharmonia Orchestra/Riccardo Muti

EMI CZS 7 67314 2 □ **ADD** □ **272:29 mins (4 discs)** □ *⊘*

It can be no coincidence that outside Russia the two outstanding interpreters of Tchaikovsky in recent years, Riccardo Muti and Claudio Abbado, both happen to be Italian. Passionate temperament may have something to do with it, but the urgent vocalising of the lyrical themes, and the natural sense of rubato necessary to carry them off without false rhetoric or sentimentality, seems to come naturally to these great exponents of Italian opera. At the zenith of his heady Philharmonia days, Muti rose most consistently to the challenge – revealing with a wealth of keenly observed detail the often experimental riches of the earlier symphonies, keeping the aspirations of the 'great three' (Nos 4, 5 and 6) fresh and flexible without any loss of expressive power.

His *Little Russian* (the nationalistic No. 2) is quite the most score-faithful of interpretations in a surprisingly quirky field, as well as the most exciting in the finale's string of leg-kicking variations on a Ukrainian folk-song (though the bass drum, as in the Fourth, is over-emphatically recorded). Unsurpassable, too, is the Fifth; again, Muti's operatic experience helps him to prove, with true conducting mastery, what a great invention the Andante cantabile really is. A powerful, intensely serious *Romeo and Juliet* fills the measure; though the absence of *Manfred*, arguably more tone poem than symphony but uniquely resourceful in terms of orchestration, proves the rule rather than the exception to the Tchaikovsky cycles; neither the Philips reissue of the bracing Markevitch series nor Temirkanov's six-CD set on RCA, fascinating alternatives both, includes it. Incidentally, if RCA ever manages separate release for Temirkanov's performances of the First and Third symphonies, remarkable for unearthing incipient melancholy beneath the Classical surface without superimposing a layer of

indiscriminate emotion, then both would be top recommendations. The same applies to the Muti Second, which has not been available on a single disc for some time. *DN*

Symphonies Nos 4–6

Leningrad PO/Yevgeny Mravinsky

DG 419 745-2 □ **ADD** □ **128:55 mins (2 discs)** □ *⊘⊘*

St Petersburg PO/Yuri Temirkanov

RCA Victor Red Seal 09026 61377 2 □ **144:07 mins (2 discs)** □ *⊘⊘⊘*

At first glance this might seem like a slot misused – instead of a top recommendation for each of the three most-recorded Tchaikovsky symphonies, the entire half-cycle offered in duplicate. What I hope it does provide is a yardstick for the two poles of Tchaikovsky interpretation, the Classically articulate (Mravinsky, of course, the great pioneer) and the sumptuously idiosyncratic (Temirkanov). Both have their followings and their virtues; and in these two opposite poles featuring the Leningrad, subsequently St Petersburg, PO in recordings over three decades apart (Mravinsky 1960, Temirkanov 1992), there are all the rare qualities necessary to make these works sound newly minted against all odds.

Conversely, one has to put up with the faults: with Temirkanov, a doom fanfare for the Fourth that stretches the St Petersburg brass beyond the call of duty; with Mravinsky, the hectic onslaught of the Fifth's finale almost missing the sense of conflict in machine-like drilling and processing. But it would be reductive to say that Mravinsky, a scrupulous rehearser of the symphonies no matter how often he'd performed them, cares only for the notes; when he finds a sense of what's behind them, as in the first movement of the *Pathétique* and the scintillating later stages of the Fourth, the mixture of passion and precision is unsurpassed. Likewise in Temirkanov's case: master of dark atmosphere in Five and Six, he asks for sustained inspiration from his players and gets it. Unlike the earlier (Wembley Town Hall!) recording, a rare opportunity wisely seized on the Russians' visit to London, the RCA engineering isn't instantly easy to like. It reflects the slightly dry but very truthful acoustic of the wonderful 1830s Petersburg Philharmonic Hall, in which the orchestra lives and breathes. That only makes one come to value all the more how much of the warmth comes from within the playing. *DN*

TCHAIKOVSKY

Symphony No. 6 in B minor (Pathétique); Violin Concerto in D

Yehudi Menuhin (violin); Berlin PO, RIAS SO, Berlin/Ferenc Fricsay

DG Dokumente 445 409-2 □ ADD mono □ 72:11 mins □ 🎵🎵

Fricsay stands alongside Toscanini and Mravinsky in reaching to the heart of Tchaikovsky's ultimate tragedy with swift emotion and ferocious articulation. Add greater inwardness of feeling and you have the complete *Pathétique*, its shattering first-movement development firmly shaped with all due concern for the pain that lies behind it, and a finale of more profoundly personal suffering than any other. Fricsay's Berlin strings are alive to every nuance, conjuring a kaleidoscope of human emotions (and the most vivacious of march-scherzos) before catastrophe strikes.

You'll need to be fairly hard-hearted to stop the player after the final descent to black oblivion; the Violin Concerto strikes up rather too soon. It makes a generous companion piece in Menuhin's fluent but not especially warm reading. The sound can be coarse at times (a few years later, DG would have it exactly right for Fricsay); vivid recent options include white-heat Ashkenazy (Decca), and the slightly more calculating Pletnev (Virgin), who, despite numerous accolades, has yet to convince me that his Russian National Orchestra is a team with a voice like Svetlanov's USSR (now Russian) State SO or Rozhdestvensky's Moscow RSO. *DN*

TCHAIKOVSKY

Variations on a Rococo Theme
see DVORAK: Cello Concerto in B minor
and PROKOFIEV: Symphony-Concerto

TCHAIKOVSKY

Violin Concerto in D
see also GLAZUNOV: Violin Concerto in A minor

TELEMANN:

Concertos in A minor and B flat for Two Recorders
see Collection: Concerti di flauti

TELEMANN

Ouvertures in C, D & B flat

The English Concert/Trevor Pinnock

Archiv 437 558-2 □ 76:52 mins □ 🎵🎵🎵

The four orchestral *Ouvertures* of Bach have unjustly overshadowed the 130-plus of

---

Telemann. These three, one long published, the others newly transcribed, reveal great wit and individuality. In the familiar C major suite, oboes pretend to be trumpets; 'sleep' is depicted by lazy, lingering last notes. The performance shows Baroque oboe- and bassoon-playing of the highest order, purposefully articulated, immaculately in tune.

Two hunting-horns add a sizzling coarse edge to the tone quality in the second *Ouverture*, and the playing of these notoriously hazardous instruments is similarly first rate – virtually crack-free, flexible and unfailingly in tune.

The third suite reverts to the solo group of three oboes and bassoon, beginning with a French overture which becomes a jocose gigue in echo between wind quartet and strings. The following movements are astonishingly imaginative and varied, including the drowsiest of Airs, a vigorously Vivaldian 'Combattans' and a Passepied with a teasingly ambiguous pulse.

Pinnock's phrasing is always purposeful without becoming quirky, and he imparts great rhythmic energy from the harpsichord in the middle of The English Concert.

This is a delightful disc, full of colour and melodies which linger in the memory long after the music has stopped. *GP*

TELEMANN

Trumpet Concerto
see Collection: Baroque Trumpet Music

TIPPETT

Concerto for Double String Orchestra; Fantasia Concertante on a Theme of Corelli; Piano Concerto; Piano Sonatas Nos 1 & 2; String Quartet No. 1

Yehudi Menuhin, John Masters (violin), Derek Simpson (cello), John Ogdon (piano); Edinburgh Quartet, Moscow CO/Rudolf Barshai, Bath Festival Orchestra/Michael Tippett, Philharmonia Orchestra/Colin Davis

EMI CMS 7 63522 2 □ ADD □ 125:31 mins (2 discs) □ 🎵🎵

This mid-price compilation of classic Tippett performances from the early Sixties is exceptionally good value, offering as it does the composer's own blazingly passionate account of the Corelli Fantasia, on any reckoning one of the greatest works in the British string-orchestra repertoire and served here as never since by the virtuosity of Menuhin and his fellow soloists. This is an ecstatic, quite transcendental reading and should be in any collection.

The popular Double Concerto, no less a classic of the string repertoire, is exceptionally powerfully projected (though with real lyric meditation in the beautiful slow movement) by the weighty combination of the Moscow and Bath orchestras in Barshai's urgent, committed reading. And John Ogdon's premiere recording of the Piano Concerto is still in many ways the best, with an inimitable sense of spreading, light-suffused landscape in the floating vistas of the broad opening movement. Ogdon is excellent, too, in the first two piano sonatas, especially the severe, mosaic-like No. 2, so radical-seeming when it first appeared, marking as it did an abrupt change of direction from Tippett's lyric style to a starker, more confrontational music. The sound is rather dry in the Edinburgh Quartet's sturdy account of the First String Quartet, but otherwise comes up superbly, the CD transfer doing something to clarify the Piano Concerto's intricate textures. There is no better anthology of Tippett's early work in the orchestral and instrumental fields. *CM*

TOCH
Five Pieces for Wind and Percussion
see WEILL: Violin Concerto

TRUSCOTT

Suite in G; Elegy; Symphony in E

National SO of Ireland/Gary Brain

Marco Polo 8.223674 □ 60:49 mins □ ❷❷❷

The late Harold Truscott, one of the most formidably learned British writers on music this past half-century, had a uniquely discouraging beginning as a composer: his own father, taking his early compositional attempts as a sign of insanity, had him committed to a mental institution. Later, he studied with Herbert Howells and became a noted teacher, but was better known in his lifetime as a writer and broadcaster than for his own compositions. The core of his *oeuvre* encompassed 17 piano sonatas (sadly none of the several LP recordings by Peter Jacobs is available on CD). There are some fine chamber works (look out for another Marco Polo disc, with Czech performers, including Truscott's First Clarinet Sonata, surely one of the best ever written in this genre) and a few orchestral scores, almost none of which he heard played in his lifetime.

He never, for example, heard the ecstatic, wind-swept *Elegy* (1943), which emerges in this world premiere performance and recording as a searing masterpiece of English string writing. Truscott's only completed

symphony (1949), which has a submerged programme based on Christ's Passion, first suggests parallels with Nielsen and Robert Simpson, then echoes Mahler in the mocking central Scherzo, and finally Bruckner in the gaunt grandeur of the long Adagio finale: not 'influences' but the necessary allusions of a well-stocked mind. The late Suite in G has ironic wit, lyricism and drastic concision in equal measure. Sterling, utterly committed performances by Gary Brain and his Irish orchestra; the symphony is the great work, but the *Elegy* alone would make this disc a real discovery, worth the attention of any collector of British music. *CM*

TUBIN

Symphonies Nos 3 & 8

Swedish RSO/Neeme Järvi

BIS CD-342 □ 62:46 mins □ ❷❷❷

The Estonian composer Eduard Tubin (1905–82) was driven out of his country by the Soviet occupation in 1944 and spent the rest of his life in exile in Sweden, virtually unknown outside his native and adopted lands until the dawn of the CD era and the championship of his fellow-Estonian Neeme Järvi. Now Tubin's 11 symphonies (the last unfinished), two operas and many other works are available, mostly on BIS; he has been 'discovered' as one of the major symphonists of the Baltic region. Certainly, his deeply sincere, finely crafted music will appeal to anyone who enjoys Sibelius or Holmboe. Whether it quite has their profundity or individuality is open to question; and not all the symphonies are equally impressive. But the two on this disc are among his finest inspirations. The Third (1940–2) is clearly the genuine article from the opening bars. The tense, dramatic first movement gives way to a dancing Scherzo with a meltingly beautiful violin solo for Trio, and then an optimistic, march-like finale with a surprisingly English air and triumphal coda. Premiered during Estonia's struggle with the Nazi invaders, one can see why it was so enthusiastically received, and its spirit remains potent today. No. 8 (1966) is an altogether darker and more dissonant work, two slowish movements enclosing two scherzos. The tragic mood – and the influence of Shostakovich – becomes unmistakable in the powerful finale. Järvi directs performances of utter commitment in good-quality BIS sound. *CM*

VARESE

Amériques; Offrandes; Hyperprism; Octandre; Arcana

Phyllis Bryn-Julson (soprano); French National Orchestra/Kent Nagano

Erato 4509-92137-2 □ 60:48 mins □ ❷❷❷

Varèse's life was an uncompromising struggle for new worlds of the imagination and new means of producing sound. He conceived music as a marriage of science and magic, conjuring a sonic cosmos studded with crystalline forms and 'intelligent' sounds moving in space. In 1919 a warehouse fire consumed almost everything he had composed up to his thirties. In the rest of his life only about a dozen works survived his angry self-criticism, depression and frustration with conventional instruments long enough to get completed. Every one is a classic of our century. All his works of the Twenties – his most productive decade – are on this disc. Nagano brings out superbly the sonic refinement, rhythmic subtlety, transparent percussion writing and sculpted lyricism of the two ensemble pieces; and the song diptych *Offrandes* has never sounded more fragile, more beautifully Debussian. But there's a fatal lack of aggression and visceral punch in Nagano's approach to the two big orchestral frescos, *Amériques* and *Arcana*, superbly though he illuminates their supernova textures. Here Boulez (mid-price Sony) is stronger – but there are yet more stunning versions if you want Varèse to blow your hi-fi system. In *Arcana*, try Chailly on Decca (coupled with Prokofiev's Third Symphony and Mosolov's *Iron Foundry*); and *Amériques*, also on Decca, is titanically well done by Christoph von Dohnányi and the Cleveland Orchestra, coupled equally appropriately with Ives's Fourth Symphony. *CM*

VARESE

Amériques
see also IVES: Symphony No. 4

VARESE/CARTER

Varèse: Déserts; Ecuatorial; Hyperprism

Carter: A Symphony of Three Orchestras

Ensemble InterContemporain, Choeurs de Radio France, New York Philharmonic/Pierre Boulez

Sony SMK 68334 □ ADD □ 48:34 mins □ ❷❷

Varèse's *Déserts*, four stark, granitic episodes for large ensemble with three taped interpolations manipulating various natural sounds, is one of the first, and still the greatest, combinations of orchestra and electronics. Its premiere, at Paris's Théâtre des Champs-Elysées in 1953, caused the greatest scandal the hall had seen since the first performance of *The Rite of Spring*. I was astounded to discover – for it's nowhere admitted on case or notes – that Boulez simply plays the instrumental sections without the tape. They're very well played, and Varèse did sanction such a procedure – but surely only as a counsel of despair: it's like performing Beethoven's Ninth Symphony without the chorus. The only complete recording remains Robert Craft's pioneering CBS version, not at present available. But this disc is still an outright recommendation, for *Ecuatorial*, Varèse's setting of a Mayan prayer to the powers of nature, is one of his very greatest works, a tremendous evocation of jungle vastness and ancient ritual with its frenzied choral writing and weird, swooping duets for ondes martenots. Boulez pierces its sonic fabric as never before. That little volcano, *Hyperprism*, is pungently done too. There is an older, sturdy version of *Ecuatorial* by Maurice Abravanel and the Utah Symphony on Vanguard Classics, valuably coupled with Varèse's otherwise-unrecorded last work, *Nocturnal*, and a performance of *Amériques* that was good in its day but now outclassed by more recent accounts. Boulez, instead, offers one of Elliott Carter's toughest works: the *Symphony of Three Orchestras* is quite short but spans the heights and depths of orchestral space in an extraordinarily freewheeling manner, creating some very unusual instrumental combinations and fearsome tuttis on the way. A must for any contemporary music collection. *CM*

VAUGHAN WILLIAMS/ELGAR

Vaughan Williams: Fantasia on a Theme of Thomas Tallis; Fantasia on Greensleeves

Elgar: Introduction and Allegro; Serenade in E minor; Elegy, Op. 58; Sospiri

Allegri Quartet, Sinfonia of London, New Philharmonia Orchestra/John Barbirolli

EMI CDC 7 47537 2 □ ADD □ 58:00 mins □ ❷❷❷

There are many fine recordings of Fantasia on a Theme of Thomas Tallis, but for me this is the greatest performance of all. Barbirolli's searingly spiritual account of 1963 seems to penetrate right to the heart of this most mystical of Vaughan Williams's works, and the string-playing has a radiance surely never equalled on disc. And it comes, at mid-price, with what must be one of the finest-ever recordings of Elgar's *Introduction and Allegro*. No one, it seems to me, has ever got as much juice out of this work, with its magnificently resonant string writing, and the final climax (replete with Barbirolli's paroxysmal groans, which only add to the experience) is quite overwhelming. The balance of quartet (here the fine Allegri Quartet) and string orchestra is most sensitively handled. The shorter pieces are all delightfully done; the Elgar Serenade is particularly stylish. These recordings are jewels of the EMI catalogue and every enthusiast for British music should possess this disc. If you must have the main Vaughan Williams and Elgar items in up-to-date sound, Christopher Warren-Green and the London Chamber Orchestra on Virgin provide probably the most outstanding modern version. *CM*

VAUGHAN WILLIAMS

Film Music: 49th Parallel – Prelude; Story of a Flemish Farm – Suite; Coastal Command – Suite; Three Portraits from The England of Elizabeth

RTE Concert Orchestra/Andrew Penny

Marco Polo 8.223665 □ 67:39 mins □ 🎵🎵🎵

The close connection between Vaughan Williams's wartime film music and his symphonies is patent in the noble, long-spanned melody of the *Forty-Ninth Parallel* Prelude, depicting the snowy wastes of the Canadian Rockies and like a hopeful major-key version of the opening of *Sinfonia antartica*. Then turn to the track called 'The Dead Man's Kit' from *Story of a Flemish Farm* to hear presages of the glacial finale of Symphony No. 6: in fact, the composer admitted that the symphony began with discarded ideas from the film score. Perhaps best of all, however, is in the superbly invigorating score for *Coastal Command*, a fine example of patriotic semi-documentary full of flying-boats, aerial combat and U-boats. Here the title music is first cousin to the Galliard of the Sons of the Morning from *Job*, while the 'Battle of the Beauforts' movement brings pre-echoes of the Scherzo and finale of the Ninth Symphony. Surprisingly substantial and thoroughly characteristic, this music is performed with obvious enthusiasm by the RTE Orchestra in a very lively recording. *CM*

VAUGHAN WILLIAMS

Job: a Masque for Dancing; The Wasps – Overture & incidental music

LPO/Adrian Boult

Belart 461 122-2 □ AAD mono □ 69:32 mins □ 🎵

A ballet of symphonic stature and gravity inspired by William Blake's visionary engravings for the Book of Job, Vaughan Williams's *Job: a Masque for Dancing* is quite simply one of his greatest works, spanning his full expressive range – from the serene rhapsody of Elihu's Dance (shades of *The Lark Ascending*) to the grandeur of God's music, the invigorating stride of the angelic Galliard, the profound quietude of opening and close, and the dissonance and graphic violence of the music associated with Satan, so prophetic of the grim Fourth Symphony. Adrian Boult recorded it twice: his second version (currently on Everest Classics) is paradoxically in poorer (though stereo) sound than in this 1955 mono version, which is of the same vintage as his pioneering Decca cycle of the symphonies. No conductor has revealed as much in this wonderful score, or with such passion and intelligence. There's no valid reason to look further, but if you must have modern stereo sound, Barry Wordsworth on Collins offers a real sonic spectacle, and a useful coupling in Holst's *Perfect Fool* ballet music. Boult's coupling, of similar Fifties vintage, is *The Wasps* – almost complete (the Kitchen Utensils lack the Trio of their march). Some of the other numbers deserve to be as well known as the famous overture. *CM*

VAUGHAN WILLIAMS/FOULDS

Vaughan Williams: Piano Concerto

Foulds: Dynamic Triptych, Op. 88

Howard Shelley (piano); RPO/Vernon Handley

Lyrita SRCD 211 □ 57:05 mins □ 🎵🎵🎵

Vaughan Williams's Piano Concerto (1931) was long neglected – and heard only in the composer's less effective version for two pianos, its large stretches having proved too much for the original dedicatee, Harriet Cohen. It has recently been revalued as one of his most powerful and characteristic works. Its sinewy polyphony, ecstatic slow movement and massive, sometimes almost baleful orchestral tuttis align it with *Job* and Symphony No. 4, to which it was close coeval.

Howard Shelley has recorded it twice, and this, his earlier version, is in some respects preferable to his later one for Chandos – there is a greater fire and sense of urgency to the playing, and the recording, one of Lyrita's finest, is cleaner and more vivid. The coupling is equally fascinating: John Foulds's concerto-like *Dynamic Triptych* (1929) is a work of amazing inventiveness, its toccata-like first movement based on an unusual modal scale, its finale an exciting study in ever-changing rhythms. Between these comes a slow movement of overwhelming Romantic lyricism, full of prophetic touches (including quarter-tones in the strings). There is no rival version. *CM*

VAUGHAN WILLIAMS

Symphonies Nos 1–9; Flos campi; Serenade to Music

Joan Rodgers, Alison Barlow, Alison Hargan (soprano), William Shimell (baritone), Christopher Balmer (viola); Liverpool Philharmonic Choir, Royal Liverpool PO/Vernon Handley

EMI Eminence CDBOX VW1 □ DDD/ADD (No. 7 only) □ **393:34 mins (6 discs)** □ 🎵🎵

It's true, and precious, that each generation brings new insights to and discovers new treasures in the Vaughan Williams symphonies. But it's equally true that any contemporary conductor must glean after Barbirolli over a stubble that Boult has reaped. There's little room for improvement on the humanity and understanding of those great musicians and friends of the composer. (The same applies to Elgar, with the added force that the composer himself was first in the field with matchless interpretations of his symphonies, whereas Vaughan Williams recorded only one of his.) Neither Boult nor Barbirolli quite produced an integral cycle, however (Boult's first Ninth was for Everest, not Decca), whereas the current catalogues show three: by Vernon Handley, Leonard Slatkin (RCA) and Bryden Thomson (Chandos). All are consummate interpreters, offering technically assured performances (and more than that) in state-of-the-art sound. The order in which I've listed them is also my order of preference, though Handley pips Slatkin by only a small margin. Perhaps his rapport with the RLPO, and the ruggedness he finds in Vaughan Williams's architecture, without ever straining the music's natural sense of flow, gives him a slight edge over the American conductor. He is strongest in Symphonies Nos 2 to 5 and in 7 and 9; some of these are individual choices below. *A Sea Symphony* (No. 1) has undue balance problems, with the soloists rather distant, and the performances of

Nos 8 and (oddly) 6 fail to engage the emotions as strongly as the rest. No. 9, a long-misunderstood work Handley has virtually made his own, is magnificent, but Slatkin here, unexpectedly perhaps, is even more revelatory. Yet Handley's set is the more competitive at price-level too, and must remain the current first choice. *CM*

VAUGHAN WILLIAMS

Symphony No. 1 (A Sea Symphony)
see also **CHORAL & SONG**: VAUGHAN WILLIAMS: A Sea Symphony

VAUGHAN WILLIAMS

Symphonies Nos 2 (A London Symphony) & 8 in D minor

BBC SO/Andrew Davis

Teldec British Line 4509-90858-2 □ **76:54 mins** □ 🎵🎵🎵

In his renowned exchange with Mahler, Sibelius spoke of the purity of form and profound inner logic which marked his symphonic ideal, but the other countered with 'No, the symphony must be like the world, all-embracing'. These two creeds may seem irreconcilable, but Vaughan Williams possessed the breadth of vision and intellectual flexibility to encompass both, something which has not always been acknowledged, and it is one of the strengths of this outstanding disc that the all-encompassing Second Symphony, with its picturesque episodes and bold use of the vernacular, is as powerfully symphonic in its urgency as the purer, dialectical Eighth.

The orchestra plays splendidly for Davis, and is captured with warmth and brilliance. This enables the Second Symphony's finale to build to a dramatic peak which I have rarely heard equalled, and throughout the performance ecstatic interludes and picturesque episodes are always felt as part of a powerful symphonic span.

The Eighth also benefits from Davis's impressive overview. The opening variations are confirmed as one of the composer's finest symphonic achievements, and the finale reveals its true mettle – not the casual romp of some interpretations, but a determined outburst of energy and joy for which conductor and engineers have created the perfect sound, weighty yet crystalline.
Anthony Payne

Symphonies Nos 3 (A Pastoral Symphony) & 4 in F minor

Alison Barlow (soprano); Royal Liverpool PO/Vernon Handley

EMI Eminence CD-EMX 2192 □ 65:39 mins □ 🎵🎵

This disc brings us remarkably impressive accounts of two of the greatest of all 20th-century symphonies, probably the most violently contrasted in any symphonic canon since Beethoven.

The *Pastoral Symphony* is a work of extraordinary daring. Containing three slow to moderately paced movements and only a minute of really quick music, it articulates a world of haunting calm.

Far from being the work of easy pastoralism Warlock famously mistook it for, it is a war symphony clinging unforgettably to the sanity of landscape amid the horrors of Flanders. Handley draws outstanding playing from the RLPO, luminous in its shades of silver and grey, and he performs a difficult feat in providing motion and contrast without disrupting a work of static visionary planes.

The Fourth Symphony presents fewer problems, but its mechanistic structuralism has to be carefully handled. Again Handley triumphs – I have rarely heard the final pages delivered with such heady brutality, while the cool, other-worldly lyricism which provides the main contrasts is hypnotically delivered.

A performance in the very highest class that recalls the composer's own overwhelming treatment. *Anthony Payne*

Symphony No. 4
see also HOLST: The Planets

Symphony No. 5; Flos campi

Christopher Balmer (viola); Liverpool Philharmonic Choir, Royal Liverpool PO/Vernon Handley

EMI Eminence CD-EMX 9512 □ 61:30 mins □ 🎵🎵

Handley doesn't quite banish memories of Barbirolli's classic recording with the Philharmonia, still in my view the most profound for mystery and chill at the heart of certainty. But this is a strong and dramatic reading, not allowing the symphony's spiritual overtones and patent connection to the opera *The Pilgrim's Progress* ever to degenerate into fuzzy-edged benevolence. Not that there's any lack of warmth: the way Handley makes the music soar at the appearance of the E major second subject really causes a catch of the

breath. This is a sterling and deeply satisfying reading of a marvellous work. This mid-price issue is made the more attractive by the coupling with the seldom (and rarely successfully) recorded *Flos campi*, one of Vaughan Williams's most individual and passionate works, inspired by verses from the Song of Solomon, with its concerto-like viola part and ecstatic wordless chorus. Difficult of balance, and needing refined interpretation to harmonise its deeply English response to oriental imagery, both poetic and musical, it is almost perfectly done here, with Christopher Balmer an eloquent soloist. Warm and spacious recording. *CM*

Symphony No. 6 in E minor; Tuba Concerto in F minor

Patrick Harrild (tuba); LSO/Bryden Thomson

Chandos CHAN 8740 □ 47:23 mins □ 🎵🎵🎵

Given that the Sixth is one of Vaughan Williams's most dramatic symphonies, widely viewed after its 1948 premiere as a monitory prevision of nuclear holocaust, surprisingly few modern performances quite seem able to bring it off. Command of the ardour, menace and baleful violence of the first three movements (Andrew Davis, Vernon Handley, Previn) doesn't guarantee ability to sustain the miasmic tension of that sphinx-like finale, whose undulating, almost expressionless lines convey ultimate elegiac pathos while never rising above pianissimo. The composer implicitly denied the post-Hiroshima scenario, relating this finale to Shakespeare's *Tempest*: 'We are such stuff as dreams are made on, and our little life is rounded with a sleep.' But the music recalls his dreaming Job, beset with frightful visions, and 'The Dead Man's Kit' sequence in his *Flemish Farm* film score: in whatever form, death is evoked here. Iron discipline is needed in performance, but Slatkin (like Kees Bakels on Naxos) seems to achieve it at the expense of the other movements' tensions. Boult, on mid-price EMI (coupled with Symphony No. 4), remains a strong recommendation, though even his finale lacks something. Bryden Thomson, despite the slightly cavernous Chandos sound, here delivers the most cogent performance of his cycle; the first movement opening is a little ponderous, but from the mechanistic march-rhythms that herald the second group all goes splendidly, and there is a rapt, frozen beauty to the finale. The Tuba Concerto, otherwise not available, is an attractive and unusual coupling, with Patrick Harrild a soloist of pachydermic bravura, though the disc is still somewhat short measure. *CM*

VAUGHAN WILLIAMS

Sinfonia antartica (Symphony No. 7); Serenade to Music

Alison Hargan (soprano); Liverpool Philharmonic Choir, Royal Liverpool PO/Vernon Handley

EMI Eminence CD-EMX 2173 □ 56:47 mins □ *🎵🎵*

Handley's *Antartica* is a powerfully atmospheric, strongly hewn reading with no doubts whatever about the fundamentally symphonic nature of the score that Vaughan Williams worked up from his film music for *Scott of the Antarctic*. Human endeavour and vast, brooding, inimical landscape are kept in judicious balance. Especially impressive is his shaping of the long central movement, 'Landscape', founded on music depicting Scott and his party toiling up an immense glacier. The tragedy of the three big movements is nicely offset by the animal life of the 'penguin' Scherzo and the English lyricism of the Intermezzo. The wordless contributions of chorus and soloist (a splendidly pure Alison Hargan) are spine-chillingly done, halfway between voice of nature and lament. EMI's sonics do the work proud. Although the exquisite *Serenade to Music* is never quite as ethereal and plastic with a full chorus, rather than the group of 16 soloists for whom it was originally envisaged, this version is also most beautifully played, shaped and sung, and can perfectly well stand as a first choice among the currently competing versions. There is, however, a fine 16-voice version from Matthew Best on Hyperion, which also contains the best alternative recording of *Flos campi*, should you already have Symphonies Nos 5 and 7 in other couplings. *CM*

VAUGHAN WILLIAMS

Symphonies Nos 8 in D minor & 9 in E minor; Flourish for Glorious John

Philharmonia Orchestra/Leonard Slatkin

RCA Victor Red Seal 09026 61196 2 □ 62:39 mins □ *🎵🎵🎵*

Leonard Slatkin's always engrossing Vaughan Williams series for RCA achieves signal success with the Ninth, and last, Symphony, completed shortly before the composer's death. Initially seriously underestimated as merely recycling familiar gestures, the work is

nowadays more justly valued as one of Vaughan Williams's most profound and troubled utterances, the visionary finale opening out new spiritual vistas. There's perhaps no ideal recorded version: Adrian Boult's two (on Everest and mid-price EMI) each define a deeper humanity, and Previn (also on RCA, coupled with Symphony No. 6) has extraordinary atmosphere. But Slatkin's resplendent sound and clarification of texture bring out all the darker elements of the work. His hard-driven Scherzo, the saxophones a trio of demented lemurs, is unparalleled for its diablerie, and Vaughan Williams's last symphonic coda is both inspiring and sinister at the same time.

I find Slatkin's account of the elusive, divertimento-like Eighth Symphony less involving than the classic Barbirolli and Boult LP performances, but the uproarious finale, with all its bells, 'phones and 'spiels, has never sounded better. The short fanfare for Barbirolli, not available elsewhere, is in much the same celebratory style. Top-notch sound throughout. *CM*

VAUGHAN WILLIAMS

The Wasps Overture
see WALTON: Symphony No. 1

VERACINI

Overtures Nos 1–4 & 6

Musica Antiqua Köln/Reinhard Goebel

Archiv 439 937-2 □ 70:45 mins □ *🎵🎵🎵*

A real discovery. On paper, the Italian virtuoso violinist-composer Francesco Maria Veracini (1690–1768) seems to have been one of many such figures that graced the early 18th century. Yet, if we are to take these overtures, probably composed in 1716, as being entirely representative of his style, he certainly deserves far more recognition than hitherto.

Anecdotal evidence, some of which may well have been apocryphal, suggests that he was a larger-than-life personality, and the music performed here bears this out. Working within the confines of a limited set of tonalities (B flat major, F major and, in the final Overture, G minor), Veracini allows his musical imagination free rein, steadfastly avoiding the predictable. Each of the overtures follows an entirely individual sequence of movements, and in some cases, such as the Gavotte of No. 2, the extended working out of thematic material transcends the simple origins of the dance. Perhaps the most surprising and attractive music of all comes in the final overture, where the conventional three-movement format of the concerto is supplemented by a primitive minuet in which all the orchestral forces play in unison. In this premiere recording of five of the complete set of six overtures, Reinhard Goebel and his excellent Musica Antiqua Köln deliver breathtakingly vivid performances in which a no-holds-barred approach to tempo and articulation matches the extravagant conception of the music itself. *EL*

VIEUXTEMPS/BRUCH

Vieuxtemps: Violin Concerto No. 5 in A minor

Bruch: Scottish Fantasy; Violin Concerto No. 1 in G minor

Jascha Heifetz (violin); New SO of London/Malcolm Sargent

RCA Victor Red Seal RD 86214 □ ADD □ 65:06 mins □ ⚫⚫⚫

Violinist of the Century (and very possibly of all time!) Jascha Heifetz made this celebrated recording of the Fifth Violin Concerto by Henri Vieuxtemps, one of the seminal figures of the Franco-Belgian school of 19th-century violin-playing, in May 1961, exactly 100 years after it was composed. This concentrated and fearsomely difficult work is permeated by an uneasy introspection and moody intensity, and is the finest of Vieuxtemps's works in the genre. Alas, it is no longer played as frequently as it should be, in an age which tends to sneer at the heart-on-sleeve Romantic traditions it typifies. Heifetz's performance is a monument to everything which his playing enshrined: formidable virtuosity, heart-easing lyricism, and a tone quality of utterly distinctive radiance, plus an illustrious and noble approach to the music itself, raising it to unexpected levels of seriousness. Yet this disc, recorded at Walthamstow Assembly Hall, London, also includes matchless accounts of Bruch's G minor Violin Concerto, and Heifetz's legendary performance of the *Scottish Fantasy*, which, despite major excisions from the text, may well be the greatest single example of the highest art of violin-playing ever preserved on disc. Orchestral support from the New Symphony Orchestra of London under Sargent is impeccably disciplined, and CD transfers of these stereo masters has added both lustre and warmth to the original LP sound. If you have no other Heifetz recording in your collection, may I implore you to acquire this one? *MJ*

VILLA-LOBOS

Guitar Concerto; 12 Études; 5 Preludes

Julian Bream (guitar); LSO/André Previn

RCA Victor Gold Seal 09026 61604 2 □ ADD □ 68:40 mins □ ⚫⚫

The Guitar Concerto, though the best known, is only one of the fabulously prolific Brazilian composer's many concertos. Unfortunately, there's been no recording of the stunning Cello Concerto No. 2 since Aldo Parisot's long-deleted LP account, but the five colourful piano concertos, recorded by Cristina Ortiz on a Decca two-CD set, are well worth investigating. The Guitar Concerto which Villa-Lobos wrote for Segovia is comparatively an intimate, small-scale piece, but full of irresistibly characteristic ideas from a composer who understood and loved the instrument. As for the solo Études and Preludes, they're perhaps *the* essential 20th-century guitar repertoire, and Bream's performances are classics of their kind. These have never been bettered for rhythmic gaiety, soulful sentiment and sheer delight in the instrument's sonorities. The recording is beautifully vivid and realistic, and pleasantly bright in the concerto, where Previn proves an ideal accompanist. A bargain at mid-price. Regrettably, there are no current recommendable versions of the complete *Chôros* and *Bachianas Brasileiras* cycles, which contain perhaps Villa-Lobos's finest music. Look out, though, for the disc in EMI's Composers in Person series, where he conducts the choral Tenth *Chôros*, a work of spirited barbarism, and Victoria de los Angeles in her immortal rendering of the Fifth *Bachiana Brasileira* for voice and five cellos. *CM*

VIVALDI

Bassoon Concertos; Concertos for Wind and Strings

Danny Bond (bassoon); Academy of Ancient Music/Christopher Hogwood

L'Oiseau-Lyre 436 867-2 □ 58:01 mins □ ⚫⚫⚫

No disc could more thoroughly discredit Stravinsky's mindless remark about Vivaldi: 'a dull fellow who could compose the same form over… and over.' Every one of these 18 movements reveals some novelty to surprise and delight. Hogwood's choice is extraordinarily colourful, from solo bassoon and strings – three of no fewer than 39 extant concertos for this charming grandfather of the wind – to a brilliant palette of virtuoso violin and oboes, dazzling horns, cello, bassoon and strings, enriched further with a varied continuo – archlute and organ as well as harpsichord.

Hogwood makes musical points all the more effectively by understating them, subtly shaping phrases and dynamics to create a remarkable sense of direction which most would be hard put to discover from the bare written page. Recording quality is soft-edged, reflecting the warmth and transparency of period instruments. An eye-opening selection, highly recommended. *GP*

VIVALDI

12 Concerti, Op. 4 (La Stravaganza)

I Solisti Italiani

Denon CO-75889/90 □ 104:59 mins (2 discs)
□ 𝟘𝟘𝟘

Vivaldi has been mocked for standardising the late-Baroque concerto, and certainly his 600-odd examples have many features in common. But having established a norm, he can then surprise the ear, constantly wandering out of the way ('extra-vagare') – hence *La stravaganza*. Although on the face of it standard solo concertos, some introduce a trio of soloists; some have four movements, others three; some introduce bizarre harmonies, others are disarmingly predictable.

I Solisti Italiani play on modern-style instruments, demonstrating clearly that, in the last analysis, authenticity of spirit is more important than authenticity of equipment. Playing without a conductor, they generate a remarkably fluid ensemble. Even the most hypnotically regular pulse is flexible – the powerful last movement of Concerto No. 5 is allowed a moment of reflection before the end. There are challenging demands for solo virtuosity, every one met here by violinists from the ensemble sharing the honours. But, for me, the slow movements are the most memorable. Generally, they're taken quite reflectively, sometimes the violin singing a lyrical aria above the simplest of bass-lines, elsewhere artful, as in No. 12, where a repeating bass, strongly implying an eight-bar phrase, is subtly compressed into six. *GP*

VIVALDI

6 Concerti, Op. 10

Giovanni Antonini (recorder); Il Giardino Armonico

Teldec Das Alte Werk 9031-73267-2 □ 48:48 mins
□ 𝟘𝟘𝟘

Il Giardino Armonico is a pioneering ensemble in Italy, where period performance

has been slow to take off. The ensemble is anything but cautious, though: these are some of the most vivid sound pictures you're ever likely to hear. In the first of this set of six recorder concertos, *La tempesta di mare*, the storm at sea is terrifying as huge waves of string sound tower up and break beneath the solo recorder. No less dramatic is *La notte*, night haunted by fantastic dreams – strings sandpaper-dry – until sleep finally comes with recorder and accompaniment almost motionless.

More blinding colours are in store with sopranino recorder representing the goldfinch in glittering runs and sensual vibrato. In contrast, the Fifth Concerto, 'all the instruments muted', is incredibly honeyed.

This isn't comfortable background Vivaldi but very assertive playing indeed. Over the top? You may think so, yet I can't assume that, having conceived these descriptive pieces so vividly, Vivaldi would have settled for less. Warm, reassuring orchestral sounds seem bland after experiencing the huge palette of colours which these players have mixed. Several further discs already evoke similar qualities, with slightly less encouragement to extremes. I look forward to more. *GP*

VIVALDI

Concerto in due cori
see Collection: Concerti di flauti

VIVALDI

Concerto for Two Trumpets
see Collection: Baroque Trumpet Music

VIVALDI

L'estro armonico, Op. 3

Simon Standage, Elizabeth Wilcock, Micaela Comberti, Miles Golding (violin), Jaap ter Linden (cello); The English Concert/Trevor Pinnock

Archiv 423 094-2 □ 100:16 mins (2 discs) □ 𝟘𝟘𝟘

The fanciful title of these 12 concertos, published in 1711, probably best translates as 'The Musical Inspiration'. Their publication is significant: they are in eight part-books, suggesting that they were probably intended for one-to-a-part performance throughout. This is Pinnock's choice, and the chamber scale is very effective indeed. The contrast between full 'orchestral' sound and solo episodes comes partly from the scoring and partly from careful balancing where Vivaldi himself has written 'solo' and 'tutti'.

The concertos are organised into four groups, each beginning with a work for four solo violins. One is particularly familiar, transcribed by Bach for four harpsichords.

Its texture is wonderfully rich, as Vivaldi divides violas below the four independent violins and, in the slow movement, gives each of the soloists a different figuration simultaneously to create a mysteriously shimmering sound. In the Allegro movements, Pinnock's team generates a fine sense of that pulsing urgency which is a hallmark of Vivaldi.

A tempting alternative, despite occasional moments of uneasy intonation, is L'Oiseau-Lyre's mid-price reissue from the early Eighties of Hogwood and the Academy of Ancient Music. *GP*

The Four Seasons; Violin Concertos, RV253 (La tempesta di mare) & RV180 (Il piacere)

CO of Europe/Marieke Blankestijn (violin)

Teldec 4509-91683-2 □ 59:06 mins □ ⦿⦿⦿

The brilliant young Dutch violinist Marieke Blankestijn plays a superb old violin by Matteo Goffriller (which is owned by a bank) on this interesting recording of *The Four Seasons* plus the next two concertos as published by Vivaldi in his Op. 8.

This was a good idea both historically as well as musically, for the two concertos – entitled *La tempesta di mare* (The Storm at Sea) and *Il piacere* (Pleasure) – are vintage Vivaldi. The title of the whole set, *Il cimento dell'armonia e dell'inventione*, might be translated as 'The contest between harmony and invention', or between the science of composition and inspiration, in which effort Vivaldi was eminently successful.

This recording includes some extraordinary playing, such as the lonely slow movement in the first concerto illustrating a dog barking at the moon (played on the viola).

If you like your *Four Seasons* on modern instruments, this is an inspired version. Those preferring original instruments might try Christopher Hogwood with the Academy of Ancient Music, which uses a slightly earlier manuscript than that published in Amsterdam in 1725. Other recommended performances include Tafelmusik with Jeanne Lamon (Sony Vivarte), or Nikolaus Harnoncourt (Teldec). *HC Robbins Landon*

Sinfonia, RV149
see Collection: Baroque music

Wind Concertos
see ALBINONI: Wind Concertos

Prelude to Act I of Die Meistersinger von Nürnberg; Rienzi Overture; A Faust Overture; The Flying Dutchman Overture; Prelude and Liebestod from Tristan und Isolde; Tannhäuser Overture

Cincinnati SO/Jesús López-Cobos

Telarc CD-80379 □ 76:55 mins □ ⦿⦿⦿

Rienzi Overture; Tannhäuser Overture; Prelude to Act I of Lohengrin; Prelude to Act III of Tristan und Isolde; Prelude to Act I of Die Meistersinger von Nürnberg; Prelude and close of Act III of Parsifal

New Queen's Hall Orchestra/Barry Wordsworth

Eye of the Storm EOS 5001 □ 144:03 mins (2 discs for the price of one) □ ⦿⦿⦿

Radically polarised in both style and musical ideal, these compilations of orchestral preludes and extracts from Wagner's music dramas each have a great deal to commend them. Jesús López-Cobos and the Cincinnati SO provide performances of striking accomplishment and grandeur, and Telarc's state-of-the-art twenty-bit digital technology ensures sumptuous and spacious sound of demonstration quality.

The readings of the *Meistersinger*, *Tannhäuser* and *Rienzi* overtures are hugely impressive; the Cincinnati brass resound magnificently across the sound field, and López-Cobos, clearly a Wagnerian of some stature and experience, draws expressive and cultivated response from the large string section at his command. There is rapt intensity, too, in his electrifying account of the Prelude and Liebestod from *Tristan*, and the performance of Wagner's independent concert overture based on Goethe's *Faust* is aptly probing and demonic in character. This is an audiophile offering of exceptional quality and distinction, though more adventurous listeners should seek out the admirable two-disc set from Eye of the Storm, with Barry Wordsworth and the New Queen's Hall Orchestra. This novel release offers two different performances of each work; the aim is to avoid placing any artistic limitations on the spontaneity and flexibility of interpretation, and at the same time to re-create an orchestral sound which might well have been familiar during the early years of this century by employing instruments of the period. Sceptics should note that such conditions do indeed make for an astonishing and dramatic listening experience, and the interaction of unexpected and unfamiliar instrumental sonorities on these familiar works will prove of inestimable interest to committed Wagnerians. Two splendid issues; I shouldn't want to be without either! *MJ*

Wagner: Siegfried Idyll

Schoenberg: Verklärte Nacht

Strauss: Metamorphosen

Sinfonia Varsovia/Emmanuel Krivine

Denon CO-79442 □ **74:28 mins** □ 🌑🌑🌑

Immediately impressive is the very high level of performance attained by the Sinfonia Varsovia under Emmanuel Krivine. Wagner's musical birthday greeting for his wife Cosima (the couple were finally married on 25 August 1870, following a protracted, bitter and all-too-public scandal) was first heard early on Christmas morning 1870 at the Villa Tribschen, Wagner's retreat on the shores of Lake Lucerne. Cosima's diary recounts the episode in detail; Wagner had assembled the musicians on the staircase, and the music filled the house with sanctified joy. Krivine's account is quite magnificent; the playing is warm, cultivated and affectionate, and recorded sound is first class. No less impressive on this disc entitled 'Beyond Wagner' are his readings of Schoenberg's *Verklärte Nacht* – based on Richard Dehmel's text charting human confession, reconciliation and transformation – and Richard Strauss's valedictory tribute to the war-ravaged city of Dresden, his great essay for 23 solo strings, *Metamorphosen.** This programme has been recorded by other, somewhat more acclaimed orchestra/conductor partnerships (James Levine and the Berlin Philharmonic have taped these works for DG with far less convincing results), yet never with comparable rapture, intensity and vision, and Denon's pristine, ideally balanced recording imparts rare intimacy to these exceptional readings from Krivine and the Poles. An essential purchase. *MJ*

**David Nice adds:* No work, except perhaps Britten's *War Requiem*, has more need of the right occasion than Strauss's *Metamorphosen*. It found exactly that in Karajan's 1947 Vienna version – replete, surely, with a response as heartfelt and grief-stricken as the composer's own to the then-recent devastations. There has been no performance since – certainly not either of Karajan's later recordings – to touch it, so wait for this classic's inevitable return.

Walton: Symphony No. 1 in B flat minor

Vaughan Williams: The Wasps Overture

LSO/André Previn

RCA Victor Gold Seal GD 87830 □ **ADD**
□ **52:14 mins** □ 🌑🌑

Whether presaging the tensions of an approaching world war (as used to be said) or reflecting anger and despair at the end of a love affair (as the composer averred late in life), Walton's First Symphony remains his most powerful and masterfully constructed orchestral work, one of the defining masterpieces of British music in the Thirties. It excited tremendous enthusiasm at the time, and it's been well served on disc ever since Hamilton Harty's recording with the LSO for Decca in 1935, the year of its first complete performance.

Now available on Biddulph, the Harty is still regarded by some critics as the finest ever. Walton himself recorded the symphony, and Boult; there are excellent current versions from Ashkenazy, Handley, Mackerras, Rattle and Slatkin, among others. But many would agree that André Previn's 1966 recording – perhaps the most outstanding of his classic LPs with the LSO from the late Sixties – remains the definitive account. The superbly engineered recording captures the crackling electricity of this high-tension performance. The razor-sharp ensemble even in the trickiest passages, the brimstone malice of the Scherzo and the urgency that powers the intoxicating triumph of the finale, are unmatched anywhere (not even by Previn himself in his lower-pressure re-make with the RPO for Telarc). Vaughan Williams's robustly lyrical *The Wasps* Overture makes an attractive makeweight in this CD reissue. (As this book goes to press we hear RCA have temporarily withdrawn this disc but intend reissuing it with a different number.) *CM*

Viola Concerto; Symphony No. 2: Johannesburg Festival Overture

Lars Anders Tomter (viola), English Northern Philharmonia/Paul Daniel

Naxos 8.553402 □ **61:27 mins** □ 🌑

The opening bitter-sweet melody of Walton's gloriously lyrical Viola Concerto must surely be regarded as one of the most memorable thematic ideas in the 20th-century repertoire. Its romantic ardour is projected with obvious affection by the Norwegian virtuoso Lars Anders Tomter, whose superb performance of the work ranks as one of the undoubted highlights of this first instalment in Naxos's eagerly awaited Walton cycle. Tomter has a particular empathy for Walton's idiom. His playing is intense, yet avoids any hint of over-indulgence, and he is supported by the English Northern Philharmonia under Paul Daniel, who come to the fore in the central Scherzo, a movement delivered with breathtaking rhythmic precision by both soloist and orchestra.

Daniel and his players make an equally impressive showing in the Second Symphony. The interpretation emphasises the darker elements of the score, sometimes at the expense of the music's brilliance, with the result that the finale perhaps lacks some of the malicious humour that is implied in Walton's caustic send-up of 12-note composition. In this respect George Szell and the Cleveland Orchestra, on Sony Essential Classics, offer a more uninhibited approach, performing the work with greater virtuosity and with more apparent urgency.

Nonetheless, Daniel's performance is extremely involving and he enjoys the benefits of a superior recording made in Leeds Town Hall that achieves an admirable balance between warmth and clarity of detail. For all these reasons this present release must be regarded as an outstanding bargain. *EL*

WARLOCK

Capriol Suite; Serenade
see **CHORAL & SONG**: WARLOCK: The Curlew

WAXMAN

Carmen Fantasie
see PAGANINI: Violin Concerto No. 1

WEBER

Clarinet Concertos Nos 1 in F minor & 2 in E flat; Concertino for Clarinet and Orchestra in E flat

Paul Meyer (clarinet); RPO/Günther Herbig

Denon CO-79551 □ 50:00 mins □ ❷❷❷

Weber's clarinet concertos have become staples of the instrument's repertoire, and with good reason, since each contains an abundance of fine melodies, and provides the soloist with ample opportunity for virtuoso display. Denon's issue, featuring the young French artist Paul Meyer, is an exceptional one. Meyer's performances are unfailingly eloquent and distinguished, and his fine control of phrasing and dynamic levels is allied to a generously expansive, richly burnished tone

and seemingly effortless technical agility. Günther Herbig, a master of dramatic incident, ensures that orchestral support from the RPO is arrestingly powerful; Herbig never loses sight of the fact that Weber was the founding-father of the German Romantic opera tradition, and invests this music with congenial good spirits and no lack of theatrical incident when needed. The recording itself is likewise admirable, since Denon's engineers have achieved a most realistic balance between soloist and orchestra, and have provided an entirely natural sense of perspective and realism. Magnificent performances, with playing that's as urbane, witty and pleasing as the music itself. A winner, though authenticists should perhaps consider Antony Pay's Virgin CD, in which he plays the solo parts and directs the Orchestra of the Age of Enlightenment. These, too, are superb accounts, the more characterful for the darker timbre of Pay's replica of an early 19th-century seven-key instrument, and the period sonority and approach advocated by the OAE. *MJ*

WEBER

Overtures: Peter Schmoll und seine Nachbarn; Turandot – Overture & March; Silvana; Abu Hassan; The Ruler of the Spirits; Jubel-Ouvertüre; Der Freischütz; Preciosa; Euryanthe; Oberon

Philharmonia Orchestra/Neeme Järvi

Chandos CHAN 9066 □ 75:27 mins □ ❷❷❷

Although the *Oberon* and *Freischütz* overtures are frequently performed as independent concert works (both are excellently played here, with Järvi drawing highly charged and splendidly heroic response from the Philharmonia, with deliciously plangent solo horn contributions in the former), several of the remaining works are but rarely encountered nowadays. *Peter Schmoll and his Neighbours*, Weber's earliest stage work, composed during his 15th year and produced in 1803, is, not surprisingly, the least memorable of these overtures, despite several attractive melodies taken from the opera itself. The slim *Turandot* extracts come from one of the 26 incidental scores Weber composed; this one, to a five-act drama by Schiller, dates from 1809. *Abu Hassan*, complete with appropriate Turkish janissary effects, appeared in 1812, a year after the magnificent concert overture *Ruler of the Spirits* had been completed. Paradoxically, Weber's finest creations in this genre coincided with plots of extraordinary convolution and near absurdity in some instances, perhaps explaining why his major operas are seldom staged today, the sole exception being the seminal Romantic opera *Der Freischütz* of 1824. Its overture, like that of *Euryanthe*, is a true orchestral *tour de force*, and both are admirably delivered here. Neeme Järvi's high-voltage readings never want for intimacy or enraptured insight, and the verve and passion of the Philharmonia's playing seldom falters. The Chandos recording is warm and reverberant, making this an especially pleasing compilation. *MJ*

WEBERN/BACH

Webern: Passacaglia, Op. 1; Six Pieces, Op. 6; Five Pieces, Op. 10; Symphony, Op. 21; Variations, Op. 30; Im Sommerwind

Bach (arr. Webern): Ricercar a 6 from The Musical Offering

Cleveland Orchestra/Christoph von Dohnányi

Decca 444 593-2 □ **67:59 mins** □ *②②*

It's difficult to imagine Anton Webern's principal orchestral works better done than this. There's nothing 'abstract' or desiccated in Dohnányi's view of the music, and the Cleveland's playing is always warmly expressive. Dohnányi is continuously alive to the subtle, elusive poetry of these scores, from the lush Straussian textures of the early tone poem *Im Sommerwind*, through the tiny, tremulous aphorisms of the Op. 10 pieces for chamber orchestra, to the severe, crystalline but passionate architecture of the 12-note Symphony and Variations. To hear Webern's unique, pointillistic orchestration of Bach's six-part ricercar from *The Musical Offering* in this context is to be reminded that his art was deeply rooted in the polyphonic practices of the Baroque masters, and even earlier. Dohnányi's account of the intense Op. 1 Passacaglia and of the Op. 6 Orchestral Pieces – almost Mahlerian here in their original version for large orchestra – are especially dramatic.

Decca's fine recording captures the full range of texture and dynamics. This is my unhesitating first choice in this repertoire, though Claudio Abbado on DG directs the Vienna PO in performances as fine, and perhaps a touch more *echt*-Viennese. But he omits *Im Sommerwind* for a less than satisfactory account of Schoenberg's *A Survivor from Warsaw*. Karajan, too, on a mid-price three-disc set of the Second Viennese School (see p323) is a surprisingly eloquent advocate for some of these pieces. *CM*

WEBERN

Passacaglia, Op. 1; Five Movements, Op. 5; Six Pieces, Op. 6; Symphony, Op. 21
see SCHOENBERG: Pelleas und Melisande

WEILL/BUSONI/SCHOENBERG

Weill: Symphonies Nos. 1 & 2

Busoni: Berceuse élégiaque

Schoenberg: Chamber Symphony No. 2

BBC SO/Gary Bertini, New Philharmonia Orchestra/ Frederik Prausnitz

EMI Matrix CDM 5 65869 2 □ ADD □ **79:19 mins** □ *②②*

Kurt Weill's two symphonies frame his composing career in the Weimar Republic and offer an effective illustration of the way his musical style changed from Expressionism towards embracing a greater degree of objectivity. The First Symphony, completed in 1921, is clearly indebted to Schoenberg's First Chamber Symphony in both its chromatic harmonic language and in its one-movement structure. But even in this early work, Weill pays oblique comment to the contemporary political situation in Germany, drawing his inspiration from projected incidental music to Becher's Expressionist play about the social revolution that will inevitably follow a terrible war.

In contrast, the Second Symphony, composed between 1933 and 1934, when Weill became a refugee from Nazi Germany, appears more restrained, even though funereal elements clearly pervade the slow introduction and central Largo movement. The influence of popular music is also crucial, with great prominence given to the wind instruments and the solo trumpet.

Among the currently available versions of these fascinating works, the pioneering 1967 recordings made by Gary Bertini and the BBC Symphony Orchestra lead the field in terms of urgency and commitment of playing. Their long overdue appearance on CD is further enhanced by the generous inclusion of the marvellous *Berceuse élégiaque* by Weill's composition teacher, Busoni, and a fine performance of Schoenberg's Second Chamber Symphony. *EL*

WEILL/HINDEMITH/TOCH

Weill: Violin Concerto

Hindemith: Septet for Wind

Toch: Five Pieces for Wind and Percussion

Christian Tetzlaff (violin); Soloists of the Deutsche
Kammerphilharmonie

Virgin VC 5 45056 2 □ 58:08 mins □ 🕗🕗🕗

The biggest work on this unusual and intelligently chosen programme is also the highlight
of the disc: Weill's sardonic, fragile and
disquieting Violin Concerto of 1924. It receives
a performance of rare refinement: Tetzlaff rises
to its virtuoso demands without compromising
the spectral atmosphere and ambiguous half-
lights so necessary to the first two movements.
The wind soloists aid him with playing of
remarkable colouristic range, and when all the
performers let rip in the finale's manic dance
one hears the consistency of the 'serious' Weill:
this movement, despite the occasional tinge of
L'histoire du soldat and its nostalgic homage to
Busoni, is clearly the progenitor of his Second
Symphony's saltarello finale.

Hindemith and Toch were among Weill's
leading contemporaries in the early Twenties:
Weill's Concerto is, for instance, directly
comparable with some of Hindemith's
Kammermusik concertos of the same time.
These two composers are represented here,
however, by much later works. Hindemith's
Wind Septet, typically complete in its mastery
of the instruments, is a good-natured, slightly
too formulaic product of his full maturity, but
seldom enough heard to make this first-rate
performance welcome. Little of Toch's music
has ever made it on to disc; these Five Pieces
(1959) are deft, witty, inventive and somewhat
poker-faced, and open out from an austere
quartet of woodwind to a large body of wind
and percussion. An interesting reminder of a
composer with whom we have still to come to
grips. But it's the Weill that makes this such a
valuable disc. *CM*

WILLIAMS

The Spielberg/Williams Collaboration – Excerpts from Raiders of the Lost Ark; Always; ET; Sugarland Express; Jaws; Empire of the Sun; Indiana Jones and the Temple of Doom; 1941; Indiana Jones and the Last Crusade; Close Encounters of the Third Kind

Toots Thielemans (harmonica); American Boychoir,
Tanglewood Festival Chorus, Boston Pops
Orchestra/John Williams

Sony SK 45997 □ 65:23 mins □ 🕗🕗🕗

This stimulating and vividly recorded
collection makes it very clear why John
Williams is the most successful Hollywood
film composer of the present day. Here is the
big-orchestra sound that descends in equal
measure from Walton and Korngold, an
unfailing knack for memorable tunes,
glittering colour and atmosphere – and, of
course, the right pictures to blazon his name
across the big screen, especially his epics for
Lucas and Spielberg. Williams understands
exactly what the medium demands and
provides it with unfailing professionalism and
enjoyable flair. The cunning of his eclecticism
is awesome: every tune, every bar has an
ancestry in other composers, yet Williams's
sound and élan are unmistakable. And when
he uses specific models, how apt they are: the
Jaws theme, for instance, a steal from
Revueltas's snake-killing poem *Sensemayá*.
Williams must be about the most resourceful
composer of marches alive today. So many
tracks are in march and Trio form, the march
conveying heroic energy, the Trio romantic
aspiration: but how varied they are, from the
Indiana Jones theme through the oriental
march of the slave children in *The Temple of
Doom* to 'Exulate Justi' from *Empire of the
Sun* and the larger-than-life American swagger
of the march from *1941*: lousy picture, great
score. Yet he can pull out every Romantic stop
in the post-Mahlerian love music of *Always*,
while the final rhapsodic compilation of
excerpts from *Close Encounters* is a kind of
tone poem in which Ligeti meets 'Wish Upon
a Star'. Great music, no; great of its kind, yes.
Superbly played and recorded. *CM*

ZIMMERMANN

Canto di speranza: Cello Concerto; Oboe Concerto; Trumpet Concerto (Nobody knows de trouble I see)

Heinrich Schiff (cello), Heinz Holliger (oboe), Håkan
Hardenberger (trumpet); SWF SO Baden-
Baden/Michael Gielen

Philips 434 114-2 □ 71:03 mins □ 🕗🕗🕗

Enthusiasts for Zimmermann's Trumpet
Concerto 'Nobody knows de trouble I see',
who were inspired by Håkan Hardenberger's
persuasive account at the 1993 Proms, will

welcome this disc, setting the work in context with Zimmermann's contemporary concertos for oboe and cello. Hardenberger claims he is now asked to perform the piece frequently 'as, sadly, its message becomes increasingly appropriate'; it was written as a reaction to racial hatred, and differing stylistic elements are fused in 'brotherly unity'. Although formally organised by a 12-tone row, the musical ideas are heavily infused with jazz, and a separate combo is specified.

The Oboe Concerto, the first of Zimmermann's works to utilise slimmed-down forces, is admirably played by Heinz Holliger (the juxtaposition in the Rhapsody of anguish and serenity is particularly effective). Heinrich Schiff brings equal expertise to the *Canto di speranza* for cello and small orchestra and the Cello Concerto. *Deborah Calland*

COLLECTION: AMERICAN ORCHESTRAL MUSIC

Carter: Variations for Orchestra; Schuller: Spectra; Babbitt: Correspondences; Cage: Atlas eclipticalis

Chicago SO/James Levine

DG 431 698-2 □ 68:23 mins □ 𝄞𝄞𝄞

The real meat in this important collection of Americana of the Fifties and Sixties is provided by Elliott Carter's Variations for Orchestra, a synoptic work which absorbs 20th-century stylistic traits as disparate as those of Schoenberg and Berg on the one hand, and Ives and Conlon Nancarrow on the other. At the same time, Carter never loses sight of his characteristic preoccupation with notions of acceleration and deceleration. Texturally, the Variations are actually a good deal more straightforward than most of his music – they were commissioned by one of America's lesser orchestras (the Louisville Orchestra). The Chicago SO, of course, is a virtuoso band and has given memorable performances of the work under Solti. Levine's account, if not quite in that class, will do very well.

For the rest, Gunther Schuller's *Spectra* is a spatially, if not always subtly, conceived piece; Milton Babbitt's *Correspondence* pits a string orchestra against a synthesized electronic tape. The pointillist whisperings of John Cage's *Atlas eclipticalis* were graphically derived from an astronomical atlas, and the piece can be played simultaneously with the composer's *Winter Music* if the conductor so chooses (Levine doesn't). First-class performances and recording. *Misha Donat*

COLLECTION: THE BANKS OF GREEN WILLOW

Butterworth: The Banks of Green Willow; Two English Idylls; Moeran: Lonely Waters; Whythorne's Shadow; Bridge: There is a Willow Grows Aslant a Brook; Bax: Three Pieces for Orchestra

Ann Murray (mezzo-soprano); English CO/Jeffrey Tate

EMI CDM 7 64200 2 □ 68:02 mins □ 𝄞𝄞

George Butterworth's tragic death in the First World War left us with an orchestral legacy of just four short pieces. They are unique in their magical poetry and individual sensibility, their idyllic charm and pastoral serenity subtly enriched by the shadows that drift across Butterworth's emotional landscape. The resulting emotional ambivalence continues to fascinate, as Tate's devoted and sensitive interpretations of the three idylls testify. In luminous and steadily paced performances with the ECO he remains aware of the darker undercurrents that sometimes stain the surface of the music. If the very deliberateness of his approach prevents the loveliness from being enhanced by those tiny, urgent contrasts which yield true magic, he still touches the heart.

One feels no such reservations about his masterly reading of Frank Bridge's *There is a Willow*. This flawless little masterpiece plunges with postwar intensity into the dark world of which Butterworth has become gently aware, and it receives playing of a haunted stillness. So too does EJ Moeran's *Lonely Waters*, which occupies similar territory, while *Whythorne's Shadow*, a charmingly Warlockian essay combining neo-Elizabethan and post-Delian styles, is sweetly characterised. The Bax pieces fare beautifully too: engaging music, this, showing the composer's early style at its freshest. *Anthony Payne*

COLLECTION: BAROQUE MUSIC

Pachelbel: Canon & Gigue; Handel: Arrival of the Queen of Sheba; Vivaldi: Sinfonia, RV 149; Purcell: Chacony in G minor; Concertos by Albinoni, Avison & Haydn

The English Concert/Trevor Pinnock

Archiv 415 518-2 □ 64:52 mins □ 𝄞𝄞𝄞

It's clever, though by no means uniquely so, to invent a three-part canon over 28 ostinato repetitions of a two-bar bass. Pachelbel's Canon and Gigue are by far his most celebrated work, although he was very prolific. No less worthy are dozens of chorale-based and non-liturgical pieces for organ, 17 harpsichord suites, and a mass of sacred choral and instrumental music. Pinnock's lucid and unaffected performance satisfies the need for Pachelbel's Canon in a collection of Baroque recordings. Hopefully, it may also stimulate a demand for more of his other music – at the time of writing, only two discs celebrate his choral music, though there are a further 45 versions of the Canon available!

Other pieces here are no less imaginative: a mixture of bowed and pizzicato strings in a Vivaldi sinfonia, sounding remarkably like mandolins within a string ensemble; a stately 'Arrival of the Queen of Sheba' from Handel's *Solomon*; a rare treat from Charles Avison – a concerto arranged from keyboard music by Domenico Scarlatti; some sparkling playing by Pinnock himself in a Haydn concerto for harpsichord (Hob. XVIII:11); in all, an enjoyable mix of essential 'pops' and rarer offerings. *GP*

COLLECTION: BAROQUE TRUMPET MUSIC

Works by Stradella, Biber, Vivaldi, Albinoni, Telemann & Handel

Crispian Steele-Perkins (trumpet); Tafelmusik/Jeanne Lamon

Sony SK 53365 □ 68:56 mins □ 🎵🎵🎵

The limited notes of the natural trumpet served as a positive challenge to composers' inventive powers. The opening Stradella sonata here, for eight strings and trumpet, contains memorably tuneful phrases, and adds such appealing tricks as echoes and dialogue with the strings. The second movement, an Aria, includes a sudden key-shift, absurdly simple yet so captivating that I used a hitherto undiscovered 'track repeat' facility on my CD player!

John Thiessen joins Steele-Perkins as second trumpet in a Biber sonata and four duets where the limits are remarkably challenged by keys foreign to the natural scale of the trumpets – and stretched by a clever lipping down of a D to a slightly misty C sharp.

Five 'Airs from Vauxhall Gardens' take Handelian operatic 'lollipops' and present them on a surviving original slide trumpet – no mere musicological curiosity but a musical delight and a striking tonal contrast with the natural instrument.

The excellent recording balance with the neat strings of Tafelmusik is not achieved simply by clever engineering but by a view which Steele-Perkins has pioneered – that the Baroque trumpet can, and should, be quiet enough to match solo strings without losing any of its natural lustre. *GP*

COLLECTION: CONCERTI DI FLAUTI

Concertos by Telemann, Heinichen, Marcello, Schickhardt & Vivaldi

Amsterdam Loeki Stardust Quartet, Academy of Ancient Music/Christopher Hogwood

L'Oiseau-Lyre 436 905-2 □ 57:17 mins □ 🎵🎵🎵

All the appealing components of Baroque concertos – fast speed and harmonic pulse, impulsive sequences, memorable ritornello themes, hypnotic repetitions – are enhanced by up to four swirling recorders.

Heinichen's Concerto a 8 in C contrasts opening energy with the simplest of textures in a unison Pastorell. Schickhardt, in D minor, has the musical-clock sound of a recorder quartet creating its own tuttis and florid episodes above a continuo bass. Elsewhere (G major) fast-tongued repeated notes bound carefree through an exhilarating Allegro.

Telemann is at his most tuneful in two concertos for a pair of treble recorders. The best is saved for the end, a Vivaldi concerto of kaleidoscopic colours – two solo violins, solo cello and organ, obbligato recorders and strings, full of surprise gestures coming on the ear, *in due cori*, from all sides.

Solo intonation is remarkable, those buzzing ghosts that recorder ensembles generate all in tune with their respective chords. Balance is poised both by careful engineering and sensitive playing, the AAM restrained but still vibrant in support of their soft-voiced soloists.

The rare repertoire for these uncommon forces is a revelation. I can't recall hearing a jollier disc. Don't miss it. *GP*

COLLECTION: FRENCH ORCHESTRAL MUSIC

Satie: Parade; Milhaud: Le boeuf sur le toit; Auric: Ouverture; Françaix: Concertino for Piano and Orchestra; Fetler: Contrasts for Orchestra

Claude Françaix (piano); LSO, Minneapolis SO/Antal Dorati

Mercury Living Presence 434 335-2 □ ADD □ 67:00 mins □ 🎵🎵

Satie's ballet *Parade*, composed for Diaghilev during the First World War, provoked almost as much controversy as Stravinsky's *The Rite of Spring* a few years before. The music may be less dissonant, but Satie's idiom was just as bewildering. The score opens portentously with a chorale and fugue, but moves without warning to suggestions of circus music and American ragtime. Satie's orchestra is equally unconventional, with prominent solos allotted to typewriter, siren, foghorn and revolver.

Antal Dorati and the LSO make the most of Satie's spectacular theatrical effects, and they are equally exuberant in Milhaud's slapstick Twenties ballet *Le boeuf sur le toit*. The Auric *Ouverture* is of slightly later provenance and doesn't quite reach the same level of thematic memorability as Françaix's perennially fresh Concertino, delivered here in the confident hands of the composer's daughter. Marvellous playing and recording make this a highly desirable release, even if the inclusion of Paul Fetler's gritty *Contrasts for Orchestra* seems rather out of place here. *EL*

COLLECTION: HUNGARIAN CONNECTIONS

Liszt: Mephisto Waltz No. 1; Hungarian Rhapsody No. 2; Bartók: Hungarian Sketches; Romanian Folk Dances; Weiner: Csongor és Tünde; Kodály: Háry János Suite

Chicago SO/Georg Solti

Decca 443 444-2 □ 71:44 mins □ ⓐⓐⓐ

These live recordings reveal the Hungarian-born maestro in unusually genial mood. Kodály's *Háry János* can rarely have sounded more exhilarating with some irresistible pointing of the dance rhythms in the catchy Intermezzo, and riotous humour in the 'Battle of Napoleon'. The *Mephisto Waltz* is characteristically hard-driven, but this is exactly the sort of music that can accommodate such an approach. At the opposite end of the emotional spectrum, Solti conjures up a wonderfully rapt atmosphere in the more reflective numbers of the Bartók works. Finally, for those who prize interesting discoveries, the short but brilliantly orchestrated scherzo by Leo Weiner (1885–1960) whets the appetite to hear more from this undeservedly neglected composer. *EL*

COLLECTION: RUSSIAN MUSIC

Rimsky-Korsakov: The Snow Maiden Suite; The Golden Cockerel Suite; Dubinushka; Liadov: Kikimora; Baba-Yaga; The Enchanted Lake; A Musical Snuffbox; Shostakovich: Symphony No. 1; Prokofiev: Symphony No. 1 (Classical); Glinka: A Life for the Tsar – ballet music; Kabalevsky: The Comedians Suite; Khachaturian: Masquerade – Waltz & Galop

Philharmonia Orchestra, RPO/Efrem Kurtz

EMI CZS 7 67729 2 □ ADD □ 147:25 mins (2 discs) □ ⓐ

EMI's commitment to the Russian mainstream repertoire in the late Fifties and early Sixties yielded extraordinary riches, allied to natural sound which makes most of today's recordings sound artificial; the performances of this century's least-fêted great conductor, Efrem Kurtz (born St Petersburg 1900), stand right at the top of a distinguished list. It is certainly tempting to label this present compilation as the most delightful Russian treasury in the catalogues, for every track is stamped with Kurtz's aristocratic elegance of phrasing and the polished story-telling of supreme Philharmonia (or Royal Philharmonic) musicians. It also happens to provide us with top recommendations in several fields.

Rimsky-Korsakov: The Philharmonia woodwind provide characterful voices of nature in the innocently delightful *Snow Maiden* Suite, while the brass, heralded by a suitably penetrating trumpet cock-crow, dominate the satirical, sombre world of *The Golden Cockerel*. If the *Tsar Saltan* Suite were here too, this would be a perfect cross-section of orchestral music from the operas; but ample compensation for the absence of Saltan's March is the irresistible *Dubinushka*, surely the jolliest revolutionary song ever written and orchestrated by Professor Rimsky in 1905 as a gesture of support for his students.

Liadov was a typical Russian in that he produced a small body of exquisite work. The three fastidiously orchestrated tone poems are here, the essence of Russian fantasy, and there is no better testament to Kurtz's sleight-of-hand wizardry than the immaculately tailored flight of Baba-Yaga, dissolving in the most magical final chord on disc.

The impish-melancholy mood of the young Shostakovich seems to grow out of this tradition; in one of the very best recordings of the First Symphony, Kurtz sharpens the wit and keeps late-Romantic swoonings in focus. Another, sprightlier First, Prokofiev's, keeps unselfconsciously within Classical bounds; again, note Kurtz's self-effacing lightness in the finale. Finally, a century of dance music from Glinka, Khachaturian and Kabalevsky shows the conductor in the characterful ballet mode for which he was most famous. Unsurpassable star ratings would create a galaxy. *DN*

COLLECTION: RUSSIAN CELLO MUSIC

Tchaikovsky: Variations on a Rococo Theme; Pezzo capriccioso; Nocturne, Op. 19/4; Andante cantabile; Glazunov: Two Pieces, Op. 20; Chant du ménéstrel; Rimsky-Korsakov: Serenade, Op. 37; Cui: Deux morceaux, Op. 36

Steven Isserlis (cello); CO of Europe/John Eliot Gardiner

Virgin Ultraviolet CUV 5 61225 2 □ 64:00 mins □ *⊘*

This compilation of Russian works for cello and orchestra is of particular interest, since Isserlis dismisses the heavily edited version of Tchaikovsky's Variations on a Rococo Theme which is normally heard on disc and in the concert hall, and plays an edition which comes a good deal closer to realising the composer's own ideals for the piece, namely that it should re-kindle something of the transparency and poise associated with an era which Tchaikovsky much admired.

Of course, if you already own Rostropovich's stunning 1969 DG recording of Dvořák's Cello Concerto (now on DG Originals, see p265), with Karajan and the Berlin Philharmonic, you'll also possess one of the greatest versions of the Tchaikovsky variations ever committed to disc, and probably won't feel disposed to explore alternatives. However, Steven Isserlis plays the work with breathtaking assurance and a fine sense of rococo modesty and decorum, not that he is unwilling to probe the emotionalism of the work when the occasion demands. Of particular note are the remaining works, much more than mere makeweights, which occupy this issue. Tchaikovsky's fine *Pezzo capriccioso*, is a stylish and delightful virtuoso work, though the famed *Andante cantabile* is known, of course, in a huge variety of transcriptions, of which this is but one example. Alexander Glazunov's Two Pieces, Op. 20, and the *Minstrel's Song*, Op. 71, are occasionally heard in the concert hall, though the Cui and Rimsky offerings are far less familiar and should come as a more than welcome surprise.

This impressively engineered CD also boasts the exacting attentions of John Eliot Gardiner, who directs the Chamber Orchestra of Europe and provides superb support for Steven Isserlis, surely one of the finest of contemporary cellists, who manages to make this repertoire seem entirely his own. A bewitching and rewarding release. *MJ*

COLLECTION: EIN STRAUSSFEST II

Works by Johann Strauss I & II, Josef Strauss & Eduard Strauss

Cincinnati Pops Orchestra & Chorale/Erich Kunzel

Telarc CD-80314 □ 68:05 mins □ *⊘⊘⊘*

An excellently played collection of Strauss family bon-bons in a recording which is superlatively brilliant and detailed, thanks to Telarc's cutting-edge recording technology and, in several instances, the extra-musical intervention of such things as steam locomotives, gunfire and similar effects. The Cincinnati Pops Orchestra (that city's fine Symphony Orchestra, *senza* its first-chair players, and heard performing lighter repertoire than normal) is, by any reckoning, a high-calibre ensemble; under their German-born music director Erich Kunzel it plays with palpably Viennese flair and refinement throughout this programme, taped in the attractive ambience of Cincinnati's historical Music Hall. Kunzel invests the fast polkas with impressive dash and verve; his players, too, clearly enjoy themselves and enter willingly into the light-hearted spirit of the enterprise, and their response certainly wouldn't disgrace their more illustrious Austrian rivals in its rhythmic vitality and poise. There's swagger and pomp aplenty, too, in the *Jubilee Festival March* by Josef Strauss, and the mock-serious orientalism of Johann Jr's stirring *Egyptian March*. The perennial *Emperor Waltzes, Music of the Spheres* and *Wine, Woman and Song* are affectionately played, and the disc is of particular significance to specialist audiophiles, whose equipment should find plenty to cope with, due to the vast dynamic range of Telarc's sonics. But beware – many of the special effects here could cause serious speaker damage if playback levels are high, so keep an eye on the volume control! *MJ*

COLLECTION: TESTIMONIES OF WAR

Blacher: Dance Scenes; Alla marcia; Chiarina; Partita; Sonatine No. 2; Three Psalms; Weill: Zu Potsdam unter den Eichen; Choral-Fantasie; plus works by Goldschmidt, Milhaud, Vaughan Williams & Harrington Shortall

Sylvie Lechevalier (piano), etc; Berlin RSO, LPO/Noam Sheriff, etc

Largo 5130 □ 116:46 mins (2 discs) □ *⊘⊘⊘*

Among the plethora of commemorative projects inspired by the fiftieth anniversary of the liberation of Europe, the present collection, masterminded by the scholar David Drew, deserves a special place. Central to the whole enterprise is a timely exploration of the work of the German composer Boris Blacher (1903–75), who bore eloquent witness to the trials and tribulations of survival under the Nazis. Up to now, Blacher's reputation has rested on a few lightweight orchestral pieces, including the exuberant Variations on a Theme of Paganini, but a cross-section of works featured here suggests a figure of much greater depth and stature.

In this respect the starkly defiant psalm settings for baritone and piano, written in 1943 in the wake of official censorship from the Nazi party, and the emotionally equivocal Partita for strings and percussion provide the most powerful illustration of Blacher's capacity to transmit the feelings of loneliness in the face of oppression. A deep sense of unease also pervades the pre-war *Alla marcia* and *Dance Scenes*, where Blacher, in opposition to rampant nationalism, deliberately employs a cosmopolitan musical language owing much to Stravinsky.

Apart from Blacher, this enthralling set contains further major discoveries including the brief but ineffably poignant *Fanfare for Those Who Will Not Return* by Harrington Shortall, and two previously unknown psalm settings by Berthold Goldschmidt dating from 1935, the year the composer fled from the Nazis. Such inspired programme planning, coupled with committed performances and outstanding liner notes, make this an urgent recommendation by any standards. *EL*

Index of Nicknamed Works

BBC Music Magazine & *CD*
SPECIAL OFFER!

All the convenience of Monthly Home Delivery
<u>plus</u> almost 25% OFF the regular price

There couldn't be a better time to make sure that you don't miss a single issue of *BBC Music Magazine*, together with its unique monthly CD.

<u>Because now, for a limited time only, you can guarantee delivery of each issue whilst saving almost 25% OFF the normal price!</u>

Think of it – all the passion, colour and excitement of the world's greatest music brought home to you (as only the BBC can do) through the lively pages of *BBC Music Magazine*, plus the 'complete work' CD which accompanies every issue.

Usually, you would expect to pay more for delivery to your door. But through this special introductory offer you will pay appreciably less.

So don't delay – simply call our credit card hotline on +44 (0)1483 733719. Your complete satisfaction is guaranteed.

GUARANTEE: If you are not satisfied with your *BBC Music Magazine* subscription at any time, simply cancel and you will receive a full refund for any remaining unshipped issues.

BBC music MAGAZINE

C D B K

Subscription Hotline +44 (0)1483 733719